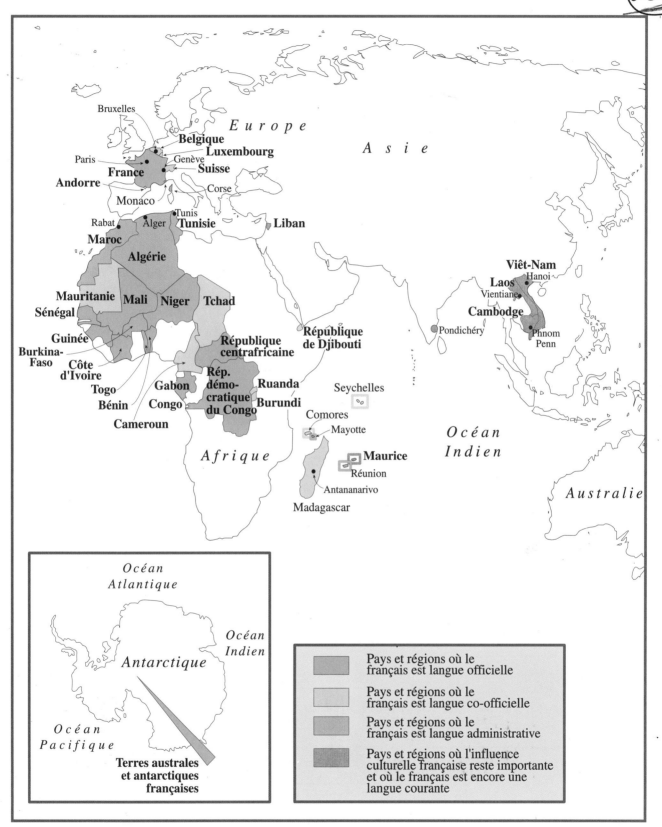

Bruxelles

E u r o p e

Belgique
Luxembourg

Paris
Genève
Suisse
France

A s i e

Andorre

Monaco

Corse

Tunis
Rabat
Alger **Tunisie**
Maroc

Liban

Algérie

Viêt-Nam
Hanoi
Laos
Vientiane
Cambodge
Phnom
Penn

Mauritanie **Mali** **Niger** **Tchad**
Sénégal

Pondichéry

Guinée

République
de Djibouti

Burkina-
Faso
Côte
d'Ivoire

République
centrafricaine

Togo
Bénin

Rép.
démo-
cratique
du Congo

Gabon
Congo

Ruanda
Burundi

Seychelles

Océan
Indien

Australie

Cameroun

Comores

Afrique

Mayotte

Maurice
Réunion

Antananarivo

Madagascar

Océan
Atlantique

Océan
Indien

Antarctique

Océan
Pacifique

Terres australes
et antarctiques
françaises

Pays et régions où le
français est langue officielle

Pays et régions où le
français est langue co-officielle

Pays et régions où le
français est langue administrative

Pays et régions où l'influence
culturelle française reste importante
et où le français est encore une
langue courante

France

Angleterre

MER DU NORD

Pays-Bas

Allemagne

LA MANCHE

Dunkerque
Calais
Lille
Valenciennes

NORD-PAS-DE-CALAIS

Belgique

Luxembourg

Amiens

PICARDIE

Metz

Reims

LORRAINE

ALSACE

Nancy
Strasbourg

Meuse
Rhin
V O S G E S

Cherbourg
Le Havre
Rouen

HAUTE-NORMANDIE

Seine

Caen

BASSE-NORMANDIE

Saint-Malo

⊙ **Paris**
Versailles
ÎLE-DE-FRANCE

CHAMPAGNE-ARDENNE

Troyes

Seine

Moselle

Mulhouse

Brest

BRETAGNE

Fougères
Rennes

Le Mans

PAYS DE LA LOIRE

Angers

Orléans

Blois   Chambord
Tours

BOURGOGNE

Dijon

Saône

Besançon

FRANCHE-COMTÉ

J U R A

Suisse

St-Nazaire
Nantes
Chinon
Azay-le-Rideau

Loire

Chenonceaux

CENTRE

Bourges

Chalon-sur-Saône

Nevers

Loire

Poitiers

La Rochelle

POITOU-CHARENTES

LIMOUSIN

Limoges

Vichy

Clermont-Ferrand

Rhône
Annecy

Lyon

RHÔNE-ALPES

Italie

OCÉAN

ATLANTIQUE

Périgueux

AUVERGNE

Saint Étienne

Grenoble

A L P E S

Bordeaux

M A S S I F   C E N T R A L

Rodez

Garonne

AQUITAINE

MIDI-PYRÉNÉES

Rhône

PROVENCE-ALPES-CÔTE-D'AZUR

Avignon

Nîmes
Montpellier   Tarascon
Béziers

Monte-Carlo

Monaco

Biarritz
Bayonne
Pau

Toulouse

Carcassonne
Narbonne

Aix-en-Provence

Grasse

Nice

P Y R É N É E S

LANGUEDOC-ROUSSILLON

Marseille

Toulon

Cannes

Espagne

Perpignan

Andorre

MER MÉDITERRANÉE

0   75 km

©1993 Magellan Geographix^SM Santa Barbara CA

CORSE

Ajaccio

THÈMES

FRENCH FOR THE GLOBAL COMMUNITY

Jane Harper ▪ Madeleine Gélineau Lively ▪ Mary K. Williams

Tarrant County College

Heinle & Heinle
Thomson Learning™

United States • Australia • Canada • Denmark • Japan • Mexico • New Zealand
Philippines • Puerto Rico • Singapore • Spain • United Kingdom

The publication of THÈMES was directed by the Heinle & Heinle College Foreign language Publishing Team:

Wendy Nelson, Senior Acquisition Editor
Stephen Frail, Marketing Manager
Esther Marshall, Senior Production & Development Editor Supervisor
Tom Pauken, Developmental Editor

Also participating in the publication of this program were:

Publisher	**Vincent P. Duggan**
Director of Photography	**Jonathan Stark**
Photo Researchers	**Jeff Freeland, Bénédicte Ferru**
Associate Marketing Manager	**Kristen Murphy-Lojacono**
Senior Manufacturing Coordinator	**Mary Beth Hennebury**
Project Manager	**Christine E. Wilson, IBC**
Compositor	**Pre-Press Company, Inc.**
Interior Designer	**Tom Zimerle**
Illustrator	**Jane O'Conor**
Cover Designer	**Cyndy Patrick**
Text Printer/Binder	**World Color**

Heinle & Heinle Publishers
20 Park Plaza
Boston, MA 02116

web	**www.thomsonrights.com**
fax	1-800-730-2215
phone	1-800-730-2214

UK/EUROPE/MIDDLE EAST:
Thomson Leaning
Berkshire House
168-173 High Holborn
London, WCIV 7AA, United Kingdom

LATIN AMERICA:
Thomson Learning
Seneca, 53
Colonia Polanco
11560 México D.F. México

JAPAN:
Thomson Learning
Placeside Building, 5F
1-1-1 Hitotsubashi, Chiyoda-ku
Tokyo 100 0003, Japan

AUSTRALIA/NEW ZEALAND:
Nelson/Thomson Learning
102 Dodds Street
South Melbourne
Victoria 3205 Australia

ASIA (excluding Japan):
Thomson Learning
60 Albert Street #15-01
Albert Complex
Singapore 189969

SPAIN:
Thomson Learning
Calle Magallanes,
28015-Madrid
España

CANADA:
Nelson/Thomson Learning
1120 Birchmount Road
Scarborough, Ontario
Canada MIK 5G4

Library of Congress Cataloging-in-Publication Data

Lively, Madeleine.
   Thèmes : French for the global community / Madeleine Lively, Jane Harper, Mary Williams.
     p. cm.
   Includes index.
   ISBN 0-8384-8233-3 (student edition)—ISBN 0-8384-8207-4 (instructor's annotated edition)
    1. French language—Textbooks for foreign speakers—English. I. Harper, Jane, 1942–
   II. Williams, Mary. III. Title.
PC2129.E5 L584 1999
—dc21   99-047126

Printed in the United States of America

ISBN: 0-8384-8233-3 (student text)

2 3 4 5 6 7 8 9 03 02 01 00

Contents

	Communicative Objectives	Thematic Objectives	Vocabulary	Structures
Chapitre 1: Mes interactions avec les autres 1				
1er Thème: 4	Using appropriate greetings and introductions in a variety of social interactions	Observing differences in casual vs. more formal French	• Greetings and leave-taking • Introductions	
2e Thème: 10	Ordering food and drink in a café	Observing politeness and natural hesitation in speech	• Café food and drink • Fixed expressions for social amenities	• Indefinite articles
3e Thème: 18	Expressing interests and opinions	Identifying what you like and do not like to do	• Likes and dislikes • Class interactions	• Subject pronouns • **Être** • **De** • Questions with intonation • **-er** verbs (introduction)
Chapitre 2: Moi, mon travail et mes loisirs 32				
1er Thème: 35	Giving information about who you are and where you are from	Examining the degree to which you are willing to give information about yourself	• Nationalities and languages • Months • Numbers 1–39	• Gender of nationalities and professions
2e Thème: 48	Exchanging information about professions and the workplace	Observing relations between careers and personal goals	• Professions	• **-er** verbs • Negation with **ne...pas**
3e Thème: 61	Telling how you spend your time away from work or school	Examining some factors that influence preferences in leisure activities	• Interests and pastimes • The workplace • Days of the week	• Yes/no questions • Adverbs of frequency • Degrees of intensity • Verb + infinitive
Chapitre 3: Mes relations interpersonnelles: Les domaines de la vie 77				
1er Thème: 80	Talking about your family and friends and what you do together	Identifying and qualifying the relationships between you and the people close to you	• Familial and social relations • Expressions with **avoir**	• Possessive adjectives • **Avoir**
2e Thème: 92	Describing people you know	Identifying and evaluating the characteristics that you associate with people	• Numbers 40–100 • Physical and psychological traits	• Descriptive adjectives • Noun/adjective agreement
3e Thème: 103	Talking about your routine activities	Identifying ways that people contribute to the community	• Leisure activities • Expressions with **faire**	• **Faire**

	Communicative Objectives	Thematic Objectives	Vocabulary	Structures
Chapitre 4: La vie en ville 119				
1ᵉʳ Thème: 123	Discussing routine errands and telling where in town you go for shopping and services	Examining places about town in terms of their importance to you and their contribution to image of the city	• Places in the community • Temporal expressions • Common activities associated with community life	• **Aller** • Contractions with **à** • Adverbs of frequency • **Futur immédiat**
2ᵉ Thème: 138	Giving directions for getting about town	Examining the notion of *quartier* and how the various areas of a city reflect the needs and interests of the community	• Giving directions	• Contractions with **de** • Prepositions of location • Imperatives
3ᵉ Thème: 152	Scheduling appointments and discussing schedules	Integrating the notion of *quartier* in describing American cities to French-speaking people	• Telling time	Information questions: • **Qui, quand, comment, pourquoi, où, qu'est-ce que** • **Prendre, apprendre, comprendre, reprendre**, etc. • Demonstrative adjectives
Chapitre 5: La vie quotidienne: Les responsabilités et la recherche d'un équilibre 171				
1ᵉʳ Thème: 176	Identifying, prioritizing, and scheduling daily routines and responsibilities	Examining indicators of stress associated with time and schedules	• Daily routines • Expressions of necessity	• Pronominal verbs (reciprocals, infinitives, imperatives) • **Il faut, il est nécessaire de, avoir besoin de** + infinitive
2ᵉ Thème: 191	Discussing academic schedules and responsibilities	Examining academic and career objectives and discussing their importance	• School courses	• Comparative expressions • **Devoir**
3ᵉ Thème: 206	Describing the ways that you spend your time off	Examining how leisure activities balance weekday routines	• Expressions for thanks and holidays	• **Jouer à/de** • Superlative expressions • **Sortir / partir / servir / dormir / se sentir**
Chapitre 6: Les expériences passées: Notre formation pour l'avenir 227				
1ᵉʳ Thème: 231	Discussing previous work and educational experiences	Identifying work and educational experiences and articulating their relevance to the workplace	• Temporal adverbs	• **Passé composé** (with **avoir**, negative, interrogative) • **Pendant** and **il y a** + expressions of time
2ᵉ Thème: 245	Talking about previous personal experiences	Identifying life experiences (outside the contexts of work and school) that have contributed to your personal development	• Skills required in the workplace	• **Passé composé** (with **être**) • **-ir** verbs
3ᵉ Thème: 266	Talking about previous work and educational experiences as they enhance career opportunities	Relating your own skills, knowledge, and interests to those defined in some specific job offerings	• Professions	• **Passé composé** (with pronominal verbs)

	Communicative Objectives	Thematic Objectives	Vocabulary	Structures
Chapitre 7: Mon voyage autour du monde 279				
1ᵉʳ Thème: 283	Describing features of nature and geography	Defining your goals for leisure travel and associating them with various geographic settings	• Colors • Geographical expressions • Topography • Sites and monuments	• Geographic prepositions • Definite articles with geographic nouns
2ᵉ Thème: 294	Describing weather conditions and seasons	Associating preferences in leisure activities with different weather, seasons, and places in the world	• Weather • Seasons	• The pronoun **y**
3ᵉ Thème: 306	Determining and expressing preferences in hotel accommodations	Planning your own world tour, identifying sites and experiences that relate to your personal travel goals	• Additional sports and pastimes	• **Vouloir** and **pouvoir** • **-re** verbs • superlative (cont.)
Chapitre 8: La cuisine: Diversité géographique et culturelle 325				
1ᵉʳ Thème: 328	Talking about selecting and purchasing food items off the shelf	Examining associations between geographic regions and foods that are identified with them	• Foods	• **Imparfait**
2ᵉ Thème: 344	Ordering a meal in a restaurant	Examining the cultural influences on regional cuisines	• Meals • Culinary items • Common expressions **à table**	• Partitive
3ᵉ Thème: 357	Using expressions of quantity with reference to foods	Identifying the significance that you attribute to certain foods based on the role they play in your memories	• Expressions related to tastes and eating habits • Quantities	• Direct object pronouns • Pronoun **en**
Chapitre 9: Les souvenirs: Les gens et les événements de la vie 379				
1ᵉʳ Thème: 382	Narrating past events in your life	Identifying the events of your life that have created lasting memories	• Important occasions	• **Imparfait** vs. **passé composé**
2ᵉ Thème: 393	Talking about people you remember and activities you have just completed	Identifying the people who have made lasting impressions in your memories	• Descriptive adjectives	• **venir, devenir, revenir, se souvenir (de)** • **venir de** + infinitive
3ᵉ Thème: 404	Describing different stages of your life: where you were living, your routine activities, what was going on around you	Looking back on the different stages of your life, describing them in terms of their personal significance for you	• Parts of the body and ailments	• Indirect object pronouns

	Communicative Objectives	Thematic Objectives	Vocabulary	Structures
Chapitre 10: Choisir un logement: Le goût et les besoins 421				
1er Thème: 425	Prioritizing features of housing in terms of desirability and un-acceptability	Identifying the variety of considerations that determine choices in housing	• Types of housing • Rooms of the house	• Negative expressions
2e Thème: 439	Determining personal preferences in rooms and furnishings	Associating features of your lifestyle with features of housing	• Household furnishings • Amenities associated with homes	• Future tense
3e Thème: 453	Discussing plans and aspirations	Examining your plans and interests and how they influence your choices in where you want to live	• Life changes	• **Si** clauses with present and future tenses • **voir** and **croire**
Chapitre 11: Le budget: Les dépenses et les priorités 471				
1er Thème: 475	Identifying budgetary categories and adding a tentative or polite tone to statements	Identifying and categorizing the ways you choose spend your income	• Terms related to savings and expenses	• Conditional mood
2e Thème: 488	Expressing need in relation to day-to-day expenses	Prioritizing your expenses and spending goals	• Clothing	• Il faut and il vaudrait mieux + infinitive
3e Thème: 498	Hypothesizing decisions based on given situations	Examining views of personal tendencies in relation to budgeting and spending	• Personal possessions	• Si clauses with imperfect and conditional verbs
Chapter 12: À la découverte du monde francophone 515				
1er Thème: 520	Expressing necessary conditions for comfort while traveling	Evaluating the attractions of major cities in terms of the quality of life they offer tourists and residents	• Weather and geog (review) • Describing places (review)	• Subjunctive
2e Thème: 531	Expressing preferences and recommendations for travel	Gaining insight into heritage and culture to be gained through sightseeing experiences	• Entertainment in the city (review)	• Subjunctive (cont.)
3e Thème: 540	Discussing sites of historical, artistic, and cultural significance in Paris	Identifying the historical processes that influence the construction of landmark sites in a city	• Architecture (review) • Places in the city (review)	• **Ouvrir, couvrir, découvrir, offrir, souffrir** • **Connaître, reconnaître** • **Connaître** vs. **savoir**

Preface to the Student Edition

Thèmes is an elementary-level program for learners of French preparing themselves for their professional as well as social roles in the global community. It is designed not only to help you acquire the language but also to help you understand the cultural assumptions of the Francophone world, the cultural norms of these diverse societies and their growing importance in the global community.

Thèmes is an integrated learning system that comprises a variety of interconnected components. As a student, you will interact with various parts of this system as you quickly develop the ability to communicate your own ideas in French. The components are mutually supportive, each one enhancing the language development in the other parts of the system while providing its own unique opportunities for language growth.

The **Textbook** provides the organizing structure for the learning system. The twelve chapters have been constructed around themes, three interrelated themes per chapter. The listening sections (identified with a cassette icon) are available on the **Text Tapes.**

The *Cahier de travaux pratiques: activités écrites et orales,* your workbook and lab manual, provides additional opportunities for listening, reading, and writing development and practice, and is a critical tool for developing your ability to communicate in French. Regular use of the *Cahier* (ideally, every day) will give you the frequent, repeated exposure that is the most effective way to learn a foreign language. Each chapter of the *Cahier* corresponds directly to the **Textbook.** The listening sections are available on the **Laboratory Tapes/CDs.**

Internet Activities, which include auto-corrected language quizzes, plus cultural expansion activities for each chapter, are available at the *Thèmes* website at http://themes.heinle.com

The **CD-ROM** is for use outside of class to practice grammar and vocabulary, listening, reading, writing and pronunciation, all within the context of an internship in a multinational communications firm.

The **composition software program** referred to throughout the *Cahier* and recommended for use with this course of study is *Système-D: Writing Assistant for French.* This process-writing program includes the following tools:
   —Bilingual dictionary of more than 10,000 entries complete with examples of usage and audible pronunciation
   —Reference grammar , including 250,000 conjugated verb forms and examples of correct use
   —Index to functional phrases
   —Sets of thematically related vocabulary items
   —Word processor and spell checker
Your language lab may have a site-license for *Système-D*, or you can purchase a personal copy either through your bookstore, or directly from Heinle & Heinle (http://www.heinle.com).

Portfolios: The FAQs
Le portefeuille de compétences

What is a portfolio?
A portfolio is a collection of documents that serves as a record of your knowledge. It is a record of what you know, what you know how to do, and what you know how to communicate.

Why do people develop portfolios?
- To have a reminder of what they have learned
- To document what they can do
- To have a record of how their views develop over time
- To help them articulate their knowledge

How do I go about developing a portfolio for this course?
- First, get a ring binder with some pocket pages to help you keep all of your portfolio documents together.
- As you proceed in the course, file everything that you feel demonstrates your ability to use French effectively.
  1. The textbook activities marked with a icon
  2. Documents that show how you use French in out-of-class interests, for example, correspondence with Francophone penpals or e-pals
  3. Requests for information from Francophone businesses or Internet sites
  4. Personal comments on Francophone movies that you see
  5. A record of peer tutoring sessions you have done, French club events you have attended or organized
  6. Tape recordings of some of your writing to practice oral expression of your own ideas
  7. An annotated list of articles you have read or Internet sites that you consult
- Review the contents of your portfolio periodically. This is a critical step, because these reviews serve to remind you of your best work in French and help you keep it fresh in your mind.
- Revise your filing system from time to time, as your interests, experience, and knowledge expand to encompass new areas.

From the Authors:
Suggestions for Student Success with Thèmes

Thèmes differs from most beginning-level textbooks in that it is geared to **all** learners—adults and traditional students alike—with a shift in language focus from the dorm to the work environment. The program stresses the features of French needed by all learners for everyday communication; and contexts reflect business and social interactions common to everyday life. Recognizing that many students drawn to language study are not necessarily language majors and may not have traditional goals for their language learning, *Thèmes* accommodates selective learning, allowing you to meet your personal learning objectives beyond those of the course syllabus. To achieve these objectives, and achieve success in learning French, the authors suggest the following:

1. **Take advantage of the learning opportunities provided you.** Go to class. Do your assigned homework. Listen to your tapes and CD's. Watch the videos. Practice in the workbook. Spend time in the Language Acquisition Center. Make good use of available resources.

2. **Study often in short time periods.** Several study sessions of 30 minutes are generally much more productive than one three-hour marathon.

3. **Vary your study activities.** You have a variety of learning materials available to you with *Thèmes*. Use several of them each day in brief sessions. You can concentrate during longer study sessions if you work with a variety of types of activities and materials.

4. **Study with a friend out of class.** Most of the in-class activities in the *Thèmes* Textbook have been designed for the interaction of two people. Find a friend (or make one) in your French class. Practice the text activities, taking turns playing each role.

5. **Practice aloud.** Read aloud the exercises in your text. Do the activities aloud with your study partner. Repeat phrases and respond to questions in your audio and video materials. Get accustomed to hearing your own voice speaking French.

6. **Don't be afraid to make mistakes.** Language development is very much a process of trial and error, followed by correction and refinement. You are expected to make errors—in pronunciation, in vocabulary, in structure—during the language acquisition process. Gradually, with practice, you will gain control of those that are most relevant for you—hence, those that you use most often.

7. **Pay attention, but relax, in class.** Anxiety can impede your ability to concentrate and can block the processes needed for language acquisition. The class activities are designed to engage your thought without stimulating panic. Everyone who has learned to speak a second language has done so through trial and error!

8. **Visualize everything.** Try to see in your mind every object, place, person, situation, or activity that is referred to in French. Work at picturing the scene rather than at translating the words into English.

9. **Surround yourself with French.** Rent video movies in French. Go to see French films in the theaters. Listen to French music on CD. Look at the pictures and titles and captions in French magazines and newspapers. Watch for French labels on clothes, toiletries, and foods. Become aware of information about francophones in the international news. Look up websites in French on topics that interest you. Heighten your awareness of the amount of French with which you come into contact daily.

10. **Basically, enjoy the process.** Acquiring skills in a language, learning about other people and their thoughts and beliefs and ideas and accomplishments, and opening your mind to other ways of viewing the world are exciting, exhilarating, enlightening, and entertaining experiences. Enjoy!

For Monte, Glen, Mom

Acknowledgments

We would like to express our sincere thanks and appreciation to our wonderful team at Heinle & Heinle Publishers: to Vince Duggan for encouraging us to take on this project; to Wendy Nelson for her strategic guidance and for her steady faith in our ideas and philosophies; to Amy Baron, Beth Tranter, and Tom Pauken, our developmental editors, for their attention to detail; to Esther Marshall for her superb organizational ability and for her calm, consistent push toward completion; to Jonathan Stark for his photography and video work. We also offer our sincere appreciation to Charles H. Heinle for his consistent belief in the value of our work.

We are grateful for the comments and suggestions made by our colleagues who reviewed this work during the draft stages:
Lucy Aghazarian, *Community College of Philadelphia*
James Davis, *University of Arkansas*
Richard Donato, *University of Pittsburgh*
Glenn Fetzer, *Calvin College*
Jean Fouchereaux, *University of Southern Maine*
Emily Guignan, *Washington University*
Sylvie Debevec Henning, *Plattsburg State University of New York*
Carolyn L. Jacobs, *Houston Community College*
Katherine Kulick, *College of William and Mary*
Mary de López, *Univeristy of Texas-El Paso*
Ann Lutkus, *University of Rochester*
Éliane McKee, *Buffalo State College*
Daniel M. Mengara, *Montclair State University*
Ana María Myers, *Polk Community College*
Mari H. O'Brien, *Wright State University*
Charline Sacks, *Nassau Community College*
Marie Smith, *Florida Community College-Jacksonville*
Robert Terry, *University of Richmond*
Fred Toner, *Ohio University*
Anita Jones Vogely, *Binghamton University*
Sharon Wilkinson, *West Virginia University*
Bonnie L. Earnest Youngs, *Carnegie Mellon University*

As always, we are especially indebted to the students of French at Tarrant County College Northeast Campus who continue to shape our ideas about learning and learning materials by their candid, good-natured responses to our classroom and internet activities.

We offer a special note of appreciation to our dear, long-time friends in France—the family of Alfred and Marguerite Stengel, the family of André and Monique LeStrat, and Dominique Jacquot and Geneviève LaCroix—who have taught us much about French language, history, art, culture, customs, and ways of thinking by opening their homes, their lives, and their minds to us through the last twenty plus years.

We also wish to thank our families for their support and encouragement during this long process, especially Monte, Glen, and Mom, whose belief in us kept us on target.

jh, mgl, mkw

MES INTERACTIONS AVEC LES AUTRES

Communicative Objectives

- To use appropriate greetings and introductions in various social interactions
- To order food and drink in a café
- To express interests and opinions

OUVERTURE EN VIDÉO:
On fait connaissance

La mise en scène: *Setting the scene*
Soyez les bienvenus: *Consider yourselves welcome.*

La mise en scène°: (anticipating)

Soyez les bienvenus°. Welcome to your study of French with the textbook THÈMES. In *Chapitre 1* you will learn to handle social interactions, such as meeting and greeting other people, ordering something in a café, talking about where you are from, and expressing opinions about activities and interests. The video component of this course provides rich cultural observations while you learn listening strategies and useful expressions based on the theme of the chapters.

You will have three Francophone guides from different parts of the world to take you through the course. The video segment of this chapter will allow you to meet your guides and hear how they introduce themselves. You will also get an opportunity to observe other French-speaking people meeting and greeting one another while you listen in on their conversations in a café setting.

A. **Les salutations.** As you observe French-speaking people meeting and greeting each other, you begin to realize the differences between formal and casual styles of address. Consider the groups of people listed in the following grid, and determine if you might expect them to use formal or casual styles of address with one another.

Groups of people interacting	Formal	Casual
A group of college students addressing one another		
A student addressing a professor		
A business executive calling on a colleague		
A husband and wife addressing each other		
A teacher addressing a student		
A parent addressing a child		
A shopper and a salesperson addressing each other		
Pet owners speaking to their pet		

Les paroles et le sens: (process listening)

On se présente. When you are meeting people, it is very important to listen carefully to their names and to be able to recognize and use their names. A person's name is very significant to the individual, and we want to be attentive to that important detail. However, a French name can sound very different and unfamiliar, and even if it looks similar to an English name, it will sound different when pronounced in French. In this course, you will become familiar with quite a few typical French names. We start off by meeting our three French-speaking guides who will take us on video tours throughout the course.

B. Nos guides s'appellent... Listen to your three guides introduce themselves, and determine which name you hear them give.

À propos des stratégies: One of the most difficult aspects of learning French is understanding the spoken language. At this point in your studies, you should not expect to understand the French you hear in this video. Your purpose here should be to become visually acquainted with scenes and situations in French-speaking places, to get to know your guides, and to get used to the sounds of the French language, its intonation, and its rhythm. The prompts on the video will guide you in good listening strategies, beginning with recognizing the sounds of certain key words and phrases and matching them with their written forms.

Votre guide parisien

1. First, what do you hear your Parisian guide give as his name?
   a. Jean-Yves   b. Xavier   c. Roger

Votre guide québécoise

2. Next, you meet your Canadian guide. What name do you hear her give?
   a. Angélique   b. Véronique   c. Monique

Votre guide de Guadeloupe

3. Your Caribbean guide gives her name as _____?
   a. Christine   b. Céline   c. Claudine

C. Nos guides se présentent. As you listen again to your French-speaking guides greet you and introduce themselves, see if you can identify which greeting and which expression they use to give their name. Put a check mark in the appropriate column in the grid. The same expression can be used by more than one person.

	Parisian guide	Canadian guide	Caribbean guide
Permettez-moi de me présenter...			
Je m'appelle...			
Moi, je m'appelle...			
Bonjour!			
Eh bien, salut!			

On y réfléchit°: (thematic integration)

D. *Tu ou Vous...* **question de rapport.** Now that you've begun to notice the various levels of formality used when different groups of people interact with one another, think about your relationships with people you know. (1) List three people who would expect you to address them casually. In French, you would use informal greetings and the **tu** form with this group. (2) List three more people who would expect you to be more formal with them. With this group, you would use more elaborate introductions and greetings and the **vous** form when speaking French.

On y réfléchit: Thinking about it/ Reflecting upon it

Objective: To use appropriate greetings and introductions in various social interactions

PRÉSENTATION

SALUTATIONS

Scène 1
—Salut, Anne. Ça va?
—Oui, ça va bien. Et toi?
—Pas mal, merci.

Scène 2
—Bonjour, madame. Comment allez-vous?
—Je vais bien, merci. Et vous, monsieur?
—Très bien, merci.

A. Bonjour, les amis. *(Hello, friends.)* Turn to several of your classmates and use the greetings modeled in **Scène 1.** Though men prefer a handshake, women can practice either the style of greeting with a brief kiss on each cheek, called **la bise,** or a handshake. Then practice using the style of greeting modeled in **Scène 2.**

PRÉSENTATIONS

Scène 3
—Salut, je m'appelle Laure Beauchamps. Et toi, tu t'appelles comment?
—Moi, je m'appelle Éric Berger.
—Bonjour, Éric. Voilà mon amie Sylvie Rousseau. Sylvie, Éric.

Scène 4
—Monsieur Pochet, je voudrais vous présenter Monsieur Jacques Carrier.
—Monsieur Carrier, Jean-Claude Pochet, le directeur du bureau.
—Bonjour, monsieur. Enchanté.

B. **On se présente.** *(We introduce ourselves.)* In groups of three, take turns introducing one member of your group to the other. Use the style of introduction modeled in **Scène 3.** Be sure to include a variety of greetings (from **Scène 1** as well) with your introductions.

C. **Les présentations au bureau.** *(Introductions at the office.)* In groups of three, imagine that you are meeting someone new at the office. Use titles and last names to make the introductions in the style modeled in **Scène 4.** Include a variety of greetings (from **Scène 2** as well).

Note Culturelle

The appropriate degree of formality, or "register," can vary greatly from one context or culture to another, making it sometimes difficult to decide between the use of **tu** or **vous** when speaking French. For example, among students, **tu** might be used with everyone, even those not acquainted with each other. Likewise, it might be used among all fellow workers. But in certain professional situations and particularly among and with people of older generations, **vous** is the pronoun of choice. British social interactions tend to be more formal than those of Americans. Similarly, the French tend to be more reserved than the people from Québec. If you are unsure of which form of address to use, listen to the native speakers and follow their lead.

On prend congé

Scène 5
—Allez, au revoir, Anne.
—Au revoir, Nicole. À bientôt.

Scène 6
—Pardon, monsieur, j'ai un rendez-vous.
—Eh bien, au revoir, madame. À demain.

D. **On prend congé.** *(We take leave of one another.)* Turn to several of your classmates and say good-bye to them, using the conversations in **Scènes 5** and **6** as models.

Scène 7

—Salut, Jean-Luc. Tu vas bien?

—Euh, assez bien, mais je suis fatigué. J'ai mal dormi.

Scène 8

—Pardon, monsieur, vous êtes Claude Roget du bureau Microsoft?

—Oui, madame.

—Bonjour, monsieur, je suis Annelise Tremblay.

—Enchanté de faire votre connaissance, madame.

Scène 9

—Bonjour, monsieur. Comment vous appelez-vous?

—Je m'appelle Claude Roget.

—Roget, avec un «t»?

—Oui, mademoiselle, R-O-G-E-T.

—Très bien. Et votre prénom?

—C'est Claude.

E. **On pratique les conversations.** Practice the situations in the **Expansion, Scènes 7** and **8** with your classmates. Your instructor will help you learn to spell your name a little later for practicing **Scène 9.**

STRATÉGIES D'ANALYSE

1. Look back at the photos that illustrate each **scène (1–9),** where a variety of greetings, introductions, and farewells are going on. Which situations would you label as casual? Which as more formal? How did you decide?

2. Now look at the lines of dialogue under the photos of the casual and formal exchanges. In which cases is the word **vous** used for *you* and in which ones is **tu** or **toi** used instead?

3. Which scenes depict greetings? Which ones introductions? Farewells? How did you decide? Do any of them include small talk or additional information?

PRÉCISIONS

- The French make careful distinctions between formal and casual situations when speaking to others. The subject pronoun **tu** is used when speaking to close friends, family members, children, and pets. French speakers generally use **vous** in more formal situations, as when speaking to people outside the family and to those in older generations or in positions of authority.

  Salut, Jean-Luc. Tu vas bien?
  Bonjour, madame. Vous allez bien?

A good rule of thumb is to use **tu** with people whom you address with a first name and **vous** with people whom you address with a title (and sometimes their last name).

• **Vous** is always used when speaking to more than one person, whether the people are being addressed in a formal or a casual situation.

Salut, Éric et Sylvie. Vous allez bien?
Bonjour, Monsieur et Madame Duclos. Vous allez bien?

F. **Salutation ou présentation?** For each of the nine scenes depicted in the **Présentation** (pages 4 and 5) and the **Expansion** (page 6) sections, identify (1) which functions (greeting, introduction, etc.) occur in each scene, and (2) whether the interaction is formal or casual. In the following grid, mark the appropriate cells to indicate the function(s) and level of formality used by the speakers in each scene. Mark the cells with a "C" for casual or an "F" for formal.

Functions	Scène 1	Scène 2	Scène 3	Scène 4	Scène 5	Scène 6	Scène 7	Scène 8	Scène 9
Greetings	C								
Introductions									
Farewells									
Extra information									

G. **On fait connaissance.** In groups of three, get to know some of your classmates. Using some of the expressions you've been practicing, exchange names and greetings, and ask how things are going. Try to vary your comments as much as possible by referring to the photo captions and to the **Expressions de politesse** on page 9 of this **Thème** for guidance.

Modèle: —*Salut. Je m'appelle Beth. Tu t'appelles comment?*
                —*Bonjour. Je m'appelle Patrick. Comment ça va?*
                —*Pas mal, merci. Et toi?*

H. **Ça continue.** In groups of three, expand your conversation to include introductions and farewells. Practice a casual conversation and then a formal one, being careful to use **tu** and **vous** appropriately. Consult the photo captions and the **Expressions de politesse** for ideas.

Modèle: Étudiante: *Salut, Patrick, ça va?*
                Étudiant: *Oui, assez bien, Amy. Et toi?*
                Étudiante: *Très bien, merci. Patrick, voilà mon ami Kevin. Kevin, Patrick.*
                Étudiant: *Bonjour, Kevin, comment ça va?*
                Étudiant: *Bonjour, Patrick. Ça va pas mal, merci. Et toi?*
                Étudiant: *Assez bien, merci. Eh bien, au revoir, Kevin. À bientôt, Amy.*

Modèle: Étudiante: *Bonjour, monsieur. Comment allez-vous?*
Étudiant: *Je vais assez bien, madame. Et vous?*
Étudiante: *Très bien, merci. Monsieur La Grange, je voudrais vous présenter Joe Conner. Monsieur Conner, Jean La Grange.*
Étudiant: *Enchanté, monsieur. Comment allez-vous?*
Étudiant: *Je vais très bien, merci, monsieur. Enchanté de faire votre connaissance.*
Étudiant: *Ah, excusez-moi, j'ai un rendez-vous. Au revoir, madame, monsieur.*

Note Culturelle

People greet each other differently in different cultures, depending on how well they know each other. In general, French people tend to be more formal than Americans, and they use titles with each other far more frequently, such as in **Bonjour, madame; Enchanté, monsieur; Au revoir, mademoiselle.** Not using titles at the end of short utterances sounds somewhat abrupt to the French.

When meeting and greeting each other, as well as when taking leave of each other, the French make physical contact, usually with a handshake for friends and business associates, though the French handshake is briefer than its equivalent in the U.S., more like a quick handclasp. In France, it is just as common for young people and for French women to shake hands as it is for men, and it is done just as frequently.

Close friends and family members exchange a brush on each cheek, accompanied by a light kiss (generally in the air), when they meet and take leave of each other. This is known as **la bise** and is popular between women and in mixed groups. Men usually prefer a warm handshake.

Did you notice as the alphabet was read that the letters *g* and *j* sound reversed? That is, in French, the letter **g** is pronounced [zhay] and **j** is pronounced [zhee].

Prononciation: L'alphabet français

Like English, written French uses the Roman alphabet. In French, however, diacritical marks (accents) may appear in combination with some letters; these are discussed later in this chapter. You will hear a recording of the French alphabet; repeat each letter aloud.

Vous pouvez épeler votre nom, s'il vous plaît? *(Would you please spell your name?)* Stand and circulate among your classmates, asking each to spell his/her first **(prénom)** and last name **(nom de famille).** Be sure to write the spellings down as you listen, so you can check your accuracy when finished.

LEXIQUE

Expressions de politesse

Pour saluer
Bonjour.
Salut.
Ça va?
Tu vas bien?
Comment ça va?
Comment allez-vous?
Vous allez bien?

Pour répondre aux salutations
Bonjour.
Salut.
(Oui,) ça va. Et toi?
Pas mal, merci.
Ça va (assez) bien, merci.
Je vais (très) bien, merci. Et vous?

Pour faire la connaissance de quelqu'un
Tu t'appelles comment?
Comment vous appelez-vous?
Vous êtes (Éric Berger)?
Et votre prénom?

(Moi,) je m'appelle (Éric Berger).

(Oui,) je suis (Éric Berger).
C'est Éric.

Pour présenter quelqu'un
Voici mon ami(e) (Sylvie).
Je voudrais vous présenter
    (Madame Annelise Courbier).

Bonjour, (Sylvie).
Enchanté(e) de faire votre connaissance.

Pour prendre congé
Au revoir.

À demain.
À bientôt.

Pour donner d'autres informations
Je suis fatigué(e).
J'ai mal dormi.
J'ai un rendez-vous.

Objective: To order food and drink in a café

PRÉSENTATION

Scène 1
—Voilà un café. On prend quelque chose°?
—Bonne idée°! Allons-y°!

Scène 2
—Mademoiselle, s'il vous plaît°?
—Oui, monsieur, j'arrive°.

Scène 3
—Vous désirez?
—Je désire un café au lait, s'il vous plaît.

Scène 4
—Je vais prendre un citron pressé. Et toi, Marc?
—Moi, je voudrais... euh... non! Je préfère une boisson alcoolisée. Donnez-moi une bière mexicaine, s'il vous plaît.

Scène 5
—Voilà un express pour monsieur, et...
—Non, mademoiselle, un citron pressé pour moi et un café au lait pour mademoiselle.
—Ah, pardon. Et une bière pour vous, monsieur?

Scène 6
—Oui, mademoiselle, merci.
—Je vous en prie, monsieur.

On prend quelque chose?: *Shall we get something (to eat or drink)?*
Bonne idée!: *Good idea!* **Allons-y!:** *Let's go!* **s'il vous plaît:** *please.*
j'arrive: *I'm coming.*

1. Look at **Scène 2.** What expression is used to get someone's attention?
2. Looking at **Scènes 3** and **4,** identify at least three expressions that are used for ordering something in a café.
3. What polite expression do French speakers add after asking a favor or placing an order? **(Scènes 3** and **4)**
4. What expression can be used for hesitating in order to gain time to think? **(Scène 4)**
5. Which expression (from **Scène 5**) is used to apologize when a mistake has been made?
6. What do the French say to thank someone? And to respond to an expression of thanks? **(Scène 6)**

PRÉCISIONS

- To get the attention of other people, you can use their title: **monsieur, madame,** or **mademoiselle**.
- Several different expressions for ordering something in a café include:

Je désire...	**Je vais prendre...**
Donnez-moi...	**Pour moi...**
Je voudrais...	**Je préfère...**

- A polite expression for adding a "please" to a request or an order is **s'il vous plaît**.
- When people need to hesitate in order to gain time to think, they can say **euh...** or **voyons...**
- When someone makes a mistake, they say **Pardon**.
- One of several ways to answer a "thank you," **Merci,** is with **Je vous en prie**.

À propos du vocabulaire: S'il vous plaît and **Pardon** can also be used as attention getters, much the same as in English when we say, "Excuse me, please..."

Vocabulaire: Qu'est-ce qu'on prend?

Les boissons chaudes

un café au lait

un café

un café-crème

un cappucino

un express

un thé citron

un thé nature

un thé au lait

un chocolat

Drinks called by their brand names,
like *Coca*, *Perrier*, *Évian*, and *Orangina*,
are capitalized.

Les boissons froides

un Coca
un Perrier
une eau minérale
un Évian
une limonade
un Orangina
un jus de fruits
un citron pressé
une orange pressée

eau gazeuse: *carbonated water*
eau plate: *non-carbonated water*

Les boissons alcoolisées

un kir
un verre de blanc
un verre de champagne
une bière mexicaine
un verre de rosé
un verre de rouge
un demi
une bière allemande
une bière canadienne

Quelque chose à manger:
Something to eat

Quelque chose à manger°

un sandwich au jambon
une omelette au jambon
un sandwich au fromage
un croque-monsieur
une omelette nature
une omelette au fromage
un croque-madame
un panini
un croissant
une salade mixte
un éclair
une salade niçoise

Structure: L'article indéfini

OBSERVATIONS

Je voudrais une bière.   *I would like a beer.*
Je voudrais un croissant.   *I would like a croissant.*
Je voudrais un café.   *I would like a (cup of) coffee.*

STRATÉGIES D'ANALYSE

1. Which word in each sentence indicates *a*?
2. What is the difference between the two spellings of the word for *a*?

PRÉCISIONS

- In French all nouns are either masculine or feminine. Most of those referring to people are easy to understand.

  un homme   *a man*   **une** femme   *a woman*

- Others are less evident.

  un café   *a coffee*   **une** bière   *a beer*

- Where *a* or *an* is used as the indefinite article in English, French generally uses **un** or **une.**

  Je voudrais **un** verre de vin.   *I would like **a** glass of wine.*
  Un Perrier pour moi.   *A Perrier for me.*
  Une bière pour moi, s'il vous plaît. *A beer for me, please.*

- **Un** is used before masculine nouns and **une** before feminine nouns. Observing which article is used with a noun can help identify the gender of the noun.

  Je voudrais **un** café noir.   *I would like **a** black coffee.*
  Je voudrais **une** bière mexicaine.   *I would like **a** Mexican beer.*

A. **On passe la commande.** *(Let's place the order.)* With your partner, practice ordering the following drinks. Remember to include either **un** or **une** before the name of the drink you ask for. You may consult the list of drink choices in the drawings on pages 11 and 12 for guidance on which article to use with each drink. You and your partner should order a drink from each column. Use the suggested expressions in your requests.

Je désire...	Je voudrais...	Pour moi...	Donnez-moi...	Je vais prendre...	Je préfère...
... Coca	... verre de blanc	... bière	... demi	... eau minérale	... jus de fruits
... limonade	... cappucino	... chocolat	... bière allemande	... verre de rouge	... verre de champagne
... kir	... thé citron	... café au lait	... café crème	... boisson alcoolisée	... citron pressé
... thé nature	... boisson chaude	... Évian	... expresso	... orange pressée	... Perrier

1er Modèle:	1er partenaire:	*—Je désire **un Coca,** s'il vous plaît.*
	2e partenaire:	*—Moi, je désire **une limonade,** s'il vous plaît.*
2e Modèle:	1er partenaire:	*—Je voudrais **un verre de blanc,** s'il vous plaît.*
	2e partenaire:	*—Et moi, je voudrais **une boisson chaude,** s'il vous plaît.*

B. **On prend la commande.** *(I'll take the order.)* Now, with your partner, take turns playing the role of a waiter or waitress and a customer in a café. Refer to **Scènes 1–6** on page 10 for ideas. Don't forget to use several polite expressions for beginning and ending your requests and comments.

Modèle:	Serveur:	*Madame, vous désirez?*
	Cliente:	*Je désire (Je voudrais, Donnez-moi, etc.) un Perrier (un café crème, un thé nature, etc.), s'il vous plaît.*
	Serveur:	*Voilà un Perrier (un café crème, un thé nature, etc.) pour madame.*
	Cliente:	*Merci, monsieur.*
	Serveur:	*Je vous en prie, madame.*

serveur is *a waiter;* **serveuse,** *a waitress.* **Garçon** can also be used for waiter, but is becoming outdated, being considered less politically correct.

C. **On prend quelque chose?** In groups of three or four (a waiter and two or three customers), join some friends at a café and order something to eat and drink from a waiter or waitress. Take turns taking the lead to (1) suggest getting something to drink and eat, (2) call the server to your table, and (3) elicit orders from everyone. Be sure to (4) thank your server, who will (5) verify the orders by repeating them and respond to your thanks. Use **Scènes 7** and **8** as a model.

Scène 7
—On prend quelque chose?
—Oui, bonne idée! Je voudrais une eau minérale, un Perrier.
—Et tu voudrais quelque chose à manger°?
—Voyons... je vais prendre une omelette au fromage.

Scène 8
—Et pour toi, Marie-Laure?
—Moi, je préfère un sandwich au jambon, avec une salade mixte.
—Et comme boisson°?
—Une bière allemande, s'il vous plaît.
—Très bien.

manger: *to eat*
comme boisson: *as a drink*

Chapitre 1

PRONONCIATION: Rythme et accentuation

French is a less tonic language than English. In English, a stressed syllable may appear at the beginning, middle, or end of a word. Imagine how difficult it is for a student of English to understand the tonic variations in the following sentences:

> Your French is **PER**fect!   Per**FECT** your French!
> You speak French to per**FEC**tion!

In French, only the final syllable of words or phrases is emphasized. The other syllables carry an equal weight when pronounced. Compare the use of stress in the two languages by reading the samples below:

> English: I would LIKE to INtroDUCE my COLLeague.
> French: BonJOUR! Enchanté de faire votre connaiSSANCE.

Additionally, in English the voice tends to "fall" at the end of words in a list; the opposite is true of French where the voice rises at the end of words in a list until you reach the last item, which falls. Schematically, then, the two languages might look like this:

I would like a ham sand ↓wich, a sal ↓ad, and some lemon ↓ade, please.

Je voudrais un sandwich au jam ↑bon, une sa ↑lade, et une limo ↓nade, s'il vous plaît.

À vous! With a partner, practice what you've just learned about French rhythm and accentuation by reading the dialogue below.

—Bonjour, monsieur.
—Bonjour, madame. Comment allez-vous?
—Je vais bien, merci.
—Comment vous appelez-vous?
—Je m'appelle Marguerite Dupont.
—Moi, je suis Yannick Bresson.
—Enchantée de faire votre connaissance.
—C'est un plaisir, madame.

LEXIQUE

Expressions pour le café

Pour suggérer quelque chose
On prend quelque chose?
Allons-y!

Pour offrir quelque chose
Vous désirez?
Tu voudrais quelque chose?
Et pour toi?
Et pour vous?
Et comme boisson?

Pour attirer l'attention
Mademoiselle? Madame? Monsieur?
S'il vous plaît?
Pardon?
Excusez-moi?

Pour hésiter
Euh...
Voyons...

Expressions de politesse
Ah, pardon, mademoiselle/madame/monsieur.
S'il vous plaît.
Merci, monsieur.
Je vous en prie, madame.

Pour répondre à une suggestion
Bonne idée!
Très bien.

Pour passer la commande
Je vais prendre...
Je désire...
Pour moi,...
Moi, je préfère...
Donnez-moi...
Je voudrais...

Pour répondre
Oui, monsieur, j'arrive.

~~ Café du Jour ~~

BOISSONS CHAUDES

un express	*black coffee*
un café crème	*coffee with cream*
un café au lait	*coffee with hot milk*
un cappucino	*capuccino*
un thé nature	*plain tea*
un thé citron	*tea with lemon*
un thé au lait	*tea with milk*
un chocolat	*hot chocolate*

BOISSONS FROIDES

un Coca	*Coke*
une eau minérale	*mineral water*
un Perrier (eau gazeuse), un Évian (eau plate)	*carbonated water non-carbonated water*
une limonade	*lemon-flavored carbonated beverage*
un citron pressé	*fresh-squeezed lemonade*
une orange pressée	*fresh-squeezed orange juice*
un Orangina	*orange-flavored carbonated drink*
un jus de fruits	*fruit juice*

BOISSONS ALCOOLISÉES

un verre de rouge	*a glass of red wine*
un verre de blanc	*a glass of white wine*
un verre de rosé	*a glass of rosé wine*
un kir	*a before-dinner drink of white wine with cream of cassis liqueur*
un verre de champagne	*a glass of champagne*
un demi	*a glass of draft beer*
une bière (mexicaine, canadienne, allemande)	*a beer (Mexican, Canadian, German)*

SANDWICHES

un sandwich au jambon	*a ham sandwich*
un sandwich au fromage	*a cheese sandwich*
un panini	*a hot, "wrapped" sandwich with a variety of grilled ingredients, as selected by the client*
un croque-monsieur	*a hot ham and cheese sandwich, topped with grilled cheese*
un croque-madame	*a hot ham and cheese sandwich, topped with a fried egg*

OMELETTES

une omelette au jambon	*a ham omelet*
une omelette au fromage	*a cheese omelet*
une omelette nature	*a plain omelet*

SALADES

une salade mixte	*a tossed salad*
une salade niçoise	*a mixed salad with tuna, eggs, and olives, typical of the south of France and named after the city of Nice*

ET AUSSI

des frites	*French fries*
un croissant	*a croissant*
un éclair	*a chocolate éclair (pastry)*

3ᴱ THÈME: Parlons des intérêts

Objective: To express interests and opinions

originaire: *originally*

Anne-Sophie est ma meilleure amie.
Elle est d'Atlanta, mais elle est originaire°
   de Québec.
Elle adore voyager à Paris et parler français.
Elle aime le vin français et la cuisine italienne.
Elle préfère la musique classique.

Voici mon ami Jean.
Il désire être acteur.
Il aime jouer au tennis.
Il déteste les maths.
Il adore les voitures de sport et l'Internet.
Il préfère la musique reggae.

STRATÉGIES D'ANALYSE

1. Look at the photographs. What would you guess the relationship to be between the two people in each picture?
2. Now look at the captions. Using any words that look similar to English words that you know (cognates), tell what kinds of information are being given about each photo.

Structure: Les pronoms sujets

OBSERVATIONS

—Bonjour, Jean-Luc. **Tu** vas bien?
—Euh, assez bien, mais **je** suis fatigué. J'ai mal dormi.

—Bonjour, **je** m'appelle Laure Beauchamps. Et toi, **tu** t'appelles comment?
—Moi, **je** suis Éric Berger.

—Bonjour, monsieur. Comment allez-**vous**?
—**Je** vais bien, merci. Et vous, madame?
—Très bien, merci.

—Bonjour, monsieur. Comment vous appelez-**vous**?
—**Je** m'appelle Claude Roget.

1. Study the four conversational exchanges. Can you find two different ways of saying *you*? What do you know about the two people in each conversation based on how they say *you*?

2. What pronoun do we use in French to refer to ourselves? What happens to this pronoun before a vowel?

3. Now look again at the captions under the drawings in the **Présentation**. Which pronoun replaces the name of Anne-Sophie? Which one refers to Jean?

PRÉCISIONS

• The subject of a verb represents the "doer" of the action. It can be identified either by using the name of the doer or by using a pronoun as a substitute for the name. French uses the following subject pronouns:

	Singular			Plural
1st:	**je (j')**	*I*	**nous**	*we*
2nd:	**tu**	*you (informal)*	**vous**	*you*
3rd:	**il**	*he/it*	**ils**	*they*
	elle	*she/it*	**elles**	*they*
	on	*one/people/we (colloquial)*		

• The subjects of verbs are generally thought of as belonging to one of three "persons."
1st person: When the doer of the verb is the same as or includes the *speaker*, the subject pronoun and verb belong to the first-person category. First-person pronouns include **je** and **nous**.

   *Moi? **Je** m'appelle Claude.*   *Nous? **Nous** allons très bien, merci.*

2nd person: When the doer of the verb is the same as or includes the *person spoken to*, the subject and verb belong to the second-person category. Second-person pronouns include **tu** and **vous**.

   *Bonjour, Claude. Comment vas-**tu**?*   *Toi et Marc, comment allez-**vous**?*

3rd person: When the doer of the verb is the same as or includes the *person spoken about*, the subject and verb belong to the third-person category. Third-person pronouns include **elle, il, on, ils,** and **elles.**

   *Mon amie, **elle** adore voyager.*   *Marc et Jean, **ils** désirent une bière.*
   *Marc, **il** préfère la musique jazz.*   *Monsieur et Madame Duclos, **ils** vont*
                                      bien?
   *En France **on** parle français.*   *Lisette et Marie, **elles** parlent français.*

A. **Mon ami et moi...** Imagine that you are going to tell your partner about the activities of some of your acquaintances as well as yourself. Begin each statement with one of the expressions given, then decide which subject pronoun you would use to continue talking about the person.

Modèles: Moi
Moi, **je**...

Mon ami et Luc
Mon ami et Luc, **ils**...

1. Toi / Nous / Moi / Mon ami
   (handwritten above: Tu   Nous   Je   Il)
2. Mon amie et moi / Éric / Éric et Lisette / Julie et Mireille
3. Le directeur du bureau / Ton collègue et toi / Madame Tremblay / Toi et moi
4. Luc, Marie-Laure et toi / Marie-Laure et Christine / Le professeur / Les amies

Structure: Le verbe être

OBSERVATIONS

Je **suis** de San Francisco.
I am from San Francisco.

Nous **sommes** de San Francisco.
We are from San Francisco.

Tu **es** de Richmond?
You are from Richmond?

Vous **êtes** de Seattle?
You are from Seattle?

Éric **est** de Chicago.
Eric is from Chicago.

Paul et Marc **sont** de Miami.
Paul and Marc are from Miami.

Anne **est** de New York City.
Anne is from New York City.

Jeanne et Pauline **sont** d'Orlando.
Jeanne and Pauline are from Orlando.

STRATÉGIES D'ANALYSE

1. Look at the forms of the verb *to be* in English in the preceding examples. Are they based directly on their infinitive, *to be*?
2. Now look at the forms of the verb **être** in French. Do some of them also look very different from their infinitive, **être**? Which ones?

PRÉCISIONS

The forms of the verb *être (to be)* are irregular in French (just as those of *to be* are in English).

je **suis**	*I am*	nous **sommes**	*we are*
tu **es**	*you are*	vous **êtes**	*you are*
il **est**	*he/it is*	ils **sont**	*they are*
elle **est**	*she/it is*	elles **sont**	*they are*
on **est**	*one is/people/we are*		

Éric et Anne-Marie sont de Paris.

B. **Je suis de...** Say where the people are from by completing each sentence with the appropriate form of **être.**

Modèle: Je *suis* de New York.

1. Moi, je _____ de Fort Lauderdale.
2. Catherine Deneuve, elle_____ de Paris.
3. Paul McCartney et Ringo Starr, ils _____ de Liverpool.
4. Mon/Ma meilleur(e) ami(e) et moi, nous _____ de Montréal.
5. Tu _____ de Londres?
6. Vous _____ de Strasbourg?
7. Le professeur de français _____ de Bordeaux.

Structure: La préposition de

OBSERVATIONS

Monique est **de** Paris.	*Monique is **from** Paris.*
Jean-Luc est **d'**Ottawa.	*Jean-Luc is **from** Ottawa.*
Carlos est **de** Madrid.	*Carlos is **from** Madrid.*

STRATÉGIES D'ANALYSE

1. What word do the French use before a city name to express *from*?
2. What happens if the city name begins with a vowel?

- The preposition **de** means *from* when it comes before the name of a city.

Vous êtes **de** Miami?	*You are **from** Miami?*
Je suis **de** Dallas.	*I am **from** Dallas.*

- Before a city name beginning with a vowel sound, the **de** contracts to **d'**.

Tu es **d'**Atlanta?	*You are **from** Atlanta?*

- The **de** also contracts to **d'** before the word **où** in the question, *"From where . . . ?"*

D'où êtes-vous?	***Where** are you **from**?*
D'où est ton ami?	***From where is** your friend?*

Note that since **ma famille** is only one family it uses the third-person singular of the verb: **Ma famille est...** (My family *is* . . .)

C. D'où est ton ami(e)? Say where the following people are from, using the appropriate form of **être** and the preposition **de**.

Modèles: moi   *Je **suis de** Detroit.*
             ma famille   *Ma famille **est d'**Ottawa.*

États-Unis: *United States*

1. moi / mes grands-parents / les Chicago Bulls / le président des États-Unis°

grand-mère: *grandmother*

2. toi et ta famille / les acteurs de cinéma / ma meilleure amie / ma grand-mère°

3. mon professeur favori / ma famille et moi / les Washington Redskins / Oprah Winfrey

Structure: Les questions

OBSERVATIONS

Tu es de Denver?	*You are from Denver?*
Vous êtes d'IBM?	*You are from IBM?*
Tu t'appelles comment?	*What is your name?*
Ça va bien?	*It's going all right?*

STRATÉGIES D'ANALYSE

If you heard these sentences, how could you tell that they were questions?

• One way that the French ask questions is by intonation, that is, by raising the voice at the end of an utterance in a questioning manner. You can identify written questions of this type by the question mark at the end of the sentence, as in English.

Ça va?	*Is it going all right?*
Vous êtes M. Carrier d'IBM?	*You are Mr. Carrier from IBM?*
Et votre prénom?	*And your first name?*
Vous êtes de Chicago?	*You are from Chicago?*

D. **Vous êtes de... ?** Find out from as many of your classmates as possible what town they are from. Your goal is to find the largest number of different hometowns.

> **Modèle:** —*D'où êtes-vous? Vous êtes de Seattle?*
> —*Non, je suis de Memphis.*

E. **On pose des questions.** Find out the following information from your partner, using the intonation style. Use the questions that you have already been practicing in this chapter. Find out:

1. How it's going.
2. What her/his name is.
3. If he/she is tired.
4. If he/she wants something (to eat or drink).
5. If he/she prefers coffee or tea.
6. If he/she is from Orlando.

Vocabulaire: Des verbes d'opinion

J'**aime** dîner au restaurant.	*I **like** to have dinner out.*
J'**adore** voyager.	*I **love** to travel.*
Je **désire** parler français.	*I **want** to speak French.*
Je **déteste** étudier les sciences.	*I **detest** studying science.*
Je **préfère** étudier le français.	*I **prefer** to study French.*
Paul **aime** travailler sur l'Internet.	*Paul **likes** to work on the Internet.*
Il **adore** jouer au foot°.	*He **adores** playing soccer.*
Il **désire** être ingénieur.	*He **wants** to be an engineer.*
Il **déteste** voyager.	*He **hates** to travel.*
Il **préfère** étudier les maths.	*He **prefers** to study math.*

J'aime jouer au foot.

foot *soccer*

Monique **aime** la musique populaire.	*Monique **likes** popular music.*
Elle **adore** la musique rock.	*She **adores** rock and roll.*
Elle **désire** une voiture de sport.	*She **wants** a sports car.*
Elle **déteste** le cinéma.	*She **hates** the movies.*
Elle **préfère** les concerts.	*She **prefers** concerts.*
Et toi? Tu **aimes** le shopping?	*And you? Do you **like** shopping?*
Tu **adores** le cinéma?	*Do you **love** the movies?*
Tu **désires** être professeur?	*Do you **want** to be a professor?*
Tu **détestes** le football américain?	*Do you **detest** football?*
Tu **préfères** jouer au tennis?	*Do you **prefer** to play tennis?*

STRATÉGIES D'ANALYSE

1. Look at the verbs in boldface type in the sentences (**aime, adore, désire, déteste, préfère**). What is the subject of the verb when the verb ends in **-s**? What subjects can be used when the verb does not end in **-s**?

2. Look again at the first two sets of sentences. In each of these sentences, there is a second verb immediately following the verb of opinion. These second verbs are all in the infinitive form (the "to do something" form). Can you find any other infinitives in the rest of the sentences?

3. Besides opinions about activities, what other likes and dislikes are mentioned in these examples?

PRÉCISIONS

- You can express an opinion in French by using the following verbs:

adorer	*to adore, to be crazy about*
aimer	*to like, to love*
désirer	*to want, to desire*
détester	*to detest, to hate*
préférer	*to prefer, to like better*

- The object of an opinion can be named by using a noun after the verb.

J'adore la **musique** classique.	*I adore classical **music.***
J'aime la **cuisine** mexicaine.	*I like Mexican **food.***
Je désire un **citron pressé.**	*I want a **lemonade.***
Je déteste le **shopping.**	*I hate **shopping.***
Je préfère le **cinéma.**	*I prefer the **movies.***

- The French can also state their opinion about activities by using a second verb after the opinion verb. Note that it is the second verb that names the activity. The second verb is always in the infinitive form.

J'adore **voyager.**	*I love **to travel.***
J'aime **dîner** au restaurant.	*I like **to have dinner** at a restaurant.*
Je désire **parler** français.	*I want **to speak** French.*
Je déteste **jouer** au foot.	*I hate **to play** soccer.*
Je préfère **travailler** sur l'Internet.	*I prefer **to work** on the Internet.*

- These verbs look alike and sound alike in the **je, il,** and **elle** forms. The **tu** form also sounds like the others although it is spelled with an **-s** on the end.

J'**aime** la musique jazz.	*I **like** jazz.*
Il **aime** la musique classique.	*He **likes** classical music.*
Elle **aime** la musique reggae.	*She **likes** reggae.*
Tu **aimes** la musique rock?	*Do you **like** rock?*

F. J'aime... Ask your partner his/her opinion about the following activities. Then express your own. Use each opinion verb **(aimer, adorer, désirer, détester, préférer)** at least once in your statements. Consult the phrases in **Expressions d'opinion** (page 27) for ideas in personalizing your comments. Take turns with your partner asking the questions.

Modèle 1: 1er partenaire: *Tu aimes étudier les maths?*
2e partenaire: *J'adore étudier les maths, et toi?*
1er partenaire: *Je préfère étudier le français.*

Modèle 2: 1er partenaire: *Tu désires voyager à Rome?*
2e partenaire: *Oui, j'aime Rome. Et toi?*
1er partenaire: *Moi aussi°, mais je préfère voyager à Paris.*   **aussi:** *also, too*

1. étudier les maths
2. voyager à Paris
3. dîner au restaurant
4. travailler

5. travailler sur l'Internet
6. parler espagnol
7. jouer au foot

G. Tu aimes... ? Now compare your interests and those of your partner by filling in the chart. Be sure to vary your use of the opinion verbs **(aimer, adorer, désirer, détester, préférer).**

Modèle: —*Moi, j'adore la musique reggae. Et toi?*
—*Moi aussi, j'aime la musique reggae.*

moi			mon/ma partenaire
J'adore		la musique reggae	**Il/Elle aime**
		les voitures classiques	
		la bière mexicaine	
		les concerts de rock	
		voyager	
		le shopping	
		jouer au foot	
		le vin français	

PRONONCIATION: Les signes diacritiques

The following five diacritical signs (accent marks) are used when writing in French. It is important when learning vocabulary that you memorize the placement of these signs, since words written without them are considered misspelled. Sometimes, these signs alone distinguish two or more words that have otherwise identical spellings but very different meanings, as in the homophones **ou** *(or)* and **où** *(where)*. Also, as you become more familiar with French orthography, the diacritical marks will help you to pronounce French words correctly.

L'accent aigu (´) is used only over the vowel **e** ➜ **é**, as in *présenter* and *café*.

L'accent grave (`) appears above the vowels **a, e,** and **u** ➜ **à, è, ù,** as in the sentences: *Où est ton père? Ah, le voilà!*

L'accent circonflexe (^) may appear above all French vowels ➜ **â, ê, î, ô, û,** as in the following words: *pâtisserie, forêt, île, hôpital, coûte.*

La cédille (ç) appears only below the letter **c** ➜ **Ç, ç** and is used to distinguish a hard *c* sound ([k], as in *café*) from its soft pronunciation ([s], as in *Ça va?*).

Le tréma (¨) is rarer than the others, but may appear above one vowel of a series to indicate that the vowels are to be pronounced separately, as in the words *Noël = No-ël* and *maïs = ma-is.*

> The **accent circonflexe** is often used to indicate the omission of an "s" in the original Latin. Many of these words kept the "s" in the English version.

Note: Diacritical signs are sometimes omitted in capitalization: Émile Zola, Emile Zola.

À vous! Repeat after your instructor each of the following phrases that you've already learned, paying special attention to the appearance and pronunciation of the diacritical marks.

Répétez, s'il vous plaît!
Bonjour! Ça va?
À bientôt!

Qu'est-ce que tu préfères?
Un citron pressé.
Moi, non. Je déteste ça!

Éric, je te présente Thérèse.
Enchanté. Vous êtes française?
Non, américaine.

Répondez à la question!
Un moment. Je réfléchis° sur le modèle.

> **réfléchir:** *to think*

LEXIQUE

Expressions d'opinion

Pour donner une opinion

j'aime...	*I like . . .*	tu détestes...	*you hate . . .*
il adore...	*he adores . . .*	tu préfères...	*you prefer . . .*
elle désire...	*she wants . . .*		

Pour compléter une opinion

la musique	*music*	dîner au restaurant	*to have dinner out*
classique	*classical*	voyager	*to travel*
jazz	*jazz*	parler français	*to speak French*
rock	*rock*	étudier	*to study*
reggae	*reggae*	les maths	*math*
populaire	*popular*	les sciences	*science*
les sports (m.)	*sports*	le français	*French*
le foot(ball)	*soccer*	jouer...	*to play . . .*
le football américain	*football*	au foot(ball)	*soccer*
le tennis	*tennis*	au football américain	*football*
le cinéma	*movies*	au tennis	*tennis*
les concerts (m.)	*concerts*	être...	*to be . . .*
le shopping	*shopping*	professeur	*a professor/teacher*
les voitures (f.) de sport	*sports cars*	ingénieur	*an engineer*
la cuisine italienne	*Italian food*	acteur / actrice	*an actor/actress*
le vin français	*French wine*	travailler	*to work*
la bière mexicaine	*Mexican beer*		

ÉCOUTONS: On fait connaissance

Imagine that we have stopped in at a sidewalk café in Paris and asked three people to tell us a little bit about themselves. Listen to their monologues, and fill out the two charts to indicate your comprehension of what they are saying. Read the charts before listening to acquaint yourself with the context.

A. On identifie le monologue. Listen for the phrases or the information that appear on the left side of the chart. Place a checkmark in the box under the column of the monologue in which that phrase or information occurs.

	Monologue #1	Monologue #2	Monologue #3
Greeting used			
Bonjour			
Salut			
How name is given			
Je suis...			
Je m'appelle..			
Mon nom est...			
Permettez-moi de me présenter...			
Preferences			
Likes cars			
Likes music			
Wants to travel			
Likes movies			

B. On cherche les détails. Now listen to the monologues again, this time for additional details. Read the chart first, and then listen and write your answers in **English**.

	1st speaker	Her best friend	2nd speaker	3rd speaker
Name of person		Virginie	Jacques Dumas	
Where person is from				
Drink ordered	tea with lemon			
Food ordered				
Profession (desired)				engineer
Preferred pastime		playing piano		

Ah! Voilà les boissons.

INTÉGRATION: Rendez-vous au café

Role-play the scenario in a group of three.

Scenario: You and a friend arrive at a café and run into another friend whom one of you knows. After introductions are made, discuss what you will order. Then tell each other some details about yourself and the new acquaintances: where people are from and things that they like as well as some things they may not like. Finding and commenting on interests you have in common will enhance the interactive nature of your conversation.

Student A: Greet the friend you run into and introduce your two friends to each other. Say what you would like to eat and drink. Tell each friend at least three things about the other (for example, where he/she is from, what kind of music or forms of entertainment he/she likes, some activities he/she likes or doesn't like, etc.).

Students B and C: Greet your friend and respond appropriately to the introductions. Tell what you would like to eat and drink. One of you should take the lead organizing the orders and the other can place the orders with an imaginary waiter. Ask and respond to questions and statements about where everyone is from and what kinds of things and activities you like, finding similarities and differences among your interests. «**Moi aussi, je...**» and «**Marc aussi, il...**» can be useful for saying "Me, too, I . . ." and "Marc too, he . . ." whereas «**Pas moi, je préfère...**» can enable you to point out differences, "Not me, I prefer . . .".

N.B. You will earn points for making this conversation as realistic and interactive as possible and for using the conversational strategies and courtesies presented in the chapter. You should ask questions and, when answering questions, you should give more than **oui** or **non** in your answer (for example, **Non, je n'aime pas la musique classique. Je préfère la musique reggae.**) Don't forget the French expressions **euh, voyons,** etc., to signal that you are thinking about your question or answer.

INTERACTIONS EN CLASSE

Beginning in *Chapitre 2,* some of the activities will be written in French. Most of the words in the direction lines will be obvious to you because of their resemblance to English. The following list previews some expressions you will see. They are divided into sections that reflect the processes of gathering information, reflecting on the information to establish your opinions about it, and discussing your ideas with others.

Jumelage *(Matching).* Beside the randomly ordered list of expressions in French, there is an alphabetized list of their English counterparts. Match the English expressions with their French equivalents.

ACQUISITION DES INFORMATIONS

3	Regardez les dessins	1	*Consult the chart*
1	Consultez le tableau	2	*Examine the survey*
6	Étudiez le modèle	3	*Look at the drawings*
2	Examinez le sondage	4	*Read the text*
4	Lisez le texte	5	*Request information*
5	Demandez des informations	6	*Study the model*
7	Employez les images	7	*Use the images*

DÉVELOPPEMENT DES OPINIONS

3	Rangez par ordre de priorité	1	*Add an example*
2	Analysez	2	*Analyze*
8	Évaluez	3	*Arrange in order of priority*
12	Écrivez un paragraphe	4	*Choose a response*
7	Déterminez	5	*Compare*
5	Comparez	6	*Detail*
4	Choisissez une réponse	7	*Determine*
11	Réfléchissez sur	8	*Evaluate*
9	Faites une liste	9	*Make a list*
1	Ajoutez un exemple	10	*Prepare a report*
10	Préparez un rapport	11	*Reflect on/Consider/Think about*
6	Détaillez	12	*Write a paragraph*

DISCUSSION

____	Rapportez	1	*Communicate your ideas*
____	Discutez	2	*Complete*
____	Négociez	3	*Decide together*
____	Décrivez la photo	4	*Describe the photo*
____	Indiquez	5	*Discuss*
____	Donnez une opinion	6	*Explain your opinion*
____	Expliquez votre opinion	7	*Give an opinion*
____	Complétez	8	*Indicate*
____	Mentionnez	9	*Mention*
____	Communiquez vos idées	10	*Negotiate*
____	Dites à votre partenaire	11	*Practice in a team*
____	Décidez ensemble	12	*Recount/Tell about*
____	Suggérez	13	*Report*
____	Travaillez en groupe	14	*Suggest*
____	Pratiquez en équipe	15	*Tell your partner*
____	Racontez	16	*Work in a group*

MOI, MON TRAVAIL ET MES LOISIRS

Communicative Objectives

- To identify, prioritize, and schedule daily routines and responsibilities
- To discuss academic schedules and responsibilities
- To describe the ways that you spend your time off

Thematic Objectives

- ✓ To examine indicators of stress and educational experiences
- ✓ To identify life experiences (outside of the context of work and school) that have contributed to your personal development
- ✓ To relate your own skills, knowledge, and interests to those defined in specific job offerings

OUVERTURE EN VIDÉO:
On s'identifie

La mise en scène

A. On s'identifie. In *Chapitre 2* you learn to identify yourself to others. Consider which items in the following chart you might include if you were asked to stand up before the class and give a brief personal introduction. Decide, too, which details you would prefer not to share.

Name	Current or anticipated profession
Phone number	Field of study
Address	Marital status
Where you're from	Age
Leisure time activities	Current or anticipated salary
What languages you speak	Religion

Les paroles et le sens

In this lesson, you will learn to express who you are, where you are from, and what you do, or plan to do, as a profession. Watch or listen to the video to hear how some French speakers identify themselves.

B. Votre guide de Paris. First you will learn more details about Xavier, your guide from Paris. Before you watch the video, read the questions to prepare yourself for the information you will need. Listen to Xavier tell about himself, and then answer the questions.

1. Which word does Xavier use to describe his marital status?
   a. marié   b. célibataire

2. Your Parisian guide also gives his profession. Which word do you hear him mention?
   a. journaliste   c. professeur
   b. avocat

C. Votre guide du Canada. Monique, your guide from Canada, tells you where she is from and something about her ancestors from France.

1. What word do you hear Monique use to identify her nationality?
   a. française   c. canadienne
   b. québécoise

2. She also talks about the professions of her ancestors and some members of her family. Which three of the following professions do you hear her mention?
   a. cultivateurs   d. médecin
   b. ingénieurs   e. infirmière
   c. musicien

D. Votre guide des Caraïbes. Now we will go to the Caribbean to learn more about your hostess from there.

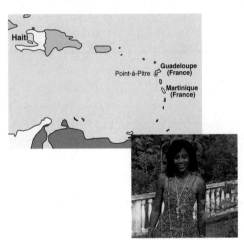

1. Which Caribbean island does Christine say she is from?
   a. Martinique   c. Guadeloupe
   b. Haïti

2. Which word do you hear her use to identify her profession?
   a. professeur   c. avocate
   b. coiffeuse

3. Christine also gives her marital status. Which term do you hear?
   a. mariée   b. célibataire

E. De nouveaux amis. Now that you know something about your guides, let's meet some members of your film crew from Canada and see what they tell us about themselves. Look at the chart. Beside the name of each person, put the letter of his/her profession and marital status, as indicated below.

Profession		État civil	
I	Ingénieur	M	marié(e)
C	Comédienne	C	célibataire
M	Maquilleuse	D	divorcé(e)
EC	Éclairagiste de cinéma	CON	conjoint(e)

Nom	Profession	État civil
James		
Brigitte		
Normand		
Marie-Christine		

On y réfléchit

F. On invite de nouveaux amis. Think back over the seven people who have just introduced themselves on the video. Consider which ones you might like (1) to join you as your guest at a party, (2) to be a guest speaker in your French class, and (3) to invite you to be a guest in their home. Check the appropriate columns.

Name	I'd like to have as my party guest	I'd like to have as a speaker in French class	I'd like to be invited to visit their home
Xavier, français, journaliste			
Monique, québécoise, étudiante			
Christine, guadeloupéenne, professeur			
James, ontarien, éclairagiste de cinéma			
Brigitte, québécoise, maquilleuse			
Normand, ingénieur de son°			
Marie-Christine, comédienne°			

ingénieur de son: *sound engineer* **comédienne:** *actress*

Objective: To give information about who you are and where you are from

PRÉSENTATION: Un coup d'œil sur le thème

Scène 1
—Ah! C'est un permis de conduire international. Quelle est votre nationalité?
—Je suis américain.

Scène 2
—Votre passeport, s'il vous plaît, mademoiselle. Ah, vous êtes du Québec? Vous parlez anglais?
—Oui, je parle anglais et français.

Scène 3
—Vous payez par carte de crédit?
—Oui, voici ma carte Visa.
—Et quel est votre numéro de téléphone, madame?

Stratégies

Many French words have counterparts in English that closely resemble them. These similar words are called *cognates.* Look at the following examples.

French	English
nationalité	nationality
université	university
américain	American
collègue	colleague

Sometimes the cognates are sufficient to tell you what someone is talking about, even if you don't understand everything that is being said.

1. Look at the photographs above. What kinds of identification do you expect a person to show in these three situations?
2. Now skim the captions to find the French expressions for these pieces of identification.
3. Skim the captions again to find other cognates. Look only for cognates; don't try to read every word.
4. The long dash at the beginning of a line in the captions indicates a change of speaker in the conversation. Based on the information in the photographs along with cognates that you can decipher, give a one-sentence description of what is happening in each conversation.

À propos des stratégies: You have probably guessed the English cognate for THÈMES. And the meaning of **identité** is easy to guess, thanks to its cognate *identity.* This kind of inferring is an especially important tool for understanding as you begin learning a language.

POUR DÉVELOPPER VOTRE FRANÇAIS

Vocabulaire: Pour parler de la nationalité

OBSERVATIONS

Ils sont nord-américains.

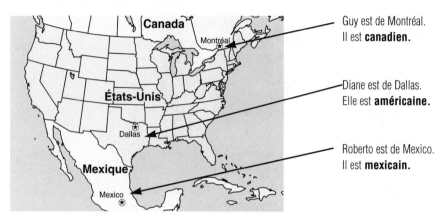

Guy est de Montréal.
Il est **canadien.**

Diane est de Dallas.
Elle est **américaine.**

Roberto est de Mexico.
Il est **mexicain.**

Ils sont européens.

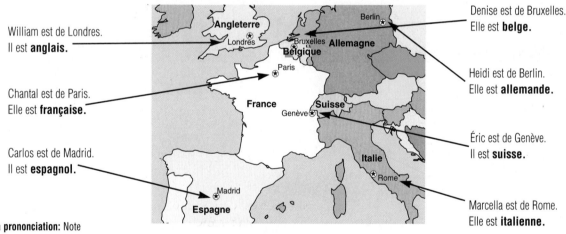

William est de Londres.
Il est **anglais.**

Chantal est de Paris.
Elle est **française.**

Carlos est de Madrid.
Il est **espagnol.**

Denise est de Bruxelles.
Elle est **belge.**

Heidi est de Berlin.
Elle est **allemande.**

Éric est de Genève.
Il est **suisse.**

Marcella est de Rome.
Elle est **italienne.**

À propos de la prononciation: Note that the addition of an **-e** normally causes a silent final consonant to be pronounced. Example: **anglais, anglaise.**

Ils sont africains.

Mohamed est de Casablanca.
Il est **marocain.**

Assika est de Dakar.
Elle est **sénégalaise.**

Ils sont asiatiques.

Ling est de Beijing.
Elle est **chinoise.**

Koji est de Tokyo.
Il est **japonais.**

STRATÉGIES D'ANALYSE

1. Which words indicate nationality? Point out some that are similar in form.
2. What difference in capitalization can you find between English and French?

PRÉCISIONS

- To give a person's nationality, use an adjective, often formed from the name of the country.

    Marco est **italien.**   Je suis **espagnol(e).**
    *Marco is **Italian.***   *I am **Spanish.***

- To tell which city someone is from, use the preposition **de** and the name of that city.

    Il est **de** Rome.   Je suis **de** Madrid.
    *He is **from** Rome.*   *I am **from** Madrid.*

- Adjectives that indicate nationality in French are not capitalized as they are in English.

    Guy est **canadien.**   Chantal est **française.**
    *Guy is **Canadian.***   *Chantal is **French.***

Structure: L'accord des adjectifs

OBSERVATIONS

Guy est de Montréal.   Michelle est de Toronto.
Il est **canadien.**   Elle est **canadienne.**

Rémi est de Nice.   Chantal est de Paris.
Il est **français.**   Elle est **française.**

Ali est de Casablanca.   Aïcha est de Rabat.
Il est **marocain.**   Elle est **marocaine.**

Guy et Michelle sont **nord-américains.**
Rémi et Chantal sont **européens.**
Ali et Aïcha sont **africains.**

STRATÉGIES D'ANALYSE

1. Do you notice any differences in the words used to give the nationality of males and females?
2. What letter is on the end of nationalities that refer to females?
3. What ending is added to words describing the nationality of more than one person?
4. If a group of people includes both males and females, do we use the masculine or the feminine form of the plural?

PRÉCISIONS

Gender distinctions in language are a fundamental difference between French and English.

- Adjectives can be used to describe someone's nationality. In French, an adjective agrees in gender and number with the noun it modifies.

Hans est **allemand.**   Marina est **allemande.**   Ils sont **allemands.**

- The feminine form of many French adjectives is made by adding **-e** to the masculine form.

David est **américain.**   Kimberly est **américaine** aussi.
Marc est **français.**   Monique est **française** aussi.
Ibrahim est **sénégalais.**   Ashrat est **sénégalaise** aussi.

- Some masculine adjectives end in an unaccented **-e.** The same form is used to modify both masculine and feminine nouns.

Éric est **suisse.**   Brigitte est **suisse** aussi.
Boris est **russe.**   Moira est **russe** aussi.

- The feminine form of adjectives ending in **-ien** is **-ienne.**

Guy est **canadien.**   Michelle est **canadienne** aussi.
Marco est **italien.**   Marcella est **italienne** aussi.

- The plural ending of most French adjectives is **-s.** It can be added to masculine or feminine forms. If an adjective already ends in **-s,** it does not need another **-s.**

Serge est **français.**   Aurélie est **française.**
Serge et Marc sont **français.**   Aurélie et Brigitte sont **françaises.**

- Groups that include both males and females require the masculine plural form.

Marco et Marcella sont **italiens.**

A. Ils sont d'où? Use the maps on page 36 to help you locate the cities. Then give the nationality of each of the following people.

Vocabulaire supplémentaire: Your friends and colleagues may be of nationalities other than the ones presented in this chapter. This **Vocabulaire supplémentaire** provides additional vocabulary you may use if you wish.

russe	russe
hollandais	hollandaise
irlandais	irlandaise
israélien	israélienne
vietnamien	vietnamienne

Modèle: Arlette est de Paris. Elle est *française.*

1. Jean-Claude est de Montréal. Il est... *Canadien*
2. Francine est aussi de Montréal. Elle est... *canadienne*
3. Aïcha et Ibrahim sont de Dakar. Ils sont... *sénégalaise*
4. Francesca est de Rome. Elle est... *Italienne*
5. Yasmina est de Casablanca. Elle est... *Marocaine*
6. Gilberto est de Mexico. Il est... *Mexicain*
7. Javier est de Madrid. Il est... *Espagnol*
8. Gérard est de Bruxelles. Il est... *Belge*
9. Sandra et Marina sont de Berlin. Elles sont... *Allemandes*

B. Je vous présente... You are working as an interpreter at an international party. Introduce the following people to your employer, telling the city they come from and their nationality. Switch roles with your partner.

Modèle: Christine et Albert (belge, Liège)
—*Je vous présente Christine et Albert. Ils sont belges. Ils sont de Liège.*
—*Enchanté(e) de faire votre connaissance.*

1. André et Marie-Christine (français, Toulouse) *e*
2. Jean-Claude et Sylvie (canadien, Trois-Rivières) *s*
3. Valérie (belge, Liège)
4. Patricia (anglais, Londres) *e*
5. Carlos et Cristina (espagnol, Ségovie) *s*
6. Frederick (allemand, Cologne)
7. Mario et Sophia (italien, Milan) *s*
8. Guy et Marie-Ange (français, Nantes) *es*
9. Yasmina (sénégalais, Dakar)
10. Marc (suisse, Montreux)

Vocabulaire: Pour discuter les langues du monde

OBSERVATIONS

Jean-Luc est français.	Il parle français.
Mario est italien.	Il parle italien.
Hiroki est japonais.	Il parle japonais.
Carlos est espagnol.	Il parle espagnol.

STRATÉGIES D'ANALYSE

1. In English, the names of languages are capitalized. Are they capitalized in French?
2. Compare the names of nationalities with the names of languages. What do you notice?

PRÉCISIONS

- The names of languages are often identical to the masculine singular form of the names of nationalities.

  Georges est **français**.   Il parle **français**.
  Christopher est **anglais**.   Il parle **anglais**.

- However, some languages are spoken in several countries, and some countries have more than one official language.

  Derek est **américain**.   Il parle **anglais**.
  François est **canadien**.   Il parle **français** et **anglais**.
  René est **belge**.   Il parle **français** et **flamand**.
  Bernard est **suisse**.   Il parle **français**, **italien** et **allemand**.

NOTE CULTURELLE

Flamand (*Flemish*) is one of the languages spoken in Flanders. Since the region lies along international borders, it has been divided by its more powerful neighbors—France, Belgium, and the Netherlands—throughout its history.

Flamand is one of the seven regional languages spoken in France—over 100,000 French speak and/or understand it. The other six regional languages are: **occitan**, spoken in the south of France; **alsacien** and **lorrain**, spoken in Alsace-Lorraine; **breton**, spoken in Brittany; **corse**, spoken in Corsica; **catalan**, spoken in the eastern part of the Pyrenees; and **basque**, spoken in the western part of the Pyrenees.

C. Qu'est-ce qu'ils parlent? Look at the sentences and the maps in the **Observations** on page 36. Take turns with your partner telling each person's nationality and, therefore, which language(s) he or she probably speaks.

> **Modèle:** *Chantal est française. Elle parle français.*

D. On parle... You and your partner have decided to work at a translation company. Tell your partner which city each employee is from, what the nationality of each person is, and which language(s) he or she speaks.

> **Modèle:** Charles, Londres
> *Charles est de Londres. Il est anglais, et il parle anglais.*

1. Jean-Claude
   Bruxelles
2. Marc
   Genève
3. Hiroki (*m.*)
   Tokyo
4. Jean-Yves
   Montréal
5. Ling (*f.*)
   Beijing
6. Charles
   Londres
7. David
   New York City
8. Elke (*f.*)
   Bonn

Vocabulaire: Pour donner l'état civil d'une personne

OBSERVATIONS

—Quel est votre **état civil**? Vous êtes **marié**?
—Non, je suis **célibataire.**

—Marie-Christine est **célibataire** aussi?
—Non, non. Marie-Christine est **mariée.**

—Jacques et Marianne? Ils sont **mariés**?
—Non, mais ils sont **conjoints.** Ils habitent ensemble° dans un appartement à Toulouse.

habitent ensemble: *live together*

—Et quel est **l'état civil** de Luc?
—Luc? Il est **divorcé.**

STRATÉGIES D'ANALYSE

1. What sort of personal information does one's **état civil** refer to?
2. Look at all the boldfaced words in the preceding sentences. Use the context of the conversation, the words you recognize, and a process of elimination to guess what the word **célibataire** means.
3. What about the word **conjoint?** Can you tell by the comment that follows it what the word **conjoint** means?
4. How does the spelling of **marié** change when it describes different people?
5. Can you guess how the word **divorcé** would be spelled if it were describing a woman?

PRÉCISIONS

- One's marital status (**état civil**) is an important aspect of one's identity for French-speaking people. The terms used to identify marital status are:

célibataire	*single*
conjoint(e)	*unmarried, living as a couple*
marié(e)	*married*
divorcé(e)	*divorced*
veuf (veuve)	*widowed*

- Like the adjectives of nationality, the adjectives describing marital status agree in gender and number with the person they modify.

Georges est **marié.**   Louise est **mariée.**
Mes parents sont **divorcés.**

E. **Quel est votre état civil?** In the time allotted to you, find out the marital status of as many of your classmates as possible. Anyone who prefers to keep this information private can answer: «**S'il vous plaît, cette information est privée.**»

Modèle 1: —*Quel est votre état civil?*
—*Moi, je suis marié(e).*

Modèle 2: —*Quel est votre état civil?*
—*S'il vous plaît, cette information est privée.*

Vocabulaire: Pour compter et donner la date (les chiffres et les mois)

OBSERVATIONS

0 1 2 3 4 5 6 7 8 9

À propos de la prononciation: The "t" of **et** is never pronounced.

0	zéro	16	seize	31	trente et un
1	un, une	17	dix-sept	32	trente-deux
2	deux	18	dix-huit	33	trente-trois
3	trois	19	dix-neuf	34	trente-quatre
4	quatre	20	vingt	35	trente-cinq
5	cinq	21	vingt et un	36	trente-six
6	six	22	vingt-deux	37	trente-sept
7	sept	23	vingt-trois	38	trente-huit
8	huit	24	vingt-quatre	39	trente-neuf
9	neuf	25	vingt-cinq		
10	dix	26	vingt-six		
11	onze	27	vingt-sept		
12	douze	28	vingt-huit		
13	treize	29	vingt-neuf		
14	quatorze	30	trente		
15	quinze				

1. janvier	4. avril	7. juillet	10. octobre
2. février	5. mai	8. août	11. novembre
3. mars	6. juin	9. septembre	12. décembre

STRATÉGIES D'ANALYSE

1. Which numerals look different from the English in their handwritten forms?
2. Does any number have both a masculine and a feminine form?
3. Are the names of the months capitalized in English? in French?

- Remember to use the masculine form **un** before a masculine noun and the feminine form **une** before a feminine noun.

- When writing dates numerically in French, give the day first, then the month.

  21/3 = March 21   **25/12** = December 25

- When expressing dates conversationally, also state the day before the month. (Note that there is no word equivalent to "of" in English.)

  Mon anniversaire est **le vingt et un mars.**   **21/3**
  Noël est **le vingt-cinq décembre.**   **25/12**

- When giving the first day of a month, use the word **premier.**

  Demain? C'est **le premier** septembre.

- Use **en** to say *in* or *during* a month.

  Mon anniversaire est **en** juin.

- The names of the months are not capitalized in French.

F. Quelle est la date? Give the following dates in French.

  Modèle: 16/8   *le seize août*

1. 21/3   5. 15/1
2. 8/4   6. 4/8
3. 18/9   7. 1/2
4. 1/7   8. 5/6

G. C'est quand, les fêtes? Use the calendar to give the date(s) when each of the following holidays takes place.

  Modèle: Noël *C'est le 25 décembre.*

1. le jour de l'An

2. la Saint-Valentin

3. la fête nationale française

4. la fête nationale américaine

5. la fête du travail française

H. **Ton anniversaire, c'est quand?** Ask your classmates when their birthdays are. Find out whose birthday is the nearest to today's date.

> **Modèle:** —C'est quand ton anniversaire?
> —Mon anniversaire est le quinze janvier.

I. **C'est moi.** Give your partner the information requested. Your partner will ask for and write down your information, then verify it with you. Then switch roles.

> **Modèle:** —Nom?   —Jack Silverman.
> —Date de naissance°?   —le 21 avril.
> —État civil?   —Célibataire.
> —Adresse?   —13 avenue Kennedy.

Date de naissance: *Date of birth*

Né(e) le...: *born on . . .*

PRONONCIATION: Les consonnes finales

Often the final consonants of French words are *silent;* this is the case for many words you have already learned, such as **anglais, juillet,** and **préférer.** But, you might ask, what about **espagnol, août,** and **professeur,** whose final consonants *are* pronounced?

The answer is that there are few foolproof rules regarding the pronunciation of final consonants. In this respect, French is similar to English. Think of the many ways that the combination "-ough" is pronounced in the English words *bough, cough, dough,* and *through!* In French, the pronunciation of sounds at the end of a word often depends on the word that follows it. An example of this is the **liaison** (discussed in the next **Thème**), which gives the language a more fluid rhythm by linking groups of words together phonetically.

Fortunately, as you acquire more vocabulary, you will become sensitive to such exceptions and recognize patterns that will guide you in pronouncing new words.

In the meanwhile, here are some helpful hints:
- If a word ends in **-e** or **-es,** the preceding consonant is pronounced. There are very few exceptions to this "rule." Compare the sounds of the following pairs of words:

hollandais	hollandaise	avocats	avocates
allemands	allemandes	chaud	chaude
étudiant	étudiante	intelligents	intelligentes

- The consonants **c, r, f,** and **l** *are usually pronounced* at the end of words. To remember this, think of the English word "CaReFuL."

  > Luc est ingénieur à Québec.
  > Cédric est professeur au Sénégal.
  > Charles Chawaf est veuf.

  The following are notable exceptions, since the final consonants of each are not pronounced: **porc** (pork); **blanc;** and words ending in **-ail (travail)** or **-eil (réveil,** alarm clock).

- A more detailed explanation of the sound **[r]** appears in *Chapitre 5.* For now, note that: **[r]** is *not* pronounced in **-er** verb infinitives, when it sounds instead like **-é: présenter, manger.** The same is *usually* true for the combination **-er** at the end of a word containing two or more syllables: **boulanger** (baker), **banquier, Perrier, février.** In most other cases, **[r]** *is* pronounced: **kir, cher, ingénieur, bonjour, éclair.**

- **Borrowed words** usually retain the final consonant sound in pronunciation (such as **l'Internet, le campus, le tennis,** and **le parking).**

À vous! With a partner, practice what you've just learned about final consonant pronunciation by reading the following phrases:

1. Elle parle anglais et créole.
2. Je désire une salade de tomates.
3. Je te présente Martine.
4. Didier Berger est veuf.
5. Quelle est la date de la fête?
6. Votre passeport, s'il vous plaît.
7. Mon anniversaire est le huit juin.
8. Isabella est italienne.
9. Il y a un parking sur le campus?
10. J'aime un bon vin sec.

POUR DÉVELOPPER VOS IDÉES

Thematic objective: To examine the degree to which you are willing to give information about yourself

Présentation: Les pièces d'identité

POUR SAISIR L'ESSENTIEL *(In order to get the main point)*: Day-to-day activities require us to provide various kinds of personal information. In this section, you examine the types of identification you use and how sensitive you consider that information.

Begin by looking at the passport. Make two lists, and label them **Informations privées** and **Informations non privées.** As you identify the types of information given on the passport, add them to the appropriate list. Then answer the question, "Would you agree to have your passport published in a textbook?"

À propos des stratégies: The activity directions in this section use cognates, graphic cues, and some translations to help you understand them. Try to guess their meanings or consult the *Interactions en classe* on page 30 before asking for an English translation.

J. **Quelles pièces d'identité est-ce que vous possédez** *(possess)*? Faites une liste des pièces d'identité que vous possédez. Voici des suggestions:

	oui	non
une carte d'étudiant		
un permis de conduire		
un passeport		
des cartes de crédit		
une carte de sécurité sociale		

Note that the direction lines in the **Pour développer vos idées** section are in French. You will be surprised at how much French you understand, even this early in your studies. The **Interaction en classe** at the end of **Chapitre 1** will help you with some of the basic French vocabulary.

K. **Les informations sur les pièces d'identité.** Quelles sortes d'informations personnelles sont sur vos pièces d'identité? Discutez la question avec vos camarades de classe.

> **Modèle:** les cartes d'étudiant
> —*Les informations sur **les cartes d'étudiant** sont **le nom** et **le numéro de sécurité sociale.***
> —*Et sur **les permis de conduire,** les informations sont...*

À propos du vocabulaire: Notice that the word **informations** is plural in French when it refers to more than one item of information.

les pièces d'identité	les informations
les cartes d'étudiant	le nom
les permis de conduire	le prénom
les passeports	l'adresse
les cartes de crédit	la description physique
	la date de naissance
	le sexe
	le numéro de téléphone
	la profession
	l'état civil
	la nationalité

L. Participer à un sondage *(survey)?* À quel point *(To what extent)* acceptez-vous de donner des informations personnelles pour un sondage dans un magazine? Complétez ces deux phrases pour indiquer vos sentiments. Utilisez la liste *Les informations privées?* comme guide.

Modèle: En général, j'accepte de donner...
Et en général, je n'accepte pas de donner...

*En général, j'accepte de donner **un nom** et **une adresse**.*
*Les informations que je n'accepte pas de donner sont **une date de naissance** et...*

Les informations privées?

un nom	un état civil
une adresse	une description physique
un numéro de téléphone	des intérêts
une date de naissance	une profession
un lieu de naissance	un numéro de carte de crédit

M. Privé ou non? Discutez vos phrases de l'exercice précédent avec votre partenaire. Cherchez un consensus.

Modèle: —*Les informations que je refuse de donner sont...*
—*Et pour moi, elles sont... / Moi, je ne refuse pas de donner...*
—*Alors pour nous les informations très privées sont... et les moins privées° sont...*

moins privées: *less private*

2ᴱ THÈME: Ma profession

Objective: To exchange information about professions and the workplace

PRÉSENTATION: Un coup d'œil sur le thème

Comme journaliste, j'interviewe beaucoup de personnes célèbres—Je prépare des reportages que je présente à la télévision. J'aime bien mon travail°, même si je ne gagne pas beaucoup d'argent°.

le travail: *work*
ne gagne... argent: *don't earn a lot of money*

Je suis étudiante. Mes études sont mon travail. J'assiste à mes cours°, et je prépare mes devoirs°. La discipline est essentielle pour les étudiants.

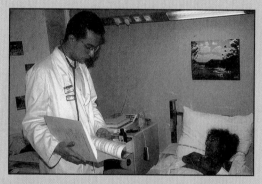

En général, les médecins aident les autres. Ils examinent la situation et donnent des conseils°. C'est un travail satisfaisant.

assiste à mes cours: *attend classes*
devoirs (m.): *homework*
donnent des conseils: *give advice*

Stratégies

1. Notice the title of the **Thème.** What do you think it is about?
2. Examine each photograph to decide what the situation is. Then skim through the caption to identify cognates.
3. Use each caption to identify one detail that the person gives about his or her work.
4. Start a list of expressions that you want to be able to use when you finish the chapter. (File them in your portfolio.)

Your personal portfolio: The activities in this text have been designed to help you develop the language you will need to express your personal views on a variety of topics. Selected assignments in which you elaborate your ideas are identified (with 📁) for inclusion in your portfolio, which will serve you as a reference work.

POUR DÉVELOPPER VOTRE FRANÇAIS

Vocabulaire: Pour parler des professions

We identify closely with our profession or job or primary life activity/responsibility. In fact, we are often described with the name of our occupation.

OBSERVATIONS

Gérard Depardieu est **comédien.**
Gérard Depardieu is an actor.

Catherine Deneuve est **comédienne** aussi.
Catherine Deneuve is an actress also.

Luciano Pavarotti est **chanteur.**
Luciano Pavarotti is a singer.

Barbra Streisand est **chanteuse** aussi.
Barbra Streisand is a singer also.

À propos du vocabulaire: Although most cognate expressions provide clues to the meaning of French words, some pairs of cognates (called **faux amis** or *false friends*) do not have parallel meanings. For example, **comédien(ne)** refers to an *actor* rather than a *comedian.*

STRATÉGIES D'ANALYSE

1. Do profession names, like nationalities, change gender to reflect the person being named?
2. What letter do feminine forms end in?
3. Do you notice any other changes from some masculine forms to their feminine counterparts?

PRÉCISIONS

- Professions, like adjectives of nationality, are marked with gender and number. Here are the most common groups of masculine and feminine endings. Note the similarities in form with the adjectives you've already learned.

masculin	**féminin**
un commerçant	une commerçan**te**
un musicien	une musicie**nne**
un chanteur	une chanteu**se**
un couturier	une coutur**ière**

• Remember that masculine forms ending in an unaccented **-e** do not need an additional **e** for feminine forms.

un artiste	une artiste
un dentiste	une dentiste

• As with adjectives, plural nouns are normally formed by adding **-s**.

Ils sont avocat**s**.	Elles sont avocate**s**.

• Certain professions have traditionally been associated with males, and language has not always changed along with modern society. Some names of professions do not have a feminine form. You may add the word **femme** before the profession name to distinguish a female from a male.

un médecin	une **femme** médecin
un professeur	une **femme** professeur
un écrivain	une **femme** écrivain

• Note that when a noun, a name, or **il/elle** is used in stating a profession, the article is omitted in French.

Gérard Depardieu est **comédien**.	*Gérard Depardieu is **an** actor.*
Céline Dion est **chanteuse**.	*Céline Dion is **a** singer.*
Je vous présente Alex. Il est **artiste**.	*This is Alex. He's **an** artist.*

Les arts

Some professions center around the arts.

Il est artiste.

Elle est musicienne.

Il est couturier.

A. On est célèbre. Working with a partner, name two well-known people (one male and the other female) in each of the following artistic professions.

Modèle: comédien
Un comédien célèbre est Gérard Depardieu.
Une comédienne célèbre est Catherine Deneuve.

1. comédien
2. chanteur
3. couturier

4. musicien
5. artiste

Other professions provide service to individuals or to the public in general.

Les services publics et privés

Il est militaire.

Elle est avocate.

Elle est agente de police.

Elle est médecin.

Elle est infirmière.

Il est chef de cuisine.

The following are some other service professions:

astronaute	*astronaut*	pharmacien(ne)	*pharmacist*
banquier(-ère)	*banker*	politicien(ne)	*politician*
journaliste	*journalist*	instituteur(-trice)	*teacher*

B. **On est bien vu.** Working with a partner, rate the attractiveness of the following professions based on prestige.

Modèle: *À mon avis°, les médecins sont très prestigieux. C'est numéro 5. Et les professeurs sont prestigieux. C'est numéro 4.*

À mon avis: *In my opinion*

peu prestigieux **1 2 3 4 5** *très prestigieux*

1. les médecins
2. les infirmières
3. les pharmaciens
4. les journalistes
5. les banquiers
6. les politiciens
7. les chefs de cuisine
8. les professeurs/instituteurs
9. les avocats
10. les agents de police

A variety of professions fall under the general heading of business or commerce.

Les affaires

Il est informaticien°.

Elle est femme d'affaires.

Elle est commerçante.

informaticien: *specialist in some aspect of computer science*

À propos du vocabulaire: The following list provides the names of several other professions you may wish to use.

Vocabulaire supplémentaire

écrivain	*writer*
dentiste	*dentist*
architecte	*architect*
agent(e) de voyages	*travel agent*
agent(e) immobilier	*real estate agent*
coiffeur(-euse)	*hair stylist*
ingénieur	*engineer*
mécanicien(ne)	*mechanic*
vendeur(-euse)	*salesperson*
caissier(-ère)	*cashier*
pompier(-ère)	*firefighter*

assez intéressant(e): *rather interesting*

The following are some other business professions:

cadre	*executive*
comptable	*accountant*
homme d'affaires	*businessman*
secrétaire	*secretary*

C. **Des professions intéressantes.** Decide on how interesting you would anticipate each of the following professions to be. Then compare your expectations with those of your partner.

Modèle: commerçant
Je pense que la profession de commerçant est assez intéressante°. C'est numéro 3.

peu intéressante 1   2   3   4   5   très intéressante

1. commerçant
2. secrétaire
3. informaticien
4. homme/femme d'affaires
5. avocat
6. comptable
7. banquier
8. professeur
9. médecin
10. agent de police

D. Je vous conseille... Suggest some appropriate professions for the following people, based on their interests. Take turns with your partner.

Modèle: —Christian adore la musique et désire chanter.
—*Je recommande la profession de musicien.*

1. Christian adore la musique et désire chanter.
2. Amina désire étudier l'informatique.
3. Nathalie adore les maths.
4. Bruno aime les aventures.
5. Jean-Claude adore parler.
6. Francine désire beaucoup de responsabilités.
7. Robert est très indépendant et créatif.
8. Guy aime examiner et présenter des idées.

E. Ce qui est important. Decide how important certain aspects of a job are to you. Then, using the grid, compare your values to those of your partner, using a scale from 1 to 5 where 1 = **peu important** and 5 = **très important**.

Modèle: —*Je pense que la stabilité financière est très importante, numéro 5. Mon partenaire pense que la stabilité financière est importante aussi, numéro 4.*

moi		mon/ma partenaire
5	la stabilité financière	4
	une situation intéressante	
	un poste prestigieux	
	un horaire souple°	
	des collègues sympathiques	
	les vacances payées	
	un bureau privé	
	des voyages intéressants	

un horaire souple: *a flexible schedule*

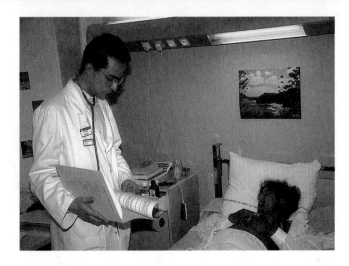

E. Des professions comme ça. Working with a partner, name at least one profession where you would expect to find each of the characteristics in Exercise E and at least one profession where you would not expect to find each characteristic. Name at least six different professions.

	Oui	Non
1. la stabilité financière	*médecin*	*artiste*
2. une situation intéressante		
3. un poste prestigieux		
4. un horaire souple		
5. des collègues sympathiques		
6. les vacances payées		
7. un bureau privé		
8. des voyages intéressants		

Structure: Les verbes en -er

OBSERVATIONS

M. Chaumont **travaille** seul°.

Sophie **parle** avec des clients.

seul(e): *alone*

Je **téléphone** aux clients.
I call clients by phone.

Tu **travailles** en équipe?
Are you working in a team?

Il **rapporte** les résultats.
He reports the results.

Elle **examine** les budgets.
She is examining the budgets.

On **aime** travailler ici.
People like to work here.

Nous **assistons** aux cours.
We attend classes.

Vous **interviewez** les candidats?
Do you interview the candidates?

Ils **présentent** les détails.
They present the details.

Elles **donnent** des conseils.
They give advice.

STRATÉGIES D'ANALYSE

1. Look at the verbs in boldface. What different French verb endings can you find?
2. What seems to determine the changes in verb endings?
3. Which verb tense (present, past, or future) is expressed in the examples?
4. Which has more ways of expressing the present tense, English or French?

PRÉCISIONS

- In French, as in English, verbs are conjugated to agree with their subjects. Many verbs have regular patterns of conjugation. Infinitives ending in **-er** make up the largest group of verbs in French. Once you learn the present-tense endings, you can conjugate any regular verb whose infinitive ends in **-er**.

To form the present tense, drop the **-er** from the infinitive and add the endings **-e, -es, -e, -ons, -ez,** or **-ent.** The ending is determined by the subject of the sentence.

<table>
<tr><td colspan="2" align="center">**parler**</td></tr>
<tr><td>je parl**e**</td><td>nous parl**ons**</td></tr>
<tr><td>tu parl**es**</td><td>vous parl**ez**</td></tr>
<tr><td>il/elle/on parl**e**</td><td>ils/elles parl**ent**</td></tr>
</table>

- Four of the forms sound the same.
- If the verb begins with a vowel sound, the **e** in **je** is dropped and an apostrophe is added.

j'aime   j'adore

- Remember that the one present-tense form in French corresponds to three ways of expressing the present tense in English.

Je parle à Christine.	*I **speak** to Christine.*
Je parle à Christine.	*I **am speaking** to Christine.*
Parlez-vous français?	***Do** you **speak** French?*

- If a sentence contains two verbs, conjugate the first verb only.

J'**aime** travailler ici.
Marie-Claire **préfère** travailler seule.
Ils **désirent** travailler en équipe.

À propos de la prononciation: Note that, while the **-s** in **nous, vous, ils,** and **elles** is normally silent, it is pronounced as a **z** before a vowel sound.

nous aimons	vous aimez
/nouzaimons/	/vouzaimez/
ils aiment	elles aiment
/ilzaiment/	/ellezaiment/

À propos de la structure: French speakers use the pronoun **on** more frequently than the pronoun **nous**. **On** travaille en équipe ici. **We** *work as a team here.*

À propos de la prononciation: Note that the final **r** in **-er** infinitives is not pronounced. The ending has the same sound as the letter **é** in **café.**

G. **Qu'est-ce qu'ils font?** *(What do they do?)* Replace the subject of each sentence with the words in parentheses and make the necessary changes in the italicized verbs. Taking turns with your partner, tell each other what people in the following professions do on the job.

1. Les secrétaires *téléphonent* aux clients. (Mme Chaumont / je / nous / vous)
2. Mme Raspail *prépare* les budgets. (le comptable / vous / les femmes d'affaires)
3. Les comptables *examinent* les budgets. (je / tu / ils / nous)
4. M. Giraux *donne* des conseils aux employés. (vous / nous / je / ils)
5. Les journalistes *rapportent* les nouvelles. (je / M. Dupont / nous / tu)
6. Mme Margot *interviewe* des gens célèbres. (nous / vous / les journalistes / tu)

H. **Le premier jour.** It's your first day on your new job and your boss tells you what some of your responsibilities are. Take notes, then repeat what you're supposed to do. Then switch roles with your partner.

> **Modèle:** —*Vous préparez les budgets.*
> —*Je prépare les budgets.*

téléphoner aux clients
donner des conseils aux clients
préparer les budgets
examiner les budgets
assister aux meetings

parler avec des clients
interviewer des personnes célèbres
rapporter les résultats
présenter des idées
préparer des vidéos

I. **Mon nouveau boulot** (*My new job*). You're writing to a friend to let him know how your new job is going. Tell him one of your responsibilities that you like, one that you prefer, and a third that you dislike.

> **Modèle:** *Je suis journaliste. J'aime préparer les budgets, mais je préfère inter-*
> *viewer les personnes célèbres. Je n'aime pas assister aux meetings.*

Structure: La négation

OBSERVATIONS

François prépare les crêpes. Il **ne** travaille **pas** en équipe; il travaille seul.

STRATÉGIES D'ANALYSE

1. Which words seem to make a statement negative?
2. Where do those words appear in a sentence (in relation to the verb)?

PRÉCISIONS

- To make a statement negative, add **ne** before the verb and **pas** after the verb.

Je **ne** travaille **pas** à l'université.	Nous **ne** préparons **pas** le rapport.
*I **don't** work at the university.*	*We're **not** preparing the report.*
Tu **ne** présentes **pas** le budget?	Vous **ne** consultez **pas** le patron?
*You're **not** presenting the budget?*	*Are you **not** consulting the boss?*

- When **ne** precedes a verb beginning with a vowel sound, the **e** is dropped and an apostrophe is added.

> Elles **n'**assistent **pas** aux cours ici.
> They **don't** attend classes here.

> Il **n'**examine **pas** l'agenda.
> He's **not** examining the agenda.

- If the phrase contains two verbs, **ne** and **pas** are normally placed around the conjugated verb.

> Tu **ne préfères pas** travailler ici?

> Je **n'aime pas** examiner les budgets.

- Use **de (d')** rather than **un, une**, or **des** after a negative verb.

> Il prépare une vidéo.
> Elle donne des conseils aux
>   employés.

> Il ne prépare pas **de** vidéo.
> Elle ne donne pas **de** conseils aux
>   employés.

J. **Pourquoi pas?** *(Why not?)* You've asked your friend for advice about what sort of job you should look for. Tell your friend what objections you have to each suggestion given to you. Then switch roles with your partner.

> **Modèle:** politicien(ne)
> —*Tu devrais° être politicien(ne).*
> —*Mais je n'aime pas parler avec beaucoup de gens.*

devrais: *should*

comptable	examiner les budgets
avocat(e)	donner des conseils
chanteur(-euse)	chanter
secrétaire	parler au téléphone
cadre	parler avec les clients
médecin	étudier les sciences

K. **Voilà ce qu'on fait.** Write two sentences about each profession, telling one activity that an individual in the profession normally does and one activity that he or she does not do. Select one item from each of the three columns. Take turns with your partner reading your sentences.

> **Modèle:** un(e) journaliste
> *Un journaliste interviewe **des** personnes célèbres. Il ne consulte pas **de** clients.*

un(e) commerçant(e)	préparer	de/des budgets
un(e) journaliste	examiner	de/des clients
un médecin	consulter	de/des collègues
un(e) couturier(-ère)	donner	de/des conseils
un(e) comptable	interviewer	de/des rapports
un(e) avocat(e)	aider	de/des candidats
un professeur	présenter	de/des personnes célèbres

PRONONCIATION: La liaison 📼

Previously, you learned that the final consonant of most French words, when pronounced alone, is silent. To create a smoother sounding flow to the language, however, groups of words are often linked together by a **liaison.** Simply put, the liaison means that you will pronounce the final consonant of a word if it is followed by a vowel sound, as you do in the following:

Vous_êtes musicienne?   Nous_aimons le reggae.   Il y a huit_étudiants.

Liaisons may be divided into three types:

1) mandatory (*liaisons obligatoires*)
In the following instances, the liaison is *always* required:
• an article + a noun or an adjective beginning with a vowel sound

      un éclair   les astronautes   des intérêts

• a subject pronoun + a verb beginning with a vowel sound

      Elles aiment les sports.

• after the verb form **est**

      Mon professeur est italien.

2) forbidden (*liaisons interdites*)
There is *never* a liaison made in the following cases:
• after any proper name

      Jean//est de Nice.   Paris//est la capitale de la France.

• after any singular noun

      du chocolat//allemand   C'est une position//intéressante.

• after the conjunction **et** (*and*)

      Sylvie et//Anne sont québécoises.

3) optional (*liaisons facultatives*)
Sometimes, to render speech more formal (public speeches, poetry readings, etc.), other liaisons are made which are neither mandatory nor forbidden, but which are stylistic in nature. You will learn more about this type of liaison in *Chapitre 8* and as you continue to study French.

À vous! With a partner, take turns reading the following phrases aloud. In the examples to the left, be sure to make the liaison; in those to the right, no liaison is made.

1. les informations
2. des agents de police
3. un écrivain russe
4. Vous examinez les budgets?
5. Nous assistons à la classe.
6. Ils travaillent en équipe.

7. des voyages
8. un café crème
9. les vacances payées
10. Louis est médecin.
11. Elle parle français et anglais.
12. Vous détestez le shopping.

POUR DÉVELOPPER VOS IDÉES

Thematic objective: To observe relations between careers and personal goals

Présentation: La qualité de notre travail

POUR SAISIR L'ESSENTIEL: Since most people spend much of their time at work, it is worthwhile to consider personal tastes and priorities in making career decisions. The following activities will guide you through a few of the initial steps of the process.

Look at the survey results in the following chart and note the range in the levels of confidence placed in these professionals. List the four professions in order based on your opinion of their trustworthiness, putting the most trustworthy one first. How do your opinions compare to those in the survey?

Qui a le moins de crédibilité?

Moins de confiance / Plus de confiance

Politiciens	Hommes d'affaires	Journalistes	Policiers
72,6%	7,8%	7,8%	7,7%

75% des francophones interrogés ont le moins de confiance en les politiciens.

À propos de la culture: Notice that commas mark decimals in French. You read 7,6% as **sept virgule six pour cent.**

L. Préférences. Complétez les phrases pour parler des activités que vous aimez et des activités que vous n'aimez pas dans un emploi.

communiquer avec le public
organiser des projets
écouter les clients
parler au téléphone

travailler seul(e)
interviewer des
   personnes célèbres
travailler le week-end
préparer des budgets

donner des conseils°
travailler en équipe
aider les autres
voyager
(autres idées???)

conseils (m.): *advice*

1. J'adore...
2. J'aime...
3. J'aime bien...

4. Je n'aime pas beaucoup...
5. Je n'aime pas...
6. Je déteste...

Modèle: J'adore *communiquer avec le public.*
          J'aime...

M. Les valeurs au travail. Complétez la phrase en mentionnant (par ordre d'importance) trois attributs que vous désirez dans un emploi. Utilisez les suggestions dans la liste pour stimuler vos idées.

- la responsabilité
- le prestige
- la sécurité financière
- un bon salaire
- le succès
- l'aventure
- une ambiance calme

- un travail intéressant
- l'occasion de voyager
- l'occasion d'aider les autres
- le contact avec le public
- des collègues sympathiques
- la satisfaction personnelle
- (autres idées???)

Modèle: Pour moi, les attributs importants sont *la responsabilité, un bon salaire* et *la satisfaction personnelle*.

N. On consulte un(e) camarade. Échangez vos phrases des exercices précédents avec votre partenaire. Prenez des notes *(Take notes)*. Considérez les préférences et valeurs de votre partenaire, et suggérez une carrière appropriée.

Modèle: —Vous aimez *donner des conseils* et *aider les autres*. Et un attribut important pour vous est *la responsabilité*. Mais vous n'aimez pas *travailler seul(e)*. Alors vous pouvez *(you can)* être *avocat(e)*.

3ᴱ THÈME: Mes passe-temps

Objective: To tell how you spend your time away from work or school

PRÉSENTATION Un coup d'œil sur le thème

Mes passe-temps préférés? J'aime la lecture°, la musique jazz et j'aime beaucoup passer une soirée° avec des amis.

la lecture: *reading*
passer une soirée: *spend the evening*

Quelquefois°, après une journée° difficile au travail, je préfère passer la soirée tout seul°, à regarder une vidéo ou à écouter un disque compact. Mais le week-end, j'aime dîner avec des amis.

Moi, je n'aime pas être seule. J'aime toujours être avec mes amis. Nous passons la soirée à danser dans un club ou dans un bar. C'est bien amusant.

always
fun

Quelquefois: *Sometimes*
une journée: *a day*
tout(e) seul(e): *all alone*

Stratégies

1. Use the strategies that you practiced with **Un Coup d'œil sur le thème** for the first two **Thèmes.**

   • Look at the title to get a general impression of the topic.

   • Examine the photographs and guess what each situation is about.

   • Skim the captions, looking for cognates and familiar vocabulary.

   • Write a one-sentence summary of the **Coup d'œil.**

2. Categorize the leisure time activities and tell whether, for you, they fall under the category of **J'aime** or **Je n'aime pas beaucoup.**

POUR DÉVELOPPER VOTRE FRANÇAIS

Vocabulaire: Pour parler des jours de la semaine

OBSERVATIONS

lundi	cours
mardi	rapports
mercredi	cours, budget
jeudi	
vendredi	cours, travail
samedi	travail
dimanche	match de foot

À propos du vocabulaire: An example of **faux amis** is the verb **assister**, *to attend.* **Nous assistons aux cours le lundi, le mercredi et le vendredi.**

Je travaille **le vendredi** et **le samedi.**
*I work **every Friday** and **Saturday.***

Tu travailles **le dimanche?**
*Do you work **Sundays?***

On examine les budgets **mercredi.**
*We're going over the budgets **on Wednesday.***

Nous assistons aux cours **le lundi, le mercredi** et **le vendredi.**
*We attend classes on **Mondays, Wednesdays,** and **Fridays.***

Vous présentez les rapports **mardi?**
*Are you presenting the reports **on Tuesday?***

Ils ne travaillent pas au bureau **dimanche;** ils jouent au foot.
*They are not working at the office **on Sunday;** they are playing soccer.*

STRATÉGIES D'ANALYSE

1. What is the first day of the week on French calendars?
2. What do you notice that is similar about the way the days of the week and the months are written in French?
3. What difference in meaning does the article **le** make before the name of a day of the week?

PRÉCISIONS

- The first day of the week on French calendars is Monday.
- The days of the week are not capitalized in French.
- Use **le** before a day of the week to mean an action occurs on that day *every* week.

On travaille **le samedi.**
*We work **every Saturday.***

On travaille **samedi.**
*We're working **on Saturday.***

A. Mes activités. Tell which days you routinely do and don't do each of the following activities.

Modèle: travailler
Je travaille le vendredi, le samedi et le dimanche.
Je ne travaille pas le lundi, le mardi, le mercredi et le jeudi.

1. travailler
2. assister aux cours
3. assister au cours de français
4. étudier
5. jouer aux sports / faire du sport
6. regarder la télé
7. dîner avec des amis
8. rester chez moi

Vocabulaire: Pour parler des loisirs

Observations

Elles **dansent** sur la place.
*They **are dancing** in the plaza.*

Les enfants **célèbrent** les jours de fête.
*The children **celebrate** the holidays.*

J'**invite** des amis chez moi le samedi.
*I **invite** friends to my place on Saturdays.*

Tu **regardes** la télévision?
*Do you **watch** TV?*

Il **chante** dans une chorale le jeudi.
*He **sings** in a chorus on Thursdays.*

Elle **assiste** aux concerts de jazz.
*She **attends** jazz concerts.*

On **retrouve** des amis au café.
*We **meet** friends in a café.*

Nous **passons** la soirée chez les Dupont samedi.
*We're **spending** the evening at the Duponts' on Saturday.*

Écoutez-vous de la musique?
*Do you **listen** to music?*

Ils **restent** à la maison dimanche.
*They **are staying** home this Sunday.*

Elles **jouent** aux cartes le jeudi.
*They **play** cards on Thursdays.*

> **À propos de la structure:** Note that we use the plural form *les* with the name of the family to indicate that these are multiple members of the family. The family name is not made plural.
> **les Dupont**   the Duponts

B. **Quand je ne travaille pas le dimanche . . .** Taking turns, tell your partner how frequently you participate in the following activities when you do not work on Sundays. Use the following adverbs to express degrees of frequency. Record the results of your discussion on a grid.

rarement	*rarely*
de temps en temps	*from time to time*
souvent	*often*

> **À propos de la structure:** The adverbs **rarement** and **souvent** come immediately after the verb. **De temps en temps** comes at the beginning or the end of the statement.

Modèle: —*Quand je ne travaille pas le dimanche, je chante souvent dans une chorale.*
             —*De temps en temps, j'invite des amis chez moi.*

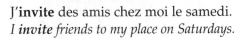

	rarement	de temps en temps	souvent
téléphoner à un(e) ami(e)			
regarder la télévision			
fréquenter les musées			
assister à des concerts			
chanter dans une chorale			moi + partenaire
inviter des amis/amies chez moi		moi	
dîner au restaurant			
rester à la maison			

Modèle: *Mon/Ma partenaire et moi, nous dînons souvent au restaurant.*

Structure: Verbe + infinitif

OBSERVATIONS

Nous **aimons fréquenter** les expositions.
*We **love to go to/attend** art exhibits.*

J'**aime bien danser** dans les clubs.
*I **like to dance** in the clubs.*

Est-ce que tu **aimes jouer** aux cartes?
*Do you **like to play** cards?*

Paul **déteste dîner** au restaurant.
*Paul **hates to eat** out at a restaurant.*

M. et Mme Lévêque **aiment bien dîner** au restaurant.
*Mr. and Mrs. Lévêque **like to eat** out at a restaurant.*

Nous **préférons rester** à la maison.
*We **prefer** to stay at home.*

Vous **aimez mieux regarder** la télé ou une vidéo?
*Do you **prefer watching** TV or a video?*

Jean et Claude **adorent dîner** à la maison.
*Jean and Claude **love to dine** at home.*

STRATÉGIES D'ANALYSE

1. Each of these sentences contains two different verbs. Which one of these verbs conjugates (changes form to agree with the subject)?
2. What form is the second verb in? Does it change its form as the subject of the sentence changes?

PRÉCISIONS

À propos de la structure. A few -er verbs require spelling changes in the stem of certain forms to reflect changes in pronunciation: **préfère, préfères, préfère, préférons, préférez, préfèrent.**

- When two verbs are used together in a sentence, the first verb conjugates to agree with the subject. The second verb stays in the infinitive form.

  J'**aime inviter** des amis chez moi.　　Nous **préférons rester** à la maison.
  *I **like to invite** friends to my place.*　　*We **prefer to stay** at home.*

- To make a negative statement, put the **ne** and **pas** around the conjugated verb.

  Je **n'**aime **pas** danser dans les clubs.
  *I **don't** like to dance in the clubs.*

- Use the following expressions to tell to what degree you like or dislike something. They range from the strongest positive emotion to the strongest negative emotion.

À propos de vocabulaire: The French use the unqualified **aimer** to express love for a person. Whenever a form of the verb **aimer** is qualified (with **bien, assez bien**, etc.) it indicates an expression of the verb *to like*.

J'aime	*I love (a person)*
J'adore	*I adore*
J'aime beaucoup	*I like a lot*
J'aime	*I like, I love (an activity or noun)*
J'aime bien	*I like quite a lot*
J'aime assez bien	*I like rather well*
Je n'aime pas beaucoup.	*I don't like . . . a lot.*
Je n'aime pas	*I do not like*
Je n'aime pas du tout	*I do not like at all, I dislike*
Je déteste	*I hate, I detest*

D. **Moi, après le travail, j'aime...** On the following chart, mark whether you like to do each activity after work. Then share your responses with a partner.

Modèle:　　—*Aimes-tu jouer aux cartes après le travail?*
　　　　　　　—*Non, je n'aime pas jouer aux cartes.*

moi			mon/ma partenaire	
oui	**non**		**oui**	**non**
		passer la soirée dans les bars		
		danser dans les clubs		
		inviter des ami(e)s chez moi		
		regarder la télévision		
		assister à des concerts		
		dîner au restaurant		
		téléphoner à des ami(e)s		
		préparer le dîner à la maison		
		écouter de la musique		
		rester à la maison		

Vocabulaire supplémentaire

aller au cinéma	*to go to the movies*
dormir	*to sleep*
lire	*to read*

E. Après le travail, nous aimons... Compare your responses in Exercise D with those of your partner by completing the Venn diagram to show activities that only you like, those that only your partner likes, and those that you both like. Prepare to report your comparisons to the class.

Modèle: *Moi, j'aime... et...*
Mon/Ma partenaire aime... et...
Mon/Ma partenaire et moi, nous aimons... et...
Nous n'aimons pas...

Moi   **Nous deux**   **Mon/Ma partenaire**

F. Vous êtes social(e)? Take this magazine survey to find out whether you or your partner is more interested in social activities. Rate each activity, then compare your results.

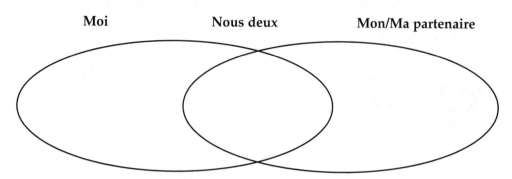

danser dans les clubs _____	J'aime beaucoup… 1
regarder la télé _____	J'aime… 2
inviter des ami(e)s chez moi ___	J'aime bien… 3
assister à des concerts _____	J'aime assez bien… 4
rester à la maison _____	Je n'aime pas beaucoup…5
parler au téléphone _____	Je n'aime pas… 6
jouer en équipe _____	Je n'aime pas du tout… 7
écouter de la musique _____	
jouer aux cartes _____	
chanter dans une chorale _____	

Résultats:
Les activités sociales m'intéressent beaucoup: moins de 27
Les activités sociales m'intéressent: 27–36
Les activités sociales m'intéressent un peu: 37–43
Les activités sociales ne m'intéressent pas du tout: plus de 43

G. Mes loisirs préférés. In your portfolio write at least five sentences about how you prefer to spend your leisure time. Use the information about yourself that you have given in the preceding exercises to stimulate your ideas.

Structure: L'interrogation

Interview: Céline Dion

Bonjour, Céline. Vous allez bien?

Vous êtes canadienne?

Est-ce que vous habitez Montréal?

Vous parlez français et anglais, n'est-ce pas?

Vous aimez chanter?

Est-ce que vous voyagez beaucoup?

Est-ce que vous préférez la cuisine française ou la cuisine québécoise?

Interview: le Président

Bonjour, M. le Président.

Comment allez-vous?

Parlez-vous avec le président du Mexique mercredi?

Présentez-vous les détails du budget en janvier ou en février?

Parlez-vous français et anglais?

Le vice-président et vous, voyagez-vous souvent en Europe?

STRATÉGIES D'ANALYSE

1. In the sample sentences, questions have been expressed four different ways. Can you identify all four?

2. What differences can you find in the ways that the questions are stated in the two different interviews? Can you guess a reason for these differences?

PRÉCISIONS

- There are four ways to ask yes/no questions in French. You've already learned to ask a question by using a rising intonation at the end.

  Vous jouez au tennis?   Ils sont canadiens?

- A very common way of asking a question is to add **est-ce que** before the subject. Note that when **que** precedes a vowel sound, the **e** is dropped and an apostrophe is added.

  Est-ce que vous dînez souvent au restaurant?
  Est-ce qu'il aime chanter?

- Another way to ask a question is to invert the subject and verb.

  Parlez-vous français?   **Êtes-vous** italien?
  Comment **allez-vous**?   **Êtes-vous** professeur?
  Comment vous **appelez-vous**?

  Except for certain fixed expressions, French speakers tend to use inversion much less frequently because it is considered rather formal.

- If you expect the answer to a question to be yes, you can simply add **n'est-ce pas** to the end of a statement.

  Tu es américain, **n'est-ce pas**?   Elle joue de la guitare, **n'est-ce pas**?

H. On pose des questions. Make questions out of each of the following statements two different ways.

> **Modèle:** François écoute de la musique.
> *Est-ce que François écoute de la musique?*
> *François écoute de la musique, n'est-ce pas?*

1. François écoute de la musique.
2. Vous chantez dans une chorale.
3. On retrouve les amis au Café Matisse.
4. Ils jouent aux cartes le mercredi.
5. Nous restons à la maison.
6. Martin et Céline regardent la télé.
7. Tu aimes sortir avec des amis.
8. Nous passons la soirée chez Gilbert.
9. Elles désirent regarder une vidéo.
10. On travaille ici en équipe.

I. Il est français, n'est-ce pas? You and your friend are at an international convention. You think you've already met some of the people there, but you ask your friend questions about them to be sure. (Remember, if you're verifying information, use **n'est-ce pas.** If you're less sure of the information, use **est-ce que** or intonation to ask the question.) Then switch roles.

> **Modèle:** *M. Chaumont est suisse, n'est-ce pas?*
> *Est-ce qu'il parle italien?*

?	?	?

M. Chaumont
suisse
parle français et
   allemand
comptable
aime les sports

Mme St. Onge
canadienne
parle français et anglais
comédienne
écoute souvent de la
   musique classique

M. Nouraddine
de Casablanca
parle français et arabe
homme d'affaires
danse souvent dans les clubs
ne joue pas aux cartes

?	?

M. et Mme Clavel
français
parlent français et anglais
professeurs
chantent dans une chorale
adorent regarder les vidéos

Mlle Nguyen
vietnamienne
parle français et vietnamien
infirmière
assiste souvent à des concerts
aime le shopping

PRONONCIATION La liaison et les chiffres 📼

In this chapter's first **Thème,** you learned that the final consonant of French words is generally silent, unless followed by a vowel sound. The same is true when pronouncing numbers, with a few notable exceptions:

When a number word is isolated in speech, the final consonant is pronounced only for the numbers 5 through 10:

cinq	six	sept	huit	neuf	dix
/k/	/s/	/t/	/t/	/f/	/s/

Note that the /p/ of *sept* is silent, but that the /t/ and /f/ of *sept* and *neuf* are **always** pronounced.

The final consonant of all other numbers pronounced alone is silent:

un   deux   trois   . . .   vingt

When a number is followed by a word beginning with a vowel sound, a liaison is made:

un infirmier   deux étudiants   trois omelettes   dix-huit heures

When followed by a word beginning with a consonant sound, no liaison is made:

un pharmacien   deux secrétaires   trois collègues   dix dollars

Note that the /t/ of *vingt* is always pronounced when followed by a vowel sound and in the numbers 21–29, whether followed by a vowel or consonant sound. Thus:

vingt   vingt amis   vingt et un   vingt-deux   vingt-cinq   vingt-huit   ...

À vous! With a partner, take turns reading the following words and phrases aloud, remembering to pronounce final consonants where appropriate.

1. J'ai vingt-neuf ans.
2. trente-six
3. trois
4. dix bières
5. C'est le neuf janvier.
6. vingt
7. un avocat
8. vingt-deux
9. Il a trente-deux ans.
10. cinq
11. Il y a neuf restaurants.
12. C'est le dix-sept juillet.

POUR DÉVELOPPER VOS IDÉES

Thematic objective: To examine some factors that influence preferences in leisure activities

Présentation: Le choix des passe-temps

POUR SAISIR L'ESSENTIEL: While most people in the United States identify with their work, leisure activities often reflect their passions. Whether they are "health nuts," "sports fans," "opera buffs," or enthusiasts of any other stripe, leisure activities help people balance their lives and give expression to their personal interests. In this section you will look at some factors that influence your choices in leisure activities.

First look at the ads here and on page 70 for entertainment places around Paris.
1. Decide what kind of entertainment they offer.
2. List them in the order of their appeal for you, putting the most interesting place first.
3. Write a couple of sentences in French explaining your first and last choices.

Cinéma

LE BALZAC
1, rue Balzac
01.45.61.10.60
M° George V
14h à 24h
Place: 42 F
Mer et Lun, 32 F
3 salles

> **Modèle:** Pour moi, *Squash Club Quartier Latin* est numéro un, parce que j'adore nager. Et *cité de la musique* est numéro cinq, parce que je n'aime pas beaucoup la musique jazz.

Opéra National de Paris
Ballet de l'Opéra National de Paris

«Giselle»

Ballet en deux actes
Représentations jusqu'au 13 juillet,
19h 30
Opéra-Garnier
01.44.73.13.00
Places: 30 à 305 F/12 à 47 euros

KARAOKE

Stars Planète

66, av. des Champs-Élysées (8e)
01.53.75.26.26
tlj-tous les jours avec D.J.
Resto, bar-cocktails
Dîner à partir de 100F
Consommations à partir de 55F/8 euros
190 places

Squash Club Quartier Latin

*19, rue de Pontoise (5e)
M° Maubert ou Jussieu
01.43.54.82.45 ou 01.43.25.31.99*

*Du lundi au jeudi de 8h à 24h
Vendredi de 8h à 22h
W.E., de 9h30 à 19h*

*Gym, musculation, piscine 33m, aquagym,
sports de combat, squash, sauna, jacuzzi*

cité de la musique
23 mai — 20h

jazz

François Jeanneau, dir. artistique
Conservatoire de Paris
M° Porte de Pantin
01.44.84.44.84

J. Solitude ou société? Le choix d'activités dépend souvent de notre compagnie, des personnes avec nous. Complétez les phrases pour expliquer vos préférences.

Quand je suis seul(e), j'aime...
Quand je suis avec des amis, j'aime...
Quand je suis en famille, j'aime...

> **Modèle:** Quand je suis seul, j'aime *écouter des disques compacts.*

K. Compensation ou célébration? Quelquefois, ce sont nos émotions qui déterminent le choix d'activité. Complétez les phrases pour expliquer vos préférences.

Après une journée difficile, j'aime...
Après une journée super, j'aime...

> **Modèle:** Après une journée difficile, j'aime *rester à la maison.*

L. Des préférences en commun. Comparez vos idées des exercices précédents avec vos camarades de classe. Trouvez des personnes qui partagent vos préférences.

> **Modèle:** —Après une journée difficile, j'aime... Et toi?
> —*Moi aussi, j'aime... après une journée difficile.* or
> —*Moi non. Après une journée difficile, je préfère...*

ÉCOUTONS: Je me présente

You will hear three monologues in which some people identify themselves by giving personal information such as where they are from, what their jobs are, and how they spend their leisure time. Their photos are on the grids below.

A. **On identifie le monologue.** Look at the three photos on the grids and note as many details as possible about the people in them. Then listen to the monologues. As you listen, match the monologues to the photos by writing the number of each monologue (#1, #2, or #3), under the corresponding photo.

B. **On cherche les détails.** Now study the grid next to the photo you identified as #1. Determine what information you will need to find out about the person(s) being discussed. Then listen to the recording of monologue #1 again, listening specifically for the information you need for the grid. Write your answers in *English*. Follow the same procedure for monologues #2 and #3.

	Nationality	Profession	At least 2 of her 4 leisure activities	Regular day for going out with friends
 Monologue #____				

	Nationality	Profession	Leisure activities	At least 3 of their 5 languages	Marital status
 Monologue #____					

Nationality	Profession	2 Leisure activities	Marital status	Day vacation ends
 Monologue #____				

INTÉGRATION:
Les correspondants internationaux

Corresponding with penpals or e-pals from other countries can broaden your knowledge and understanding of other cultures. The following e-pal profiles come from the Internet.

A. **Choisir un correspondant.** Use these steps to choose an e-pal from the candidates represented.

1. Skim through the cards to identify the kinds of information requested. Which are most important to you in choosing a penpal?
2. Read the sections that you chose as most important. Decide which of the applicants you would prefer to correspond with. Identify the specific information that influenced your decisions for or against each applicant.
3. Now, go through each card carefully, reading all of the information provided. Does any of the additional information cause you to change your mind about your choices?
4. If you could add a section to the form, what additional information would you ask for?

À propos: Notice that surnames and the names of cities in forms and mailing addresses are in all capital letters. What other conventions do you notice that are different from those you are accustomed to?

le basket: *basketball*
le foot(ball): *soccer*
le droit: *law*
étrangers (m.): *foreigners*
recevoir: *to receive (as a guest)*

Nom: SOUCHET	**Fiche no:** 7456
Prénom: Éric	**Sexe:** M
Adresse: Route de Belleville 74380 LUCNIGES	**Nation:** France
Email: esouche@webser.com	**Langue(s):** français/anglais
Région: Lyon et la région	

Université: Paris 5	**Études:** droit

Loisirs: cinéma, musique, lecture	
Sports: basket, foot	

Je voudrais correspondre avec: des Canadiens et des Américains

Notes:

Nom: GIRARD	**Fiche no:** 7935
Prénom: Valérie	**Sexe:** F
Adresse: 18, rue Yves Lefèvre 34970 LATTES MAURIN	**Nation:** France
Email: vgirard@webser.com	**Langue(s):** français/italien
Région: Sud de la France	

Université: Université Paul Valéry	**Études:** arts

Loisirs: musique rock, musée, cinéma	
Sports: ski, tennis	

Je voudrais correspondre avec: des étrangers.

Notes: J'aime les États-Unis, surtout la Floride et la Californie. *Je peux recevoir mon correspondant.*

Nom: BEASSE	**Fiche no:** 7469
Prénom: Virginie	**Sexe:** F
Adresse: 17, rue St-Antoine	**Nation:** France
35700 RENNES	**Langue(s):** français/espagnol
Email: vbeasse@webser.com	
Université: Université de Rennes	
Études: sciences de l'éducation	
Loisirs: lecture, voyages, jardin	
Sports: vélo	
Je voudrais correspondre avec: des étrangers.	
Notes: Je suis professeur de maths dans une école où les enfants sont âgés de 11 à 15 ans. *Je peux recevoir mon correspondant.*	

Nom: CLÉMENT	**Fiche no:** 541
Prénom: David	**Sexe:** M
Adresse: 37, rue de la Charité	**Nation:** France
10100 ROMILLY SUR SEINE	**Langue(s):** français/espagnol
Email: dclement@webser.com	
Université:	
Études: hôtellerie	
Loisirs: cinéma, voyages, cuisine	
Sports: fléchettes, footing	
Je voudrais correspondre avec: des Anglais et des Américains	
Notes: préférence pour famille sans animaux domestiques. *Je peux recevoir mon correspondant.*	

le jardin: *garden*
le vélo: *cycling*
fléchettes (f.): *darts*
sans: *without*

B. **Discussion.** Discuss your answers to the reading questions in Exercise A, *Choisir un correspondant* with your partner. Did you base your decisions on the same information? Would you change your approach to selecting a penpal based on what you learn from your partner? Use the *Formule de discussion* to help you formulate your sentences.

Formule de discussion:
—Pour moi, les informations importantes sont l'âge, l'adresse, les langues, les études, les loisirs, les sports, les remarques, la possibilité de rendre visite à° mon/ma correspondant(e).
—Je (ne) voudrais (pas) correspondre avec...

  parce qu'il/elle (ne) parle (pas)...
  parce qu'il/elle (n')habite (pas) à...
  parce qu'il/elle (n')étudie (pas)...
  parce qu'il/elle (n')aime (pas)...
  parce qu'il/elle (n')est (pas)...
  parce qu'il/elle (ne) peut (pas) recevoir des (de) correspondants

rendre visite à: *visit*

C. Ma fiche de correspondant. Create your own **Fiche de correspondant.**

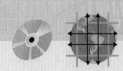

http://themes.heinle.com

LEXIQUE DE BASE

LEXIQUE D'EXPANSION

Les nationalités, les origines et les langues

nord-américain(e)	North American	britannique	British
américain(e)	American	hollandais(e)	Dutch
canadien(ne)	Canadian	irlandais(e)	Irish
mexicain(e)	Mexican	israélien(ne)	Israeli
européen(ne)	European	russe	Russian
allemand(e)	German	vietnamien(ne)	Vietnamese
anglais(e)	English		
belge	Belgian		
espagnol(e)	Spanish		
français(e)	French		
italien(ne)	Italian		
suisse	Swiss		
africain(e)	African		
marocain(e)	Moroccan		
sénégalais(e)	Senegalese		
Asiatique	Asian		
chinois(e)	Chinese		
japonais(e)	Japanese		

Les états civils

célibataire	single
conjoint(e)	living together as a couple
divorcé(e)	divorced
marié(e)	married
veuf/veuve	widowed

Les chiffres

voir la page 42

Les mois

janvier	January
février	February
mars	March
avril	April
mai	May
juin	June
juillet	July
août	August
septembre	September
octobre	October
novembre	November
décembre	December

Chapitre 2

les arts — **the arts**

artiste — artist
chanteur(-euse) — singer
comédien(ne) — actor/actress
couturier(-ière) — fashion designer
musicien(ne) — musician

écrivain, femme écrivain — writer

les services publics et privés — **public and personal services**

agent(e) de police — police officer
astronaute — astronaut
avocat(e) — lawyer
banquier(-ère) — banker
infirmier(-ère) — nurse
journaliste — journalist
médecin, femme médecin — doctor
militaire — serviceman/woman
pharmacien(ne) — pharmacist
politicien(ne) — politician
pompier(-ère) — firefighter
professeur, femme professeur — professor

agent(e) de voyages — travel agent
agent(e) immobilier(-ère) — real estate agent
coiffeur(-euse) — hair stylist
dentiste — dentist

les affaires — **business sector**

cadre — business executive
commerçant(e) — shopkeeper
comptable — accountant
homme/femme d'affaires — businessman/woman
informaticien(ne) — computer expert
secrétaire — secretary

architecte — architect
caissier(-ère) — cashier
mécanicien(ne) — mechanic
vendeur(-euse) — salesperson

assister aux cours/meetings — to attend classes/meetings
donner des conseils — to give advice
étudier un projet — to study a project
examiner les budgets — to examine the budgets
interviewer des candidats — to interview candidates
parler avec les clients — to speak with clients
préparer les vidéos — to prepare videos
présenter les détails — to present the details
rapporter les résultats — to report the results
téléphoner aux clients — to call customers
travailler en équipe — to work on a team
travailler seul(e) — to work alone
voyager — to travel

Les loisirs

assister à des concerts	to attend concerts	aller au cinéma	to go to the movies
chanter dans une chorale	to sing in a choir	dormir	to sleep
danser dans un club	to dance at a club	lire	to read
dîner au restaurant	to have dinner at a restaurant; eat out		
écouter de la musique	to listen to music		
célébrer les jours de fête	to celebrate special days		
fréquenter les expositions	to go to exhibits		
inviter des amis	to invite friends over		
jouer aux cartes	to play cards		
passer la soirée	to spend the evening		
regarder la télé(vision)	to watch TV		
rester à la maison	to stay home		
retrouver des amis au café	to meet friends at the café		
sortir avec des amis	to go out with friends		
téléphoner à des amis	to call friends		

Les préférences

adorer	to love
aimer	to like, to love
aimer beaucoup	to like a lot
aimer bien	to like quite a lot
aimer assez bien	to like rather well
ne pas aimer beaucoup	to not like much
ne pas aimer	to not like
ne pas du tout aimer	to not like at all, to dislike
détester	to detest, to hate

Les jours de la semaine

lundi	Monday
mardi	Tuesday
mercredi	Wednesday
jeudi	Thursday
vendredi	Friday
samedi	Saturday
dimanche	Sunday

Pour nuancer une idée

beaucoup	a lot
un peu	a little
pas du tout	not at all
toujours	always
souvent	often
quelquefois	sometimes
de temps en temps	from time to time
rarement	rarely
ne... jamais	never

MES RELATIONS INTERPERSONNELLES:
Les domaines de la vie

Communicative Objectives

- To talk about your family and friends and what you do together
- To describe people you know
- To talk about your routine activities

Thematic Objectives

- ✓ To identify and qualify the relationships between you and the people close to you
- ✓ To identify and evaluate the characteristics that you associate with people
- ✓ To identify ways people contribute to the community

OUVERTURE EN VIDÉO:
On présente sa famille

La mise en scène

A. **La famille de Christine.** In *Chapitre 3* you will talk about your family and friends and what you do together. On the video, Christine, your guide from Guadeloupe, and her extended family are enjoying a meal at a special family gathering. Before meeting them on screen, familiarize yourself with the members of Christine's family by studying her family tree. As you examine it, anticipate what each person's relationship to Christine is. On Christine's family tree, write in the word *in English* for each person's relationship to Christine, for example, *husband, father,* or *cousin.* (Hint: Each "row" of photos represents a different generation.)

La famille de Christine

Jean
(père)

Andréa
(mère)

Léonita
(belle-mère)

Relationship to Christine (in English):

Yveline
(cousine)

Katia
(belle-sœur)

Vidian
(frère)

Christine   Lucien
(mari)

Laurie
(nièce)

Pierre-Éric
(neveu)

Valérie
(nièce)

Luggie
(fille)

B. **Christine décrit** *(describes)* **sa famille proche** *(her immediate family).* The first people you will meet are Christine and her husband and daughter, whom she describes with affection. Look at their images on the segment of the video without the soundtrack. From what you observe on the video, what terms can you anticipate that Christine might use to describe them?

1. The age of Christine's daughter Luggie is probably
   a. six years old.   b. ten years old.   c. sixteen years old.

2. The color of Luggie's eyes appears to be
   a. blue.   b. green.   c. brown.

3. Christine probably describes her daughter as
   a. athletic.   b. adorable.   c. ambitious.

4. Christine probably describes her husband as
   a. tall and handsome.   b. short but strong.   c. muscular and athletic.

Les paroles et le sens

C. Les descriptions de sa famille. Now listen to Christine talk about Lucien and Luggie. Listen for and identify the key words Christine uses to describe her husband and daughter.

1. Christine says her daughter's age is
   a. *six ans.*   b. *dix ans.*   c. *seize ans.*

2. Christine describes the color of Luggie's eyes as
   a. *bleus*   b. *verts*   c. *marron*

3. How does Christine describe her daughter's nature?
   a. *athlétique*   b. *adorable*   c. *ambitieuse*

4. How does Christine describe her husband Lucien?
   a. *grand et beau*   b. *petit mais fort*   c. *musclé et athlétique*

How do your answers correspond to what you anticipated in Exercise B?

D. Qu'est-ce que c'est que «la famille»? Christine also talks about what family means to her. She mentions some groups of family members that make up her immediate and extended families. On the following chart, check off the family members you hear Christine mention.

mari	sœurs	petits-enfants	neveux
femme	parents	mère	nièces
enfant	beaux-parents	père	oncles
frères	grands-parents	tantes	cousins

On y réfléchit

E. Now that you've met Christine's family members at their family dinner, think about your own family members who gather together on special holiday occasions. Look at the list of the family members and copy onto a sheet of paper the words that represent at least four special members of your family. Next to each of those four words, write the first name of a person who has that relationship to you.

Modèle: oncle / *Uncle Joe*

mari	sœur	petit-enfant	neveu
femme	parent	mère	nièce
enfant	beau-parent	père	oncle
frère	grand-parent	tante	cousin

1ER THÈME: Ma famille, mes amis et mes collègues

Objective: To talk about your family, friends and colleagues, and what you do together

PRÉSENTATION: **Un coup d'œil sur le thème**

ma meilleure amie: *my best friend (f)*

bavarder: *to chat*

Quand je désire parler de ma vie ou de mes amours, je téléphone à ma meilleure amie°, Céline. On fréquente un petit café près de l'appartement. Nous aimons prendre un café et passer du temps à bavarder°.

avoir: *to have*

heureusement: *fortunately*

quand on a besoin d'aide: *when someone needs help*

À propos de la prononciation: The **c** and **t** in **respect** are silent. This word ends with a vowel sound in French.

Je travaille dans un bureau, et je commence à avoir° des responsabilités assez importantes. Heureusement°, ma patronne est sympathique. Elle est toujours là quand on a besoin d'aide°. J'ai beaucoup de respect pour Madame Chenier.

she is always fair when someone needs help

femme: *wife* In less casual speech, use the word ***épouse.***

fils (m.): *sons*

jeune: *young*

heureux: *happy*

J'aime bien passer la soirée en famille. Ma femme° et moi avons deux enfants. Nos fils° sont très jeunes°. Laurent a trois ans, et son petit frère a deux ans. Nous sommes très heureux° ensemble.

À propos de la prononciation: fils is spelled the same for singular and plural. Notice that the **l** is silent, but the **s** is pronounced.

Stratégies

1. Identify the three kinds of relationships mentioned in the title of the **Thème.**

   - Match each photograph in the **Coup d'œil** with one of the three relationships.
   - Identify the words or phrases from the captions that correspond to the people in the photographs and match them to the three relationships in the title.

2. Summarize each of the captions in English. Then work with a partner and compare your summaries. Did you both get the same general idea from each caption?

3. Take notes on any vocabulary that you may want to use to talk about people in your life.

POUR DÉVELOPPER VOTRE FR[...]

Structure: Les adjectifs possessi[...]

OBSERVATIONS

1. J'apprécie beaucoup **ma** famille. J'aime **mon** père, **ma** mèr[...]
   deux frères.
   *I really value **my** family. I love **my** father, **my** mother, **my** sister, an...mes*
   brothers.

2. La famille de Philippe n'habite pas ici. **Son** père et **sa** mère habiter[...]
   Baltimore, **son** frère travaille à Montréal et **ses** trois sœurs sont à l'u[...]
   sité à Berkeley.
   *Philip's family doesn't live here. **His** father and **his** mother live in Baltimore, h[...]*
   *brother works in Montreal, and **his** three sisters are at the university in Berkeley.[...]*

3. La famille de Claudine habite à Paris. **Son** père travaille pour IBM et **sa**
   sœur est étudiante à la Sorbonne.
   *Claudine's family lives in Paris. **Her** father works for IBM and **her** sister is a*
   student at the Sorbonne.

4. **Mon** frère et moi, nous sommes les premiers étudiants universitaires de
   notre famille. **Notre** sœur et **nos** cousins travaillent.
   *My brother and I are **our** family's first university students. **Our** sister and **our***
   cousins work.

5. Christine est **mon** amie.
   *Christine is **my** friend.*

[caption on photo:] ...ille de Claudine habite à Paris.

STRATÉGIES D'ANALYSE

1. Find the various ways of expressing *my* in the first sentence. What seems
   to make the difference between using **ma** and **mon**? When is the form **mes**
   used?

2. Look at items 2 and 3. How do you say "his father"? "her father"?
   If you saw **sa mère** with no reference to anybody, could you tell whether it
   meant "his mother" or "her mother"?

3. How do we express the notion of *our* (in item 4)?

4. In item 5, Christine is feminine. Note the possessive adjective used to
   express *my*. Why do you think this form is used?

La sœur de Claudine est étudiante à la Sorbonne.

[handwritten notes:]
my = ma / mon, mes
your = ta / ton, tes
her/his = sa/son, ses
our = notre, nos
your = votre, vos
their = leur, leurs

PRÉCnership or relationship by using possessive adjectives. In
ive adjective (like any other adjective) agrees in gender and
* W e noun it modifies.

	Singular			Plural
	masculine	feminine before consonants	feminine before vowel sounds	
	mon frère	**ma** sœur	**mon** amie	**mes** cousins
(fam.)	**ton** frère	**ta** sœur	**ton** amie	**tes** cousins
/her/its	**son** frère	**sa** sœur	**son** amie	**ses** cousins
ur	**notre** frère	**notre** sœur	**notre** amie	**nos** cousins
your	**votre** frère	**votre** sœur	**votre** amie	**vos** cousins
their	**leur** frère	**leur** sœur	**leur** amie	**leurs** cousins

* The possessive adjective agrees with the noun it modifies.

sa sœur = either *his sister* or *her sister* (Use the feminine form because **sœur** is feminine.)

son frère = either *his brother* or *her brother* (Use the masculine form because **frère** is masculine.)

* If a feminine noun begins with a vowel (or vowel sound), use the same form as in the masculine: **mon, ton,** and **son.**

Mon amie Anne-Marie est étudiante ici.
Ton éducation est importante.

A. J'apprécie. Tell your partner about values among your family, colleagues, and friends.

fiers: *proud*

Modèle: notre/nos/enfants
Dans notre famille, nous sommes fiers° de nos enfants.

1. Dans notre famille, nous sommes fiers de...

notre	maison
nos	voitures
	enfants
	grand-père
	voyages
	héritage

valeurs (f.): *values*

| | valeurs° |

2. Au travail, mes collègues sont fiers de...

leur	patron/patronne
leurs	employés

ordinateurs (m.): *computers*

| | ordinateurs° |
| | ponctualité |

3. Mes amis et moi, nous apprécions bien...

notre   voiture
nos   week-ends
            éducation
            université
            parcs
            amitié°
            profs
            bars

une amitié: *friendship*

Marc est fier de sa nouvelle voiture.

4. Moi, j'apprécie bien...

mon   famille
ma   amis
mes   collègues
          éducation
          ordinateur
          téléphone
          week-ends

5. Mon/Ma meilleur(e) ami(e) apprécie bien...

son   famille
sa   enfants
ses   professeur de...
         collègues
         héritage

Vocabulaire: Pour identifier les membres de la famille

It is easy to see the relationships among family members when they are in a family tree.

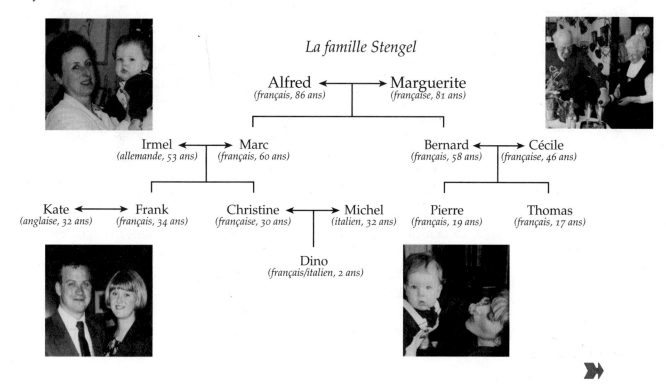

La famille Stengel

Alfred ←→ Marguerite
(français, 86 ans)   *(française, 81 ans)*

Irmel ←→ Marc   Bernard ←→ Cécile
(allemande, 53 ans) *(français, 60 ans)*   *(français, 58 ans)* *(française, 46 ans)*

Kate ←→ Frank   Christine ←→ Michel   Pierre   Thomas
(anglaise, 32 ans) *(français, 34 ans)*   *(française, 30 ans)* *(italien, 32 ans)*   *(français, 19 ans)* *(français, 17 ans)*

Dino
(français/italien, 2 ans)

À propos du vocabulaire: Note that in family relationships based on law rather than blood lines, the French language shows a casual attitude. In blood-line relationships, however, the language is precise. Ambiguous language such as **belle-sœur** for either *sister-in-law* or *stepsister* (legal relationship) reflects this casual approach as opposed to the precision shown in **demi-sœur**, *half-sister*.

À propos du vocabulaire: To indicate an "ex-relative" in French, add "ex-" to the title as in English, e.g., **une ex-femme, un ex-mari.**

Marguerite est la femme d'Alfred. C'est la mère de Marc et de Bernard et la grand-mère de Frank, de Christine, de Pierre et de Thomas. C'est l'arrière-grand-mère de Dino.

Alfred est le mari de Marguerite. C'est le père de Marc et de Bernard et le grand-père de Frank, de Christine, de Pierre et de Thomas. C'est l'arrière-grand-père de Dino.

Marc est le fils de Marguerite et d'Alfred. C'est le frère de Bernard, le mari d'Irmel, le père de Frank et de Christine et le grand-père de Dino. C'est l'oncle de Pierre et de Thomas et le beau-frère de Cécile.

Christine est la fille d'Irmel et de Marc et la sœur de Frank. C'est la mère de Dino. C'est la cousine de Pierre et de Thomas et la nièce de Bernard et de Cécile. C'est la petite-fille de Marguerite et d'Alfred. C'est la conjointe de Michel.

Dino est le fils de Christine et de Michel. C'est le petit-fils d'Irmel et de Marc et l'arrière-petit-fils de Marguerite et d'Alfred. C'est le neveu de Frank.

Michel est le conjoint de Christine. C'est le père de Dino.

Vocabulaire supplémentaire

une belle-mère	*mother-in-law or stepmother*
un beau-père	*father-in-law or stepfather*
une belle-sœur	*sister-in law or stepsister*
un beau-frère	*brother-in law or stepbrother*
une belle-fille	*daughter-in-law or stepdaughter*
un beau-fils	*son-in-law or stepson*
une demi-sœur	*half-sister*
un demi-frère	*half-brother*

STRATÉGIES D'ANALYSE

1. Study the relationship of Marguerite to other people in the family tree. Whose wife is she? Whose mother is she? Whose grandmother? Whose great-grandmother? Now read the first paragraph in the margin. Find the French words for wife, mother, grandmother, great-grandmother.

2. Study the relationship of Alfred to other people in the family tree. Whose husband is he? Whose father? Whose grandfather? Whose great-grandfather? Now read the second paragraph to find the French words that describe these relationships.

3. Using a similar strategy with Marc, find the French words for son, brother, uncle, and brother-in-law.

4. Using a similar strategy with Christine, find the French words for daughter, sister, cousin, niece, and granddaughter.

5. Now use the same strategy with Dino to discover the French words for grandson, great-grandson, and nephew.

PRÉCISIONS

- In French, the word **parent** is used to mean *relative* as well as the English cognate *parent*.

  Tous mes **parents** habitent en Alsace.   *All my relatives live in Alsace.*

- The following French words specify family relationships.

un mari, un époux	*husband*	un neveu	*nephew*
une femme, une épouse	*wife*	une nièce	*niece*
un père	*father*	un grand-père	*grandfather*
une mère	*mother*	une grand-mère	*grandmother*
un fils	*son*	un petit-fils	*grandson*
une fille	*daughter*	une petite-fille	*granddaughter*
un frère	*brother*	un arrière-grand-père	*great-grandfather*
une sœur	*sister*		
un(e) cousin(e)	*cousin*	une arrière-grand-mère	*great-grandmother*
un oncle	*uncle*		
une tante	*aunt*		

B. **La famille de Frank.** Complete the following statements based on the family tree, using Frank as a reference point.

1. Kate est *sa fiancée*.
2. Dino est *son neveu*.
3. Marc est _____.
4. Bernard est _____.
5. Alfred est _____.
6. Marguerite est _____.
7. Cécile est _____.
8. Pierre et Thomas sont _____.
9. Christine est _____.

C. La famille de Marguerite et d'Alfred. Complete the following statements using Marguerite and Alfred as a reference point.

1. Irmel et Cécile sont *leurs belles-filles*.
2. Marc et Bernard sont _____.
3. Frank est _____.
4. Christine est _____.
5. Pierre et Thomas sont _____.
6. Dino est _____.

D. La famille de Dino. Complete the following statements using Dino as a reference.

1. Alfred est *son arrière-grand-père*.
2. Marguerite est _____.
3. Irmel est _____.
4. Marc est _____.
5. Frank est _____.
6. Christine est _____.
7. Michel est _____.

Vocabulaire: Pour parler de nos activités avec les autres (avec des verbes en -er)

Les Martin **passent** du temps en famille.

M. Dufour **invite** une amie à dîner.

Les jeunes **participent** aux projets communautaires.

Vous **bavardez** avec vos amis?

E. Mes amis et moi. Create at least five sentences using elements from each column. Make the verb you select for each sentence agree with its subject. Read your sentences to your partner.

Modèle: *Mes amis et moi, nous passons du temps ensemble à l'université.*

je	adorer	fréquenter les musées
tu	aimer (bien)	dîner au restaurant
mon ami(e)	détester	passer du temps au café
mes amis et moi	bavarder	rester à la maison
vous	parler	
Paul et Marc	chanter	avec les ami(e)s
Anne et Christine	passer du temps	avec les profs
mon père et moi	ensemble	avec la famille
mes amis	fréquenter	avec les collègues au travail
Monique	inviter (une personne)	
toi et moi		à la maison
mon professeur		au café
mon professeur et moi		à l'université
		au travail
		les musées
		les cinémas
		les expositions
		les restaurants
		à dîner
		au cinéma/au musée/au restaurant
		à danser

Structure: Le verbe avoir

We use the verb **avoir** *(to have)* to indicate ownership of things and relationships among people, as well as in special expressions.

OBSERVATIONS

J'ai un frère et deux sœurs.
I have a brother and two sisters.

Tu as un demi-frère intéressant.
You have an interesting half-brother.

Nous avons beaucoup de nièces et de neveux.
We have many nieces and nephews.

Vous avez une belle-mère ravissante.
You have a gorgeous mother-in-law.

Il a sommeil.
He is sleepy.

Ils ont faim.
They are hungry.

Elle a l'intention d'aller au cinéma.
She intends to go to the movies.

Elles ont l'habitude de rester à la maison.
They are accustomed to staying at home.

Madeleine **a l'air malade.**

STRATÉGIES D'ANALYSE

1. Obviously, the verb **avoir** is irregular in its formation. Do any of its present-tense forms look at all like the infinitive? Which ones?

2. The verb **avoir** is used in a number of idiomatic expressions that do not correspond directly between French and English. Find four of these expressions in the sentences.

PRÉCISIONS

- The conjugation of **avoir** is irregular.

j'**ai**	nous **avons**		je n'**ai** pas	nous n'**avons** pas
tu **as**	vous **avez**		tu n'**as** pas	vous n'**avez** pas
il/elle/on **a**	ils/elles **ont**		il/elle/on n'**a** pas	ils/elles n'**ont** pas

- The verb **avoir** is used in many common idiomatic expressions.

J'ai	**faim.**	*I am*	*hungry.*
	soif.		*thirsty.*
	sommeil.		*sleepy.*
	froid.		*cold.*
	chaud.		*hot.*
	raison.		*right.*
	tort.		*wrong.*
	de la chance.		*lucky.*

Tu as envie de rester ici?
Do you feel like staying here?

Il a l'intention de parler avec son patron.
He intends to talk with his boss.

Nous avons besoin de consulter notre avocat.
We need to consult our lawyer.

Ils ont l'habitude de dîner ensemble le vendredi soir.
They are accustomed to having dinner together on Friday evenings.

Vous avez l'air fatigué.	*You look tired.*
content.	*happy.*
triste.	*sad.*
optimiste.	*optimistic.*
pessimiste.	*pessimistic.*
malade.	*sick.*

F. **Ma famille.** Tell your partner who the members of your family are by giving their relationship to you.

Modèle: *J'ai un père, une belle-mère, deux frères et une demi-sœur.*

1ᴱᴿ THÈME: Ma famille, mes amis, mes collègues

G. Non, tu as tort. Take turns answering the following questions with your partner. Use **avoir** expressions in your responses.

> **Modèle:** —Est-ce que tu désires un Perrier?
> —*Oui, s'il te plaît. J'ai soif.*
> ou —*Non, merci. Je n'ai pas soif.*

1. Est-ce que tu désires un sandwich?
2. Est-ce que tu désires un Coca?
3. Est-ce que tu voudrais un chocolat?
4. La capitale des États-Unis est New York City, n'est-ce pas?
5. La capitale de la France est Paris, n'est-ce pas?
6. Est-ce que les enfants ont besoin d'un pull-over?
7. La capitale du Canada est Toronto, n'est-ce pas?
8. Ton enfant a envie de se coucher°?
9. Est-ce que tu désires une eau minérale?
10. Le professeur aime le français, n'est-ce pas?

se coucher: to go to bed

H. Elle a l'air... With your partner, fill in the blanks with the name of a class member.

1. _____ a l'air fatigué.
2. _____ a l'air content.
3. _____ a l'air triste.
4. _____ et _____ ont l'air malade.
5. _____ et _____ ont l'air intelligent.

I. J'ai besoin de... Working with your partner, choose an expression from the following list to complete each sentence.

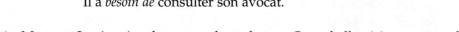

(avoir) besoin de	l'habitude de	envie de	l'intention de

> **Modèle:** Deux agents de police arrivent à l'appartement de mon cousin. Il a *besoin de* consulter son avocat.

1. Ma tante Louise aime beaucoup la sculpture. Quand elle visite une grande ville, elle a _____ visiter les musées.
2. Quand mon collègue Georges est au bureau, il n'a pas le temps de parler avec sa femme. Alors, il n'a pas _____ téléphoner à la maison.
3. Mon mari et moi, nous regardons une vidéo ensemble tous les week-ends. Nous avons _____ regarder un film classique.
4. Je déteste mon travail. Je n'ai pas _____ rester dans cette entreprise.
5. Mon patron travaille beaucoup et il est fatigué. Il désire rester à la maison samedi et dimanche. Il n'a pas _____ travailler ce week-end.
6. Mes amis et moi, nous aimons célébrer les anniversaires. Nous avons _____ fêter les occasions spéciales ensemble.

Est-ce que j'ai besoin de consulter mon avocat?

À propos de la structure: Note that we use the infinitive form of the verb after **de**. **J'ai envie de** *rester* à la maison.

PRONONCIATION: L'élision 🎞️

L'**élision** in French is similar to a contraction in English; it means that a vowel at the end of a word (usually **-a** or **-e**) is dropped when the following word begins with a vowel sound. Elisions occur in spoken and written French; in the latter, an apostrophe (') is used to mark the omission of the vowel.

Sometimes, elision is required, as is the case with the pronouns **je** and **que,** the singular definite articles **(le, la)**, the negative **ne,** and the possessive **de** in the following examples:

je → j'	**J'**ai soif.	
que → qu'	**Qu'**est-ce que c'est?	
le → l'	**l'**oncle	
la → l'	**l'**omelette	
ne → n'	Vous **n'**avez pas froid?	
de → d'	Le père **d'**Hélène est Marc.	

À propos du vocabulaire;
Since the definite articles **(le, la)** of nouns beginning with a vowel sound are elided **(l')**, the gender of such nouns may be somewhat more difficult to remember. To help you memorize which nouns are masculine or feminine as you learn new vocabulary, try using the indefinite articles **(un, une)** instead, as these are never subject to elision.

Other times, elisions are a sign of a more informal or colloquial register of language. This type of elision is more common in spoken French than in written forms. In these cases, vowels other than **-a** or **-e** might be omitted:

Tu as faim? → **T'**as faim?

In certain expressions, vowels might be dropped that do not precede a vowel sound. Again, this is more common in spoken French than in written forms:

Je veux bien! → **J'**veux bien!

À vous! With a partner, practice pronouncing the following sentences that contain elisions:

1. J'habite l'avenue Leclerc.
2. L'ami d'Antoine travaille à l'université.
3. Qu'est-ce que vous racontez?
4. Nous visitons l'exposition d'Ingres au Louvre.
5. Elle n'a pas d'ordinateur.
6. Tu n'as pas l'adresse d'Olivier?

1ᴱᴿ THÈME: Ma famille, mes amis et mes collègues

POUR DÉVELOPPER VOS IDÉES

Thematic objective: To identify and qualify the relationships between you and the people close to you

Présentation: La qualité de nos rapports avec les autres

POUR SAISIR L'ESSENTIEL: A survey was conducted in the Montréal area to determine the quality of relationships among people in the workplace. Read through the categories and numbers. Judging from this survey, would you guess **Québécois** to be easy or difficult to get along with? Explain your reasoning.

Which choice best describes your relationships with people at work or school?

Sondage: *Survey*

SONDAGE°

En général, comment sont vos rapports avec vos collègues au travail?

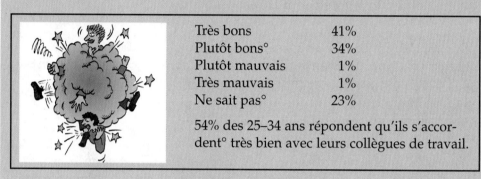

Très bons	41%
Plutôt bons°	34%
Plutôt mauvais	1%
Très mauvais	1%
Ne sait pas°	23%

54% des 25–34 ans répondent qu'ils s'accordent° très bien avec leurs collègues de travail.

Plutôt bons: *Rather good*

Ne sait pas: *Do not know*

s'accordent: *agree, get along*

J. **Mes rapports avec les autres.** Décrivez vos rapports avec les autres en complétant les phrases.

> **Modèle:** Mes rapports avec mes collègues au travail sont *plutôt bons.*

 très bons
plutôt bons

 plutôt mauvais
très mauvais

1. Mes rapports avec mes collègues au travail sont...
2. Mes rapports avec ma famille sont...

voisins (m.): *neighbors*

3. Mes rapports avec mes voisins° sont...
4. Mes rapports avec mes amis sont...

K. **Nos sentiments envers** (*toward*) **les autres.** Complétez les phrases pour donner une description de vos sentiments envers vos collègues, votre famille, vos voisins et vos amis.

j'essaie de: *I try to*

Sentiments: j'admire... / j'ai du respect pour... / j'accepte... / j'essaie de° tolérer...

> **Modèle:** En général, *j'ai du respect* pour mes collègues.

1. En général, ... (*sentiment*) ... mes collègues.
2. En général, ... (*sentiment*) ... ma famille.
3. En général, ... (*sentiment*) ... mes voisins.
4. En général, ... (*sentiment*) ... mes amis.

L. **Le partage (*Sharing*) des réflexions.** Travaillez en groupe de trois ou quatre. À tour de rôle°, décrivez la qualité de vos rapports avec les autres personnes dans votre vie. Après chaque tour du groupe, mettez-vous d'accord° sur un résumé général de vos idées en utilisant la formule appropriée. Préparez quatre résumés.

À tour de rôle: *Taking turns*
mettez-vous d'accord: *agree on*

Modèle: En général, nous avons *des rapports harmonieux* avec nos collègues.

Formule de résumé

En général, nous avons	des rapports harmonieux	avec nos collègues
	des rapports divers	avec notre famille
	des problèmes	avec nos voisins
		avec nos amis

J'aime bien passer du temps avec ma grand-mère.

M. **Les rôles des autres dans ma vie.** Complétez trois ou quatre phrases pour communiquer vos idées. Comparez vos phrases avec celles (*those*) de votre partenaire.

Modèle: —Quand j'ai des problèmes, j'aime parler avec *mon meilleur ami*.
—Et moi, quand j'ai des problèmes, j'aime parler avec *mon père*.

1. J'aime bien passer du temps avec _____.
2. Quand j'ai des problèmes, j'aime parler avec _____.
3. Quand j'ai envie de bavarder avec quelqu'un, je téléphone à _____.
4. Une personne que je respecte beaucoup est _____.
5. J'admire _____ pour son talent.
6. J'admire _____ pour sa bonne humeur.
7. J'admire _____ pour son intelligence.
8. J'admire _____ pour sa générosité.
9. J'aime regarder des vidéos avec _____.
10. J'aime bien fréquenter les boutiques avec _____.
11. J'aime bien fréquenter les bars avec _____.
12. Quand je désire fêter une occasion spéciale, je téléphone à _____.

mon petit ami/ma petite amie
mon meilleur ami
ma meilleure amie
mon ami(e)
un(e) collègue
mon patron/ma patronne
un voisin/une voisine
mon mari/mon époux
ma femme/mon épouse
mon conjoint/ma conjointe
mon père
ma mère
mon frère
ma sœur
(autres personnes)

2ᴇ THÈME: On est comme ça

Objective: To describe people you know

PRÉSENTATION: Un coup d'œil sur le thème

retraité: *retired*

Alfred Stengel, un homme intelligent et travailleur

yeux (m.) bleus: *blue eyes*
cheveux (m.) blancs: *white hair*

Alfred Stengel est français. Il habite à Haguenau en Alsace. Il est directeur retraité° du Collège Foch, une école secondaire pour les élèves de 12 à 14 ans.

M. Stengel est assez grand avec les yeux bleus° et les cheveux blancs°. À l'âge de 86 ans, il n'est pas jeune, mais il est fort, énergique et actif dans les affaires de sa communauté. Intelligent et travailleur, il est président de la chorale communautaire et l'un des directeurs de l'hôpital de Haguenau.

Époux, père, grand-père et arrière-grand-père, il

dévoué: *devoted*

est dévoué° à sa famille et bien respecté par tous les membres de sa famille.

Alfred est retraité, mais il est actif dans sa communauté.

Christine Stengel, la petite-fille d'Alfred Stengel, est française aussi. Elle habite à Colmar en Alsace où elle est infirmière à l'hôpital.

À l'âge de 30 ans, Christine est grande et svelte. Elle est belle, avec le visage° ovale, les cheveux châtain° et les yeux bleus.

Intelligente et travailleuse, comme son grand-père, elle cherche° de l'équilibre dans sa vie de mère de famille et d'infirmière. Énergique, amusante, joyeuse et pratique, Christine est bien aimée par sa famille et ses amis.

visage: *face*
châtain: *brown (hair)*

cherche: *seeks*

Christine cherche de l'équilibre dans sa vie de mère de famille et d'infirmière.

Stratégies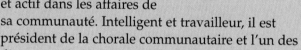

1. Make two columns. Label one "Alfred" and the other "Christine." In the first column list the adjectives used to describe Alfred; in the second, list those that describe his granddaughter. What traits do they share?

2. Which of the adjectives in your lists would you use to describe yourself?

POUR DÉVELOPPER VOTRE FRANÇAIS

Vocabulaire: Pour donner l'âge de quelqu'un

OBSERVATIONS

Moi, **j'ai vingt-deux ans.**
Mon père a **quarante-huit** ans.
Ma mère a **quarante-six** ans.
Les parents de mon père ont **soixante-neuf**
  et **soixante-sept** ans.
Les parents de ma mère sont plus âgés; ils ont
  soixante-dix-huit et **soixante-quinze ans.**

[Me] I'm 22 years old.
My dad is 48.
My mom is 46.
My father's parents are 69 and 67.

My mother's parents are older;
they are 78 and 75.

STRATÉGIES D'ANALYSE

1. In English, we identify directly with our age, indicating that we *are* our age. Example: I'm 22. Do we use the verb *to be* (**être**) in French to state our age? Which verb do we use?
2. When giving our age in English, we can use the number alone. In French, what word follows the number when referring to age?
3. Study the ages of the grandparents in the examples. Can you figure out the system of numbers used in French from 60 to 79?

PRÉCISIONS

- Use the verb **avoir** to state someone's age.

Paul **a** 19 ans. Ses sœurs **ont** 22
et 24 ans.

*Paul **is** 19. His sisters **are** 22 and 24.*

- When referring to age, use the word for years **(ans)** after the number.

J'ai 32 **ans.**

- Numbers from 40 to 69 are formed like numbers from 20 to 39.

40	quarante	50	cinquante	60	soixante
41	quarante et un	51	cinquante et un	61	soixante et un
42	quarante-deux	52	cinquante-deux	62	soixante-deux
49	quarante-neuf	59	cinquante-neuf	69	soixante-neuf

- From 60 to 79, however, French numbers are counted in a set of 20. Thus, numbers from 70 to 79 continue the sequence of numbers from the 60's.

60	soixante	74	soixante-quatorze
69	soixante-neuf	75	soixante-quinze
70	soixante-dix	76	soixante-seize
71	soixante et onze	77	soixante-dix-sept
72	soixante-douze	78	soixante-dix-huit
73	soixante-treize	79	soixante-dix-neuf

- Numbers from 80 to 100 are counted in a set of 20. The number for 80 is **quatre-vingts** (four twenties).

Note the **-s** in **quatre-vingts**. There is no **-s** when followed by another number: **quatre-vingt-deux.**

80	quatre vingts	90	quatre-vingt-dix
81	quatre-vingt-un	91	quatre-vingt-onze
82	quatre-vingt-deux	92	quatre-vingt-douze
89	quatre-vingt-neuf	99	quatre-vingt-dix-neuf
		100	cent

Note Culturelle

The numbering system of the Gauls, early inhabitants of France, was based on 20. The Romans introduced the system based on 10 (decimals) into the region. The Gauls adopted the system of their Roman conquerors, but reverted to their own when the numbers got big. The numbering systems in Belgium and Switzerland carry the decimal system through the larger numbers. They have words for 70 (**septante**), 80 (**octante**), and 90 (**nonante**).

A. Ils ont quel âge? As part of your study of possible retirement homes for your grandparents, you are checking on the ages of the residents. Take turns with your partner reading aloud the ages of the following individuals.

Modèle: Mme LeGros, 98
Mme LeGros a quatre-vingt-dix-huit ans.

1. M. LeGros, 99
2. Mme Chaumont, 77
3. M. Chaumont et M. Simard, 79
4. Mme Bellevue, 74
5. M. Bellevue, 83

6. Mme LaCroix, 91
7. M. LaCroix, 92
8. Mme Beauchamps, 94
9. M. Beauchamps, 89
10. M. et Mme Thierry, 78

Vocabulaire: Pour décrire quelqu'un (avec avoir)

OBSERVATIONS

Elle a un visage ovale.

Il a les yeux bleus.

Il a un nez impressionnant.

Il a les cheveux blonds.

Elle a les cheveux châtain°/marron° et un large sourire.

Il a les cheveux frisés.

châtain: *brown*
marron: *chestnut brown*

J'**ai** trente-deux **ans.** Quel **âge avez-vous?**
*I **am** thirty-two **years old.** How **old are you?***

Tu **as les yeux verts?**
*Do you **have green eyes?***

Son frère **a une barbe** et **une moustache.**
*His/Her brother **has a beard** and **a moustache.***

Mes sœurs et moi, nous **avons les cheveux courts.**
*My sisters and I **have short hair.***

Vous **avez le visage rond** et **le nez parfait.**
*You **have a round face** and **a perfect nose.***

Les jumelles **ont les cheveux bouclés, le visage ovale, les yeux noirs** et **le nez retroussé.**
*The twins **have curly hair, an oval face, black eyes,** and **a turned-up nose.***

STRATÉGIES D'ANALYSE

1. Which verb is used in these examples of personal descriptions?
2. In these descriptions of facial features, which comes first—the name of the body part or its description?
3. Are any of the new vocabulary words similar to English words? Which ones?

- Adjectives usually follow the noun they modify.

Elle a un visage **ovale/long/rond/carré.**	*She has an **oval/long/round/square** face.*
Elle a les cheveux **blonds/noirs/roux/bruns/marron/châtains/blancs.**	*She has **blond/black/red/brown/chestnut/white (gray)** hair.*
Elle a les cheveux **bouclés/frisés/raides/ondulés/longs/courts.**	*She has **curly/tightly curled/straight/wavy/long/short** hair.*
Il a les yeux **verts/bleus/noirs/marron.**	*He has **green/blue/black/brown** eyes.*
Il a le nez **court/pointu/retroussé.**	*He has a **short/pointed/turned-up** nose.*

- Note that the adjective **marron** is invariable in the singular and the plural.

B. **L'homme ou la femme de mes rêves.** Tell your partner about the man or woman of your dreams using the following sentences.

1. L'homme/La femme de mes rêves a _____ ans.
2. L'homme/La femme de mes rêves a les cheveux _____ et _____.

blonds	longs	bouclés
noirs	courts	frisés
roux	raides	
bruns	ondulés	
marron/châtains		

3. Il/Elle a le visage _____.

carré	rond
long	ovale

4. Il/Elle a les yeux _____.

bleus	noirs
verts	marron

5. Il/Elle a le nez _____.

court	retroussé
pointu	impressionnant

C. **L'homme ou la femme de ma vie (*suite*).** Now compare the man or woman of your dreams to the current one in your life. Complete the following sentences and read them to your partner.

Modèle: *La femme de mes rêves a les cheveux longs et blonds.*
En réalité, la femme de ma vie n'est pas comme ça.
Elle a les cheveux bleus.

L'homme/La femme **de mes rêves** a
_____ ans.
les cheveux _____.
le visage _____.
les yeux _____.
le nez _____.

L'homme/La femme **de ma vie** a
_____ ans.
les cheveux _____.
le visage _____.
les yeux _____.
le nez _____.

Structure: Les adjectifs

OBSERVATIONS

La jeune fille est **adroite.**
L'homme est **maladroit.**

Cendrillon est **jolie.**
Ses belles-sœurs sont **laides.**

Mon père est **optimiste.** Ma mère est **optimiste** aussi.
*My father is **optimistic.** My mother is **optimistic** also.*

Mon oncle est **paresseux.** Ma tante est **paresseuse** aussi.
*My uncle is **lazy.** My aunt is **lazy** too.*

Paul et Marc sont **indifférents.** Ils ne sont pas **curieux.**
Anne et Lucie sont **indifférentes** aussi. Elles ne sont pas **curieuses.**
*Paul and Marc are **indifferent.** They are not **curious.***
*Anne and Lucie are also **indifferent.** They are not **curious.***

STRATÉGIES D'ANALYSE

1. What happens to an adjective when the noun it modifies changes from masculine to feminine?
2. What happens to an adjective when the noun changes from singular to plural?
3. Can you develop a rule or explanation for the agreement of an adjective with the noun it modifies?

PRÉCISIONS

- In French, an adjective agrees in gender (masculine or feminine) and in number (singular or plural) with the noun it modifies.

  Mon patron est bien **organisé.**   Ma secrétaire est bien **organisée** aussi.

- Most frequently we add an **-e** to the masculine form of an adjective to make it feminine.

  Mon cousin est **grand.**   Ma cousine est **grande** aussi.

À propos de la prononciation:
Note that the final consonant of most adjectives is not pronounced. However, when a silent **-e** is added for feminine agreement, the final adjective is then pronounced. Example: **grand, grande**.

- Adjectives that end in an *unaccented* **-e** in the masculine keep the same form in the feminine.

Mon père est **extrême.**   Ma mère est **extrême** aussi.

Mon cousin est **optimiste.**   Ma cousine est **optimiste** aussi.

- Masculine forms that end in **-eux** generally change to **-euse** in the feminine. Some masculine forms that end in **-eur** also change to **-euse** in the feminine.

Robert est **affectueux.**   Christine n'est pas **affectueuse.**

Mon ami est **travailleur.**   Notre sœur est **travailleuse** aussi.

- Most adjectives add **-s** to form the plural (if they do not already end in **-s** or **-x**).

Paul et Marc sont **indifférents.**   Anne et Lucie sont **indifférentes** aussi.

Ils ne sont pas **curieux.**   Elles ne sont pas **curieuses.**

D. **Qui est... ?** Working with your partner, choose a famous person who demonstrates each of the following traits. Pay attention to the gender of the individual, making the adjective agree with the noun.

     Modèle: *Oprah Winfrey est travailleuse.*

1. ...est spontané(e)
2. ...est flamboyant(e)
3. ...est égoïste
4. ...est énergique
5. ...est intelligent(e)
6. ...est affectueux/affectueuse
7. ...est dynamique
8. ...est ennuyeux/ennuyeuse°
9. ...est travailleur/travailleuse
10. ...est intolérant(e)

ennuyeux/ennuyeuse: *boring*

E. **Comment décrire... ?** Working with a partner, choose one adjective from the pair of antonyms to describe each individual, based on the description. (All adjectives are given in the masculine singular form. Change the gender and/or number as necessary.)

     Modèle: Mon oncle Robert a un million de dollars américains. Il est...

                 (riche/pauvre)

                 Il est riche.

À propos du vocabulaire: Since Exs. E and F are based on antonyms, if you recognize one of the adjectives as a cognate, you can infer the meaning of the other.

1. Mon oncle donne beaucoup de son argent aux pauvres. Il est... (généreux/avare)
2. Ma tante Monique pose beaucoup de questions. Elle est... (curieux/indifférent)
3. Ma sœur a des idées fixes. Elle est... (influençable/têtu)
4. Mon patron pense toujours que tout est possible. Il est... (pessimiste/optimiste)
5. Ma cousine organise toutes ses activités en avance. Elle est... (méthodique/spontané)
6. Notre prof a beaucoup d'histoires° intéressantes. Il est... (amusant/ennuyeux)
7. Ma mère n'aime pas les hommes avec les cheveux longs et bleus. Elle est... (tolérant/intolérant)

histoires (f.): *stories*

F. Notre prof est... From each pair of antonyms, select the adjective that you think is the better description of your French professor. Then join another pair of partners, and each group can take turns comparing lists.

> **Modèle:** *À mon avis°, notre prof de français est curieux, mais mon partenaire pense° qu'il est indifférent.*

À mon avis: *In my opinion*
pense: *thinks*

À mon avis	Notre prof est...	À l'avis de mon/ ma partenaire
curieux	curieux/indifférent	*indifférent*
	méthodique/spontané	
	tolérant/intolérant	
	amusant/ennuyeux	
	intelligent/pas bien intelligent	
	modeste/égoïste	
	timide/flamboyant	
	naïf/sophistiqué	
	bien organisé/mal organisé	

G. Qualité ou défaut? Tell your partner about your best friend. Use the list of descriptive words to help you comment on some of your best friend's traits and on your perception of them.

À propos de la structure: Nouns that end in **-isme** are generally masculine. Nouns that end in **-té** and **-ance** or **-ence** are generally feminine.

> **Modèle:** sensible
> *Mon/Ma meilleur(e) ami(e) est sensible.*
> *J'apprécie sa sensibilité.*
> ou *Sa sensibilité est agaçante°.*

agaçante: *annoying.*

sensible	sa sensibilité
timide	sa timidité
fragile	sa fragilité
dynamique	son dynamisme
émotif(-ive)	son émotivité
généreux(-euse)	sa générosité
tolérant(e)	sa tolérance
persévérant(e)	sa persévérance
spontané(e)	sa spontanéité
intelligent(e)	son intelligence
optimiste	son optimisme
pessimiste	son pessimisme

H. Auto-analyse. It is usually easier to describe others than ourselves. Use the chart on the next page to help you identify your own traits. Use the numbers on each scale to indicate where in the range your personal tendencies lie.

tolérant(e)	1	2	3	4	5	intolérant(e)
travailleur(-euse)	1	2	3	4	5	paresseux(-euse)
intelligent(e)	1	2	3	4	5	pas bien intelligent(e)
optimiste	1	2	3	4	5	pessimiste
pratique	1	2	3	4	5	frivole
docile	1	2	3	4	5	dynamique
bien organisé(e)	1	2	3	4	5	mal organisé(e)
affectueux(-euse)	1	2	3	4	5	réservé(e)
influençable	1	2	3	4	5	têtu(e), obstiné(e)
méthodique	1	2	3	4	5	spontané(e)
amusant(e)	1	2	3	4	5	ennuyeux(-euse)
généreux(-euse)	1	2	3	4	5	avare
curieux(-euse)	1	2	3	4	5	indifférent(e)
gentil/gentille (kind)	1	2	3	4	5	méchant(e) (mean)
timide	1	2	3	4	5	flamboyant(e), hardi(e)
modeste	1	2	3	4	5	égoïste
rêveur(-euse)°	1	2	3	4	5	réaliste
naïf(-ive)	1	2	3	4	5	sophistiqué(e)

rêveur:
dreamer

Now select the five features you feel are most significant in your relations with people (a) in your family, (b) in your social activities, and (c) at school or work.

I. Discussion de notre auto-analyse. Report the results of your self-analysis to your partner and compare your findings.

1. Rapport à votre partenaire:
   En famille, je suis _____, _____ et _____.
   Avec mes amis, j'ai envie d'être _____ et _____.
   Quand je suis à l'école ou au travail, j'ai besoin d'être _____ et _____.

2. Avec votre partenaire, cherchez des similarités dans vos rapports avec les autres. Écrivez vos comparaisons dans un schéma *(diagram)*.

Schéma

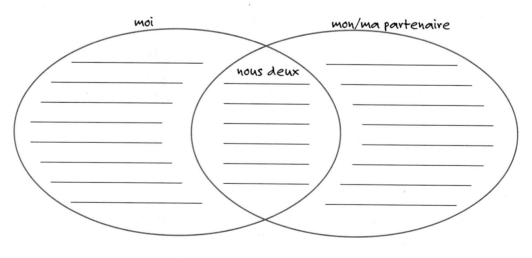

PRONONCIATION: Les voyelles *a* et *i*

À propos de la prononciation:
The pronunciation of **a** and **i** may be altered when they appear with other vowels or in combination with **-m** or **-n**. These variations are discussed in subsequent chapters.

When the French vowels **a** and **i** are not combined with other vowels or followed by a nasal consonant **(m, n)**, they are pronounced in the following manner:

- **a**   similar to the *a* sound of the English word *calm.* To pronounce it correctly, your lips should be rounded. Repeat the following words after your instructor:

      bavarder   adorer   agent

The diphthong **oi** in French is also pronounced **a** (preceded by a *w* sound), as in the English word "water":

      voilà   toi   froid

- **i**   similar to the *i* sound of the English word *elite.* Remember that **y** is pronounced the same as **i**. Now, repeat these words:

      joli   Michel   Yveline

(Did you smile when you pronounced **i**? You should, to pronounce it correctly!)

À vous! With a partner, read aloud the following sentences, paying particular attention to the pronunciation of the sounds *a* and *i:*

1. J'habite à Paris.
2. Le mari d'Isabelle s'appelle Yves.
3. La fille a un visage ovale et les yeux noirs.
4. Il est maladroit parce qu'il a sommeil.
5. J'adore la musique classique.
6. Vous avez quel âge?
7. Si tu as soif, prends une boisson!
8. Il y a trois avocats.

POUR DÉVELOPPER VOS IDÉES

Thematic objective: To identify and evaluate the characteristics that you associate with people

POUR SAISIR L'ESSENTIEL: Stereotypes are oversimplified conceptions or images (favorable or unfavorable) usually based on superficial or limited observations. Although they are often inaccurate, they are routinely presented and accepted as fact. The following joke plays with some common stereotypes about professions and nationalities.

The joke gives four pairs of stereotypes. Choose one pair and identify the stereotypical quality (or qualities) associated with the profession and the two nationalities that make the combination either heavenly or disastrous. Use the formula in the **Modèle** to organize your ideas.

À propos de la structure: You can intensify a negation by adding **du tout.** For example, you could say **Les Anglais n'ont *pas du tout* la réputation d'être...**

Modèle: Les chefs sont *créatifs et artistiques.* Les Français ont la réputation d'être *artistiques et avant-gardes.* Mais les Anglais n'ont pas la réputation d'être *imaginatifs.*

Do you agree with the stereotypical descriptions?

LES STÉRÉOTYPES

Au Paradis
les chefs sont français;
les comptables sont anglais;
les agents de police sont allemands; et
les amants sont italiens.

En Enfer
les chefs sont anglais;
les comptables sont français;
les agents de police sont italiens; et
les amants sont allemands!

À propos du vocabulaire: Refer to Ex. H on pp. 99–100 for a list of useful adjectives.

J. On dit que... *(People say . . .)* Il y a beaucoup de stéréotypes aux États-Unis. Travaillez avec un(e) partenaire pour déterminer les qualités stéréotypiques attribuées aux groupes sur la liste.

Modèle: Les écrivains sont...
On dit que les écrivains sont rêveurs.

1. Les voisins sont toujours...
2. Les blondes sont...
3. Les bibliothécaires sont...
4. Les roux/rousses sont...
5. Les belles-mères sont...
6. Les ex-femmes sont...
7. Les comptables sont...
8. Les avocats sont...
9. Les politiciens sont...
10. Les Texans sont...
11. Les gens qui ont une voiture de sport sont...
12. (Autres ???)

faux: *false*

K. Mais en réalité... Évidemment les stéréotypes sont souvent faux°. Travaillez avec un partenaire pour réfuter vos stéréotypes de l'exercice précédent. Choisissez au moins trois stéréotypes à réfuter.

Modèle: *On dit que les écrivains sont rêveurs, mais mon beau-père est écrivain et il est très réaliste et pratique.*

3ᴱ THÈME: On fait sa part°

On fait sa part: *One does his/her part*

Objective: To talk about your routine activities

PRÉSENTATION: Un coup d'œil sur le thème

Comment est-ce que je fais ma part pour ma famille? En réalité, je fais ma part dans ma famille, c'est-à-dire°, je partage les tâches ménagères° avec ma femme et ma fille. J'aide à faire la cuisine et le samedi on fait le marché° ensemble. Et en général, le dimanche, on fait une promenade ensemble. Le travail est plus agréable comme ça.

c'est-à-dire: *that is (to say)*
tâches (f.) ménagères: *household chores*
fait le marché: *go grocery shopping*

Ma femme, ma fille et moi, nous sommes heureux ensemble.

Faire sa part pour ses amis, c'est très important. Par exemple°, quelquefois° j'aide mon amie Catherine avec ses enfants. En général, j'essaie vraiment d'être libre quand mes amis ont besoin de moi.

par exemple: *for example*
quelquefois: *sometimes*

J'aime les enfants et j'aime aider mon amie.

Au bureau, tout le monde fait sa part. Pour moi, c'est souvent la paperasserie°, et je fais aussi des coups de téléphone aux clients. Mais la première chose à faire chaque jour quand j'arrive au bureau, c'est le café! Tous° mes collègues apprécient cette contribution.

paperasserie: *paperwork*

Tous: *All (pl)*

J'ai beaucoup à faire au bureau.

Stratégies

1. Use the photos to determine which paragraph is about **travail,** which is about **amis,** and which is about **famille.** If the photo is ambiguous, consult the accompanying paragraph for clarification.
2. Scan the paragraphs to find the phrases that tell what people are doing in each photograph.
3. Make a list of expressions from the paragraphs that describe activities that you do.
4. Write a one-sentence description in English of the **Coup d'œil.**

POUR DÉVELOPPER VOTRE FRANÇAIS

Structure: Le verbe faire

OBSERVATIONS

Jacqueline **fait** des courses. Elle cherche des fleurs.
*Jacqueline is running errands. She is looking
for some flowers.*

Deux par deux les enfants **font** une promenade dans
le parc.
Two by two, the children are taking a walk in the park.

Je **fais la grasse matinée** le week-end.
I sleep late on weekends.

Qu'est-ce que tu **fais**?
What are you doing?

Il **fait** de la lecture après le dîner.
He does some reading after dinner.

Qu'est-ce qu'on **fait** ce week-end?
What are we doing this week-end?

Nous **faisons** nos devoirs ensemble.
We do our homework together.

Qu'est-ce que vous **faites** samedi soir?
What are you doing Saturday night?

Mes collègues au travail **font**
rarement de la paperasserie.
My colleagues at work rarely do paperwork.

STRATÉGIES D'ANALYSE

1. The verb **faire** *(to do, to make)* is used in each of the sample sentences. Are the forms of **faire** regular or irregular in the present tense?
2. Do any of the endings of **faire** look like the endings on any other verbs that you have studied? For example, does **font** remind you of similar forms for other verbs you have studied? Which ones?
3. Can you identify an expression in the sample sentences which uses the verb **faire** but does not mean "do" or "make"? What is the idiomatic expression used in that sentence?

- The verb **faire** (*to do* or *to make*) is irregular in its conjugation.

je **fais**	nous **faisons**
tu **fais**	vous **faites**
il/elle/on **fait**	ils/elles **font**

A. **On fait...** Taking turns with your partner, restate each of the following sentences, replacing the italicized word with the words given in parentheses. Be sure to change the form of the verb to agree with the subject.

1. *Je* fais les devoirs de français. (nous / vous / tu / ils)
2. *Nous* faisons des courses. (je / tu / elles / il)
3. *Paul* fait la grasse matinée le week-end. (nous / je / tu / mes amis)
4. *Christine* fait une promenade dans le parc. (je / vous / nous / les enfants)
5. *Nous* faisons de la paperasserie au bureau. (vous / je / mon patron / mes collègues)

Vocabulaire: Pour parler de nos activités de tous les jours° (avec faire)

de tous les jours: *everyday*

Observations

Marc **fait un coup de téléphone.**
Marc is making a telephone call.

La dame **fait de la lecture** dans le parc.
The lady is doing some reading in the park.

Monique **fait la queue** pour acheter des pâtisseries.
Monique is standing in line to buy pastries.

Stratégies d'analyse

1. Appropriate translations from one language to another are rarely done word for word. Using the photos, can you determine what expression in French means *to stand in line* in English?
2. The French word **queue** literally means *tail*. Therefore, what is the literal translation for **faire la queue**? What is really meant by **faire la queue**?
3. Do you know the British expression for *standing in line* that uses part of the French expression?

PRÉCISIONS

• Many common expressions about daily activities are stated in French using **faire**.

Vocabulaire supplémentaire:

faire le nécessaire: *to do whatever it takes*

faire son possible: *to do what one can*

faire du magasinage: *to do some shopping (Québec)*

faire des courses	*to run errands*
faire de la paperasserie	*to do paperwork*
faire la grasse matinée	*to sleep late*
faire les devoirs	*to do homework*
faire de la lecture	*to do some reading*
faire la queue	*to stand in line*
faire un coup de téléphone	*to make a telephone call*
faire la sieste	*to take a nap*
faire une promenade	*to take a walk*
faire un voyage	*to take a trip*
faire du shopping	*to do some shopping*
faire sa part	*to do one's part*

B. Qui fait ça? Tell your partner who around your house, school, or workplace does the following day-to-day-activities. Create six sentences using expressions from the three columns.

surveillant(e): *supervisor*

colocataire: *roommate/housemate*

Moi, je	fais	du sport
Mes enfants	fais	de la paperasserie
Les clients	fait	des devoirs
Mon/Ma surveillant(e)°	faisons	la sieste
Mon père/Ma mère	faites	la grasse matinée
Mon époux/épouse	font	la queue au marché
Mon frère/Ma sœur	aime(nt) faire	un coup de téléphone
Mon/Ma colocataire°	déteste(nt) faire	du shopping
[nom] et moi, nous		les courses
Mes collègues		sa part au travail/
Mes amis		à la maison
Mon/Mes professeur(s)		
Mes camarades de classe		

Vocabulaire: Pour parler des activités chez soi° (avec faire)

OBSERVATIONS

chez soi: *at home*

Monique **fait le ménage.**
Monique does the housework.

Monique **fait le marché.**
Monique does the grocery shopping.

Monique et André **font la cuisine** ensemble.
Monique and André do the cooking together.

1. Using the photos and the expressions in the captions, can you determine what word means *kitchen* or *cooking*?

2. What is the French word used for *market* or *marketing*? What would you expect a **supermarché** to be?

PRÉCISIONS

Vocabulaire supplémentaire
faire la lessive: *to do the laundry*
faire du bricolage: *to putter, tinker*

- Many common expressions about household tasks are stated in French using **faire**.

faire le ménage	*to do the housework*
faire le marché	*to do the grocery shopping*
faire la cuisine	*to cook*
faire la vaisselle	*to do the dishes*
faire du jardinage	*to do some gardening*

C. Chez nous... Tell your partner who does each of the following household tasks at home.

1. Chez nous, *ma sœur fait* le ménage.
2. Chez nous, _____ le marché.
3. Chez nous, _____ la cuisine.
4. Chez nous, _____ les courses.
5. Chez nous, _____ du jardinage.
6. Chez nous, _____ ne _____ pas la cuisine.
7. Chez nous, _____ ne _____ pas le ménage.
8. Chez nous, _____ ne _____ pas la vaisselle.
9. Chez nous, _____ déteste faire du jardinage.
10. Chez nous, _____ adore faire du shopping.

D. Mes responsabilités. From time to time we all end up with household tasks to do. Use different expressions to complete the following sentences and express your feelings about these jobs. Use the infinitive form **faire** in your sentences.

1. J'aime...
2. Je n'aime pas beaucoup...
3. Je déteste...

Compare your responses to those of your partner, looking for things you have in common. Be prepared to report your findings to the class.

Modèle: *Mon/Ma partenaire et moi, nous aimons faire la cuisine, mais nous détestons faire le marché.*

Vocabulaire: Pour parler des activités sportives (avec faire)

Les hommes **font du sport.**
The men are involved in sports.

La jeune fille **fait du jogging** dans le parc.
The girl is jogging in the park.

La dame **fait une promenade** avec ses chiens.
The lady is taking a walk with her dogs.

STRATÉGIES D'ANALYSE

Words are often borrowed from one language to another. For example, **promenade** has been borrowed by English speakers from French. Can you give some examples of words that look borrowed by French speakers from English?

Vocabulaire supplémentaire

faire du tennis	*to play tennis*
faire du ski/ski nautique	*to ski/water-ski*
faire du basket	*to play basketball*
faire du foot(ball)	*to play soccer*
faire du football américain	*to play football*
faire du golf	*to play golf*
faire du hockey	*to play hockey*
faire de la planche à voile	*to go windsurfing*
faire du camping	*to go camping*

PRÉCISIONS

- Many common expressions about sports are expressed in French with **faire.**

faire du sport	*to participate in sports*
faire du vélo	*to go bikeriding*
faire de l'exercice	*to exercise*
faire une promenade	*to take a walk*
faire du jogging	*to jog*

E. **Faire du sport.** Using words from all three columns, tell your partner at least five things about your attitude toward sports.

> **Modèle:** *Mes amis et moi, nous faisons de l'exercice tous les week-ends.*

moi, je (j') mon ami(e) mon ami(e) et moi mes ami(e)s mes ami(e)s et moi mon frère ma sœur mon patron mes collègues (autres???)	faire aimer faire aimer beaucoup faire détester faire préférer faire	du sport du jogging de l'exercice une promenade du vélo (autres???)

F. **Les activités de ma vie.** Using any of the expressions with **faire,** complete the following sentences about yourself. Take turns with your partner reading your sentences.

> **Modèle:** Avant de sortir avec mes amis, *je fais le ménage.*

1. Après le cours de français, il est nécessaire de _____.
2. Le week-end, j'ai l'habitude de _____.
3. Mes amis et moi, nous _____ ensemble.
4. Avec mes collègues, je _____.
5. Ma famille et moi, nous _____.
6. Le samedi je _____ avec mes amis.
7. Le dimanche mes amis et moi, nous _____.
8. Chez moi, je _____.
9. Si *(If)* j'ai le choix entre faire du vélo et faire une promenade, je _____.

À propos de la structure:
Remember to use the infinitive after the preposition **de**.

G. **Mes priorités.** Indiquez vos préférences parmi ces activités. Recopiez toute la liste par ordre de vos priorités.

faire la grasse matinée	faire la queue	faire la cuisine
faire de la paperasserie	faire du jardinage	faire les devoirs
faire du shopping	faire du vélo	faire de la lecture
faire un voyage	faire du camping	faire le marché
faire de l'exercice	faire une promenade	(autre???)

Mes préférences, par ordre de priorité, sont:

1.   6.   11.
2.   7.   12.
3.   8.   13.
4.   9.   14.
5.   10.   15.

PRONONCIATION: Le son [e]

Similar to the vowel sound in the English word *take*, the French vowel sound represented by the phonetic symbol [e] is most commonly written **-é**. It appears in many words you already know, such as:

étudiant   répéter   persévérant   café

However, [e] may also be written:

-er (when part of a verb infinitive): mang*er*, fréquent*er*, appréci*er*
-ez : Vous travaill*ez*? Vous av*ez* les cheveux bruns.
-es : (single-syllabic words only) : l*es*, m*es*, t*es*.

Repeat the following sentences after your instructor:

1. Vous allez prier° à la mosquée°.
2. Achetez des éclairs au supermarché!
3. Éric va visiter les musées de Québec.

prier: *to pray*
mosquée: *mosque*

À vous! Taking turns with a partner, read the following tongue-twisters, paying particular attention to your pronunciation of the sound [e].

1. Les téléphones sont occupés toute la journée.
2. Il n'y a pas de télé pendant les pannes d'électricité°.
3. Je te présente ma fiancée, Félicité Béranger.
4. La générosité des employés est appréciée.

les pannes (f.) d'électricité: *power outages*

POUR DÉVELOPPER VOS IDÉES

Thematic objective: To identify ways that people contribute to the community

POUR SAISIR L'ESSENTIEL: One aspect of social interaction is community service, the ways that we do our part to improve the quality of life around us. Read the following recruitment advertisement. Which of the activities mentioned are a part of your day-to-day routine? Which would you be most interested in doing as a community service? Add at least one activity to each of the two lists. (Consult the **Lexique** for ideas.)

le temps: *time*

Votre communauté a besoin de vous!

Contribuez votre temps° et votre énergie.

Pour les personnes âgées	**Pour les jeunes**
• *Faites le ménage.*	• *Aidez les jeunes à faire leurs devoirs.*
• *Faites la cuisine.*	• *Organisez des excursions.*
• *Faites des courses.*	• *Encouragez les jeunes.*
• *Faites le jardinage.*	• *Faites des sports.*
• *Faites de la lecture.*	• *Organisez une équipe sportive.*
• *Passez du temps à bavarder.*	

Faites des excursions avec les enfants.

On fait de bonnes œuvres°?
Bien sûr°! On fait sa part pour ses voisins.

---

bonnes œuvres: *good deeds*
Bien sûr!: *Of course!*

H. **La communauté et ses besoins.** Choisissez deux des bonnes causes dans la liste suivante. Puis *(Then)* mentionnez aux moins quatre activités à faire pour chacune des deux causes. Utilisez la publicité de recrutement à la page 110 comme modèle.

Bonnes causes
- Pour les malades° à l'hôpital
- Pour les jeunes mères de famille
- Pour les handicapés
- Au resto du cœur°
- À la maison de retraite°
- Pour les enfants défavorisés°

Activités
- Faire la lessive
- Faire des courses
- Faire du jardinage
- Faire des visites
- Faire de la lecture
- Faire la cuisine
- Faire du babysitting
- Organiser des activités sportives
- Organiser une soirée musicale
- Autres???

malade: *ill (person), patient*

resto du cœur: *soup kitchen*
maison de retraite: *retirement home*
défavorisé(e): *underprivileged*

I. **Notre publicité de recrutement.** Travaillez avec votre partenaire pour créer une publicité de recrutement. Utilisez la publicité à la page 110 comme modèle.

ÉCOUTONS: Ce que nous faisons ensemble

You will hear three monologues in which some people are talking about activities they do with different groups of acquaintances. Listen first to determine the general context of each monologue. Then predict the types of activities you can expect to hear in the follow-up details. Finally, listen to identify some of the specific activities they mention.

A. **On identifie le domaine.** Listen to three people talking about upcoming activities. Determine whether they are discussing work or school projects, a family gathering, or outings with friends. Match each monologue with the letter of the phrase that best describes what is being discussed in that monologue.

_____ Monologue #1:   a. Weekend plans with a friend

_____ Monologue #2:   b. Projects at work or school

_____ Monologue #3:   c. Family gathering

B. **On anticipe les activités.** Now anticipate which of the activities in the following list you expect to hear mentioned in the continuation of each monologue. Keep in mind the context you have already determined from the introductory statements. Write either #1, #2, or #3 in front of each activity to correspond to the monologue that best matches it. Some activities may match more than one monologue; others may remain unselected.

_____ aider avec les enfants   _____ faire la grasse matinée   _____ passer du temps à bavarder

_____ aller au cinéma   _____ faire le marché   _____ prendre un café ensemble

_____ assister à des matchs sportifs _____ faire le ménage   _____ rester à la maison

_____ chanter dans une chorale   _____ faire nos devoirs   _____ téléphoner aux clients

_____ consulter le comptable   _____ fêter ensemble   _____ travailler à l'ordinateur

_____ dîner au restaurant   _____ fréquenter les bars   _____ voyager

_____ faire de la paperasserie   _____ participer aux projets

_____ faire la cuisine   communautaires

C. **On vérifie nos prédictions.** Listen to the three monologues again. This time the speakers will add some details, listing specific activities that they plan to be involved in. As you listen, locate the activities you hear in the list for Exercise B. (They are listed alphabetically.) On a clean copy of the list, mark either #1, #2 or #3 in front of each activity that you hear mentioned in the corresponding monologue.

INTÉGRATION: Notre équipe de bénévoles°

bénévoles: *volunteers*

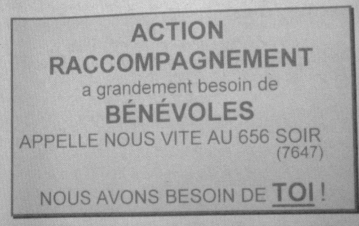

ACTION
RACCOMPAGNEMENT
a grandement besoin de
BÉNÉVOLES
APPELLE NOUS VITE AU 656 SOIR
(7647)

NOUS AVONS BESOIN DE **TOI** !

On s'organise pour les services communautaires.

Scenario: You are on the committee to select a two-member team to run your company's annual fundraising, a walk-a-thon for the local food bank. Your committee must fill the following positions on the team:

1. Someone to organize the project, schedule events and equipment, order supplies and advertising, etc.
2. Someone to recruit walkers and sponsors.

A. **Première décision: Les qualités recherchées.** Working with one or two partners, make a list of the qualifications you want to find in candidates for each of the two positions. Identify at least three qualities for each one.

Modèle: —Pour le poste d'organisateur nous cherchons une personne *responsable et pratique*. Et pour le recruteur nous avons besoin de quelqu'un de *dynamique*.

À propos du vocabulaire: Consult the vocabulary on pages 99–100 and the **Lexique** for ideas as you brainstorm for qualities.

Organisateur/Organisatrice	Recruteur/Recruteuse

B. **Deuxième décision: Comparaison des candidats.** Continue your committee work by reviewing the following descriptions of the volunteers and determining which ones have the most appropriate qualifications for the two positions. Use the **Formules de discussion** to present your ideas.

Formules de discussion

Pour proposer un candidat: À mon avis, (*Dominique Tavernier*) est un bon candidat pour le poste d'organisateur/de recruteur parce qu'il est (*organisé*).

Pour présenter un argument pour un candidat: Oui, c'est vrai. Et il a de l'expérience (*il s'occupe du budget pour le théâtre municipal*).

Pour présenter un argument contre un candidat: Je ne suis pas d'accord° parce qu'il (*n'aime pas avoir beaucoup de responsabilité*).

Je ne suis pas d'accord: *I don't agree*

Conclude your discussion by confirming the group recommendation for each position.

Pour recommander un candidat: Alors, on recommande (*nom*) pour le poste d'organisateur? Et pour le poste de recruteur est-ce que nous recommandons (*nom*)?

À propos du vocabulaire: The word **service** in the **fiche** means "department (in a business firm)." You may want to consider a volunteer's work experience as you discuss qualifications.

Fiche de Bénévole

Nom: _____ Arnaud _____   **Prénoms:** _____ Julien _____

Service: _____ Ventes _____   **Poste:** _____ Représentant _____

Expérience bénévole: _Sponsoriser des activités pour les personnes âgées_ de notre communauté

Commentaire: _Je suis dynamique et bon travailleur, mais je n'aime pas_ beaucoup faire de la paperasserie.

Fiche de Bénévole

Nom: _____ Benoît _____   **Prénoms:** _____ Martine-Françoise _____

Service: _____ Personnel _____   **Poste:** _____ Secrétaire _____

Expérience bénévole: _Organiser des excursions au zoo pour les enfants à_ l'école de ma fille

Commentaire: _J'ai l'habitude de travailler avec les jeunes. J'ai de la_ patience!

---

stagiaire: *trainee*

colonie de vacances: *summer camp*

Fiche de Bénévole

Nom: _____ Crozier _____   **Prénoms:** _____ Sophie-Louise _____

Service: _Relations Publiques_   **Poste:** _____ Stagiaire° _____

Expérience bénévole: _Travailler dans une colonie de vacances° (enfants de_ 9 à 12 ans)

Commentaire: _J'aime bien les sports et la nature. Mes amis disent_ que je suis spontanée.

Fiche de Bénévole

Nom: Sirven   **Prénoms:** Patrick

Service: Comptabilité   **Poste:** Assistant

Expérience bénévole: Travailler avec les scouts. Faire la vaisselle au restaurant du cœur. Organiser des fêtes pour des enfants malades.

Commentaire: Je suis plutôt méthodique dans mon travail. J'aime les gens, mais je suis un peu réservé.

Fiche de Bénévole

Nom: Tavernier   **Prénoms:** Dominique

Service: Achats   **Poste:** Secrétaire

Expérience bénévole: Participer aux soirées musicales à la maison de retraite°. Je m'occupe du budget pour le théâtre municipal.

Commentaire: Je suis organisé, énergique et travailleur. Je n'aime pas avoir beaucoup de responsabilité.

maison de retraite: *retirement home*

C. Troisième décision: Recommandation des candidats. The final step in your committee project is to write a memo presenting your recommendations to the CEO of your company. Use the following form as a guide for your memorandum.

Mémorandum

Date: 28/10/2000
À: Pierre Renard, PDG°
De: Le Comité de sélection
Objet: Recommandations pour l'équipe du projet communautaire des restaurants du cœur

****

Pour le poste d'**Organisateur/Organisatrice,** nous recommandons _____.
Il/Elle travaille dans notre service de _____, où il/elle est _____.

Expérience: _____

Qualités pour le poste: _____
_____

Pour le poste de **Recruteur/Recruteuse,** nous recommandons _____.
Il/Elle travaille dans notre service de _____, où il/elle est
_____.

Expérience: _____

Qualités pour le poste: _____
_____

PDG: *Président Directeur Général*

LEXIQUE DE BASE

La famille

un père	father	un beau-père	father-in-law/stepfather
une mère	mother	une belle-mère	mother-in-law/stepmother
un frère	brother	un beau-frère	brother-in-law/stepbrother
une sœur	sister	une belle-sœur	sister-in-law/stepsister
un mari/un époux	husband	un oncle	uncle
une femme/une épouse	wife	une tante	aunt
un fils	son	un petit-fils	grandson
une fille	daughter	une petite-fille	granddaughter
un(e) enfant	child	des petits-enfants	grandchildren
un(e) cousin(e)	cousin	un demi-frère	half-brother
un grand-père	grandfather	une demi-sœur	half-sister
une grand-mère	grandmother	des jumeaux/jumelles	twins
un parent	parent, relative	un neveu	nephew
		une nièce	niece

Les proches

un(e) fiancé(e)	fiancé(e)	un(e) colocataire	roommate/housemate
un(e) conjoint(e)	live-in partner	un copain/une copine	friend
un(e) petit(e) ami(e)	boyfriend/girlfriend	un(e) voisin(e)	neighbor
un(e) ami(e)	friend		
un(e) meilleur(e) ami(e)	best friend		

Les rapports au travail

un(e) collègue	colleague	un(e) employé(e)	employee
un(e) assistant(e)	assistant	un(e) employeur(-euse)	employer
un(e) surveillant(e)	supervisor	un(e) client(e)	customer
un(e) patron(ne)	boss		

Pour décrire les gens

être affectueux(-euse)	to be affectionate	être émotif(-ive)	to be emotional
amusant(e)	amusing, fun	énergique	energetic
avare	miserly, stingy	faible	weak
content(e)	happy	flamboyant(e)	flamboyant, over the top
curieux(-euse)	curious	fragile	frail
dynamique	dynamic	frivole	frivolous
égoïste	egoistic, self-centered	influençable	impressionable, easily influenced
ennuyeux(-euse)	boring, annoying	joli(e)	pretty, handsome
extrême	extreme	laid(e)	ugly
généreux(-euse)	generous	modeste	modest
gentil(le)	nice, kind	naïf (naïve)	naive
grand(e)	tall, big	paresseux(-euse)	lazy
indifférent(e)	indifferent, lacking in intellectual curiosity	pauvre	poor

À propos du vocabulaire: The difference between **des personnes** and **des gens** is like the difference between *persons* and *people* in English.

intelligent(e)	intelligent	ponctuel(le)	punctual
intolérant(e)	intolerant	réaliste	realistic
malade	sick	rêveur(-euse)	a dreamer
méchant(e)	mean, mischievous	riche	rich
méthodique	methodical	sensible	sensitive
organisé(e)	organized	sentimental(e)	sentimental
optimiste	optimistic	sophistiqué(e)	sophisticated
patient(e)	patient		
persévérant(e)	persevering		
pessimiste	pessimistic		
sincère	sincere		
spontané(e)	spontaneous		
têtu(e)	stubborn, hard-headed		
timide	timid, shy		
tolérant(e)	tolerant		
travailleur(-euse)	hard-working		
triste	sad		

Pour décrire les gens avec **avoir**

avoir les yeux bleus	to have blue eyes	avoir une moustache	to have a mustache
marron	brown eyes	avoir une barbe	to have a beard
noirs	dark eyes	avoir tort	to be wrong
verts	green eyes	avoir de la chance	to be lucky
avoir les cheveux blancs	to have gray/white hair	avoir les cheveux frisés /	to have curly hair
marron/châtains	chestnut brown hair	bouclés	
blonds	blond hair	ondulés	wavy hair
roux	red hair	raides	straight hair
courts	short hair	avoir le visage carré	to have a square face
longs	long hair	long	a long face
avoir... ans	to be . . . years old	rond	a round face
avoir l'air	to seem, look (+adj)	ovale	an oval face
avoir faim	to be hungry	avoir le nez retroussé	to have a turned-up nose
avoir soif	to be thirsty	court	a short nose
avoir sommeil	to be sleepy	pointu	a pointed nose
avoir froid	to be cold	impressionnant	an impressive nose
avoir chaud	to be hot		
avoir raison	to be right		
avoir tort	to be wrong		

Pour nuancer une idée

avoir besoin (de)	to need (to)
avoir envie (de)	to want (to), to feel like
avoir l'habitude (de)	to be in the habit (of)
avoir l'intention (de)	to intend (to)

Pour parler des activités

admirer	to admire	accepter	to accept
aider	to help	bricoler	to tinker, putter
apprécier	to appreciate, value	fumer	to smoke
assister (à)	to attend	offrir	to offer, give

bavarder	to make conversation, chat	retrouver	to meet (someone by pre-arrangement)
chanter	to sing	téléphoner (à)	to telephone
contribuer	to contribute	tolérer	to tolerate
danser	to dance		
déjeuner	to have lunch		
dîner	to have dinner		
fêter	to celebrate/party		
fréquenter	to frequent (a place)		
inviter	to invite		
jouer	to play		
participer (à)	to participate (in)		
passer du temps	to spend time		
préparer	to prepare		
regarder	to watch, look at		
rester	to stay, remain		

Pour parler des activités avec **faire**

faire	to do, make		
faire de la lecture	to do some reading	faire la lessive	to do the laundry
faire des devoirs	to do homework	faire le nécessaire	to do whatever it takes
faire un voyage	to take a trip	faire de son mieux	to do one's best
faire du shopping	to go shopping	faire du jardinage	to do some gardening
faire la cuisine	to cook	faire du magasinage	to go shopping (Québec)
faire la vaisselle	to do the dishes	faire du ski (nautique)	to (water-)ski
faire la grasse matinée	to sleep late	faire du tennis	to play tennis
faire le marché	to do the grocery shopping	faire du jogging	to jog
faire un coup de téléphone	to make a phone call	faire du basket	to play basketball
faire de la paperasserie	to do paperwork	faire du foot(ball)	to play soccer
faire le ménage	to do housework	faire du football américain	to play football
faire des courses	to do errands	faire du golf	to play golf
faire la sieste	to take a nap	faire du hockey	to play hockey
faire sa part	to do one's part (of work)	faire de la planche à voile	to go windsurfing
faire du sport	to participate in sports	faire du camping	to go camping
faire de l'exercice	to exercise	faire du bricolage	to putter
faire une promenade	to take a walk	faire son possible	to do what one can
faire du vélo	to go bikeriding		
faire la queue	to stand in line		

Les chiffres 40–100

voir les pages 93–94

combien?	how much/how many?
deux cents	two hundred
duex cent trois	two hundred three
mille	a thousand
un million	a million

LA VIE EN VILLE

Communicative Objectives

- To discuss routine errands and tell where in town you go for shopping and services
- To give directions for getting around town
- To schedule appointments and discuss schedules

Thematic Objectives

✓ To examine places about town in terms of their importance to you and their contribution to the image of the city

✓ To examine the notion of *quartier* and how the various areas of a city reflect the needs and interests of the community

✓ To integrate the notion of *quartier* in describing American cities to French-speaking people

OUVERTURE EN VIDÉO:
On découvre la ville

La mise en scène

J'aime bien habiter un quartier intéressant avec des cafés animés. C'est là où les gens se rencontrent et passent du temps ensemble.

Moi, je préfère un quartier tranquille avec de beaux parcs où on peut faire des promenades et apprécier la beauté de la nature.

NOTE **C**ULTURELLE

Cities and towns tend to organize themselves unofficially into different neighborhoods, or sectors, of the city. These are called **quartiers** in French, and each **quartier** has its own personality. Paris, which is so large, is also officially organized in **arrondissements,** which correspond loosely to our ZIP code areas. There are twenty **arrondissements** in Paris, beginning with the first, or **premier arrondissement** (1ᵉʳ), located on the Right Bank near the Louvre, and fanning out clockwise in a spiraling effect across the city. Each **arrondissement** typically has several **quartiers** within it.

A. Où on va pour... *(Where we go for . . .)* In *Chapitre 4* you will talk about the different neighborhoods of a city and what special features characterize them. You will discuss where you go in town for shopping and errands, food and dining, and sports and entertainment. On the video, you will see a variety of these places in Paris and Québec, and you will hear people talking about them. Before seeing them on screen and learning the French terms for those places, think about your own community and the places you go for various purposes. On the grid, list *in English* three to five specific places in each category where you might go.

Shopping & Errands	Food & Dining	Sports & Entertainment	On Campus

B. On anticipe le vocabulaire. Now that you have thought of some of the places you typically go to in your own community, try to match the names of some of them with their French equivalents. This will help you anticipate what you will hear on the video.

Shopping & Errands	Shopping et courses	Food & Dining	Restauration
___Shopping mall	a. Bureau de poste	___Café	a. Supermarché
___Specialty shop	b. Pharmacie	___Restaurant	b. Bar
___Post office	c. Centre commercial	___Open-air market	c. Café
___Gas station	d. Boutique	___Supermarket	d. Marché en plein air
___Pharmacy	e. Station-service	___Bar, pub	e. Restaurant

Entertainment	Amusements	On Campus	Sur le campus
___Concert hall	a. Cinéma	___Classrooms	a. Gymnase
___Park	b. Clubs	___Stadium	b. Bureaux des profs
___Museum	c. Parc	___Professors' offices	c. Laboratoires
___Movie theater	d. Salle de concert	___Cafeteria	d. Résidences
___Discotheque, dance club	e. Théâtre	___Gym	e. Cafétéria
___Theater	f. Musée	___Dormitories	f. Stade
___Clubs	g. Discothèque	___Laboratories	g. Salles de classe

Les paroles et le sens

C. On écoute des interviews. Listen to the interviews with people talking about why they like to go to cafés and about where they go for entertainment and shopping. On the grids, mark an X in the appropriate column to indicate in which interviews you hear the key phrases mentioned.

au centre commercial
aux boutiques
à boutique spécialisée
au grand mag.
à la pâtisserie

Pourquoi on va au café	#1	#2	#3	#4	#5
prendre (boire) un verre (l'apéritif) *to have drink*					
décider de notre soirée *decide how to spend evening*					
rencontrer des amis (gens) / attendre des amis *wait 4 some friends*					✓
passer un bon moment / passer du temps (agréable) *spend (a bit) (some) time* ✓					
apprécier l'ambiance (le quartier, le lieu) *enjoy the setting*					
prendre le petit déjeuner / déjeuner *eating lunch*					
voir les gens passer *watching ppl. pass by*					✓

Où on va pour s'amuser	#1	#2	#3	#4	#5	#6
au cinéma *voila un, regarder un nouveau film*						
au théâtre *voir un spectacle*						
au café						
en discothèque *danser*						
au parc *et prendre*						
en boîte						
dans les bars						
au musée *apprécier une collection d'art*						

NOTE CULTURELLE

Georges Eugène, baron Haussmann (1809–1891), is credited with giving Paris the urban organization and beauty it enjoys today, with its grands boulevards and expansive parks and gardens. He is known as one of the great **urbanistes** of the 19th century. Appointed by Napoleon III to renovate and beautify the French capital, it was Haussmann who divided Paris into its twenty **arrondissements,** a system that remains today and that has served as a model for our modern ZIP codes. **Le boulevard Haussmann,** which runs in front of the famous department store **Les Galeries Lafayette** in the **neuvième arrondissement,** bears his name.

On y réfléchit

D. **Mes préférences de quartiers.** Now that you have learned to identify characteristics of different **quartiers** of the city, think about what type of neighborhood you would choose to live in if you were to relocate this year. Then consider where you might want to live five years from now, then ten years from now. Read the following descriptions and decide which ones you would select for each of these periods of your life.

1. Voici un joli quartier historique. Il y a une ancienne cathédrale magnifique où on donne fréquemment de bons concerts, des librairies avec une grande variété de livres et des galeries d'art où on peut apprécier l'art. Les maisons de ce quartier sont d'une architecture intéressante et bien appréciée par les résidents et par les historiens. Ce quartier a beaucoup de petits commerçants qui offrent un service personnel. On aime aussi les petites boutiques spécialisées et les restaurants calmes et assez élégants.

2. Voilà un quartier qui offre tout ce qui est moderne et efficace. Il y a de grands immeubles d'appartements modernes, plusieurs avec un parking à l'intérieur. On est très bien installé avec un système de sécurité. Il y a une station de métro tout près, et aussi un grand centre commercial. Dans ce quartier, on trouve un cinéma, une grande variété de boutiques et quelques grands magasins. Là, les soirées sont bien animées, avec des cafés-terrasses, des boîtes de nuit intimes et des bars populaires.

3. Ça, c'est un bon quartier pour les jeunes familles. Il y a une bonne sélection de jolies maisons modestes en très bon état. Il y a un parc avec un beau lac où, le dimanche, on trouve beaucoup de familles qui font des promenades et des pique-niques. Ce quartier a quelques bonnes écoles, publiques et privées. Il y a aussi pour les enfants un petit théâtre tout près du parc.

4. L'université se trouve au beau milieu de ce quartier pittoresque. Il y a de grandes maisons tout près du campus où habitent beaucoup de gens qui travaillent et étudient à l'université. Les gens qui habitent ce quartier profitent du beau campus pour faire des promenades, jouer au tennis et même pratiquer le golf ou le foot sur les grands terrains. Tout autour du campus il y a beaucoup de cafés, de restaurants, de bars et de librairies où les gens du quartier et de l'université se donnent rendez-vous. On peut y trouver une ambiance à la fois intellectuelle et culturelle grâce au° grand nombre de musiciens et d'artistes qui les fréquentent.

grâce à/au: *thanks to*

Objective: To discuss routine errands and tell where in town you go for shopping and services

PRÉSENTATION: Un coup d'œil sur le thème

du moins: *at least*

Vers la Place Mandle ou le carrefour de la Crosse

gratuits: *free of charge*
loin: *far, distant*
attire les foules (f.): *attracts crowds*
prend: *takes, gets*

mène: *leads*

librairies (f.): *bookstores*

LA RUE CHARTRAINE

C'est la rue principale d'Évreux, ou du moins°, la plus fréquentée le samedi après-midi. La rue Chartraine offre aux résidents de nombreux commerces et services. Plusieurs parkings (gratuits° ou payants) ne sont pas très loin° de cette rue qui attire les foules°.

Cette rue prend° aussi son charme de sa voie pavée et de ses accès possibles vers la rivière. Elle mène° à la place du Marché et à la cathédrale.

Librairies°, photographes, cafés, banques, boutiques de vêtements ou parfumeries, tout un choix de commerces toujours à votre service.

Stratégies

1. Scan the description of **la rue Chartraine** and make a list of what it offers its residents.
2. Categorize the items on your list according to whether they are **pratique, esthétique,** or **divertissant.** Note that an item might be appropriate for more than one category.
3. Which places would be on your itinerary if you were spending a Saturday afternoon on **la rue Chartraine?**

POUR DÉVELOPPER VOTRE FRANÇAIS

Vocabulaire: Des endroits en ville°

endroits (m.) en ville: *places in the city*

OBSERVATIONS

1. Look at the labels on the buildings and other places in the city. Which ones are cognates of English words? Make a list of these cognates.
2. Now look for the names of places that are not cognates. Make a second list of these words. Which list is longer?

PRÉCISIONS

- Many of the names of buildings and other places in the city are cognates in French and English, making them easy to recognize.

un **aéroport**	*airport*	un **hôpital**	*hospital*
une **banque**	*bank*	un **hôtel**	*hotel*
une **boutique**	*boutique*	un **musée**	*museum*
un **bureau de poste**	*post office*	un **parc**	*park*
un **café**	*cafe*	une **pharmacie**	*pharmacy*
un **cinéma**	*cinema*	un **restaurant**	*restaurant*
un **centre commercial**	*shopping mall or center*	une **station-service**	*service station*
		un **supermarché**	*supermarket*
un **centre d'étudiants**	*student center*	une **synagogue**	*synagogue*

- Other places in the city are not cognates and require more attention.

un **arrêt d'autobus**	*bus stop*	une **gare**	*train station*
une **bibliothèque**	*library*	un **immeuble de bureaux**	*office building*
une **boulangerie**	*bakery*		
une **église**	*church*	une **maison**	*house*

- A few place names are **faux amis** (*false cognates*), requiring careful attention.

un **hôtel de ville**	*city hall*
une **librairie**	*bookstore*

NOTE CULTURELLE

French often adds **-erie** to a name of an item, creating a word that means a place where that item is sold.

On achète des **sandwiches** à la **sandwicherie**.
On achète des **parfums** à la **parfumerie**.
On achète de la **crème** à la **crémerie**.
On achète des **chaussettes** (*socks*) à la **chaussetterie**.
On achète des **sweaters** à la **sweaterie**.
On achète des **chemises** (*shirts*) à la **chemiserie**.
On achète des **épices** (*spices*) à l'**épicerie**.

On aime aller chez les petits commerçants: à la sandwicherie, à la parfumerie et à la chaussetterie.

A. **Il y a** (*There is, There are*)... Consultez le plan de la ville à la page 124. À tour de rôle avec votre partenaire, demandez si les endroits suivants° se trouvent° dans la ville. (Reminder: After a negative expression, use **pas de** or **pas d'**.)

les endroits suivants: *the following places*
se trouvent: *are located*

Y a-t-il: *Is there? Are there?*

Modèle 1:   —*Y a-t-il*° *un restaurant en ville?*
                   —*Oui, il y a un restaurant en ville.*

Modèle 2:   —*Y a-t-il une université en ville?*
                   —*Non, il n'y a pas d'université en ville.*

1. un café
2. une université
3. une banque
4. un cinéma
5. un supermarché

6. une gare
7. une librairie
8. un centre commercial
9. une église
10. une mosquée

Structure: Contractions avec à

OBSERVATIONS

On regarde un film **au cinéma**.

On cherche des CD **au magasin de musique**.

On apprécie l'art **au musée**.

On achète des médicaments **à la pharmacie.**

On assiste au match de foot **au stade.**

On cherche un plan de la ville **à la librairie.**

On a rendez-vous **au bureau.**

On retrouve des amis **au restaurant.**

On touche un chèque **à la banque.**

STRATÉGIES D'ANALYSE

1. Look at the captions and find two different ways of expressing the French equivalent of *in the* or *at the*.
2. What seems to make the difference between using **au** and using **à la**?

PRÉCISIONS

You have already used the preposition **à** directly before a noun to mean *to* or *in* or *at*.

Je vais à Montréal.　　　　*I am going **to** Montréal.*
Nous travaillons à Québec.　*We work **in** Québec City.*
Je suis à la porte.　　　　*I am **at the** door.*

- When **à** is followed by **la** or **l'**, there is no change in **à**.

Je vais **à la** pharmacie.　　*I am going **to the** pharmacy.*
Paul travaille **à l'**hôpital.　*Paul works **at the** hospital.*

- When **à** is followed by **le** or **les,** contractions occur.

à + le = au	Pierre va **au** parc.
	*Pierre is going **to the** park.*
à + les = aux	Georges parle *aux* clients.
	*George talks **to the** customers.*

- **À** is also used in some verbal expressions where it is not translated.

| On **assiste au** match de foot. | *They **are attending** a soccer match.* |
| **Téléphonez à** Georges demain. | ***Call** George tomorrow.* |

B. **Des courses à faire** *(Some errands to do).* Tout le monde a beaucoup de courses à faire aujourd'hui. À tour de rôle avec votre partenaire, dites où on a besoin d'aller.

> **Modèle:** Jeanne: la librairie, la banque, le café, le bureau de poste
> *Jeanne a besoin d'aller à la librairie, à la banque, au café et au bureau de poste.*

1. Jacques: le bureau de poste, la pharmacie, la station-service, le marché
2. Marguerite: le supermarché, le bureau, l'église, l'hôpital
3. Claude: le stade, l'école, le magasin, le cinéma
4. Jeannine: les courts de tennis, le restaurant, la bibliothèque, la librairie
5. Paul: l'hôtel, le café, le parc, la pâtisserie
6. Anne-Marie: le musée, la synagogue, la banque, le bureau de poste
7. Christine: la librairie, le supermarché, le centre commercial, la gare
8. Étienne: la bibliothèque, le stade, le bureau, le magasin de musique

C. **Pour acheter... ?** Dites à votre partenaire où on va pour faire chaque activité. Consultez la liste suivante pour des idées.

> **Modèle:** Pour acheter un livre
> *À la librairie.*

le restaurant	le cinéma	**la station-service**	*le musée*
le bureau de tabac		**le bureau de poste**	**l'église** le bar
la pharmacie	*le parc*	**la discothèque**	l'école la librairie
la cathédrale	*la mosquée*	LA SYNAGOGUE	la gare **la banque**
le stade	le théâtre	**l'aéroport**	le centre commercial
le centre d'étudiants	*le distributeur automatique de billets (ATM)*		

1. Pour acheter un stylo?
2. Pour prendre le dîner?
3. Pour danser?
4. Pour voir un film?
5. Pour écouter un concert?
6. Pour prendre un café?
7. Pour prendre le train?
8. Pour prier°?
9. Pour retirer° de l'argent?
10. Pour regarder des statues?
11. Pour envoyer des cartes postales?
12. Pour acheter des médicaments?

Pour prier: *To pray*
retirer: *to withdraw*

Structure: Le verbe irrégulier aller

OBSERVATIONS

—Salut, Paul. Comment **vas**-tu?
—Je **vais** bien, merci. Et toi et Georges, comment **allez**-vous?
—Ça **va** très bien. Luc et toi, est-ce que vous **allez** au cinéma avec les autres?
—Pas moi. Je **vais** au ballet à l'Opéra Garnier.

—Hi, Paul. How **are** you doing?
—I**'m doing** fine, thanks. And how **are** you and George **doing**?
—Very well. **Are** you and Luc **going** to the movies with the others?

—Not me. I**'m going** to the ballet at the Garnier Opera House.

STRATÉGIES D'ANALYSE

1. You have already used the verb **aller** in several expressions of greeting. Do you remember how to ask "How's it going?" How would you reply "I'm fine, thank you"?

2. You also know that the verb **avoir** has the form **ont** in the third-person plural (**ils/elles**) and that the verb **être** has the form **sont** in the third-person plural. Using these verbs as models, can you guess the third-person plural form of **aller**?

3. You remember the **vous** form of **aller** from the expression: «**Comment allez-vous?**» If you know that the **nous** form of **aller** is closely related to the **vous** form, can you guess how the **nous** form is spelled?

4. What would you add in the blanks to complete the verb pattern for **aller**?

   je **vais**   nous _____
   tu **vas**   vous **allez**
   il/elle/on (ça) **va**   ils/elles _____

PRÉCISIONS

• The irregular verb **aller** (*to go*) has the following forms in the present tense:

	aller	
je **vais**	nous **allons**	
tu **vas**	vous **allez**	
il/elle/on **va**	ils/elles **vont**	

The famous **Opéra Garnier,** built between 1862 and 1875, was the only major opera house in Paris until 1989, when the new **Opéra** was constructed at **la place de la Bastille.**

l'Opéra Garnier

l'Opéra de la Bastille

D. **Cet après-midi.** À tour de rôle avec votre partenaire, dites où on va cet après-midi. Remplacez les mots en italique par les mots entre parenthèses. Faites les changements nécessaires.

1. Cet après-midi *Henri* va à la bibliothèque. (Georges et Paul / nous / je / Anne-Marie)
2. Cet après-midi *Jeannette* va au centre commercial. (Jacques / vous / je / nous)
3. *Claudine et Françoise* vont au musée cet après-midi. (Sophie / tu / vous / je)
4. *Brigitte et sa sœur* vont à la banque cet après-midi. (je / nous / tu / Philippe)
5. Cet après-midi *je* vais au bureau. (nous / vous / M. et Mme Colbert / tu)
6. *Toi et moi, nous* allons à la gare cet après-midi. (je / vous / Charles et Marc / Bernadette)

E. **On va en ville.** Complétez les phrases suivantes avec les formes correctes du verbe **aller.** Lisez le dialogue avec votre partenaire.

—Salut, Jacqueline. Comment _____-tu?

—Je _____ bien, merci. Et toi, comment ça _____?

—Très bien. Je _____ à Paris ce week-end.

—Tu _____ à Paris toute seule?

—Non, mon amie Bernadette _____ en ville avec moi. Nous _____ aux musées et au théâtre.

—Vous _____ faire du shopping, n'est-ce pas?

—Très peu. Les magasins _____ être fermés vendredi et dimanche à cause de la fête.

E. **Où va-t-on?** Avec votre partenaire, faites une liste aussi longue que possible des endroits où on peut aller pour faire chaque activité. Utilisez le vocabulaire des endroits en ville pour vous donner des idées.

> **Modèle:** étudier ensemble
> *Pour étudier ensemble, on va à la bibliothèque, à la maison, au labora-*
> *toire ou au centre d'étudiants.*

1. chercher un livre
2. acheter un pull-over
3. faire un pique-nique
4. dormir
5. dîner avec des amis
6. acheter un disque compact
7. fêter un anniversaire
8. retrouver des amis
9. assister à un match de foot
10. voir un film
11. consulter un médecin

Vocabulaire: Quelques adverbes

OBSERVATIONS

Je travaille **toujours** le week-end.
*I **always** work on the weekend.*

Je prépare **souvent** des documents pour mon patron.
*I **often** prepare documents for my boss.*

Quelquefois deux ou trois de mes collègues sont aussi au bureau.
***Sometimes** two or three of my colleagues are also at the office.*

De temps en temps je suis tout(e) seul(e).
***From time to time** I am alone.*

Mon patron est **rarement** au bureau le samedi.
*My boss is **rarely** at the office on Saturdays.*

Il **n'**est **jamais** au bureau le dimanche.
*He is **never** at the office on Sundays.*

STRATÉGIES D'ANALYSE

1. Look at the boldfaced words in the sentences. How do these words modify the meaning of the sentences?
2. Where are most of these adverbs located in a sentence?

PRÉCISIONS

- You have already used a few adverbs to modify the meaning of verbs, adjectives, or other adverbs.

Je vais **bien.**	*I'm doing **fine.***
Ma patronne est **assez** sportive.	*My boss is **rather** athletic.*
Paul joue **très** bien au tennis.	*Paul plays tennis **very** well.*

- There are several adverbs you can use to indicate the range of frequency with which you do certain things, thus clarifying your meaning.

Je fais **toujours** les budgets.	I *always* do the budgets.
Marc assiste **souvent** aux meetings.	*Marc **often** attends the meetings.*
Quelquefois Jacques travaille avec nous.	***Sometimes** Jacques works with us.*
Paul est **rarement** au bureau.	*Paul is **rarely** at the office.*
Georges **ne** fait **jamais** les budgets.	*Georges **never** does the budgets.*

- You can further distinguish frequency by adding other adverbs.

Éric joue **très souvent** au tennis.	*Eric plays tennis **very often.***
Il travaille **assez rarement** le vendredi.	*He works **rather rarely** on Fridays.*
Il est **presque toujours** sur les courts de tennis.	*He is **almost always** at the tennis courts.*

- **Quelquefois** and **de temps en temps** usually come either at the beginning or at the end of a sentence. The shorter adverbs directly follow the verb.

J'arrive au bureau en retard **de temps en temps.**
Quelquefois, je suis en avance.

G. **Au travail.** Indiquez à votre partenaire avec quelle fréquence vous faites chaque activité au travail.

Modèle: faire des heures supplémentaires

0%			50%			100%
jamais	presque jamais	rarement	de temps en temps	souvent	presque toujours	toujours
				X		

*Je fais **souvent** des heures supplémentaires.*

1. faire des heures supplémentaires
2. parler au patron
3. dîner avec le patron
4. profiter des vacances
5. annuler° les vacances
6. consulter des collègues
7. consulter un agenda
8. téléphoner à un client
9. déléguer les responsabilités
10. faire des négotiations

annuler: *to cancel*

H. **Dans mon temps libre** (*my free time*)**...** Dites à votre partenaire avec quelle fréquence vous faites chaque activité dans votre temps libre.

Modèle: dîner au restaurant

jamais	presque jamais	rarement	de temps en temps	souvent	presque toujours	toujours
			X			

*Je dîne au restaurant de **temps en temps.***

1. dîner au restaurant
2. aller au café
3. jouer au tennis
4. jouer au foot
5. assister à un match de... au stade

6. faire une promenade au parc
7. apprécier l'art au musée
8. acheter un CD au magasin de musique
9. toucher un chèque à la banque
10. regarder les animaux au zoo

I. De temps en temps on fait... Écrivez au moins cinq phrases au sujet de vous-même ou de vos collègues pour décrire la fréquence de vos activités. Consultez la fiche pour stimuler vos idées.

Modèle: *De temps en temps mon ami et moi nous allons au parc pour faire une promenade.*

toujours	je	aller	au cinéma	pour...	prendre	des CD
presque toujours	tu	avoir besoin d'aller	au musée		acheter	des médicaments
souvent	mon ami(e)	avoir envie d'aller	au parc		louer	des provisions
de temps en temps	mon ami(e) et moi	avoir le temps d'aller	au bureau de poste		chercher	des livres
rarement	mon patron	avoir l'intention d'aller	à la banque			des vidéos
presque jamais	mon patron et moi		à la discothèque			un café
jamais	mon époux(-se)		au restaurant			un Coca
	mon fils		au bureau			le déjeuner
	ma fille		au centre d'étudiants			le dîner
	mes enfants		à la maison			
	on		à l'appartement			
			au café			
			à la librairie			
			à la bibliothèque			
			à la pharmacie			
			au magasin de musique			
			au supermarché			
			au magasin de vidéos			
			à la banque			
			à la pharmacie			
			à la maison			
			à la gare			
			à l'église			
			au supermarché			
			au centre commercial			

Structure: Le futur immédiat

OBSERVATIONS

—Qu'est-ce que tu **vas faire** cet après-midi?
—Je **vais aller** en ville où je **vais acheter** un livre à la librairie et **visiter** le musée.
—Et ce soir?
—Je **vais rester** en ville.
—Tu **vas dîner** au Café de la Paix?
—Non, je **ne vais pas payer** un dîner cher. Je **vais prendre** une salade à l'hôtel.

À propos de la culture: Le Café de la Paix, located across from the **Opéra Garnier** in Paris, was the first in the city to enclose its sidewalk café behind glass during cold weather. This spot is popular both with tourists and with patrons of the **Opéra.** The sidewalk café has ice cream dishes as a house specialty. At the tables inside, you can order meals.

STRATÉGIES D'ANALYSE

1. When the verb **aller** is followed by a second verb, which of the two verbs conjugates to agree with the subject? In what form is the other verb?
2. When a sentence with two verbs is negative, where is the **ne... pas** placed?
3. What is the time frame (present, past, or future) expressed by **aller** plus a second verb in the infinitive?

PRÉCISIONS

- To express an action that will occur in the not-too-distant future, use the present tense of **aller** followed by a verb in the infinitive form.

Je **vais acheter** un plan de la ville.	*I'm going to buy a city map.*
Nous **allons travailler** très tard ce soir.	*We're going to work very late tonight.*

- In the negative, the **ne** goes before and the **pas** goes after the conjugated form of **aller.**

M. Leclerc **ne va pas** dîner au restaurant avec nous ce soir.	*M. Leclerc is not going to have dinner at the restaurant with us this evening.*

J. **Ce week-end...** Dites à votre partenaire ce que vous allez faire ce week-end. Faites au moins six phrases au sujet de vos activités et de celles (*those*) de vos amis. Dites au moins deux activités que vous n'allez pas faire.

Modèle: *Christine et moi, nous allons dîner au restaurant ce week-end. Nous n'allons pas préparer le dîner chez nous.*

Moi, je	aller	acheter...	étudier...
Mon ami(e)		téléphoner à...	travailler...
Mon ami(e) et moi		faire...	préparer...
Mes ami(e)s		regarder...	organiser...
Mes ami(e)s et moi		dîner à...	(autre???)
Vous		visiter...	
Toi, tu			
Ma famille			

PRONONCIATION: Le son [ɛ]

The vowel represented by the phonetic symbol [ɛ] is pronounced like the vowel sound in the English words *set* and *said* and may be written several ways in French:

è, as in **père**   **ê**, as in **fête**   **e**, as in **merci**

Also, when not followed by **–m** or **–n**, the diphthongs **–ai** and **–ei** are pronounced [ɛ]:

lait   neige

Repeat the following words after your instructor:

> frère, très
> rêve, extrême
> interpersonnel, béret
> jamais, vaisselle
> soleil, surveillant

À propos du vocabulaire: It may be helpful to remember that the accent marking –é (**accent aigu**) literally means "sharp" accent.

Notez bien! The [e] sound introduced in the previous chapter is a somewhat sharper and higher pitched sound than [ɛ].

Repeat the following pairs of words after your instructor. Do you hear the difference between [e] and [ɛ]?

[ɛ]	[e]
lait	les
mais	mes
est	et

À vous! With a partner, read the following dialogue, paying particular attention to your pronunciation of the sound [ɛ].

On his way to the bus-stop, Didier meets his friend Chloé. They walk together and discuss their plans for the afternoon.

> —Salut, Chloé!
> —Salut, Didier! Qu'est-ce que tu fais cet après-midi?
> —Je vais au musée Picasso avec ma grand-mère. Et toi?
> —Je vais à la banque pour toucher un chèque.
> —Mais après?
> —Après, je vais passer du temps à la bibliothèque.
> —Moi aussi, j'ai besoin de faire mes devoirs!
> —Alors, pourquoi est-ce que tu vas au musée?
> —Parce que ma grand-mère habite une maison de retraite et quand il fait du soleil...
> —Elle aime sortir?
> —Oui, c'est ça!
> —Je comprends. Voici ton arrêt d'autobus...
> —Oui... Bonne journée!
> —À toi aussi. Ciao!

À propos du vocabulaire: The Italian expression for *Bye!*, which is *Ciao!*, is used internationally and is very popular in French.

POUR DÉVELOPPER VOS IDÉES

Thematic objective: To examine places about town in terms of their importance to you and their contribution to the image of the city

Présentation: Qu'est-ce qu'on attend° de sa ville?
Le pratique et l'agréable

attend: *expect*

> **POUR SAISIR L'ESSENTIEL:** This description of the **quartier Montcalm** is excerpted from a web site on Quebec. The first paragraph provides some introductory information by telling where and what it is. The next four paragraphs are essentially categorized lists.
>
> 1. Skim through the reading to identify the four categories it addresses. Write them on your paper as list headers.
> 2. Under each category heading, list the kinds of places (not their proper names) mentioned in the reading.
> 3. Compare your lists with your partner. Did either of you overlook any items?

Quartier Montcalm

à mi-chemin: *midway*

Situé à mi-chemin° entre le centre-ville de Québec et Sainte-Foy, le quartier Montcalm est principalement résidentiel.

Sur le plan culturel, le quartier bénéficie de la présence du Musée du Québec, de la Maison Henry-Stuart, du kiosque Edwin-Bélanger et des galeries d'art. Le Grand Théâtre de Québec et le Théâtre Périscope sont à proximité, dans le quartier Saint-Jean-Baptiste.

ne manque pas: *does not lack*
En plus de: *Besides, in addition to*

Le quartier ne manque pas° d'espaces récréatifs. En plus de° la présence des Plaines d'Abraham, les résidents bénéficient de parcs de voisinage, comme le parc des Braves. En matière d'installations récréatives, le centre Lucien-Borne, le YMCA et les institutions scolaires répondent aux besoins.

Pour l'éducation et l'esprit, le quartier loge les écoles Joseph-François Perrault (secondaire), Anne-Hébert (primaire), le Québec High School, le Saint-Patrick High School et l'école de musique Arquemuse ainsi que les églises Saint-Dominique, Saints Martyrs Canadiens et l'église Notre-Dame du Chemin (à sauver d'une démolition prochaine).

De plus: *Moreover*

attirent: *attract*

La fonction commerciale est surtout localisée dans les environs de l'avenue Cartier, une des artères les plus prestigieuses et animées de la ville de Québec, et du boulevard René-Lévesque. C'est un secteur très fréquenté par les résidents du quartier. De plus°, de nombreux commerces spécialisés et la vie nocturne que l'on y retrouve attirent° une clientèle régionale et touristique.

K. **Où aller pour les besoins typiques?** L'importance relative des lieux dans une ville dépend des besoins de ses habitants. Réfléchissez à vos activités de tous les jours. Pour chaque catégorie, (1) mentionnez quelques activités et (2) indiquez où vous allez normalement pour faire ces activités.

> **Modèle:**   Distractions: *Je vais souvent au café pour retrouver des amis.*
> *On va au parc pour faire un pique-nique.*
> *Nous allons au cinéma pour regarder un nouveau film.*

Catégories: Distractions • Alimentation • Services médicaux • Services municipaux • Shopping • (Autres ???)

L. **Les endroits indispensables.** Travaillant en groupe de deux ou trois, déterminez quels sont les dix endroits les plus indispensables dans votre ville. (1) Employez° les **Expressions utiles** pour proposer vos idées et (2) élaborez vos suggestions avec une activité pour chaque endroit.

Employez: *Utilisez*

> **Modèle:**   *Dans notre ville, on a besoin de supermarchés où on va chercher des provisions. Et il est nécessaire d'avoir des restaurants élégants pour fêter les occasions spéciales.*

Expressions utiles: On a (aussi) besoin de... pour... • Un autre endroit essentiel est... pour... • Il est nécessaire d'avoir... pour... • Oui, c'est vrai. • Je ne suis pas d'accord, parce qu'il n'y a vraiment pas besoin de...

M. **L'image publique de la ville.** Les différents endroits dans une ville contribuent aussi à son image publique. C'est la personnalité qu'elle présente à ses résidents et à ses visiteurs. Travaillez en groupe de deux ou trois pour faire une description «psychologique» de votre ville (ou de la ville où se trouve votre université). Mentionnez trois ou quatre aspects de sa «personnalité» et expliquez comment ils se manifestent. Cherchez de l'inspiration dans la liste suivante de **Types de villes** et dans le Lexique du *Chapitre 3*.

> **Modèle:**   —*À mon avis, c'est une ville accueillante parce que les commerçants sont très sympathiques et généreux.*
> —*Oui, et c'est une ville touristique aussi parce qu'il y a un grand parc d'attractions.*

Types de villes: accueillant ≠ hostile • touristique ≠ ennuyeux • rural ≠ urbain • sophistiqué = cosmopolite • industriel ≠ artisanal • élégant ≠ simple • historique ≠ moderne • universitaire

Préparez ensemble un résumé écrit de vos décisions.

Objective: To give directions for getting around town

PRÉSENTATION: Un coup d'œil sur le thème

PLACE DE L'HÔTEL DE VILLE

Dans ce carré de 200 × 200 mètres, les monuments prestigieux d'Évreux: l'Hôtel de Ville, le Théâtre Scène Nationale, la Maison des Arts, l'ombre portée° sur les pavés: le Beffroi° qui fête ses 500 ans cette année.

Sur cette image, la rivière qui traverse° Évreux (l'Iton) est derrière nous. Et en passant par le passage du Beffroi, on peut arriver dans un quartier commerçant d'Évreux.

l'ombre portée: *the shadow cast*
Beffroi: *belfry*

traverse: *crosses, runs through*

Stratégies

1. Identify some activities that can be done at the **place de l'Hôtel de Ville** in Évreux. Which would you most enjoy?
2. What kinds of buildings surround the city hall in your town? Would you use a scene of the area around the city hall on a postcard from your city?

POUR DÉVELOPPER VOTRE FRANÇAIS

Structure: La préposition de et l'article défini

OBSERVATIONS

Je vais **de l'**université au café pour prendre un verre avec mes amis.

Puis je vais **du** café à la banque pour toucher un chèque.

Après ça, je vais **de la** banque au bureau de poste pour envoyer des cartes postales à mes amis.

1. You have already used **au** as a contraction for the preposition **à** + the definite article **le** to mean *to the* or *at the*. Do you think that **du** is also a contraction? A contraction for what? What do you think **du** might mean in the captions to the photographs?

2. Based on your knowledge of **à** + the definite article **la** or **l'**, how do you think that **de** is used with **la** and **l'**?

PRÉCISIONS

You have already used the preposition **de** directly before a noun to mean *from, of,* or *about*.

Monique va **de** Montréal à Québec.	*Monique is going **from** Montréal to Québec.*
M. Jacquot est le secrétaire **de** mon patron.	*Mr. Jacquot is the secretary **of** my boss.*
Nous parlons **de** notre prof de maths.	*We're talking **about** our math prof.*

de +la = du

- When **de** is followed by the definite article **la** or **l'**, there is no change in **de**.

Anne va **de la** pharmacie à la banque.	*Anne is going **from the** pharmacy to the bank.*
Georges arrive bientôt **de l'**aéroport.	*George is arriving soon **from the** airport.*

- When **de** is followed by the definite article (**le, la, l', les**), contractions occur with **le** and **les**.

de + le = du	**de + les = des**
Nous allons **du** parc au café.	*We are going **from the** park to the cafe.*
Marie téléphone à la femme **du** patron.	*Marie is calling the wife **of the** boss.*
Paul parle **des** clients à Nice.	*Paul is talking **about the** customers in Nice.*

À propos de la structure: Note that the verb **téléphoner** uses *à* before the person or place being called. Examples: **Téléphonez** *à* **Paul. Téléphonons** *au* **restaurant pour réserver une table.**

À propos de la prononciation: The **s** of **des** is usually silent, but before a vowel or vowel sound, it is pronounced as a **z**. Examples: **des hôtels, des étudiants.**

A. Qui a l'adresse? À tour de rôle avec votre partenaire, lisez les phrases suivantes. Remplacez les mots en italique et faites les changements nécessaires.

1. Qui a l'adresse du *prof?* (pharmacie / librairie / restaurant / cinéma / *de* l'université)

2. Où est l'entrée principale du *musée?* (banque / église / bureau de poste / gare / bibliothèque)

3. On cherche le nom du *café.* (boutique / hôtel / parc / hôpital / supermarché)

4. Est-ce que tu as le numéro de téléphone de la *pharmacie?* (immeuble / librairie / cathédrale / musée / café)

Vocabulaire: De et les prépositions de lieu

OBSERVATIONS

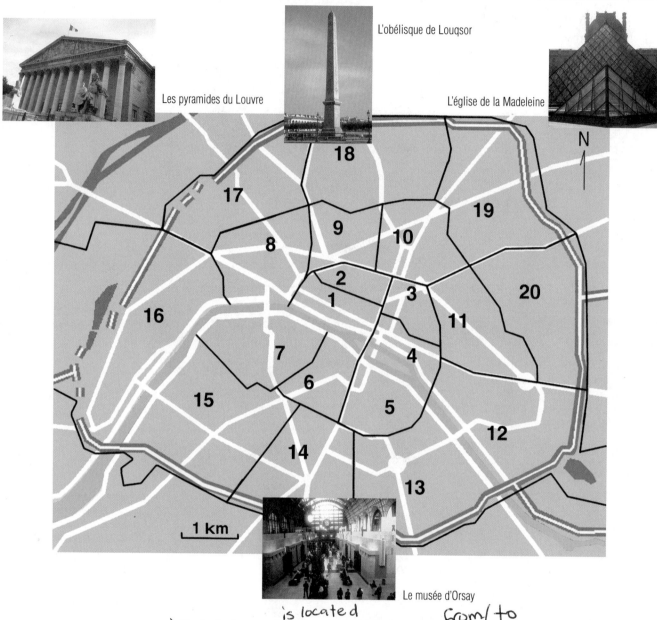

L'obélisque de Louqsor

Les pyramides du Louvre

L'église de la Madeleine

Le musée d'Orsay

is located

from/to

À Paris, le Louvre <u>se trouve</u> sur la Rive droite **de la** Seine. Le musée d'Orsay est sur la Rive gauche **de la** Seine.

Le Palais-Royal se trouve **près du** Louvre. Le palais de l'Élysée est **loin du** musée.

On peut dire que: *You can say that*

La Bibliothèque nationale est **derrière** le Palais-Royal. On peut dire que° le Palais-Royal est **devant** la Bibliothèque nationale.

ailes (f.): *wings*

Les pyramides du Louvre se trouvent **entre** les deux ailes° du musée.

L'église de l'Auxerrois est **en face du** Louvre.

Le Jeu de Paume se trouve **à côté de** l'Orangerie, **au bout du** jardin des Tuileries.

L'Orangerie est **au coin du** jardin des Tuileries **près de la** Seine.

Le musée d'Orsay se trouve **de l'autre côté de la** Seine.

L'obélisque de Louqsor se trouve **au centre de la** place de la Concorde.

autre = other
gauche = left
droite = right

NOTE CULTURELLE

Many buildings and monuments of historical interest are located in the central part of Paris. The following brief descriptions provide an introduction to this part of the city.

Le Louvre—formerly a royal palace; currently the most visited museum in France.

coin du = corner to
près du = near to close to

Les pyramides du Louvre—glass pyramids designed by I. M. Pei in the courtyard of the Louvre; the largest serves as the principal entrance to the museum.

derriére = behind

L'église de l'Auxerrois—church facing the front of the Louvre; the ringing of its bells signaled the beginning of *le massacre de Saint-Barthélemy*.

devant = infront of

entre = between

Le jardin des Tuileries—the gardens between the Louvre and the *place de la Concorde*, refurbished and reopened in 1997.

en face de = opposite to across from

à côté de = beside next

Le palais de l'Élysée—the residence and offices of the president of France.

au bout de = at end of

L'église de la Madeleine—a church built in the Roman style of the Parthenon; site of frequent choral concerts.

Le Palais-Royal—a royal palace near the Louvre, former residence of such notables as Cardinal Richelieu; currently a site of government offices and small shops.

La place Vendôme—contains a column made from the melted cannons of armies defeated by Napoléon; directly in front of the Ritz Hotel.

L'obélisque de Louqsor—monument from the tomb of Rameses II, presented as a gift to France from Egypt.

Le musée d'Orsay—former train station on the Left Bank of the Seine, currently a museum housing a large collection of Impressionist and other paintings and sculptures.

Le Jeu de Paume—museum that has traditionally housed collections not deemed worthy of being hung in the Louvre; former site of the Impressionist collection now in the Musée d'Orsay.

L'Orangerie—another museum in the corner of the Tuileries Garden, faces the *place de la Concorde*; houses the famous waterlily paintings of Monet.

La place de la Concorde—busy traffic circle around the *obélisque de Louqsor*; site of the guillotine during the French Revolution.

La Bibliothèque nationale de France (BNF)—created in 1994, located along the Seine River, it consists of four 22–story glass skyscrapers and houses more than 12,000,000 printed books, manuscripts, maps, drawings, medals, antiques, etc., combining the former **Bibliothèque nationale** created in 1926 and the **Bibliothèque de France** created in 1989.

La place Vendôme devant l'hôtel Ritz

Les colonnes de Buren dans la cour du Palais-Royal, près du Louvre

Le jardin des Tuileries entre le Louvre et le Jeu de Paume

STRATÉGIES D'ANALYSE

1. Study the map of the center of Paris on page 140. Find the places named in each sentence. Try to determine the meaning of the words in boldface by observing the relative location of the places named.

2. What happens to the preposition **de** when it follows a preposition of place such as **en face** or **au coin**?

3. Can you find any prepositions of place that are not followed by **de**?

PRÉCISIONS

- Many prepositions of place are followed by **de**.

près de	*near*
loin de	*far from*
en face de	*across from, facing*
à côté de	*next to, beside*
au coin de	*at the corner of*
au bout de	*at the end of*
au centre de	*in the middle of*
à droite de	*to the right of*
à gauche de	*to the left of*
de l'autre côté de	*on the other side of*

- The **de** after prepositions of place contracts as usual with the definite article **le** or **les**.

La bibliothèque se trouve à droite **du** musée.
The library is located to the right of the museum.

Mon bureau se trouve en face **des** bureaux de nos avocats.
My office is located across from the offices of our lawyers.

Le café est à côté **de la** banque.
The café is beside the bank.

Je travaille dans un immeuble de bureaux près **de l'**église.
I work in an office building near the church.

- Note that some prepositions of place are used without the preposition **de**.

L'hôtel se trouve **derrière** la gare.
*The hotel is located **behind** the train station.*

Il y a un beau parc **devant** l'église.
*There is a beautiful park **in front of** the church.*

Les pyramides du Louvre se trouvent **entre** les deux ailes du musée.
*The pyramids of the Louvre are located **between** the two wings of the museum.*

NOTE CULTURELLE

Paris is divided by the serpentine river, **la Seine**. When describing any location in Paris, usually the first information given is whether it is located on the Right Bank **(sur la Rive droite)** or on the Left Bank **(sur la Rive gauche)**. You can get your bearings by facing the direction that the river is flowing. **La Rive droite** is then on your right; **la Rive gauche** is on your left.

La Rive droite, with its numerous banks, department stores, theaters, and opera houses as well as the stock exchange **(la Bourse)** and **la Bibliothèque nationale**, is generally considered more sophisticated than **la Rive gauche**, home of many universities and schools, students, and artists where a more bohemian style characterizes the area. However, business, educational, and cultural centers can be found throughout the city.

In French, we have two words to describe different types of rivers. **Un fleuve** is a river that flows directly into the sea. **Une rivière** is a river (or tributary) that flows into another river. **La Seine** is **un fleuve** since it flows directly into **la Manche** (*the English Channel*), on the north coast of France.

B. **Près d'ici.** À tour de rôle avec votre partenaire, lisez les phrases suivantes. Remplacez les mots en italique et faites les changements nécessaires.

1. La place Vendôme est assez près *de l'Opéra Garnier*. (jardin des Tuileries / Louvre / église Saint-Roch / Seine)
2. Le Louvre se trouve loin *du palais de l'Élysée*. (Opéra Garnier / église de la Madeleine / cathédrale de Notre-Dame)
3. Mon ami a un appartement *en face du* Palais-Royal. (à côté de / près de / à gauche de / derrière)
4. Il y a un café *à côté de* la Madeleine. (en face de / à droite de / à gauche de / devant / derrière)
5. Y a-t-il un bon restaurant *près de* la Bourse? (en face de / à côté de / devant / derrière)

C. **Le cinéma se trouve....** À tour de rôle avec votre partenaire, décrivez les positions relatives des lieux dans chaque dessin. Écrivez au moins deux phrases pour décrire chaque dessin.

Modèle:

Le cinéma se trouve à côté du café.
Le café est tout près du cinéma.
Le cinéma est à droite du café.
Le café se trouve à gauche du cinéma.
Le cinéma n'est pas loin du café.

1.

2.

3.

4.

5.

6.

7.

8.

9.

Structure: L'impératif

OBSERVATIONS

Paris, le 15 mai

Ma chère amie Suzanne,
Tu vas adorer Paris! C'est une ville merveilleuse! À ton arrivée à l'aéroport Orly, **cherche** un taxi devant la sortie près des bagages. **Va** directement à l'hôtel Atlantis. **Fais** attention. L'entrée de l'hôtel est très petite et difficile à trouver. **Dépose** les valises dans la chambre, puis **retrouve**-moi aux Deux Magots, le café en face de l'église Saint-Germain-des-Prés.

Passons notre première soirée ensemble à Paris dans les rues de la Rive gauche.

Grosses bises,
Jacqueline

Par Avion

Suzanne Nelson
114 Santa Clara Blvd.
Los Angeles, CA 90876
USA

STRATÉGIES D'ANALYSE

1. Study the words in boldface on the postcard. Are they nouns or verbs? What function do they serve in these sentences?
2. What is the subject of each of these verbs? Is the subject expressed or understood? Do we have a similar verb construction in English? What is it called?
3. From the examples given, can you tell how these verbs are formed?
4. Which verbs would you expect to have irregular forms?

PRÉCISIONS

- Imperative verbs (command forms) are used to make requests and to give orders, suggestions, or directions.
- The three forms—**tu**, **vous**, and **nous**—are the same as the present tense (except that the **-s** of the **tu** form is dropped for regular **-er** verbs and for **aller**). Imperative verbs are used alone, with no subject pronoun, which is understood.

Present tense		*Imperative*	
tu téléphones	*you are calling*	**Téléphone.**	*Call.*
vous téléphonez	*you are calling*	**Téléphonez.**	*Call.*
nous téléphonons	*we are calling*	**Téléphonons.**	*Let's call.*

Cherche un emploi.
Look for a job.

Va à la cafétéria avec nous.
Go to the cafeteria with us.

Accompagnez-moi à la banque, s'il vous plaît.
Go with me to the bank, please.

Allez à mon bureau, s'il vous plaît.
Go to my office, please.

Travaillons ensemble.
Let's work together.

Allons au bureau de poste.
Let's go to the post office.

- Note that in the expression **Vas-y**, the imperative **tu** form retains the **-s**.

—Je veux organiser le budget.
—**Vas-y**!

I want to organize the budget.
Go on and do it!

- As you would expect, the imperative forms of **avoir** and **être** are irregular.

avoir		être	
Present tense	*Imperative*	*Present tense*	*Imperative*
tu as	**Aie!**	tu es	**Sois!**
vous avez	**Ayez!**	vous êtes	**Soyez!**
nous avons	**Ayons!**	nous sommes	**Soyons!**

Aie du courage!
Have courage!

Sois sage!
Be good! (said to a child)

Ayez de la patience!
Have patience!

Soyez à l'heure!
Be on time!

Ayons de l'énergie!
Let's have some energy!

Soyons calmes!
Let's be calm!

- The negative imperative form is regular, with **ne** before the verb and **pas** after it.

Ne parle pas anglais au patron.	*Don't speak* English to the boss.
Ne fumez pas ici, s'il vous plaît.	*Please **don't smoke** here.*
N'examinons pas les documents ce soir.	*Let's not go over* the documents *this evening.*
N'aie pas peur!	*Have no fear!*
Ne soyez pas idiots!	*Don't be stupid!*
Ne soyons pas en retard!	*Let's not be late.*

NOTE CULTURELLE

L'église Saint-Germain-des-Prés, located in the **6e arrondissement** in the heart of the Latin Quarter **(le Quartier latin)**, is one of the three oldest churches in Paris. Built in 558, it is still an active church as well as a popular site for orchestra and choral concerts. Directly across the street from **Saint-Germain-des-Prés**, on the corner of **le boulevard Saint-Germain-des-Prés**, is the famous café, **les Deux Magots**, named for the statues of two vagabonds inside the café.

D. **Dites à votre partenaire.** Utilisez l'impératif pour donner les directives suivantes à votre partenaire.

Modèle: de faire attention *Fais attention!*

1. d'étudier le plan de la ville
2. de chercher un bon restaurant
3. de donner l'adresse du restaurant à votre patron(ne)
4. d'être à l'heure
5. d'aller au cinéma avec vous
6. de ne pas fumer
7. de ne pas écouter de la musique rock
8. d'être sage
9. d'avoir de la patience
10. de ne pas avoir peur

E. **Dites à vos amis.** Utilisez les phrases de l'Exercice D pour donner les directives à votre partenaire et à son ami(e).

Modèle: de faire attention *Faites attention!*

F. **Proposez à votre partenaire.** Utilisez les phrases de l'Exercice D pour proposer des activités à votre partenaire à faire ensemble.

Modèle: de faire attention *Faisons attention!*

G. **Des conseils** *(Advice)* **importants.** Dites à votre partenaire le conseil le plus important que vous désirez donner aux individus suivants.

Modèle: aux futurs parents *Aimez l'enfant!*

1. aux professeurs
2. à votre patron
3. à votre meilleur(e) ami(e)
4. aux enfants d'un(e) de vos ami(e)s
5. à un collègue
6. aux touristes qui visitent les États-Unis
7. à votre époux(-se) ou petit(e) ami(e)
8. aux gens dans la voiture devant vous
9. à une personne qui désire parler français
10. à une personne qui entre dans la cafétéria universitaire pour la première fois

Vocabulaire: Des directions en ville

OBSERVATIONS

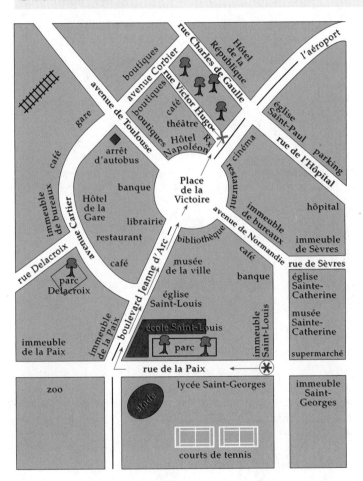

Madame: Pardon, monsieur, **savez-vous où se trouve** le théâtre Claudel?

Monsieur: Bien sûr, madame. Ce n'est pas **loin d'ici. Descendez** la rue de la Paix. **Allez tout droit jusqu'au** boulevard Jeanne d'Arc. **Tournez à droite** et **continuez jusqu'à** la place de la Victoire. **Traversez** la place. Il y a un hôtel **de l'autre côté de** la place.

Madame: Pardon, monsieur. Où est l'hôtel?

Monsieur: De l'autre côté de la place. **À côté de** l'hôtel il y a une pharmacie. Après la pharmacie, **tournez à gauche** dans la rue Victor Hugo. Le théâtre Claudel se trouve **derrière** la pharmacie. Il est **à gauche de** la rue Victor Hugo **en face du** parc.

Madame: Merci beaucoup, monsieur.

Monsieur: Je vous en prie.

STRATÉGIES D'ANALYSE

1. What did the woman say to get the attention of the man whom she asked for directions?
2. What expression did she use to find out whether he could give her directions?
3. We generally give directions in three steps. First, we give a general idea where the place is in relation to where we are (near, far). Then we give detailed directions including names of streets, intersections, and landmarks. Finally, we describe the destination in relation to what is around it. Can you find these three parts of the directions in the example?

PRÉCISIONS

- To ask directions it is necessary to get the attention of the person you expect to ask. Some possible beginnings are:

  —**Pardon,** monsieur.
  —**S'il vous plaît,** madame.

- The request for directions can be phrased in a number of ways.

Où est l'hôtel?	*Where is the hotel?*
Où se trouve la gare?	*Where is the train station located?*
Savez-vous où se trouve l'hôpital?	*Do you know where the hospital is located?*
Je cherche le musée. **Pouvez-vous m'aider?**	*I'm looking for the museum. Can you help me?*

- The first step in giving directions is to provide some general information about where the place is.

La gare **n'est pas loin d'ici.**	*The train station **is not far from here.***
Elle est **dans le nord de la ville.**	*It's **in the north part of town.***
Elle est **à dix minutes d'ici.**	*It's **ten minutes from here.***

- The second step in giving directions is to provide detailed, precise information, including landmarks, intersections, street names, and any other helpful comments.

Allez tout droit jusqu'à...	*Go straight ahead as far as . . .*
Tournez à droite/à gauche.	*Turn right/left.*
Continuez dans la rue...	*Keep going on . . . Street.*
Traversez la place/le boulevard...	*Cross the square/the boulevard . . .*
Prenez/Montez/Descendez la rue...	*Take/Go up/Go down . . . Street.*
Dépassez...	*Go past . . .*

- The final step in giving directions is to describe the exact location of the place in terms of what side of the street it is on, what is next to it/across from it/in front of it, or any outstanding landmarks that will help identify it.

  La gare se trouve **à droite/à gauche/au bout de la rue.**
  *The train station is **on the right side/on the left side/at the end of the street.***

  L'hôtel se trouve **de l'autre côté de la place, en face de l'hôpital.**
  *The hotel is **on the other side of the square, across from the hospital.***

H. **Des adresses.** Avec votre partenaire, utilisez les informations suivantes pour déterminer les adresses des bâtiments dans la rue de l'Université. (*Note:* When you give directions, take the perspective of a person who is walking or driving down the street in front of the buildings.)

Modèle: La banque se trouve en face de l'église.
Alors, l'adresse de la banque est 13, rue de l'Université.

11	13	15	17	19

rue de l'Université

12	14 *l'église*	16	18	20

1. La banque se trouve en face de l'église.
2. La pharmacie se trouve au bout de la rue, à droite de l'église.
3. Le musée est de l'autre côté de l'église.
4. La librairie est à gauche du musée.
5. Le bureau de poste se trouve en face de la librairie.
6. La bibliothèque se trouve entre la banque et le bureau de poste.
7. La station-service est au bout de la rue, à côté du bureau de poste.
8. Le supermarché est à l'autre bout de la rue, en face de la pharmacie.
9. L'hôtel se trouve à l'autre bout de la rue, à côté de la librairie et en face de la station-service.

I. **Où se trouve... ?** À tour de rôle avec votre partenaire, donnez des directions pour circuler dans la ville selon le plan à la page 147.

Modèle: de l'Hôtel de la République à la gare
La gare n'est pas loin d'ici. Montez la rue Charles de Gaulle jusqu'à l'avenue Corbier. Tournez à gauche. Allez tout droit sur l'avenue Cartier. Traversez l'avenue de Toulouse. La gare se trouve à droite de l'avenue Cartier au coin de l'avenue de Toulouse.

1. de la gare au lycée Saint-Georges
2. du lycée Saint-Georges à l'hôpital
3. de l'hôpital au musée de la Ville
4. du musée de la Ville à l'immeuble de Sèvres
5. de l'immeuble de Sèvres à l'école Saint-Louis
6. de l'école Saint-Louis à l'Hôtel Napoléon
7. de l'Hôtel Napoléon au supermarché
8. du supermarché au parc Delacroix

J. **On va à l'hôpital.** Imaginez que vous êtes à l'hôpital pour rendre visite à un(e) ami(e) malade. Vous avez besoin de transport pour rentrer chez vous. Utilisez le plan de la ville à la page 147. Écrivez un message à votre partenaire où vous donnez les directions pour aller de votre appartement dans l'immeuble de la Paix à l'hôpital.

PRONONCIATION: Le son [ə]

An unaccented **e** at the end of 2-letter words (**le, je**) or at the end of a syllable in the middle of a word (**petit**) is pronounced like the *a* in the English word *alone* except that the lips should be slightly rounded.

Repeat the following words after your instructor:

je   demi   avenue   le

À propos de la prononciation: In French, a syllable equals one vowel sound. Remember that an unaccented **e** at the end of words is usually silent. Sometimes (usually to sustain a rhythmic pattern in music or poetry), the mute **e** is pronounced [ə].

À vous! With a partner, take turns reading the following sentences. When do you pronounce [ə]? When is it silent?

1. Où est-ce que tu travailles?
2. Je n'ai pas de cigarettes.
3. Le bureau de tabac se trouve à gauche de la gare.
4. À quelle heure est-ce que Josette arrive?
5. Elle arrive à onze heures et demie.

POUR DÉVELOPPER VOS IDÉES

*Thematic objective: To examine the notion of **quartier** and how the various areas of a city reflect the needs and interests of the community*

Présentation: Les quartiers de la ville: La diversité complémentaire

POUR SAISIR L'ESSENTIEL: The word **quartier** is used technically to designate an administrative division of a city, but in casual usage it refers broadly to any area of a city that has a unity of its own. It corresponds to a range of English expressions, such as "district," "area," "neighborhood." Like the English *neighborhood*, the French **quartier** is often invested with personal and cultural significance.

The following paragraph briefly describes some of the diversity among various **quartiers** in Montreal.

1. Summarize the explanation in English.
2. Decide whether this explanation is presented in social, historical, or topographical terms.
3. Name another city that can be described in similar terms. If a similar description could be applied to the area where you live, name some of the places that might be thought of as **quartiers.**

Montréal par districts

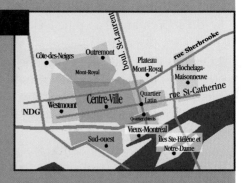

Montréal, comme plusieurs autres grandes villes, est une ville de quartiers. Mais les quartiers de Montréal sont très différents les uns des autres°. Chaque quartier a sa propre personnalité, sa propre histoire. Les différences sont visibles et palpables. Cette différence est due au fait que° Montréal débuta° à l'endroit où le Vieux-Montréal est situé maintenant mais a lentement débordé au-delà° des fortifications vers les faubourgs°. La vieille ville a continué son expansion vers le nord mais plusieurs villes et villages entourant la ville à l'ouest, au nord et à l'est se sont fusionnés° avec

les uns des autres: *from one another*

due au fait que: *due to the fact that*
débuta: *began*
lentement débordé au-delà: *slowly overflowed beyond*
vers les faubourgs: *toward the suburbs*
se sont fusionnés: *grew together*
n'existent plus: *no longer exist*

Montréal. Toutes ces petites villes et ces villages avaient leur propre histoire, leur propre style architectural, etc. Quelques-uns de ces vieux quartiers n'existent plus° ou sont complètement différents, mais plusieurs gardent leur personnalité.

K. **Les quartiers et leur rôle dans la ville.** La description sur le site Internet *Montréal par districts* comprend une liste des quartiers principaux. (1) Étudiez la liste ci-dessous pour décider quels quartiers vous voudriez avoir près de chez vous et quels quartiers vous préférez avoir assez loin de votre maison ou votre appartement. (2) Discutez un minimum de trois quartiers et donnez une raison pour chacune de vos opinions.

> **Modèle:** *Je voudrais habiter près du Vieux-Montréal à cause des magasins et des bâtiments historiques. C'est parce que j'aime bien faire du shopping et j'adore visiter des sites historiques.*

Des quartiers montréalais

Vieux-Montréal: la mecque touristique, l'hôtel de ville, restaurants, magasins, bâtiments historiques

Centre-Ville: musées, le Mont-Royal, la rue Ste-Catherine, etc.

La Ville souterraine: beaucoup de magasinage

Quartier latin et le village: bars, clubs et cafés

Plateau Mont-Royal: quartier résidentiel avec plusieurs restaurants, cafés et bars de quartier

Hochelaga-Maisonneuve: le stade Olympique, le jardin botanique, le Biodôme, etc.

Îles Ste-Hélène et Notre-Dame: le Casino de Montréal, La Ronde, la Biosphère, etc.

Côte-des-Neiges et Notre-Dame-de-Grâce: le cimetière, l'Oratoire, le campus de l'Université de Montréal, l'avenue Monkland

Outremont: restaurants, parcs, promenades

Quartier chinois: jardins, boutiques de cadeaux, marché chinois

Westmount: parcs, maisons riches et célèbres

Sud-ouest: la rue Notre-Dame, le marché Atwater, le canal Lachine, etc.

Autres districts: la petite Italie, Ahuntsic (île de la Visitation, Sault-au-Recollet, boulevard Gouin), quartier latino-américain, Parc-Extension, etc.

L. **Un quartier à mon goût** *(to my taste).* Imaginez un quartier que vous voudriez beaucoup fréquenter—c'est-à-dire, un quartier avec les distractions et les services correspondant à votre style de vie. Imaginez que vous habitez ce quartier. Quels sont les endroits près de chez vous dans ce quartier idéal? Mentionnez un minimum de cinq endroits en indiquant leur emplacement par rapport à votre maison. Consultez le Lexique et les pages 125 et 142 pour quelques mots de vocabulaire.

> **Modèle:** 1. *Il y a un parc en face de ma maison.*
> 2. *À côté de chez moi, il y a un café terrasse.*
> 3. *À droite du parc, il y a une petite librairie.*

M. **Mon quartier.** Organisez vos phrases de l'exercice précédent dans un paragraphe. Commencez le paragraphe par une introduction à votre sujet. Élaborez votre description des endroits et terminez par un petit commentaire personnel.

> **Modèle:** *J'habite un immeuble (une maison) dans un quartier pittoresque (traditionnel, moderne, calme, animé, etc.). En face de chez moi, il y a un parc où je fais des promenades. À droite du parc, il y a une librairie. J'aime la lecture et je vais souvent à la librairie. À côté de mon immeuble, il y a un café. Mes amis et moi, nous aimons prendre un verre° au café le samedi soir... J'aime bien mon quartier, c'est un lieu sympathique.*

prendre un verre: *to have a drink*

une journée: *a day*

3ᴱ THÈME: On passe une journée° en ville

Objective: To schedule appointments and discuss schedules

PRÉSENTATION: Un coup d'œil sur le thème

renommés: *renowned*

Quand on fait son premier séjour à Paris, il est absolument nécessaire de visiter les quatre sites les plus renommés° de la ville.

La tour Eiffel

était: *was*
la plus haute: *the tallest*
un ascenseur: *elevator*
ne manquez pas: *don't miss*
troisième étage: *third level*

Commencez par la tour Eiffel. Située dans le 7ᵉ arrondissement, c'est le symbole universel de la France. Au moment de son inauguration en 1889, elle était° la plus haute° construction du monde. On peut utiliser l'ascenseur° de 9h30 du matin jusqu'à 11h00 du soir. Ne manquez pas° la vue panoramique du troisième étage°.

L'Arc de triomphe de l'Étoile

souterrains: *underground, subterranean*
le Soldat inconnu: *Unknown Soldier*

Pour arriver en sécurité sur la place Charles de Gaulle, où se trouve l'Arc de triomphe, prenez un des passages souterrains°. Visitez le tombeau du Soldat inconnu° sous l'arche centrale, et prenez l'ascenseur pour monter dans l'arc pour une vue superbe de l'avenue des Champs-Élysées. Pendant l'été, il est ouvert de 9h30 du matin à 11h00 du soir du mardi au samedi.

Le musée du Louvre

Le musée du Louvre se trouve à l'est de l'Arc de triomphe. Il est impossible de tout voir en une seule visite. Mais pour les histoires que vous allez raconter chez vous, allez voir la Joconde° de Léonard de Vinci. On y trouve aussi la fameuse Vénus de Milo. N'oubliez pas que le Louvre est fermé° le mardi.

la Joconde: *the Mona Lisa*

fermé: *closed*

Notre-Dame de Paris

au beau milieu: *right in the middle*

étoile: *star*

La cathédrale Notre-Dame, au beau milieu° de la Seine, est aussi considérée comme le beau milieu de Paris. Au portail ouest, il y a une étoile° en bronze qui marque le point zéro quand on mesure la distance entre Paris et les autres villes de France, ou la distance entre la France et tout autre lieu du monde. On peut faire la visite de la cathédrale entre 8h00 du matin et 6h45 du soir.

[handwritten notes:]
am - du matin
pm - du soir
Il est...

POUR DÉVELOPPER VOTRE FRANÇAIS

Structure: L'heure

[handwritten:]
9:45am ① Il est dix heures moins le quart
9:15am ① Il est neuf heures quinze minutes
② Il est neuf heures et quart

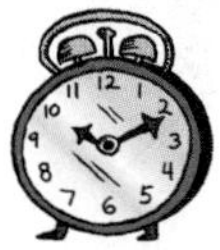

OBSERVATIONS

10:10

—Quelle heure est-il?
—Il est dix heures dix.

What time is it?
It is 10:10.

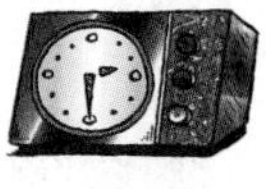

2:30

—Pardon, vous avez l'heure?
—Il est deux heures et demie.

Excuse me. Do you have the time?
It is 2:30.

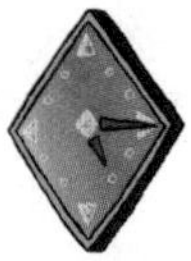

5:15

—Savez-vous quelle heure il est?
—Il est cinq heures et quart.

Do you know what time it is?
It is 5:15.

3:40

—Il est quelle heure?
—Il est quatre heures moins vingt.

What time is it?
It's twenty minutes before four.

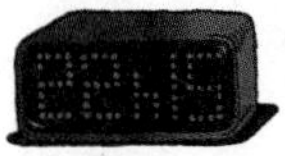

10:15

—À quelle heure part le train?
—À vingt-deux heures quinze.

What time does the train leave?
At 10:15 in the evening.

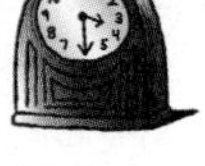

—À quelle heure commence le film?
—À quinze heures trente. Soyez à l'heure.

3:30

15!

What time does the movie start?
At 3:30 in the afternoon. Be on time.

6:00   9:45

—Quand est-ce qu'on prend le petit déjeuner à l'hôtel?
—Entre six heures et neuf heures quarante-cinq du matin. Ne soyez pas en retard.

When do we have breakfast at the hotel?
Between 6:00 and 9:45 A.M.
Don't be late.

7:00 midnight

—Quand est-ce que le dîner est servi au restaurant Chez André?
—De dix-neuf heures jusqu'à minuit.

When is dinner served at the restaurant Chez André?
From 7:00 P.M. until midnight.

STRATÉGIES D'ANALYSE

1. Tell three ways to ask someone in French what time it is.
2. Can you find two ways to express *half past the hour* in French?
3. Can you find two ways to indicate that something happens *between* two times?
4. Using the examples as a guide, can you figure out the following times?
   16h   18h30   21h15   14h10
5. How do you express *on time* and *late* in French?

PRÉCISIONS

- To ask someone what time it is, use **Quelle heure est-il?**

  or one of the related questions: **Savez-vous quelle heure il est?**
  Vous avez l'heure?
  Il est quelle heure?

- To ask at what time something happens, use **À quelle heure... ?**

  À quelle heure est-ce que tu arrives au bureau?
  (At) what time do you arrive at the office?

- To respond to this question, use the preposition **à** to give an exact time or the preposition **vers** to give an approximate time.

  —**À quelle heure** quittez-vous   *(At) what time do you leave*
  la maison?   *the house?*
  —**À 7h15.**   *At 7:15.*
  —**Vers 7h15.**   *At about 7:15.*

- To ask *when* something happens, use **Quand?**

  Quand est-ce que la bibliothèque est ouverte?
  When is the library open?

- To tell that something happens *between* two times, use either of the following:

  entre 9h **et** 10h30   *between 9:00 and 10:30*
  de 6h **à** 8h45   *from 6:00 until/to 8:45*

- To distinguish between A.M. and P.M. in informal situations, use:

du matin	8:14 A.M.	huit heures quatorze **du matin**
de l'après-midi	3:15 P.M.	trois heures et quart **de l'après-midi**
du soir	7:30 P.M.	sept heures et demie **du soir**

- In nonofficial situations, you may hear rounded quarter-hours in telling time.

9h15	10h30
Il est neuf heures quinze.	Il est dix heures trente.
Il est neuf heures **et quart**.	Il est dix heures **et demie**.

3h45	12h30
Il est trois heures quarante-cinq.	Il est midi trente.
Il est quatre heures **moins le quart**.	Il est midi **et demi**.

À propos de la structure: Since the word **heure** is feminine, the word **demie** ends in an **e** in expressions with **heure**. Since **midi** and **minuit** are masculine, **demi** after either of these expressions does not add an **e**. Examples: Il est trois heures et **demie**. Il est midi et **demi**.

- Use special terms to express *noon* (**midi**) and *midnight* (**minuit**).
- For all official or formal times, use the 24-hour clock.

Le vol arrive **à 14h08**.	*The flight arrives **at 2:08** P.M.*
Le concert commence **à 20h30**.	*The concert begins **at 8:30** P.M.*
Téléphonez-moi **à 21h** précises.	*Call me **at exactly 9:00** P.M.*

- The following are other frequently-used expressions dealing with time:

Sois/Soyez **à l'heure**.	*Be on time.*
Sois/Soyez **en avance**.	*Be early.*
Ne sois/soyez pas **en retard**.	*Don't be late.*
Je vais **passer une heure** chez le dentiste.	*I'm going to spend an hour at the dentist's office.*

A. Quelle heure est-il? À tour de rôle avec votre partenaire, demandez quelle heure il est.

Modèle: 4:25 P.M.
—*Quelle heure est-il? (Tu as l'heure?) (Sais-tu quelle heure il est?)*
—*Il est quatre heures vingt-cinq de l'après-midi.*
ou —*Il est seize heures vingt-cinq.*

1. 9:10 A.M.	3. 8:15 P.M.	5. 4:30 A.M.	7. 10:40 P.M.	9. 3:45 P.M.
2. 7:05 P.M.	4. 6:50 A.M.	6. 9:35 P.M.	8. 11:30 A.M.	10. 2:15 P.M.

B. Ça prend du temps. À tour de rôle avec votre partenaire, estimez le temps nécessaire pour faire chaque activité.

À propos de la structure: Note the spelling of **demi** in the expression for half-hour (**une demi-heure**).

Modèle: laver la voiture
Laver la voiture prend une demi-heure.

une heure	15 minutes	**une demi-heure**	*10 minutes*
deux heures et demie		20 minutes	**trois heures**
5 minutes	**un quart d'heure**		*toute la journée*

1. laver la voiture
2. préparer le dîner
3. voir un film au cinéma
4. faire une réservation à l'hôtel
5. écrire une lettre à un(e) ami(e) par courrier électronique°

6. aller à la banque
7. faire une pause-café°
8. faire une promenade de 5 km
9. chercher un livre à la bibliothèque
10. aller chercher des médicaments à la pharmacie

C. **À quelle heure... ?** Marc a deux amis américains chez lui. Il va faire le touriste avec ses amis. Étudiez **l'horaire de Marc** pour lundi. À tour de rôle avec votre partenaire, répondez aux questions.

Modèle: être au Panthéon
—*À quelle heure est-ce que Marc et ses amis vont être au Panthéon?*
—*Ils vont être au Panthéon à neuf heures quarante-cinq.*

1. prendre le petit déjeuner
2. déjeuner
3. dîner
4. faire une pause-café
5. visiter la Sainte-Chapelle
6. visiter l'église de la Madeleine
7. faire une promenade au bord de la Seine

8. être au jardin du Luxembourg
9. être au jardin des Tuileries
10. arriver à la place de la Concorde
11. faire du shopping
12. passer une heure à la cathédrale Notre-Dame
13. passer une heure dans la rue de Rivoli

lundi	l'horaire de Marc	
7h00	petit déjeuner aux Deux Magots	
7h45 *quarant cinq*	l'église Saint-Germain-des-Prés	
8h30 *trente*	l'église Saint-Sulpice	
9h00	le jardin du Luxembourg	⑧
9h45	le Panthéon	
10h30	le Boul' Mich'	
10h45	pause-café	
11h15 *onze*	la cathédrale Notre-Dame	⑫
12h30 *douze*	déjeuner dans l'île Saint-Louis	(
14h00 *quatorze*	le Palais de Justice	
14h30	la Sainte-Chapelle	⑤
15h30 *quinze*	au bord de la Seine	7
16h15 *size.*	le jardin des Tuileries	⑨
17h00 *dix-sept*	la place de la Concorde	⑩
17h30	l'église de la Madeleine	⑥
18h15 *dix-huit*	du shopping dans la rue de Rivoli	⑪ ⑬
19h30 *dix-neuf*	dîner à la Bonne Fourchette dans la rue Saint-Honoré	

Note Culturelle

Le boulevard Saint-Michel, running north-south through **la Rive gauche,** cuts through the heart of **le Quartier latin.** Since the universities in the area do not have student centers or dormitories, many of the services needed by students are satisfied by merchants on **le Boul' Mich',** as the street is known. There are numerous **cafés,** take-out **(à emporter)** and fast-food **(restauration rapide)** eat-in establishments, as well as **boulangeries, librairies, pharmacies, boutiques,** and **cinémas.**

Le Boul' Mich' se trouve au Quartier latin.
La vie au Boul' Mich' est très animée.

Structure: Les adjectifs démonstratifs ce, cet, cette, ces = "THIS"

OBSERVATIONS

Je vais rester à la maison **ce matin.**	*I'm going to stay at home **this morning.***
Cet après-midi nous allons au cinéma.	***This afternoon** we're going to the movies.*
Est-ce que tu travailles **cette semaine?**	*Are you working **this week?***

STRATÉGIES D'ANALYSE

1. What are the three different forms in French for *this?* *ce, cet, cette*
2. Based on what you have learned about nouns in French, what would you expect to cause the difference between **ce** and **cette?** *ce = consonant, cet = 2 vowels cette = feminine*
3. **Après-midi** is a masculine noun. Why do you think that the masculine demonstrative adjective **ce** adds a **t** to become **cet** before **après-midi?** *a = vowel*
4. What would you expect the plural form *these* to be? *ces*

PRÉCISIONS

-   In French, the demonstrative adjective is used to point out specific things. It changes form based on gender and number. There are three singular forms equivalent in meaning to *this* or *that* in English.

Paul va au concert **ce** soir.	*(masculine singular before a pronounced consonant)*
Téléphone-moi **cet** après-midi.	*(masculine singular before a vowel or vowel sound)*
Cette journée est très agréable.	*(feminine singular)*

ex- J'aime ce sac-ci mais je désteste ce sac-là

-ci = close to you

-la = further away

ce magazine -ci/la

- There is only one plural form, equivalent in meaning to *these* or *those* in English.

Ces musées sont intéressants.   ***These** museums are interesting.*
Je ne vais pas visiter **ces** écoles.   *I'm not going to visit **those** schools.*

- Sometimes it is important to make a distinction between *this* and *that* or between *these* and *those*. In that case, use the demonstrative adjective with the noun and add **-ci** (for *this* or *these*) or **-là** (for *that* or *those*) to the noun.

J'aime assez bien **ce café-ci**, mais je préfère **ce café-là**.
*I like **this café** fairly well, but I prefer **that café**.*

Allons voir **ce film-ci**. Je n'aime pas du tout **cette comédienne-là**.
*Let's go see **this film**. I don't like **that actress** at all.*

Ces musées-ci sont plus intéressants que **ces musées-là**.
***These museums** are more interesting than **those museums**.*

D. **Ce soir.** À tour de rôle avec votre partenaire, remplacez les mots en italique par les mots entre parenthèses. Faites les changements nécessaires.

1. Est-ce que tu vas au bureau *ce soir*? (après-midi / matin)
2. Où se trouve *ce musée*? (école / théâtre / université / bibliothèque)
3. À quelle heure commence *ce film*? (concert / conférence° / cours)
4. Savez-vous où se trouvent *ces églises*? (cinémas / musées / restaurants / cafés)
5. Savez-vous à quelle heure arrive *ce vol*°? (train / étudiants / étudiantes / profs)

une conférence: *a lecture*

un vol: *a flight*

Structure: Le verbe irrégulier prendre

OBSERVATIONS

—Je **prends** la visite guidée du musée d'Orsay à 9 heures.   *I **am taking** the guided tour of the Musée d'Orsay at 9 o'clock.*

—Ces visites **prennent** combien de temps?   *How much time do these tours **take?***

—Pas plus de deux heures, j'espère. Marc et moi, nous **prenons** le petit déjeuner ensemble à 8 heures.   *Not more than two hours, I hope. Mark and I **are having** breakfast together at 8:00.*

—Tu **comprends** les guides au musée?   *Do you **understand** the guides at the museum?*

—Assez bien. Et j'**apprends** toujours beaucoup.   *Fairly well. And I always **learn** a lot.*

STRATÉGIES D'ANALYSE

1. The conjugation of the verb **prendre** is irregular. From the forms given, can you guess the other forms of the verb to complete the conjugation?

je **prends**	nous **prenons**
tu _____	vous _____
il/elle/on **prend**	ils/elles **prennent**

2. Find two other verbs in the sample sentences that appear to conjugate like **prendre**.

3. Since **prendre** means *to take*, what would you expect **reprendre** to mean?

PRÉCISIONS

- The irregular verb **prendre** *(to take)* has the following forms in the present tense:

je **prends**	nous **prenons**
tu **prends**	vous **prenez**
il/elle/on **prend**	ils/elles **prennent**

- The base meaning of **prendre** is *to take*. But that meaning is often modified by the expression in which it is used.

Je **prends** faim.	**Prenons** le petit déjeuner au café.
I'm getting hungry.	*Let's have breakfast at the café.*
Tu **prends** soif?	Vous **prenez** un dessert?
Are you getting thirsty?	*Are you having dessert?*
Ça **prend** beaucoup de temps.	Elles **prennent** rendez-vous pour demain.
This takes a lot of time.	*They are setting an appointment for tomorrow.*

- The following verbs are conjugated like **prendre**:

apprendre	*to learn*
comprendre	*to understand*
reprendre	*to take back, resume, rehire*

E. **Prendre rendez-vous.** À tour de rôle avec votre partenaire, remplacez les mots en italique par les mots entre parenthèses. Faites les changements nécessaires.

1. Est-ce que *Georges* prend rendez-vous chez le médecin demain? (tu / vous / Marie-Claire et Dominique / Christine)

2. Est-ce que *tu* prends un dessert? (vous / nous / elles / Jacqueline)

3. *Je* comprends bien les questions. (tu / nous / Geneviève / les étudiants)

4. *Nous* apprenons beaucoup de français. (vous / les étudiants / Paul et moi / je)

5. *Le prof* reprend les documents. (je / vous / nous / Louis)

6. *Je* prends le métro. (nous / tu / les enfants / vous)

quelques bribes de: *some parts, excerpts of*

F. **Au café.** Souvent au café on peut entendre quelques bribes° des conversations aux autres tables. À tour de rôle avec votre partenaire, complétez les conversations en utilisant les formes convenables des verbes **prendre, apprendre, comprendre** ou **reprendre.**

1. —Mon professeur de biologie parle très vite. Je ne *comprends* pas ses conférences.

   —Est-ce que les autres étudiants _____ assez bien?

2. —J'ai soif. Je _____ un citron pressé. Et toi, qu'est-ce que tu _____?

3. —Ma mère va en Italie en avril. Elle _____ l'italien à l'université.

   —Et vous, est-ce que vous _____ l'italien avec elle?

4. —Tu _____ trop de café. _____ du thé cet après-midi.

5. —Est-ce que Marie-Louise _____ rendez-vous ce matin avec Jean-Claude?

   —Oui. Ils _____ le petit-déjeuner ensemble au Café de Flore.

6. —J'apprécie le travail de Marguerite. Elle _____ le temps de m'aider.

logiciel: *software program*

7. —Je n'aime pas du tout ce logiciel°. Mais je _____ les disquettes.

Structure: Des questions d'information

OBSERVATIONS

Le cristal de Baccarat est très célèbre.

À propos de la structure: You will often see **y** in sentences with the verb **aller** to complete the idea *to go someplace.*

—**Qu'est-ce que** nous allons faire cet après-midi?
—Allons regarder le cristal au musée Baccarat.
—**Où** est ce musée?
—Dans la rue du Paradis, près de la gare de l'Est.
—**Quand** est-ce que le musée est ouvert?
—De lundi à vendredi.
—**Qui** nous accompagne?
—Dominique. Elle désire aller voir le cristal aussi.
—**Pourquoi** est-ce que Christine n'y va pas avec nous?
—Parce qu'elle apprécie beaucoup le cristal. Le cristal de Baccarat est très cher, et

être tenté(e): *be tempted*

elle préfère ne pas être tentée°.

1. Using the context, can you determine how to ask each of the following information questions: *Who? What? When? Where? Why?* Look at the answer that follows each of these questions to determine what you think the question word is asking.
2. How do you expect the response to a **Pourquoi?** question to start?

PRÉCISIONS

In order to obtain information, you need to be able to ask the *Who? What? When? Where?* and *Why?* questions.
- To ask *Who?*, use **qui**.

Qui va au concert avec moi?	**Who** *is going to the concert with me?*
Qui travaille ce week-end?	**Who** *is working this weekend?*

- To ask *Where?*, use **où**.

Où est le musée?	**Where** *is the museum?*
Où se trouve un arrêt d'autobus près d'ici?	**Where** *is a bus stop near here?*

- To ask *When?*, use **quand**. Use **à quelle heure** to ask specifically about the time of an activity.

Quand est-ce que nous allons à Versailles, mercredi ou jeudi?	**When** *are we going to Versailles, Wednesday or Thursday?*
À quelle heure commence le ballet?	**(At) what time** *does the ballet start?*

- To find out *what* someone wants or is doing, use **qu'est-ce que**.

Qu'est-ce que nous allons faire cet après-midi?	**What** *are we going to do this afternoon?*
Qu'est-ce que vous voulez comme boisson?	**What** *do you want to drink?*

- To ask *Why?*, use **pourquoi**. Note that the *because* answer begins with **parce que**.

Pourquoi allez-vous à la Rive droite?	**Why** *are you going to the Right Bank?*
Parce que je préfère le bureau de change dans la rue de Rivoli.	**Because** *I prefer the money exchange on the rue de Rivoli.*

Various money exchange offices **(un bureau de change)** have different conversion rates and commission fees. You need to shop for the best exchange rate. Pay special attention to the posted rates, especially to the sell rates **(ventes)** for dollars or buy rates **(achats)**. In exchanging American dollars for French francs or Euros, look for the buy rate **(achats).**

À propos: Be sure to read what follows the blank to help you decide which question word to use.

G. Des questions. Ajoutez les mots interrogatifs nécessaires pour compléter le dialogue suivant. À tour de rôle avec votre partenaire, lisez le dialogue.

—_____ tu vas faire ce soir?

—Marc et moi, nous allons au cinéma pour voir un nouveau film.

—_____ se trouve le cinéma?

—Dans l'avenue des Champs-Élysées.

—_____ commence le film?

—À 19h30. Il y a aussi une séance à 17h10.

—_____ allez-vous dîner?

— Après le film.

—_____ allez-vous dîner, à ce nouveau restaurant à côté du cinéma?

—Non, ce restaurant-là est très cher. Je préfère prendre une pizza à emporter à la maison.

—_____ reste à la maison avec l'enfant?

—La jeune fille qui habite la maison en face de chez nous. Elle est très responsable.

PRONONCIATION: Les voyelles nasales

In French, when certain vowels are followed by **-m** or **-n** *in the same syllable,* they are nasalized. There are four nasal vowel sounds in French, represented by the following phonetic symbols:

[ã], as in *français,* **en avance,** *souvent*
[ɛ̃], as in *faim, musicien, inviter*
[ɔ̃], as in **on,** *allons, comptable*
[œ̃], as in **un,** *brun, parfum*

To pronounce the first three correctly, position your mouth as you would to pronounce the non-nasal [a], [ɛ], and [o], but force air through your nostrils while saying them. The last sound listed, [œ̃], is a nasalized version of the vowel *e* [schwa] as it sounds in **je** and **le.**

À vous! With a partner, practice reading the following sentences containing nasal vowels:

1. De temps en temps, je te rencontre au centre commercial.
2. Mon grand-père a quatre-vingt-cinq ans.
3. J'ai les cheveux bruns et les yeux marron.
4. C'est loin le magasin de vêtements? Non, c'est là au coin.
5. Quand est-ce que vous allez prendre le train pour Avignon?
6. Un bon garçon aide ses parents.

Notez bien! If the **–m** or **–n** which would otherwise cause a vowel to be nasalized is followed by a vowel sound, the preceding vowel is no longer nasalized. (This is because the **–m** or **–n** would no longer belong to the same syllable.)

Nasalized	Denasalized
un améric*ain*	une américaine
mon	monotone
an	Anne

POUR DÉVELOPPER VOS IDÉES

Thematic objective: To integrate the notion of quartier *in describing American cities to French-speaking people*

Présentation: Un plan du quartier

POUR SAISIR L'ESSENTIEL: Below are brief descriptions of three popular **quartiers** in Paris.

1. Skim through them, noting dates and any names that you recognize.
2. Skim the descriptions a second time to determine the topic of each paragraph.
3. Now read the three descriptions more carefully; list two or three facts about each **quartier.**
4. Working with a partner, compare your lists. Add information from your partner's list to your own. If you and your partner have conflicting interpretations, study the reading together to reach an agreement.
5. Based on the facts that you have listed, decide which of the **quartiers** you would most like to visit. Tell why.

Le Quartier latin

Le Quartier latin est fort marqué par la présence de l'université de Paris. Fondée par Robert de Sorbon pour les étudiants pauvres, la Sorbonne date de 1253. Au cours du temps°, elle a gagné une réputation internationale. Le quartier tient son nom du fait que° le latin était la langue universitaire jusqu'en 1793.

Si vous faites un tour du Quartier latin, ne manquez pas de visiter le Panthéon où sont inhumés° de grands esprits° de la France, tels que° Voltaire, Rousseau, Victor Hugo et Pierre et Marie Curie.

À part° les sites historiques, il y a aussi de nombreux cinémas, cafés, restaurants et librairies dans ce quartier animé.

Étudiants devant l'entrée de la Sorbonne

La basilique du Sacré-Cœur. Son clocher° pèse 18.5 tonnes.

Montmartre

Ce quartier tient son nom du Mont des Martyrs. De cette hauteur°, il domine la ville de Paris. Les touristes y sont surtout attirés° par le Sacré-Cœur, une basilique romano-byzantine, qui offre une vue panoramique de la ville. Si vous visitez Montmartre, allez à la place du Tertre pour apprécier le charme qui, à la fin du XIXᵉ siècle°, a fait de ce site le centre de la vie artistique et intellectuelle—et bohémienne—de Paris. Prenez un café dans les mêmes établissements qui ont accueilli° Hector Berlioz et Pablo Picasso.

Les Halles–Beaubourg

Le quartier des Halles était le premier marché de Paris, datant du XIIᵉ siècle. On l'appelait «le ventre° de Paris». Maintenant, au lieu du marché il y a un centre commercial, le Forum des Halles et des équipements de loisirs. C'est un lieu très populaire le samedi après-midi.

Si vous allez au Forum des Halles, traversez le boulevard Sébastopol pour une visite du Centre Pompidou. Prenez le temps d'examiner son architecture ultra-moderne (très controversée) et de visiter le Musée national d'Art moderne. Là vous allez trouver une collection impressionnante d'art moderne.

On dit que «ce *paquebot*»° *de la culture* dans le quartier des Halles a été difficilement accepté.

H. Les quartiers de ma ville. Appliquez le concept de quartiers aux secteurs de la ville où vous habitez. Identifiez les quartiers de votre ville. (1) Mentionnez au moins trois quartiers en donnant° à chacun un nom. (2) Expliquez où chaque quartier est situé dans la ville. (3) Indiquez les caractéristiques principales de chacun. (Cherchez du vocabulaire dans la liste **Types de quartier**.) Écrivez trois paragraphes avec les informations.

donnant: *giving*

Modèle: *Un quartier assez important dans ma ville est Trinity Heights. Il se trouve au nord de la ville, près de l'aéroport. C'est un vieux quartier commerçant. Il y a beaucoup de boutiques intéressantes.*

Types de quartier

- un quartier des affaires
- un quartier artisanal
- un quartier historique

- un quartier commerçant
- un quartier industriel
- un quartier touristique

- un quartier culturel
- un quartier résidentiel
- un quartier universitaire

I. Comment s'amuser dans ma ville. Quand vous avez un invité° chez vous, quels sites et quelles activités est-ce que vous recommandez? Consultez la liste des **Besoins et intérêts des touristes** et indiquez où on va dans votre ville pour les satisfaire°. Discutez au moins cinq besoins et intérêts.

invité: *guest*

les satisfaire: *to satisfy them*

Modèle: *Si vous désirez admirer l'architecture, allez au centre-ville. C'est un quartier historique. L'hôtel de ville est beau. Le théâtre Bernhardt n'est pas loin de l'hôtel de ville, et il est très moderne.*

Besoins et intérêts des touristes

- apprécier une collection d'art (moderne / impressionniste / classique / amérindien°)
- faire du tourisme
- faire une promenade
- admirer l'architecture
- déjeuner sur le pouce°
- passer un après-midi actif / nager
- acheter des souvenirs
- toucher un chèque / chercher de l'argent

- prendre des photos
- acheter des cartes postales
- envoyer des cartes postales
- faire des recherches (généalogiques)
- consulter les archives municipales
- apprécier la cuisine de la région
- assister à un concert ou à un spectacle de théâtre
- passer la soirée à danser / dans les bars

amérindien: *American Indian*

déjeuner sur le pouce: *to have lunch on the run*

J. Une visite guidée de notre ville. Travaillez en équipe de deux ou trois pour organiser une visite de votre ville. Organisez votre visite selon les questions suivantes.

1. À quelle heure est-ce que la visite commence?
2. Quel est le point de départ? (On part de... pour aller à...)
3. À quel quartier est-ce qu'on va d'abord°?
4. Décrivez un peu ce quartier.
5. Quels endroits est-ce qu'on va visiter dans ce quartier?
6. Qu'est-ce qu'on fait à chaque endroit?
7. Combien de temps est-ce qu'on va passer à chaque endroit?
8. Où et à quelle heure est-ce qu'on va déjeuner?
   [Recommencez avec des informations sur le deuxième quartier.]
9. Où et à quelle heure est-ce que la visite se termine°?

d'abord: *first*

se termine: *end*

ÉCOUTONS: Autour de la ville

These activities will help you practice listening for specific details in directions to (1) locate places on a map, (2) identify a sequence of errands, and (3) follow a route described in conversation. It is a good idea to study the map before you begin listening, so that you have a general idea of what and where the streets and buildings are.

A. **Où se trouve?** Several places in the **quartier** are not marked on the map. Among them are the five listed below. As you listen to the descriptions of where these five places are located, identify their locations on the map. Mark each unlabeled location with the appropriate letter to show which building is found there.

A. Café Deauville   **C.** Lycée Clemenceau   **E.** Parking
B. Librairie Anatole   **D.** Magasin de sport

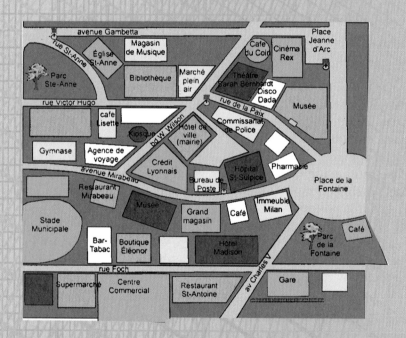

B. **Des courses partout.** *(Errands everywhere.)* In this activity, you will hear part of a conversation between friends, Michel and Stéphanie. Michel has a number of errands to do today and he lists them for Stéphanie. As you hear Michel say where he plans to go for each errand, mark a number (1, 2, 3, 4, or 5) on that location on the map to show whether it comes first, second, third, etc., on Michel's to-do list.

Before you begin listening, take a moment to locate the places on the map that are listed on the next page. Circle each one on the map so that you can find it easily when you hear it mentioned in the conversation.

> **Supermarché:** au sud du quartier, dans la rue Foch, à côté du centre commercial et près du stade
> **Bureau de poste:** au milieu du quartier, dans l'avenue Mirabeau, entre le Crédit Lyonnais et l'hôpital St-Sulpice
> **Grand magasin:** au milieu du quartier, dans l'avenue Mirabeau, en face du bureau de poste
> **Pharmacie:** à l'est de l'hôpital St-Sulpice, sur la place de la Fontaine
> **Bibliothèque:** dans le nord du quartier, dans la rue Victor Hugo, à côté du marché

À propos du vocabulaire Notice the difference between the words **un cours,** used for a course at school, and **une course,** which means *errand.* Note that while the final **-s** is not pronounced in **cours,** the **-s** is pronounced in **course** because of the final silent **-e.**

C. Quelle est la bonne route? In Exercise B you listened to Michel tell about his errands for the day. Stéphanie also has some plans. In this part of their conversation, she asks Michel for directions to a couple of places. As he describes the route, mark your map to reflect his description. (1) Mark an X to show where Stéphanie enters the **quartier** Les Monts, (2) trace a line along the route she takes, and (3) put a check on each of her two stops.

INTÉGRATION: Une brochure de notre ville

Working in groups of three or four, design either a brochure or a web site to advertise a city of your choice. (Suggestions: a common hometown, the town where your university is located, a city that all the members of your group have visited, or a hypothetical ideal city on which you can all agree.)

A. On choisit une ville. First, decide on which town or city you will advertise. If you can find no location in common among you, then create an ideal imaginary city.

B. On décrit la ville. Make a list of the various identifiable **quartiers** of the city. Tell where the **quartiers** are located in the city in relation to one another. Then describe the characteristics of each **quartier.** Also for each **quartier,** make a list of possible places that a visitor might like to see with notes about what one might find interesting in each place. Give hours that the sites are open.

C. On satisfait les besoins des touristes. As part of the brochure or web site, give information on the best places (or on a range of places) for tourists to stay overnight and to have meals.

D. On suggère une journée en ville. Suggest a one-day tour of the city. Give specifications of the suggested itinerary: what to visit in which order with an approximate schedule. Give directions as appropriate. Don't forget to indicate possibilities for meals and for spending the night.

E. On fait la publicité. Now, using the information you have compiled, design the marketing document for your chosen location. Add any photographs or slogans or logos you wish. Prepare your document for distribution to the class.

Des lieux en ville

un aéroport	airport	un bureau de tabac	tobacco shop
un arrêt d'autobus	bus stop	un court de tennis	tennis court
une banque	bank	une cathédrale	cathedral
une bibliothèque	library	une chaussetterie	sock shop
une boulangerie	bakery	une chemiserie	shirt shop
une boutique	boutique	une crémerie	creamery/dairy store
un bureau de poste	post office	une épicerie	grocery store
un café	cafe	un fleuve	river
un centre commercial	shopping center/mall	un hôtel de ville	city hall
un centre d'étudiants	student center	un lave-auto	car wash
un cinéma	movie theater	un lycée	high school
une école	school	une mosquée	mosque
une église	church	une parfumerie	perfume shop
une gare	train station	un parking	parking garage/lot
un grand magasin	department store	une pâtisserie	pastry shop
un hôpital	hospital	une sandwicherie	sandwich shop
un hôtel	hotel	une sweaterie	sweater shop
un immeuble	apartment building	une synagogue	synagogue
un immeuble de bureaux	office building	un terrain de golf	golf course
un magasin de musique	music store		
un magasin de vidéos	video store		
une maison	house		
un musée	museum		
un parc	park		
une pharmacie	drugstore		
un quartier	neighborhood		
un restaurant	restaurant		
un stade	stadium		
une station-service	gas station		
un supermarché	supermarket		
une université	university		

Pour décrire les activités en ville

acheter	to buy	annuler	to cancel
aller	to go	louer	to rent
assister à	to attend		
chercher	to look for, to get (something)		
consulter	to consult		
envoyer	to send		
faire	to do, to make		
fêter	to celebrate		
jouer (à) (de)	to play (game) (instrument)		
laver	to wash		
manger	to eat		
payer	to pay for		

prendre	to take, to have
profiter (de)	to take advantage of (benefit from)
regarder	to look at
retrouver	to meet (someone) by pre-arrangement
toucher (un chèque)	to cash (a check)
travailler	to work
visiter	to visit

Quelques adverbes temporels

de temps en temps	from time to time
ne... jamais	never
quelquefois	sometimes
rarement	rarely
souvent	often
toujours	always

Pour situer un endroit

(assez) près de	(rather) near
à côté de	next to, beside
à droite de	to the right of
à gauche de	to the left of
au bout de	at the end of
au coin de	at the corner of
de l'autre côté de	on the other side of
derrière	behind, in back of
devant	in front of
en face de	across from, facing
entre	between
loin de	far from

Pour donner des directions

aller tout droit	to go straight ahead
continuer	to keep going
dépasser	to go past
descendre la rue...	to go down . . . street
monter la rue...	to go up . . . street
prendre la rue...	to take . . . street
tourner à droite	to turn right
tourner à gauche	to turn left
traverser la place/le boulevard/le fleuve	to cross the plaza/ the boulevard/ the river

Pour poser des questions

À quelle heure?	At what time?	Combien coûte(nt)... ?	How much does (do) . . . cost?
Où?	Where?		
Pourquoi?	Why?		
Qu'est-ce que... ?	What?		
Quand?	When?		
Quelle heure est-il?	What time is it?		
Qui?	Who?		

Pour parler de l'heure

À quelle heure... ?	(At) what time . . . ?
À trois heures.	At three o'clock.
Vers trois heures.	At around three o'clock.
Il est deux heures.	It is two o'clock.
deux heures et demie.	half past two.
deux heures et quart.	a quarter after two.
deux heures moins le quart.	a quarter to two.
deux heures quarante.	two forty.
deux heures vingt.	two twenty.
Il est midi.	It's noon.
Il est minuit.	It's midnight.
Quelle heure est-il?	What time is it?
Quand... ?	When... ?
Entre... h et... h.	Between . . . and . . . .
De... h jusqu'à... h.	From . . . until . . . .

Des verbes

apprendre	to learn
comprendre	to understand
prendre	to take, to have/to set (an appointment)
reprendre	to take back, to regain, to rehire

LA VIE QUOTIDIENNE:
Les responsabilités et la recherche d'un équilibre

Communicative Objectives

- To identify, prioritize, and schedule daily routines and responsibilities

- To discuss academic schedules and responsibilities

- To describe the ways that you spend your time off

Thematic Objectives

✓ To examine indicators of stress associated with time and schedules

✓ To examine academic and career objectives and to discuss their importance

✓ To examine how leisure activities balance weekday routines

La mise en scène

Jérôme: «Être en santé, c'est d'abord et
avant tout un équilibre.»

André: «M'entretenir, c'est gérer
mon stress.»

A. On cherche un équilibre entre... In *Chapitre 5* we will examine the responsibilities we have in our daily lives and talk about how we allocate our time and manage the stress associated with our daily schedules. Jérôme tells us what being in good health, physical and mental, means to him: «**Être en (bonne) santé, c'est d'abord et avant tout un équilibre**». Can you anticipate some of the areas Jérôme might mention that play a part in the balance he suggests we seek? In English, write down three or four, then compare your list with that of your partner. Are your lists similar?

If your lists were in French, would they look somewhat like this one?

Un équilibre entre:

bénévolat: *volunteer work*

- Les études
- La musique
- Le sport
- La religion
- La famille

- Le bénévolat°
- Le travail
- Tout ce qui est social
- Activités entre amis
- Activités culturelles

B. Pour gérer son stress... André tells us that he believes that keeping in good health is linked to being able to manage stress. Can you anticipate some of the ways he might suggest? Write down in English two to four techniques you use for reducing stress. Then compare your list with that of your partner. Add to your own list any suggestions your partner has that you want to remember.

C. On anticipe le vocabulaire. Now that you have thought about some techniques used to manage stress, try to match some English terms with their French equivalents. This will help you anticipate what you will hear on the video.

Techniques for managing stress	Des techniques pour gérer son stress
_____ Have a sense of humor	a. Profiter du temps libre
_____ Be in good health	b. Se détendre
_____ Participate in sports	c. Être en [bonne] santé
_____ Take things one at a time	d. S'entraîner physiquement
_____ Make the best use of your free time	e. Avoir le sens de l'humour
_____ Do physical training and exercise	f. Prendre les choses une à la fois
_____ Relax	g. Rire
_____ Laugh	h. Faire du sport

Les paroles et le sens

D. Comment combattre le stress. Listen to the interviews with people talking about what they do to combat stress. On the grid, mark an X in the appropriate columns to indicate in which interviews you hear the key phrases mentioned.

Ce qu'on fait pour combattre le stress

Interviews ⬊ / Techniques ⬋	#1	#2	#3	#4	#5	#6
Faire du sport						
Se coucher tôt						
Se lever de bonne heure						
Se détendre						
S'énerver moins						
Sortir (avec des amis), (dans les bars)						
Écouter de la musique						
Aller au cinéma						
Faire de la peinture						
Jouer de la musique						

E. On combat le stress à l'université. Listen to some students telling what courses they take. When you hear a subject mentioned, put the number of the student you hear speaking beside the name of that subject on your grid. Some students will mention more than one subject, and some subjects will be mentioned by more than one student.

Matières	Étudiant(e) #	Matières	Étudiant(e) #
L'anglais		La linguistique	
La biologie		La littérature	
La chimie		Les mathématiques (les maths)	
La finance		La philosophie	
Le français		Les sciences	
L'histoire		Les sciences sociales	
L'informatique		La théologie	
Les langues			

NOTE CULTURELLE

In France, where education is nationalized, all the universities are controlled by the government **(ministère de l'Éducation nationale).** They do not charge tuition, and admission is open to any student who has passed the **baccalauréat** (a competitive national exam) at the end of secondary school **(lycée).**

The **bac** exam has traditionally been extremely difficult, including all subjects studied throughout secondary school. But starting in the 1980s, when only about 25% of students typically passed the exam, the French government made a commitment to increase the percentage of successful candidates. The result of that effort is reflected both in the exam results (from about 27% in 1980 to 62% in 1996) and in the subsequent number of university admissions for the first year **(premier cycle).** The national goal is an 80% pass rate.

Today, the **bac** is still dreaded as extremely difficult, though it is more accessible than it was for past generations. Many students set aside several months after finishing the **lycée** to study for the **bac** full-time, giving up work and leisure-time activities to make this big investment in their future.

Students who do not pass the **bac** either spend another several months preparing in order to retake the exam, or enroll in one of France's many technical and professional schools that are privately owned and operated. Students have to pay tuition here. Although they cannot earn traditional university degrees at these schools, they can earn professional licenses and certification that qualify them for good jobs.

Think about it: How important would it be for you to take a year studying for a big exam to get admitted to the university system? Would you give up doing many of the things you love, playing sports, going out with friends, even working a part-time job, to spend time studying?

On y réfléchit

F. **Mon propre** (*own*) **stress comme étudiant(e).** You have heard some students talking about the courses they take. Did you hear some of your courses mentioned in the list in Exercise E? Select the courses that you have already taken and that you are taking this semester. (1) Copy them in French on the chart provided. (2) Then add, in English, some of your other courses that you have not yet learned how to say in French. Watch for them as you study this chapter. (3) Finally, copy down from the video the French expressions for at least two techniques that you currently use for managing your own stress, and two others (total of four) that you would like to learn to use.

1. Subjects that I take or have taken that I now know how to say in French: **(en français)**	2. Other subjects that I want to learn how to say in French: **(in English)**	3. Les techniques que j'utilise pour gérer mon stress:	4. Autres techniques que je voudrais apprendre pour gérer mon stress:

G. On cherche l'équilibre. Students go through stressful times as they prepare for life's challenges. Consider how your life might change if you were to spend a semester or a year preparing for some major exam, such as the GRE (to get into graduate school) or the LSAT (to get into law school).

What sacrifices might you make in your own daily life, which leisure-time activities might you have to abandon for a while, and how would you manage to maintain balance and combat stress? Would the time you spend with your family be altered? Would you spend your days differently?

What kinds of changes do you expect in your lifestyle once you have completed your studies? Do you anticipate having more or less stress? More or less time for family and leisure activities? More or fewer days off? Mark an X in the appropriate columns from the video to indicate how you might change your allocation of time spent in different areas of your life in order to maintain balance when preparing for a major exam or after you have completed your degree.

DÉCOUVERTE

Although the role of leisure time varies with each individual, it is also a matter of cultural tradition. Sometimes we can gain insight into cultural values by looking at statistical data. Consider the following information based on a report published by a Statistics Agency in France. It lists the average annual number of vacation days enjoyed by various areas of the French workforce in the mid-1990s.

	Nombre moyen de jours de congé par personne
Indépendants	
Artisans, commerçants, chefs d'entreprise	21
Agriculteurs	5
Professions libérales	33
Salariés	
Cadres	35
Professions intermédiaires	35
Employés	38
Ouvriers	31
Professeurs	115
Étudiants	115

A substantial portion of this vacation time is taken during July and August. In fact, tourists are often warned not to go to Paris during this period of **grandes vacances** because many Parisians will have closed their shops and vanished to their favorite vacation spots.

1. Read the DÉCOUVERTE note. Which information do you consider most interesting, puzzling, or explainable?

2. Discuss your opinions with classmates to broaden your interpretation of the information.

1ᴱᴿ THÈME: Une journée typique

Objective: To identify, prioritize, and schedule daily routines and responsibilities

Un coup d'œil sur le thème

tout ce que: *all that*

Évidemment: *Obviously*

Il n'y a jamais assez de temps pour tout ce que° j'ai besoin de faire. Je me lève à six heures du matin, et d'habitude je me couche après minuit. J'amène ma fille à l'école à sept heures et demie, et ses cours se terminent à trois heures. Entre huit heures et deux heures, quand elle est à l'école, je travaille comme comptable dans une boutique près de chez nous. L'après-midi, j'essaie de passer quelques heures avec ma fille, parce que le soir je vais à l'université où je fais des études de commerce. Alors, je quitte la maison vers six heures du soir et, en général, je rentre après dix heures. Évidemment°, je n'ai pas beaucoup de temps pour m'amuser.

un bourreau de travail: *workaholic*

consacrer: *dedicate*

En général, je ne me considère pas comme un bourreau de travail°. Mais cette année mon emploi du temps est très chargé. Je suis étudiant en mathématiques, et le week-end je travaille dans un magasin de sport. Mes cours commencent à huit heures du matin, et d'habitude je passe les soirées à la bibliothèque. J'ai rarement le temps de sortir avec des amis. Mais je vais avoir mon diplôme en décembre, et l'année prochaine, j'ai l'intention d'avoir du temps libre. Alors je vais consacrer° plus de temps à ma famille et à mes amis.

Stratégies

1. Listen to these two people discuss their schedules.

   • Use the context to infer the meanings of new vocabulary and structures.

   • What kinds of details (what they do at different times of the day) do the two people give in their descriptions?

   • Which statements reveal their personal attitudes regarding their schedule?

2. Make a list of the expressions that you might use to talk about your schedule.

POUR DÉVELOPPER VOTRE FRANÇAIS

Structure: Le présent des verbes pronominaux

OBSERVATIONS

D'habitude, je **me réveille** à 6h30. Je reste au lit quelques instants avant de **me lever.**

Puis je **me prépare** pour aller au travail. Je prends une douche, je **me brosse** les dents et je **me rase.** En somme je fais ma toilette.

À 6h50 je réveille Annick. Pendant que je **m'habille,** elle va lever notre fille, Anne-Marie.

J'amène° Anne-Marie à la garderie° pendant qu'Annick **se prépare** pour ses cours.

En général, je suis un peu en retard quand je quitte la garderie. Il faut° **me dépêcher** pour arriver au bureau à l'heure.

Annick reste à la maison jusqu'à 9h30. Elle fait un peu le ménage avant de **s'en aller.**

Le soir, nous passons du temps avec Anne-Marie. **Nous nous amusons à** jouer avec elle après le dîner.

On couche Anne-Marie vers 8h30. Puis on **se repose** un peu avant de **s'occuper de** la vaisselle.

Une fois les tâches° domestiques terminées, Annick reprend ses devoirs, et moi, je **m'installe** avec le journal.

En fin de journée, à 11h30, on **s'embrasse. Nous nous couchons** bien fatigués.

---

amener: *to take* / **la garderie:** *daycare center* / **il faut:** *it is necessary* / **les tâches (f.):** *tasks, chores*

1ᵉʳ THÈME: Une journée typique

1. Look at the verbs that are in boldface in the examples. What is the extra word before each of these verbs? Can you figure out how this word is being used?
2. With these special verbs, what is the reflexive pronoun that renames the subject **je?** What is the reflexive pronoun that renames the subject **elle?**
3. What is the reflexive pronoun that renames the subject **nous?** What would you expect the reflexive pronoun renaming the subject **vous** to be?
4. The verb **réveiller** means *to wake up.* What do you think the difference in meaning is between **je me réveille** (in the first drawing) and **je réveille Annick** (in the third drawing)?
5. Can you find another example in the sample sentences of a verb used both *with* and *without* a reflexive pronoun? Can you explain the difference in meaning between the two sentences?

PRÉCISIONS

- Some verbs take a special form to show that the subject receives as well as performs the action of the verb. They are called *pronominal verbs.* These verbs use a *reflexive pronoun,* renaming the subject, to show this action. Since the reflexive pronoun renames the subject, it must agree with the subject in *person* and *number.*

Je me renseigne sur l'horaire des vols.
I'm getting information (informing myself) about the flight schedule.

Est-ce que **tu te rattrapes** dans ton travail?
Are you getting caught up in your work?

Il se repose après une longue journée au bureau.
He's resting after a long day at the office.

Nous nous occupons des tâches domestiques.
We are attending to the household chores.

Est-ce que **vous vous intéressez à** la cuisine chinoise?
Are you interested in Chinese cooking?

Les enfants **s'amusent** bien ensemble.
The children are having a good time together.

- Note that **me, te,** and **se** drop the **e** before a vowel or vowel sound.

Je m'inquiète; les enfants ne se calment pas.
I'm worried; the children are not calming down.

Est-ce que **tu t'ennuies**? Tu peux passer l'après-midi avec un bon livre.
Are you bored? You can spend the afternoon with a good book.

Elle s'entraîne tous les jours.
She works out every day.

Il s'énerve. Ses fils se disputent encore.
He's getting upset. His sons are arguing again.

Elles s'habituent à travailler quatre jours par semaine.
They are getting accustomed to working four days a week.

- In the negative, put the **ne** in front of the reflexive pronoun and the **pas** (or other negative form) after the verb.

Je **ne** me dépêche **pas**.	*I'm **not** in a hurry.*
Nous **ne** nous téléphonons **jamais** avant midi.	*We **never** call each other before noon.*

- These verbs are not always used with reflexive pronouns. When the subject of the sentence is not also the recipient of the action, the reflexive pronoun is not used.

Je **me** réveille à 6h30.	Je réveille ma femme à 6h45.
I wake up at 6:30.	*I wake my wife at 6:45.*
Tu **t'**habilles avant le petit déjeuner?	Tu habilles les enfants avant le petit déjeuner?
Do you get dressed before breakfast?	*Do you dress the children before breakfast?*
Paul **se** promène après le dîner.	Paul promène le chien dans le parc.
Paul takes a walk after dinner.	*Paul is walking the dog in the park.*

A. Notre journée d'aujourd'hui. À tour de rôle avec votre partenaire, dites ce qu'on fait aujourd'hui. Remplacez les mots en italique par les mots entre parenthèses. Faites les changements nécessaires.

1. *Je* me lève à 7h00. (tu / nous / vous / Jeannette / les enfants)
2. *Elle* s'habille avant le petit déjeuner. (nous / Georges / mes camarades de chambre / vous / tu)
3. *Tu* te brosses les dents après le petit déjeuner. (vous / nous / je / l'enfant / mes sœurs)
4. *Je* me dépêche pour arriver aux cours à l'heure. (tu / mes amis / vous / mes amis et moi / les étudiants)
5. *Nous* nous entraînons après les cours. (vous / tu / les garçons / mon [ma] petit[e] ami[e] / je)
6. *Je* me repose avant le dîner. (nous / tu / nos amis / vous / tout le monde)
7. *Tu* t'occupes des devoirs après le dîner. (je / nous / vous / mon [ma] camarade de chambre / les étudiants)

Note Culturelle

Notez qu'au Québec on utilise **la fin de semaine** au lieu de **le week-end**. Le plus souvent en France, on dit et écrit **le week-end**. Voici une indication des différences linguistiques entre la France et le Canada.

Les Québécois francophones ont fait d'autres changements. Par exemple, ils disent souvent **magasiner** au lieu de **faire du shopping**, l'expression utilisée en France.

Réfléchissons: À votre avis: Pourquoi est-ce que les Français utilisent l'expression anglaise/américaine pour **la fin de semaine?**

B. **À chacun ses responsabilités.** À tour de rôle avec votre partenaire, indiquez la personne qui, chez vous, est responsable pour chacune des activités.

> **Modèle:** s'intéresser à la cuisine
> *Chez moi, ma femme s'intéresse à la cuisine.*

1. s'intéresser à la cuisine
2. se réveiller de bonne heure°
3. s'occuper des enfants
4. s'occuper de la vaisselle
5. s'inquiéter quand on est en retard
6. se disputer

7. se renseigner sur les détails avant de partir en voyage
8. se promener le matin (ou le soir)
9. se dépêcher le matin
10. se préparer pour des cours
11. se reposer après le dîner
12. se coucher avant minuit

de bonne heure: *early*

C. **Comment se déroule une journée typique.** Finissez les phrases dans le modèle pour expliquer une de vos journées typiques. Utilisez les expressions données. Puis lisez le paragraphe à votre partenaire.

> **Modèle:** D'abord le matin *je me lève* et après, je!... Puis je... avant le petit déjeuner. Après le petit déjeuner, je... Puis je!... avant de m'en aller à... heures. D'habitude, je... avant midi. Pendant l'après-midi, souvent je... Quand je rentre le soir,... Alors je/nous... avant le dîner. Après le dîner, je/nous... Enfin, je/nous... vers... heures.

TENDANCES 96
Sondages Léger & Léger
TOUS DROITS RÉSERVÉS.

À quelle heure vous levez-vous le matin durant la fin de semaine?
Avant 6h	5 %	Entre 9h et 10h	14 %
Entre 6h et 7h	14 %	Entre 10h et 11h	9 %
Entre 7h et 8h	28 %	Après 11h	4 %
Entre 8h et 9h	25 %	Travaille le soir	1 %

30 % des 18–24 ans se lèvent entre 10h et 11h durant la fin de semaine.

Vous vous levez à quelle heure le week-end? Faites-vous partie de la majorité?

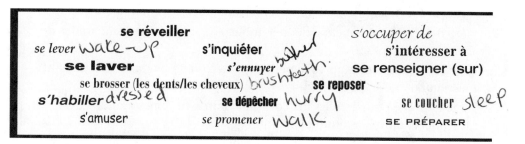

se réveiller
se lever *wake-up*
se laver
se brosser (les dents/les cheveux) *brush teeth*
s'habiller *dressed*
s'amuser

s'inquiéter
s'ennuyer *bored*
se dépêcher *hurry*
se promener *walk*

se reposer

s'occuper de
s'intéresser à
se renseigner (sur)
se coucher *sleep*
SE PRÉPARER

Structure: Les verbes pronominaux à l'infinitif

OBSERVATIONS

Je m'appelle Marguerite. Je passe mes journées à **m'occuper** de la cuisine. J'ai l'habitude de **me lever** de bonne heure pour préparer le petit déjeuner. Après le déjeuner, je préfère **me reposer** un peu avant de préparer le dîner. En général, j'aime **me coucher** à 10 heures.

Mon mari Alfred a l'habitude de **se lever** de bonne heure pour **se préparer** pour le petit déjeuner. Il a besoin de **se reposer** après le déjeuner avant de **s'occuper** des activités de l'après-midi. Il a l'habitude de **s'installer** devant la télé après le dîner et de **se coucher** vers 11 heures.

1. Look at the verbs in boldface type. Are they pronominal verbs? How can you tell?
2. These verbs are all in the infinitive form. Can you explain why?
3. Does the reflexive pronoun agree with the subject in this form?

PRÉCISIONS

- When reflexive pronouns are used with an infinitive, they still must agree with the subject of the sentence or clause.

J'ai l'habitude de **me** réveiller de bonne heure.
I usually wake up early.

Tu as besoin de **t'**intéresser à ton travail.
You need to take an interest in your work.

Si **on** désire **s'**avancer au travail, il faut continuer à **s'**améliorer.
If one wants to advance at work, it is necessary to continue to improve.

Nous avons l'intention de **nous** inscrire à un stage à Genève.
We intend to enroll in a workshop in Geneva.

Voulez-**vous vous** reposer avant le dîner?
Do you want to rest before dinner?

Mes enfants vont **s'**arranger pour arriver à l'heure.
My children are going to get organized to arrive on time.

D. **Combien de temps?** Demandez à votre partenaire combien de temps il/elle passe à chaque activité.

Modèle: s'habiller le matin
—*Combien de temps est-ce que tu passes à t'habiller le matin?*
—*Moi, je passe dix minutes à m'habiller le matin.*

1. s'habiller le matin
2. habiller les enfants
3. se préparer pour les cours
4. préparer le petit déjeuner
5. se laver les cheveux
6. laver la voiture
7. se promener
8. promener le chien
9. se regarder dans le miroir
10. regarder la télé

E. **Nos activités.** À tour de rôle avec votre partenaire, créez au moins six phrases originales en utilisant des expressions de chaque catégorie donnée.

Modèle: *Mes amis et moi, nous avons l'intention de nous préparer pour les examens.*

Moi, je Mon ami(e) Mes ami(e)s Mon ami(e) et moi Tu Vous — (Autres???)	aller désirer préférer espérer avoir besoin de avoir l'intention de avoir l'habitude de	se lever se coucher se réveiller	de bonne heure très tard avant/après midi avant/après minuit à... heures avant les autres
		se laver se laver les cheveux se brosser les dents se raser se maquiller°	tous les jours tous les deux jours° deux fois par jour° trois fois par jour le matin le soir
		se préparer (pour) s'amuser (à) se rattraper (dans)	les examens les cours la conférence
		s'arranger (pour) s'occuper (de) se renseigner (sur)	les tâches domestiques les vacances le concert
		s'inquiéter s'ennuyer se reposer se calmer se disputer	plus moins°

se maquiller: *to put on makeup* / **tous les deux jours:** *every other day* / **deux fois par jour:** *twice a day* / **moins:** *less*

Structure: Les verbes pronominaux à l'impératif

OBSERVATIONS

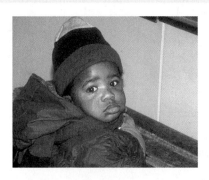

—**Calme-toi. Ne t'inquiète pas. Assieds-toi** à table et **repose-toi** un peu. Je vais téléphoner à ta mère. Elle va arriver bientôt.

STRATÉGIES D'ANALYSE

1. In the affirmative command form, does the reflexive pronoun go before or after the verb?
2. What happens to **te** when it follows the imperative verb?
3. How does the negative imperative differ from the affirmative imperative?

Chapitre 5

PRÉCISIONS

- The imperative form of a verb is used to make suggestions or to give commands. With pronominal verbs in the affirmative command form, the reflexive pronoun follows the imperative verb and is linked to it by a hyphen. (Note that **te** becomes **toi** in this position.)

Tu ne te dépêches pas assez.
You are not hurrying enough.

Dépêche-**toi** plus.
Speed up.

Quand est-ce que vous vous installez dans votre nouveau bureau?
When are you getting moved into your new office?

Installez-**vous** aussitôt que possible, s'il vous plaît.
Get settled in as soon as possible, please.

Nous nous préparons pour notre conférence au congrès professionnel.
We're getting ready for our session at the professional meeting.

Préparons-**nous** pour notre conférence au congrès.
Let's get ready for our session at the meeting.

- The following are common imperative expressions that use reflexive verbs:

Servez-vous. — *Help yourself.*
Asseyez-vous. ⎱
Assieds-toi. ⎰ *Be seated.*
Arrête-toi! — *Stop it!*
Ne t'inquiète pas. ⎱ *Don't worry.*
Ne vous inquiétez pas. ⎰

Calme-toi. ⎱ *Calm down.*
Calmez-vous. ⎰
Taisez-vous! ⎱ *Be quiet!*
Tais-toi! ⎰
Va-t'en! ⎱ *Beat it! Get out of here!*
Allez-vous-en! ⎰

- In a negative imperative, put the reflexive pronoun before the verb as usual.

Ne **vous** levez pas.
Don't get up.

Ne **t'**énerve pas.
Don't get excited.

F. Dépêche-toi! Imaginez que vous êtes instituteur(-trice) dans une garderie. En surveillant les enfants, vous observez des situations qui nécessitent votre attention. À tour de rôle avec votre partenaire, faites des phrases à l'impératif pour dire aux enfants quoi faire°. Utilisez des verbes pronominaux à l'impératif.

pour dire quoi faire: *to tell what to do*

Modèle: Lisette et Dominique parlent trop fort°. Elles doivent° se taire.
—*Lisette, Dominique. Taisez-vous!*

trop fort: *too loudly*
doivent: *ought*

1. Charles et Jean parlent trop fort. Ils doivent se taire.
2. Les enfants mangent du chocolat. Ils doivent se laver.
3. Gigi ne trouve pas sa poupée°, et elle pleure°. Elle doit se calmer.
4. Jacquot continue à dormir, et sa mère arrive. Il doit se réveiller.
5. Jacques reste trop longtemps dans les toilettes. Vous désirez qu'il se dépêche.
6. Pierrot et Lucie se disputent. Vous désirez qu'ils s'arrêtent.
7. Anne-Sophie pleure parce que son père est en retard. Vous désirez qu'elle ne s'inquiète pas.
8. Alexis parle sans cesse. Il a besoin de se taire.

une poupée: *doll* / **pleurer:** *to cry*

Structure: Les verbes pronominaux (suite)

OBSERVATIONS

Éric **parle** à ses collègues au travail. Il est nécessaire d'expliquer le nouveau projet.
Éric is talking to his colleagues at work. It is necessary to explain the new project.

Éric est très insatisfait à cause du budget. Il **se parle** à lui-même pendant qu'il travaille.
Éric is very frustrated with the budget. He is talking to himself as he works.

Éric et sa petite amie Marie-Laure **se parlent** au téléphone tous les jours après le travail.
Éric and his girlfriend Marie-Laure talk to each other on the telephone every day after work.

STRATÉGIES D'ANALYSE

1. To whom is Éric talking in the first frame? In the second? What difference do you see in the two verbs to show the difference in the receivers of the action?
2. In the last frame, who is doing the talking? Who is being spoken to?
3. What do you notice about the form of the verb in the last frame to indicate that both Éric and his girlfriend are doing the talking?
4. What do you notice in front of the verb that shows that they are both also receiving the action, hence, speaking to "each other," interacting with each other?

PRÉCISIONS

- Pronominal verbs are also used in French to indicate a reciprocal action in which two or more people interact. In English, we use the expression "each other" to accomplish this purpose. Since a reciprocal action requires at least two people, verbs are used in this way only in the plural.

Jean-Luc et Margot **se regardent.**
*Jean-Luc and Margot **are looking at each other.***

Jeannette et Étienne **se marient** à la cathédrale St-Patrick.
*Jeannette and Étienne **are getting married** in St. Patrick's Cathedral.*

Monique et sa mère **se téléphonent** tous les jours.
*Monique and her mother **telephone each other** every day.*

Mes collègues ont l'habitude de **se retrouver** au bar l'après-midi à 5h45.
*My colleagues are accustomed **to meeting** at the bar each afternoon at 5:45.*

G. Qui fait... ? À tour de rôle avec votre partenaire, indiquez qui (parmi vos proches°) fait les activités suivantes. Faites attention à la forme des verbes.

parmi vos proches: *among those close to you*

> **Modèle:** se téléphoner au moins deux fois par jour
> *Mon petit ami et moi, nous nous téléphonons au moins deux fois par jour.*

1. se téléphoner au moins une fois par jour
2. se promener tous les jours
3. s'organiser pour les cours toujours en avance
4. se lever avant 6h00
5. s'embrasser en se quittant
6. se retrouver au bar après le travail
7. se marier l'été prochain
8. se renseigner toujours avant de partir en voyage
9. ne jamais se parler

Structure: Expressions pour suggérer la nécessité

OBSERVATIONS

Pour être un bon père ou une bonne mère, **il faut** aimer les enfants. **Il est nécessaire de** bien écouter leurs problèmes et de célébrer leurs succès. On **a besoin de** s'occuper de leur éducation. **Il ne faut pas** rejeter *(reject)* leurs idées. **Il n'est pas nécessaire d'**être riche, mais **il faut** être heureux.

STRATÉGIES D'ANALYSE

1. Do you remember how to say that you *need* to do something?
2. Can you find two other ways to express a sense of obligation or necessity?
3. **Il faut** and **il est nécessaire de** have similar meanings. In the negative, however, the meanings are quite different. Based on the content of the paragraph, can you figure out the difference?

PRÉCISIONS

- In French, necessity can be suggested by the use of **avoir besoin de** + *infinitive*. Conjugate the verb **avoir** to indicate *who needs* to do something.

   Tu **as besoin d'**aller à la pharmacie.   Nous **avons besoin de** nous habiller.
   *You **need** to go to the drugstore.*   *We **need** to get dressed.*

- Expressions that convey a stronger sense of obligation are **il faut** + *infinitive* and **il est nécessaire de** + *infinitive*. These are impersonal expressions that do not change form. Note that in English an impersonal *you* (that does not refer specifically to the person being addressed) is often used, as in proverbs and sayings.

Il faut prendre le petit déjeuner pour bien travailler toute la matinée.
One must eat breakfast in order to work well throughout the morning.

Quand on est fatigué, **il faut** se reposer.
When you are tired, you have to rest.

Il est nécessaire de travailler pour gagner sa vie.
It is necessary to work to earn a living.

Pour apprendre le français, **il est nécessaire** de faire les devoirs.
In order to learn French, you must do the homework.

- In the affirmative, **il faut** and **il est nécessaire de** have very similar meanings; in the negative, however, their meanings differ greatly.

—Est-ce que je peux faire la vaisselle?
—**Il n'est pas nécessaire de** faire la vaisselle ce soir.

May I do the dishes?
It isn't necessary to do the dishes this evening.

—Est-ce que je peux tourner à droite?
—Non, non! **Il ne faut pas** tourner à droite! C'est une rue à sens unique.

May I turn right?
No! You must not turn right!
It's a one-way street.

À propos du vocabulaire: The French often answer with a double (or even a triple) **oui** or **non** for added emphasis. Example: —Tu désires aller au cinéma avec nous? —Oui, oui. On dit que le film est superbe. Example: —Est-ce que je prépare le dîner ce soir? —Non, non, non! C'est aujourd'hui ton anniversaire. On dîne au restaurant.

H. Des conseils. Vous êtes bien connu(e) parmi vos amis comme étant une personne qui écoute bien les problèmes des autres. On vous demande souvent des conseils. À tour de rôle avec votre partenaire, donnez deux ou trois conseils pour chaque situation suggérée. Utilisez les expressions suivantes dans vos conseils: **tu as besoin de, il faut, il est nécessaire de, il ne faut pas, il n'est pas nécessaire de.** Consultez les conseils donnés dans le tableau pour vous inspirer.

dormir en classe/au travail	s'intéresser à...	parler au prof
avoir de la patience	assister toujours aux cours	demander de l'aide
sortir *(to go out)* avec tes ami(e)s	étudier avec un(e) ami(e)	déjeuner avec des collègues
louer *(to rent)* une vidéo	se coucher tard	s'absenter
inviter des ami(e)s	sortir au cinéma	se coucher plus tôt

Modèle: —Je désire apprendre le français.
—*Tu as besoin d'assister toujours aux cours, de bien écouter, d'étudier tous les jours et de parler français avec tes ami(e)s. Il ne faut pas dormir en classe.*

1. Je désire apprendre l'espagnol.
2. Je veux m'amuser ce week-end.
3. Je n'ai pas de bonnes notes en mathématiques.
4. Je désire voir un film intéressant.
5. Je veux trouver un job à l'université.
6. Mon colocataire ne fait jamais le ménage.
7. Mon enfant n'aime pas se lever le matin.
8. Je veux être heureux(-euse) au travail.
9. J'ai besoin de plus d'énergie. Je suis toujours fatigué(e).
10. Je passe trop de temps toute seule. Je n'ai pas d'amis.

I. Le secret du succès au travail. Offrez à votre partenaire des conseils pour avoir du succès au travail. Donnez au moins trois directives pour ce qu'il faut faire et trois directives pour ce qu'il ne faut pas faire.

> **Modèle:** *Il faut s'intéresser au travail.*
> *Il ne faut pas se maquiller au bureau.*

J. Le secret du bonheur en famille. Offrez à votre partenaire des conseils pour être heureux en famille. Donnez au moins trois suggestions pour ce qu'il faut faire et trois suggestions pour ce qu'il ne faut pas faire. Consultez l'Exercice H.

> **Modèle:** *Il faut s'intéresser au travail de son époux/épouse.*
> *Il ne faut pas se disputer avant de se coucher.*

PRONONCIATION L'intonation française

The ability to understand and to reproduce French intonation patterns is very important, since often the characteristic rising and falling of the voice contains clues about the meaning of an utterance.

Listen as your professor pronounces each of the phrases below, paying attention to the pitch used (rising or falling) at the end of the sentence or clause.

- **Interrogative (question) sentences:**
  - **that require a yes/no answer** = *rising* intonation.

  Vous comprenez?   Marie ne travaille pas ce soir?

  - **that require an informational answer** = *falling* intonation.

  À quelle heure est-ce que vous partez? Pourquoi n'aimez-vous pas les frites?

- **Imperative (command) sentences** = *falling* intonation.

  Donnez-moi ce journal!

- **Declarative sentences**
  - **short** = *falling* intonation.

  Je suis très fatigué(e) aujourd'hui.   Ils vont jouer au hockey cet après-midi.

- **longer sentences, containing clauses** = combination of *rising*, then *falling* intonation.

  S'il n'est pas chez ses parents, il est à la piscine.

  Je dois me lever à 6 h, m'habiller et partir pour mon cours de français.

À vous! With a partner, take turns reading the dialogue below, being sure to use the appropriate intonation for each sentence.

Dominique: Salut, Yannick! Eh, dis, qu'est-ce que tu fais maintenant?

Yannick: Je vais à la bibliothèque avec Laure. En fait, je suis déjà en retard.

Dominique: Ah, je vois. Mais tu ne vas pas rester là tout l'après-midi quand même!

Yannick: Et pourquoi pas?

Dominique: Ben, je ne sais pas... Corinne et moi, nous allons au ciné voir un film.

Yannick: Quel film?

Dominque: Je ne sais pas encore. C'est elle qui veut y aller.

Yannick: Pour moi, j'veux bien, mais Laure doit rentrer avant 8h.

Dominique: C'est dommage! Le film commence à 6h30 et dure deux heures.

Yannick: Et donc, c'est impossible... un autre jour, peut-être?

Dominique: Oui, bien sûr. Allez, ciao!

Yannick: À plus tard.

POUR DÉVELOPPER VOS IDÉES

Thematic objective: To examine indicators of stress associated with time and schedules

Présentation: Le stress dans notre vie

POUR SAISIR L'ESSENTIEL: On the following page is an excerpt from a press release issued by the *Bureau de la Statistique du Québec*. Check the title to determine the subject of the article; then skim the two paragraphs to identify the main ideas. Use that information to complete the following statements.

1. The title suggests that the article is about _____ .

2. The main idea of the first paragraph is:
   a. Men tend to be more pressed for time than women.
   b. About 40% of the population is pressed for time on a daily basis.
   c. Professional people are more pressed for time than homemakers.

3. The main idea of the second paragraph is:
   a. Women are more apt than men to experience stress.
   b. About half the people surveyed feel that they are more productive now than five years ago.
   c. About half the people surveyed feel that they are more pressed for time now than they were five years ago.

Le stress associé à l'emploi du temps

Dans une publication intitulée *Les conditions de vie au Québec: un portrait statistique*, le Bureau de la Statistique du Québec (BSQ) annonce qu'une proportion importante de Québécois semblent avoir des difficultés à gérer leur emploi du temps. Dans une enquête° sur l'emploi du temps, 41,4 % des Québécois et 40,8 % des Québécoises ont affirmé «se sentir pressés par le temps° tous les jours». Le BSQ observe que la proportion des personnes «pressées par le temps tous les jours» augmente avec la hausse° du temps consacré au temps productif (travail professionnel rémunéré et activités domestiques non rémunérées).

Êtes-vous stressé(e) par le temps?

La publication précise qu'une grande proportion des Québécois ont l'impression que le manque de temps° s'est aggravé° au cours des dernières années. Le sentiment «d'être plus pressés qu'il y a cinq ans°» est partagé par 48,9% des hommes et par 50,9% des femmes. Cette perception augmente avec le temps consacré aux activités productives.

une enquête: un sondage

se sentir pressés par le temps: *to feel stressed, pressed for time*
le manque de temps: *lack of time*
s'est aggravé: *worsened*
la hausse: *rise, increase*
qu'il y a cinq ans: *than five years ago*

(adapté d'un communiqué de presse du Bureau de la Statistique du Québec)

K. Êtes-vous stressé(e) par le temps? Pour déterminer le niveau de stress dans la vie quotidienne des Québécois, le Bureau de la Statistique du Québec a présenté une liste des commentaires auxquels les participants ont indiqué **Oui** ou **Non**. Vous avez ici une adaptation de cette liste. Pour chacun des dix commentaires, indiquez à quel point il est vrai pour vous. Employez l'échelle *(scale)* suivante:

0 points = il n'est pas vrai pour vous   **2** points = il est plutôt vrai
1 point = il est un peu vrai   **3** points = il est très vrai

Enfin totalisez les points pour déterminer le niveau de stress créé par votre emploi du temps.

La liste des commentaires sur le stress

_____ **1.** J'ai l'intention d'avoir plus de temps libre l'année prochaine.

_____ **2.** Je me considère comme un bourreau de travail.

_____ **3.** J'ai tendance à me coucher tard ou à me lever tôt pour terminer mes projets.

_____ **4.** Je n'ai pas le temps de faire tout ce que j'ai besoin de faire.

_____ **5.** Je ne consacre pas assez de temps à ma famille ou à mes amis.

_____ **6.** Je voudrais accomplir° plus.

_____ **7.** Je me sens pris(e)° dans une routine quotidienne.

_____ **8.** Je sens que je n'ai pas le temps de m'amuser.

_____ **9.** Je m'énerve un peu quand je n'ai pas assez de temps.

_____**10.** J'aimerais passer plus de temps seul(e).

_____ **Total**

accomplir: *accomplish*

je me sens pris(e): *I feel caught*

> **À quel point êtes-vous stressé(e) par le temps?** Calculez vos points.
>
> 0–5 points = Il faut partager votre secret!
> 6–10 points = Votre emploi du temps est encore bien organisé.
> 11–20 points = Essayez d'équilibrer un peu votre emploi du temps.
> 21–25 points = Il faut éliminer quelques obligations de votre emploi du temps.
> 26–30 points = Vite, prenez des vacances avant d'avoir une crise de nerfs!

L. Un commentaire personnel sur mon emploi du temps. Choisissez un des commentaires de **La liste des commentaires sur le stress,** dans l'exercice K, et élaborez l'idée dans un paragraphe sur votre emploi du temps. Cherchez de l'inspiration dans les paragraphes du **Coup d'œil** de ce **Thème** à la page 176.

DÉCOUVERTE

Vacation time is often related to particular cultural "rituals." Consider these comments from the French press.

• *Traditionnellement, les mois de juillet et d'août concernent près de 40% du total annuel des séjours de vacances des Français.*

[Le Télégramme]

a vécu: *has lived*

• *Longtemps la France a vécu° ses étés sur le rythme sacré des juillettistes et des aoûtiens…*

• *Si la France, comme l'Italie et l'Espagne, conserve un fort penchant pour les vacances d'été, la raison n'a rien à faire avec l'économie: c'est à cause du soleil…*

[adapté de l'*Expansion* online]

1. Read the **DÉCOUVERTE** note. As you note the percentage of vacation trips the French take in July and August, consider popular vacation times in the United States. Are there certain times of the year that are particularly important for different portions of the population (e.g., spring break, Thanksgiving, summer)? Do people spend their vacation time differently or go to different places depending on the "occasion" of the vacation time? Do these factors appear to have any impact on the local, regional, or national economies?

2. 40% is fairly close to half the total number of vacations. One way to get a sense of the significance of the number is to think in terms of four out of every ten people you know about (not just your friends). How does this percentage compare with your perception of the number of Americans who take extended (two- to four-week) summer vacation trips?

3. What impressions come to mind as you reflect on the statements in the **DÉCOUVERTE** note? What questions are raised about vacations, culture, traditions, and the economy?

4. Discuss your impressions and questions with others in class.

2ᴱ THÈME: La vie universitaire

Objective: To discuss academic schedules and responsibilities

PRÉSENTATION: **Un coup d'œil sur le thème**

Il n'est jamais trop tard pour reprendre les études. Marguerite Coléno en est un exemple. Son emploi du temps est minuté. Entre ses «devoirs» de mère de famille et ceux d'étudiante, elle doit organiser sa vie différemment. Elle se sépare rarement de ses livres et classeurs°. De la cuisine à l'amphithéâtre°, son envie d'apprendre grandit un peu plus chaque jour. Voici quelques-unes de ses réflexions sur ce sujet:

un classeur: *file folder*
un amphithéâtre: *lecture hall*

- Après une longue réflexion sur mon travail, j'ai décidé de reprendre mes études.
- C'est parce que j'avais l'impression de ne plus avancer dans ma carrière.
- Dans mes cours, c'est la mémoire qui me demande le plus grand effort parce qu'on ne la fait pas assez travailler dans le quotidien.
- Mais il faut équilibrer son emploi du temps, alors je garde° de nombreux moments pour mes enfants et mon mari.
- Et pour les autres qui pensent à reprendre leurs études, je dis: Partir dans ce genre d'aventure permet de diversifier et d'élargir° ses connaissances° en apprenant un nouveau métier.

Marguerite Coléno reprend ses études à l'âge de cinquante ans.

garder: *keep*

élargir: *broaden*
connaissances (f.): *knowledge*

Stratégies

Consider your version of such reflections on school and life. Complete the sentences below to tell about them. You may use the expressions supplied or others you have learned.

1. Après une longue réflexion sur... [A]... je voudrais... [B]...

A	B
mon travail	*diversifier mes expériences*
mes études	*faire un plus grand effort*
mes besoins	*changer de métier*
mes options	*garder plus de temps pour...*
mes rapports avec...	
mes résultats dans mes cours	
mon emploi du temps	
(autres aspects de votre vie)	

2. J'ai l'impression de ne plus avancer dans...
   - *mes études*
   - *ma vie professionnelle*
   - *mes rapports avec...*
   - *mon travail*
   - *mes efforts de...*

3. Je garde de nombreux moments pour...
   - *mes études*
   - *mes passe-temps*
   - *diversifier mes expériences*
   - *ma famille*
   - *des activités communautaires*
   - *(autres priorités personnelles)*

4. Une (Des) chose(s) importante(s) pour m'avancer ... [A]... est (sont)... [B]...

A	B
• *dans ma carrière professionnelle*	• *la bonne mémoire*
• *dans mes études*	• *l'expérience*
• *vers mes objectifs personnels*	• *de bons rapports avec: mon patron/ mes collègues/mes professeurs*
	• *de bons résultats*
	• *la motivation*
	• *la diversification des connaissances*

POUR DÉVELOPPER VOTRE FRANÇAIS

Vocabulaire: Les études supérieures

OBSERVATIONS

le Moyen Âge: *the Middle Ages*

pouvoir: *to be able to*

Moi, je suis Anne-Marie Leclerc. J'ai 20 ans. Je suis étudiante à l'Université de Paris VIIe, la Sorbonne. Je me spécialise en **littérature** française. Puisque j'espère être prof de littérature française du Moyen Âge°, j'ai l'intention de faire mon doctorat.

Pour me préparer à cette carrière, il faut prendre des cours de **philosophie**, de **langues modernes** et de **langues mortes**, d'**histoire**, de **géographie** et de **psychologie** aussi bien que beaucoup de cours de **littérature**. On a besoin aussi de quelques cours de **pédagogie** pour pouvoir° offrir des conférences intéressantes un jour.

Mes profs à **la faculté des lettres** sont formidables; ils se préparent bien pour leurs conférences. Moi, je suis une étudiante sérieuse. Je **me renseigne** sur les cours avant de **m'inscrire**. J'organise un **emploi du temps** raisonnable. Je ne **sèche** jamais de cours. J'étudie beaucoup. Et voilà! Je ne **rate** pas les examens. Au contraire, j'ai **de bonnes notes**.

Moi, je m'appelle Derek Thompson. J'ai 32 ans. Je suis **diplômé** en **commerce** d'une université américaine. Mais il faut continuer les études toute la vie pour rester compétitif dans le milieu professionnel. Alors, je suis encore étudiant. En ce moment, je prends des cours **d'informatique.**

J'ai l'intention de prendre des cours de **comptabilité** aussi. Et j'ai besoin de faire des études de français et d'allemand parce que je voudrais travailler aux bureaux européens de ma société.

À mon âge et avec les responsabilités de ma famille, être étudiant n'est pas facile. Il faut organiser un **emploi du temps** exigeant° pour pouvoir **assister à** tous les cours, étudier et **réussir aux examens** aussi bien que travailler et avoir une vie familiale satisfaisante.

Le lundi et le mercredi j'assiste aux cours entre 18 heures et 21 heures. Je rentre à la maison vers 21h30. Le mardi après le dîner, j'étudie et je fais les devoirs. Le jeudi soir est réservé à ma famille. C'est comme ça que j'organise ma vie!

exigeant: *demanding*

STRATÉGIES D'ANALYSE

1. Can you find two ways that Anne-Marie uses to refer to colleges or schools as part of the university organization?

2. Both Anne-Marie and Derek make reference to their **emploi du temps.** Can you tell from the context of their comments what **emploi du temps** means?

3. Derek implies that he attends all his classes by using the expression **assister à tous les cours.** Look at the expression that Anne-Marie uses to talk about her attendance record: «**Je ne sèche jamais de cours.**» What do you think the verb **sécher** must mean? What clues lead you to that conclusion?

4. Two expressions about exams are given: **réussir aux examens** and **rater les examens.** Can you figure out which of these terms means *to pass* and which means *to flunk*? How can you tell?

5. Both of these individuals seem to be good students. Now reread the two monologues using the vocabulary below to help confirm your impression.

prendre des cours	*to take courses*
des conférences	*lectures*
se renseigner sur	*to get information about*
s'inscrire	*to enroll*
un emploi du temps	*a schedule*
sécher un cours	*to cut a class*
rater les examens	*to flunk the exams*
assister aux cours	*to attend classes*
réussir aux examens	*to pass exams*
des travaux pratiques	*practical/lab work*

Note Culturelle

L'enseignement supérieur en France

En France, à la fin des études au lycée (vers l'âge de 18 ou 19 ans), on passe le **baccalauréat (bac).** Si on réussit au bac, on peut entrer dans le système universitaire. En France l'éducation à l'université est gratuite (on ne paie rien). Mais il faut réussir à un examen à la fin de la première année pour pouvoir continuer les études. Soixante pour cent des étudiants échouent° à cet examen la première fois. Si on rate l'examen, il faut refaire la première année. Après la deuxième année d'études universitaires, on peut recevoir le **diplôme d'études universitaires générales.** Après deux ans de plus d'études supérieures, on peut obtenir une **licence** et, peut-être, une **maîtrise.** Il faut au moins trois ans de plus après la maîtrise pour obtenir un **doctorat.**

En France, on a le choix entre le D.E.U.G. (diplôme d'études universitaires générales), qu'on prépare à l'université traditionnelle, et le D.U.T. (diplôme universitaire de technologie), préparé dans un institut de technologie.

Réfléchissons: À votre avis: Quel sont les avantages d'un système gratuit pour les étudiants? Pour les gens du pays? Y a-t-il aussi des désavantages à ce système?

échouent: *fail*

Précisions

- In French, the schools or colleges (as administrative units of the university) are referred to as **les facultés** or **les écoles.** The following are customary groupings of academic disciplines.

Tableau des disciplines et matières universitaires

La faculté des lettres
les langues modernes
    (l'anglais, le français, l'espagnol,
    l'allemand, le japonais, le chinois,
    l'arabe, le russe, etc.)
les langues mortes (le latin, le grec)
la littérature
la philosophie
la théologie

L'école des beaux-arts
l'art dramatique
la céramique
la danse
le dessin (*drawing*)
l'histoire de l'art
la musique
la peinture
la sculpture

La faculté des sciences humaines
l'anthropologie
l'archéologie
la géographie
l'histoire
la linguistique
la psychologie
    les relations humaines
    la psychologie de l'enfant
    la technique de communication
les sciences économiques
    l'économie de la famille
    l'économie internationale
les sciences politiques
la sociologie

La faculté des sciences naturelles
la biologie
la botanique
la géologie
la physiologie

L'école des sciences exactes
l'astronomie
la chimie
l'informatique (*computer science*)
les mathématiques
la physique (*physics*)

La faculté des études professionnelles
le commerce
le comptabilité (accounting)
le droit (law)
  le droit social
  le droit fiscal
  le droit de l'enfant
  le droit international
  le droit de la famille
la gestion (management)

le journalisme
le marketing
la médecine
la pédagogie
les relations internationales
la santé (health)
  la médecine préventive
  la nutrition
  l'hygiène
  l'éducation physique et sportive

• Certain procedures are generally necessary at the beginning of a course of study.

On s'inscrit à la faculté des beaux-arts/des lettres/des sciences naturelles, etc.
You register in the school of Fine Arts/of Letters/of Natural Science, etc.

On règle les frais d'inscription.   *You pay tuition and fees.*

On se renseigne sur les cours, les horaires et les profs.
You get information about the courses, the schedules, and the profs.

On organise un emploi du temps raisonnable.
You set up a reasonable schedule.

• Most courses have several of the following components:

J'assiste à mon **cours magistral** le lundi, le mercredi et le vendredi.
*I attend my **lecture class** on Mondays, Wednesdays, and Fridays.*

Quand est-ce que tu assistes à ta **séance de travaux pratiques?**
*When do you attend your **lab session?***

Est-ce qu'on **fait l'appel** dans ton cours de comptabilité?
*Do they **call the roll** in your accounting class?*

Nous **passons** un examen tous les vendredis. Je vais **réussir à** l'examen cette semaine.
*We **take** an exam every Friday. I am going **to pass (do well on)** the exam this week.*

Je n'**échoue** pas **à** mes examens. Non, non, je ne **rate** jamais les examens!
*I don't **fail** my exams. No, no, I never **flunk** the tests!*

Est-ce que tu **as de bonnes notes?**
*Do you **make good grades?***

J'ai **la moyenne.**
*I make **the average.***

A. **À quelle faculté?** À tour de rôle avec votre partenaire, dites à quelle faculté chaque étudiant(e) prend ses cours.

Modèle: Marie-Louise prend des cours de philosophie et de langues modernes.
           Elle est étudiante à la faculté des lettres.

1. Marie-Claire prend des cours de littérature et de philosophie.
2. Jean-Luc prend des cours de chimie et de mathématiques.
3. Paul prend des cours de comptabilité et de commerce.
4. Brigitte prend des cours de géographie et d'histoire.
5. Marc prend des cours d'archéologie et de sociologie.
6. Suzanne prend des cours de biologie et de physiologie.
7. Marthe prend des cours de dessin et de peinture.
8. Madeleine prend des cours de français et d'espagnol.
9. Éric prend des cours de relations humaines et de techniques de communication.
10. Pierre prend des cours de sculpture et de céramique.

B. **Quel cours est-ce qu'on prend?** À tour de rôle avec votre partenaire, dites quel cours on prend si les phrases suivantes décrivent les activités du cours.

> **Modèle:** On étudie les victoires de Napoléon Bonaparte.
> On s'intéresse aux dates.
> *On prend un cours d'histoire.*

1. On étudie la Révolution française.
2. On examine les fonctions du corps humain.
3. On regarde les étoiles *(stars)* et les planètes.
4. On discute comment influencer le public pour acheter une certaine marque *(brand name, trademark)* de bière.
5. On cherche des objets très vieux.
6. On admire les œuvres de Renoir, de Monet, de Pissarro et de Manet.
7. On écoute les œuvres de Chopin, de Debussy et de Fauré.
8. On étudie les œuvres de Molière, de Racine et de Corneille.
9. On discute les idées de Sartre et de Camus aussi bien que celles de Platon et d'Aristote.
10. On étudie la relation entre ce qu'on mange et la qualité de vie.

C. **Ma spécialisation.** Renseignez votre partenaire sur votre spécialisation universitaire. Complétez les phrases suivantes en utilisant les mots en italique comme modèle.

1. Je vais me spécialiser en *musique* .
2. Ainsi, je fais mes études à l'école des *beaux-arts* .
3. Pour ma spécialisation, il est nécessaire de prendre ces cours obligatoires: *l'italien* , _____ et _____.
4. Comme cours en option, je m'intéresse à *la photographie* , _____ et _____.

D. **Ce que je pense.** Choisissez une matière parmi les six disciplines données dans le **Tableau des disciplines et matières universitaires** aux pages 194–195. Évaluez ces matières en termes (1) d'intérêt, (2) d'importance et (3) de difficulté pour vous. Écrivez vos six phrases, puis lisez-les à votre partenaire.

1	2	3	4	5
(ne) pas	peu	assez	plutôt	très

> **Modèle:** *Dans les sciences exactes, l'astronomie est très intéressante,*
> *mais elle est peu importante pour moi, et plutôt difficile.*

E. Je trouve mon cours... Mentionnez à votre partenaire un cours que vous prenez ce semestre. Puis, décrivez le cours avec au moins **cinq** phrases pour indiquer votre opinion et votre attitude envers ce cours. Consultez les expressions suggérées pour vous donner des idées.

Modèle: *Ce semestre je prends un cours d'informatique. Je trouve le cours magistral très intéressant parce que le prof est intelligent et précis. À la séance de travaux pratiques, on fait des exercices. C'est là que je comprends bien les leçons. Je ne sèche jamais le cours, et je fais toujours les devoirs. Alors, je ne rate pas les examens et j'ai de bonnes notes.*

trouver	le cours magistral	intéressant
	les séances de travaux pratiques	ennuyeux
	les conférences	compréhensible
	les activités	incompréhensible
	les devoirs	précis
	le prof	difficile
	les autres étudiant(e)s	facile
	mon (ma) partenaire	pratique
		(autres???)
assister à	le cours magistral	tous les jours
sécher	la séance de travaux pratiques	souvent
	le rendez-vous avec mon (ma)	de temps en temps
	partenaire	ne... jamais
étudier	l'horaire	avant de m'inscrire
	la description du cours	tous les jours
	mes notes	souvent
	le texte	de temps en temps
	la leçon	ne... jamais
		beaucoup
s'intéresser à	la matière	très peu
	le professeur	beaucoup
	un(e) étudiant(e) du cours	
faire	les devoirs	toujours
	les exercices	souvent
	les compositions	de temps en temps
	le nécessaire	ne... jamais
réussir à	les examens écrits	toujours
échouer à	les examens oraux°	souvent
rater		de temps en temps
		ne... jamais
aimer	le prof de...	
aimer bien	le cours de...	
ne pas aimer	les examens/activités/devoirs, etc.	
détester	(autres???)	

oraux (m. oral): *oral*

Structure: La place des adjectifs

branché: *connected, linked, tied*
une expérience: *experiment*

—Je prends un **bon** cours *intéressant,* un cours *obligatoire* pour ma spécialisation en médecine. Je passe de **longues** heures au laboratoire devant un **nouvel** ordinateur *superbe* branché° à un **grand** microscope *électronique.* Je fais de **vraies** experiences°, les **mêmes** expériences qu'on fait à l'hôpital. Je prends un cours de biologie.

STRATÉGIES D'ANALYSE

1. Where are French adjectives usually placed in relation to the noun they modify? (Note examples italicized in this paragraph.)
2. Note the adjectives in bold. Where are they in relation to the noun they modify?
3. Do adjectives placed in front of the noun they modify agree in gender and number as do other adjectives? How can you tell?

PRÉCISIONS

- You have already seen that French adjectives are usually placed **after** the noun they modify. They agree in gender and number with this noun.

  Je prends un cours **important** à ma spécialisation.
  I am taking a course important for my major.

  Est-ce que les cours **obligatoires** sont toujours intéressants?
  Are the required courses always interesting?

- However, the following adjectives are placed **before** the noun they modify: **grand, petit, vieux, jeune, bon, mauvais, vrai, nouveau, long, beau, joli, autre, même.**
- Many of these adjectives that precede the noun describe physical qualities.

À propos de la structure: You already know many high-frequency expressions that can serve as models to help you remember this word order. Examples: **nouveaux** riches, **nouvelle** cuisine
une **jeune** fille
mon **petit** ami
les **grands** magasins, une **grande** surface
une **bonne** idée, une **mauvaise** idée
Bon voyage.
Bon appétit.
la **même** chose
ma **belle**-mère, mon **beau**-père
les **beaux**-arts
Autres questions?

vieux	*old*	J'ai un **vieux** bureau chez moi.
nouveau	*new*	Nous avons un **nouveau** microscope au labo.
jeune	*young*	Ce **jeune** prof enseigne la chimie.
petit(e)	*small*	Retrouve-moi au **petit** laboratoire.
grand(e)	*large, big*	Quand est le **grand** examen?
beau	*beautiful*	Tu as organisé un **beau** document.
joli(e)	*pretty*	Quelle **jolie** salle de classe!

- Some of these adjectives that precede the noun describe moral qualities.

bon(ne)	*good*	Je cherche un **bon** ordinateur.
mauvaise	*bad*	C'est une **mauvaise** journée!
vrai(e)	*true, real*	J'ai besoin de **vraies** vacances.

- A few of these adjectives that precede the noun are adjectives of differentiation.

autre	*other*	Est-ce que tu prends un **autre** cours de latin?
même	*same*	Marie a le **même** prof que nous.

- The adjectives **beau, nouveau,** and **vieux** have a special masculine singular form used before nouns beginning with a vowel or silent h. The feminine form is pronounced like this special form.

mas. singular	mas. singular before vowel	feminine singular
beau	**bel**	**belle**
nouveau	**nouvel**	**nouvelle**
vieux	**vieil**	**vieille**

Tu as le **nouveau** livre pour le cours?
Tu vas acheter un **nouvel** ordinateur?
La **nouvelle** situation est un problème.

F. **Je prends un cours.** À tour de rôle avec votre partenaire, lisez les phrases suivantes. Remplacez les mots en italique par les mots entre parenthèses. Faites les changements nécessaires.

1. Je prends un *bon* cours. (intéressant / nouveau / extraordinaire / mauvais)
2. Nous passons un *grand* examen le vendredi. (petit / autre / difficile / mauvais)
3. J'ai un prof *intelligent*. (bon / précis / grand / vieux / jeune)
4. Est-ce que ton cours est dans la *petite* salle de classe? (grand / nouveau / vieux / même)

G. **Mes cours et mes profs.** À tour de rôle avec votre partenaire, décrivez vos cours et vos professeurs ou les cours et les profs à votre université. Utilisez deux adjectifs dans chaque description, l'un avant le nom et l'autre après le nom.

Modèle: prof de philosophie
Mon prof de philosophie, c'est un vieux prof énergique.

1. prof de chimie
2. prof de mathématiques
3. prof de...
4. cours de français
5. cours de...
6. laboratoire de biologie
7. laboratoire de...
8. ordinateurs dans mon cours de...
9. examens pour mon cours de...
10. devoirs pour mon cours de...

1. Read the ✦ DÉCOUVERTE note. You know from your own language that words often have cultural meanings that imply more than their dictionary definitions would indicate. Consider the transition from summer vacation to work and school. Do people in the United States recognize a particular occasion as marking the end of summer pastimes?

2. The notion of transition away from the lifestyle associated with summer back to "normal" routines is often identified with Labor Day. How is this reflected in the things people do and the ways they describe Labor Day? How would you describe the cultural significance of Labor Day in the United States to a foreigner?

3. Discuss your ideas with classmates.

Structure: Le comparatif

OBSERVATIONS

ceux: *those*

—J'aime **mieux** mon cours de psychologie **que** mon cours de sociologie. Le prof de psychologie est **meilleur que** le prof de sociologie: **plus intéressant** et **plus intelligent**. De plus, les examens de psychologie sont **moins difficiles que ceux°** de sociologie. La sociologie est **aussi importante que** la psychologie pour ma spécialisation, mais les conférences de psychologie sont **meilleures que** les conférences de sociologie. Comme *(As a)* cours en option, je recommande la psychologie.

STRATÉGIES D'ANALYSE

1. Can you summarize the information and advice in the paragraph above?

2. In making comparisons between two persons or places or things, we can describe one of them as *more than* or *less than* or *as much as* the other in any quality or trait that we choose. Can you find the French equivalents for each of these expressions?

3. In English, we can use *better* as either an adjective or an adverb. In French, we use different words. Can you find examples of these forms?

PRÉCISIONS

• In English, when comparing two *persons* or *things,* comparisons are made by either: (1) adding *-er* to an adjective (tall*er*, smart*er*, bright*er*, clean*er*, pretti*er*) or (2) using a comparison word (*more* independent, *less* optimistic, *as* sincere).

- In French, a comparison word is *always* used.

Mon père est **plus fort que** ton père.	*My father is **stronger than** your father.*
Mon prof de math est **moins timide que** mon prof de littérature.	*My math prof is **less shy than** my lit prof.*
Mon cours de biologie est **aussi intéressant que** mon cours de philosophie.	*My biology course is **as interesting as** my philosophy course.*

Similarly, in English, when comparing two *actions*, comparisons are made by:
(1) adding *-er* (fast*er*, farth*er*, lat*er*, earli*er*) or
(2) using a comparison word (*more* impatiently, *less* quickly, *as* honestly)
- In French, as with adjectives, a comparison word is *always* used with adverbs.
- Note that expressions with **plus, aussi,** and **moins** are followed by **que** with both adjectives and adverbs.

Mon prof de physique parle **plus vite que** mon prof d'espagnol.	*My physics prof **speaks faster than** my Spanish prof.*
Jean travaille **moins rapidement que** son frère.	*Jean works **less rapidly than** his brother.*
Tu parles **aussi courageusement que** notre patron.	*You speak **as courageously as** our boss.*

À propos de la structure: In French, many adverbs are formed by adding **-ment** to the feminine form of the adjective. Examples: lente**ment**, curieuse**ment**, heureuse**ment**

- The adjective **bon** (*good*) and the adverb **bien** (*well*) have irregular comparative forms.
- **Bon(ne)(s)** becomes **meilleur(e)(s),** meaning *better* as an adjective. Like any adjective, it changes form to agree in gender and number with the noun that it modifies.

J'ai de bonnes notes, mais les notes de Marc sont **meilleures** que les miennes.	*I make good grades, but Marc's grades are **better** than mine.*

- **Bien** becomes **mieux,** also meaning *better*, but as an adverb. It is invariable in form.

Je comprends assez bien le français, mais Lisette comprend **mieux** que moi.	*I understand French fairly well, but Lisette understands better than I do.*

H. **Mon (Ma) meilleur(e) ami(e) et moi.** Faites une comparaison entre vous et votre meilleur(e) ami(e). Donnez au moins cinq comparaisons en employant quelques adjectifs du tableau à la page suivante. Utilisez les trois formes du comparatif **(plus, moins, aussi).**

Modèle: *Moi, je suis impulsif, énergique, réaliste, content et indépendant. Christine, ma meilleure amie, est **plus** impulsive et **plus** énergique **que** moi, mais elle est **moins** réaliste et **moins** contente **que** moi. Elle est **aussi** indépendante **que** moi.*

agressif(-ve)	égoïste	intelligent(e)	pessimiste
compétent(e)	frivole	intéressant(e)	réaliste
content(e)	généreux(-euse)	joli(e)	sérieux(-euse)
courageux(-euse)	heureux(-euse)	libéral(e)	sincère
curieux(-euse)	impatient(e)	obstiné(e)	spontané(e)
drôle	impulsif(-ve)	optimiste	sportif(-ve)
dynamique	indépendant(e)	patient(e)	superstitieux(-euse)

I. Plus ou moins. Écrivez six phrases de comparaison entre deux de vos ami(e)s ou de vos collègues. Utilisez les trois formes du comparatif **(plus, moins, aussi).**

> **Modèle:** *Georges est **aussi** intelligent **que** Marc, mais Marc étudie **mieux que** lui. Ainsi, Marc a de **meilleures** notes **que** Georges.*

J. Comparaison des cours. Dites à votre partenaire au moins quatre comparaisons de deux cours à votre université.

> **Modèle:** *(1) Le cours de littérature française est plus intéressant que le cours d'histoire des États-Unis, mais (2) il faut étudier plus sérieusement avant un examen de littérature que d'histoire. (3) Le prof d'histoire est aussi intelligent que le prof de littérature, mais (4) il est moins drôle.*

Structure: Le verbe **devoir**

OBSERVATIONS

—S'il te plaît, Maman. Je voudrais regarder la télé.
—D'abord tu **dois** faire tes devoirs.

—Pourquoi est-ce que tu te dépêches?
—Je **dois** retrouver Marc au café dans cinq minutes.

—S'il te plaît, nous avons besoin de 200 francs.
—Dommage. Vous me **devez** déjà 300 francs.

STRATÉGIES D'ANALYSE

1. In the present tense, the verb **devoir** can have two possible meanings. Use the drawings and the captions to determine which two have the same meaning of **devoir**. What does **devoir** mean in these two situations? What form of the main verb follows **devoir** in each of these sentences?
2. What appears to be the context in the third drawing? Can you tell what **devoir** means in this situation?
3. Look at the **vous** form of **devoir** in the third example. Based on your familiarity with many French verbs, what do you think that the **nous** form of **devoir** is? Can you complete the conjugation chart?

je **dois**	nous _____
tu **dois**	vous **devez**
il/elle/on _____	ils/elles **doivent**

PRÉCISIONS

- The irregular verb **devoir** indicates obligation or necessity. Followed by an infinitive, it tells what one *must, has to, should,* or *is supposed to* do.

je **dois**	nous **devons**
tu **dois**	vous **devez**
il/elle/on **doit**	ils/elles **doivent**

Je **dois** m'occuper de ce projet pour demain.
*I **must** take care of that project for tomorrow.*

Tu **dois** te lever bientôt.
*You **have to** get up soon.*

Il **doit** finir l'examen avant de partir.
*He **is supposed to** finish the exam before leaving.*

Vous **devez** vous coucher avant minuit.
*You **should go** to bed before midnight.*

Elles **doivent** arriver au bureau avant 9 heures.
*They **are supposed to** arrive at the office before 9 o'clock.*

- **Devoir** can also mean *to owe.*

Tu **dois** combien d'argent à tes amis?
*How much money **do** you **owe** your friends?*

Je **dois** 30 euros à Madeleine.
*I **owe** Madeleine 30 euros.*

M. **On doit prendre un cours de...** Voici une liste des spécialisations de quelques étudiants. À tour de rôle avec votre partenaire, donnez au moins un cours obligatoire à votre université pour chaque spécialisation.

Modèle: Georges et moi: la physique
—*Georges et moi, nous nous spécialisons en physique.*
—*Pour une spécialisation en physique, vous devez prendre un cours de mathématiques.*

1. Anne-Marie: la chimie
2. Paul: la littérature américaine
3. Georges et Robert: la biologie
4. Christine et Claudine: le journalisme
5. Moi: l'informatique
6. Serge et moi: l'art dramatique
7. Louis et vous: la philosophie
8. Toi: la comptabilité
9. Hubert: les relations internationales
10. Marie-Ange: l'histoire

PRONONCIATION La lettre **r**

In French, the sound [r] is produced in the back of the mouth, at the point where the tongue and throat meet. To pronounce this sound correctly, try this:

First, prepare to pronounce the English [h], as in the word *hot*
Now, without changing the position of your tongue, say *rose*.

You should feel a slight vibration, similar to what you feel when you gargle or clear your throat.

Repeat the following words after your professor:

Rouen	le riz	la bière	mercredi
rouge	avoir	peur	regarder

The letter **r** is not pronounced in the infinitive forms of **-er** verbs (**quitter, regarder,** etc.) nor at the end of most nouns ending in **-er** or **-ier** (**boulanger, métier,** etc.). Some exceptions do exist, most notably words of only one syllable (**cher, mer, fer** *[iron]*, etc.).

À vous: With a partner, practice pronouncing the following sentences.

1. Le père de Robert est professeur d'art dramatique.
2. Où se trouve le bureau du professeur de géographie?
3. Est-ce que tu préfères faire du sport ou du théâtre?
4. Je vais préparer une carrière en gestion°.

POUR DÉVELOPPER VOS IDÉES

Thematic objective: *To examine academic and career objectives and to discuss their importance*

Présentation: Les études et leur rôle dans la vie

POUR SAISIR L'ESSENTIEL: Here is another portion of the interview with Marguerite Coléno, a fifty-year-old woman who is returning to school to complete her university degree.

1. Read the interviewer's questions and identify Marguerite Coléno responses to them.
2. Based on the information in the interview, how would you describe Mme Coléno? Write two or three sentences telling what you think she is like. For each trait you identify, tell what information leads you to your conclusion.

Modèle: *Madame Coléno a l'air artiste parce que c'est une ancienne styliste dans une grande maison de couture°, et elle prend des cours de théâtre, de psychanalyse et de peinture.*

Le bonheur de reprendre ses études

Qu'est-ce qui vous a décidée à reprendre vos études?

Marguerite Coléno: Je l'ai fait naturellement, après une longue réflexion sur mon travail. J'avais l'impression de ne plus avancer.

Après tant d'années, est-ce que cette reprise demande un gros effort?

MC: La mémoire est la plus difficile, parce qu'on ne la travaille pas assez dans le quotidien. Mais l'expérience acquise au fil des ans° et la maturité m'ont aidée avec des matières comme la littérature et le cinéma, la psychanalyse, la sociologie, le théâtre, la peinture.

Comment a réagi votre famille?

MC: Je garde de nombreux moments pour mes enfants et mon mari. Quand ils rentrent à la maison, j'essaie de ne pas avoir le nez dans un livre. Ils sont plutôt fiers de mes résultats.

Marguerite Coléno, cinquante ans, ancienne styliste° dans une grande maison de couture, mariée, deux enfants, n'a pas eu peur d'essayer cette nouvelle expérience.

Qu'aimeriez-vous dire° à ceux qui ont envie de reprendre leurs études?

MC: Je leur dirais que tout est possible. C'est une question de motivation. On parle de plus en plus de temps libre, de réduction du temps de travail. Partir dans ce genre d'aventure permettra de diversifier et d'élargir ses connaissances en apprenant, pourquoi pas, un nouveau métier.

J. **À vous l'interview.** Travaillez en groupe de trois ou quatre et interviewez vos partenaires sur leurs réflexions. Après les interviews, déterminez quelles questions évoquent les réponses les plus similaires. Lesquelles évoquent le plus de diversité dans les réponses? Employez la **Formule de rapport sur les réponses en groupe** à la fin de cet exercice pour rapporter les résultats.

Modèle: —Pourquoi êtes-vous étudiant(e) à l'université?
—Parce que je cherche à *préparer une carrière.*

1. —Pourquoi êtes-vous étudiant(e) à l'université?
   —Parce que je cherche à...
   ... préparer une carrière. *Kat*
   ... avancer dans ma carrière. *Sonia*
   ... m'améliorer (pour être une personne plus intelligente, intéressante, mieux éduquée, cultivée, raffinée).
   ... m'amuser. *Dragan*
   ... (autres raisons???)

2. —Quelle sorte d'effort est nécessaire pour avoir de bons résultats dans vos études?
   —En général, je dois...
   ... bien aménager mon emploi du temps.
   ... diminuer/minimiser mon temps de travail.
   ... montrer de la motivation.
   ... dormir moins.
   ... sortir/célébrer moins.
   ... laisser de côté°...

3. —Quand vous parlez de vos ambitions, quelle est la réaction de votre famille et de vos amis/collègues?
   —Ils sont surpris.
   Ils sont plutôt fiers.
   Ils m'encouragent.
   Ils me découragent.
   Ils pensent que je prends de bonnes décisions.
   Ils pensent que je ne prends pas de bonnes décisions.
   Ils pensent que c'est une perte de temps°.

4. —Quelle est votre réaction envers un(e) ami(e)/collègue qui voudrait reprendre ses études?
   —Vas-y! Tout est possible.
   C'est une question de motivation.
   Il y a des avantages et des inconvénients°.
   C'est important pour avancer dans sa carrière. *Sonia*
   C'est une bonne façon de° s'améliorer. *Dragan, Kat*

laisser de côté: *put aside, forgo*

une perte de temps: *a waste of time*

des avantages (m.) et des inconvénients (m.): *pros and cons*
c'est une bonne façon de: *it's a good way to*

Formule de rapport sur les réponses en groupe:

La question pour laquelle notre groupe a les réponses les plus similaires est la question numéro *deux*, qui demande «*Quelle sorte d'effort est nécessaire pour avoir de bons résultats dans vos études?*» Nous sommes presque tous d'accord que: *En général, je dois bien aménager mon emploi du temps.* La question qui provoque le moins de réponses similaires est: «*Quand vous parlez de vos ambitions, quelle est la réaction de votre famille et de vos amis/collègues?*»

3ᴱ THÈME: Le temps libre

Objective: To describe the ways that you spend your free time

PRÉSENTATION: **Un coup d'œil sur le thème**

Vu par les femmes : un sondage La Redoute/IFOP

Je rêve de: *I am dreaming about*
choisir chez moi: choisir d'un catalogue ou de l'Internet

être livrée à domicile: *have purchases delivered to the house*

mettre moins de temps pour me rendre: *to take less time en route*

70% Je rêve de° choisir chez moi° les articles dont j'ai besoin.

58% Je rêve d'avoir plus de temps pour m'occuper de moi.

61% Je rêve d'avoir une activité sportive.

75% Je rêve d'être livrée à domicile°.

76% Je rêve de gagner une journée de temps libre.

22% Je rêve de mettre moins de temps pour me rendre° au travail.

30% Je rêve de m'occuper de ma famille et de mes amis.

N°22 **missWeb** JUILLET 98

Stratégies

The chart represents the results of a survey done by the department store **La Redoute** in conjunction with the polling service **IFOP**.

1. Notice the play on words in **le temps libéré** contrasted with **le temps libre.** Since you know that **le temps libre** means *leisure time,* can you guess the meaning of **le temps libéré** and why it is used here?

2. Which statements underscore the fact that the survey was sponsored by a department store?

3. Copy the statements from the survey that reflect your own priorities for getting and using leisure time. Alter the wording as necessary to reflect your ideas.

Modèle: Je rêve *souvent* d'avoir une journée de temps libre.
Je *ne* rêve *pas* d'avoir une activité sportive.
Je *ne* désire *pas* choisir chez moi les articles dont j'ai besoin.
Je préfère aller en ville faire du shopping.

POUR DÉVELOPPER VOTRE FRANÇAIS

Vocabulaire: Le verbe jouer

OBSERVATIONS

Je suis étudiante et j'assiste à mes cours cinq jours par semaine. Je fais mon travail sérieusement. Mais, de temps en temps, j'ai besoin de me reposer. Qu'est-ce que je fais? Je **joue du piano.** Cela me calme.

Moi, j'étudie le marketing à l'université pendant la semaine et je travaille dans un supermarché le samedi. Le dimanche, c'est pour moi. Je passe presque toute la journée sur le terrain de golf. Oui, c'est vrai. Je **joue au golf** le dimanche. Cela me relaxe.

Nous avons beaucoup de stress dans la vie. Un grand-père travaille sept jours sur sept°. Il passe beaucoup de temps et dépense beaucoup d'énergie pour son épouse, ses enfants et ses petits-enfants. Nous avons besoin d'un peu de temps pour nous. Le jeudi matin nous **jouons aux cartes** ensemble.

sept jours sur sept: *seven days out of seven*

STRATÉGIES D'ANALYSE

1. What two prepositions are used following the verb **jouer**?
2. From the examples given, can you generalize an explanation of when each preposition is appropriate?

PRÉCISIONS

• The verb **jouer** (*to play*) is followed by the preposition **de** before the name of a musical instrument. The usual contractions are made with the definite article **(le, les).**

Dans un groupe de jazz, on joue **du piano, du saxophone, de la clarinette, de la trompette, de la guitare, de la basse** et **de la batterie.** Quelquefois on joue aussi **de la flûte** et **du trombone.** Est-ce qu'on joue **du violon** et **du violoncelle?**

In a jazz group someone plays **the piano, the saxophone, the clarinet, the trumpet, the guitar, the bass,** *and* **the drums.** *Sometimes someone also plays* **the flute** *and* **the trombone.** *Does somebody play* **the violin** *and* **the cello?**

- The verb **jouer** *(to play)* is followed by the preposition **à** before the name of a sport or game. The usual contractions are made with the definite article **(le, les).**

À l'université il y a des équipes qui jouent **au basket, au football, au football américain, au volley, au baseball, à la balle-molle°** et **au tennis.** Y a-t-il des équipes qui jouent **aux échecs** ou **aux cartes?**

At the university there are teams that play **basketball, soccer, football, volleyball, baseball, softball,** *and* **tennis.** *Are there teams that play* **chess** *or* **cards?**

balle-molle: *softball (au Québec)*

A. En commun. À tour de rôle avec votre partenaire, utilisez le verbe **jouer** pour dire ce que les gens de chaque groupe font en commun.

Modèle: Van Cliburn, Elton John, Jerry Lee Lewis, Sarah Mclachlan
Ils jouent du piano.

1. Willie Nelson, Sheryl Crow, Bruce Springsteen, André Segovia, Carlos Santana
2. Greg Norman, Tom Watson, Arnold Palmer, Fuzzy Zoeller, Tiger Woods
3. Drew Bledsoe, Dan Marino, Troy Aikman, Emmitt Smith, Brett Favre
4. Midori, Itzak Perlman, Isaac Stern
5. Dennis Rodman, Shaquille O'Neal, Jason Kidd, Rebecca Lobo
6. Steffi Graf, Monica Seles, Pete Sampras, Michael Chang, Martina Hingis, Lindsay Davenport
7. Wynton Marsalis, Al Hirt
8. Wayne Gretzky, Eric Lindros, Vladimir Jagr, Brett Hull
9. Roger Clemens, Mark McGwire, Sammy Sosa, Pedro Martinez, Ken Griffey, Jr.

NOTE CULTURELLE

509, c'est le nombre de terrains de golf en France. Ce chiffre place l'Hexagone [la France] au sixième rang mondial. On compte 7.082 joueurs pour un parcours° au Japon et 1.573 aux États-Unis, mais en France il n'y en a que 514. De plus en plus de terrains de golf ont du mal à rester rentables°: le prix de revient° d'un seul trou° est évalué à 1 million de francs et presque autant pour son entretien°. (Un parcours a 18 trous.)

Réfléchissons: À votre avis: Où est-ce qu'il faut attendre le plus longtemps pour jouer au golf: en France, aux États-Unis ou au Japon?

un parcours: *golf course* / **rentable:** *profitable* / **prix de revient:** *total cost* / **un seul trou:** *a single hole* / **son entretien:** *its upkeep/maintenance*

Structure: Les verbes sortir, partir, dormir, servir et se sentir

OBSERVATIONS

—Qu'est-ce que tu fais ce week-end?
—Je **sors** avec Pierre. Nous allons dîner dans un restaurant en ville.

—Quand est-ce que les vacances commencent?
—Demain. Mon frère et moi, nous **partons** immédiatement pour Paris.

—Pendant les vacances, je **dors** beaucoup plus que d'habitude. Je **dors** presque toujours dans le train. Quand le train roule, je **me sens** bien.

—Où est-ce que vous mangez?
—Nous préférons les petits restaurants. Mais on **sert** du bon café partout *(everywhere)*, même *(even)* à la gare.

STRATÉGIES D'ANALYSE

1. Can you find the expression that means *to go out* with someone?
2. That verb can also be used to mean *to leave*. Which other verb also means *to leave*?
3. Do you know a word in English for *residence hall* that is derived from the French word meaning *to sleep*?
4. Based on the similar forms of other verbs in this group, can you complete the present tense conjugation of the verb **dormir?**

je ———	nous ———
tu ———	vous **dormez**
il/elle/on **dort**	ils/elles **dorment**

5. Can you find the expression that means *to feel*? How does this verb differ from the others in this group?

PRÉCISIONS

These five verbs—**sortir, partir, dormir, servir, se sentir**—belong to a special group of verbs that follow a similar pattern in their conjugations.

- In the plural forms, they simply drop the **-ir** infinitive ending before adding the expected **-ons, -ez,** and **-ent** endings to the stem.

sortir *to go out, to leave*	**partir** *to depart, to leave*	**dormir** *to sleep*	**servir** *to serve*
nous **sortons**	nous **partons**	nous **dormons**	nous **servons**
vous **sortez**	vous **partez**	vous **dormez**	vous **servez**
ils/elles **sortent**	ils/elles **partent**	ils/elles **dorment**	ils/elles **servent**

- The singular forms, however, are unique. They drop the final consonant of the stem in addition to the **-ir** ending from the infinitive before adding a new set of singular endings: **-s, -s,** and **-t.**

je **sors**	je **pars**	je **dors**	je **sers**
tu **sors**	tu **pars**	tu **dors**	tu **sers**
il/elle/on **sort**	il/elle/on **part**	il/elle/on **dort**	il/elle/on **sert**

- The verb **se sentir** (*to feel*) conjugates like the others, but includes the reflexive pronoun.

je **me sens**	nous **nous sentons**
tu **te sens**	vous **vous sentez**
il/elle/on **se sent**	ils/elles **se sentent**

- Note the difference in pronunciation between the third person singular **(il/elle/on)** and third person plural **(ils/elles)** forms. The final **-ent** ending in the plural gives sound to the consonant preceding that ending.

il **dort**	ils **dorment**	elle **sort**	elles **sortent**

B. **À quoi ça sert?** *(What's that good for?)* À tour de rôle avec votre partenaire, formulez la question pour demander comment on utilise chaque objet ou idée. Travaillez ensemble pour suggérer une réponse, si possible.

À propos de la structure: Note that the verb in the expression **À quoi sert/servent… ?** is made plural if the subject is plural.

> **Modèle:** les vacances
> —À quoi servent les vacances?
> —Les vacances servent à se reposer.

1. les vacances
2. une fête
3. le week-end
4. les feux d'artifice°
5. le champagne
6. les chansons
7. les fleurs
8. la musique
9. le travail
10. ce truc°

les feux (m.) d'artifice: *fireworks*

ce truc: *that "thing-a-ma-jig," that "whatcha-ma-call-it"*

le sommeil: *sleep*

C. **Tout le monde dort.** Renseignez votre partenaire sur les habitudes de sommeil° des personnes mentionnées. Consultez les expressions données dans la fiche pour des idées. Employez le verbe **dormir** comme dans le modèle.

> **Modèle:** *Moi, je dors souvent au cinéma.*

Moi, je	souvent	(très) tard
Mon/Ma petit(e) ami(e)	rarement	dans les cours
Mon/Ma petit(e) ami(e) et moi	très peu	au cinéma
Mes ami(e)s	d'habitude	au ballet
Mes ami(e)s et moi	beaucoup	au théâtre
Mon/Ma conjoint(e) et moi	de temps en temps	à l'église
Mes parents	presque toujours	à l'opéra
Ma sœur	ne… jamais	devant la télé
Mon frère		le samedi matin
Mon enfant		le dimanche après-midi
Mes enfants		le week-end
Est-ce que tu… ?		le lundi
Est-ce que vous… ?		

D. **Tout le monde sort.** À tour de rôle avec votre partenaire, dites qui parmi vos proches sort (ou ne sort pas) pour faire chaque activité mentionnée. Travaillez ensemble pour expliquer la raison de cette action, si possible.

À propos de la culture: Les enfants français disent souvent **fais dodo** quand ils veulent exprimer l'idée de *go to sleep, go 'night-night.'* «**Fais dodo**» est aussi le titre d'une chanson française traditionnelle pour les enfants.

> **Modèle:** de la maison pour fumer à l'extérieur
> *Mon frère et moi nous sortons de la maison pour fumer à l'extérieur.*
> *(Chez nous, il ne faut pas fumer dans la maison.)*

1. de la salle de classe pour fumer à l'extérieur
2. de la salle de classe pour chercher un Coca
3. souvent de l'autoroute pour chercher des toilettes
4. rarement (ou souvent) en avance de la salle de classe
5. rarement seul(e)
6. souvent ensemble
7. tous les samedi soirs
8. d'habitude le week-end
9. au cinéma une fois par mois (par semaine)
10. souvent dans un bar avec les ami(e)s

Vocabulaire: Les verbes qui signifient *to leave*

OBSERVATIONS

—Mes parents vont **partir** pour la Martinique demain. Pendant quinze jours la maison est à moi.
—Tu as de la chance! On peut organiser une fête chez toi?
—Ah non! En ce qui concerne la maison, Maman est exigeante. Chez nous il faut **sortir** pour fumer une cigarette.
—C'est vrai?
—Absolument. Elle dit qu'elle va **quitter** mon père s'il fume dans la maison.
—Alors, faire la fête chez toi n'est pas une bonne idée.

STRATÉGIES D'ANALYSE

1. The three words in bold can all be translated in English as *to leave*. Can you figure out any differences in the ways that these three verbs are used in French?
2. Which one of these verbs is used with a direct object?
3. What kind of word follows the other two verbs?

PRÉCISIONS

In French there are three verbs that mean *to leave*: **sortir, partir,** and **quitter.** However, each of these verbs has a special interpretation.

- **Sortir** means *to leave* in the sense of *to go out*. **Sortir** is followed by the preposition **de** to tell *from where* one is leaving.

> Les toilettes? Quand tu **sors de** la salle de classe, va à gauche. Les toilettes sont juste avant les portes principales, à droite.
> *The restrooms? When you **leave** the classroom, go left. The restrooms are just before the main doors, on the right.*

- **Sortir** is sometimes accompanied by the preposition **avec** when it is used to express the idea of *to go out socially* (on a date or with friends).

  Denis **sort** regulièrement **avec** Louise. Ils aiment bien **sortir avec** leurs amis.
  Denis goes out regularly with Louise. They like to go out with their friends.

- **Sortir** can be followed by **pour** to tell *why* one is going out.

  Je **sors pour** fumer une cigarette.
  I'm going out to smoke.

- **Partir** means *to leave* in the sense of *to depart* or *to go away*. Like **sortir, partir** is followed by the preposition **de** to tell *from where* one is leaving. It can also be followed by the preposition **pour** to tell *for which destination* one is leaving.

  Nous **partons de** Paris dans huit jours pour aller à Genève.
  We are leaving Paris in a week to go to Geneva.

  Moi, je **pars pour** Strasbourg ce soir après le concert.
  As for me, I'm leaving for Strasbourg this evening after the concert.

- The verb **quitter,** on the other hand, always takes a direct object that names the place or person being left.

  Jacqueline **quitte** le café pour rentrer au travail.
  Jacqueline is leaving the cafe to return to work.

  Geneviève **quitte** son mari après dix ans de mariage.
  Geneviève is leaving (quitting) her husband after ten years of marriage.

E. **Qui sort?** À tour de rôle avec votre partenaire, complétez les conversations que vous entendez autour de vous au café. Utilisez les formes convenables de **sortir, partir** ou **quitter.**

> **Modèle:**   —Qu'est-ce que Brigitte va faire?
> —Elle va _quitter_ son fiancé Bernard pour aller aux États-Unis avec un musicien américain. Bizarre!

1. —Qu'est-ce que Marie va faire?

   —Elle va _____ son mari pour partir à Rome avec un artiste italien.

2. —Jean-Claude et Françoise _____ pour Nice demain.

   —Combien de temps vont-ils passer sur la Côte d'Azur°?

3. —Éteignez° la lumière quand vous _____ des toilettes, s'il vous plaît.

4. —Georges et sa femme arrivent de Montréal ce week-end. On organise une fête pour samedi soir.

   —Dommage. Paul et moi, nous _____ pour les Alpes vendredi.

5. —Robert passe trop de temps avec sa secrétaire. Ils _____ ensemble dans un bar tous les après-midi.

   —Marie-Claire doit _____ cet homme. Il ne comprend pas ce que c'est d'«être fidèle°».

6. —Avec qui est-ce que Dominique _____ maintenant?

   —Avec un étudiant en droit de Cannes. Il est intelligent, et beau aussi!

la Côte d'Azur: *the Riviera*

éteignez: *imperative form of* **éteindre:** *to extinguish, to turn off (lights)*

d'être fidèle: *to be faithful, loyal*

7. —Mon camarade de chambre déteste les cigarettes.

—Je comprends. Chez nous il faut _____ de la maison pour fumer.

8. —Les vacances commencent demain.

—Oui, et je _____ immédiatement pour la Côte d'Azur.

Structure: Le superlatif

—Pour moi, le stress est **le plus prononcé** avant un examen oral.
—Pas pour moi. Je souffre **le plus** avant un examen écrit.
—Moi, je suis **le plus stressé** quand je dois préparer une thèse.
—Oh, vous les jeunes. Le stress **le plus sérieux** arrive avec une famille et un travail. Vous êtes à la période la moins stressante de votre vie.

STRATÉGIES D'ANALYSE

1. Superlatives indicate that one person or thing within a group of three or more has the most or least of a quality. What two-word phrase in French appears to mean *the most*?

2. Can you find the one adverbial expression (describing a verb) among these superlatives?

PRÉCISIONS

In English, when comparing *more* than two persons or things, comparisons are made by either:

(1) adding -*est* to the adjective (tall*est*, smart*est*, bright*est*, clean*est*, pretti*est*) or

(2) using a term to express the maximum or minimum capacity or quality (*the most* unusual, *the least* expensive).

• In French, the superlative term **(le plus, le moins)** is *always* used.

M. LeBrun est le professeur **le plus intéressant** de l'école des beaux-arts.
*Mr. LeBrun is **the most interesting** professeur in the school of fine arts.*

Le cours **le moins difficile** de la faculté des sciences naturelles est la biologie.
*The **least difficult** course in the school of natural sciences is biology.*

• When comparing two persons or things, **que** is used with the comparative form. When comparing *more* than two persons or things, **de** is used with the superlative form.

Le château de Fontainebleau est plus grand **que** le château de Chenonceaux.
*Fontainebleau Castle is larger **than** Chenonceaux Castle.*

Le château de Chambord est **le** plus grand **de** tous les châteaux de la vallée de la Loire.
*Chambord Castle is **the** largest **of** all the Loire Valley castles.*

- The placement of the superlative form *before* or *after* the noun corresponds to the normal placement of the adjective.

> **Le plus bel hôtel** à Haguenau est aussi **le plus grand hôtel** de la ville.
> *The most beautiful hotel in Haguenau is also the city's largest hotel.*

> Paul travaille pour **la société la plus importante** à l'économie de la région.
> *Paul works for the most important company to the economy of the region.*

Note that with an adjective that follows the noun, an extra definite article is inserted:

> **la** société **la** plus importante

Similarly, in English, when comparing three or more **actions**, comparisons are made either by:
(1) adding *-est* (the fast*est*, the farth*est*, the lat*est*, the earli*est*) or
(2) using a term to express the maximum or minimum quality (*the most impatiently, the least honestly*).

- In French, the superlative of the adverb is formed by simply adding **le** before the comparative form of the adverb. The preposition **de** is used to indicate *in* or *of* the group.

> **Des** trois étudiants c'est Marc qui parle **le plus vite**.
> *Of the three students it's Marc who speaks the fastest.*

> Tous les hommes jouent bien au tennis, mais c'est Pierre qui joue **le mieux du** groupe.
> *All the men play tennis well, but it's Pierre who plays the best in the group.*

F. Contre le stress. En groupes de trois, comparez avec les autres votre participation aux activités suivantes pour diminuer le stress.

Modèle: aller à la plage
—*Pour diminuer le stress, quelquefois je vais à la plage.*
—*Vous allez à la plage* **plus** *souvent* **que** *moi. Je ne vais jamais à la plage.*
—*Et moi, je vais à la plage* **le plus** *souvent de nous tous. Pour diminuer le stress, généralement je vais à la plage tous les jours.*

0	1	2	3	4
jamais	rarement	quelquefois	souvent	généralement

1. aller au cinéma
2. regarder la télé
3. dormir huit heures
4. dîner au resto
5. prendre un Coca

6. prendre une bière
7. fumer une cigarette
8. faire une promenade
9. téléphoner à mes parents
10. nager dans une piscine°

une piscine: *swimming pool*

G. Le plus important. À tour de rôle avec votre partenaire, indiquez ce que vous trouvez le plus important pour passer de bonnes vacances.

> **Modèle:** une chambre tout(e) seul(e), une salle de bains dans la chambre, des toilettes privées
> *Pour moi, la chose la plus importante, c'est d'avoir des toilettes privées.*

1. une chambre tout(e) seul(e), une salle de bains dans la chambre, des toilettes privées
2. être à la plage, au centre-ville, isolé(e) dans les montagnes
3. un bon restaurant, une discothèque animée, une librairie
4. un terrain de golf, un terrain de tennis, une piscine
5. beaucoup de fleurs, beaucoup d'ascenseurs°, beaucoup de taxis   **un ascenseur:** *elevator*
6. une variété de boutiques, une variété de restaurants, une variété de bars
7. un téléviseur, un téléphone, un mini-bar dans la chambre
8. être tout(e) seul(e), avec des ami(e)s, avec la famille
9. l'accès au métro, l'accès au train, l'accès à l'aéroport
10. visiter de grands magasins, des théâtres, des musées

Vocabulaire: Pour fêter et remercier

OBSERVATIONS

—Bonne fête!
—Joyeux anniversaire!
—Merci mille fois.

—Joyeux Noël.
—Merci. C'est gentil.

—Bonne année!
—Bonne et heureuse année à toi aussi!

STRATÉGIES D'ANALYSE

1. Find two expressions used to show gratitude.
2. Find two ways to wish someone a happy birthday.
3. Find two ways to wish someone a happy new year.

Holidays, birthdays, and other celebrations provide an opportunity to express thanks or good wishes to someone. The following expressions are frequently used for these occasions.

- **Pour remercier**

Merci bien.
Merci beaucoup.
Merci mille fois.
Je vous remercie.
Vous êtes (Tu es) bien aimable.
Vous êtes (Tu es) trop gentil(le).

Pour accepter des remerciements

De rien.
Il n'y a pas de quoi.
Je vous en prie. Je t'en prie.
Pas de quoi.
À votre service.

- **Pour féliciter**

Fécilitations.
Mes félicitations.
Bravo!

Pour accepter des félicitations

Merci.
Merci. C'est gentil.
Merci beaucoup.
Merci mille fois.

- **Pour souhaiter**

Bonne et heureuse année!	*Happy New Year!*
Bon anniversaire/Joyeux anniversaire!	*Happy Birthday!*
Joyeux Noël!	*Merry Christmas!*
Joyeuses Pâques.	*Happy Easter.*
Bonne fête des mères/pères.	*Happy Mother's/Father's Day.*
Bonne fête de (St. Valentin) .	*Happy (Valentine's) Day.*

H. **Bonne fête.** À tour de rôle avec votre partenaire, dites ce qu'on peut dire dans chaque situation.

Modèle: Votre ami vous offre un cadeau d'anniversaire.
On peut dire: Merci, c'est gentil.

1. Votre ami vous offre des fleurs comme cadeau d'anniversaire.
2. Vous êtes avec vos amis à minuit le 31 décembre.
3. Vous portez du café à votre mère qui reste au lit le dernier dimanche de mai.
4. Vous offrez un cadeau à un enfant de quatre ans le 25 décembre.
5. Vous offrez des fleurs et des chocolats à votre petite amie le 14 février.
6. Vous offrez une carte de vœux° à un ami qui fête son anniversaire de naissance°.
7. Vous offrez des fleurs à des amis qui fêtent leurs noces d'or (leur 50ᵉ anniversaire de mariage).
8. Vous offrez un cadeau à votre père le dernier dimanche de juin.

une carte de vœux: *greeting card*
un anniversaire (de naissance): *birthday*

NOTE CULTURELLE

Il y a onze jours de congé officiels en France. Six de ces jours fériés sont des fêtes religieuses. Les cinq autres fêtes sont civiles.

Réfléchissons: À votre avis: Pourquoi est-ce que la majorité des fêtes officielles en France sont des jours religieux chrétiens?

Nom de la fête	Date	Type	Ce qu'on dit	Ce qu'on fait
le Jour de l'An	Le 1er janvier	civile	«Bonne et heureuse année»	On offre aux amis de petits cadeaux appelés «étrennes», souvent des bonbons.
Pâques	Varié, un dimanche et lundi en mars ou avril	religieuse	«Joyeuses Pâques»	On offre aux enfants des œufs, le plus souvent en chocolat ou en sucre. On va à la messe (à l'église).
la Fête du Travail	le 1er mai	civile		On défile dans les rues.
la Fête de la Victoire	le 8 mai	civile		On fait des cérémonies militaires.
l'Ascension	le 6e jeudi après Pâques	religieuse		On va à la messe.
la Pentecôte	dimanche et lundi 10 jours après l'Ascension	religieuse		On va à la messe. Souvent on quitte les grandes villes pour aller à la campagne.
la Fête nationale française	le 14 juillet	civile		On regarde des défilés (*parades*) militaires et des feux d'artifice. (À Paris le défilé est sur l'avenue des Champs-Élysées.)
l'Assomption	le 15 août	religieuse	«Bonne fête» (à toutes les filles nommées Marie)	On va à la messe.
la Toussaint	le 1er novembre	religieuse		On place des fleurs sur les tombeaux dans les cimetières.
l'Armistice	le 11 novembre	civile		On fait des cérémonies militaires. Souvent il y a des concerts.
Noël	le 25 décembre	religieuse	«Joyeux Noël»	On fait le repas du réveillon après la messe de minuit. Le Père Noël apporte des cadeaux, surtout aux enfants.

PRONONCIATION Les consonnes doubles **ss** et **ll**

A few exceptions exist, notably words that would be homophones of others if the **ll** were pronounced [j]: **la ville; mille.**

By now, you've probably noticed that the French letter **s** sounds like the English **z** when it appears between two vowels as in the words **maison, visiter,** and **musée.** The combination **ss,** however, is always pronounced [s]: **pessimiste, assez, nécessaire.** The French **l** is usually pronounced the same as in English, except for the combinations **ille, ail(le)** and **eil(le)** when the **ll** is pronounced [j].

	Sounds like the *y* in
fille [fi:j]	happy
travaille [trava:j]	fly
vieille. [vjEj]	say

À vous! With a partner, read the following conversation between Benoît and Cécile, paying particular attention to your pronunciation of **s, ss, l,** and **ll.**

Benoît: J'ai besoin de travailler! D'abord, je vais faire de la paperasserie.
Cécile: C'est bien, mais tu devrais chercher l'équilibre entre le travail et les loisirs...
Benoît: Oui, Cécile, je sais, mais j'essaie toujours d'être le meilleur employé que possible.

avec eux: *with them*

Cécile: Et ta famille? Est-ce que tu passes beaucoup de temps avec eux°?
Benoît: Bien sûr! En fait, cet après-midi, nous allons assister à un match de baseball ensemble.
Cécile: Et tu n'es pas fatigué de travailler ainsi tout le temps?

faire la grasse matinée: *to sleep in*

Benoît: Pendant la semaine, oui, mais le week-end, je fais toujours la grasse matinée°!
Cécile: Moi aussi, j'adore rester au lit le samedi. Le dimanche, je vais à la messe.

POUR DÉVELOPPER VOS IDÉES

Thematic objective: To examine how leisure activities balance weekday routines

Présentation: Sondage sur le temps libre

POUR SAISIR L'ESSENTIEL: The article on the following page presents the results of a survey done by **IFOP** (L'Institut Français d'Opinion Publique et d'Études de Marchés) and the department store **La Redoute.**

1. Read the two questions and decide how you would answer them.
2. Next look at how the women surveyed would spend extra free time. What are the three most popular choices? What are the three least popular choices?
3. Categorize all the choices in these three groups: (1) **Avoir du temps pour les autres,** (2) **Avoir du temps pour soi,** (3) **Avoir du temps pour les activités préférées.** Notice that some choices may fall into more than one category.

Vu par les femmes : un sondage La Redoute/IFOP

La Redoute propose une nouvelle communication publicitaire qui a l'objet d'écouter des femmes et de répondre à leurs aspirations. Pour le premier sondage (en collaboration avec l'institut IFOP), on a interviewé des femmes (20–60 ans) qui travaillent et qui ont des enfants. Le principe?... explorer le concept du «temps libéré».

Question: *Avez-vous besoin de plus de temps?*

Une majorité de ces femmes actives de moins de 50 ans ont répondu affirmativement; plus de 67% des femmes interrogées ont indiqué qu'elles se sentent frustrées vis-à-vis du temps libre. 33% des femmes interrogées déclarent consacrer trop de temps à leur travail et 22% trop de temps au trajet pour s'y rendre°.

58% (surtout les 35–49 ans) pensent ne pas avoir assez de temps pour s'occuper d'elles-mêmes et dans une même proportion de leurs ami(e)s. Quand elles sont mariées avec des enfants, elles désirent également consacrer plus de temps à leurs enfants (47%) et leur conjoint (46%).

76% des femmes interrogées désirent se libérer une journée supplémentaire par semaine.

Question: *Que feriez-vous avec plus de temps?*

Passer plus de temps à se détendre et à s'amuser. Avoir plus de temps pour les autres: les enfants d'abord.

La majorité des femmes désirent en priorité:

s'occuper de leurs enfants	92%
voir les ami(e)s	89%
inviter des ami(e)s chez soi	78%
passer du temps en famille	77%

Mais les femmes ne s'oublient° pas. Elles désirent aussi avoir plus de temps pour:

s'amuser	90%
apprendre	84%
voyager	83%
s'occuper de son corps°	78%

Les femmes à Paris préfèrent la lecture (89%), à l'exception des 25–34 ans, qui préfèrent à 84% le sport contre 55% des 50–60 ans.

S'occuper de la maison en général intéresse 68% des femmes interrogées; celles qui habitent des villages préfèrent jardiner ou bricoler (71%).

À noter que l'oisiveté° reste minoritaire; 49% des femmes à Paris ont choisi de ne rien faire (seulement 26% pour les 50–60 ans). Dormir est le choix d'une femme sur deux, surtout les 20–24 ans (68%).

s'oublier: *forget about themselves*

s'occuper de son corps: *to take care of their body*

le trajet pour s'y rendre: *the commute to get there*

l'oisiveté (f.): *idleness*

I. **Trouver le temps.** Quand vous trouvez du temps libre dans votre emploi du temps, qu'est-ce que vous aimez en faire? Complétez les phrases pour les différentes circonstances. Consultez la liste des **choix rapportés dans le sondage IFOP La Redoute** à la page précédente pour stimuler votre réflexion.

Les phrases à compléter:
(1) Quand je trouve quelques heures de libre, j'aime...
(2) Quand je gagne un après-midi de libre, j'aime...
(3) Quand je gagne une journée de libre, j'aime...
(4) Quand je gagne un week-end de libre, j'aime...

> **Modèle:** Quand je trouve quelques heures de libre, j'aime *aller au gymnase pour m'entraîner un peu.*

À propos du vocabulaire: Ne négligez pas les activités que vous avez étudiées dans les chapitres précédents. Consultez les lexiques.

Les choix rapportés dans le sondage IFOP La Redoute
- ne rien faire
- dormir
- faire du sport
- m'occuper de la maison
- jardiner / bricoler
- faire de la lecture
- passer du temps en famille
- jouer avec mes enfants
- voir mes amis
- m'occuper de mon corps
- recevoir *(to receive guests)*
- voyager

J. **Réflexions sur mon emploi du temps.** Réfléchissez sur votre emploi du temps pour compléter au moins cinq des phrases suivantes.

1. Je me sens... (*souvent/rarement*) pressé(e) par le temps.
2. Quand j'ai besoin d'économiser du temps, je (ne)... (pas).
3. J'ai l'impression de perdre mon temps° quand je...

perdre mon temps: *to waste my time*

4. Je me sens frustré(e) quand je dois passer du temps à...
5. Il est surtout difficile de trouver assez de temps pour...
6. Pour équilibrer mon emploi du temps, j'ai besoin de trouver... (Mentionnez une quantité de temps.)
7. Pour équilibrer mon emploi du temps, j'ai besoin de... (Mentionnez une activité.)
8. La priorité numéro un dans mon emploi du temps, c'est...
9. Le meilleur moment de ma journée, c'est...
10. Je voudrais passer (beaucoup/un peu) plus de temps à...
11. Je voudrais passer (beaucoup/un peu) moins de temps à...
12. Je voudrais avoir plus de temps pour... (*moi/les autres/mes activités préférées*).

K. **Mes priorités.** Choisissez trois de vos phrases de l'exercice précédent. Pour chaque phrase, développez un paragraphe où vous expliquez un peu vos priorités concernant votre emploi du temps. Écrivez trois ou quatre phrases par paragraphe pour élaborer vos idées.

Synthèse des idées sur les DÉCOUVERTES. Based on your examination and discussions of the **Découverte** notes throughout the chapter, what are your initial impressions of **les grandes vacances** in France? What comparisons or contrasts do you notice between French and American cultures?

ÉCOUTONS: Une journée difficile

You will hear two telephone conversations in which people are talking about demands on their daily schedules. First, determine the general mood of each speaker. Then identify who does the activities that are making demands on their time. Finally, identify a person you know in your own life who handles demands on his or her time in a similar manner to each speaker that you hear in these conversations.

A. On identifie l'humeur. Listen to each of the people talking in the two telephone conversations and determine what each one's general mood is during the conversation. Match each speaker with the letters of the two or three phrases that best describe his or her frame of mind. Read through the choices before listening to the tape.

Conversation #1, Guy Martin: _____
Conversation #1, Marie-Christine: _____
Conversation #2, Guy Martin: _____
Conversation #2, Louise Girard: _____

a. pressé(e) par le temps
b. calme
c. stressé(e)
d. découragé(e)
e. désire aider
f. ne veut pas aider, mais accepte
g. compatissant(e) (*sympathetic*)
h. non-compatissant(e)

B. On identifie les actions et les acteurs. Now listen again to the conversations and try to identify who does the actions mentioned. On the list, match each action with the person who does it or who is responsible for getting it done. Write the letter **G**, for Guy, **M-C** for his wife Marie-Christine, or **L** for his colleague Louise, in front of the appropriate action. Some actions may be matched to more than one person and others may remain unselected. Read through the choices before listening.

G = Guy Martin   **M-C** = his wife, Marie-Christine   **L** = his colleague, Louise

____ travailler au bureau
____ faire les devoirs
____ demander l'aide d'un collègue
____ déjeuner
____ se laver les cheveux
____ prendre un jour de congé
____ emmener le bébé chez le médecin
____ travailler sur le campus
____ réserver les hôtels et les vols d'avion
____ passer un examen
____ prendre rendez-vous chez le médecin
____ se renseigner sur les horaires d'un congrès

____ déjeuner avec des collègues
____ aller à une séance de travaux pratiques
____ s'habiller
____ s'occuper de l'organisation d'un meeting au bureau
____ s'occuper de la voiture
____ téléphoner à l'école
____ donner des coups de téléphone
____ s'occuper du bébé pendant l'examen
____ parler avec la garderie
____ se rattraper
____ se dépêcher pour rentrer à la maison

C. On fait des associations. Now reflect on the personalities of the three characters in these telephone conversations. Can you think of someone you know who reacts similarly when extra demands are made on his or her time? Name that person and make a statement about how he/she resembles one of our characters.

Modèle: *Ma petite amie ressemble à Marie-Christine parce qu'elle n'a jamais assez de temps pour assumer toutes ses responsabilités. Elle est souvent paniquée.*

ÉLABORATION DE PERSPECTIVE

The following excerpts are from an editorial in *Expansion* magazine, a French periodical that treats business and economy. As you read them, bear in mind the ideas you discussed in the **Découverte** activities.

Fini les grandes vacances de l'économie

diminue: *is diminishing*
activité: *business*

Le grand sommeil de l'été, vieille habitude française, diminue°. Mais nous sommes encore loin de ces pays où l'activité° ignore les vacances.

Il est clair que ce modèle a commencé à évoluer. Dans un certain nombre de secteurs, les entreprises ferment toujours pendant les mois de juillet et août. Mais d'autres sociétés, de plus en plus nombreuses, préfèrent préserver la continuité de l'activité, donc l'étalement° des congés.

un étalement: *spreading*

il y a vingt ans: *twenty years ago*

défauts (m.): *faults*

Même s'il est beaucoup moins profond qu'il y a vingt ans°, le grand sommeil de l'été continue de distinguer la France des autres pays développés, et reste considéré comme un de nos défauts° nationaux.

Roy-Uni = Royaume-Uni: *United Kingdom*

LA FRANCE RESTE DU CÔTÉ DES PAYS LATINS

+3% États-Unis
−4,5 % Roy.–Uni
−8 % Japon
−10 % Allemagne
−26 % France
−40 % Espagne
−49 % Italie

Production des industries manufacturières de sept grands pays en août 1995

Écart de production entre le mois d'août et la moyenne des autres mois de l'année (en %)

Source: OCDE

fracture estivale: *summer break*

La fracture estivale°, caractéristique des nations autour de la Méditerranée, n'existe pas aux États-Unis, et très peu en Europe du Nord ou au Japon.

[adapté de l'*Expansion* online]

1. Read the excerpts from the article «**Fini les grandes vacances de l'économie**». In these passages, the author touches on the tension between national traditions and the internationalization of commerce. What seems to be his attitude on the subject? How can you tell?

2. Examine the figures in the graph comparing the industrialized countries in terms of differences in productivity during August as opposed to the rest of the year. Do any of these figures surprise you? Do they suggest how the internationalization of commerce might influence national and regional customs?

3. Discuss your insights with your classmates, taking notes on their interpretations of the material.

4. Write a paragraph in English with the following components:

- a thesis statement, summarizing your impressions;
- several sentences in which you offer support for your impressions based on the information here and in the **Découverte** notes;
- a conclusion, in which you tell what additional information you would like to have on the subject.

INTÉGRATION

Your company has recently gone through a wellness evaluation process. Based on the findings of high stress levels among the employees, management has decided to send the committee to the French subsidiary of the company to do a similar review at that site. Working in groups of three or four, design and conduct a survey to find out the major stress factors in the lives of your associates and their preferred ways to relieve these stresses.

A. On s'auto-analyse. First, individually, list the major stress factors in your own life. Categorize these stresses in terms of various aspects of your life. Give at least three examples of causes of stress in each category.

Modèles:	la vie personnelle	*Je suis fatigué(e).*
	la vie familiale	*J'ai trop de travail à la maison.*
	la vie scolaire	*J'ai peur des examens de math.*

Then, for each category, list three to five ways that you attempt to alleviate the stress or to rebalance your life.

| | la vie professionnelle | *quitter le bureau pour déjeuner dans un bon restaurant* |
| | la vie sociale | *aller voir de bons films au cinéma* |

B. On compare les listes personnelles. In your group, compare your personal stress factors and the activities that you use to regain your balance. Determine the four or five stresses in each category that you consider to be the most significant.
   Now study your anti-stress measures. Make a list of the five top choices for each category.

C. On prépare un sondage. Prepare a survey to ask individuals about the frequency or intensity of their stresses and their anti-stress activities. Set up a scale of 1–5 to record their responses.

jamais	rarement	quelquefois	souvent	toujours
1	2	3	4	5

D. On pose des questions. Get responses from at least five individuals per member of the group. If necessary, you may assist non-French speakers with the language or rephrase the questions in English for them.

E. On décrit les résultats. Write a narrative description of the results of your survey. Tell what stressors you found to be the most pronounced in your survey sample. Comment on the most popular ways of relieving these stresses.

LEXIQUE DE BASE

LEXIQUE D'EXPANSION

Pour parler des activités quotidiennes

s'amuser	to have a good time	s'améliorer	to improve oneself
se brosser (les dents/ les cheveux)	to brush (teeth/hair)	s'arranger	to get organized
se coucher	to go to bed	s'asseoir	to sit down
se dépêcher	to hurry	s'avancer	to advance
s'embrasser	to kiss (each other)	se calmer	to calm down
s'entraîner	to work out	se disputer	to argue, to quarrel
s'habiller	to get dressed	s'en aller	to go away
s'inscrire	to register, to enroll	s'énerver	to get upset
s'installer	to get settled	s'ennuyer	to be bored
s'intéresser à	to be interested in	s'habituer (à)	to become accustomed (to)
s'organiser	to get organized	s'inquiéter	to be worried
se laver	to wash (up)	s'occuper (de)	to attend to
se lever	to get up	se maquiller	to put on makeup
se marier	to get married	se raser	to shave oneself
se parler	to talk to each other		
se préparer	to get ready		
se promener	to take a walk		
se regarder	to look at each other		
se renseigner (sur)	to get information (about)		
se reposer	to rest		
se retrouver	to meet		
se réveiller	to wake up		
se taire	to get quiet, to hush		
se téléphoner	to call each other		

Pour suggérer la nécessité

avoir besoin (de)	to need
devoir	to have to, must, should
il est nécessaire (de)	it is necessary (to)
il faut	it is necessary, one must
il ne faut pas	one must not
il n'est pas nécessaire (de)	it is not necessary (to)

Pour parler des disciplines et matières universitaires

la faculté des lettres	School of Language and Literature		
la littérature	literature	la théologie	theology
la philosophie	philosophy		
les langues modernes	modern languages		
les langues mortes	classical languages		
l'école des beaux-arts	School of Fine Arts		
la musique	music	la céramique	ceramics
la peinture	painting	la danse	dance
l'art dramatique	drama	le dessin	drawing
l'histoire de l'art	art history	la sculpture	sculpture

la faculté des sciences humaines	School of Social Sciences	l'anthropologie	anthropology
l'archéologie	archeology	la géographie	geography
l'histoire	history	les relations humaines	human relations
la linguistique	linguistics		
la psychologie	psychology	la psychologie de l'enfant	child psychology
les sciences économiques	economics		
		la technique de communication	speech and communication theory
les sciences politiques	political science		
la sociologie	sociology	l'économie de la famille	family economics
la faculté des sciences naturelles	School of Natural Sciences	l'économie internationale	international economics
la biologie	biology		
la géologie	geology	la botanique	botany
		la physiologie	physiology
l'école des sciences exactes	School of Exact Sciences		
		l'astronomie	astronomy
la chimie	chemistry	la physique	physics
l'informatique	computer science		
les mathématiques	mathematics		
la faculté des études professionnelles	Professional Schools		
le commerce	business	le droit social	social law
le comptabilité	accounting	le droit fiscal	tax law
le droit	law	le droit de l'enfant	child law
la gestion	management	le droit international	international law
le journalisme	journalism	le droit de la famille	family law
le marketing	marketing	la médecine préventive	preventive medicine
la médecine	medicine		
la pédagogie	pedagogy	la nutrition	nutrition
les relations internationales	international relations	l'hygiène	(public) health
la santé	health	l'éducation physique et sportive	physical education and sports

Pour parler des cours

un emploi du temps	schedule	les frais d'inscription	tuition and fees
un cours (magistral)	(lecture) course	l'appel	roll call
(une séance de) travaux pratiques	lab (session)	rattraper le travail en retard	to catch up on late work
de bonnes notes	good grades		
une conférence	lecture		
les devoirs	homework		
passer un examen	to take a test		
échouer à un examen	to fail a test		

rater un examen	to flunk a test		
réussir à un examen	to pass or do well on a test		
avoir la moyenne	to make average grades		

<h3>Pour faire des comparaisons</h3>

aussi... que	as . . . as
le meilleur	the best (as adjective)
le mieux	the best (as adverb)
le moins	the least
le plus	the most
mieux	better (as adverb)
moins... que	less . . . than
plus... que	more . . . than

<h3>Pour parler des instruments de musique</h3>

la batterie	drums	la basse	string bass
la guitare	guitar	la clarinette	clarinet
le piano	piano	le saxophone	saxophone
la trompette	trumpet	la flûte	flute
le violon	violin	le trombone	trombone
		le violoncelle	cello

<h3>Des verbes</h3>

dormir	to sleep
jouer à	to play a sport or game
jouer de	to play a musical instrument
partir	to leave, to go away
quitter	to leave (a person or place)
servir	to serve
sortir	to leave, to go out, exit

LES EXPÉRIENCES PASSÉES:
Notre formation pour l'avenir

Communicative Objectives

- To talk about previous work and educational experiences
- To talk about previous personal experiences
- To talk about previous work and educational experiences as they enhance career opportunities

Thematic Objectives

- ✓ To identify work and educational experiences and articulate their relevance to the workplace
- ✓ To identify life experiences (outside the contexts of work and school) that have contributed to your personal development
- ✓ To relate your own skills, knowledge, and interests to those defined in specific job offerings

OUVERTURE EN VIDÉO:
On fait une demande d'emploi

La mise en scène

a reçu: *received*
un poste: *a job*

Voilà Yannick, le petit ami de la sœur de Xavier, notre guide à Paris. Yannick a reçu° son diplôme universitaire (sa licence) l'année dernière. Il a fait une spécialisation en économie et maintenant il cherche un poste°.

Listening strategies

Since understanding spoken French is considerably more difficult than understanding the written language, it is helpful to start a listening task by observing some clues to help determine the context of the segment. Visual clues can assist you in identifying the speakers, what their relationship to each other is, and how they react to each other. Additionally, clues can sometimes indicate the topic and tone of the conversation. In the first part of this video lesson, the sound track has been replaced by a voice-over track to guide you in making observations that will assist you in anticipating the context and content of the segment you will hear later.

A. On fait des observations. You are about to watch a video in which some young people are discussing the job search process. In preparation, preview the following questions. Then watch the video to find answers to these questions.

1. What does Yannick seem to be working on? It appears that he is
   a. filling out a job application form.   c. typing his résumé.
   b. writing a letter to apply for a job.

2. How is Yannick writing the document he is working on? Yannick is writing
   a. on a computer.   b. on a typewriter.   c. with pen and ink.

3. In this segment, one person is giving advice and the other(s) is (are) receiving the advice. It appears that
   a. Xavier is giving advice to his sister Aude and to Yannick.
   b. Aude is giving advice to her boyfriend Yannick.
   c. Yannick is giving advice to his girlfriend Aude.

4. What seems to be Yannick's mood? Yannick appears to be
   a. enthusiastic.   b. impatient.   c. discouraged.

B. On remarque (*We notice*) le ton et les gestes. Now watch the segment again, this time with its original sound track, but do not try to understand the language yet. Listen and watch for clues in gesture, tone, and intonation in order to prepare you to understand the conversation the next time you listen. As you watch, try to answer the next two questions.

1. Can you tell by her gestures, tone, and intonation whether Aude is making specific suggestions or giving general encouragement?
   a. Specific suggestions   b. General encouragement
2. At the end of the segment, what does the tone in Yannick's voice indicate about his frame of mind?
   a. He is greatly encouraged and eager to proceed.
   b. He is still despondent and reluctant to start.

Les paroles et le sens

C. On écoute. Listen to the video segment again. This time you are going to work on discriminating the sounds you hear for certain key expressions you will encounter in this chapter.

1. As Xavier introduces this segment on Yannick's job search, he tells us about Yannick's university degree and his major field of study. What do you hear him say about Yannick's major? Xavier tells us that Yannick
   a. a reçu sa licence en marketing.
   b. a fait une spécialisation en économie.
   c. cherche un poste dans la gestion.

2. Yannick enumerates several things that he has done in his job search. Which of the things listed here do you *not* hear him mention?
   a. ... j'ai lu toutes les petites annonces.
   b. ... j'ai eu des entretiens.
   c. ... j'ai écrit des lettres de ma plus belle écriture.

3. In her efforts to encourage Yannick, Aude enumerates the qualities, the experiences, and training that will serve him in his future career. Which of the following do you *not* hear her mention?
   a. T'as une très bonne formation.   d. Tu as fait un très bon stage.
   b. Tu parles trois langues.   e. Tu te présentes bien.
   c. T'as le soutien de ta famille.

4. Aude mentions that the company where her grandfather's friend works is looking for someone in sales. How do you hear Yannick react to the idea of working in sales rather than in management?
   a. Ah, non, non, la gestion, ça m'intéresse pas.
   b. Ah, les ventes, ça m'intéresse beaucoup.
   c. Ah, non, non, les ventes, ça m'intéresse pas.
   d. Je veux entrer dans les ventes.

5. What do you hear Yannick say that interests him about working for an international firm?
   a. Ça m'intéresse, le voyage.   c. Ça m'intéresse, les vacances.
   b. Ça m'intéresse, la gestion.   d. Ça m'intéresse, le salaire qu'ils offrent.

6. Finally, Aude lists the three essential steps Yannick must take to apply for and land a job: writing a letter of introduction as a job applicant, sending the résumé (CV), and being invited in for an interview. In which order does she recommend that they be done?
   a. ... tu écris une lettre de candidature, peut-être que tu seras contacté pour un entretien et tu envoies ton CV.
   b. ... tu envoies ton CV, tu écris une lettre de candidature et peut-être que tu seras contacté pour un entretien.
   c. ... tu écris une lettre de candidature, tu envoies ton CV et peut-être que tu seras contacté pour un entretien.

DÉCOUVERTE

Did you notice how Yannick proclaimed that he had written in his very best handwriting (**ma plus belle écriture)?** Did you think it was strange not to type the cover letter to his résumé? Actually, he was just doing what potential employers expect. In France, the CV is typed, but the cover letter is traditionally handwritten so that it can be subjected to analysis by a handwriting expert, a graphologist. Here is a bit of information offered by *Le magazine de l'emploi:*

Il faut savoir que° la France est le seul pays du monde à utiliser des méthodes de sélection ou d'évaluation de profil° sur la base d'analyse graphologique°. [n° 18, mars–avril, p. 14]

And ***CV Magazine*** warns, «[…] *une lettre manuscrite° est donc une opération extrêmement importante, qui risque fort d'être déterminante dans l'acceptation ou le refus de votre candidature°.*» [n° 1, 1996, p. 86]

The practice may be due to change, though. It is hotly contested these days. The article from ***Le magazine de l'emploi*** goes on to say, «... *c'est légalement douteux et surtout pas professionnel.*»

Il faut savoir que: *It must be noted that*
un profil: *the personal data provided by the job applicant*
une analyse graphologique: *handwriting analysis*
manuscrite: *handwritten*
une candidature: *application*

1. Read the **DÉCOUVERTE** note. Then decide what *you* consider the main point of interest in the information and ideas presented. Each person in the class may have a different opinion about this.

2. Identify the phrases that support your perception of the main point.

3. Discuss your opinions with classmates to broaden or reinforce your interpretation.

On y réfléchit

D. **On fait son choix.** Now think back over some of Yannick's qualifications and preferences for his career and compare them with your own. Choose completions for the following statements and tell your partner. You may want to select more than one completion for some statements.

Parmi mes atouts: *My potential for success includes*

1. Parmi mes atouts°,
   - j'ai une très bonne formation.
   - je fais une spécialisation en _____.
   - je parle _____ (deux, trois?) langues.
   - j'ai le soutien de ma famille.
   - j'ai fait un très bon stage.
   - je me présente bien.

2. Mes intérêts? _____, ça m'intéresse.
   - La gestion
   - Les ventes
   - L'éducation
   - La médecine
   - Le droit
   - La comptabilité
   - La communication
   - Le voyage
   - Les vacances
   - Le salaire
   - (autre ???)

1ᴱᴿ THÈME: Mes atouts dans le domaine du travail

Objective: To talk about previous work and educational experiences

PRÉSENTATION: Un coup d'œil sur le thème

Carrières

Spécialiste financier dans une entreprise internationale

Chef d'équipe graphiste
dans une entreprise publicitaire

Ingénieur développement logiciel° dans le domaine de la bureautique°

Responsabilités

- Contrôler° les budgets des divers services de l'entreprise
- Préparer des rapports annuels pour des succursales° dans le monde entier

- Planifier des programmes de publicité, en respectant les besoins et les budgets des clients
- Gérer° l'équipe de graphistes

- Analyser les besoins du marché
- Développer de nouveaux produits et contrôler leur performance

À propos: In this chapter you will look at some of the ways your experiences in school, on the job, or "out in the world" prepare you for a career. You will find it helpful to review your portfolio entries from **Chapitre 1** (careers and work-related tasks), **Chapitre 2** (academic courses), and **Chapitre 4** (personality and character traits) as you elaborate your ideas.

Contrôler: *Monitor, Inspect, Verify*
une succursale: *branch office*

Gérer: *Direct, Organize*

À propos du vocabulaire: You learned the word **marché** in earlier chapters; here you can expand its use into a business context. You can also use the context of product development to make sense of the expression **cycle de vie**. Take a guess, then compare your interpretation with others'.

un logiciel: *software*
bureautique: *office functions*

Stratégies

1. Use the page layout (in addition to the skills you have already studied) to help you quickly identify the focus of the *Coup d'œil.*
2. How does the material on the right side of the page relate to that on the left?

3. Scan the *Responsabilités* to make two lists, one with actions, the other showing the objects, or recipients, of the actions. Be sure to align your lists so that you can easily see the correspondence between each action and its object.

> **Modèle:** <u>Action</u>   <u>Object of the action</u>
>   prepare   (yearly) reports

4. Scan each responsibility again, looking for any information that might alter or expand the interpretation you gave it in the preceding step.
5. Brainstorm with your partner to identify academic courses or work experiences in other fields that might help qualify someone for the careers and tasks presented in the reading. Are any of your own academic or work experiences mentioned on your brainstorming lists?

POUR DÉVELOPPER VOTRE FRANÇAIS

Structure: Le passé composé avec avoir

OBSERVATIONS

Mme Leclerc et Mme Piaget sont assises à la table. Mme de la Force est debout.

L'été dernier les deux professeurs d'anglais au lycée **ont travaillé** en équipe pour préparer leurs cours.

Elles **ont organisé** le travail.

Elles **ont examiné** les livres ensemble.

Mme Leclerc **a regardé** des vidéos.

Mme Piaget **a cherché** des photos et **a créé** des posters intéressants pour les salles de classe.

Mme de la Force, un prof américain, **a expliqué** quelques détails de la vie aux États-Unis.

Elles **ont classé** leurs documents ensemble.

*Last summer the two high school English teachers **worked** as a team to prepare their courses.*

*They **organized** the work.*

*They **studied** the books together.*

*Mme Leclerc **looked at** videos.*

*Mme Piaget **looked for** pictures and **created** interesting posters for the classrooms.*

*Mme de la Force, an American teacher, **explained** details of life in the United States.*

*They **filed** their documents together.*

STRATÉGIES D'ANALYSE

1. Each of the word groups in boldface is in the **passé composé,** a past tense in French. How many words are required to form this past tense?
2. Which of the words that make up each compound past tense verb changes to agree with the subject?
3. The meaning of the verb is carried by the past participle. From the examples given, can you figure out how to form the past participle of regular **-er** verbs?

PRÉCISIONS

The **passé composé** (*compound past tense*) is used to tell what happened or what someone did.

- The **passé composé** consists of two parts:

  (1) the auxiliary verb, which is conjugated to agree with the subject, and
  (2) the past participle of the verb, which provides the meaning.

- Most verbs use **avoir** as the auxiliary verb.

J'**ai** tapé les messages.
I typed the messages.

Nous **avons** précisé les idées.
We have clarified the concepts.

Tu **as** préparé les rapports?
Did you prepare the reports?

Vous **avez** développé un produit rentable.
You have developed a profitable product.

Il **a** organisé les programmes.
He has planned the programs.

Est-ce qu'elles **ont** rangé le stock?
Did they put up the inventory?

- To form the past participle of **-er** verbs, remove the **er** from the infinitive and add **-é.**

infinitive	past participle ending	past participle
par**ler**	**-é**	par**lé**
travai**ller**	**-é**	travail**lé**

J'**ai approvisionné** le rayon des parfums.
*I **stocked** the perfume counter.*

Nous **avons téléphoné** aux clients.
*We **have telephoned** the customers.*

Tu **as accumulé** 40 heures de travail.
*You **have accumulated** 40 hours of work.*

Vous **avez réparé** le télécopieur.
*You **fixed** the fax machine.*

Il **a tapé** les rapports pour l'équipe?
***Did** he **type** the reports for the team?*

Ils **ont coordonné** les activités.
*They **coordinated** the activities.*

Elle **a créé** les présentations.
*She **has created** the presentations.*

Elles **ont changé** de société.
*They **have changed** companies.*

On **a installé** Microsoft Office.
*We **have installed** Microsoft Office.*

- Note the variety of possible meanings in English for verbs in the **passé composé** in French.

J'**ai renseigné** les clients.

*I **informed** the customers.*
*I **have informed** the customers.*
*I **did inform** the customers.*

A. Au travail. À tour de rôle avec votre partenaire, mentionnez une activité que quelqu'un de chaque profession a probablement faite au travail hier. Utilisez les idées données ou ajoutez vos idées.

> **Modèle:** *Un journaliste a interviewé des personnes célèbres.*

1. un(e) journaliste
2. un professeur
3. un(e) secrétaire
4. un médecin
5. un(e) avocat(e)
6. un(e) comptable
7. un(e) religieux(-euse)
8. un(e) pharmacien(ne)
9. un(e) banquier(-ère)
10. un(e) politicien(ne)

classer des documents
rapporter les nouvelles
coordonner les activités
consulter ses collègues
préparer un budget
consulter des clients
examiner des malades
donner des informations
préparer des examens
interviewer des personnes célèbres
taper des rapports
donner des interviews
gagner beaucoup d'argent

ont été faites: *were done*

B. Qui a fait ce travail? Il est possible que les activités mentionnées dans l'exercice précédent ont été faites° par des personnes de professions différentes. Suivez le modèle pour composer au moins cinq phrases où vous nommez deux professionnels qui ont fait la même activité au travail. Puis, à tour de rôle avec votre partenaire, lisez vos phrases.

> **Modèle:** *Un avocat et un comptable ont consulté des clients.*

déjà: *already*

C. Ce que j'ai déjà° fait au travail. Cochez (✓) les activités dans la liste suivante que vous avez déjà faites au travail. Puis, mentionnez à votre partenaire les activités que vous avez cochées.

> **Modèle:** *Moi, j'ai renseigné des clients, j'ai travaillé à la caisse et j'ai pris des messages.*

laisser: *to leave*

moi	les activités au travail	mon/ma partenaire
	coordonner les activités d'un groupe	
✓	renseigner des clients	
	stocker des rayons	
✓	travailler à la caisse	
✓	laisser° des messages	
	surveiller des enfants	
	parler aux clients par téléphone	
	classer des documents	
	taper des rapports	
	nettoyer une cuisine ou un bâtiment	
	installer des machines	
	accumuler plus de 40 heures de travail par semaine	

D. **Ce que nous avons en commun.** Utilisez la fiche de l'Exercice C pour faire une comparaison de vos expériences de travail et de celles *(those)* de votre partenaire. Décidez quelles activités vous avez tous les deux° en commun.

tous les deux: *both*

Modèle: *Mon partenaire et moi, nous avons travaillé à la caisse et nous avons pris des messages.*

ou *Mon partenaire et moi, nous n'avons rien fait en commun au travail.*

NOTE CULTURELLE

Presque tout le monde accepte qu'une connaissance des langues étrangères est un avantage pour un homme ou une femme d'affaires. De nos jours, **45%** des **cadres français** sont capables de s'exprimer **en anglais ou en allemand.** Les Français sont les mauvais élèves de la classe européenne. **68%** des **Grecs** et des **Portugais** et **60%** des **Espagnols** parlent l'anglais

ou l'allemand. En France, les moins appliqués en langues étrangères sont les directeurs du personnel: seulement 1,3% d'entre eux parlent couramment l'anglais. Les meilleurs sont les contrôleurs financiers, dont 20% parlent bien l'anglais et 74% parlent correctement l'allemand.

Réfléchissons: À votre avis: Voyez-vous un problème en France le fait

que seulement 1,3% des directeurs du personnel parlent une langue étrangère? Avec une Europe unie, est-ce que les sociétés françaises vont avoir plus ou moins de problèmes? À votre avis, est-ce que l'aspect financier est plus important que les employés?

Structure: Le passé composé à la forme négative

OBSERVATIONS

Ma secrétaire **n'a pas trouvé** la lettre que vous cherchez. Elle **n'a pas encore classé** ses documents cette semaine.

Non, je **n'ai pas vérifié** les stocks. J'ai passé toute la journée devant mon ordinateur.

Nous **n'avons pas développé** de produits rentables depuis longtemps.

STRATÉGIES D'ANALYSE

1. Where does the **ne... pas** go to indicate the negative in the **passé composé?**
2. Where in relation to the negative does the past participle come?

- To make a verb negative in the **passé composé**, place the two parts of the negative (**ne... pas**) around the auxiliary verb. Then add the past participle afterward.

Je **n'ai pas** élaboré les détails.
*I did **not** expand on the details.*

Tu **n'as pas** classé les documents.
*You have **not** filed the documents.*

Il **n'a pas** rangé les livres.
*He did **not** straighten up the books.*

Nous **n'avons pas** assuré la qualité.
*We have **not** guaranteed the quality.*

Vous **n'avez pas** noté le rendez-vous.
*You did **not** make a note of the meeting.*

Ils **n'ont pas** réparé le répondeur.
*They have **not** repaired the answering machine.*

E. Ce que je n'ai pas encore fait. En utilisant la liste de l'Exercice C à la page 234, dites à votre partenaire quelles activités vous n'avez pas encore faites au travail.

À propos de la structure: Remember that after a negative we use **de** rather than the indefinite articles **un(e)** and **des**, but the definite articles **le, la,** and **les** remain the same.

Modèle: *Je n'ai pas encore coordonné les activités d'un groupe. Je n'ai pas encore installé les machines.*

Structure: Le passé composé à la forme interrogative

—**Est-ce que j'ai terminé** le travail dans votre bureau?
—**As-tu installé** tous les logiciels?
—Pas encore. Georges va installer Excel demain. J'ai déjà installé tous les autres.
—**Il a travaillé** ici aussi longtemps que toi?
—Non, mais il a étudié l'informatique à l'université.

1. How many different ways of asking questions can you find in the dialogue?
2. Can you describe how to ask a question in each way?

- To ask a *yes/no* question in the **passé composé**, use intonation, **est-ce que, n'est-ce pas,** or inversion. With inversion, the **pronoun** subject is inverted with the auxiliary verb; then the past participle is added afterward. Inversion is not used when **je** is the subject.

Est-ce que j'ai accumulé plus de 40 heures?
Have I accumulated more than 40 hours?

As-tu travaillé comme livreur?
Have you worked as a delivery person?

Georges **a-t-il** installé PowerPoint sur ton ordinateur?
Did Georges install PowerPoint on your computer?

Avons-nous assuré la liaison des projets?
Have we assured the linking of the projects?

Avez-vous organisé le travail de votre équipe?
Have you organized the work of your team?

Ont-ils surveillé le projet?
Did they supervise the project?

Structure: La négation avec jamais

OBSERVATIONS

—Avez-vous jamais° créé des présentations professionnelles?
—Non, **je n'ai jamais créé** de présentations professionnelles. Mais j'ai développé beaucoup de présentations sur mon ordinateur pour mes cours à l'université.

—Avez-vous jamais travaillé comme serveur dans un bar?
—Non, **je n'ai jamais travaillé** comme serveur. Mais l'été dernier j'ai travaillé à la caisse dans un restaurant.

jamais: *ever*

STRATÉGIES D'ANALYSE

1. Find the two sentences that indicate that someone has *never* done something. What two words are necessary to express *never* in these sentences?
2. Can you explain the difference between expressing *ever* and *never* in French?

PRÉCISIONS

• Use **ne... pas** with a verb to give it the simple negative meaning of *not*.

Je **ne** travaille **pas** le lundi.
*I do **not** work on Mondays.*

Il **n'a pas** changé de société.
He hasn't changed companies.

• Use **ne... jamais** with a verb to mean *never*.

Je **ne** travaille **jamais** quand je suis malade.
*I **never** work when I am sick.*

Il **n'a jamais** coordonné les horaires.
*He has **never** coordinated the schedules.*

• Used alone (without **ne**), **jamais** means *ever*.

As-tu **jamais** commandé de la marchandise?   *Have you **ever** ordered goods?*

F. Où as-tu travaillé? Demandez à votre partenaire s'il/si elle a jamais fait les boulots° suivants. Quand vous entendez une réponse affirmative, demandez pour quelle société votre partenaire a travaillé.

> **Modèle:** vendeur(-euse)
> — *As-tu jamais travaillé comme vendeur(-euse)?*
> — *Non, je n'ai jamais travaillé comme vendeur(-euse).*
> — *As-tu jamais travaillé comme caissier(-ère)?*
> — *Oui, j'ai travaillé comme caissier(-ère).*
> — *Où ça?*
> — *Dans un supermarché.*

1. vendeur(-euse)
2. livreur(-euse)
3. réceptionniste
4. secrétaire
5. caissier(-ère)
6. serveur(-euse)
7. télévendeur(-euse)
8. chauffeur

Vocabulaire: Des expressions qui indiquent le passé

OBSERVATIONS

Hier soir j'ai dîné avec Henri dans un joli petit restaurant. On a passé une très belle soirée.

Il y a quatre ans j'ai commencé mes études universitaires. Et me voici—diplômée.

J'ai travaillé **pendant deux mois** sur ce projet. Il est enfin terminé.

STRATÉGIES D'ANALYSE

In French the **passé composé** is used to indicate that something happened in the past. You can use a variety of phrases to be more specific about *when* in the past the event occurred. From the context of the captions, can you figure out the meaning of the words in boldface?

PRÉCISIONS

- We use expressions such as the following to specify *when in the past* something happened:

hier (matin, après-midi, soir)	*yesterday (morning, afternoon, evening)*
samedi dernier	*last Saturday*
le week-end dernier	*last weekend*
la semaine dernière	*last week*
le mois dernier	*last month*

l'année dernière	last year
il y a (deux jours, trois mois, deux ans, longtemps)	(two days, three months, two years, a long time) ago
pendant (longtemps, une heure, six mois, trois ans)	during, for (a long time, one hour, six months, three years)
en 1990	in 1990
il y a huit jours	one week ago
il y a quinze jours	two weeks ago

À propos du vocabulaire: The French count both the first and the last day of one-week and two-week segments of time (**huit jours, quinze jours**).

G. Il y a longtemps. Travaillez avec votre partenaire pour déterminer la séquence des activités suivantes. Puis numérotez les phrases pour indiquer leur ordre. Commencez par le passé lointain° (1) et continuez jusqu'au passé le plus proche (10).

le passé lointain: *the distant past*

_____ A. L'année dernière j'ai travaillé 15 heures par semaine dans une société près de l'université.

_____ B. Ce matin j'ai acheté un journal pour consulter les petites annonces.

_____ C. Il y a quatre mois j'ai quitté mon boulot pour consacrer° plus de temps à mes études.

consacrer: *devote, allocate*

_____ D. Il y a deux ans j'ai décidé de me spécialiser en arts graphiques.

_____ E. Pendant deux ans j'ai considéré une variété de spécialisations.

_____ F. La semaine dernière j'ai sollicité une lettre de recommandation de mon meilleur prof.

_____ G. Il y a longtemps j'ai décidé d'aller à l'université.

_____ H. Hier soir j'ai organisé les éléments pour ma lettre de candidature.

_____ I. Le week-end dernier j'ai analysé toutes les œuvres dans mon dossier.

_____ J. Il y a quatre ans j'ai commencé mes études universitaires.

H. Quand as-tu... ? Demandez à votre partenaire quand il/elle a fait les activités suivantes. Votre partenaire, à son tour, vous posera les mêmes questions.

> **Modèle:** travailler comme réceptionniste
> —*Quand as-tu travaillé comme réceptionniste?*
> —*J'ai travaillé comme réceptionniste il y a deux ans.*
> ou —*Je n'ai jamais travaillé comme réceptionniste.*

1. visiter une exposition dans un musée
2. assister à un concert
3. taper un rapport pour un cours
4. préparer une présentation
5. téléphoner à un(e) ami(e)
6. ranger sa chambre ou son appartement ou sa maison
7. travailler comme serveur(-euse)
8. acheter une voiture
9. accumuler plus de 40 heures de travail pendant une semaine
10. installer un nouveau logiciel sur l'ordinateur

À propos de la structure: Note that in item #6 the possessive adjective must change its form to agree with the subject of your question.

Structure: Le passé composé des verbes irréguliers

OBSERVATIONS

Scène 1
Ce matin j'**ai fait** mon possible pour être à l'heure à la grande réunion.

Scène 2
Mais, à la fin, j'**ai été** en retard.

Scène 3
Et pendant le meeting, mon répondeur **a pris** vingt messages. Alors, j'**ai eu** trop de travail pour rentrer à la maison à l'heure.

STRATÉGIES D'ANALYSE

1. Can you tell what tense the verbs in boldface are in? How do you know?
2. Can you tell from the context of the sentences what these verbs mean? Do you remember the infinitive forms of these verbs?

PRÉCISIONS

- In order to use irregular verbs in the **passé composé,** you only need to learn one new form of each verb, the past participle.

infinitive	past participle	
avoir	**eu**	J'ai **eu** trente messages ce matin.
être	**été**	Tu as **été** en retard aujourd'hui.
faire	**fait**	Il a **fait** son possible.
prendre	**pris**	Nous avons **pris** les suggestions du patron.
apprendre	**appris**	Vous avez **appris** les formules pour le budget.
comprendre	**compris**	Ils ont **compris** les demandes des clients.

I. Quand as-tu... ? Dites à votre partenaire la dernière fois que vous avez fait les activités suivantes.

Modèle: être chez tes parents
—*Quand as-tu été chez tes parents?*
—*J'ai été chez mes parents la semaine dernière.*

1. être chez tes parents
2. avoir des invités chez toi

par cœur: *by heart*

3. apprendre de la poésie par cœur°
4. prendre un cours de maths

5. jouer au basket-ball
6. faire le ménage chez toi
7. prendre le petit déjeuner avec tes ami(e)s
8. être en retard pour le travail
9. avoir un week-end sans° devoirs

sans: *without*

10. prendre le dîner seul(e) au restaurant

PRONONCIATION: Les sons [u] et [y]

In French, the vowel sound represented by the phonetic symbol [u] is the same as that in the English words *who* and *food* and is written **ou** as in **nous** and **trouver.** By contrast, the sound [y], written **u,** is unlike any English vowel. To pronounce it correctly, round your lips and say *ee.* This is the sound you hear in words like **tu** and **une.**

Repeat the following pairs of words after your instructor, paying attention to your pronunciation of the sounds [u] and [y]:

[u]	[y]
tout	tu
vous	vue
l'amour	le mur
joue	jus
sourd°	sûr
loup°	Luc

sourd(e): *deaf*
un loup: *wolf*

À vous! With a partner, take turns reading these sentences that feature the sounds [u] and [y].

1. Est-ce que tu as trouvé un boulot?
2. Je ne sais pas. J'attends toujours un coup de téléphone du bureau.
3. Excusez-moi, madame... où se trouve le musée?
4. Tournez dans la rue Hubert et continuez tout droit.
5. Où vas-tu? À l'université?
6. Non, je n'ai plus de cours aujourd'hui.

POUR DÉVELOPPER VOS IDÉES

Thematic objective: To identify work and educational experiences and articulate their relevance to the workplace

Présentation: Les expériences sur le marché du travail

POUR SAISIR L'ESSENTIEL: Nathalie is writing a **lettre de candidature** to accompany her CV, or résumé. Since she is responding to an ad in the newspaper, she highlights those experiences that best address the skills required.

- Read the newspaper ad and make a list of words or phrases that suggest what qualities are being sought.
- Read the excerpt from Nathalie's letter and make a second list of the phrases she uses to indicate her preparedness for the position.
- Match the qualifications that Nathalie mentions in her letter with those sought in the ad. If you were the personnel director for DiaCom International, would you consider giving her an interview? Why (not)?

En plus de: *Besides*

service: *department*

Cie°: *the abbreviation for Compagnie*

comprennent: *include*

Mes études m'ont bien préparée pour ce poste. Je suis diplômée en psychologie et communication, et j'ai pris des cours du soir en informatique où j'ai appris à utiliser WordPerfect et Excel. En plus de° mes cours, j'ai fait un stage d'un an dans le service° des Relations Publiques à Damar Cie°, où j'ai renseigné les clients sur les nouveaux produits. Pendant ce temps, j'ai eu l'occasion de mettre en pratique mes compétences dans le domaine de la communication.

Mes expériences comprennent° aussi des travaux d'étudiant. J'ai travaillé comme hôtesse d'accueil dans un restaurant, un travail qui a exigé une bonne présentation...

DiaCom International
recherche: Spécialiste en marketing, vente
Poste: vendeur (vendeuse) spécialiste pour la vente de systèmes produits informatiques.
Mission: Vous préparez les activités de vente, les contacts client, les présentations, les stratégies commerciales.
Profil: Diplômé(e) universitaire (orientation économie ou psychologie), vous avez de l'expérience dans le domaine de ventes ou de relations publiques. La connaissance des applications classiques MS-Office (Word, Excel, Access) est exigée. Autonome, vous prenez volontiers des initiatives. Une présentation excellente est importante. D'excellentes aptitudes de communication en anglais et en français sont exigées, la pratique de l'allemand représente un atout. Rémunération en rapport avec le profil.
REF.07.D/M

DÉCOUVERTE

The CV (*curriculum vitae*) is similar to a résumé. It is usually accompanied by a cover letter **(lettre de candidature),** in which the applicant expands on the experiences that highlight his/her qualifications for the job. So, you might wonder, why write a letter that just repeats what is already in the CV? Here's the answer given in *CV Magazine*:

> [...]*Une bonne lettre [...] c'est une lettre qui montre que vous avez compris ce que demande ou ce qu'est l'entreprise°, met en évidence vos points forts par rapport à cette entreprise, montre votre motivation et votre envie de créer un lien avec cette entreprise... Et ceci, bien sûr, dans une présentation impeccable et un style direct et personnel.*

> CV MAGAZINE, N° 1, 1996, p. 70.

ce que demande ou ce qu'est l'entreprise: *both the nature of the company and the qualifications sought in applicants*

1. Read the DÉCOUVERTE note. Determine what you consider to be the main point. Note that each person in the class may have a different opinion about this.

2. Identify the phrases that support your perception of the main point.

3. Discuss your opinions with classmates to broaden or reinforce your interpretation.

J. **Mes travaux d'étudiant.** Identifiez vos expériences sur le marché du travail et indiquez les dates où vous avez fait ces travaux. Vous pouvez organiser les informations dans un tableau selon le modèle. Consultez le lexique à la fin du chapitre pour du vocabulaire utile.

Modèle:

DATE	EMPLOYEUR	POSTE	RESPONSABILITÉS
1999	IBM	assistant dans le service des ventes	· vérifier les stocks · coordonner le travail des vendeurs · taper des rapports
1997–1998	Martin & Associates (le bureau de mon père)	employé polyvalent°	· prendre des messages téléphoniques · faire des livraisons · faire des photocopies · classer les dossiers
1996	Pizzeria Deluxe (restaurant)	cuisinier	· préparer les pizzas · nettoyer la cuisine · prendre des commandes au téléphone

À propos de la communication: Notice the four categories of information that you give in the **tableau.** In a CV (or résumé) you could organize the data by date, employer, or the title of your position, whichever looks most impressive and gives the most balanced presentation.

un employé polyvalent: *an employee who does a variety of jobs*

K. **Rapport des expériences.** Faites des phrases pour rapporter vos expériences. Pour chaque expérience, indiquez au moins une de vos responsabilités. (Ce sont des phrases pour votre lettre de candidature.)

Modèles: *J'ai travaillé pour Pizzeria Deluxe comme cuisinier en 1996. J'ai préparé les pizzas.*

À l'âge de dix-huit ans, j'ai travaillé comme employé polyvalent dans le bureau de mon père. J'ai pris des messages téléphoniques et j'ai fait des livraisons.

À propos de la communication: Don't try to memorize the list of suggestions in Exercise L; just learn those that help you communicate your own experiences.

ce que vous y avez appris: *what you learned in them*

L. **Les études.** Faites une liste des cours que vous voudriez mentionner dans votre CV. Pour au moins deux cours que vous avez déjà pris, essayez de donner une description générale de ce que vous y avez appris°. Consultez le modèle et les suggestions.

Modèle: —*Dans mon cours d'anglais (avec le professeur Johnson), j'ai appris à communiquer clairement mes idées.*

—*Dans mon cours de psychologie (avec le professeur Delorme), j'ai commencé à comprendre l'importance des gestes dans la communication.*

Suggestions pour vos descriptions générales

J'ai appris à...

- préciser des concepts
- organiser mes idées
- communiquer clairement mes idées
- organiser un projet important
- travailler en équipe
- coordonner les activités d'un groupe
- équilibrer mon emploi du temps

J'ai commencé à...

- apprécier l'importance de l'environnement
- apprécier la diversité des pays et des peuples
- comprendre les rapports entre la géographie et la société
- comprendre l'importance des gestes dans la communication
- apprécier l'importance de l'autodiscipline
- comprendre le rôle du gouvernement dans notre société
- apprécier l'importance d'une bonne culture générale

---

chacun(e): *each one*
marché du travail: *job market*

M. **Communiquer nos expériences aux autres.** Dans une interview avec votre partenaire, rapportez trois ou quatre de vos expériences professionnelles et éducatives (prises des deux activités précédentes). Pour chacune°, mentionnez comment elle contribue à votre préparation pour le marché du travail°. En écoutant votre partenaire, indiquez les expériences que vous trouvez les plus appropriées pour son CV.

À part: *Besides*

Je voudrais avoir fait ça:
I would like to have done that.

Expressions utiles: Où as-tu travaillé?
Qu'est-ce que tu as fait là?
À part° mes expériences comme…
En plus de mes cours…
Ça, c'est intéressant!
Je voudrais avoir fait ça°.
Tu as pris de bons cours?
Qu'est-ce que tu as appris (dans ce cours)?
À mon avis, les meilleures expériences pour ton CV sont ton travail à… et…

Objective: To talk about previous personal experiences

Un coup d'œil sur le thème

un entraîneur: *coach*
valorisante: *valuable*

En contribuant à l'éducation des enfants, j'ai beaucoup appris moi-même.

Être entraîneur° a été une expérience valorisante° pour moi.

Il y a trois ans, j'ai eu l'occasion de travailler comme bénévole avec les enfants de notre église. C'est une expérience que je recommande.

De 1998 à 1999 j'ai été entraîneur pour l'équipe de football de ma communauté. À mon avis, cette expérience a enrichi ma vie°.

a enrichi ma vie: *enriched my life*
Ce que j'ai fait: *What I did*

Ce que j'ai fait°:
J'ai planifié des excursions. Et quand nous sommes sortis en groupe, j'ai pris la responsabilité du bien-être° des enfants.

Ce que j'ai fait:
J'ai réussi à solliciter le soutien financier des commerçants locaux pour notre équipe.

le bien-être: *well-being*

Ce que j'en ai appris°:
J'ai appris l'importance de la fiabilité° et de la confiance en soi.

Ce que j'en ai appris:
J'ai cultivé la capacité de motiver les autres.

Ce que j'en ai appris: *What I learned from it*

fiabilité: *reliability*

Ce que j'ai fait:
J'ai organisé des projets, et j'ai encouragé la participation des parents.

Ce que j'ai fait:
J'ai aidé les joueurs à résister au stress.

Ce que j'en ai appris:
J'ai développé mon sens de l'organisation ainsi que° le sens des contacts.

Ce que j'en ai appris:
J'ai développé une sensibilité aux besoins psychologiques de l'équipe.

ainsi que: *as well as*

Stratégies

1. Examine the typefaces and the layout of the information in the *Coup d'œil.* Can you tell what the different sections of information are about?
2. Scan the reading to identify the sections that have a cause-and-effect relationship with one another. What are their titles? Skim them to decide which represent the "cause" and which the "effect."

3. Now read the narrator's introductory comments to determine the contexts for their responsibilities. For example, was the young woman traveling with her family? Was the young man playing college sports?
4. Reread the sections that tell the narrators' responsibilities and how they benefited from their involvement. Explain how such duties might contribute to the development of the skills and aptitudes mentioned.
5. Do you have any of these or similar skills? How did you acquire them?
6. Take notes on the phrases that you might use to tell about your own experiences.

POUR DÉVELOPPER VOTRE FRANÇAIS

Vocabulaire: Des verbes en -ir pour décrire un changement dans l'apparence physique

OBSERVATIONS

Roland **grossit** pendant les vacances d'été.

Vivianne **rougit** quand elle chante devant un groupe de gens.

Je **grossis** chaque année pendant les vacances de Noël.
*I **gain weight** during the Christmas holidays each year.*

Tu **rougis** facilement.
*You **blush** easily.*

Il **blanchit** de peur.
*He **is turning white** from fear.*

Souvent nous **maigrissons** pendant une crise personnelle.
*Often we **get thin** during a personal crisis.*

Vous **grandissez** vite.
*You **are growing up** fast.*

Ils **vieillissent** sous nos yeux.
*They **are getting old** before our eyes.*

STRATÉGIES D'ANALYSE

1. Do any of these new verbs in boldface remind you of other French words that you have learned?
2. How were those words used?

PRÉCISIONS

• Some verbs that describe a change in physical appearance end in **-ir** in the infinitive form. These verbs are often based on the feminine forms of related adjectives.

finir	fini	J'**ai fini** l'emploi du temps. *I **have finished** the schedule.*
choisir	choisi	Il **a choisi** un partenaire. *He **chose** a partner.*
servir	servi	Claire **a servi** le café dans le salon. *Claire **served** the coffee in the living room.*

F. La dernière fois... ? Dites à votre partenaire la dernière fois que vous avez fait les choses suivantes. Puis, décrivez la situation.

À propos du vocabulaire: Review the expressions for indicating *when* in the past in *1er Thème* of this chapter.

Modèle: rougir
—*Quand est la dernière fois que tu as rougi?*
—*J'ai rougi hier soir quand j'ai oublié le nom de ma cousine.*

1. rougir
2. gagner à un match de tennis
3. blanchir
4. choisir un film classique en vidéo
5. dormir jusqu'à midi
6. servir un bon dîner
7. accueillir quelqu'un à l'aéroport
8. ne pas réussir à un examen

À propos de la structure: Infinitives in the negative are preceded by both **ne** and **pas** (**ne pas réussir**). Remember to put these two words on either side of the auxiliary verb when using the **passé composé.**

Structure: Le passé composé avec être

OBSERVATIONS

Erlène **est restée** trois jours chez Monique et André.

Erlène, Monique et André **sont allés** visiter le château à Fontainebleau.

Erlène **a rangé** sa chambre avant son départ.

Erlène **est allée** à Samois-sur-Seine pour passer un séjour° chez Monique et André. Elle **est partie** de la gare de Lyon à Paris à 8h31 et **est arrivée** à Fontainebleau à 9h14. Monique a accueilli Erlène à la gare. Les trains arrivent toujours à l'heure exacte en France. Erlène **est restée** trois jours chez Monique et André. Ensemble ils **sont allés** à Barbizon, et puis ils **sont rentrés** à Fontainebleau pour visiter le château et pour faire le marché. Avant de rentrer à Paris, Erlène a rangé sa chambre.

*Erlène **went** to Samois-sur-Seine to visit Monique and André. She **left** the Gare de Lyon in Paris at 8:31 and **arrived** in Fontainebleau at 9:14. Monique greeted Erlène at the station. Trains always arrive exactly on time in France. Erlène **stayed** three days at Monique and André's house. Together they **went** to Barbizon, and then they **returned** to Fontainebleau to visit the castle and to do the grocery shopping. Before returning to Paris, Erlène straightened up her room.*

un séjour: *a stay, a visit*

À propos de la culture: Trains leave from and arrive at their stations precisely on time in France, a legacy from Napoléon III.

2E THÈME: Mes expériences personnelles

Je **suis allé(e)** à Genève.	Nous **sommes parti(e)s** à 22 heures.
I went to Geneva.	*We left at 10 p.m.*
Es-tu **sorti(e)** avec Marc?	**Êtes**-vous **resté(e)(s)** le week-end?
Did you go out with Marc?	*Did you stay the weekend?*
Il **est entré** dans la bibliothèque.	Ils **sont montés** au deuxième étage.
He entered the library.	*They went up to the third floor.*
Elle **est arrivée** en retard.	Elles **sont descendues** au sous-sol.
She arrived late.	*They went down to the basement.*

STRATÉGIES D'ANALYSE

1. These verbs in boldface are in the **passé composé.** However, they do not use **avoir** as the auxiliary verb. What is the auxiliary verb marked in bold?

2. What happens to the past participle when **être** is used as the auxiliary verb?

NOTE CULTURELLE

Barbizon, une petite ville près de Fontainebleau, est célèbre pour avoir servi de lieu de séjour à des artistes célèbres, comme **Rousseau, Corot, Diaz, Dupré, Millet** et **Troyon,** vers la fin du XIXe siècle et au début du XXe siècle. Aujourd'hui à Barbizon il y a beaucoup de touristes qui cherchent de beaux tableaux peints et vendus par des artistes contemporains.

Réfléchissons: Si vous allez à Barbizon, quel genre de tableau est-ce que vous désirez y *(there)* trouver pour vous-même: un naïf, un impressionniste, un classique, un moderne, un réaliste?

PRÉCISIONS

À propos de la structure: You will learn which verbs use **être** as their auxiliary in the next section.

You have learned to conjugate verbs in the **passé composé** using **avoir** as the auxiliary verb: **(j'ai travaillé, nous avons choisi).**

• Certain verbs are conjugated with **être** rather than **avoir** as the auxiliary.

• The past participle of these verbs must agree with the *subject* in *number* and *gender.*

Il est parti.	Ils sont partis.
Elle est parti**e.**	Elles sont parti**es.**

• The past participle of verbs conjugated with **être** is actually functioning like an adjective agreeing with its subject. Sometimes the English equivalent meaning reflects this usage.

Elle **est morte.**	*She **died.** (or) She **is dead.***

- The negative and interrogative forms of verbs conjugated with **être** are formed the same way as verbs conjugated with **avoir**. In the negative, place the two parts of the negative (**ne... pas**) around the auxiliary verb.

> Elle **n'est pas** partie en taxi, elle est partie en métro.
> *She did**n't** leave by taxi; she left by subway.*

- When asking a question using inversion, invert the subject pronoun with the auxiliary verb.

> **Sommes-nous** arrivés à l'heure?   ***Have we** arrived on time?*
> Claudine, **es-tu** sortie avec Pierre?   *Claudine, **did you** go out with Pierre?*

 ote Culturelle

En France on appelle le niveau où on entre dans un bâtiment le **rez-de-chaussée°**. Les Français commencent à numéroter les étages au-dessus° du rez-de-chaussée. Ainsi **le premier étage** en France est celui qu'on appelle *the second floor* aux États-Unis. Après ça, il y a **le deuxième étage** (*the third floor* aux États-Unis), **le troisième étage** (*the fourth floor*), etc. **Le sous-sol** se trouve sous° le rez-de-chaussée.

Réfléchissons: À quel étage se trouve votre chambre à coucher? Et votre salle de classe?

rez-de-chaussée: *groundfloor*
au-dessus: *above*
sous: *below*

G. **Nous sommes sortis.** À tour de rôle avec votre partenaire, lisez les phrases suivantes. Remplacez les mots en italique par les mots entre parenthèses. Faites les changements nécessaires.

1. *Nous* sommes sortis de l'université. (je / vous / tu / mes amis / Monique)
2. *Paul* est allé au cinéma avec nous. (André et Monique / vous / tu / Christine)
3. *Je* suis arrivé(e) à l'heure. (nous / tu / André / vous / ils)
4. Après le film, *nous* sommes rentrés à la maison. (je / tu / vous / Monique / mes amis)
5. *Pierre* est parti de la maison. (vous / je / tu / Christine et Marc / nous)
6. *Je* ne suis pas allé(e) au cinéma avec les autres; *je* suis resté(e) à la maison. (nous / vous / Jean-Claude / tu / Anne-Marie et Sophie)

Vocabulaire: Des verbes avec être

OBSERVATIONS

La maison d'*être*

1. Après le travail M. Clovis **est allé** directement de son bureau à la maison.
2. Il **est arrivé** à la maison un peu fatigué.
3. Il **est entré** dans la maison par la porte principale.

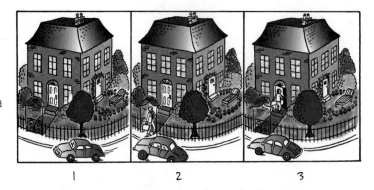

4. Puis il **est sorti** au jardin pour admirer ses fleurs.
5. Après une demi-heure de repos tout seul dans le jardin, M. Clovis **est retourné** à la maison.
6. Il **est rentré** dans la maison par la porte arrière.

7. Il **est descendu**° à la cave chercher une bouteille de vin pour le dîner.
8. Il **est tombé** dans l'escalier, se cognant la tête°. Mais il a réussi à protéger la bouteille de vin!
9. Un peu désorienté, il **est revenu**° à la salle à manger pour dîner avec la famille.

10. Pendant le dîner il **est tombé**° malade.
11. Il **est monté** à sa chambre.
12. Le médecin **est venu**°.

13. Pauvre M. Clovis! Il **est resté** au lit pendant deux jours pour se reposer.
14. Mais malgré° les efforts du médecin, il **est mort°**.
15. Son âme° **est partie** de son corps.

13   14   15

16

16. Son âme **est née** de nouveau au paradis.

Il est descendu: *He went down* **se cognant la tête:** *hitting his head* **il est revenu:** *he came back* **il est devenu:** *he became* **malgré:** *in spite of* **est venu:** *came* **il est mort:** *he died* **Son âme:** *His soul*

STRATÉGIES D'ANALYSE

Can you figure out anything that these verbs have in common that might place them into this special category?

PRÉCISIONS

You may want to use one of the following **aide-mémoire** to help you remember which verbs are in this set.

- They are verbs that express motion or movement from one place to another.
- They are the verbs that are used to tell the story of **la maison d'être**.
- They are verbs that do not take a direct object.
- The first letters of these verbs spell **DR. & MRS. VANDERTRAMP.**

Descendre	Je suis **descendu(e)** du train.	*I got off the train.*
Rentrer	Je suis **rentré(e)** à minuit.	*I came home at midnight.*
Monter	Je suis **monté(e)** dans le taxi.	*I got into the taxi.*
Rester	Je suis **resté(e)** au bureau.	*I stayed at the office.*
Sortir	Je suis **sorti(e)** avec mes amis.	*I went out with my friends.*
Venir	Je suis **venu(e)** à l'école à 7 heures.	*I came to school at 7:00.*
Aller	Je suis **allé(e)** au cinéma.	*I went to the movies.*
Naître	Je suis **né(e)** en 1979.	*I was born in 1979.*
Devenir	Je suis **devenu(e)** malade.	*I became ill.*
Entrer	Je suis **entré(e)** dans le théâtre.	*I entered the theater.*
Retourner	Je suis **retourné(e)** à Paris en 1995.	*I returned to Paris in 1995.*
Tomber	Je suis **tombé(e)** devant le café.	*I fell in front of the café.*
Revenir	Je suis **revenu(e)** à la salle de classe.	*I came back to the classroom.*
Arriver	Je suis **arrivé(e)** avant toi.	*I arrived before you.*
Mourir	Je suis **mort(e)** de peur.	*I died of fright.*
Partir	Je suis **parti(e)** avant midi.	*I left before noon.*

raconter: *to recount, to tell (a story)*
chaque fois: *each time*

H. **La maison d'*être*.** À tour de rôle avec votre partenaire, racontez° à nouveau l'histoire de **la maison d'*être*,** mais changez chaque fois° le rôle principal comme suggéré dans la liste suivante. Faites les changements nécessaires.

> **Modèle:** Mme Clovis
> *Mme Clovis est allée directement de son bureau à la maison.*
> *Elle est arrivée à la maison par la porte principale.*

1. Mme Clovis
2. M. et Mme Clovis
3. Moi
4. M. Clovis et moi

cette fois-ci: *this time*

I. **La maison d'*être* (suite).** Écrivez l'histoire de **la maison d'*être*,** et cette fois-ci°, c'est vous qui jouez le rôle principal, avec **Je** comme sujet des verbes.

souligner: *to underline*
surligner: *to highlight*

J. **Notre maison d'*être*.** Avec votre partenaire, écrivez une nouvelle histoire originale pour **la maison d'*être*.** Soulignez° (ou surlignez°) tous les seize verbes qui utilisent **être** au **passé composé**.

PRONONCIATION: Les sons [o] et [ɔ]

The French vowel represented by the phonetic symbol [o] is similar to the sound in the English word *boat*. It is most commonly written **au** or **eau**, as in the words **chaud** and **beau**. It may also be written **o** when at the end of a syllable, as in the words **trop** or **photo**. The sound [ɔ], called an *open o*, is written **o** and is similar to the vowel of the English word *awe*, except that the lips should be rounded when pronouncing it.

Repeat the following words after your instructor, paying attention to your pronunciation of the sounds [o] and [ɔ]:

[o]	[ɔ]
faux	formation
grossir	obéir
mot	mort
l'eau	l'hôpital

À vous! With a partner, take turns reading these sentences that feature the sounds [o] and [ɔ].

1. Aujourd'hui, il faut organiser mes notes.
2. Mon collègue est au téléphone.
3. Le chauffeur s'appelle Paul.
4. J'ai un problème avec mon ordinateur.
5. Madame de Beauséant est morte.
6. Nous sommes sortis avec nos amis au restaurant.

POUR DÉVELOPPER VOS IDÉES

Thematic objective: To identify life experiences (outside the contexts of work and school) that have contributed to your personal development

Présentation: La vie personnelle contribue à nos talents

POUR SAISIR L'ESSENTIEL: In this excerpt from a **lettre de candidature,** Richard tells how the skills he developed on his trips abroad with the city choir contribute to his qualifications for the workplace.

1. Read the excerpt from the letter and make a list of the experiences that you think might be valuable to him in his job search.
2. Next read the advertisement for the job to identify the qualifications sought for the position. Do any of Richard's qualities match those sought by the company? If you were the personnel director for Hôtels Essor, would you consider giving him an interview? Why (not)?

En plus de mes expériences professionnelles, j'ai organisé plusieurs séjours à l'étranger pour la chorale municipale de ma ville. Pendant ces voyages, j'ai réussi à trouver des solutions à plusieurs malentendus°, et j'ai développé une sensibilité aux besoins des voyageurs. Puisque° je suis né à la Jamaïque, où j'ai habité jusqu'à l'âge de treize ans, je parle couramment anglais. Nous avons quitté Kingston en 1990, mais nous y sommes retournés chaque année pour les vacances. Grâce à° ces visites annuelles, je connais très bien les Caraïbes.

Hôtels Essor

Poste: Responsable des relations publiques dans le domaine de l'hôtellerie et restauration, basé aux îles Caraïbes.

Mission: Vous établissez un bon rapport entre le service de l'hôtel et la clientèle. Vous analysez personnellement les questions/plaintes° et offrez des solutions. Vous préparez des rapports pour le chef de service.

Profil: Diplôme universitaire ou l'équivalent. Vous avez une excellente aptitude à la communication, une bonne présentation et une grande facilité de contact. Vous êtes bilingue français/anglais, l'espagnol est un avantage.

REF: JL33

un malentendu: *misunderstanding*

Puisque: *Since, Given that*

une plainte: *complaint*

Grâce à: *Thanks to*

2ᴱ THÈME: Mes expériences personnelles

deux cent cinquante-sept   257

K. **Encore des compétences.** Indiquez (✓) à quel point vous avez les compétences ou qualités énumérées dans la liste.

Non, pas du tout.	Oui, un peu.	Compétences/Qualités	Oui, plutôt.	Oui, beaucoup.
		• la confiance en moi		
		• la fiabilité°		
		• la persévérance		
		• la facilité de contacts		
		• un sens des priorités		
		• un sens de l'organisation		
		• la capacité de résister au stress		
		• la capacité de motiver les gens		
		• la capacité d'équilibrer mon emploi du temps		
		• la capacité de négocier un consensus		
		• la capacité de m'adapter à des situations diverses		
		• (autres ???)		

fiabilité: *reliability*

 L. **Les leçons de la vie.** Réfléchissez sur les compétences et les qualités que vous avez en bonne quantité. (Celles dans les colonnes «Oui, plutôt.» et «Oui, beaucoup.» de l'Exercice K.) Essayez de déterminer comment vous avez appris ou développé ces qualités. Cherchez au moins deux expériences, à part° le travail et les études, qui ont contribué à vos compétences générales. Écrivez deux ou trois paragraphes de trois ou quatre phrases où vous expliquez (1) la situation, (2) ce que vous avez fait et (3) la compétence que vous en avez gagné°. Consultez les suggestions **Activités de la vie personnelle** pour stimuler vos réflexions.

à part: *besides*

que vous en avez gagné: *that you gained from it*

Modèle 1: *Il y a trois ans, quand ma mère est tombée malade, j'ai dû m'occuper de la maison et de mes deux sœurs. J'ai eu beaucoup de responsabilités pour la première fois de ma vie. Grâce à cette expérience, j'ai développé un sens de l'organisation et des priorités. Maintenant j'ai une meilleure capacité de résister au stress et j'apprécie mieux l'importance de la fiabilité.*

Modèle 2: *L'année dernière, j'ai fait un voyage avec deux amis. Nous sommes allés en Allemagne, et nous sommes restés chez des amis. J'ai rencontré beaucoup de gens, et j'ai eu beaucoup de nouvelles expériences. Pendant le voyage, j'ai appris à m'adapter à des situations diverses. Et j'ai gagné de la confiance en moi.*

À propos de la structure: The **passé composé** is used to tell what happened or what someone did. We use it to say what happened, when it started, when it ended, or how long it lasted.

There is another verb form used to tell about things that used to happen, things that were happening, or to describe how something was in the past. You'll learn that form later.

À propos de la communication: Don't try to memorize the list of suggestions; just learn those that help you communicate your own experiences.

Activités de la vie personnelle

Événements personnels
grandir
maigrir
grossir
tomber malade
apprendre

Communauté
organiser, participer à,
assister à, contribuer à,
aller
~~~~~~
festivals communautaires
projets municipaux
symphonie
musée
théâtre

Sports
commencer à faire,
apprendre à,
gagner un trophée
~~~~~~
jouer au football
faire du volley
faire du cyclisme
faire de la gymnastique
nager

Église/Clubs
participer à, aider, animer
~~~~~~
chorale
colonie de vacances
scouts

Voyage
aller, retourner, visiter,
passer les vacances à,
faire un voyage

Bénévolat
organiser, participer à, aider,
contribuer à
~~~~~~
resto du cœur
hôpital
enfants défavorisés

M. **On raconte ses expériences.** Choisissez une de vos expériences à communi-quer° aux autres. Avant la classe, pratiquez en lisant° votre paragraphe sur une cassette pour perfectionner votre prononciation et votre style. (Essayez de mémoriser cette petite anecdote en français.) En classe, travaillez en groupe de trois ou quatre, et racontez° votre expérience à vos partenaires.

communiquer: *tell*
en lisant: *by reading*

raconter: *recount, tell*

DÉCOUVERTE

You may already realize that your experiences away from work and school are valuable for your job search. French employers often draw significant inferences about personality and character from the ways candidates spend their leisure time. *«Les loisirs ou centres d'intérêt prennent aussi une place importante dans le CV. On imagine la personnalité d'un candidat avec ses loisirs. […] Jogging, lecture, voyage, etc. sont significatifs: ils désignent quelqu'un qui s'intéresse à sa santé, cultivé et aimant faire des voyages.»*

[CV MAGAZINE, N° 1, 1996, p. 11.]

1. Read the DÉCOUVERTE note. Then decide what you consider to be the main point of interest in the information and ideas presented. Each person in the class may have a different opinion about this.

2. Identify the phrases that support your perception of the main point.

3. Discuss your opinions with classmates to broaden or reinforce your interpretation.

3ᴱ THÈME: Mes expériences par rapport à une carrière

Objective: To talk about previous work and educational experiences as they enhance career opportunities

PRÉSENTATION: Un coup d'œil sur le thème

Stratégies

1. Before you look at the following ads, brainstorm with classmates to list the kinds of information you look for in employment ads.

Marianne recherche un nouveau poste.

Yves pense à changer de travail.

Secrétaire

Poste offert: Secrétaire de direction pour le groupe d'aide humanitaire «SCHR» dépendant de la Croix Rouge, Oxfam, etc. Basé à Genève.

Mission: Vous êtes chargé(e) de

- développer des stratégies d'action
- d'assister aux réunions
- de promouvoir° l'organisation et la collecte de fonds

Profil:

supermarché du cœur

- avoir 5 ans d'expérience dans le travail humanitaire
- être diplômé — *Médecins sans frontières*
- maîtriser anglais écrit et parlé

Contacter Jean-Marc COBAULT, 15 rue Moulin, 75009 PARIS, REF: 917.L/G

Afrique Francophone

Directeur(trice) commercial marketing exportation
Perspectives:
- Vous animez une équipe de 4 à 6 commerciaux.
- Vous initiez° des études de marchés et analysez les besoins de la clientèle.
- Vous définissez et vous assurez la mise en place° de la stratégie pour les différents segments de clients du marché public.

Qualification et Expérience:
- Âge 35 ans *travail chez Globaltronics*
- Formation universitaire, expérience 5 ans réussie en équipe de vente
- Sens commercial, autonome°, bon(ne) négociateur(trice) ✓
- Goût des voyages, très bon français et anglais

Adresser lettre, CV et photo à:
Service de Recrutement
18, rue Gustave Eiffel
13010 Marseille
REF 005.G2

---

promouvoir: *to promote* / **initiez:** *initiate* / **mise en place:** *establishment* / **autonome:** *able to work independently*

2. Examine the ad that Marianne is studying. Identify the major categories of information in it.

3. How well do these categories of information meet your expectations?

4. What are the corresponding sections in the advertisement for the job in Africa?

5. Marianne and Yves have marked up their ads, noting the points that are most relevant for them. Based on the items marked, infer some of the qualifications they might have for the positions that interest them. Writing complete sentences, make a list of the qualifications you identify.

   Modèle: *Yves a beaucoup voyagé.*

6. Work with your partner to embellish your statements. Give your imagination free rein for this exercise.

   Modèle: *Yves a beaucoup voyagé. Il a fait des voyages à Hong Kong, à Berlin et à Londres. L'année dernière il est allé à Madrid. Il a assisté à plusieurs conférences importantes. Il a beaucoup appris.*

7. Can any of the sentences that you created with your partner be adapted to describe your own experiences? If so, be sure to keep a copy of them.

POUR DÉVELOPPER VOTRE FRANÇAIS

Structure: Le passé composé des verbes pronominaux

OBSERVATIONS

Isabelle **s'est occupée** des enfants le week-end dernier.

Jean-Louis **s'est servi** fréquemment de l'Internet le semestre passé pour son cours de marketing.

Je **me suis installé(e)** au bureau.
I got settled at the office.

Nous **nous sommes rattrapé(e)s** dans notre travail.
We got caught up in our work.

Tu **t'es renseigné(e)** sur les dates?
Did you get the information about the dates?

Il **s'est occupé** des messages du patron.
He attended to the messages from the boss.

Elle **s'est** vite **habituée** à travailler quatre jours par semaine.
She got quickly accustomed to working four days a week.

Vous **êtes-vous** bien **amusé(e)(s)?**
Did you have a good time?

L'année passée ils **se sont entraînés** ensemble au gymnase près du bureau.
Last year they worked out together at the gym near the office.

Elles **se sont préparées** pour les interviews.
They prepared themselves for the interviews.

STRATÉGIES D'ANALYSE

1. Do these sentences refer to activities in the present, past, or future? What gives you that information?
2. What is the auxiliary verb in these examples, **avoir** or **être**?
3. Where have you already used **être** as the auxiliary verb in the **passé composé**?
4. Can you tell what happens to the past participle with these pronominal verbs in the **passé composé**?

PRÉCISIONS

À propos du vocabulaire: Note that since **se tromper de** means, in general, to be mistaken about something, it takes on a more specific meaning from its context.

- Pronominal verbs use **être** as their helping verb in the **passé composé**. In most cases, the past participle agrees with the pronoun (**me, te, se, nous, vous**).

Oh là là! Je **me suis trompé(e)** de numéro de téléphone.
Oh dear! I dialed the wrong telephone number.

Est-ce que tu **t'es chargé(e)** de trouver un restaurant pour le déjeuner d'affaires?
Did you take responsibility for finding a restaurant for the luncheon meeting?

Elle **s'est informée** sur les nouveaux produits pendant sa première semaine dans l'entreprise.
She acquainted herself with the new products during her first week with the company.

Nous **nous sommes appliqué(e)s** à finir le projet en avance.
We dedicated ourselves to finishing the project ahead of schedule.

Comment est-ce que vous **vous êtes préparé** pour l'examen final?
How did you prepare for the final exam?

Ils **se sont** vite **adaptés** aux nouvelles méthodes.
They quickly adapted to the new methods.

A. Nous nous sommes occupés du projet. À tour de rôle avec votre partenaire, lisez les phrases suivantes. Remplacez les mots en italique avec les mots entre parenthèses et faites les changements nécessaires.

1. *Je* me suis réveillé(e) ce matin avant six heures. (vous / nous / tu / Jeannette)
2. *Nous* nous sommes dépêchés pour arriver à l'heure au bureau. (je / vous / tu / Paul et Marc)
3. *Jeannette* s'est installée immédiatement devant son ordinateur. (tu / vous / je / Marc et moi)
4. *Tu* t'es occupé(e) du nouveau projet. (nous / je / Paul / vous)
5. Est-ce que *vous* vous êtes préparé(e) pour la présentation à votre groupe? (Nicole / tu / nous / Jeannette et Paul)
6. *Nous* nous sommes appliqués pour finir la présentation en avance. (vous / tu / Jeannette / je)

B. Ma journée jusqu'à maintenant. Cochez (✓) les activités dans la liste suivante que vous avez déjà faites avant d'arriver au cours de français aujourd'hui. Ensuite, à tour de rôle avec votre partenaire, racontez les activités que vous avez cochées pour décrire votre journée d'aujourd'hui jusqu'à maintenant.

Modèle: *Avant d'arriver au cours aujourd'hui, je me suis réveillé(e) à 6h30.*

✓ se réveiller à ? heures
☐ s'habiller
☐ se dépêcher
☐ se laver
☐ s'occuper des tâches domestiques
☐ s'occuper des enfants
☐ se préparer pour les cours
☐ s'installer devant l'ordinateur

☐ s'installer à une table dans un café
☐ s'entraîner
☐ se renseigner sur les actualités°
☐ s'énerver
☐ se promener
☐ s'inscrire à un cours
☐ se servir du courrier électronique
☐ se rattraper dans le travail

les actualités (f.): *news of the day*

C. Comment nous nous sommes occupé(e)s... Travaillez avec votre partenaire pour compléter la fiche suivante. Utilisez la liste de l'exercice précédent pour faire une comparaison entre vos activités avant le cours et celles de votre partenaire.

Modèle: *Moi, je me suis occupé(e) des tâches domestiques.*
Mon (Ma) partenaire s'est entraîné(e).
Tous les deux, nous nous sommes installés devant l'ordinateur.

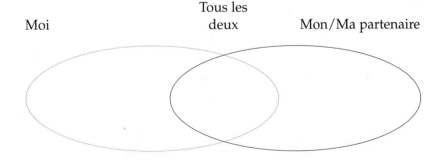

Moi   Tous les deux   Mon/Ma partenaire

À propos du vocabulaire: Refer to the **Lexique** in *Chapitre 5* for vocabulary using pronominal verbs.

Remember that not all verbs are pronominal. It is possible that you will include some verbs in your paragraph that do not require the extra pronoun.

D. **Ma journée jusqu'à maintenant (suite).** Écrivez un paragraphe pour décrire vos activités d'aujourd'hui avant d'arriver au cours. Utilisez au moins cinq verbes pronominaux différents dans vos phrases. À tour de rôle avec votre partenaire, lisez vos phrases.

> **Modèle:** *Ce matin je me suis réveillé(e) à six heures précises. Je me suis entraîné(e) jusqu'à sept heures. Puis, je me suis lavé(e) et je me suis habillé(e) avant de prendre le petit déjeuner. Je me suis occupé(e) de la vaisselle et ensuite j'ai fait mes devoirs avant de quitter la maison pour aller à l'université.*

à la fois: *at a time*

E. **On vérifie....** Relisez votre paragraphe à votre partenaire, une phrase à la fois°. Votre partenaire va répéter vos activités d'aujourd'hui pour vérifier les détails.

> **Modèle:** —*Ce matin je me suis réveillé(e) à six heures précises.*
> —*Ah, bon! Ce matin tu t'es réveillé(e) à six heures précises.*

entendre: *to hear*
des bribes (f.): *excerpts*

F. **Des conversations au café.** Vous êtes à une table dans une terrasse de café avec votre partenaire. Vous pouvez entendre° quelques bribes° des conversations des autres clients dans le café, mais vous n'entendez pas tout. Il est nécessaire de tirer des inférences pour tout comprendre. À tour de rôle avec votre partenaire, complétez les conversations suivantes.

Conversation 1:

1. —Pourquoi est-ce que tu es arrivé en retard ce matin?
   —Parce que je ___*me suis*___ occupé des enfants. Ma femme est à Lyon, chez ses parents.

Conversation 2:

2. —À quelle heure est-ce que tu _____ réveillé(e) ce matin?
   —À 7h45. Alors je _____ dépêché(e) pour arriver à l'heure!

Conversation 3:

3. —Regarde! Qui est la femme qui _____ installée à la table avec Jean-Claude?
   —Aucune idée°.

Aucune idée: *No idea*

Conversation 4:

4. —Pourquoi est-ce que vous _____ si bien habillé(e) aujourd'hui?
   —Vous trouvez? J'ai rendez-vous cet après-midi avec de nouveaux clients.

Conversation 5:

5. —Quand est-ce que tu vas te préparer pour la présentation devant le patron?
   —C'est déjà fait. Je _____ installé(e) devant mon ordinateur hier soir à 7 heures. Enfin, je _____ couché(e) à minuit, une fois mon travail fini.

Conversation 6:

6. —Tu vas faire un voyage avec ta mère?
   —Mais oui. Nous _____ organisé(e)s la semaine dernière. Nous allons passer deux semaines en Europe.

Conversation 7:

7. —Paul aime son nouveau boulot?

   —Pas du tout. L'année dernière il _____ habitué à travailler trois jours par semaine. Maintenant il travaille quatre jours et tous les week-ends. Il n'est pas content.

Conversation 8:

8. —Comment est-ce que vos collègues ont trouvé si vite ces informations?

   —Ils _____ servis du courrier électronique.

Note Culturelle

En France, si on fait un compliment à quelqu'un sur son apparence physique, ses talents, etc., la bonne réponse n'est pas **Merci**. Une phrase qui reflète le compliment, telle que **Vous trouvez?** ou **Tu trouves?** est préférable.

G. La mise en pratique. Utilisez les expressions de la fiche suivante pour décrire quelques activités et événements au passé. Écrivez au moins une phrase avec chaque verbe.

   Modèle: *Mes collègues se sont adaptés aux nouvelles technologies.*

je tu vous nous mon ami(e) mes ami(e)s mes ami(e)s et moi ma famille ma famille et moi mes collègues mes collègues et moi le professeur le professeur et moi mes camarades de classe	s'adapter	• à un emploi du temps flexible • au travail en équipe • aux nouvelles technologies • à la vie universitaire • à beaucoup de travail • à avoir des enfants à la maison
	se charger	• de l'éducation des enfants (de...) • du budget de l'entreprise/la maison • des préparatifs pour le déjeuner d'affaires/le voyage à... • de la présentation au groupe/à la classe
	s'occuper	• des devoirs pendant le week-end dernier • d'un projet personnel • des enfants hier soir • des tâches domestiques • de la présentation pour le cours
	se servir	• du courrier électronique (pour communiquer avec...) • de l'aide de... • d'un aide-mémoire dans mon cours (de...)

Structure: Le passé composé des verbes pronominaux à la forme négative

OBSERVATIONS

—Vous êtes en retard. Est-ce que vous vous êtes occupé des enfants ce matin?

—Non, **je ne me suis pas occupé** des enfants. Le problème, c'est que **je ne me suis pas levé** quand le réveille-matin° a sonné.

le réveille-matin: *alarm clock*

—Est-ce que tu t'es servie du courrier électronique pour communiquer avec ta famille?

—Non, **je ne me suis pas servie** du courrier électronique cette fois-ci. J'ai téléphoné.

STRATÉGIES D'ANALYSE

1. Where do the **ne** and **pas** go in negative statements with pronominal verbs?
2. Where does the reflexive pronoun go?
3. Does the past participle still agree with the reflexive pronoun?

PRÉCISIONS

• To negate a pronominal verb in the **passé composé**, put **ne** before and **pas (encore)** or **jamais** after the helping verb. The reflexive pronoun goes immediately before the helping verb, staying closer to the verb than the negative form **ne**.

Elle **ne s'est pas** dépêchée, et elle est arrivée en retard.
*She did**n't** hurry, and she arrived late.*

Ils **ne se** sont **jamais** absentés du cours.
*They have **never** been absent from class.*

H. **Je ne me suis pas habitué(e) à...** À tour de rôle avec votre partenaire, lisez les phrases suivantes. Remplacez les mots en italique par les mots entre parenthèses et faites les changements nécessaires.

1. *Je* ne me suis pas encore habitué(e) à la vie universitaire. (vous / tu / nous / mon/ma camarade de chambre)
2. *Robert* ne s'est pas bien amusé ce week-end. (tu / je / nous / vous / mes amis)
3. *Nous* ne nous sommes pas occupé(e)s du budget la semaine dernière. (le patron / les comptables / je / vous)
4. *Vous* ne vous êtes pas encore absenté(e) de ce cours. (le prof / les étudiants / nous / tu)
5. *Je* ne me suis pas dépêché(e) ce matin. (mes enfants / mon/ma conjoint(e) / vous / nous)
6. *Vous* ne vous êtes pas adapté(e) à un emploi du temps flexible. (je / tu / nous / Geneviève et Dominique)

I. **Ce qu'on n'a pas fait.** Dites à votre partenaire qui parmi vos proches n'a pas fait les choses suivantes. Servez-vous des expressions **ne... pas, pas encore, jamais.**

> **Modèle:** s'énerver au travail/en classe
> *Ma surveillante° ne s'est jamais énervée au travail.*

surveillant(e): *supervisor*

1. s'énerver au travail/en classe
2. s'amuser pendant le week-end
3. s'habituer à la vie universitaire
4. se dépêcher pour arriver au travail/en classe à l'heure
5. s'occuper de ses devoirs samedi soir
6. s'amuser pendant les vacances l'été dernier
7. se dépêcher pour arriver en avance à un rendez-vous
8. s'entraîner dans un gym
9. s'absenter de ce cours
10. se reposer le week-end dernier

J. **Qui ne s'est jamais... ?** Trouvez quelqu'un parmi vos camarades de classe qui n'a jamais fait les choses suivantes. Demandez la signature de la personne que vous identifiez pour chaque numéro.

> **Modèle:** —*Est-ce que tu t'es jamais occupé(e) d'un client furieux au travail?*
> —*Non, je ne me suis jamais occupé(e) d'un client furieux.*
> —*Alors, signe ici, s'il te plaît.*
> ou —*Bien sûr, je me suis déjà occupé(e) d'un client furieux.*
> —*Merci quand même°.*

Merci quand même: *Thanks anyway.*

1. s'occuper d'un client furieux au travail
2. se réveiller en retard
3. se coucher dans un train
4. s'entraîner dans un gym
5. se servir du courrier électronique
6. s'adapter au travail en équipe
7. s'énerver au travail
8. s'appliquer aux études supérieures
9. s'occuper des enfants d'un(e) collègue
10. se charger d'un budget

PRONONCIATION: Les sons [œ] et [ø]

To pronounce correctly the French vowel sound represented by the symbol [œ]:
    Round your lips as if to say the English word *open*;
    Pronounce *a* as in *aid*.
This sound may be written **eu** or **œu**, as in the words **leur** and **sœur**.
    At the end of a word, **eu, eue,** and **eux** are pronounced [ø], a vowel similar to that in the English word *foot*.

Repeat the following words after your instructor, paying particular attention to your pronunciation of the vowels [œ] and [ø].

[œ]	[ø]
cœur	ennuyeux
heure	cheveux
immeuble	neveu
meilleur	mieux
seul	queue

À vous! Read the following sentences with a partner.
1. J'ai les yeux bruns et les cheveux blonds.
2. Mon neveu est paresseux.
3. Ma sœur va chez le coiffeur.
4. Jacques, c'est le meilleur vendeur que je connais.
5. Elle a fait la queue pendant deux heures.
6. J'ai peur d'être ennuyeux.

POUR DÉVELOPPER VOS IDÉES

Thematic objective: To relate your own skills, knowledge, and interests to those defined in some specific job offerings

Présentation: La vie personnelle contribue à nos compétences

POUR SAISIR L'ESSENTIEL: The following employment ads are categorized into five sectors.

1. Identify these five sectors and rate each of them according to its appeal for you. Use expressions like these for the rating:
   • *Ça m'intéresse beaucoup.*
   • *Ce n'est pas mal.*
   • *Je ne voudrais pas travailler dans ce domaine.*
2. Of the six jobs described in these ads, which would you most like to have (either for the summer or as a career)? Identify the positive qualities of the job(s) that you have selected.

3. Identify the requirements for the job(s) that you selected. Which ones do you currently possess? Will you obtain other qualifications during the next few years (either through your education or through other experiences)?

4. Skim through the remainder of the ads to find expressions to describe an ideal job. Make a list of these expressions for your portfolio.

5. Skim the ads again to find expressions that describe your general qualifications for work. Make a list of these expressions for your portfolio.

Secteur Tourisme

Professeur d'aérobic

Mission: Travailler dans un contexte de tourisme, loisirs et vacances.

Profil:
- Être en bonne forme
- Disposer d'une expérience professionnelle réussie
- Avoir une excellente présentation
- Être âgé(e) de 18 à 25 ans
- Parler couramment anglais

Rémunération intéressante

Adresser votre CV et deux photos.
REF FN.562

Directeur(trice) pour un centre de vacances/séjours linguistiques pour les enfants et adolescents âgés de moins de seize ans. Nous proposons des activités telles que séjours ski, randonnées, soirées linguistiques.

Qualifications recherchées:
- Faire preuve de° fiabilité
- Parler anglais et allemand couramment
- Expérience réussie avec les jeunes personnes
- Bonnes connaissances des sports
- Bonne culture générale

Adresser lettre, CV et photo.
REF LM.091

faire preuve de: *demonstrate*

Secteur Domicile

Gardienne d'enfant

Famille espagnole habitant la Grèce recherche une gardienne expérimentée pour leur enfant (2 ans).

Il faut:
- Fournir d'excellentes références professionnelles
- Être non fumeuse
- Aimer le bord de la mer et être bonne nageuse
- Avoir une bonne culture

Adresser lettre, CV et 4 coupons réponse°.
REF 1357

Informatique

Informaticien(ne)s recherché(e)s pour maintenance d'ordinateurs dans un cadre scolaire

Mission: Vous êtes chargé(e) de la réparation et de l'entretien° de 50 appareils de type IBM. Vous installez les nouveaux logiciels et contrôlez la vérification antivirus.

Profil: Vous avez:
- de bonnes connaissances des derniers logiciels et de l'Internet
- la capacité de régler votre emploi du temps
- le sens de l'organisation

Adresser lettre, CV et 2 coupons réponse°.
REF PR.551

un entretien: *upkeep*

coupon réponse: *postal coupons (for return postage)*

MÉTIERS SCIENCES HUMAINES

Historien d'entreprise

Mission: Vous constituez les archives de la société; recueillez des documents et témoignages qui servent à rapporter les étapes de développement de la société; vous travaillez avec des cadres pour exploiter vos connaissances dans la publicité et dans les décisions internes de l'entreprise.

Qualités nécessaires:
- Rigueur de méthode
- Esprit d'analyse et de synthèse pour étudier et faire parler les documents°
- Souci de la vérité°
- Bonne culture générale
- Mémoire
- Curiosité
- Goût de lecture

Adresser lettre et CV.
REF MC.5546

Métiers de Commerce

Entreprise d'exportation cherche un **Chargé d'études:**

Vous rassemblez° les documents et les informations nécessaires à déterminer l'influence des campagnes publicitaires et des nouveaux emballages° sur la vente de nos produits.

Profil:
- Diplômé en sciences économiques
- Rigueur et organisation pour mener les analyses
- Esprit d'analyse et de synthèse pour traiter les informations
- Goût de voyages

Adresser lettre et CV.
REF LH.7801

rassembler: *to gather, assemble*
un emballage: *packaging*

étudier et faire parler les documents: *study the documents and "make them tell their stories"*
le souci de la vérité: *concern for truth*

K. **Le premier pas vers** *(step toward)* **un emploi.** Examinez les petites annonces dans ce chapitre afin de° choisir l'emploi que vous trouvez le plus intéressant ou le plus approprié à vos compétences. Ensuite, faites une liste des compétences et des qualités recherchées pour le poste. Enfin, examinez votre liste et cochez (✔) celles que vous possédez. (Cherchez les petites annonces aux pages 242, 257, 269 et 272.)

L. **On cherche à se vendre** *(To convince people of one's ability, qualities).* Pour chacune des qualifications que vous avez cochées dans l'exercice précédent, écrivez un paragraphe où vous expliquez comment vous avez gagné cette compétence ou comment vous avez développé cette qualité. Précisez la qualification et détaillez ce que vous avez fait pour l'avoir.

M. **On s'entraide** *(Help one another).* Demandez à votre partenaire d'examiner vos paragraphes et de faire des suggestions. En examinant les paragraphes de votre partenaire, vérifiez (1) la clarté de son expression et (2) la force de ses assertions. Puis, (3) vérifiez l'exactitude de la grammaire. Après avoir examiné les paragraphes, utilisez les expressions suivantes pour discuter les idées. Enfin, refaites vos paragraphes pour les perfectionner°.

Expressions pour commenter les idées:

Ça, c'est clair. ↔ Je ne comprends pas bien cela.

Ça, c'est bon, parce qu'on cherche une personne… ↔ Ici le rapport est moins évident.

Stratégies

As you proofread your partner's paper, focus on the use of the **passé composé,** since this is new and apt to present the greatest problems. Use the following checklist of potential problems as a guide.

1. choice of auxiliary verb **(avoir / être)**
   *J'**ai** fait un stage… / Je **suis** allé(e) à…*

2. agreement of auxiliary verb with the subject

3. agreement of past participle with subject (if the auxiliary is **être**)
   *Nous sommes arrivé**s** en…*

4. pronoun agrees with subject
   *Je **me** suis adapté(e) à…*

If you notice a mistake, just circle it and write the number from this list of potential problems as a reference.

1. *J'ai allé à…*

DÉCOUVERTE

The cover letter for the CV is sometimes called a **lettre de motivation.** *Le magazine de l'emploi* explains it this way:

La lettre de motivation permet° d'évaluer votre intérêt et votre enthousiasme à intégrer un certain type d'entreprise [pour] y exercer certaines fonctions à un niveau de responsabilité bien défini°. À partir de° l'annonce que vous avez sélectionnée dans la presse, vous devez dans votre lettre décrire succinctement où, quand, comment et dans quelles circonstances vos différentes fonctions passées (en accord avec celles décrites dans l'annonce) vous ont amené° au niveau de responsabilités ou de connaissances actuelles°.

[n° 18, mars–avril 1997, p. 14]

permet: *lets (the reader)*

exercer certaines fonctions à un niveau de responsabilité bien défini: *to perform certain duties at a well-defined level of responsibility*
À partir de: *Beginning from*
vous ont amené: *have led you*
actuelles: *current*

1. Read the DÉCOUVERTE note. Then decide what you consider to be the main point of interest in the information and ideas presented. Each person in the class may have a different opinion about this.

2. Identify the phrases that support your perception of the main point.

3. Discuss your opinions with classmates to broaden or reinforce your interpretation.

Synthèse des idées sur les découvertes. Based on your examination and discussions of the **DÉCOUVERTE** notes throughout the chapter, draw a (some) general conclusion(s) about French attitudes, values, or procedures in recruiting and hiring new employees.

ÉCOUTONS: L'interview professionnelle

You will hear two telephone interviews with people applying for the position described in the advertisement below. First, listen for the applicants' specific qualifications for the job of concierge. Then consider more general qualities that they exhibit (or fail to exhibit) during the interviews. Finally, decide which of the two applicants you would hire, based on the information in the ad and the responses in the interviews. Begin by reading the employment advertisement.

Hôtel Mercure International

recherche assistant(e) concierge
à mi-temps pour le nouvel hôtel.

Responsabilités:

- Vous accueillez la clientèle, et vous êtes responsable de leur confort dès leur arrivée jusqu'à leur départ.
- Vous les renseignez sur les services de l'hôtel (garage, blanchisserie, commande de repas, boutiques, etc.)
- Vous vous informez sur les attractions et les autres services du quartier. Et vous donnez des conseils selon les besoins des clients.
- Vous êtes responsable du personnel qui travaille dans le hall (bagagistes, voituriers, grooms°).

Qualifications et expériences:

- Vous avez une bonne présentation et un bon sens des relations humaines.
- Vous avez au moins 20 ans.
- Vous êtes bilingue français/anglais. (Une deuxième langue étrangère est fort recommandée.)
- Vous êtes courtois(e) et discret/discrète.
- Vous avez une expérience d'au moins un an dans le domaine de tourisme.

Contacter Tom Legrand Tél. 04.87.28.02.54

---

groom: *bellman*

A. **On identifie les qualifications.** Écoutez ces entrevues téléphoniques et identifiez (✓) les qualifications mentionnées pour chaque candidat(e).

Qualifications ⇨ Candidat(e) ⇩	Parle anglais	Parle une troisième langue	Diplôme universitaire	Expérience dans le domaine du tourisme
Mme Tremblay				
M. Galbert				

B. **On fait l'évaluation préliminaire.** Considérez toutes les informations données dans les conversations téléphoniques avec les candidats. Écoutez non seulement les paroles mais aussi leur façon de parler. Faites attention à ce qu'ils disent et aussi à ce qu'ils ne disent pas. Puis, indiquez (✓) vos impressions sur la fiche.

Candidat(e) ⇨ Degré ⇨	Mme Tremblay peu / assez / beaucoup / trop	M. Galbert peu / assez / beaucoup / trop
Confiance en soi		
Compétence		

Bonne
  présentation
  téléphonique		

Ambition		
Flexibilité		
Votre commentaire *personnel:*		

C. On prend la décision. Pour chaque candidat(e), faites deux listes. Dans la première liste, écrivez les «Pour», les arguments en faveur de cette personne. Dans la deuxième liste, écrivez les «Contre», les arguments contre l'embauche de ce candidat/cette candidate. Enfin, décidez le meilleur candidat/la meilleure candidate.

Modèle:

Louise Tremblay		*Serge Galbert*	
Pour	**Contre**	**Pour**	**Contre**

ÉLABORATION DE PERSPECTIVE

1. Read the **lettre de candidature** on the next page and the "how-to" suggestions surrounding it, noting any information or ideas that relate to your discussions of the **Découverte** notes.

2. Examine the passages that you noted to determine their significance for your conclusions regarding the **Découverte.** Writing complete sentences (in English), articulate your perceptions, so that you can communicate them clearly in class discussion. Remember to include references to verbiage in the **lettre de candidature** to support your assertions.

3. Discuss your insights with your classmates, taking notes on their interpretations of the material.

4. Write a paragraph with the following components:
   - a thesis statement, summarizing your views
   - several sentences in which you offer detailed support for your views
   - a conclusion, in which you tell what additional information you would like to have on the subject

Vos coordonnées
(prénom, nom,
adresse, téléphone)

Date et lieu d'envoi

Les coordonnées du recruteur ou
de l'annonce

Le début de la lettre :
«Madame», «Monsieur» ou
«Messieurs» si vous ne
connaissez pas le sexe du
destinataire

L'introduction. Par exemple:
«Je vous propose ma
candidature pour le poste
de… »
«Veuillez trouver ci-joint
mon dossier° de candidature
au poste de… »

En deux ou trois
paragraphes, développez
les informations qui
vont concrètement
répondre au besoin
de l'entreprise:

Votre formation

Votre expérience,
mentionnant vos capacités
et qualités

Vos petits boulots

Vos langues

Vos loisirs et centres
d'intérêt

Une ou deux lignes pour
proposer une rencontre

Une formule de politesse
simple

Martine RUIS
15, rue St.-Jean
21000 DIJON
Tél.: 03 80 21 45 42

Dijon, le 18 février 2000

Maurois & Cie
28, rue de la Chouette
44000 NANTES
À l'attention de Madame KRIEG

Madame,

J'ai le plaisir de vous adresser ma candidature pour le poste de…

Diplômée de l'École Supérieure de Commerce de Rennes, j'ai des connaissances approfondies° en gestion financière. Pendant mes études j'ai eu l'occasion de préparer plusieurs budgets. Grâce à cette expérience j'ai appris à faire attention aux détails dans des projets importants.

De 1997 à 1999, j'ai géré une équipe de représentants chez Drouet (agence immobilière). J'ai profité de cette occasion pour développer le sens des contacts et apprendre à gérer le travail des autres.

Mes loisirs, aussi, ont contribué à ma capacité de travail. J'aime les sports, surtout le football. Alors, de 1998 à 1999 j'ai été entraîneur pour l'équipe de football de ma communauté. Pendant cette période, j'ai réussi à encourager le support financier des commerçants locaux pour notre équipe. Grâce à mes efforts, j'ai développé une grande capacité à motiver les autres.

Je reste à votre disposition pour un prochain contact.

Veuillez agréer, Madame, mes meilleures salutations.

Martine Ruis

La signature
(Éviter les signatures trop grandes ou
trop petites, que les graphologues
analyseront avec suspicion.)

Veuillez trouver ci-joint mon dossier: *Please find attached (to this letter) my file /* **connaissances**
approfondies: *substantial knowledge*

INTÉGRATION

You and your partner hope to find summer employment at one of the French-owned Club Med vacation sites. Although you have not seen any postings of job opportunities at Club Med, you have decided to investigate the possibilities. Compile and categorize your educational, work, language, and travel experiences as preparation for making application with the organization.

A. **On énumère des postes possibles.** A Club Med vacation site is a self-contained location with all housing, meals, sports, and entertainment provided. First, working with your partner, make a list of job possibilities in such a spot. (Examples: **réceptionniste à l'hôtel, femme de chambre** (housekeeper), **comptable, diététicien, serveur, barman, spécialiste en tennis, musicien, prof de dance, gardien à la piscine, liaison en relations publiques, animateur d'activités sportives/sociales, assistant en administration**)

B. **On détermine ses intérêts.** From your list, select one or more jobs for which you may have some qualifications.

C. **On détermine les besoins du poste.** Working with your partner, make a list of qualities you would expect to be required or preferred by Club Med for each job that interests you.

D. **On spécifie ses qualifications.** Beside each entry in your list of expected qualities needed for the job, write one or more examples of activities from your background (education, work, language, travel) that you feel would satisfy the requirement. Review your list with your partner, who may have other suggestions for you.

E. **On spécifie ses qualités personnelles.** Now make a list of personal qualities or attributes that you believe would be desirable in the vacation atmosphere (Examples: **sportif, amical, honnête**)

F. **On écrit une lettre de candidature.** Write a letter **(Lettre de candidature)** to Club Med in which you present yourself as a possible employee for the next summer.

LEXIQUE DE BASE

LEXIQUE D'EXPANSION

Pour décrire les tâches au travail ou à l'école

s'adapter (à)...	to adapt oneself, get used to . . .	accumuler des heures	to accumulate hours
aux nouvelles technologies	the new technologies	gérer une équipe	to lead a (work) team/crew
à un emploi du temps flexible	a flexible schedule	contrôler les budgets	to monitor budgets
au travail en équipe	teamwork	cultiver la capacité de...	to cultivate the ability to . . .
analyser les besoins	to do a needs analysis	planifier une excursion,	to plan an excursion,
s'appliquer (à)...	to apply oneself . . .	des programmes	programs
à finir le projet	to finishing the project		
aux études	to studies		
au travail	to work		
apprécier l'importance de...	to understand (and appreciate) the importance of . . .		
choisir un logiciel	to choose a software program		

Déjà vu

classer des documents, des dossiers	to file documents, files	équilibrer son emploi du temps	to balance one's schedule
commander du matériel, du stock	to order supplies, stock	gagner de l'argent	to earn money
communiquer ses idées	to communicate one's ideas	s'absenter du travail	to be absent from work
consulter des collègues	to consult colleagues	s'amuser le week-end	to enjoy oneself on the weekend
coordonner le travail	to coordinate the job	s'énerver au travail	to get upset at work
créer des présentations	to create presentations	s'entraîner au gym	to work out at the gym
développer...	to develop . . .	s'habituer à la vie universitaire	to get accustomed to university life
des produits	products	s'informer sur...	to get information on . . .
des présentations	presentations	les nouveaux produits	the new products:
mon sens de l'organisation	my sense of organization	la clientèle	the clientele
une sensibilité à...	a sensitivity to . . .	s'occuper (de)...	to busy oneself with; to attend to . . .
organiser un projet	to organize a project	des devoirs	one's homework
préciser des concepts	to specify/clarify concepts	des enfants	the children
prendre des messages	to take messages	d'un projet	a project
préparer des rapports	to prepare reports	se charger (de)...	to take charge of, to take responsibility for . . .
ranger les produits, le stock	to put up the stock, organize the inventory	de l'éducation des enfants	the children's education
renseigner les clients	to provide information to clients	du budget	the budget
se servir (de)...	to make use of . . .	se dépêcher	to hurry (up)
de l'assistance de...	the aid of . . . ; __'s help	se préparer (pour)	to get ready (for)
du courrier électronique	e-mail	les examens de fin de classe	final exams
surveiller les employés	to supervise employees	l'entretien	the interview
taper les rapports	to type reports	se reposer pendant le week-end	to rest during the weekend
travailler à la caisse	to work the cash register	stocker la marchandise	to stock (an area)
vérifier les stocks	to check the inventory		

choisir...
  ses cours
  des cartes de vœux
  de travailler tard
  d'installer ce nouveau logiciel

to choose . . .
  one's courses
  some greeting cards
  to work late
  to install this new software program

établir...
  de bons rapports
  une bonne réputation
  un budget

to establish. set up . . .
  good relations
  a good reputation
  a budget

finir...
  son travail
  ses devoirs
  les courses
  d'étudier

to finish . . .
  one's work
  one's homework
  the errands
  studying

réfléchir (à)...
  à ce que tu fais
  à sa spécialisation
  à une carrière
  à ses besoins financiers

to think (about), reflect (on) . . .
  what you're doing
  one's major
  one's career
  one's financial needs

réussir... (à)
  aux examens
  dans ses projets personnels
  à l'interview
  dans les relations avec les autres

to succeed; to do well; to pass (a test)
  to pass one's exams
  to succeed at one's personal projects
  to do well . . . on an interview,
  in one's relations with others

obéir (à)...

  à ses parents
  aux lois
  aux conseils

to obey (someone or
  something) . . .
  one's parents
  the laws
  advice

réagir (à)...
  gracieusement
  spontanément
  avec intelligence
  avec calme
  avec patience
  à la bonne /mauvaise
    nouvelle

to react (to) . . .
  graciously
  spontaneously
  intelligently
  calmly
  patiently
  to the good/bad news

grandir — to get big, grow up
grossir — to get fat, gain weight
maigrir — to get thin, lose weight
rougir — to turn red, blush
vieillir — to grow older
blanchir — to turn pale
mincir — to slim down
rajeunir — to make appear younger

je suis allé(e) — I went
je suis arrivé(e) — I arrived
je suis entré(e) (dans) — I entered (into)
je suis monté(e) — I went up(stairs)
je suis parti(e) — I left, departed
je suis rentré(e) — I returned home
je suis resté(e) — I stayed, remained
je suis retourné(e) — I returned, went back
je suis sorti(e) — I went out, exited
je suis tombé(e) — I fell (down)

je suis descendu(e) — I went down(stairs)
je suis devenu(e) — I became
il/elle est mort(e) — he/she died, is dead
je suis né(e) — I was born
je suis revenu(e) — I came back
je suis venu(e) — I came

Les compétences et qualités au travail

la connaissance des besoins	a knowledge of the needs	la capacité de (d')...	the ability to . . .
du marché	of the market	d'équilibrer son emploi	balance one's schedule
financiers	financial needs	du temps	
personnels	personal needs	de s'adapter à des	adapt to different situations
la capacité de (d')...	the ability to . . .	situations diverses	
négocier un consensus	negotiate an agreement	la facilité des contacts	the quality of "having a way
motiver les gens	motivate people		with people"
résister au stress	bear up under stress	la fiabilité	reliability
la confiance en soi	confidence in oneself	la persévérance	perseverance
une bonne présentation	the quality of presenting oneself		
	well in demeanor as well as dress		
un sens de l'organisation	a sense of organization		
un sens des priorités	a sense of priorities		

Pour préciser une idée

à part	besides	ainsi que...	as well as . . .
dans le service de	in the department of	grâce à...	thanks to . . . , as a result of . . .
en plus de	besides, in addition to		

MON VOYAGE AUTOUR DU MONDE

Communicative Objectives

- To describe features of nature and geography
- To describe weather conditions and seasons
- To determine and express preferences in hotel accommodations

Thematic Objectives

✓ To define your goals for leisure travel and associate them with various geographic settings

✓ To associate preferences in leisure activities with different weather, seasons, and places in the world

✓ To plan your own world tour, identifying sites and experiences that relate to your personal travel goals

La mise en scène

In *Chapitre 7* you will define your idea of scenic beauty in terms of environmental features and associate those features both with places around the world and with the leisure activities you enjoy on vacation. The video segment focuses on presenting and helping you recognize key expressions that are useful for talking about your perceptions of scenic beauty.

You will view some scenes from the three vastly different Francophone sites that you have been studying: Guadeloupe, Québec, and France. As you first see the scenes without their soundtrack, you will be asked to make visual observations that will help you anticipate some phrases. In this first viewing of the video, be prepared to check off mentally some of the main elements you notice that are being featured. They are listed on the right of your screen in English. In most cases, there are several correct choices.

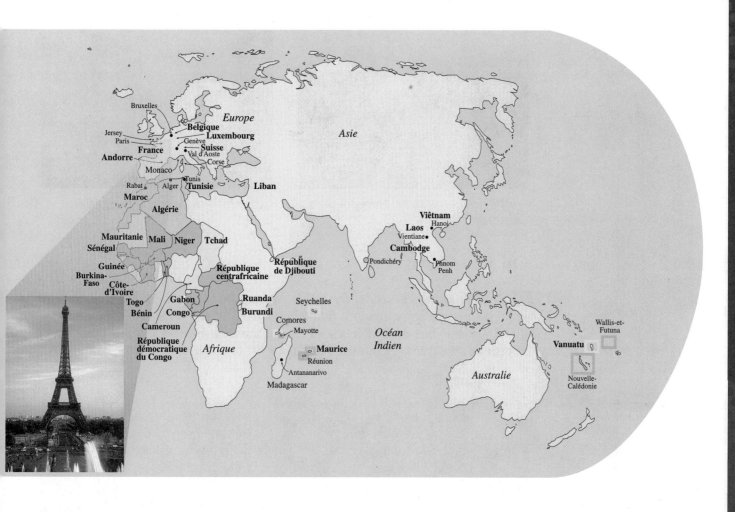

A. On se prépare. Examine the three photographs of well-known sites in Guadeloupe, Québec, and France. Then identify the geographic and/or touristic features on the following list that you would associate with each of the three sites. Mark *G* for Guadeloupe, *Q* for Québec, and/or *F* for France next to each item. Each item may be associated with more than one of the three sites.

1. cityscape
2. European-style architecture
3. winter weather
4. snowy weather
5. spring weather
6. tropical
7. nature
8. monument
9. exotic
10. cosmopolitan
11. historic
12. fountains
13. gardens
14. forest

B. On anticipe le vocabulaire. Watch the video segment that has been recorded without a soundtrack. You will be asked to identify descriptive elements from a list on the screen to help you anticipate the French you will hear on your second viewing.

Les paroles et le sens

C. On écoute. As you listen to the video soundtrack, work on discriminating the sounds you hear used to talk about the places you see.

Mes intérêts pour mon voyage

Faire une excursion pour admirer le paysage le long des grands fleuves de la France.

Apprécier la beauté du coucher du soleil dans les Caraïbes.

On y réfléchit

D. Réfléchissons. Consider the sights you saw and the expressions you heard. From the groups of expressions that follow, make a list of at least ten elements that represent your own interests for leisure travel. Use «**Mes Intérêts pour mon voyage**» as the title for your list. Keep your list to use in activities later in this chapter.

vue panoramique	beauté de la neige	sites touristiques célèbres
bord de mer	charmante et historique	capitale mondiale
île tropicale	architecture influencée	magasins et restaurants
excursions en bateau	par l'Europe	Côte d'Azur
bateau à voile	joie de vivre	casino de Monte Carlo
planche à voile	pratiquer un sport	la ville la plus ensoleillée
sports nautiques	ski de fond	cathédrale Notre-Dame de Paris
un temps superbe	patin	proximité de l'Italie
ciel clair et bleu	hockey sur glace	influence italienne
jamais mauvais	visiter des sites	architecture
coucher du soleil	historiques	cuisine provençale
la plage	faire un tour en calèche	les plages
palmiers	apprécier la solitude	Alsace
très belle forêt dense	illuminée par nuit	influence de la culture
végétation tropicale	participer aux fêtes	allemande
arbres fascinants	Carnaval	beauté des forêts
sons exotiques	festival de Mardi Gras	villages pittoresques
jardin exotique	cuisine régionale	la ville la plus touristique
grande variété de fleurs	célèbres stations de ski	du monde
merveilleuses couleurs	grands fleuves	Arc de Triomphe
faire des promenades	vie quotidienne	musée du Louvre
ambiance de calme et de luxe	petits villages de montagne	tour Eiffel
solitude reposante	randonnées	

lieux (m.): *places*

Objective: To describe features of nature and geography

PRÉSENTATION: Un coup d'œil sur le thème

Les Alpes sont un des sites préférés des vacanciers. On admire surtout les sommets blancs éternels des glaciers. La beauté majestueuse de ces montagnes est une des plus grandes splendeurs de la nature.

Honfleur est une ville pittoresque dans le nord de la France, sur la côte de Normandie. Avec son port et ses rues paisibles°, elle garde son charme et attire beaucoup de touristes.

paisibles: *peaceful*

Les îles tropicales de la mer des Caraïbes attirent° les amateurs de somptueuse végétation. Avec leurs forêts denses et leurs belles fleurs sauvages°, elles offrent une solitude sereine pour les vacances.

attirent: *attract*

fleurs (f.) sauvages: *wildflowers*

Les voyages touristiques: Qu'est-ce qu'on recherche? Pour chaque photo, indiquez trois raisons pour visiter le lieu représenté. Voici quelques suggestions.

Quelques objectifs pour les voyages

Aventure	Repos, tranquillité	**Dépaysement°**
Enrichissement culturel	**Exotisme**	**Tourisme**
Se faire des souvenirs°		*Rencontrer des gens intéressants*
Beauté naturelle	**Apprendre des choses intéressantes**	**???**

dépaysement (m.): *change of scenery*

se faire des souvenirs: *to create memories*

POUR DÉVELOPPER VOTRE FRANÇAIS

Vocabulaire: Des expressions pour décrire la nature

OBSERVATIONS

Les couleurs

bleu(e)	rouge	violet(te)
jaune	noir(e)	rose
vert(e)	gris(e)	

blanc(he)

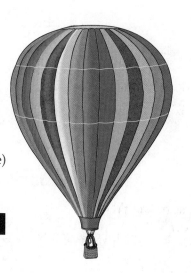

J'apprécie beaucoup la beauté du feuillage d'automne. Les couleurs—rouge, jaune et orange—sont étonnantes. Quelle merveille!

Le mont Blanc, la montagne la plus haute des Alpes, a l'air éternel. C'est incroyable!

Les fleurs exotiques des îles tropicales attirent les touristes. Elles sont roses, blanches, rouges et bleues—de toutes les couleurs. Voilà de magnifiques fleurs jaunes. Quelle beauté! Je n'ai jamais rien vu d'aussi beau de ma vie.

STRATÉGIES D'ANALYSE

1. Many words about nature are cognates in French and English. What new words in the examples can you identify based on their resemblance to English?

2. Which expressions in these captions are used to show astonishment or delight?

PRÉCISIONS

- Since many geographical terms are cognates, you will be able to figure out their meanings readily.

une montagne rocheuse	*a rocky mountain*
une plante exotique	*an exotic plant*
le feuillage d'automne	*autumn foliage*
la végétation dense	*dense vegetation*
une rivière	*a river, a tributary*
une île tropicale	*a tropical island*
une jungle	*a jungle*

- A few terms are not quite so easy to identify:

des plages ensoleillées	*sunny beaches*
une forêt pluviale	*a rain forest*
des chutes (d'eau)	*(water)falls*
des collines	*hills*
un fleuve	*a major river (that flows to the sea)*
le bord de mer	*the seashore*

À propos de la structure: The circumflex (^) over a letter generally means that an "s" was left out as the Latin word became French. When French became a written language, grammarians carefully put in a circumflex to show where the "s" had originally been. The "s" was retained in some of these words in English. Examples: **île** = *isle, island;* **forêt** = *forest;* **côte** = *coast.*

A. Des voyages appropriés. Dites à votre partenaire quelle ambiance est préférable (à votre avis) pour chaque occasion.

> **Modèle:** un voyage de noces°:
> lieux: la forêt dense/le désert/les chutes d'eau
> *Moi, je considère les chutes d'eau préférables pour un voyage de noces.*

1. un voyage de noces:
   la jungle/une plage ensoleillée/les montagnes
2. des vacances avec des enfants de moins de 10 ans:
   le désert/un village au bord de la mer/le lac
3. un week-end avec des ami(e)s:
   une région pluvieuse/une plage au bord de la mer/une forêt tropicale
4. une journée avec des parents âgés:
   une excursion pour voir les montagnes Rocheuses/le feuillage d'automne/les chutes du Niagara
5. un père et ses deux fils (âgés de 14 et 15 ans):
   un parc d'amusement (d'attractions)/le lac/la plage
6. trois sœurs (âgées de 25, 27 et 30 ans):
   un parc d'amusement (d'attractions)/un village au bord de la mer/le désert
7. vous et votre partenaire:
   une grande ville/un petit village/la jungle

voyage de noces: *honeymoon trip*

À propos du vocabulaire: Le voyage de noces refers to the wedding trip taken by newlyweds, **les nouveaux mariés. La lune de miel** *(the honeymoon)* refers to the early period of bliss at the beginning of a marriage.

B. Quelle vue splendide! Étudiez les photos déjà présentées dans ce chapitre. Décrivez une de ces photos à votre partenaire. Votre partenaire va deviner° ce que vous décrivez et va réagir à cette photo.

deviner: *to guess*

> **Modèle:** —*Je regarde une photo d'une plage ensoleillée où des gens s'amusent bien.*
> —*Voilà la photo. C'est fantastique!*

Structure: L'article défini avec les noms géographiques

L'Europe francophone m'intéresse beaucoup. Avez-vous visité **la** France, **la** Suisse ou **la** Belgique? Les villes de Paris, Genève et Bruxelles sont magnifiques.

L'Afrique francophone m'intéresse plus. Je voudrais visiter **la** Côte-d'Ivoire, **le** Sénégal et **la** Tunisie.

Les Français aiment beaucoup visiter **les** États-Unis, par exemple, **le** Texas, **la** Californie, **la** Floride, **l'**état de New York et **l'**Arizona (à cause du Grand Canyon).

Stratégies d'analyse

1. The definite article is used in French with some geographic names but not with others. Find the place names in the examples that do *not* take definite articles and determine what they have in common.

2. Can you identify the gender of the other geographic names in the examples from their definite articles? Are there any genders that you cannot identify from their definite articles?

3. What is the final letter in the names of the places that you can determine are feminine?

4. Based on your answer to question #3, can you guess the genders of **l'Europe, l'Afrique,** and **l'Arizona?**

Précisions

- In general, use a definite article with the names of continents, countries, provinces, and states.

  Est-ce que vous trouvez **l'Afrique** francophone ou **l'Europe** francophone plus intéressante?
  *Do you find francophone **Africa** or francophone **Europe** more interesting?*

  Moi, je n'ai pas encore visité **la Suisse, la Côte-d'Ivoire, le Sénégal** et **la Tunisie.**
  *[Me] I have not yet visited **Switzerland, the Ivory Coast, Senegal,** and **Tunisia.***

- In general, do *not* use an article with city names. Some exceptions are **La Nouvelle-Orléans, Le Havre,** and **Le Caire.**

  J'aime beaucoup **La Nouvelle-Orléans,** mais je préfère passer mes vacances à **Paris.**
  *I love **New Orleans,** but I prefer to spend my vacations in **Paris.***

À propos de la structure: Note that **Tahiti** is also an exception in that it does not use a definite article.

- The names of continents, countries, provinces, and states ending in **e** in French are usually feminine; those ending in letters other than **e** in French are usually masculine. Some notable exceptions are **le Mexique** and **le Maine** (which end in **e** but are masculine) and **Tahiti** (which does not end in **e** but is feminine).

La Russie et **le Mexique** ont vu beaucoup de changements à la fin du XXe siècle.
Russia and Mexico saw many changes at the end of the twentieth century.

Structure: Les prépositions avec les noms des villes

OBSERVATIONS

Nous allons **à** Paris.
*We are going **to** Paris.*

Nous sommes **à** Paris.
*We are **in** Paris.*

Luc est **de** Paris.
*Luc is **from** Paris.*

STRATÉGIES D'ANALYSE

1. Which preposition do we use with the name of a city to indicate *in* or *to* the city?
2. Which preposition is used to say *from* the city?

PRÉCISIONS

- With city names, use **à** to express *to* or *in*.

  Cet été nous allons passer nos vacances **à** Paris, **à** Strasbourg, **à** Nice et **à** Cannes.
  *This summer we are going to spend our vacation **in** Paris, **in** Strasbourg, **in** Nice, and **in** Cannes.*

- Use **de** with city names to mean *from*.

  Nous allons d'abord **à** Paris. Puis, nous allons en train **de** Paris à Strasbourg. Nous avons un vol **de** Strasbourg à Nice. Marc a loué une voiture pour aller **de** Nice à Cannes.
  *We are going first to Paris. Then, we are going by train **from** Paris to Strasbourg. We have a flight **from** Strasbourg to Nice. Marc has rented a car to go **from** Nice to Cannes.*

À propos de la structure: In the rare case when the name of a city includes a definite article, **à** and **de** precede the definite article, as in **à La Nouvelle-Orléans**. If the city name is masculine, as in **Le Havre**, the **à** and **de** contract with the definite article as usual: **au Havre**.

C. Où se trouve... ? Décidez avec votre partenaire dans quelle ville se trouvent les célèbres lieux touristiques mentionnés.

se tromper: to be mistaken

À propos du vocabulaire: The real name of the **statue** is *La Liberté éclairant le monde* (Liberty lighting the world) but in popular use it is shortened to *la statue de la Liberté*.

Note that while the name of Mexico, the country, is **le Mexique**, the name of Mexico City is simply **Mexico** in French.

Modèle: —*L'Acropole est à Rome, n'est-ce pas?*
—*Je pense que tu te trompes°. L'Acropole se trouve à Athènes.*
—*Oh oui, tu as raison.*

l'Acropole
la tour Eiffel
la statue de la Liberté
le Buckingham Palace
le musée Prado
la chapelle Sixtine
l'Hermitage
le Kremlin

Hong Kong	Madrid
Rome	Saint-Pétersbourg
Moscou	Paris
New York	Mexico
Londres	Athènes

D. Quelle langue est-ce qu'on parle à... ? Dites à votre partenaire quelle langue on parle dans les villes mentionnées.

Modèle: Pékin
À Pékin on parle chinois.

1. Mexico
2. Bruxelles
3. La Nouvelle-Orléans
4. Berlin
5. Moscou

6. Londres
7. Genève
8. Francfort
9. Le Havre
10. Chicago

Structure: Les prépositions avec les noms de pays, de provinces et d'états

OBSERVATIONS

Je vais **en** Suisse.	Je travaille **en** Suisse.	Je suis **de** Suisse.
Nous allons **en** France.	Nous travaillons **en** France.	Nous sommes **de** France.
Ils vont **en** Californie.	Ils travaillent **en** Californie.	Ils sont **de** Californie.
Je vais **au** Canada.	Je travaille **au** Canada.	Je suis **du** Canada.
Juan est **au** Mexique.	Il travaille **au** Mexique.	Il est **du** Mexique.
Je vais **au** Texas.	Je travaille **au** Texas.	Je suis **du** Texas.
Je suis **aux** États-Unis.	J'habite **aux** États-Unis.	Je suis **des** États-Unis.
Paul est **aux** Antilles.	Il habite **aux** Antilles.	Il est **des** Antilles.

STRATÉGIES D'ANALYSE

1. What French word do we use to express *in* or *to* a feminine country or region? To express *in* or *to* a masculine country or region?

2. How do we express *in* or *to* countries that are plural?

3. In French how do we say *from* a feminine country? *From* a masculine country? *From* a plural country?

PRÉCISIONS

- For countries or regions in the singular, expressing *in*, *to*, and *from* depends on the gender of the geographical name. We use **en** before feminine names (generally those that end in **-e** in French) and **au** before masculine names to say *in* or *to*. We use **de (d')** before feminine names and **du** before masculine names to say *from*.
- With the names of plural countries or regions, we use **aux** to indicate *to* or *in* and **des** to say *from*.
- Masculine countries and regions that begin with a vowel or vowel sound are preceded by **en** or **d'**.

> Je travaille **en** Iran, mais je ne suis pas **d'**Iran.
> Ma famille habite **en** Oklahoma.

À propos de la structure: Note the difference in expressing *at* or *to* before a province or country name and before a city name.

Ma cousine habite dans l'état de New York, **à** Albany. Moi, j'habite **à** New York.

Lise fait un voyage **à** Montréal, **au** Québec. Moi, je préfère aller **à** Québec.

Marc étudie l'espagnol **à** Cuernavaca, **au** Mexique. Je n'ai pas visité Cuernavaca, mais je suis déjà allé **à** Mexico.

NOTE CULTURELLE

Les vacances sont importantes pour les Français. Il y a presque 400 tour-opérateurs en France qui organisent des excursions touristiques. L'organisation la plus grande est Nouvelles Frontières. Le Club Méditerranée est aussi très important.

Quand les Français bouclent° leurs valises pour franchir° les frontières, leurs destinations favorites sont **les Antilles** (43%) et **l'Amérique du Nord** (38%). Les palmiers et le sable blanc de **Tahiti** attirent chaque année 11% des touristes tricolores°.

Réfléchissons: Pourquoi pensez-vous que la destination favorite des Français pour les vacances (hors de France) soit les Antilles? Qu'est-ce qui attire les Français aux Antilles?

boucler: *to buckle, to close*
franchir: *to cross*
tricolore: *reference to France (with its three-colored flag—* **bleu/blanc/rouge***)*

La destination préférée des Français pour leurs vacances est les Antilles. Ils aiment beaucoup le soleil et la plage.

Les Français s'intéressent beaucoup aux États-Unis aussi. La culture du Texas pique leur curiosité.

E. **Mon itinéraire.** Détaillez pour votre partenaire votre itinéraire pour les voyages suggérés. Utilisez la préposition appropriée pour chaque pays.

Modèle: Suisse / Belgique / France / Angleterre / Canada / États-Unis
D'abord, je vais ___*de*___ Suisse ___*en*___ Belgique.
Ensuite, je vais _____ Belgique _____ France.
Puis, je vais _____ France _____ Angleterre.
Alors, je vais _____ Angleterre _____ Canada.
Enfin, je vais _____ Canada _____ États-Unis.

1. États-Unis / Canada / Angleterre / France / Belgique / Suisse
2. États-Unis / Mexique / Espagne / Italie / Suisse / Russie
3. Canada / France / Allemagne / Autriche / Italie / Espagne
4. Canada / Espagne / Tunisie / Algérie / Sénégal / Égypte
5. États-Unis / Antilles / France / Italie / Égypte / Sénégal
6. Antilles / Mexique / États-Unis / Japon / Chine / Russie
7. France / Algérie / Tunisie / Sénégal / Égypte / Tahiti

F. Leçon de géographie. Décidez avec deux partenaires où dans le monde se trouvent les célèbres lieux touristiques mentionnés. Utilisez la préposition appropriée pour chaque région géographique. Notez qu'il y a souvent plus d'une bonne réponse.

Modèle: Étudiant(e) #1: La Vallée de la Mort est en Afrique, n'est-ce pas?
Étudiant(e) #2: Je pense que tu te trompes. C'est le désert du Sahara qui est en Afrique.
Étudiant(e) #3: La Vallée de la Mort se trouve aux États-Unis, mais dans quel état?
Étudiant(e) #2: Je pense qu'elle se trouve dans l'état de Nevada.

Lieux touristiques	*Régions géographiques*	
La Forêt-Noire	Europe	Canada
Le Grand Canyon	Italie	Asie
Le désert du Sahara	Allemagne	États-Unis
Stonehenge	Inde	Mexique
Les chutes du Niagara	Afrique	Floride
La Grande Muraille	Arizona	Amérique
Le Tadj Mahall	Angleterre	Pérou
La Tour Penchée	Chine	
Le Cap Canaveral		
Téotihuacán		
Machu Picchu		

To complement this review of French vowel sounds, you might wish to refer to *Chapitres 3*, *4*, and *6* of your text and workbook where a more detailed guide to pronunciation for each sound appears.

PRONONCIATION: Révision des voyelles

À vous. Repeat each word after your instructor.

[a]	voile, Carnaval, plage	[ɔ]	tropical, sport, solitude
[e]	été, répéter, variété	[œ]	fleurs, vendeur, seul
[ɛ]	clair, neige, carrière	[ø]	bleu, mieux, coiffeuse
[ə]	je, promenades, avenir	[u]	couleurs, tour, Louvre
[i]	proximité, historique, quotidien	[y]	excursion, vue, étude
[o]	bateau, mauvais, mot		

POUR DÉVELOPPER VOS IDÉES

Thematic objective: To define your goals for leisure travel and associate them with various geographic settings

Présentation: Un tour au bout du monde

Valérie Lefranc et Fabien Maurice, deux amateurs de cyclisme et d'aventure, ont décidé de faire le tour du monde à vélo. Afin de° partager leurs expériences avec tout le monde, ils ont développé un site Internet, où ils présentent leurs motivations et leurs préparatifs, et où on peut suivre leur route.

Afin de: *In order to*

POUR SAISIR L'ESSENTIEL:

1. Examinez la carte dans la lecture suivante (le site Internet). Quels lieux sur la route vous semblent les plus intéressants? Les plus reposants? Les plus incroyables°? Les plus difficiles à traverser? Les plus impressionnants?

incroyables: *incredible*

un but: *goal, objective*

2. Lesquels des trois objectifs décrits dans la lecture correspondent à vos buts° personnels pour les voyages touristiques?

3. Parcourez° le texte et faites une liste des expressions utiles pour exprimer vos propres objectifs pour les voyages (minimum 6 expressions).

Parcourez: *Skim*

4. Relisez les paragraphes. Voudriez-vous partir en voyage avec Fabien et Valérie? Pourquoi (pas)?

L'itinéraire du tour du monde à vélo

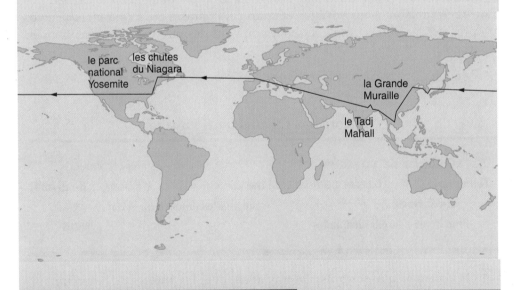

le parc national Yosemite • les chutes du Niagara • la Grande Muraille • le Tadj Mahall

Deux vélos pour un tour du monde

L'aventure, ce mélange° de peur et de confiance, a toujours existé dans notre esprit. Nous avons commencé notre tour du monde en Amérique du Nord en orientant chaque soir nos vélos dans la direction du soleil couchant.

un mélange: *mixture*

---

battre un record: *to break a record*
dans le but de: *dans l'intention de*

mal décrit: *poorly described*
préconçues: *preconceived*
la sagesse: *wisdom, sagacity*

nous-mêmes: *ourselves*

en éveil: *alert* / **disponible:** *available, free*

Les objectifs du projet
- À la recherche de l'aventure
- À la recherche de connaissances
- À la recherche de nos limites

À la recherche de l'aventure

Nous ne partons pas dans l'intention de battre un record° ni de gagner un trophée, mais plutôt dans le but de° regarder, d'écouter, de toucher et de goûter.

Changer de panorama, de climat, d'environnement social; prendre de nouvelles habitudes. Voilà nos motivations pour cette formidable aventure.

À la recherche de connaissances

Nous cherchons aussi dans ce voyage à voir de nos propres yeux les réalités d'un monde souvent mal décrit°. Nous espérons laisser derrière nous nos idées préconçues° pour mieux comprendre les différences entre notre société et celles des pays que nous traversons. Cela va nous permettre de gagner de la sagesse° et de meilleures connaissances pour notre avenir.

À la recherche de nos limites

Ce tour du monde va nous permettre de partir à la découverte de nous-mêmes°. Il va sans doute être difficile, mais les difficultés comptent très peu comparées à tout ce que nous allons découvrir: la joie d'être libres, de rester en éveil°, d'être disponibles°, ouverts à chaque expérience.

G. **Les lieux et leurs attractions.** Consultez les expressions dans le tableau **Encore des raisons pour voyager,** et faites cinq phrases qui montrent *(show)* vos propres raisons pour voyager. Indiquez où vous désirez voyager et mentionnez pourquoi.

> **Modèle:** *Je voudrais aller en Chine pour voir de mes propres yeux la Grande Muraille.*

Encore des raisons pour voyager

Changer de paysage		*Voir de mes propres yeux...*
Écouter...	**Laisser derrière moi mes...**	
		Changer de climat
Goûter...	*Changer d'environnement social*	
Prendre de nouvelles habitudes		**Autres ???**

H. **On communique ses buts.** En travaillant avec les phrases de l'exercice précédent, posez des questions à votre partenaire pour trouver où il/elle voudrait aller et pourquoi. En écoutant ses réponses, décidez si vous allez ajouter ces lieux à votre propre liste.

> **Modèle:** *—Où est-ce que tu voudrais aller pendant ton voyage?*
> *—D'abord, je voudrais aller en Chine.*
> *—En Chine? Pourquoi?*
> *—Je voudrais y aller pour voir la Grande Muraille de mes propres yeux.*

I. **On établit des priorités.** (1) Faites une liste de vos objectifs pour un voyage autour du monde. Consultez les tableaux **Encore des raisons pour voyager** (page 292) et **Quelques Objectifs pour les voyages** (page 283) pour trouver des suggestions. (2) Organisez votre liste par ordre de vos priorités. (3) Pour chacun des objectifs sur votre liste, mentionnez au moins un lieu à visiter et indiquez pourquoi on y va.

DÉCOUVERTE

The following sets of couplets come from a poem called *«Invitation au voyage»*, in which the author, Charles Baudelaire (1821–1867), describes the appeal of different places. Notice how he makes commonplace vocabulary in short phrases evoke images, scents, and moods.

1

Les plus rares fleurs
Mêlant° leurs odeurs

mêler: *to mix*

ᏮᎧᏮᎧᏮ

2

Les riches plafonds°,
Les miroirs profonds

le plafond: *ceiling*

ᏮᎧᏮᎧᏮ

3

Là, tout n'est qu'ordre et beauté,
Luxe, calme et volupté.

ᏮᎧᏮᎧᏮ

4

Vois sur ces canaux°
Dormir ces vaisseaux°

canaux (m.): *canals (The singular form is* **canal.**)
vaisseaux (m.): *vessels, boats*

ᏮᎧᏮᎧᏮ

1. Make two columns. Label one of them "Expressions that appeal to the senses." Label the other "Expressions that evoke moods." Now as you reread the couplets in the DÉCOUVERTE note, categorize words and phrases as appropriate. Are there some expressions that you think should be in both columns?

2. Read the couplets again. As you do, flip through the pages of the *Ouverture* and this *Thème* to find photos that the couplets describe. (Each person in the class may have a different opinion about these.)

3. Identify which words in the couplets cause you to associate them with the particular photos you have selected.

4. Decide which of the couplets best describe(s) the trip around the world that you would like to take.

2ᴱ THÈME: Dans mes plus beaux rêves° de voyage...

Objective: To describe weather conditions and seasons

PRÉSENTATION: Un coup d'œil sur le thème

je me détends: *I am relaxing*

dos: *back*

Dans mes plus beaux rêves de voyage, je me détends° sur une plage ensoleillée au bord de la mer Méditerranée. Pour moi, l'essentiel c'est le repos, le soleil, la chaleur.

Dans mes plus beaux rêves de voyage, je suis sur une île tropicale. J'ai les cheveux au vent et le soleil dans le dos°. À mon avis, l'important c'est le dépaysement, la nature, des journées (et des soirées!) pleines d'activité.

Dans mes plus beaux rêves de voyage, je passe des journées dans des lieux que je n'ai jamais visités. Je fais du tourisme pour mieux connaître le monde et ses habitants. Ce qui compte°, c'est apprendre quelque chose de nouveau.

Ce qui compte: La chose importante

Les rêves de voyage

Regardez les images et lisez les commentaires. Quel narrateur (ou Quelle narratrice) voudriez-vous accompagner en voyage?

Pensez au voyage idéal pour vous. Quelle image avez-vous de ce voyage? Est-ce qu'elle ressemble à une des photos de ce chapitre? Où êtes-vous dans votre voyage de rêve? Décrivez un peu la scène. Que faites-vous? Qu'est-ce qui importe° pour votre voyage?

Qu'est-ce qui importe: *What is important*

POUR DÉVELOPPER VOTRE FRANÇAIS

Vocabulaire: Les saisons et le temps

OBSERVATIONS

Les mois d'été sont **juin, juillet** et **août.** Le plus souvent, **en été** il fait chaud. On va à la plage aussi souvent que possible.

Les mois d'automne sont **septembre, octobre** et **novembre.** D'habitude, **en automne** il commence à faire frais. On fait du cyclisme **en automne.** L'automne, c'est une bonne saison pour les randonnées.

Les mois d'hiver sont **décembre, janvier et février. En hiver,** il fait froid. On cherche des montagnes couvertes de neige pour faire du ski.

Les mois de printemps sont **mars, avril et mai. Au printemps** il commence à faire doux. Au printemps il fait un temps agréable pour les promenades.

STRATÉGIES D'ANALYSE

1. Most of the names of the months are recognizable as cognates in English. From the months, determine the names of the four seasons.
2. Each of the captions contains a weather expression using the verb **faire** to describe temperature. Based on the months and seasons, figure out what each weather expression probably means.

PRÉCISIONS

- The four seasons are:

l'été	*summer*	**l'hiver**	*winter*
l'automne	*fall*	**le printemps**	*spring*

- Use **en** to express *in* before **été, automne,** and **hiver,** which begin with a vowel (or vowel sound). With **printemps,** which begins with a consonant, use **au.**
- Many expressions that describe weather conditions use the verb **faire.** Some expressions make general evaluation statements about the weather.

Il fait beau.	*The weather is beautiful.*
mauvais.	*bad.*
Il fait un temps magnifique.	*The weather is magnificent.*
fantastique.	*fantastic.*
incroyable.	*unbelievable.*
moche.	*ugly.*
lourd.	*heavy, oppressive.*
déprimant.	*depressing.*
insupportable.	*unbearable.*
misérable.	*miserable.*

- Others are used to report temperature conditions.

Il fait chaud.	*It is hot.*
froid.	*cold.*
frais.	*cool.*
doux.	*mild.*

- Still others describe specific conditions.

Il fait du soleil.	*It is sunny.*
Il fait du vent.	*It is windy.*
Il fait du brouillard.	*It is foggy.*

Vocabulaire: Les saisons et le temps (suite)

OBSERVATIONS

Quel temps fait-il aujourd'hui?
Le ciel est couvert.
Il y a des nuages.
C'est nuageux.
Il n'y a pas de soleil.
Il pleut.
Il fait 15 degrés.
Il fait un temps épouvantable.

Quel temps fait-il?
Il fait très froid.
Il neige.
Il y a du vent.
Il y a du verglas partout.
La route est verglacée.
Il fait moins 5 degrés.
Il fait mauvais.

1. Note that the same weather conditions can be described in a variety of ways. How many different ways is *cloudy* described in the first drawing?

2. Which expressions with the second drawing indicate the cold climate without using the word for cold?

Précisions

- A variety of expressions can be used to talk about the weather.

Il pleut.	*It's raining.*
Il neige.	*It's snowing.*
Le ciel est couvert.	*The sky is overcast.*
C'est nuageux.	*It's cloudy.*
Il y a des nuages.	*It's cloudy; there are clouds.*
Il y a du vent.	*It's windy.*
Tout est couvert de verglas.	*Everything is iced over.*
La route est verglacée.	*The road is icy.*

À propos de la culture: Francophone countries use the Celsius scale to indicate temperature.
- To convert Celsius temperatures to Fahrenheit, divide by 5, multiply by 9, and add 32. [$F = (C/5 \times 9) + 32$]
- To convert Fahrenheit temperatures to Celsius, subtract 32, multiply by 5, and divide by 9. [$C = (F - 32) \times 5/9$]

- Temperatures can also be specified.

Il fait 0 degré (Celcius).	*It is 32 degrees (Fahrenheit).*
Il fait 20 degrés (Celcius).	*It is 68 degrees (Fahrenheit).*

A. Quel temps fait-il? Pour chaque mot qui décrit le temps dans le tableau suivant, donnez à votre partenaire trois conditions spécifiques qui sont, à votre avis, des exemples de ce type de temps. Complétez la fiche ensemble avec les détails de votre discussion.

Modèle: moche
Il fait un temps moche quand il pleut, il fait froid et il fait du vent.

Moi 3 conditions	Évaluation	Mon/Ma partenaire 3 conditions
Il pleut/Il fait froid/Il fait du vent	moche	
	1. magnifique	
	2. déprimant	
	3. beau	
	4. incroyable	

B. Nous sommes d'accord. Maintenant déterminez si vous et votre partenaire êtes d'accord ou pas d'accord au sujet de vos évaluations du temps.

> **Modèle:** *Mon/Ma partenaire et moi, nous sommes d'accord qu'il fait un temps moche quand il pleut et quand il fait du vent. Mon partenaire est contente quand il fait froid, mais pas moi.*

Structure: Le temps

OBSERVATIONS

Hier

Hier il a fait beau. Il a fait chaud. Il y a eu du soleil. Il a fait 20 degrés.

Aujourd'hui

Ce matin il continue à faire beau, mais moins chaud qu'hier. Cet après-midi nous allons avoir des nuages. Pour l'instant, il fait 18 degrés, mais à 14 ou à 15 heures la température va commencer à tomber.

Demain

Demain il va faire beaucoup plus frais. Il va faire 14 degrés dans l'après-midi après une température de 8 degrés à l'aube°. Le ciel va être couvert pendant toute la journée.

l'aube (f.): *dawn*

STRATÉGIES D'ANALYSE

1. Note the tense of the verbs that we use to give a weather report from yesterday.
2. Is today's weather report from the morning news or the evening news? How can you tell?
3. How can you tell that the third report is a forecast for the future, even if you did not have the word **demain** for tomorrow?

PRÉCISIONS

- To report past weather, as with other events of the past, use the **passé composé.**

Il a fait frais hier.	*It was cool yesterday.*
Il a plu.	*It rained.*
Il n'a pas neigé.	*It did not snow.*

- To forecast weather, you can often use the **futur immédiat** to indicate future time. Conjugate the verb **aller** to provide the sense of future time, then add the infinitive to give the meaning.

Il **va faire** du vent.	*It's going to be windy.*
Il **va pleuvoir.**	*It's going to rain.*

C. **La météo autour du monde.** Dites à votre partenaire quel temps il a fait hier, quel temps il fait aujourd'hui et quel temps il va faire demain dans trois villes de trois pays différents. Vous devez chercher vos informations dans les journaux, sur l'Internet ou à la télé avant d'arriver en classe.

Modèle: *À Strasbourg en France il a fait beau **hier**. Il a fait du soleil. Il n'y a pas eu de nuages. Il a fait 17 degrés.*

Aujourd'hui il fait un peu plus frais. En ce moment, il fait 14 degrés; il va faire 15 degrés cet après-midi. Nous allons avoir des nuages au moment du coucher du soleil.

Demain il va faire encore plus frais; il va faire 12 degrés au maximum. Le ciel va être couvert pendant toute la journée. Il va pleuvoir de temps en temps dans l'après-midi.

Vocabulaire: Le temps

OBSERVATIONS

—Comme il fait chaud!
—Oui, la chaleur est terrible!

—Comme il fait froid!
—Oui, je gèle°!

je gèle: *I'm freezing*

STRATÉGIES D'ANALYSE

You recognize the expression for *it's hot*. Can you determine which word is the noun form meaning *the heat*?

PRÉCISIONS

- We can make associations between certain weather descriptions and a noun that generalizes the weather condition.

Il fait chaud.	**la chaleur**	Il fait chaud.	**l'humidité**
Il fait du soleil.		Il fait lourd.	
		Le ciel est couvert.	
Il fait froid.	**le froid**	Il pleut.	
Il neige.			
Il gèle.		Il pleut.	**la pluie**
		Le ciel est couvert.	

D. **Comme il fait... !** À tour de rôle avec votre partenaire, pratiquez des façons de répondre à des commentaires au sujet du temps. Consultez le tableau précédent et les expressions d'évaluation du temps (**Précisions,** p. 297) pour vos associations et commentaires.

> **Modèle:** —Comme il fait lourd!
> —*Ah, oui. L'humidité est abominable.*

1. Comme il fait lourd!
2. Comme il fait chaud!
3. Comme il fait froid!
4. Comme il pleut!
5. Comme il neige!

E. **Une correspondance à travers les années.** Depuis plus de 20 ans *(For more than 20 years),* Alfred et Marguerite Stengel (de la ville de Haguenau, en France) correspondent régulièrement *(regularly)* avec une amie américaine. À tour de rôle avec votre partenaire, lisez à haute voix *(aloud)* les extraits des lettres écrites par Alfred et Marguerite. Puis, répondez aux questions qui suivent.

Haguenau, le 8 février 1993

Bien chère Jane,
Chez vous, au Texas, le printemps doit déjà s'annoncer. Heureux pays! Ici l'hiver continue à se faire remarquer. Après un janvier rigoureux dans ses débuts est venue une fin de mois aux températures printanières. Depuis le début février, c'est à nouveau la rigueur. De tout l'hiver, pas de neige, ce qui est inhabituel pour notre province...

Bons baisers.
Papi

Haguenau, le 24 octobre 1993

Chère petite Jane,
Aujourd'hui c'est dimanche, un dimanche pluvieux et froid. Depuis au moins quatre semaines il ne cesse de pleuvoir et nous ne voyons plus le soleil. En règle générale, il y a 6 à 8 degrés de moins que la normale saisonnière. C'est affreux. Tout est mouillé°. Nous ne pouvons pas aller au jardin, même pas pour chercher de la salade...

Grosses bises.
Mamie et Papi

Haguenau, le 10 avril 1994

Chère fille du Texas,
Chez nous le temps est toujours aussi froid et mauvais. Depuis que vous avez quitté Haguenau, nous avons eu deux jours de beau temps vrai. Nous ne voyons jamais le soleil. Il fait froid, il pleut chaque jour et pour changer il tombe, surtout dans le Vosges°, très souvent de la neige et même dans la plaine il y a souvent des chutes de neige. Des tempêtes sont notre lot quotidien. De semaine en semaine, la météo nous promet une amélioration° du climat. Mais aucun changement n'est en vue...

Grosses bises et bonnes semaines remplies de bonheur.
Mamie et Papi

Haguenau, le 15 janvier 1995

Bien chère fille du Texas,
Nous voilà en plein hiver avec de la neige, du vent froid et des températures basses (jusqu'à dix degrés au-dessous de° zéro). Mais nous ne devons pas trop nous plaindre°, c'est un climat de saison. Nous nous consolons avec l'idée que dans deux mois tout aura disparu et nous aurons des températures plus clémentes...

Nos bons baisers.
Mamie et Papi

Haguenau, le 2 février 1995

Chère fille du Texas.
Ton papi et ta mamie, de France vont tous les deux bien, malgré un temps abominable. Il a plu ces derniers temps presque sans s'arrêter. Dans notre pauvre France de nombreuses régions sont inondées. Plus près de nous, à la suite des neiges° dans les Vosges, beaucoup de rivières du Haut-Rhin et de l'Alsace débordent. Actuellement le niveau des eaux baisse. La Bretagne, la Normandie et les Ardennes sont toujours sous les eaux. Les gens circulent en bateau dans les rues. Tour de la Hollande où plus de 200.000 personnes ont dû être évacuées. Nous l'avons échappé bel...

Bon baisers de nous deux.
Mamie et Papi

---

aucun: *no, not any*
mouillé: *wet*
les Vosges: montagnes entre la France et l'Allemagne
une amélioration: *an improvement*
au-dessous de: *below*
nous ne devons pas trop nous plaindre: *we shouldn't complain too much*
la neige: *snow*

1. Consultez une carte de France. Où se trouve l'Alsace? Trouvez deux villes en Alsace qui ont plus d'habitants qu'Haguenau. Où se trouvent les Vosges?
2. Chaque lettre a une date. Faites une liste chronologique des dates. Puis résumez (dans vos propres termes) le temps décrit dans chaque lettre.

3. Qu'est-ce que vous pensez? Quel temps fait-il généralement en hiver en Alsace? Quand est-ce qu'il commence à faire froid, d'habitude? Jusqu'à quand est-ce qu'il fait froid au printemps?

4. Comparez le temps en hiver à Haguenau au temps hivernal (d'hiver) chez vous.

Structure: Le pronom y

À propos de la culture: Évidemment, le temps est un sujet de grand intérêt parmi les gens de tous les pays, y compris *(including)* les Français. On en parle beaucoup du temps, parce qu'il influence beaucoup la vie quotidienne, et on en discute souvent dans la correspondance.
Réfléchisons: Dans les lettres d'Alfred et Marguerite, comment est-ce qu'ils décrivent le temps? Est-ce qu'ils donnent simplement les faits? Est-ce qu'ils mentionnent des détails? Est-ce qu'ils parlent de leurs réactions personnelles au temps? Qu'est-ce que vous pensez: les descriptions d'Alfred et Marguerite ressemblent-elles plus à la météo ou à de la poésie?

OBSERVATIONS

—Allez-vous **à Londres** ce week-end?
—Oui, j'**y** vais avec Marc.

*Are you going **to London** this weekend?*
*Yes, I'm going **(there)** with Marc.*

—Vous travaillez **dans les jardins botaniques,** n'est-ce pas?
—Non, mais ma sœur **y** travaille.

*You work **in the botanical gardens,** don't you?*
*No, but my sister works **there**.*

—Est-ce qu'on vend beaucoup de souvenirs **à la plage?**
—À mon avis on **y** vend trop de souvenirs.

*Do they sell many souvenirs **on the beach?***

*In my opinion they sell too many souvenirs **there**.*

—Qui a voyagé **en France** avec toi cet été?
—Marcelle **y** a voyagé avec moi.

*Who traveled **to France** with you this summer?*
*Marcelle traveled **there** with me.*

—Vas-tu souvent **au lac?**
—Mais non. Je n'**y** vais jamais.

*Do you often go **to the lake?***
*Oh no. I never go **(there)**.*

—Pourquoi préférez-vous rester **chez vos parents?**
—Je préfère **y** rester parce que ça ne coûte rien.

*Why do you prefer to stay **with relatives?***

*I prefer to stay **there** because it doesn't cost anything.*

—Est-ce que tu t'intéresses **aux plantes exotiques?**
—Oh oui, je m'**y** intéresse beaucoup.

*Are you interested **in exotic plants?***

*Oh yes, I am very interested **in them**.*

STRATÉGIES D'ANALYSE

1. What do you think the function of the pronoun **y** might be? What does it replace in a sentence?

2. Where does **y** seem to go in relation to the verb in a sentence?

3. If the statement is in the past tense, does the pronoun **y** precede the auxiliary verb or the past participle?

4. If the statement is negative, where does **y** go in relation to the verb?

5. Where does **y** go if there is a conjugated verb followed by an infinitive in the sentence?

6. Does **y** always mean *there?*

PRÉCISIONS

- The pronoun **y** is used to replace an expression formed by a preposition of place such as **à, dans, en, sur** or **chez** + a noun. Note that **y** goes immediately in front of the verb.

  Vous allez souvent **à Strasbourg** pendant les vacances?
  Oui, nous **y** passons de beaux séjours.

  Vous restez en général **chez votre cousin?**
  Oui, nous **y** restons au moins deux fois par an.

- In the **passé composé, y** immediately precedes the auxiliary verb.

  Qui a voyagé **en Afrique** avec vous?
  Jean-Paul **y** a voyagé avec moi.

- With a negative expression, **y** immediately precedes the verb.

  Est-ce que tu travailles **à l'université?**
  Non, je n'**y** travaille pas.

  Êtes-vous allés **en France** cet été?
  Non, nous n'**y** sommes pas allés cet été. Mais nous espérons **y** aller cet hiver.

- When two verbs are used together (a conjugated verb + an infinitive), **y** precedes the infinitive.

  Pourquoi est-ce que tu préfères habiter **chez tes parents?**
  Je préfère **y** habiter parce que ça ne coute rien.

- Although **y** often takes on the meaning of *there* in English, it is also used as a substitute for prepositional phrases that are not related to location.

  Est-ce que vous vous intéressez **aux forêts pluviales?**
  Oui, je m'**y** intéresse beaucoup.

F. As-tu l'intention d'y aller? Demandez à votre partenaire où il/elle a l'intention d'aller ce week-end.

> **Modèle:** —*As-tu l'intention d'aller au cinéma ce week-end?*
> —*Oui, j'ai l'intention d'y aller.*
> ou —*Non, je n'y vais pas.*

au cinéma	au jardin botanique	au café
	au match de foot	à la plage
au théâtre	*au ballet*	à la campagne
au bord de la mer	**à la montagne**	au lac

G. **J'y suis allé(e).** En employant quelques-unes des expressions suivantes, posez cinq questions à votre partenaire, qui va vous répondre.

> **Modèle:** —*Toi et ta famille êtes-vous jamais allés dans les montagnes Rocheuses?*
> —*Oui, nous y sommes allés, et nous voulons y retourner.*
> —*Pendant quelle saison est-ce que vous y êtes allés?*
> —*Nous y sommes allés en été.*

toi	aller	à la plage
vous		dans les montagnes Rocheuses
toi et ton époux/épouse		dans le Sahara
toi et ton/ta conjoint(e)		au lac Champlain
tes/vos ami(e)s		dans une forêt (tropicale/dense)
toi et tes ami(e)s		dans les îles Caraïbes
votre/ta famille		au jardin botanique
tes/vos collègues		aux chutes du Niagara
tes/vos enfants		en ville

H. **Je voudrais y aller.** Donnez à votre partenaire une comparaison entre deux lieux où vous voudriez passer des vacances. Ensuite, votre partenaire va indiquer à quel lieu il préfère aller avec vous.

> **Modèle:** —*J'aime bien les vacances à la plage de Cancún, mais aussi les vacances à Manhattan à New York City. À la plage on peut se reposer, se bronzer et nager. En ville on peut aller aux théâtres, aux musées et à une grande variété de bons restaurants.*
> —*Moi aussi, j'aime bien la plage. Mais j'aime mieux New York. Je préfère y aller parce que j'adore aller aux théâtres.*

PRONONCIATION: Révision des voyelles nasales

Before beginning this practice section on the French nasal vowels [ã], [ɔ̃], [ɛ̃], and [œ̃], you may wish to review page 162 where their pronunciation is described.

Repeat each word after your instructor.

[ã] employé; grand; santé
[ɔ̃] ponctuel; tomber; condition
[ɛ̃] moins; infirmière; pain
[œ̃] un; lundi; brun

À vous! Taking turns with a partner, read the following sentences, focusing on your pronunciation of the nasal vowels.

1. Lundi, j'ai acheté un nouveau parfum.
2. En été, je vais rendre visite à mes parents.
3. Nous avons eu une séance très longue.
4. Il s'intéresse aux sciences.
5. Elle est moins inquiète maintenant.
6. C'est bon le pain avec de la confiture!

POUR DÉVELOPPER VOS IDÉES

Thematic objective: To associate preferences in leisure activities with different weather, seasons, and places in the world

Présentation: À chaque activité son époque

Voyage au bout du monde

À propos du vocabulaire: In this reading, **la marche** is walking (as a sport or outdoor activity). Some etymologists believe that the command "Mush!" (used with sled dogs) comes from the French verb **marcher.**

POUR SAISIR L'ESSENTIEL:

«Aventure au bout du monde» est un site Internet où on peut trouver des informations pratiques pour les voyages. Les conseils suivants font un extrait fascinant de ce site.

1. Organisez les six activités proposées dans la lecture en deux listes pour indiquer vos préférences. Le titre de la première liste est «**Je voudrais faire…** ». La deuxième liste s'appelle «**Je ne voudrais pas faire…** ».

2. Pour chaque activité, expliquez pourquoi vous (ne) voudriez (pas) la faire.

   Modèle: *Je ne voudrais pas faire de randonnées dans le Sahara, parce que je n'aime pas le désert. Il y fait trop chaud. J'aime mieux les randonnées dans la forêt.*

3. Indiquez votre degré d'intérêt pour chaque activité.

   Modèle: *Je m'y intéresse beaucoup/bien/assez bien/peu/très peu.*
   ou *Je ne m'y intéresse pas du tout.*

4. Comparez les activités dans votre liste de préférences avec celles de votre partenaire. Expliquez pourquoi vous aimez ces activités. Enfin, choisissez une activité que vous voudriez faire ensemble.

récolte des dattes: *date harvest*
propices: *favorable*
à la marche: aux randonnées
sèche: *dry*
une baleine: *whale*
tandis que: *while, on the other hand*

Randonnées dans le Sahara: Octobre est un bon mois pour visiter le plus grand désert du monde. Il y fait encore un peu chaud pendant la journée mais les nuits sont douces, et en plus c'est la période de la récolte des dattes°. Quant aux mois d'hiver, la chaleur est agréable le jour, mais la nuit il fait plutôt froid. Par contre, il n'y a que peu de vent.

Trekking au Népal: Mi-octobre à mi-mars est la meilleure époque, le ciel est clair et les températures pendant la journée sont propices° à la marche°.

Découverte de l'Amazonie: De juin à octobre on se dirige vers le sud afin d'éviter les violents orages.

Descente du fleuve Niger: Si l'on veut effectuer la totalité du trajet sur les gros bateaux de la Compagnie Malienne de Navigation, la période adéquate se situe entre juillet et fin novembre.

Safari photo dans les réserves d'animaux: Au Kenya, janvier–février, à la fin de la saison sèche°, semble l'idéal. En Inde, on voyage entre janvier et mai selon les réserves.

Observations des baleines°: Au Québec les meilleures observations se font entre fin août et fin septembre, tandis qu'au sud de l'Argentine c'est entre juillet et novembre.

I. **Scènes de mon voyage au bout du monde.** Vous avez déjà considéré votre voyage touristique en termes généraux. Maintenant réfléchissez-y de nouveau afin de préciser les images de vos rêves de voyage. Commencez par déterminer les attributs physiques des scènes que vous imaginez. Décrivez deux scènes. Basez vos descriptions sur ces questions, et organisez vos idées comme dans le schéma.

Questions pour stimuler les idées:

1. Où êtes-vous dans ce rêve?
2. Quel temps fait-il dans la scène que vous imaginez? Mentionnez aux moins deux aspects du temps.
3. Comment est le paysage? Mentionnez au moins trois aspects du paysage.
4. Qui est là? Qu'est-ce qu'on fait? Mentionnez aux moins trois aspects de ces questions—même si vous êtes la seule personne dans l'image.

Schéma de ma scène de voyage

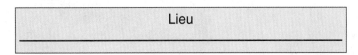

Lieu

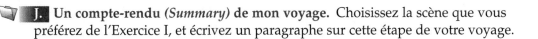

Temps	Paysage	Actions
1.	1.	1.
2.	2.	2.
3.	3.	3.

À propos du vocabulaire: Refer to the **Coup d'œil** sections in **1er** and **2e Thèmes** for vocabulary and ideas. You can also draw vocabulary for leisure activities from the **Lexiques** in **Chapitres 2** and **5.** And, of course, remember to refer to your portfolio entries as you collect your thoughts for this activity.

J. **Un compte-rendu** *(Summary)* **de mon voyage.** Choisissez la scène que vous préférez de l'Exercice I, et écrivez un paragraphe sur cette étape de votre voyage.

K. **On fait des comparaisons.** Décrivez vos deux scènes à votre partenaire. Faites vos descriptions aussi riches que possible. En écoutant les descriptions de votre partenaire, décidez laquelle de ses scènes vous préférez. Expliquez pourquoi en faisant une comparaison assez détaillée des attributs des deux scènes.

Modèle: —*J'aime mieux la scène à Cozumel que la scène aux Alpes en Suisse. À mon avis, le soleil est meilleur que la neige, et la plage est plus jolie que les montagnes. Il est moins intéressant de visiter des boutiques que de marcher au bord de la mer.*

3ᴱ THÈME: Mon tour du monde

Objective: To determine and express preferences in hotel accommodations

Un coup d'œil sur le thème

veux: voudrais

en même temps: *at the same time*

Quand je voyage, j'aime faire du tourisme. Je veux° apprendre quelque chose de nouveau et, en même temps°, me faire des souvenirs.

la Cité interdite: *the Forbidden City (in Beijing)*

Alors, je vais commencer mon tour du monde en Italie. Bien sûr, je vais visiter la chapelle Sixtine—un des plus beaux trésors artistiques du monde. Et puisque je me passionne pour l'histoire, je veux voir de mes propres yeux le colisée à Rome (imaginer les combats terribles des gladiateurs). Après Rome on va à Pise s'émerveiller devant la Tour penchée. Puis je vais faire une excursion en gondole sur les canaux de Venise, où on peut admirer la grande variété de l'architecture vénitienne. À la fin de mon séjour en Italie, je vais mieux connaître notre civilisation occidentale.

Après l'Europe, je vais continuer mon voyage en Chine. Là, je vais voir la Cité interdite°, imaginer les merveilles de la vie des empereurs. On va visiter la place Tian'anmen à Pékin pour réfléchir sur l'histoire des révolutions dans ce grand pays. Et il faut absolument faire une excursion à Badalin pour se promener le long de la Grande Muraille. Avant de quitter la Chine, je veux mieux comprendre les peuples et les cultures de l'Orient.

Puisque j'aime l'aventure et la nature aussi bien que l'histoire et l'architecture, je veux passer quelques semaines en Afrique. Je vais faire un safari photo dans une réserve d'animaux. Ça va être une expérience exceptionnelle: les animaux exotiques et le paysage grandiose. Je ne vais jamais oublier ces images.

à ne pas manquer: *not to miss*

une étape d'un voyage: *leg of a trip*

📁 Les expériences à ne pas manquer°
Parcourez les étapes° de ce voyage. Choisissez les lieux que vous voudriez visiter et les expériences que vous voudriez partager. Faites des listes où vous organisez ces lieux et expériences selon vos objectifs personnels. Cherchez des suggestions dans le tableau **Quelques objectifs pour les voyages** à la page 283.

POUR DÉVELOPPER VOTRE FRANÇAIS

Vocabulaire: À l'hôtel

insonorisé: *soundproofed*
un double vitrage: *double-paned windows*
une moquette murale: *wall-to-wall carpet*
ailes (f.): *wings*
un sèche-cheveux: *hair dryer*

OBSERVATIONS

Hôtel Louvre-Concorde****luxe
Place A. Malraux
75001 Paris
Tél: 01.42.61.56.01
Métro: Palais-Royal

Au cœur de Paris, face à l'Opéra, entre le musée du Louvre et les jardins du Palais-Royal, il se situe au centre des trésors artistiques de la capitale, des boutiques parisiennes et du quartier des affaires.

Hôtel Zéphyr***
31 bis, bd Diderot
75012 Paris
Tél: 01.43.46.12.72
Métro et R.E.R.: Gare de Lyon

À 100m de la gare de Lyon, hôtel entièrement rénové. 90 chambres climatisées et insonorisées° avec salle de bains, TV couleur, mini-bar, téléphone direct. Petit déjeuner buffet et room service. Restaurant, bar, 200 m² de salles de réunion.

Hôtel Mercure Paris-Montmartre***
3, rue Caulaincourt
75018 Paris
Tél: 01.42.94.17.17
Métro: Place de Clichy

Situé place de Clichy, au pied de la Butte Montmartre. 308 chambres insonorisées, équipées de salle de bains, téléphone direct, télévision, radio, mini-bar. Petit déjeuner buffet. Bar «Le Montmartre» ouvert de 12h à 2h du matin. 500 m² de salons pour réunions et réceptions.

Hôtel Campanile Gobelins**
17, avenue d'Italie
75013 Paris
Tél: 01.45.84.95.95
Métro: Place d'Italie

Entièrement neuf, il offre 123 chambres modernes et confortables avec double vitrage° et moquette murale°, dans 2 ailes° bâties autour d'un jardin intérieur. Les chambres sont équipées avec une salle de bains complète, TV couleur, téléphone direct. Pas de restaurant. Petit déjeuner servi en cafétéria.

Hôtel de Maine**
16, rue Maison-Dieu
75014 Paris
Tél: 01.43.22.00.67
Métro: Gaieté

À 500m de la gare Montparnasse, l'hôtel, entièrement rénové, propose 31 chambres équipées de salles de bains ou douche avec sèche-cheveux°. TV couleur, téléphone direct et mini-bar dans les chambres.

1. The location of a hotel is especially important in a large city. Make a list of the expressions from the listings of these Paris hotels that give information about location.

2. The size of a hotel may be important if you are booking for a group. Find any information that tells something about the size of these hotels.

3. Make a list of amenities that you would find in the rooms of the hotels.

4. Based on your study of these listings, what do you think the stars after the name of each hotel mean?

5. Which one of the signs would you hang on your hotel door if you wanted to sleep late? If you wanted to indicate that you would be out of your room for a few hours?

NOTE CULTURELLE

En France on utilise un système d'étoiles pour indiquer le niveau de luxe des hôtels.

Les hôtels les plus luxueux sont marqués de **quatre étoiles,** qui indiquent que ces hôtels offrent beaucoup de commodités°, tels que grande salle de réception bien meublée, parking couvert, piscine, ascenseur, téléphone direct, téléviseur et mini-bar dans toutes les chambres, salles de bains et W.-C. privés dans toutes les chambres, restaurant qui sert tous les repas, bar.

Un hôtel **trois étoiles** offre moins de ces commodités, mais toutes les chambres sont bien équipées et confortables. La plupart° des chambres ont une salle de bains. Il y a un ascenseur et un restaurant.

Un hôtel **deux étoiles** est confortable. Trente pour cent des chambres ont une salle de bains. Dans les grandes villes, on trouve généralement un téléphone, un téléviseur et un mini-bar dans les chambres. Il y a une salle à manger où on peut prendre le petit déjeuner, mais, le plus souvent, il n'y a pas de restaurant.

Dans un hôtel **une étoile,** il y a au moins dix chambres avec lavabo°. Le plus souvent, on partage les W.-C. et les douches/bains avec les autres clients de l'hôtel.

commodités (f.): *amenities*
La plupart: *Most*
un lavabo: *sink, basin*

A. **Je cherche un hôtel...** À tour de rôle avec votre partenaire, décrivez l'hôtel et la chambre que vous désirez pour votre voyage à Paris. Donnez au moins quatre préférences pour l'hôtel et quatre préférences pour la chambre. Indiquez aussi où vous préférez prendre le petit déjeuner.

Modèle: *Je cherche un hôtel situé dans un quartier historique près des musées. Je désire un hôtel trois étoiles avec un restaurant.*

Je cherche une chambre confortable et insonorisée avec salle de bains et TV couleur. Je préfère une chambre au deuxième étage près de l'as-censeur, une chambre qui donne sur la cour°.

Je préfère prendre le petit déjeuner dans la salle à manger.

donne sur la cour: *faces the courtyard*

chercher/désirer/préférer	un hôtel/une chambre/le petit dejeuner
dans un quartier d'affaires	climatisée
historique	insonorisée
moderne	confortable
culturel	moderne
résidentiel	rénovée
animé	bien meublé(e)°
tranquille	avec salle de bains
avec un ascenseur°	W.-C.
un restaurant	sèche-cheveux
un bar	radio
un grand salon	TV couleur
un petit salon intime	téléphone direct
des salles de réunion	mini-bar
deux étoiles	double vitrage
trois étoiles	moquette murale
quatre étoiles	coffre-fort°
quatre étoiles luxe	au premier étage
situé près des théâtres	deuxième étage
des restaurants	troisième étage
des musées	quatrième étage
des cinémas	près de l'ascenseur
des boutiques	loin de l'ascenseur
des grands magasins	qui donne sur la rue
d'un parc	qui donne sur la cour
de l'aéroport	dans ma chambre
de la gare	dans la salle à manger
du centre-ville	en cafétéria

bien meublé(e): *well-furnished*

ascenseur: *elevator*

un coffre-fort: *safe*

Structure: Le présent des verbes réguliers en -re

OBSERVATIONS

En Martinique on **vend** des vêtements sur les plages.

Erlène **rend** visite à la coiffeuse chaque semaine.

À propos de la prononciation: Note that, with **-re** verbs in the present, though the **-d** is *not* pronounced in the singular forms, the **-d** *is* pronounced in all the plural forms. Remember not to pronounce the final **-ent** in the third-person plural form.

J'**attends** toujours jusqu'à la dernière minute.
*I always **wait** until the last minute.*

Tu ne **perds** pas patience?
*Aren't you **losing** patience?*

Dans les îles Caraïbes, on **entend** beaucoup de musique reggae.
*In the Caribbean islands, one **hears** a lot of reggae music.*

Nous **répondons** à vos questions.
*We **are answering** your questions.*

Vous **perdez** votre temps.
*You **are wasting** your time.*

Les étudiants **se détendent** devant la télé après les cours.
*The students **relax** in front of the TV after classes.*

1. The words in boldface present the third regular conjugation of verbs. What are the endings in the plural forms? Are these plural endings similar to or different from the regular verbs that you have already seen (those with an **-er** infinitive and those with an **-ir** infinitive)?

2. Look at the endings for the singular forms. What do you notice that is unusual?

PRÉCISIONS

You are already using regular verbs with infinitives ending in **-er** (verbs like **travailler** and **parler**) and in **-ir** (verbs like **finir** and **choisir**).

- There is a third set of regular verbs whose infinitives end in **-re**. To conjugate these verbs, remove the **-re** to get the stem, then add a regular set of endings.

infinitive	*stem*		
ren**dre**	rend	je ren**ds**	nous rend**ons**
		tu ren**ds**	vous rend**ez**
		il/elle/on rend	ils/elles rend**ent**

B. À l'hôtel. À tour de rôle avec votre partenaire, remplacez les mots en italique par les mots entre parenthèses. Faites les changements nécessaires.

1. *J'*attends un coup de téléphone de la réception de l'hôtel. (nous / vous / Sophie / les étudiants)

2. *Nous* entendons la télévision de la chambre à côté. Les chambres de cet hôtel ne sont pas insonorisées. (on / notre prof / vous / Éric et Paul)

3. *Vous* perdez votre temps. L'hôtel est complet; il n'y a plus de chambres libres. (nous / tu / on / les étudiants)

4. Est-ce que *les employés* répondent aux questions à la réception? (le patron / la réceptionniste / nous / vous)

5. Où est-ce que *Marc* se détend à l'hôtel? (Sophie et Guy / vous / tu / on)

C. Les mots perdus. Vous êtes à la terrasse d'un café et vous entendez quelques conversations de gens qui passent devant le café. De temps en temps, il y a un mot que vous ne comprenez pas, mais avec votre connaissance du français vous pouvez deviner° les mots perdus. Complétez les phrases suivantes avec la forme convenable du verbe qui convient.

deviner: *guess*

1. —Après le divorce de ses parents, où va Louis pour les vacances de Noël?
   —Il _____ visite à sa mère avant Noël et à son père entre Noël et le Nouvel An. *(rendre/perdre/vendre)*

2. —J'ai expliqué mille fois à mon mari pourquoi je ne veux pas passer les vacances chez ses parents!
   —Vous _____ votre temps. Il y va toujours. *(attendre/perdre/entendre)*

3. —J'ai l'intention d'acheter une nouvelle voiture.
   —Alors, vous _____ votre Peugeot? Ça m'intéresse beaucoup. *(répondre/rendre/vendre)*

4. —Je suis arrivée au café pour mon rendez-vous avec Marc, mais il n'est pas arrivé à l'heure. Je suis partie après dix minutes. Je ne (n') _____ personne! Qu'est-ce qu'il était fâché! *(attendre/entendre/rendre)*

5. —Calme-toi, Chérie! Tu _____ patience trop facilement avec les enfants.
   (vendre/répondre/perdre)

6. —Où est-ce qu'on _____ le meilleur jazz du monde?
   (entendre/répondre/attendre)

   —Je pense que c'est à La Nouvelle-Orléans en Louisiane aux États-Unis ou, peut-être, à Montreux en Suisse.

7. —Je m'inquiète parce que mon fils ne _____ pas à mes questions.
   (rendre/perdre/répondre)

   —Quel âge a-t-il?

   —Quinze ans.

   —Cela s'explique. Ce n'est pas étonnant.

Structure: Le passé composé des verbes réguliers en -re

OBSERVATIONS

Mamie est arrivée à la fête à moto.

L'anniversaire de Mamie°

Hier soir, toute la famille **a rendu** visite à notre grand-mère pour fêter ses 80 ans°. On **a attendu** après le dîner (jusqu'à la dernière minute!) pour lui annoncer la mauvaise nouvelle. Quelle horreur! On n'**a** jamais **entendu** d'excuses comme ça! Nous **avons répondu** à ses protestations jusqu'à minuit. Mais enfin, elle **a perdu** la bataille. Le lendemain° j'**ai vendu** sa motocyclette.

Mamie (f.): *familiar name for Grandmother; Granny.*

fêter ses 80 ans: *celebrate her 80th birthday*

lendemain: *the following day*

STRATÉGIES D'ANALYSE

1. Examine the verbs in this paragraph. In what time frame do you think that this scenario takes place? Why?

2. How are these verbs similar to others you have used? How are they different?

PRÉCISIONS

- In the **passé composé,** the past participle of **-re** verbs is formed by removing the **-re** and adding **u** to the stem.

infinitive	*past participle*	
per**dre**	per**du**	**J'ai perdu** ma montre à la plage. **I lost** my watch at the beach.

D. **On a vendu...** À tour de rôle avec votre partenaire, remplacez les mots en italique par les mots entre parenthèses. Faites les changements nécessaires.

1. *On* a vendu des Cocas sur la plage. (les serveurs / je / nous / vous)

2. *J'ai* perdu 15 euros dans le parc. (tu / nous / vous / Sylvie)

3. *Le réceptionniste* a répondu à toutes les questions. (le prof / tu / vous / nous)

4. *Nous* avons attendu le serveur un quart d'heure. (je / vous / les étudiants / tu)

5. *Je* n'ai pas entendu la musique hier soir. (nous / tu / vous / le patron)

6. Quand est-ce que *vous* avez rendu visite à votre grand-mère? (tu / Marie-Claude / les enfants / nous)

Structure: Le superlatif (suite)

OBSERVATIONS

De tous mes amis, Christophe est **le plus sérieux**. Il prend les cours **les plus difficiles de** notre groupe. Il a **les meilleures notes de** tous les étudiants dans ses cours. Il passe **le moins de temps** à faire du sport et à s'amuser. Il profite **le mieux de** ses congés parce qu'il assiste à des stages d'informatique.

*Of all my friends, Christopher is the **most serious**. He takes **the most difficult** courses **of** our group. He gets **the best grades of** all the students in his classes. He spends **the least time** in sports and play. He makes **the best of** his vacations because he attends computer camps.*

STRATÉGIES D'ANALYSE

1. In each comparison in these sentences, how many people or things are being compared? Two? More than two?
2. We have already made comparisons of two objects using **plus** and **moins**. What words are used before these two words to indicate that more than two items are being compared?
3. How do we say *the best* when describing an action? When describing people, places, or things?

PRÉCISIONS

- In French, the superlative forms (those used in comparisons of more than two) are the same as the comparative forms (**plus, moins, meilleur,** and **mieux**), except that the definite article (**le, la, les**) is also used.

  Strasbourg est une **grande** ville.   *Strasbourg is a **big** city.*
  Marseille est **plus grande que** Strasbourg.   *Marseille is **bigger than** Strasbourg.*
  Paris est **la plus grande** ville **de** France.   *Paris is **the biggest** city **in** France.*

- Note that in French, **de** means *in* or *of* after a superlative.

  la plus grande ville **de** France

- When adjectives are used, the article agrees with the noun.

  La montagne **la plus haute** des Alpes est le mont Blanc.
  *The **highest** mountain in the Alps is Mont Blanc.*

  Les mois **les plus froids** sont janvier et février.
  *The **coldest** months are January and February.*

- Note that when an adjective follows the noun it modifies, you repeat the definite article in the superlative form.

À propos de la structure: You may wish to review the placement of adjectives in *Chapitre 5.*

E. **À mon avis...** Dites à votre partenaire votre opinion sur les lieux suivants. Faites au moins deux comparaisons de chaque groupe. Servez-vous des adjectifs dans la liste **Pour décrire les lieux** pour trouver des idées.

> **Modèle:** une plage ensoleillée, une forêt dense, une montagne couverte de neige
> *Une plage ensoleillée est le lieu le plus romantique.*
> *Une forêt dense est le lieu le plus mystérieux.*
> *Une montagne couverte de neige est le lieu le moins chaud.*

1. La Nouvelle-Orléans, Québec, Miami
2. les fleurs de printemps, le feuillage d'automne, les neiges d'hiver
3. une grande ville, un village au bord de la mer, un petit village à la campagne°
4. des îles tropicales, des montagnes couvertes de neige, des chutes d'eau
5. la France, le Canada, les États-Unis
6. la tour Eiffel, la Tour penchée, la statue de la Liberté

à la campagne: *in the country*

Pour décrire les lieux

* petit(e)/grand(e)	* pittoresque
* froid(e)/chaud(e)	* romantique
* animé(e)/tranquille	* reposant(e)
* historique/moderne	* haut(e)
* agréable/désagréable	* mystérieux(-euse)
* intéressant(e)/ennuyeux(-euse)	* ensoleillé(e)
* fréquenté(e)	

Structure: Les verbes irréguliers **vouloir** et **pouvoir**

OBSERVATIONS

Je **veux** visiter le Tadj Mahall.
*I **want** to visit the Taj Mahal.*

Tu **veux** y aller avec moi?
*Do you **want** to go there with me?*

Il **veut** des souvenirs.
*He **wants** some souvenirs.*

Nous **voulons** voir la Forêt-Noire.
*We **want** to see the Black Forest.*

Voulez-vous aller au Grand Canyon cet été?
***Do you want** to go to the Grand Canyon this summer?*

Ils ne **veulent** pas passer le week-end au lac.
*They **don't want** to spend the weekend at the lake.*

À propos de la structure: Je voudrais *(I would like)* is considered a more polite form than **je veux** *(I want)*.

1. Look at the **nous** and **vous** forms of the verb **vouloir** *(to want)*. How do we get the stem for these forms?

2. Using the verb **vouloir** *(to want)* as a model, can you complete the following sentences with **pouvoir** *(can or may)*, which has similar forms?

   Je _____ prendre les billets d'avion.   Nous _____ visiter la cathédrale.

   Tu _____ aller à Nice avec moi?   Vous _____ organiser l'itinéraire.

   On _____ se reposer à la plage.   Ils _____ choisir l'hôtel.

PRÉCISIONS

- The verb **vouloir** *(to want)* has an irregular conjugation.

je **veux**	nous **voulons**
tu **veux**	vous **voulez**
il/elle/on **veut**	ils/elles **veulent**

- Use **vouloir** to indicate that someone wants something.

Je **veux** un Coca, s'il vous plaît.	*I want a Coke, please.*
Je **veux** respirer l'air frais des montagnes.	*I want to breathe the fresh air in the mountains.*

- We use the idiomatic expression **vouloir bien** in casual conversation to mean *OK, sure, with pleasure.*

—Tu **veux** aller au parc avec nous?	*—Do you want to go to the park with us?*
—Oui, je **veux bien.**	*—Yes, sure.*

À propos du vocabulaire: Pouvoir is the verb that the common expressions **on peut** (one can) and **peut-être** (maybe) come from.

- The verb **pouvoir** *(can or may)* has the same irregular conjugation as **vouloir**.

je **peux**	nous **pouvons**
tu **peux**	vous **pouvez**
il/elle/on **peut**	ils/elles **peuvent**

- We use the verb **pouvoir** to mean both *can* (to be able to) and *may* (to have permission to).

J'ai beaucoup de stress au bureau, mais je **peux** me reposer au lac.
I have lots of stress at the office, but I can rest at the lake.

Normalement je travaille jusqu'à 18 heures, mais demain je **peux** partir à 15 heures pour aller au lac avec toi.
Usually I work until 6 o'clock, but I have permission to leave at 3:00 tomorrow to go to the lake with you.

À propos du vocabulaire: We say *«Je peux?»* to ask permission as a form of excusing ourselves, for example, before stepping in front of someone.

- In the **passé composé, pouvoir** has the meaning *to succeed in.*

> Après deux heures de coups de téléphone, j'**ai pu** trouver un hôtel avec une chambre libre.
> *After two hours of telephone calls, I **succeeded** in finding a hotel with a vacancy.*

F. **Où veux-tu aller?** Quelquefois nous avons des buts différents pour les vacances. Dites à votre partenaire où vous voulez aller pour faire chacune° des activités suivantes. Mentionnez au moins deux autres lieux possibles.

chacune: *each one*

Modèle: —faire des sports nautiques
—*Où veux-tu aller pour faire des sports nautiques?*
—*Pour faire des sports nautiques, moi, je veux aller en Guadeloupe.*
   Mais on peut aussi aller à Cozumel ou à Monte Carlo. Et toi?

1. faire des sports nautiques
2. apprécier la nature
3. faire du ski dans les montagnes
4. visiter les musées
5. admirer l'architecture
6. trouver la meilleure plage pour se bronzer
7. faire de l'alpinisme
8. faire du shopping
9. se reposer
10. faire une randonnée à vélo

PRONONCIATION: Révision des consonnes finales

Reminders:
- the final consonant of a word ending in mute **-e(s)** is always pronounced:

   mauvais → mauvaise   lourd → lourde

- While most final consonants are silent in French unless followed by a word that begins with a vowel sound, the letters **c, r, f,** and **l** are generally pronounced (remember **"careful"**):

   lac   chaleur   bref   social

- The **r** of **-er** verb infinitives is never pronounced. The sound pronounced is **-é**:

   quitter   se dépêcher

- The final **l** is not pronounced when it appears in the combinations **-ail** and **-eil**:

   travail   soleil

To complement this review, you might wish to refer to **Chapitre 2** of your text and workbook where general guidelines for final consonant pronunciation are outlined.

À vous! Taking turns with a partner, read the following sentences. When are final consonants pronounced? When are they silent?

1. L'Afrique, c'est le plus grand continent du monde.
2. Aujourd'hui, il fait du soleil. Demain, il va neiger.
3. Le lac du parc n'est pas très profond.
4. Il a pris sa photo devant l'hôtel à côté d'un palmier.
5. J'ai horreur des bateaux! J'ai souvent le mal de mer.
6. Il y a neuf terrains de golf sur cette île.

POUR DÉVELOPPER VOS IDÉES

Thematic objective: To plan your own world tour, identifying sites and experiences that relate to your personal travel goals

Présentation: Les lieux les plus passionnants du monde

POUR SAISIR L'ESSENTIEL:

Retournons au site Internet d'«*Aventures du bout du monde*». On y trouve des renseignements sur des lieux touristiques dans le monde.

1. Dans chaque section de la lecture, cochez (✓) les sites et les activités que vous trouvez intéressants—ou même passionnants—et mettez un *X* à côté des sites et des activités que vous trouvez peu amusants ou plutôt ennuyeux.

2. De tous les sites et activités mentionnés dans la lecture, choisissez les cinq meilleurs pour votre tour du monde.

marchandage est de rigueur:
bargaining is a must
bijoux (m.) en or, en argent et en ambre (m.): *gold, silver, and amber jewelry*
ours (m.): *bear*
motoneige (f.): *snow mobile*
raquettes (f.): *snowshoes*
broderies (f.): *embroidery*
fausse: *fake*
inoubliable: *unforgettable*

Netscape: A VOIR À FAIRE

Location: http://www.abm.fr

 Égypte
A voir, à faire
Le Caire (vieux quartiers, mosquées, musées Copte et d'Art égyptien) et ses environs (Gizeh avec son sphinx et ses pyramides); Alexandrie (rade, musées); la vallée des Rois et la vallée des Reines; Temples de Louxor et Karnak; le Mont et le monastère Ste Catherine (Sinaï); oasis du désert de Libye; vallée du Nil (croisières en bateau); Mer Rouge (plages et surtout plongée); Canal de Suez. 50% de réduction à l'entrée des sites sur présentation de la carte internationale d'étudiant.

 Artisanat/achats
Choix varié d'artisanat de toutes sortes dans les souks où le marchandage est de rigueur° avec des bijoux en or, en argent et en ambre,° (fausses) antiquités, papyrus, tapisseries, gallabeyas (costume local), épices, essences de fleurs et de parfums.

 Gréce
A voir, à faire
Athènes (Acropole, Agora, monuments byzantins, musées archéologique et byzantin); vestiges grecs ou romains (Corinthe, Delphes); monastères du Mont Athos et des Météores; randonneè sur le Mont Olympe. Sur les îles essentiellement la Crête (randonnées dans les gorges de Samaria) et pour leurs monuments Delos, Corfou, Rhodes. Plages et activités nautiques dans de très nombreuses îles des Cyclades, ou encore dans les îles Ioniennes (Corfou) pour beaucoup nettement moins fréquentées. Vie nocturne particulièrement animée dans tous les coins touristiques.

 Artisanat/achats
Céramiques, poteries, broderies,° (fausses) antiquités, bijoux, argenterie et huile d'olive.

 Québec
A voir, à faire
Le Québec est d'abord une destination nature aussi bien en été qu'en hiver. Balades et découvertes des paysages, des forêts, des lacs (dont le lac St Jean), des fleuves et rivières (le St Laurent et ses affluents), des parcs et réserves naturelles (Laurentides, Gaspésie . . .), ou encore de la côte Atlantique et des îles de la Madeleine. Faune et flore très variées avec de nombreuses espèces surtout les baleines (à la fin de l'été dans l'estuaire du St Laurent), et les ours.° Pour l'hiver large choix d'activités avec notamment ski, motoneige,° ou balades en raquettes.° Passer un hiver au Québec est aussi une expérience intéressante et inoubliable° pour qui n'est pas habitué aux hivers rigoureux et au rythme de vie que cela implique.

 Artisanat/achats
Artisanat amérindien (veste de peau, mocassins), sculptures sur bois, raquette à neige, bons vêtements d'hiver ou de randonnée, sirop et sucre d'érable.

 Australie
A voir, à faire
Vaste choix. Pour ne citer que l'essentiel: Alice Spring (au cœur du désert), Ayers Rock (le plus grand monolithe du monde), parcs nationaux, sites aborigènes, Grande Barrière (plongée, plages, surf), mines d'or ou d'opales, l'Australie historique (notamment dans l'état de Victoria), Sydney et sa baie.

 Artisanat/achats
Artisanat aborigène notamment peintures, boomerangs et dejeridus. Également les opales sous toutes leurs formes.

La cathédrale Notre-Dame de Paris
Est-ce qu'elle vous charme? Vous vous intéressez à son architecture gothique? À son art? À son expression spirituelle? À son histoire légendaire? Fait-elle partie de votre itinéraire?

G. On commence ses projets. Commencez à planifier votre propre tour du monde. (1) Choisissez trois pays, provinces ou régions que vous voulez visiter. Chacun des trois doit être dans un continent différent. (2) Pour chaque pays, faites une liste des villes et des sites que vous ne voulez pas manquer. Mentionnez au moins trois lieux pour chaque pays.

Pays 1	Pays 2	Pays 3

Lieux d'intérêt
1.
2.
3.
…

Lieux d'intérêt
1.
2.
3.
…

Lieux d'intérêt
1.
2.
3.
…

H. C'est le meilleur lieu pour… Pour chaque lieu sur vos listes de l'Exercice G, prenez des notes générales où vous décrivez ce qu'il y a d'extraordinaire ou expliquez un peu pourquoi vous vous y intéressez.

I. Échange d'itinéraires. Discutez avec un(e) partenaire vos idées pour votre tour du monde. Pendant la discussion, choisissez au moins trois des sites mentionnés par votre partenaire à ajouter à votre propre itinéraire.

J. J'envisage mon tour du monde. Écrivez une dissertation de cinq paragraphes sur votre tour du monde. Dans le premier paragraphe, identifiez vos objectifs pour un voyage touristique. Dans les trois paragraphes suivants, décrivez trois étapes du voyage. Terminez votre récit avec une conclusion générale. Consultez le **Coup d'œil** (page 306) comme modèle.

DÉCOUVERTE

Here are some additional couplets from the poem «*L'invitation au voyage*», by Baudelaire. Notice that the difference in the final consonants in **couchants** and **champs** does not disrupt the rhyme. **Champs** and **chants** sound identical. Other words that would rhyme with them include **entend, vent, étonnant, dans,** and **sent.** The pronunciation changes that have taken place in French over the centuries have caused many different spellings to be pronounced alike.

mouillés: *damp*
brouillés: *muddled*

revêtent les champs: *cloak the fields*

1
Les soleils mouillés°
De ces ciels brouillés°

⟨⟩

2
Les soleils couchants
Revêtent les champs°

⟨⟩

Do either of these couplets seem to describe the scenes you imagined for your travels in this *Thème*?

SYNTHÈSE DES DÉCOUVERTES

Read back through the couplets presented here and on page 293. Notice the spelling patterns that rhyme. Brainstorm with classmates to find other sets of different spellings that rhyme in French.

Once you have made lists of rhyme patterns, look back through the descriptive phrases you have studied in this chapter—particularly those that you have written in your portfolio—to begin your own set of lists of rhyming words. In each set of rhymes, be sure to include words that evoke the mood(s) and the flavor(s) that you associate with leisure travel. Collect a minimum of five sets of rhyming words, with at least three items in each set.

Modèle: Set 1: *champs, chant, entend, vent, étonnant, dans, sent*

ÉCOUTONS: Chez l'agent de voyage

You will hear two conversations between a travel agent and someone trying to plan a trip. First, listen just to get an overview of each traveler's profile. Then listen for the travelers' specific preferences and objectives for their vacation trips. Finally, decide which of the two vacations trips you would select for yourself, based on your own preferences and objectives in travel.

A. On identifie les voyageurs. Écoutez les conversations, et indiquez le voyageur dans chaque situation. Écrivez *MS* pour Madame Savard et *PB* pour Patrick Benoît.

Âge	Budget	Priorités	Destination
45–65 ans _____	Limité _____	Repos _____	Rester en France _____
20–30 ans _____	Généreux _____	Aventure _____	Quitter la France _____

B. On identifie les qualifications. Écoutez une deuxième fois les conversations. Cette fois-ci, identifiez les intérêts et les objectifs mentionnés par chaque voyageur.

Besoins et préférences ⇨ Voyageur ⇩	Le tourisme	L'aventure	L'exotisme	Le sport	Le repos	L'enrichissement culturel	Rencontrer des gens intéressants	La beauté naturelle	Se faire des souvenirs
Mme Savard									
Patrick Benoît									

C. On prend la décision. Réfléchissez aux deux voyages recommandés par Monique Delacroix. Indiquez quel voyage vous préférez, et cochez (✓) tous les éléments qui ont influencé votre décision.

Je choisirais:
I would choose

Je choisirais° le voyage ___ **a)** au Club Med en Guadeloupe ou ___ **b)** sur la Côte d'Azur.

Je choisirais ce voyage... :

à cause du tourisme	à cause de l'aventure	à cause de l'exotisme	à cause du sport	à cause du repos	à cause de l'enrichissement culturel	pour rencontrer des gens intéressants	à cause de la beauté naturelle	pour se faire des souvenirs

L'invitation au voyage
Charles BAUDELAIRE (1821–1867)
LES FLEURS DU MAL

Mon enfant, ma sœur,
Songe à la douceur
D'aller là-bas vivre ensemble!
Aimer à loisir,
Aimer et mourir
Au pays qui te ressemble!
Les soleils mouillés
De ces ciels brouillés
Pour mon esprit ont les charmes
Si mystérieux
De tes traîtres yeux
Brillant à travers leurs larmes.

Là, tout n'est qu'ordre et beauté,
Luxe, calme et volupté.

Des meubles luisants,
Polis par les ans,
Décoreraient notre chambre;
Les plus rares fleurs
Mêlant leurs odeurs
Aux vagues senteurs de l'ambre,
Les riches plafonds,
Les miroirs profonds,
La splendeur orientale,

Tout y parlerait
À l'âme en secret
Sa douce langue natale.

Là, tout n'est qu'ordre et beauté,
Luxe, calme et volupté.

Vois sur ces canaux
Dormir ces vaisseaux
Dont l'humeur est vagabonde;
C'est pour assouvir
Ton moindre désir
Qu'ils viennent du bout du monde.
Les soleils couchants
Revêtent les champs,
Les canaux, la ville entière,
D'hyacinthe et d'or;
Le monde s'endort
Dans une chaude lumière.

Là, tout n'est qu'ordre et beauté,
Luxe, calme et volupté.

Pour ébaucher une perspective

1. Read through the poem, highlighting the lines you find most appealing.

2. Look for images to illustrate the poem. You might use photos or drawings from magazines, from your own albums, or you may want to take photographs. Find at least two images for each stanza and one for the refrain (seven in all).

3. Find a piece of music that you would use to interpret the mood of the poem.

4. Record on video your recitations of the poem, accompanied by the music and images you have chosen for your interpretation.

NOTE CULTURELLE

La sensualité que vous remarquez dans ce poème de Baudelaire est caractéristique de son œuvre. En fait, Napoléon III a déclaré que certains poèmes dans les *Fleurs du mal* représentaient un outrage à la moralité publique et aux bonnes mœurs°. Le poète et ses éditeurs ont été condamnés à payer une amende, et ils ont perdu leurs droits civils. De plus, le tribunal a ordonné la suppression de certains poèmes de cette collection. Mais, comme disent les Français, «Autres temps, autres mœurs». En 1998 la Bibliothèque nationale a payé 3,2 millions de francs pour les épreuves de l'édition originale des *Fleurs du mal*.

Réfléchissons: Depuis toujours, la recherche de l'équilibre entre les droits des artistes et la moralité publique est un problème cactus. Pouvez-vous mentionner d'autres artistes (écrivains, musiciens, philosophes, etc.) qui sont confrontés à un gouvernement ou à un public hostile?

mœurs: *customs, moral behavior*

INTÉGRATION

A. Négocier un itinéraire. Form groups of four. Imagine that this group is your team of traveling companions for your world tour. Your task is to develop the itinerary for your world tour, deciding on five stops for your group. Take turns describing to your group the three sites that you would personally choose to include on your world tour, using your notes from the *Idées* section of *3ᵉ Thème* (page 317). Be as convincing as possible so that your group will decide on one of your sites to visit.

B. Organiser un itinéraire. As a team, develop a written itinerary that you can leave at home with family members and/or colleagues at work. Decide on the sequence and locations of your stops, how long you will spend at each site, and at least three activities you will do there. Tell which mode of transportation you will use to get to each destination.

C. Laisser un message sur le répondeur *(answering machine).* Imagine that your trip is well under way and that you need to check in with someone at home or the office. Because of the time difference, no one answers the phone, so you must leave a message on the voice mail. Make an audio recording of your personal message.

1. Tell how your trip is going and how you are feeling.
2. Mention your favorite place that you have visited thus far, what you did there and what you specifically liked about it.
3. Mention how the weather was there. Tell what you did one day when the weather was bad.

4. Tell where you are now, what you are seeing or doing there, and how the weather is.

5. Mention one other site you plan to visit before coming home and what you intend to see or do there.

6. Send any personal messages you wish.

D. **Écrire une lettre à un(e) collègue.** Write a letter home to a family member or colleague.

1. Include the information from your telephone message in Exercise C.

2. Also mention the most beautiful site you've seen, the best meal you've had, what you found the least interesting, and what you found to be the most fascinating (or educational or mysterious or romantic, etc.)

3. Make one comment on where the weather was either the nicest, warmest, sunniest, coldest, or worst.

4. Tell when you will be arriving home.

LEXIQUE DE BASE   LEXIQUE D'EXPANSION

Pour décrire la nature

un feuillage	foliage	une plante exotique	exotic plant
une montagne (rocheuse)	(rocky) mountain	la végétation dense	dense vegetation
une île tropicale	tropical island	une colline	hill
une rivière	river	une vallée	valley
un fleuve	major river to the sea	une vue panoramique	panoramic view
un jardin botanique	botanical garden	un coucher de soleil	sunset
une plage ensoleillée	sunny beach	un soleil couchant	setting sun
une chute (d'eau)	waterfall	un palmier	palm tree
au bord de la mer	at the seashore	un arbre fascinant	fascinating tree
un désert	desert	un son exotique	exotic sound
une forêt	forest	merveilleuses couleurs	marvelous colors
un lac	lake	une ambiance calme et luxueuse	calm, luxurious ambiance
le paysage	countryside		
une ville pittoresque	picturesque city	la solitude reposante	restful solitude
à la campagne	in the country	une chaîne de montagnes	mountain range
		une côte	coast

Pour indiquer des régions géographiques

une carte géographique	geographical map
une ville	city
un village	village
un pays	country
un état	state
une province	province
un continent	continent
le monde	the world
le monde francophone	French-speaking world
au bout du monde	at (to) the end of the world
autour du monde	around the world

Pour parler avec des verbes en -re

attendre	to wait (for)
perdre	to lose
perdre (son) temps	to waste (one's) time
perdre patience	to lose patience
rendre visite à	to visit, pay a visit to (a person)
vendre	to sell
répondre à	to answer (someone or something)
se détendre	to relax
entendre	to hear

Les saisons

en été (m.)	in the summer
en automne (m.)	in the autumn, fall
en hiver (m.)	in the winter
au printemps	in the spring

la météo	weather report	Il y a du soleil.	It's sunny.
Il fait...	The weather is . . .	du vent.	It's windy.
beau	beautiful	du verglas.	It's icy.
mauvais	bad	du brouillard.	It's foggy.
chaud	warm, hot	des nuages.	It's cloudy.
froid	cold	Il fait un temps...	The weather is . . .
frais	cool	incroyable	unbelievable
doux	mild	déprimant	depressing
du soleil	sunny	insupportable	unbearable
du vent	windy	superbe	superb
Il fait un temps...	The weather is . . .	abominable	abominable
magnifique	wonderful, marvelous	Le ciel est nuageux.	It's cloudy.
moche	ugly	Tout est couvert de glace.	It's icy.
lourd	heavy, oppressive		
épouvantable	miserable, awful		
Le ciel est couvert.	It's cloudy.		
Il pleut.	It's raining.		
Il neige.	It's snowing.		
la pluie	rain		
la neige	snow		
la chaleur	heat		
le froid	cold		
l'humidité (f.)	humidity		
La route est verglacée.	The road is icy.		
Il fait... degrés.	It is . . . degrees.		

bon(ne)	good
meilleur(e)	better
le (la) meilleur(e)	the best
bien	well
mieux	better
le mieux	the best

vouloir	to want something
Je veux bien.	OK, sure, with pleasure
pouvoir	can (to be able to), may (to have permission to)
J'ai pu...	I succeeded in . . .

LA CUISINE:
Diversité géographique et culturelle

Communicative Objectives

- To talk about selecting and purchasing food items off the shelf

- To order a meal in a restaurant

- To use expressions of quantity with reference to foods

Thematic Objectives

✓ To examine associations between geographic regions and foods that are identified with them

✓ To examine the cultural influences on regional cuisines

✓ To identify the significance that you attribute to certain foods based on the role they play in your memories

OUVERTURE EN VIDÉO:
La cuisine: Grand intérêt du monde francophone

On fait des courses (d'alimentation): *We go grocery shopping*

On fait des courses°

On fait des courses (d'alimentation): *We go grocery shopping*

On commence par les légumes?

On fait la queue au rayon de viande pour acheter le gigot.

La mise en scène

In *Chapitre 8* you will examine the relationship between geographic regions and food, observe cultural influences on regional cuisine, and identify the significance that you attribute to foods based on the role they play in your memories. This video segment focuses on key expressions that are useful for talking about foods, both in their "grocery store" or "market" form and in their prepared state, such as on a menu or served at a meal. As you learn to talk about foods, notice how often the origin or preparation of foods typical of a certain region is pointed out.

You will see some scenes in a supermarket and a pastry shop in France, as well as a planning session for a special dinner party.

A. **L'anniversaire de Maman.** Watch the video segment in which Xavier and his two sisters, Aude and Élisabeth, are planning a special birthday dinner for their mother. Before we listen to their planning session, let's anticipate what we can expect them to put on the menu for this formal family dinner, and consequently, on their shopping lists. Check off at least four items you think they'll most likely decide on.

hors d'œuvre	finger foods	birthday cake
pizza	French fries	soda
hamburgers	leg of lamb	beer
tuna fish sandwiches	apple pie	wine
salad	chocolate eclairs	champagne

B. **On anticipe le vocabulaire.** Now let's watch the video segment of Aude and Élisabeth doing their shopping. Watch it first without the soundtrack to get some visual clues about which food items they include on their shopping list. Check off any items in the list on the next page you see them select.

lettuce	artichokes	celery
mushrooms	tomatoes	carrots
asparagus	spinach	zucchini squash
chicken	leg of lamb	salmon
sirloin steak	lobster	soda
mineral water	beer	baguettes (loaves of bread)
chocolate eclairs	3-layer praline cake	1-layer chocolate cake

Les paroles et le sens

C. **On écoute.** As you watch the video segment again, this time with its sound-track, work on discriminating the sounds you hear used to talk about the foods you see.

On y réfléchit

D. **Mes plats préférés.** Do you have some favorite foods among the international cuisines with which you are familiar? Add some other dishes that you know to the following chart.

French	Mexican	Italian	Chinese
crêpes	flan	fettucine	moo goo gai pan
coq au vin	enchiladas	spaghetti	egg drop soup
???	???	???	???
Spanish	**Polish**	**German**	**Thai**
???	???	???	???

Et comme entrée, pourquoi pas des truites en gelée ou du pâté de chez le traiteur? On peut aller chez Fauchon sur la place de la Madeleine.

E. **Des aliments que j'apprécie.** Now think of the ingredients in some of your favorite food preparations in general. Have you learned the words for any of them in French yet? Check off the items you recognize in the chart that are among the foods you like.

Plats principaux	Légumes	Desserts	Boissons
viande	courgettes	éclair	eau minérale
gigot	tomates	gâteau au chocolat	jus de fruit
jambon	laitue	gâteau praliné	bière
poulet	champignons	fromage	vin blanc
poisson	brocolis	sorbet	vin rouge
truite	artichauts		champagne

1ᴱᴿ THÈME: Spécialités de la région

Objective: To talk about selecting and purchasing food items off the shelf

PRÉSENTATION: Un coup d'œil sur le thème

une assiette: *plate*

Que ce soient: *Whether it be*
la moutarde... dijonnais: *Dijon mustard*
le confit: *preserved (meat)*
une truffe: *truffle*
à la [mode] niçoise: *in the style of the city of Nice*

se déguste: *is tasted*

La France, cinq fois plus petite que le Québec, renferme une histoire culinaire si riche en traditions qu'il est impossible de vous la présenter sur une seule assiette°. C'est un buffet gastronomique où chaque région a ses traditions, ses spécialités, ses cultures et ses styles de préparation.

Que ce soient° les moutardes du pays dijonnais°, les confits° et les truffes° du Périgord, le cassis de Bourgogne

Que ce soit un plat préparé à la niçoise°, à la parisienne, à la normande ou à la bretonne

Que ce soient les vins d'Alsace, des Côtes du Rhône, les grands Beaujolais ou les Bourgognes, les rosés de Provence, le Champagne

Que ce soient les fromages, du camembert doux et ivoire au roquefort persillé sur un plateau de plus de 500 variétés

La France se déguste° de ville en village, de la mer au sommet des Alpes.

Une table à la française. Trouvez-vous des produits que vous connaissez dans cet inventaire d'aliments français? Avez-vous goûté quelques-uns de ces produits? En avez-vous acheté? Organisez vos réponses en trois listes, en ajoutant d'autres produits alimentaires de la France ou du monde francophone que vous connaissez.

Aliments français que je connais	Aliments français que j'ai déjà goûtés	Aliments français que j'ai déjà achetés ou préparés
moutarde de Dijon truffes salade niçoise	moutarde de Dijon salade niçoise	salade niçoise

Vocabulaire: Les aliments chez les petits commerçants

OBSERVATIONS

a. un millefeuille
b. une religieuse
c. un petit pain
d. une tartelette aux fraises
e. un palmier
f. un pain de campagne
g. un croissant
h. un éclair
i. une baguette
j. une tarte aux pommes
k. un pain complet
l. un gâteau au chocolat

a. des épinards
b. des petits pois
c. des tomates
d. des oignons
e. des asperges
f. des choux-fleurs
g. des choux de Bruxelles
h. de la salade
i. des carottes
j. des haricots verts
k. des pommes de terre
l. des champignons

Chéri,

Rappelle-toi que ce soir les Martin viennent dîner chez nous. Moi, je travaille aujourd'hui pendant ton jour de congé. S'il te plaît, va acheter des provisions pour ce soir. J'ai l'intention de servir une soupe à l'oignon gratinée, des côtelettes de veau aux légumes, une salade, des fromages et un dessert. J'ai besoin de:

- *salade,*
- *pommes de terre,*
- *carottes,*
- *choux de Bruxelles,*
- *un assortiment de fromages,*
- *pain,*
- *fraises et framboises comme dessert.*

Ah, oui, j'ai aussi besoin de côtelettes!! Va chez les petits commerçants si tu en as le temps. Les produits sont plus frais. Merci mille fois. À 18 heures.
Bises.
Marie-Claude

a. du Roquefort
b. du Port Salut
c. du chèvre
d. du Brie
e. de l'Emmenthal

a. un rôti de porc   d. des côtelettes de
b. un poulet   veau
c. un gigot   e. du bœuf (biftek)

1. What do you think the relationship is between Marie-Claude and the person to whom she wrote the note? What clues did you use to come to your conclusion?

2. Where does Marie-Claude prefer to shop, at the supermarket or at the individual neighborhood stores? Why?

3. Using the pictures of the items sold in the small shops, determine how many stops a person would have to make to buy the items on Marie-Claude's list.

PRÉCISIONS

Vocabulaire d'expansion

un pain au chocolat	roll with a strip of chocolate through it
un pain de mie	loaf of white bread (usually sliced)
un pain de seigle	rye bread
un pain aux céréales	multi-grain bread

- In France, the small neighborhood stores that specialize in one or a few kinds of foods are still common. Many people prefer to buy from the specialty shops rather than at a supermarket and because the produce is usually fresher, the food items are generally prepared on location, the shopkeepers are usually friendlier and more likely to know the customers, who prefer to shop daily.

- A bakery may specialize in bread **(une boulangerie)** or in pastries **(une pâtisserie)**, or it may be a combination of both **(une boulangerie-pâtisserie).** Since most French people buy fresh bread every morning, there are usually a number of these shops in every neighborhood.

- The following items are usually available at a **boulangerie:**

du pain	bread	un croissant	croissant
une baguette	French bread	un pain complet	whole-wheat bread
des petits pains	rolls		

Vocabulaire d'expansion

un baba au rhum	rum pastry
un gâteau aux amandes	almond cake
une tarte aux myrtilles/bluets	blueberry pie (**myrtilles** in France, **bluets** in Québec)
un biscuit	cookie
(à soda)	cracker

- Items usually available at a **pâtisserie** are:

une tarte...	pie	un millefeuille	layers of puff pastry and cream
aux cerises	cherry pie		
aux fraises	strawberry pie	une religieuse	type of cream puff
au citron	lemon pie	un éclair	chocolate eclair
une tartelette...	individual tart	un gâteau...	cake
aux framboises	raspberry tart	au chocolat	chocolate cake
aux abricots	apricot tart	praliné	praline

- Many French prefer to buy their fruits and vegetables at an open-air market **(un marché en plein air)** rather than at a supermarket. The produce is generally fresher and often a better price.

- Each market has its specialties depending on its suppliers. The following fruits and vegetables are commonly available:

Vocabulaire d'expansion

des concombres (m.)	cucumbers
des endives (f.)	endives
des aubergines (f.)	eggplants
des brocolis (m.)	broccoli
des choux (m.)	cabbage
des poivrons verts (m.)	green peppers
de l'ail (m.)	garlic
des radis (m.)	radishes
du maïs	corn
des ananas (m.)	pineapples
des poires (f.)	pears
du raisin	a bunch of grapes

Des légumes		Des fruits	
des asperges (f.)	asparagus	des abricots (m.)	apricots
des carottes (f.)	carrots	des bananes (f.)	bananas
des champignons (m.)	mushrooms	des cerises (f.)	cherries
des épinards (f.)	spinach	des citrons (m.)	lemons
des haricots verts (m.)	green beans	des fraises (f.)	strawberries
des oignons (m.)	onions	des framboises (f.)	raspberries

des petits pois (m.)	peas	des oranges (f.)	oranges
des pommes (f.) de terre	potatoes	des pamplemousses (m.)	grapefruit
de la salade	lettuce	des pêches (f.)	peaches
des tomates (f.)	tomatoes	des pommes (f.)	apples
des courgettes (f.)	zucchini squash		

- A cheese shop **(une fromagerie)** obviously specializes in cheese. It may also sell yogurt, butter, cream, and milk.

du yaourt	yogurt	du camembert	a popular cheese from Normandy
du beurre	butter		
de la crème	cream	du Brie	a mild, semi-soft cheese
du lait	milk	du Roquefort	a strong, blue cheese
du fromage	cheese	du chèvre	goat cheese
		de l'Emmenthal	Swiss cheese with holes, also made in France

Vocabulaire d'expansion
de la Raclette
  a special fondue-type dish with melted cheese
de la Gourmandise
  a packaged dessert cheese containing kirsch, a cherry-flavored liqueur
du Boursin
  a packaged soft cheese containing herbs and garlic

- At the butcher shop **(la boucherie)** you can buy fresh meat, such as:

du bœuf	beef	du jambon du pays	ham on the bone/ cured ham
du veau	veal		
du porc	pork	des côtelettes (f.)	cutlets, chops
de l'agneau (m.)/	lamb	du bifteck	steak
du gigot	leg of lamb	du rosbif	roast beef

A. Où va-t-on... ? Dites à votre partenaire où on va pour acheter ces aliments.

Modèle: du pain
  —*Où va-t-on pour acheter du pain?*
  —*Pour acheter du pain, on va à la boulangerie.*

1. un croissant
2. des bananes
3. du fromage
4. des pommes
5. des pommes de terre
6. du veau
7. des petits pains
8. du brie
9. une tarte aux fraises
10. du porc

B. Chez les petits commerçants. C'est à vous et à votre partenaire de faire le marché. Voici la liste des aliments que vous cherchez. Avant de partir de la maison, organisez vos courses. Faites quatre listes en indiquant où on va pour faire les achats.

des cerises
du pain complet
des croissants
des côtelettes de veau
du beurre
des asperges

des pommes de terre
du camembert
des framboises
des champignons
du jambon de pays
des petits pains

du lait
une tarte aux pommes
des tomates
des bananes
des petits pois
des abricots

des fraises
des pommes
des carottes
du brie
des pêches
des oignons

à la boulangerie-pâtisserie	à la boucherie	à la fromagerie	au marché

Structure: Les aliments chez les petits commerçants (suite)

OBSERVATIONS

a. des carottes
au citron
b. un poulet rôti
c. du saumon
fumé
d. une quiche

e. du pâté
f. du saucisson
g. des saucisses (f)
h. du jambon

a. du homard
b. des huîtres (f)
c. du poisson
d. des crevettes (f)

a. des pâtes (f)
b. du riz
c. des céréales (f)
d. du sucre
e. du poivre
f. du sel
g. du vinaigre

h. de l'huile
i. de l'eau minérale
j. du jus de fruit
k. de la confiture
l. de la moutarde
m. du thé
n. du café

STRATÉGIES D'ANALYSE

1. Which of these shops seems most like a grocery store or a general store?
2. Which one do you think has the most pleasant aromas? Why?
3. Would you like to work in one of these stores? Why or why not?

PRÉCISIONS

- In France **une charcuterie** sells prepared pork products essentially. However, some **charcuteries** are also **traiteurs** and function like a delicatessen in the U.S. Some of the items typically available in **une charcuterie** include the following:

du jambon	*ham*
du saucisson	*salami*
des saucisses	*sausages*
du pâté	*pâté (a meat spread)*
du saumon fumé	*smoked salmon*
des quiches	*quiches*
des salades niçoises	*"chef" salads made with tuna and other seafood (typical of the Mediterranean coast area around Nice)*
des carottes râpées	*grated carrots*

- In some **charcuteries** you can also buy other items, such as:

du poulet rôti	*roasted chicken*	de l'eau minérale	*bottled water*
du pain	*bread*	du vin	*wine*
des fromages	*cheeses*		

- Fish is bought at a fish market, **une poissonnerie.** The following may be some of the choices available:

du poisson	*fish*	du thon	*tuna*
du saumon	*salmon*	du homard	*lobster*
de la sole	*sole*	des crevettes (f.)	*shrimp*
de la truite	*trout*	des huîtres (f.)	*oysters*

À propos de la prononciation: Pay attention to the aspirate **h**, as in **homard, haricots, hollandais(e), hors-d'œuvre,** compared to the **h** in **huile** and **huîtres.**

- Packaged grocery products are sold at **une épicerie,** including the following staples:

des épices (f.)	*spices*	du riz	*rice*
du sel	*salt*	des pâtes (f.)	*pasta*
du poivre	*pepper*	du café	*coffee*
de la moutarde	*mustard*	du thé	*tea*
de la mayonnaise	*mayonnaise*	de la confiture	*jam*
des céréales (f.)	*cereal*	du miel	*honey*

C. **Où va-t-on pour acheter... ?** Dites à votre partenaire où on va pour acheter les aliments suivants.

Modèle: des crevettes
—*Où va-t-on pour acheter des crevettes?*
—*Pour acheter des crevettes, on va à la poissonnerie.*

1. du poisson
2. de la moutarde
3. du pâté
4. de l'huile et du vinaigre
5. du sel et du poivre
6. un homard
7. du saumon fumé
8. du riz
9. des huîtres
10. des céréales

D. **Chacun son goût.** (*Each to his own taste*). Imaginez que vous préparez le dîner chez vous pour trois ou quatre amis. Qu'est-ce que vous choisissez quand vous allez faire les courses dans un marché? D'abord, indiquez votre choix parmi les possibilités ci-dessous dans chaque catégorie.

moi	des aliments	mon/ma partenaire
du saumon fumé	des huîtres, du saumon fumé, des crevettes	
	du bifteck, des côtelettes de porc, du veau, du poisson	
	des pommes de terre, du riz, des pâtes	
	des haricots verts, des carottes, des petits pois, des asperges	
	du pain de campagne, des petits pains, une baguette	
	du brie, du camembert, du roquefort, du chèvre	
	un gâteau au chocolat, une tarte aux fraises, des éclairs	

E. Une comparaison des goûts. Maintenant comparez vos choix à ceux de votre partenaire.

Modèle: —*Chez moi, je voudrais servir du saumon fumé.*
—*Moi, je choisis de servir des crevettes chez moi.*

tous les deux: *both of us*   ou   —*Moi aussi; tous/toutes les deux°, nous allons servir du saumon fumé.*

F. On fait à nouveau les courses. C'est à vous et à votre partenaire de faire le marché. Vous avez une longue liste d'aliments variés. Avant de commencer, catégorisez les achats selon l'endroit où on va pour les acheter. Organisez les aliments en de nouvelles listes. Puis cochez (✓) les aliments que vous deux avez l'intention d'acheter pour ce soir.

des huîtres	une baguette	du riz	du chèvre
des pommes de terre	des céréales	des crevettes	du sel
du vinaigre	du brie	des oignons	des champignons
des petits pains	des bananes	une tarte aux fraises	de l'Emmenthal
du beurre	un homard	des yaourts	du sucre
un gâteau au chocolat	de la moutarde	des abricots	des côtelettes de porc
du saumon fumé	du poivre	un éclair	un millefeuille

au marché	à l'épicerie	à la poissonnerie	à la fromagerie/ crémerie	à la boucherie	à la charcuterie	à la boulangerie-pâtisserie

Note Culturelle

En France, comme aux États-Unis, il y a de plus en plus de femmes qui travaillent. Ainsi, travaillant plus d'heures par semaine, les Françaises passent moins de temps à la sélection et la préparation des repas pour la famille. **Le supermarché** est devenu de plus en plus populaire dans la culture française. Avec un arrêt au supermarché, on peut trouver tout ce qui est nécessaire pour préparer le dîner: de la viande, des légumes, des fruits, des fromages, du vin, de l'eau, du pain, un dessert.

Réfléchissons: À votre avis: Où est-ce que vous préférez faire les courses pour les provisions? Aimez-vous mieux aller chez les petits commerçants ou au supermarché? Quels avantages et désavantages trouvez-vous en faisant les courses au supermarché?

- As in the United States, **le supermarché** has sections or counters or aisles **(des rayons)** labeled to help customers locate items throughout the store. These sections are organized in the same divisions as at **les petits commerçants** and carry the same names.
- **Le supermarché** has other **rayons** where additional products are displayed, such as:

le rayon volaille

du poulet	*chicken*
du canard	*duck*
de la dinde	*turkey*

le rayon produits surgelés

de la viande	*meat*
des légumes	*vegetables*
de la glace	*ice cream*
du sorbet	*sorbet/sherbet*
de la pizza	*pizza*

le rayon boissons

de l'eau minérale	*mineral water*
du jus de fruits	*fruit juice*
du vin rouge	*red wine*
du vin blanc	*white wine*
de la bière	*beer*
du Coca	*soda, cola*

- Many French people who shop at **le supermarché** once a week or so also patronize **les petits commerçants** in their neighborhood for fresh bread, pastries, fruits, and vegetables.

G. Ce que j'aime beaucoup et ce que je n'aime pas du tout. Vous allez comparer vos préférences avec celles de votre partenaire dans les fiches Venn suivantes.

1. D'abord, faites des listes pour indiquer vos préférences en viandes, poissons, légumes, fruits, fromages, pâtisseries et boissons.
2. Puis, indiquez les choses que vous n'aimez pas du tout manger.
3. Enfin, comparez vos listes à celles de votre partenaire. Avez-vous plus de choix similaires ou différents? Trouvez tous les choix que l'un de vous aime beaucoup et l'autre n'aime pas du tout.

À propos du vocabulaire: The most important vocabulary concerning foods *for you* are the names of things that you especially like and those that you really do not care for. Pay special attention to the names of foods in these two groups.

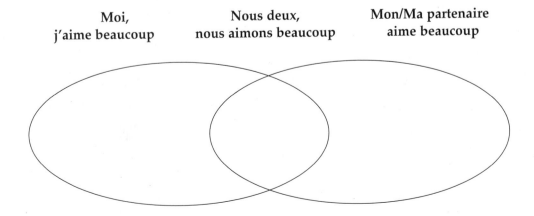

Moi,
j'aime beaucoup

Nous deux,
nous aimons beaucoup

Mon/Ma partenaire
aime beaucoup

On cherche les différences d'opinion

Ce que j'aime beaucoup et mon/ma partenaire n'aime pas du tout	Ce que mon/ma partenaire aime beaucoup et je n'aime pas du tout

Structure: L'imparfait

OBSERVATIONS

—À l'âge de 6 ans, je **prenais** toujours le petit déjeuner.
*At the age of six, I **would** always **eat** breakfast.*

—Qu'est-ce que tu **prenais,** des céréales ou des œufs au bacon?
*What **would** you **have,** cereal or bacon and eggs?*

—Des œufs au lard. En ce temps-là, ma mère **préparait** le petit déjeuner tous les jours.
*Bacon and eggs. In those days, my mother **used to make** breakfast every day.*

—Ma famille et moi, nous **étions** tous à table ensemble.
*My family and I **were** all at the table together.*

—Ta famille et toi, vous **preniez** tous les repas ensemble?
***Would** your family and you **eat** all your meals together?*

—Non, mes deux frères **arrivaient** toujours trop tard pour le dîner.
*No, my two brothers **would** always **arrive** too late for dinner.*

STRATÉGIES D'ANALYSE

1. Look at the words in boldface. How do they function in the sentence: do they name the subject, state the action, or describe an object?
2. Using the English equivalents given, determine what time frame these verbs describe (present, past, or future time).
3. You have already learned to tell about a past event with the **passé composé** (**J'ai parlé français avec mon prof au supermarché ce matin**). How does the new verb tense look different from the **passé composé?**
4. Copy the verbs from the sentences onto a sheet of paper. Then underline or highlight what you think the endings for this new tense are.

PRÉCISIONS

• The imperfect tense (**l'imparfait**) is used to describe *what one used to do or what things used to be like.*

Je **jouais** du piano; je **répétais** toujours avant le petit déjeuner.
*I **used to play** the piano; I **would** always **practice** before breakfast.*

Nous **prenions** du bœuf; maintenant nous sommes végétariens.
*We **used to eat** meat; now we are vegetarians.*

On **servait** le coq au vin ici.
*They **used to serve** coq au vin here.*

Quand j'**avais** huit ans, j'**allais** au cinéma le samedi.
*When I **was** eight, I **would go** to the movies every Saturday.*

Pendant ma jeunesse, j'**étais** souvent malade.
*During my youth, I **was** often sick.*

Il **faisait** froid et sombre; il n'y **avait** pas de lumière.
*It **was** cold and dark; there **were** no lights.*

- To form the imperfect tense, start with the **nous** form of the present tense. Drop the **-ons** ending, then add the imperfect endings: **-ais, -ais, -ait, -ions, -iez, -aient.**

nous aim~~ons~~	j'aim**ais**	nous aim**ions**
	tu aim**ais**	vous aim**iez**
	il/elle/on aim**ait**	ils aim**aient**

- The imperfect tense of any regular verb is formed this way, regardless of the infinitive form of the verb.

parler	nous parl~~ons~~	je parl**ais**, etc.
finir	nous finiss~~ons~~	je finiss**ais**, etc.
rendre	nous rend~~ons~~	je rend**ais**, etc.

- The imperfect tense of any irregular verb (except **être**) is also formed this way.

avoir	nous av~~ons~~	j'av**ais**, etc.
faire	nous fais~~ons~~	je fais**ais**, etc.
dire	nous dis~~ons~~	je dis**ais**, etc.
aller	nous all~~ons~~	j'all**ais**, etc.
prendre	nous pren~~ons~~	je pren**ais**, etc.

- The verb **être** has an irregular stem, **ét-,** but the endings are the same as for other verbs.

être	nous sommes	j'ét**ais**
		tu ét**ais**
		il/elle/on ét**ait**
		nous ét**ions**
		vous ét**iez**
		ils/elles ét**aient**

- When you hear or see one of the following time expressions referring to the past, you can anticipate the use of the imperfect tense, furthering the idea of repeated or habitual actions in the past or how things used to be:

quand j'étais petit(e)	*when I was little*
quand j'étais jeune	*when I was young*
quand j'avais ___ ans	*when I was ___ years old*
pendant ma jeunesse	*in my youth*

à cette époque	*at that time*
en ce temps-là	*at that time*
autrefois	*formerly, in the past*
d'habitude	*generally, as a habit*
fréquemment	*frequently*
souvent	*often*
toujours	*always*
tous les jours	*every day*
une fois par semaine	*once a week*
le lundi, le mardi...	*on Mondays, Tuesdays . . .*
chaque lundi...	*every Monday . . .*
le matin, l'après-midi, le soir	*mornings, afternoons, evenings*

H. À l'âge de dix ans... Cherchez des informations de la vie de votre partenaire quand il/elle avait dix ans. Puis, racontez à un(e) autre étudiant(e) au moins cinq choses au sujet de votre partenaire.

> **Modèle:** faire du sport
> —*À l'âge de dix ans, jouais-tu aux sports?*
> —*Oui, je jouais au foot et au basket avec mes amis.*

1. faire du sport
2. jouer de la musique
3. habiter où
4. parler des langues étrangères
5. aimer aller à l'école
6. être bon en maths
7. étudier beaucoup
8. se disputer avec ses frères et sœurs
9. déjeuner ou dîner en famille
10. être content(e)

I. Quand j'étais jeune... Écrivez des phrases où vous décrivez un peu votre vie quand vous étiez plus jeune (à six ans, à dix ans, à quinze ans, à vingt ans, comme vous voulez). Vous pouvez dire, par exemple:

où vous habitiez / avec qui vous habitiez / si vous habitiez un appartement ou une maison / si vous habitiez en ville ou à la campagne / où vous alliez à l'école / si vous aimiez l'école / les matières que vous préfériez / les matières que vous n'aimiez pas beaucoup / qui était votre instituteur/institutrice préféré(e) / qui était votre meilleur(e) ami(e) / comment était votre meilleur(e) ami(e) / vos activités et celles de votre meilleur(e) ami(e) / vos activités le week-end / vos intérêts (sport, musique, cinéma, animaux...) / si vous travailliez / où vous travailliez / ce que vous désiriez être en tant qu'adulte

J. C'était la fête de... Comparez les traditions de votre famille avec celles de la famille de votre partenaire. (1) D'abord, avec votre partenaire, décidez quelle fête discuter. (2) Puis, en utilisant la liste ci-dessous comme guide, faites une comparaison entre les activités de vos deux familles.

> **Modèle:** Étudiant(e) 1: *À Noël, chez nous, ma mère servait toujours une dinde.*
> Étudiant(e) 2: *Chez nous, on fêtait Hanoukka avec des beignets de pommes de terre.*
> Étudiant(e) 1: *Nous avions un grand arbre illuminé dans le salon.*
> Étudiant(e) 2: *Et chez nous, on allumait la menorah.*

1. ce qu'on préparait et servait comme repas
2. à quelle heure on servait les repas

3. qui prenait les repas en famille
4. comment on décorait l'appartement ou la maison
5. quelle musique on écoutait
6. qui rendait visite à la famille
7. où on allait en famille
8. ce qu'on s'offrait comme cadeaux
9. ce que vous aimiez le plus de cette fête
10. ce que vous n'aimiez pas du tout de cette fête

PRONONCIATION: La liaison obligatoire (révision)

As you learned in *Chapitre 2*, a liaison is required in French:

1. between an article and a noun or adjective beginning with a vowel sound:
   un‿assortiment   les‿aliments   des‿oranges   des‿anciens‿amis
2. between a subject pronoun and a verb beginning with a vowel sound:
   Nous‿avons mangé des crêpes Suzettes.   Ils‿habitent à Dakar.
3. after the verb form **est** when followed by a vowel sound:
   Elle est‿avocate.

In addition to these cases, several other instances require a liaison:

4. between an adjective and a noun beginning with a vowel sound:
   Bon‿appétit!   Mon petit‿ami s'appelle Claude.
5. between a verb form and a subject pronoun in inversion:
   Quand revient-il?   Que fait-on?
6. after monosyllabic adverbs, like **trop, très,** and **pas:**
   Je n'ai pas‿assez d'argent. C'est très‿intéressant!

À vous! Referring to the chart below that shows which consonants are pronounced during liaison, practice reading the following sentences with a partner.

Written form	Pronunciation	
s, x, z	z	des‿abricots; aux‿universités; chez‿elle
d, t	t	un grand‿homme; Lit-il le journal?
n	n	On‿est quel jour aujourd'hui?
p	p	Vous êtes trop‿optimiste!
r	r	au premier‿étage

1. Je vais avoir un gâteau aux amandes pour fêter mon anniversaire.
2. Ils ont d'excellentes employées chez eux.
3. Il n'est pas encore arrivé? Il est très en retard!
4. Pourquoi ne répond-elle jamais au téléphone?
5. Le meilleur endroit pour étudier, c'est à la bibliothèque.
6. Elle ne me plaît pas beaucoup. Elle est trop égoïste.

POUR DÉVELOPPER VOS IDÉES

Thematic objective: To examine associations between geographic regions and foods that are identified with them

Présentation: Chaque région a son talent...

POUR SAISIR L'ESSENTIEL: Chaque région de la France a ses spécialités alimentaires. Quelquefois elles reflètent la situation géographique du lieu, comme les plats avec des fruits de mer près de la mer. Parfois, c'est l'influence culturelle des pays voisins, comme la combinaison de saveurs espagnoles, provençales et italiennes autour de la Méditerranée. La lecture à la page suivante présente une carte annotée de la France culinaire.

1. Préparez des titres pour trois catégories: «J'aime bien... », «Je n'aime pas beaucoup... » et «Je voudrais essayer... ».

2. Parcourez la lecture pour trouver des aliments pour chaque catégorie.

   Modèle:

J'aime bien:	Je n'aime pas beaucoup:	Je voudrais essayer:
• la cuisine au beurre et à la crème	• le homard	• le canard

3. Quelle région préférez-vous visiter pour un tour gastronomique? À votre avis, quels aliments sont les plus attrayants?

K. **Des spécialités régionales aux États-Unis.** Quelles sont les spécialités régionales des États-Unis? Commencez par faire une liste des spécialités régionales que vous connaissez aux États-Unis. Puis comparez votre liste avec celle de votre partenaire. Ensuite, réfléchissez ensemble pour créer une liste plus complète. Pour chaque élément dans votre nouvelle liste, indiquez l'aliment et la région ou le lieu où il est réputé. Essayez de déterminer les influences géographiques ou culturelles qu'on peut observer dans ces spécialités régionales. Par exemple, est-ce que le climat semble être un facteur? La proximité de la mer? Les fleuves et rivières? Les montagnes, les collines, les plaines? Les pays voisins? La proximité d'un port ou d'un aéroport?

   Modèle:

Ma liste de spécialités régionales		
Aliments	**Lieu**	**Influences**
• les oranges et les pamplemousses	• Floride	• le soleil, le climat
• le homard	• Maine	• la proximité de la mer
• les saucissons	• Michigan	• l'héritage polonais

L'Ouest. La **Normandie** avec sa cuisine au beurre et à la crème est surtout réputée pour ses produits laitiers: beurre, lait, fromage, crème. La cuisine y est souvent riche. Les pommes sont une autre spécialité normande; on en fait la célèbre tarte Tatin, du cidre (alcoolisé) et du **Calvados** (cidre distillé).

En **Bretagne** les crêpes font partie de la cuisine quotidienne, et les repas sont aussi pleins de poissons comme les coquilles Saint-Jacques et le homard.

La **Touraine**, pays du grand gourmand Pantagruel (personnage de Rabelais), nous propose des andouilles (saucisses fabriquées avec des tripes).

Comme témoignage° de la qualité de leur cuisine, ces régions nous donnent les termes culinaires *à la rouennaise* (de la ville de Rouen), qui indique «avec du canard», et *à la normande*, évidemment c'est-à-dire «avec pommes».

Le Sud-Ouest. Une des spécialités de cette région est le cassoulet, un mélange de haricots et de plusieurs viandes. On le trouve surtout à **Carcassonne** ou à **Toulouse.** Naturellement, en passant par ce côté de la France, il faut s'offrir aussi un peu du célèbre fromage fabriqué exclusivement dans les caves à **Roquefort.** La région de Bordeaux est mondialement connue pour ses grands vins. Et n'oublions pas les excellentes truffes du **Périgord.** On les appelle «diamants noirs» tant elles sont précieuses. Parmi les contributions de cette partie du pays sont les termes *à la périgourdine*, signifiant «un plat avec des truffes» et *à la bordelaise*, qui veut dire «fait avec le vin de **Bordeaux**».

Le Nord. L'**Île de France** se pique de° ses fromages exceptionnels, tels que le brie et le coulommiers. En **Picardie,** on régale les gourmets et les gourmands avec des moules° et des frites. Et **Paris**? Qu'est-ce qu'elle contribue à cette corne d'abondance qu'est la France? Évidemment, ce sont ses grands chefs cuisiniers!

sur la cuisine française dans le terme *à la lyonnaise*, qui veut dire «préparé avec des oignons».

L'Est. La **Bourgogne** nous offre ses merveilleux escargots et son bœuf charolais. Les **Ardennes** y ajoutent du jambon et du saucisson. Et en **Lorraine,** on nous prépare des quiches avec du lard°. Il est impossible d'ignorer la **Champagne** qui a donné son vin pétillant à toutes nos occasions spéciales. En **Alsace** (fortement influencée par sa voisine, l'Allemagne) on aime surtout les bières, la charcuterie et, bien sûr, la choucroute. Peu surprenant, alors qu'en principe le terme *à l'alsacienne* signifie qu'un plat contient du chou, de la choucroute ou bien, du saucisson.

Le Sud-Est. C'est le goût de la **Méditerranée**! L'huile d'olive, l'ail, les légumes et, évidemment, les poissons donnent leur richesse aux plats de ces régions: la bouillabaisse (une soupe composée de divers poissons et assaisonnée avec de l'ail et de l'huile d'olive), la ratatouille (un mélange d'aubergines°, de courgettes et de tomates cuites à l'huile d'olive) et la piperade (une omelette aux tomates et aux poivrons).

Ces régions se font remarquer dans le lexique culinaire par les termes *à la niçoise*, «avec des olives, des tomates et des anchois°» et *provençale*, qui veut dire «avec des tomates, de l'ail et de l'huile d'olive».

MER DU NORD
Pays-Bas
Allemagne
Grande-Bretagne
Dunkerque
Calais
Belgique
NORD-PAS-DE-CALAIS
Lille
Valenciennes
Luxembourg
MANCHE
Cherbourg
Amiens
HAUTE-NORMANDIE
Le Havre
Rouen
PICARDIE
Reims
Metz
Caen
Seine
LORRAINE
ALSACE
Saint-Malo
BASSE-NORMANDIE
Versailles
★ Paris
ÎLE-DE-FRANCE
CHAMPAGNE-ARDENNE
Nancy
Strasbourg
Brest
Fougères
Troyes
Mulhouse
BRETAGNE
Rennes
Le Mans
Orléans
BOURGOGNE
Besançon
St-Nazaire
PAYS-DE-LA-LOIRE
Angers
Blois
Chambord
Dijon
FRANCHE-COMTÉ
Suisse
Nantes
Chinon
Tours
Chenonceaux
Azay-le-Rideau
Bourges
Nevers
Chalon-sur-Saône
CENTRE
Poitiers
La Rochelle
LIMOUSIN
Vichy
Annecy
POITOU-CHARENTES
Limoges
Clermont-Ferrand
Rhône
Lyon
RHÔNE-ALPES
Italie
OCÉAN ATLANTIQUE
Périgueux
AUVERGNE
Saint Étienne
Grenoble
Bordeaux
MASSIF CENTRAL
PROVENCE-ALPES-CÔTE-D'AZUR
AQUITAINE
Garonne
Rodez
MIDI-PYRÉNÉES
Avignon
Monte-Carlo
Biarritz
Bayonne
Pau
Toulouse
Nîmes
Montpellier
Tarascon
Grasse
Aix-en-Provence
Monaco
Nice
Carcassonne
Narbonne
Toulon
Cannes
PYRÉNÉES
Béziers
Marseille
LANGUEDOC-ROUSSILLON
Espagne
Andorre
Perpignan
0   75 km

Du Centre aux Alpes… L'**Auvergne** est renommée° pour sa charcuterie et ses fameux fromages bleus. Dans les Alpes ce sont les gratins de pommes de terre, les raclettes et les fondues de gruyère qui règnent°. Et les grands chefs de **Lyon** laissent leur empreinte°

---

comme témoignage de: *as testimony, proof of*
se piquer: *to be proud of*
moules (f.): *mussels*
renommé: *renowned, famous*
régner: *reign*

laisser leur empreinte: *leave their mark, influence*
lard: *bacon*
aubergine: *eggplant*
anchois: *anchovies*

L. Des festivals régionaux. Examinez ce que vous savez des régions et de la culture des lieux sur votre liste de l'Exercice K. Quels lieux voudriez-vous visiter pour leur festival annuel? Nommez au moins trois lieux et pour chacun indiquez à quels festivals vous voudriez assister.

M. Un tour gastronomique. Travaillez en groupe de trois ou quatre pour organiser un tour gastronomique des États-Unis. Indiquez (1) les lieux, (2) la saison ou le mois où vous visitez chaque lieu, (3) les attributs géographiques de chaque lieu et (4) la cuisine ou l'aliment que vous allez fêter. Traitez au moins trois lieux.

dépliant: *folded brochure*

N. Une publicité. Créez un dépliant° publicitaire pour votre tour gastronomique des États-Unis. Cherchez des expressions utiles dans votre dossier pour le *Chapitre 7.* Donnez les informations suivantes:

1. Quelles villes ou régions est-ce qu'on va visiter?
2. Quand est-ce qu'on va aller dans chaque endroit?
3. Quelles sont les attractions principales de chaque étape du tour?
4. Quelle cuisine ou quel aliment va-t-on apprécier?
5. Quels instituts, agences, sociétés commerciales, etc. vont contribuer à la publicité du tour?

NOTE CULTURELLE

Parfois un aliment est si profondément associé à la culture locale qu'on le fête avec des festivals, des défilés et des jeux. C'est ainsi qu'on célèbre l'érable° au Québec. Voici un paragraphe du site Internet de l'Institut Québécois de l'Érable:

«Depuis trois cents ans que les Québécois font du sirop d'érable, l'érable fait partie de l'histoire de ce peuple. Les Amérindiens en faisaient la cueillette° déjà bien avant eux. [...] Les histoires anciennes, les chansons, l'artisanat sont tous marqués par ce noble végétal. Les fêtes actuelles° rassemblent chaque année un nombre important de citoyens du Québec mais attirent aussi des gens de partout dans le monde».

Réfléchissons: Quelles villes ou régions américaines célèbrent un aliment avec des festivals? Quels sont les aliments fêtés?

érable (m.): *maple*
la cueillette: *harvest*
actuelle: *de nos jours, à présent*

DÉCOUVERTE

As you have observed, regional specialties are often character-ized by products that are manufactured in or near the area. Examples include **saucisse** and **choucroute** in Alsace, as well as **roquefort** cheese made near the city of Roquefort. Look for ingredients produced in or near Brussels (Belgium) mentioned in this recipe for **poulet à la bruxelloise.**

Poulet à la bruxelloise
Pour 4 personnes.
1 poulet de 1200 g
100 g de beurre
1/2 litre de bière brune
4 cuillerées à soupe de genièvre°
6 échalotes°
1 tasse de crème fraîche
sel
poivre

genièvre (m.): *gin*
échalotes (f.): *shallots*

1. Read the list of ingredients for **poulet à la bruxelloise** in the DÉCOUVERTE. Then decide which one(s) you would expect to characterize a Germanic cuisine. Try to identify the attributes of that/those product(s) that you associate with a Germanic region.

2. Would it be possible to make this dish with products available in your local stores? If not, could you simplify the recipe using products readily available in your area?

3. Working in a group of three or four, discuss with classmates how you would describe this dish in a restaurant menu in English so that its main character-istic would be obvious to an American.

Objective: To order a meal in a restaurant

PRÉSENTATION: Un coup d'œil sur le thème

La jambalaya est-ce un plat créole ou cajun? Selon les Louisianais, c'est une question de préparation.

un colon: *colonist*

Au fil du temps: *Over time*

le gombo: *okra or gumbo (a seafood stew, often thickened with okra or filé)*

génial: *ingenious*

épicé: *spicy*

La cuisine louisianaise est vraiment un mélange de styles, mais on y distingue deux héritages en particulier: le créole et le cajun. La cuisine créole est surtout populaire aux environs de la Nouvelle-Orléans. Selon le chef louisianais John Folse,* les colons° aristocrates de l'Europe sont arrivés dans les pays accompagnés de leurs chefs. Ces maîtres de la cuisine classique de l'Europe ont adapté leurs recettes aux produits du Nouveau Monde. Au fil du temps°, ils ont aussi été influencés par les saveurs africaines et antillaises des îles Caraïbes. On souligne les similarités entre la paella, plat espagnol, et la jambalaya, entre la bouillabaisse de Marseille et les soupes au gombo°.

La cuisine cajun, par contre, est une création des Acadiens. Le chef Folse la décrit comme le reflet de leur aventure historique: C'est la cuisine d'un peuple génial° et créatif, un peuple qui sait s'adapter et survivre. Ces anciens habitants de la Nouvelle-Écosse, au Canada, ont été forcés par les soldats anglais d'abandonner leurs maisons. Beaucoup de ces Acadiens (Cajuns) ont enfin terminé leur migration en Louisiane. Pas de luxe pour les exilés; les Cajuns favorisent les repas qui consistent d'un seul plat bien robuste, un mélange de viande, de fruits de mer et de légumes.

En général, on contraste ces deux traditions ainsi: La cuisine créole est à base de crème et de beurre. La cuisine cajun est à base de porc, surtout le lard. Les tomates sont populaires pour les plats créoles, mais les plats cajuns sont plutôt épicés°. Et qu'est-ce qu'elles ont en commun? Selon les Louisianais, c'est «la sainte Trinité» de la cuisine louisianaise: le poivron vert, l'oignon et le céleri.

The Evolution of Cajun and Creole Cuisine. Chef John Folse & Company

La cuisine
Quelles ethnies ou quels héritages se distinguent dans les cuisines de votre région? Quels ingrédients ou aliments sont typiques des différents types de cuisine?

POUR DÉVELOPPER VOTRE FRANÇAIS

Vocabulaire: Les repas

OBSERVATIONS

a. de la confiture
b. du beurre
c. des tartines
d. un croissant
e. du café
f. du lait chaud

a. des céréales
b. du jus d'orange
c. des œufs plats et du lard
d. du café
e. du lait froid

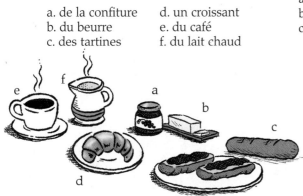

En France, le matin on mange léger° au petit déjeuner.

Au Canada et aux États-Unis, généralement on prend un petit déjeuner plus copieux° qu'en France.

léger: *lightly*
copieux: *copious, large*

a. une tranche de pizza
b. une salade niçoise
c. des frites
d. un sandwich au jambon

e. une omelette
f. de la soupe
g. un panini

À midi, certains Français choisissent un déjeuner rapide dans un restaurant fast-food.

a. de la soupe à l'oignon
b. du saumon aux haricots verts et carottes
c. de la salade
d. un plateau de fromages
e. du sorbet
f. du café

D'autres Français préfèrent un déjeuner traditionnel à midi.

STRATÉGIES D'ANALYSE

1. What do the French call breakfast?

2. If you know that **jeûner** means *to fast* and that the prefix **dé-** is similar to *dis-* in English, what do you think **le petit déjeuner** means? With which meal does the French language declare that the daily fasting is over?

3. Can you find anything in common between breakfast in France and breakfast in Canada or the United States?

4. How does **un déjeuner rapide** compare with your usual lunch?

Précisions

- The French usually have a light breakfast, **le petit déjeuner,** consisting of a hot beverage and bread with butter and jam.

du café	*coffee*
du café au lait	*coffee with hot milk*
du café noir	*black coffee*
un express	*an espresso*
du thé	*tea*
du thé au lait	*tea with hot milk*
du thé citron	*tea with lemon*
du thé nature	*plain tea*
du chocolat	*hot chocolate*

À propos du vocabulaire: In English we say *seafood*, the French say **des fruits de mer** *(fruits of the sea).*

À propos de la culture: Canadians refer to the three meals of the day as:
—**le déjeuner** (since there is nothing **petit** about it, due, perhaps, to the cold climate?)
—**le dîner**
—**le souper** (ou **le dîner**)

- Many French now have a fast-food lunch, **le déjeuner rapide,** with a more traditional meal in the evening, **le dîner.** Others continue the tradition of having the main meal of the day at noon, **le déjeuner,** with a lighter meal in the evening, **le dîner** or **le souper.**
- The traditional French main meal, whether at noon or in the evening, is served in courses, generally in the following order:

  (1) l'entrée: de la soupe, des crudités, du pâté ou de la terrine, des œufs durs
  (2) le plat principal: de la viande, du poisson ou des fruits de mer, avec des légumes
  (3) de la salade
  (4) du fromage
  (5) un dessert: une tartelette, du gâteau, du sorbet, de la glace ou un fruit
  (6) du café

- Drinks may be served with a meal. Coffee is served *with* **le petit déjeuner,** but never until *after* **le déjeuner** or **le dîner.**

A. Le petit déjeuner. Discutez avec votre partenaire de vos préférences pour le petit déjeuner. Dites: (1) à quelle heure vous prenez le petit déjeuner,
(2) où vous prenez le petit déjeuner,
(3) si vous préférez un petit déjeuner à la mode française ou à la mode américaine/canadienne,
(4) la boisson que vous prenez le matin.

B. Le petit déjeuner le week-end. Maintenant discutez avec votre partenaire de vos préférences pour le petit déjeuner le samedi ou le dimanche. Notez les différences entre votre repas typique pendant la semaine et le week-end.

Vocabulaire: Les menus à prix fixe

OBSERVATIONS

À propos de la culture: Most places of business are listing their prices both in French francs and in Euros in anticipation of the European Common Market change-over to a common monetary system.

On peut passer une soirée très agréable dans un bon restaurant.

Le Menu Quick est ouvert tous les jours, sept sur sept.

Chez Nous
un restaurant de tradition
ouvert de 12h à 14h30, de 17h à 23h
fermé le dimanche

Menu à 199F/30 Euros

Entrée: choix de
Soupe à l'oignon gratinée
Potage aux champignons
6 escargots
Moules provençales gratinées
Pâté de lapin
Assiette de crudités

Plat principal: choix de
Filet de saumon à la florentine
Côtelette de porc aux abricots
Steak au poivre à la bordelaise
Côtelettes de veau à la crème

salade verte

plateau de fromages

dessert
Crème caramel
Tarte aux pommes
Coupe de 3 glaces
en hiver: Tarte Tatin

boisson non-comprise

15% service compris

Le Menu Quick
pour votre vie chargée
ouvert de 11h à 24h - 7 jours sur 7

**59F
9Euros**

Menu

1
soupe du jour
œuf dur mayonnaise
crudités

2
omelette aux champignons frites
poulet rôti frites
saumon grillé

3
tarte du jour
glace (vanille ou chocolat)

1/2 bouteille d'eau minérale
ou un verre de vin

Service compris
Boisson comprise

À propos de la culture: Tarte Tatin is a traditional, hot, caramelized apple pie, usually served in France during the winter.

STRATÉGIES D'ANALYSE

1. Which one of these restaurants would you choose:
   —when you are in a hurry? —when someone else is paying the bill?
   —when looking for elegance? —at noon?
   —when you are paying the bill? —with a friend in the evening?

2. What seasonal change can you find in one of the menus?

- In France, restaurants must offer a fixed-price menu (**un menu à prix fixe**) in addition to their regular menu. A **prix fixe** meal is usually considerably less expensive than ordering the dishes from the regular menu (**à la carte**).
- When ordering from **un menu à prix fixe**, look to see whether the price includes a beverage (**boisson comprise**) and the 15 percent tip (**service compris**).
- The preparation of a dish is sometimes described by a reference to a region where the mode of preparation originated or has been particularly popular.

provençale	*from Provence*	*tomato-based sauces spiced with herbs*
chantilly	*from Chantilly*	*served with whipped cream*
bordelaise	*from Bordeaux*	*sauces prepared with Bordeaux wine*
florentine	*from Florence, Italy*	*served or made with spinach*
madère	*from Madeira, Spain*	*sauces prepared with Madeira wine*
antillaise	*from the Antilles*	*as in Guadeloupe or Martinique tradition*
hollandaise	*from Holland*	*sauce made with egg yolks and lemon, often served on poached eggs and vegetables*

C. Un menu à prix fixe, s'il vous plaît. Avec votre partenaire, décidez à quel restaurant aller pour le dîner vendredi soir, *Chez Nous* ou le *Menu Quick*. Puis, dites à un serveur imaginaire ce que vous avez l'intention de commander.

Modèle: —*Allons au* Menu Quick *vendredi soir. Ça ne coûte pas cher.*
—*Je préfère aller au* Chez Nous. *La cuisine est traditionnelle, et les plats sont bien préparés.*
—*Bien sûr, si tu veux payer.*

—*Monsieur, je vais commencer avec des moules provençales gratinées. Puis, comme plat principal, je voudrais des côtelettes de veau à la crème, s'il vous plaît.*
—*Pour moi, comme entrée, je voudrais de la soupe à l'oignon gratinée, et ensuite, du saumon à la florentine. J'adore les épinards.*

Structure: Le partitif

OBSERVATIONS

Le matin j'achète **des** croissants à la boulangerie en face de l'appartement.
*Every morning I buy **some** croissants at the bakery across from the apartment.*

Le matin je prends **du** thé citron. Marc prends toujours **du** café noir.
In the morning I have tea with lemon. Marc always has black coffee.

Moi, je voudrais **de la** salade de crevettes. Est-ce que tu as choisi?
*As for me, I would like **some** shrimp salad. Have you made a selection?*

Avez-vous **de l'**huile et **du** vinaigre pour la salade?
*Do you have **(any)** oil and vinegar for the salad?*

J'ai toujours **des** pommes dans le frigo, mais aujourd'hui je n'ai pas **de** poires. Je n'ai pas acheté **d'**abricots non plus.
*I always have **(some)** apples in the refrigerator, but today I don't have **any** pears. I have not bought **any** apricots either.*

STRATÉGIES D'ANALYSE

1. In the sentences, find four ways to say *some*.
2. Can you identify the criterion that determines which form to use: **du, de la, de l'**, or **des**?
3. What happens to **du, de la,** or **des** after a negative?
4. What is the English equivalent after a negative?

PRÉCISIONS

- You have been using two types of articles:

  1. the definite articles (*the* in English): **le, la, l'**, and **les**.
  2. the indefinite articles (*a, an,* or *some* in English): **un, une,** and **des**.

- A third type of article, the partitive, is used to indicate a certain amount (a part) of something, but not the whole. In English, this concept is sometimes expressed by the use of *some* or *any*.
- The partitive is formed by using **de** plus the definite article: **du, de la, de l', des**. (Remember that **de + le = du** and that **de + les = des**.) The partitive articles become **de** or **d'** after a negative expression.

Avez-vous **du** saumon fumé aujourd'hui?
*Do you have (**any**) smoked salmon today?*

Je voudrais **de l'**eau minérale, s'il vous plaît.
*I would like (**some**) mineral water, please.*

Donnez-moi **des** cerises et **des** fraises, s'il vous plaît.
*Give me (**some**) cherries and (**some**) strawberries, please.*

- Note that the partitive is used in French whether or not the *some* or *any* is expressed in English.

Nous avons **du** pâté, mais nous n'avons pas **de** saumon fumé.
We have pâté, but we do not have smoked salmon.

D. **Allons au marché.** À tour de rôle avec votre partenaire, lisez les phrases suivantes. Remplacez les mots en italique par les mots entre parenthèses. Faites les changements nécessaires.

1. Allons au marché. Je cherche des *fraises* et des *framboises*. (pommes, abricots / citrons, bananes / melon, cerises / oranges, raisin)
2. Allons au marché. Je voudrais acheter des *pommes de terre*. (tomates / carottes / haricots verts / épinards)
3. Allons à la boulangerie. Je vais acheter des *baguettes*. (pain complet / croissants / petits pains)
4. Allons à la pâtisserie. Je voudrais servir une *tarte aux cerises* ce soir. (gâteau au chocolat / tartelettes aux framboises / tarte aux fraises / éclairs)
5. Allons à la crémerie. J'ai besoin d'acheter du *beurre*. (lait / crème / roquefort / brie / yaourt)

E. Dans mon omelette... Dites à votre partenaire les ingrédients que vous voulez pour votre omelette personnelle. Vos choix d'ingrédients: champignons, oignons, poivrons verts, tomates, jambon, fromage, thon, fines herbes.

> **Modèle:** —*Qu'est-ce que vous voulez dans votre omelette?*
> —*Dans mon omelette je voudrais du jambon, du fromage et des tomates, s'il vous plaît.*

une épaule: *(pork) shoulder*

F. Sur ma pizza... Dites à votre partenaire les ingrédients que vous choisissez le plus souvent pour votre pizza personnelle. Vos choix d'ingrédients: épaule°, saucisse, fromage, sauce tomate, tomates, champignons, oignons, olives vertes, olives noires, câpres°, anchois°, un œuf.

câpres (f.): *capers*
anchois (m.): *anchovies*

le Grand Marnier: *French liqueur with orange flavor*

Je vais m'acheter une crêpe. Voyons... Qu'est-ce que je vais prendre sur ma crêpe?

Donnez-moi une crêpe flambée au Grand Marnier°, s'il vous plaît.

la compote de pommes: *apple sauce*
la cannelle: *cinnamon*
le Calvados: *French liqueur made from apples, produced in Normandy*

G. Sur ma crêpe... Dites à votre partenaire les ingrédients que vous voulez pour votre crêpe. Votre choix d'ingrédients: jambon, fromage, chocolat, sucre, confiture de fraises, confiture de framboises, confiture de pêches, compote de pommes°, cannelle°, Grand Marnier, Calvados°.

Vocabulaire: À table

OBSERVATIONS

À propos de la culture: Note that the fork and spoon are placed with bowl down, which would seem upside-down in an American setting. Because of this placement, the silver markings by the factory are inside the bowl of these pieces.

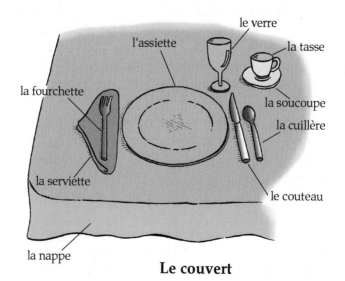

Le couvert

Stratégies d'analyse

1. Look at the silverware on the table. Do you see any differences in the normal placement of silverware in a French table setting from the way tables are usually set in the United States?

2. This table is set for a formal dinner. Do the place settings look sparse to you? What other items might be at each place for a formal American dinner?

Précisions et Note culturelle

- En France, pour un dîner traditionnel on sert un plat à la fois. Les plats sont généralement servis dans l'ordre suivant: l'apéritif°, l'entrée, le plat principal avec légumes, la salade, le fromage, le dessert, le café, le pousse-café° (ou le digestif).

- On prépare la table simplement pour chaque plat. Par exemple, si on sert une soupe comme entrée, on met une cuillère à soupe à chaque couvert, mais si on sert des crudités comme entrée, on met une fourchette et un couteau devant chaque personne.

- On remet les couverts (assiettes, fourchettes, couteaux, etc.) après chaque plat. Puis, on met les couverts nécessaires pour le plat suivant: fourchette et couteau pour un bifteck frites, par exemple, ou cuillère pour un sorbet.

Réfléchissons: Qu'est-ce que vous en pensez? Quelle table est-ce que vous préférez, une table américaine avec trois fourchettes, deux couteaux, trois cuillères et trois verres ou une table française avec des couverts simples que l'on remplace?

un apéritif: *before-dinner drink*

pousse-café: *after-dinner drink*

H. On met la table. Pour compléter les phrases suivantes, choisissez les mots convenables de la liste donnée.

* assiette	* nappe
* couteau	* serviette
* cuillère	* soucoupe
* cuillère à café	* tasse
* flûte°	* verre
* fourchette	

une flûte: *a tall slender champagne glass*

1. Mettez la table pour moi, s'il vous plaît. Je voudrais utiliser la _____ en lin° que j'ai achetée à Bruxelles.

2. J'ai des _____ en lin que j'ai achetées avec la nappe. L'ensemble va bien aller avec les assiettes de Limoges. Nous avons besoin de quatre couverts.

3. Je veux utiliser ma porcelaine d'Haviland. Mettez une grande _____ au centre de chaque couvert.

4. Nous allons commencer le dîner avec des crudités. Mettez une _____ à gauche et un _____ à droite de l'assiette.

5. Après les crudités, je vais servir de la soupe à l'oignon gratinée. Mais ne mettez pas les _____ à table avec les fourchettes et les couteaux. On met les _____ après les crudités et avant la soupe.

le lin: *linen*

6. Nous avons besoin de deux _____ à chaque place: un _____ à vin et un _____ à eau.

7. Nous allons servir du champagne avant le dîner. Mettez les _____ à champagne sur la table basse dans le salon.

8. Je vais servir du café après le dîner. S'il vous plaît, mettez quatre _____ et _____ sur le buffet dans la salle à manger. N'oubliez pas les petites _____.

NOTE CULTURELLE

—*Une table réservée à partir de 20h00, s'il vous plaît.*
—*Pour combien de personnes?*
—*Pour quatre, s'il vous plaît.*

En France on réserve une table au restaurant *à partir de 20 heures* (ou une autre heure désirée) parce qu'avec la réservation on a la table pour la soirée. On ne va pas être pressé pour terminer le dîner.

- Les expressions suivantes sont aussi utiles à table:

Une table pour deux, s'il vous plaît.	*A table for two, please.*
Deux couverts, s'il vous plaît.	*A table for two, please.*
Deux menus (prix fixe), s'il vous plaît.	*Two (fixed price) dinners, please.*
Bon appétit.	*Have a nice dinner.*
Passez-moi le... , s'il vous plaît.	*Pass me the . . . , please.*
Encore du (de la)... ?	*More . . . ?*
Merci, non, ça suffit.	*No, thank you, that's plenty.*
Terminé(e)(s)?	*Finished?*
Le service est compris?	*Is the service charge included?*
L'addition, s'il vous plaît.	*The check, please.*

Réfléchisssons: Pourquoi est-ce qu'on demande une table pour le dîner à 20 heures, pas à 8 heures? À votre avis, combien de temps est-ce qu'on passe à table pour le dîner en France?

PRONONCIATION: La liaison interdite (révision)

As you learned in *Chapitre 2*, a liaison should *not* be made:

1. after a proper name:
   Bernard// a deux chiens.   Marseilles// est un port au sud-est de la France.

2. after the conjunction **et:**
   Robert// et // Anne   On arrive et // on attend

3. after a singular noun:
   du poulet épicé   une chanson//harmonieuse

In addition to these cases, you should not make a liaison:

4. before an aspirate **h** (You will learn about this in *Chapitre 10*):

   deux// homards   *des// haricots verts*

5. after the interrogative word **quand** (when):

   Quand// est-elle partie?

À vous! Practice reading the following sentences with a partner, being sure *not* to make a liaison where it is prohibited.

1. On a pleuré quand on a appris que Jean est mort.
2. Tristan et Yseut étaient des amants.
3. M. Duval est un politicien ambitieux et optimiste.
4. Quand avez-vous rendu visite à Jules et Armine?
5. C'est un plat assez facile à préparer.
6. Marc et Élyse sont allés ensemble à Alger et à Dakar.

POUR DÉVELOPPER VOS IDÉES

Thematic objective: To examine the cultural influences on regional cuisines

Présentation: Un mélange culturel et culinaire

POUR SAISIR L'ESSENTIEL: La cuisine louisianaise reflète la particularité de son histoire. Plusieurs cultures distinctes ont contribué à cette richesse gastronomique. Arrivés de l'Europe, de l'Afrique, des Antilles, du Québec, aristocrates et réfugiés, les immigrés ont apporté leurs propres idées culinaires à la base de cuisine déjà développée par les Amérindiens de la région. Étudiez la chronologie et la carte suivantes pour mieux comprendre cette histoire unique.

1. Examinez la carte, en notant bien les quatre parties du monde marquées en gris. Puis parcourez la chronologie en cherchant l'identité des gens qui sont venus de ces quatre régions du monde. Enfin, pour chaque groupe, indiquez une de leurs contributions à l'évolution de la cuisine louisianaise.

Parties du monde	Gens	Contribution
1. *la Louisiane*	*les Amérindiens*	*le filé, le maïs, les fruits de mer*
2.		
3.		
4.		
5.		

2. Réfléchissez sur vos perceptions de la cuisine louisianaise. Faites une liste des noms et des adjectifs les plus appropriés pour décrire cette cuisine.

À propos de la culture: Acadie was an area of Canada colonized by the French. It corresponds roughly to modern-day Nova Scotia and New Brunswick. In 1713 it was ceded to the English, who tried to force the French colonists to swear allegiance to the British crown. The Acadians who refused were harshly treated and, in 1755, forced out of their homes. Villages were burned and families separated. This massive deportation is referred to as **le Grand Dérangement**. Henry Wadsworth Longfellow wrote a moving account of this tragedy in his long poem *Evangeline*.

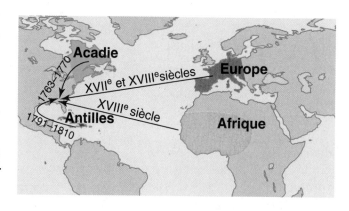

Les influences diverses sur la cuisine louisianaise

le filé: *ground sassafras leaves, used to thicken soups*

un esclave: *slave*

jambalaya: plat à base de riz et de viande ou de fruits de mer
paella: plat à base de riz et de viande ou de fruits de mer
bouillabaisse: une soupe à base de fruits de mer

ancien: *former*
en quête de: *in search of*

Avant l'arrivée des Européens	Les Amérindiens habitaient la région. Leurs aliments comprenaient déjà des fruits de mer, du maïs et du filé°.
1682	Cavelier de La Salle a occupé la région au nom de la France. Il l'a nommée la Louisiane en l'honneur du roi Louis XIV.
Au début du XVIIIᵉ siècle	Avec le développement du système agricole basé sur les plantations, on a amené des Africains comme esclaves°. Les Africains ont apporté le gombo à cette région.
Fin du XVII–le XVIII siècle	Un nombre important de colons européens sont arrivés, et ils ont amené leurs chefs au nouveau monde. C'est la naissance de la culture assez raffinée des Créoles. On dit que la jambalaya° est basée sur la paella° et que les soupes qu'on appelle gombos sont basées sur la bouillabaisse°.
1762	La Louisiane a été cédée à l'Espagne.
1763–1770	Les Acadiens, déportés de leur pays par les Anglais, ont commencé à s'installer en Louisiane. Après quelque temps, on les a appelés les Cadiens ou les Cajuns. Arrivés comme réfugiés, ils ont fait une cuisine simple, mais robuste.
1791–1810	Les anciens° propriétaires de plantations ont été chassés des îles Caraïbes par les esclaves en quête de° leur liberté. Ils ont ajouté des saveurs antillaises à la cuisine de la région.
1800	Les Français ont repris la Louisiane à l'Espagne.
1803	Napoléon Bonaparte a vendu ce territoire aux États-Unis pour la somme de quinze millions de dollars.

I. **La diversité autour de nous.** Réfléchissez sur la diversité des cuisines dans votre région ou dans une autre région que vous connaissez. Quelles sont les cultures ou les ethnies° représentées dans cette diversité? Quels aliments ou saveurs associez-vous avec ces cuisines, par exemple, le riz, les fruits de mer, les fruits tropicaux, les piments? Connaissez-vous des restaurants ou des marchés spécifiques où on peut trouver ces aliments? Classez vos informations dans un tableau. N'oubliez pas d'indiquer la région dans le titre du tableau.

ethnie (f.): *ethnicity*

Modèle:

Tableau sur la diversité culinaire dans la région de *la Nouvelle-Orléans*

Restaurant, Marché, etc.	Culture/Ethnie	Aliments
Antoine's	*Créole*	*riz, gombo, fruits de mer*

J. **À la recherche des influences.** Travaillez en groupe de trois ou quatre pour discuter les tableaux que vous avez créés pour l'exercice précédent. Aidez vos partenaires à compléter leurs tableaux en donnant des informations aussi complètes que possible.

Modèle: —J'ai étudié la diversité culinaire ici près de l'université. Il y a plusieurs restaurants mexicains où les plats ont des haricots, des oignons et des tomates. Je pense que la cuisine mexicaine emploie souvent des piments.
—N'oubliez pas le restaurant vietnamien au coin de la rue West et de l'avenue Penn.
—Oh oui, c'est vrai. Il s'appelle Chez Yien. Quelles saveurs sont typiques de la cuisine vietnamienne?

DÉCOUVERTE

Are regional products popular because they are plentiful in an area, or are they produced in abundance because they are popular with the locals? This is perhaps a "chicken-or-egg" question. In any case, regional specialties are often characterized by products that are abundantly available in the area. Notice the kinds of ingredients mentioned in this recipe for **riz à l'antillaise.**

Riz à l'antillaise
Pour 4 personnes.
Ingrédients:
250 g de riz
30 g de beurre
60 g de chair de noix de coco°
1 citron
4 tranches d'ananas
3 cuillerées à soupe de jus d'ananas
4 cuillerées à soupe de crème fraîche
4 cuillerées à soupe de bouillon instantané
1 cuillerée à café de curry
poivre de cayenne
sel

chair de noix de coco: *coconut meat*

1. Read the list of ingredients for **riz à l'antillaise** in the DÉCOUVERTE. Then decide which ingredients you would expect to characterize Caribbean cuisine from the Antilles. Try to identify the attributes of that/those product(s) that you associate with tropical islands.

2. Would it be possible to make this dish with products available in your local supermarket? Could you simplify this recipe using products from your supermarket?

3. Working in a group of three or four, discuss with classmates how you would rename this dish so that the main feature of its preparation would be obvious to an American.

3ᴱ THÈME: À chacun son goût

Objective: To use expressions of quantity with reference to foods

PRÉSENTATION: Un coup d'œil sur le thème

Pendant les fêtes d'hiver, je pense beaucoup à ma grand-mère et aux vacances que nous passions chez elle. Elle habitait dans le Maine, et il neigeait assez souvent en décembre. J'adorais sa grande maison, la cuisine pleine de petits gâteaux, et j'aimais surtout le beau sapin° de Noël décoré avec des bonbons. Quand on entrait dans la maison, on sentait l'arôme du pain d'épices° que ma grand-mère préparait chaque année. Quand j'étais jeune, je pensais que la fête commençait avec ce premier goût de pain d'épices. C'était une scène délicieuse.

sapin: *fir tree*

un pain d'épices: *gingerbread*

J'ai rarement le temps de faire la cuisine, mais je fais toujours un gâteau pour l'anniversaire de ma fille. Je me rappelle les gâteaux que ma mère préparait pour mon anniversaire quand j'étais petite. Chez nous, on n'organisait pas de grandes fêtes pour les anniversaires, alors le gâteau était encore plus important. D'habitude, c'était un grand gâteau à la noix de coco. Quelquefois Maman ajoutait du colorant alimentaire jaune ou rose. J'aimais beaucoup ce truc°, et je le fais pour ma fille aussi. Ma mère préparait toujours avec beaucoup de soin mon gâteau. Je regardais attentivement comme elle y parsemait° la noix de coco parce que je savais alors qu'elle terminait la tâche. Enfin, quand elle posait les bougies°, elle me demandait toujours, «Chérie, quel âge as-tu cette année? Oh là là, que tu grandis!» Et bien sûr, je fais de même avec ma fille.

un truc: *trick*

parsemait: *sprinkled*

une bougie: *(birthday) candle*

Et vous? Comment est-ce que les aliments figurent dans vos souvenirs? De quels aliments vous souvenez-vous du temps de votre enfance? Comment sont les scènes que vous vous rappelez?

POUR DÉVELOPPER VOTRE FRANÇAIS

Vocabulaire: Des expressions de quantité

OBSERVATIONS

K

Kougelhopf
Gâteau originaire d'Alsace
(servi souvent au petit déjeuner en Alsace)

250 g. farine° - 15 g. levure° - 1 œuf - 1 cuillerée à café° de sel - 25 g. sucre- 1 dl° lait - 80 g. de raisins secs° - 100 g. beurre.
Garniture: 100 g. d'amandes effilées - 8 à 10 grosses amandes brutes - 50 g. sucre glace.

Préparer un levain°. Lorsqu'il est fait, mélanger les ingrédients petit à petit. Pour obtenir une pâte bien élastique et molette, bien fouetter à la main. Faire lever au chaud. Bien beurrer un moule à Kougelhopf et appliquer au fond de chaque côté un raisin ou une moitié d'amande. Faire lever la pâte une deuxième fois dans le moule. Cuire à four° bien chaud.

Kugelhopf

---

la farine: *flour*
la levure: *yeast*
une cuillerée à café: *teaspoonful*
dl: *deciliter or ¹⁄₁₀ of a liter*
raisins secs (m.): *raisins*
le levain: *leaven*
le four: *oven*

STRATÉGIES D'ANALYSE

1. What kind of document do you think that «**Kougelhopf**» is: a memorandum, a letter, a grocery list, a recipe, a poem, or a short story?

2. Find the expressions that you think refer to measurements. Knowing that France uses the metric system, can you guess the meaning of any of them?

PRÉCISIONS

- You have already learned some general expressions of quantity.

Nous avons **un peu de** temps libre ce week-end. Je voudrais lire le journal.
*We have **a little** free time this weekend. I would like to read the paper.*

J'ai **très peu de** beurre. Tu peux aller à la crémerie cet après-midi?
*I have **very little** butter. Can you go to the dairy this afternoon?*

Nous avons **beaucoup de** pommes. Je peux faire une tarte.
*We have **lots of** apples. I can make a pie.*

- We use other expressions to signify quantities of sufficiency.

J'ai acheté un kilo de rosbif. C'est **assez de** viande pour huit personnes?
*I bought a kilo of roast beef. Is that **enough** meat for eight people?*

Ne mange pas **trop de** pain. On va servir le dîner bientôt.
*Don't eat **too much** bread. Dinner will be served soon.*

J'ai préparé **beaucoup trop de** soupe. J'ai doublé la recette.
*I have made **far too much soup**. I doubled the recipe.*

- We use another group of expressions to indicate measures of volume.

Veux-tu **un verre de** lait?
*Do you want **a glass of** milk?*

Merci, non, mais je voudrais **une tasse de** café.
*No, thank you, but I would like **a cup of** coffee.*

Il y a a **un litre de** lait dans le frigo. Il se trouve derrière **la bouteille de** vin.
*There is **a liter of** milk in the fridge. It is behind **the bottle of** wine.*

On a besoin d'**un décilitre de** lait pour cette recette.
*You need **one-tenth of a liter of** milk for this recipe.*

J'ai acheté **une boîte de** thé au supermarché.
*I bought **a box of** tea at the supermarket.*

J'ai besoin d'**une cuillère à café de** sel et d'**une cuillère à soupe de** sucre.
*I need **a teaspoon of** salt and **a tablespoon of** sugar.*

- Since France is on the metric system, measures of weight are in kilo(gram)s and grams rather than in pounds and ounces.

Donnez-moi **300 grammes de** fraises et **200 grammes de** cerises, s'il vous plaît.
*Give me **300 grams of** strawberries and **200 grams of** cherries, please.*

Marc a apporté **un kilo de** chocolats.
*Marc brought **a kilo of** chocolates.*

À propos de la culture: The only countries that have not formally adopted the metric system of measurement are Liberia, Burma, and the United States.

- Of course, we also use numbers and approximate numbers to tell how many.

  Six personnes vont dîner chez nous vendredi soir.
  Six people are going to have dinner at our place Friday evening.

  J'ai besoin d'**une douzaine d'**œufs et d'**une dizaine de** pommes.
  *I need **a dozen** eggs and **about ten** apples.*

- Sometimes we indicate quantity based on size or shape or presentation.

  Je voudrais **une tranche de** saumon fumé.
  *I'd like **a slice of** smoked salmon.*

  J'ai commandé **une côtelette de** veau.
  *I have ordered **a veal cutlet**.*

  Il y a **un bout de** pain et **un morceau de** beurre sur l'assiette.
  *There is **a crust of** bread and **a piece of** butter on the plate.*

  J'ai vu **une assiette de** pâtisseries dans la salle à manger.
  *I saw **a plate of** pastries in the dining room.*

  Il y a **un plateau de** fromages à côté d'**une corbeille de** fruits dans la cuisine.
  *There is **a platter of** cheese next to **a basket of** fruit in the kitchen.*

- Note that we use **de** (or **d'**) with an expression of quantity before a noun.
- To ask a question about quantity, we use **combien de**...? (how many . . . how much . . . ?).

A. **Combien?** Vous et votre partenaire vous vous retrouvez à une terrasse de café. Vous pouvez entendre un peu de conversation des gens qui passent devant vous. Travaillez ensemble pour deviner les autres mots de ces conversations.

> **Modèle:** —J'ai invité huit personnes à dîner chez moi ce soir. J'ai acheté un kilo de rosbif. C'est *assez de* viande pour huit?
> (un plateau de, un litre de, assez de)

1. —Pour faire une tarte aux pommes avec ta recette, j'ai besoin de (d') _____ pommes? (combien de, trop de, un demi-litre de)
2. —Après le concert samedi soir, tout le monde peut revenir chez moi.
   —Tu peux servir _____ fromages, du pain, des fruits et du vin. (une tasse de, un plateau de, une bouteille de)
3. —Je vais acheter une baguette à la boulangerie.
   —Et moi, je vais à la charcuterie acheter deux bonnes _____ jambon. (tranches de, corbeilles de, tasses de)
4. —Qu'est-ce que tu vas préparer pour le dîner ce soir?
   —J'ai des _____ porc dans le frigo. On ajoute de la soupe et des haricots verts, et voilà un bon dîner. (verres de, corbeilles de, côtelettes de)

5. —Je suis fatigué.

—Moi aussi. Allons au café pour prendre une _____ thé. (bouteille de, tasse de, tranche de)

6. —Est-ce que nous avons _____ jus d'orange à la maison?

—Je ne sais pas. (une tranche de, assez de, une assiette de)

7. —Il y avait une _____ personnes dans le salon.

—Mais, c'est une petite maison! (vingtaine de, bouteille de, tasse de)

8. —Quand tu fais du sorbet aux fraises, mets de côté° des fraises entières pour une belle présentation.

mets de côté: *put on the side*

—Combien?

—Comme tu veux. _____ personnes vont être à table? (un litre de, 200 grammes de, combien de)

B. **Pour faire un kougelhopf.** Vous avez déjà à la maison les ingrédients pour la garniture° d'un kougelhopf. Avec votre partenaire, consultez la recette à la page 358. Ensuite, organisez les autres ingrédients nécessaires dans des listes appropriées pour faire les courses chez les petits commerçants. Indiquez dans vos listes la quantité de chaque ingrédient que vous avez besoin d'acheter.

la garniture: *the decoration*

à l'épicerie	à la fromagerie/crémerie
200 grammes de farine	

Structure: Le pronom en

OBSERVATIONS

—Tu veux **de la** glace?   *Do you want **any** ice cream?*
—Oui, j'**en** veux, s'il te plaît.   *Yes, please, I want **some**.*

—Qui a **des** pâtisseries?   *Who has **some** pastries?*
—Moi, j'**en** ai.   *I have **some**.*

—Tu as acheté **un kilo de** cerises?   *Did you buy **a kilo of** cherries?*
—J'**en** ai acheté deux kilos.   *I bought two kilos **(of them)**.*

—Nous avons **combien de** jus d'orange?   ***How much** orange juice do we have?*
—Nous **en** avons un litre.   *We have a liter **(of it)**.*

—Est-ce que tu manges **beaucoup de** poisson?   *Do you eat **a lot of** fish?*
—Non, je n'**en** mange pas beaucoup.   *No, I don't eat much **(of it)**.*

1. In the sentences, **en** is a pronoun replacing a noun or noun expression. What word introduces these nouns replaced by **en?**
2. Can you find one example where the **de** contracts with another word? Which word?
3. Where does **en** go in the sentence in relation to the verb?
4. What does **en** seem to mean?

PRÉCISIONS ···

-   In order to avoid repetitive (and boring) speech and writing, we often use pronouns to replace nouns. The pronoun **en** replaces a noun introduced by the preposition **de** or by a number.

—Vous voulez **un kilo de** fraises?	*Do you want **a kilo of** strawberries?*
—Oui, j'**en** veux **un kilo,** s'il vous plaît.	*Yes, I want **a kilo of them,** please.*
—Tu as mangé **deux** pommes?	*Did you eat **two** apples?*
—Non, j'**en** ai mangé *trois.*	*No, I ate **three of them.***

-   When the pronoun **en** replaces a noun introduced by a partitive (**du, de la, de l', des**), the English equivalent is *some* or *any.*

—Tu as **des** millefeuilles?	*Do you have **(any)** millefeuilles?*
—Non, je n'**en** ai pas.	*No, I don't have **any.***
—Tu veux **du** sorbet?	*Do you want **(any)** sorbet?*
—Oui, j'**en** veux.	*Yes, I want **some.***

-   When the pronoun **en** replaces a noun introduced by an expression of quantity, there is often no English equivalent used.

—Est-ce que le bébé a **assez de lait?**	*Does the baby have **enough milk?***
—Oui, il **en** a **assez.**	*Yes, he has **enough (of it.)***
—Nous avons **combien de céréales?**	***How much cereal** do we have?*
—Nous **en** avons **beaucoup.**	*We have **a lot (of it).***
—Est-ce que tu manges **beaucoup de bœuf?**	*Do you eat **a lot of beef?***
—Non, je n'**en** mange pas **beaucoup.**	*No, I don't eat **much (of it).***

-   When the pronoun **en** replaces a noun in a verbal expression that requires the use of **de,** the English equivalent is usually *of it* or *of them.*

—Qui va **s'occuper du dîner?**	*Who is going **to take care of dinner?***
—Moi, je vais m'**en** occuper.	*Me. I'm going to take care **of it.***

—Avez-vous **besoin de pâtisseries?**   *Do you **need** any **pastries?***
—Oui, j'**en** ai besoin.   *Yes, I need some **of them.***

• The pronoun **en** goes in front of the verb (just like the pronoun **y**).

—Est-ce que nous avons **du jambon?**   *Do we have **any ham?***
—Oui, nous **en** avons assez.   *Yes, we have enough **(of it).***

C. **Combien de fois... ?** Dites à votre partenaire combien de fois (par jour, par semaine ou par mois) vous mangez chaque aliment. Utilisez **en** dans vos réponses.

Modèle: des œufs
—*Combien de fois par semaine est-ce que tu manges des œufs?*
—*J'en mange une fois par semaine.*

À propos du vocabulaire: Be careful to change **manges** to **prends** when mentioning drinks instead of foods.

1. des œufs   6. du lait
2. du bœuf   7. des céréales
3. du poisson   8. du chocolat
4. du café   9. du fromage
5. du Coca   10. des desserts

D. **Dans ma cuisine.** Dites à votre partenaire la quantité de chaque aliment que vous avez dans votre cuisine. Utilisez **en** dans vos réponses.

Modèle: du lait
—*Combien de lait as-tu dans ta cuisine?*
—*J'en ai un litre.*

1. du lait   6. du beurre
2. des pommes   7. du fromage
3. des bananes   8. du chocolat
4. des céréales   9. de la glace
5. du café   10. de l'eau minérale

E. **Qui s'occupe de... ?** Discutez avec votre partenaire de la responsabilité de chaque personne chez vous.

Modèle: du dîner
—*Chez toi, qui s'occupe du dîner?*
—*Chez moi, c'est mon conjoint qui s'en occupe. Et chez toi?*
—*Chez moi, je m'en occupe.*

1. du dîner   5. de la vaisselle
2. du petit déjeuner   6. des enfants
3. des courses   7. du transport
4. du vin

Structure: Les pronoms d'objet direct (le, la, l', les)

OBSERVATIONS

—Est-ce que Marie veut ma recette de kougelhopf? | *Does Marie want my recipe for kougelhopf?*
—Oui, elle **la** veut. | *Yes, she wants it.*

—Est-ce que tu as ma recette de kougelhopf? | *Do you have my recipe for kougelhopf?*
—Oui, je **l'**ai. | *Yes, I have it.*

—Et tu as mes recettes de pâtisseries pour la fête? | *And you have my pastry recipes for the party?*
—Je **les** ai aussi. | *I have them too.*

STRATÉGIES D'ANALYSE

1. We use pronouns to replace nouns. What are the new pronouns in these sentences?
2. The new pronouns in these sentences are **la, l'**, and **les**. If **la** is feminine singular, what do you expect the masculine singular form to be?
3. Where do these direct object pronouns go in relation to the verb in the sentences?

PRÉCISIONS

À propos de la structure: Be careful to distinguish between a direct object pronoun (**le, la, l', les**) and the object pronoun **en**. Remember that the direct object is used directly with the verb whereas **en** replaces a noun expression that begins with **de**.

- A direct object answers *Whom?* or *What?* after the verb of a sentence. You can recognize a direct object in French since there is *never* a preposition (**à, de, pour, avec,** etc.) between the verb and the object. The direct object is used directly with the verb.

  —Qui prépare le dîner? | *Who is making dinner?*
  —Dominique **le** prépare. | *Dominique is preparing it.*

- In French we use **le, la, l'**, and **les** to replace a person or thing that is the direct object of the verb. In the singular, **le** (*he, it*) is masculine, **la** (*she, it*) is feminine; either **le** or **la** becomes **l'** before a vowel sound. **Les** (*them*) replaces all plural nouns.

  —Tu aimes les haricots verts? | *Do you like green beans?*
  —Oui, je **les** aime beaucoup. | *Yes, I like them a lot.*

- The direct object pronoun goes directly in front of the verb.

—Qui étudiait le menu avec toi?
—Marc l'étudiait avec moi.

Who was studying the menu with you?
Marc was studying it with me.

- If the conjugated verb is followed by an infinitive, the direct object pronoun goes before the infinitive.

—Qui veut voir le film avec moi?
—Moi, je veux **le** voir avec toi.

Who wants to see the movie with me?
Me. I want to see it with you.

F. **Je les aime.** Dites à votre partenaire si vous aimez ou détestez les aliments suivants. Utilisez des pronoms dans vos réponses aux questions de votre partenaire.

Modèle: les escargots
—*Est-ce que tu aimes les escargots?*
—*Oui, je les aime beaucoup.*
ou —*Non, je ne les aime pas du tout.*
ou —*Non, je les déteste.*
ou —*Je ne sais pas. Je n'en ai jamais mangé.*

1. les escargots
2. les huîtres
3. les crevettes
4. les moules
5. le veau
6. les champignons
7. le chou-fleur
8. le pâté
9. la soupe à l'oignon
10. le chèvre
11. le roquefort
12. le camembert
13. les framboises
14. les fraises
15. la glace

PRONONCIATION: La liaison facultative

As mentioned in **Chapitre 2,** optional liaisons (*liaisons facultatives*) are sometimes made where neither required nor prohibited in order to render speech more formal or stylized (in public speeches, singing, poetry readings, etc.). The following represent cases where liaison is a question of individual taste:

1. between a plural noun and the adjective following it, when the adjective begins with a vowel sound:
   des arbres exotiques   *des livres intéressants*

*Remember that there is *never* a liaison between a singular noun and its adjective!
   un plat// épicé

2. after all verb forms, when followed by a vowel sound:
   Nous faisons un effort!   *Je suis allé(e)*   *Il travaillait à l'usine.*

À vous! With a partner, practice reading the following poetic verses. Make both required and optional liaisons.

1. Tout à coup des accents inconnus à la terre
   Du rivage charmé frappèrent les échos;
   Le flot fut attentif, et la voix qui m'est chère
   Laissa tomber ces mots...

   (Alphonse de Lamartine, *Le Lac*)

2. Les grands bois et les champs sont de vastes asiles
   Libres comme la mer autour des sombres îles.

   (Alfred de Vigny, *La Maison du Berger*)

3. Est-elle brune, blonde ou rousse?—Je l'ignore.
   Son nom? Je me souviens qu'il est doux et sonore
   Comme ceux des aimés que la Vie exila.

   (Paul Verlaine, *Mon Rêve familier*)

4. Tous ces jours passeront; ils passeront en foule
   Sur la face des mers, sur la face des monts,
   Sur les fleuves d'argent, sur les forêts où roule
   Comme un hymne confus des morts que nous aimons.

   (Victor Hugo, *Soleils couchants*)

POUR DÉVELOPPER VOS IDÉES

Thematic objective: To identify the significance that you attribute to certain foods based on the role they play in your memories

Présentation: Des goûts du passé

POUR SAISIR L'ESSENTIEL:

Marcel Proust a écrit une série de livres où il raconte ses souvenirs de jeunesse. Dans le premier de ces livres, il explique que le goût d'un petit gâteau (une madeleine) lui rappelle des visites chez sa tante, qui habitait à Combray. Le paragraphe ci-dessous est basé sur cet extrait où il décrit un peu la scène et mentionne des habitudes qui font partie du passé.

Utilisez cette méthode pour saisir l'essentiel de ses souvenirs.

1. Parcourez° d'abord le paragraphe pour identifier les images principales du souvenir.
2. Puis relisez°-le avec un partenaire pour faire deux listes. Dans la première, indiquez les **éléments de la scène;** dans la deuxième, indiquez les **actions habituelles.**

Parcourez: *Scan* / **relisez:** *reread*

Et tout d'un coup le souvenir m'est apparu°. C'était le goût du petit morceau de madeleine° que ma tante Léonie m'offrait après l'avoir trempé° dans son thé. C'est ce qu'elle faisait le dimanche matin à Combray quand j'allais lui dire bonjour dans sa chambre. Et dès que° je me suis rappelé le goût du morceau de madeleine que ma tante me donnait, aussitôt la vieille maison grise sur la rue, où était sa chambre, est apparue comme un décor de théâtre avec la maison, la ville, la place où on m'envoyait avant déjeuner, les rues où j'allais faire des courses, les chemins qu'on prenait s'il faisait beau. Tout cela a pris forme dans mon esprit. Toutes ces images sont sorties de ma tasse de thé.

(Basé sur un extrait *Du côté de chez Swann* de Marcel Proust)

le souvenir m'est apparu: *the memory appeared to me*
une madeleine: *a small sponge cake, baked in a shell-shaped mold*
après l'avoir trempé: *after having dipped it*
dès que: *as soon as*

G. Des arômes du passé. Réfléchissez aux aliments qui par leur arôme ou leur goût évoquent des souvenirs de vos traditions familiales, vos coutumes avec certains amis ou, peut-être, des habitudes personnelles. Essayez d'imaginer quelques éléments de la scène pour la décrire. Utilisez les questions dans le tableau suivant ainsi que les informations dans votre dossier d'activités **Quand j'étais jeune...** et **C'était la fête de...** (page 338) dans le *1ᵉʳ Thème* de ce chapitre pour stimuler vos idées. Organisez vos idées en suivant le modèle du tableau ci-dessous.

le lieu	les circonstances	les personnes	les actions
Où se passait cette tradition ou coutume? (Chez des parents? À l'école? Dans un café spécial?)	**Comment était la scène?** (Il faisait beau? Il pleuvait? Il neigeait? La salle était sombre et triste? Elle était chaleureuse et gaie?) **Quel âge aviez-vous?** (Vous étiez très jeune? Plutôt jeune? Vous aviez quinze ans? Seize ans?)	**Est-ce qu'il y avait d'autres personnes présentes?** (La famille proche? Un ami particulier? Des voisins?) **Comment étaient ces autres personnes?** (Elles étaient contentes? Fières? Gentilles? Impatientes?)	**Qu'est-ce qu'on faisait?** (On préparait un repas spécial? On offrait des cadeaux?) **Quelle était la fréquence de cette habitude ou tradition?** (Tous les mois? Tous les ans? Chaque semaine?)

H. Rapporter des souvenirs. En groupe de deux ou trois, communiquez votre souvenir basé sur le goût, l'arôme, la préparation ou la présentation d'un aliment. En écoutant les souvenirs de vos partenaires, posez des questions spécifiques pour apprendre autant de détails que possible.

me rappelle: *reminds me (of)*
m'apprendre: *to teach me*
alliez: *used to go*

Modèle: —L'arôme du melon me rappelle° une de mes habitudes préférées de ma jeunesse. J'avais huit ans, et mon père et moi faisions les courses ensemble le samedi. Mon père avait beaucoup de patience, et il essayait de m'apprendre° à apprécier les bons fruits et légumes. J'adorais sentir les melons. C'était une odeur facile à distinguer.
—Ah oui, c'est un bon souvenir? Et est-ce que vous alliez° chez les petits commerçants ou au supermarché pour faire les courses?
—... (réponse)
—Où est-ce que tu habitais?

I. **Réflexion écrite.** Écrivez un ou deux paragraphes (sept phrases au minimum) où vous racontez un souvenir «alimentaire». N'oubliez pas d'indiquer vos sentiments à l'égard de ce souvenir.

DÉCOUVERTE

This recipe is identified as African. Since Africa is the second largest continent (after Asia), the name of the dish stretches the term "regional" to cover a lot of ground.

Coq sauté à l'africaine
Pour 4 personnes. Ingrédients:

une feuille de laurier: *bay leaf*
aubergines (f.): *eggplants*
cacahuètes décortiquées: *shelled peanuts*

une gousse d'ail: *garlic clove*
une branche de thym: *sprig of thyme*

1 poulet de 1 kg 300	1 feuille de laurier°
10 g de farine	2 aubergines°
2 dl de vin blanc sec	50 g de cacahuètes décortiquées°
½ litre de bouillon de volaille	3 cuillerées à soupe d'huile
2 oignons	1 pincée de poivre de cayenne
3 gousses d'ail°	sel
1 branche de thym°	poivre

1. Read the list of ingredients for **coq sauté à l'africaine** in the DÉCOUVERTE. Then decide which ingredient(s) you would expect to characterize African cuisine. Try to identify the attributes of that/those product(s) that you associate with Africa.

2. Would it be possible to make this dish with products available in your local supermarket?

3. Working in a group of three or four, discuss with classmates how you would rename this dish so that the main feature of its preparation would be evident to an American.

SYNTHÈSE DES DÉCOUVERTES

Based on your examination and discussions of the DÉCOUVERTE notes throughout the chapter, compare how French and Americans identify the main features of a dish on a menu or in a recipe title.

Hint: Consider these examples of French dishes:

Soupe à l'oignon

Omelette aux fines herbes, Quiche florentine

Steak au poivre à la bordelaise, Poulet à la bruxelloise

Salade niçoise

Tarte aux pommes

You will hear two voice mail **(boîte vocale)** messages in which people talk about their dining plans. First, identify the dishes and/or food items you hear discussed in each message. Then, express your own preferences in the food selections.

A. **On identifie les aliments.** Écoutez les messages suivants et sous chaque catégorie encerclez° les aliments mentionnés.

encerclez: *circle*

Message n° 1:

Catégories d'aliments ⇨	Le plat principal	Les légumes *(au moins deux des trois mentionnés)*	Le dessert *(au moins un des deux mentionnés)*	Aussi *(au moins un des deux mentionnés)*
Specific foods asked for ⇨	a. ham b. roast beef c. leg of lamb d. chicken breast e. veal chops f. lobster g. trout h. pizza	a. peas b. mushrooms c. green beans d. salad e. potatoes f. wild rice g. asparagus h. spinach	a. chocolate eclairs b. fruit pie c. caramelized custard d. praline cake e. fruit sorbet f. ice cream	a. cheese b. onion soup c. shrimp cocktail d. escargots (snails) e. bread f. wine g. coffee h. raw vegetables and dip

Message n° 2:

Catégories d'aliments ⇨	Le plat principal	Les légumes *(au moins deux des trois mentionnés)*	Le dessert	Aussi *(au moins deux des trois mentionnés)*
Specific foods mentioned ⇨	a. ham b. roast beef c. leg of lamb d. chicken breast e. veal chops f. lobster g. trout h. pizza	a. peas b. mushrooms c. green beans d. salad e. potatoes f. wild rice g. asparagus h. spinach	a. chocolate eclairs b. fruit pie c. caramelized custard d. praline cake e. fruit sorbet f. ice cream	a. cheese b. onion soup c. shrimp cocktail d. escargots (snails) e. bread f. wine g. coffee h. raw vegetables and dip

B. **On prend la décision.** Réfléchissez aux deux dîners décrits dans les messages. Décidez quel dîner vous préféreriez. Ensuite, indiquez les aliments qui ont influencé votre décision: cochez (✓) chaque aliment mentionné dans les messages que vous aimez et mettez un (x) à côté de ceux que vous n'aimez pas.

Je choisirais le **(a.)** ____ premier dîner **(b.)** ____ deuxième dîner.

Je choisirais ce dîner... :			
à cause du plat principal	**à cause des légumes**	**à cause du dessert**	**à cause d'autre chose**
____a. de la pizza	____a. des épinards	____a. des éclairs	____a. du café
____b. du poulet	____b. des asperges	____b. du gâteau praliné	____b. du vin
____c. de la truite	____c. de la salade	____c. du sorbet aux fruits	____c. des escargots
____d. du rôti de bœuf	____d. des haricots verts	____d. de la tarte aux fruits	____d. du fromage
____e. du homard	____e. du riz sauvage	____e. de la glace	____e. des baguettes
____f. du gigot	____f. des petits pois	____f. de la crème brûlée	____f. des crevettes
____g. des côtelettes de veau	____g. des champignons		____g. des crudités avec sauce
____h. du jambon	____h. des pommes de terre		____h. de la soupe à l'oignon gratinée

ÉLABORATION DE PERSPECTIVE

1. The following menu highlights the culinary specialties from several areas of the Francophone world. Working in a group of two or three, determine the main features of each dish. As you work through the menu, fill in the chart showing the associations you make between the places in the name of the dishes and the products used in their preparation.

provençale	tomatoes, garlic, olive oil
niçoise	
roquefort	
africaine	
bruxelloise	
florentine	
normande	
bordelaise	
chantilly	
madère	
antillaise	

La Fête française

Le menu

l'entrée

6 escargots à la provençale
salade niçoise
œuf dur roquefort

le plat principal

coq à l'africaine
poulet à la bruxelloise
escalope de veau à la
provençale
saumon à la florentine
côtelette de porc à la
normande

brochette de bœuf à la
bordelaise

le dessert

fraises à la chantilly
pêches au madère
glace à la vanille à
l'antillaise

1/2 bouteille d'eau
minérale

75 FF/12 Euros - tout compris

2. Referring to your portfolio notes for Exercise K, *Thème 1*, **Des spécialités régionales aux États-Unis**, in the *1ᵉʳ Thème* fill in the chart for regions of the United States and products that you associate with them.

Wisconsin	cheese, cream, butter

3. Continuing to work with your group, create a menu similar to the one for **La Fête française** to highlight regional specialties of the United States. Use the names of the regions in the names of the dishes on your menu. Examples: Hawaiian Chicken (for chicken prepared with pineapple), Asparagus à la Wisconsin (for asparagus prepared with cream or cheese).

4. Discuss what this style of labeling dishes contributes to your perceptions of the relationships among food, geography, and culture.

INTÉGRATION

A. Établir des priorités. Quelles sont vos priorités quand vous choisissez un nouveau restaurant pour une occasion spéciale? Indiquez l'importance des attributs dans le tableau en utilisant numéro 1 pour le plus important.

Attribut	Ordre de priorité
charme du nom du restaurant	
décor/ambiance	
prix	
qualité de la cuisine	
sorte de cuisine (italienne, mexicaine, classique, nouvelle)	
spécialités de la maison	
quartier de la ville	
divertissements (musique, danse, spectacle, bar, etc.)	
???	

LECTURE: RESTAURANTS RECOMMANDÉS

Voici quelques critiques de restaurants extraites de la revue *Pariscope*. En lisant les critiques, notez les qualités que vous trouvez surtout attrayantes.

Caveau François Villon
64, rue de l'Arbre Sec, 75001 Paris
Tél +33 01.42.36.10.92 Fermé samedi midi, dimanche et lundi midi. Accueil jusqu'à 1h du matin. Cartes de crédit: VISA, AMEX
Une joyeuse ambiance règne toujours dans ce charmant bistrot des Halles décoré d'amusantes peintures moyenâgeuses et avec de belles caves du XVème siècle où un troubadour agrémente les dîners d'un joli répertoire de chansons françaises. Délicieuse cuisine de Patrick Collin, jovial patron de cet endroit authentique, qui nous régale par exemple d'une superbe cuisine néo-classique. Unique menu-carte à 155 FF (24 euros).

La Poule au Pot
9, rue Vauvilliers, 75001 Paris
Tél +33 01.42.36.32.96 Fermé lundi et au déjeuner. Accueil de 19h à 6h du matin. Cartes de crédit: VISA, AMEX
Les Rolling Stones, Dire Straits, Mastroianni, Prince, Bruce Springsteen et une foule de stars et de personnalités illustres du monde entier ont signé le livre d'or de ce charmant bistrot des Halles, qui séduit tant par son cadre authentique que par sa belle cuisine classique française avec pot-au-feu, la célèbre poule au pot, le soufflé au Grand Marnier et autres plats immuables°. Carte: environ 260 FF (40 euros). Menu à 160 FF (24 euros).

immuables: *fixed, unchanging*

Karlov

197, rue de Grenelle, 75007 Paris

Tél +33 01.45.51.29.21 Fermé au déjeuner et le dimanche. Accueil jusqu'à minuit.
Cartes de crédit: VISA, AMEX

Un décor luxueux évocateur de l'ancienne Russie accueille les amateurs de cuisine et de musique russe. Avec au programme de la soirée, l'excellent trio Arbat pour nous bercer de belles mélodies. Carte: environ 400 FF. Menu à 270 FF (41 euros) vin compris en semaine.

La Tour d'Argent

15, quai de la Tournelle, 75005 Paris

Tél +33 01.43.54.23.31 - Fax +33 01.44.07.12.04 Fermé lundi. Accueil jusqu'à 22h.
Voiturier. Cartes de crédit: VISA, AMEX, DC

L'illustre restaurant parisien de Claude Terrail n'a rien perdu de son charme au fil des ans. Et c'est toujours un vrai bonheur de s'installer dans sa luxueuse salle perchée au 5ème étage, avec vue sur la Seine et Notre-Dame. Et si la carte composée par Bernard Guilhaudin a conservé les grandes spécialités de la maison comme les quenelles de brochet André Terrail, les pêches flambées à l'eau de vie de framboise, et bien entendu le célèbre caneton Tour d'Argent, elle s'est enrichie de plats inventifs.

Carte des vins fastueuse et service de classe. Carte: environ 1.100 FF (167 euros).
Menu à 375 FF (57 euros) au déjeuner.

[*Pariscope*, Nov., 1997, (www.pariscope.fr)]

B. **Évaluer les qualités des restaurants.** Pour chaque attribut mentionné dans la liste, écrivez le nom du restaurant décrit dans la lecture qui correspond le mieux à vos goûts. Expliquez pourquoi.

Modèle: charme du nom du restaurant

À mon avis, le nom «Caveau François Villon» a beaucoup de charme parce qu'il évoque l'histoire et la poésie.

Attribut	Restaurant
Modèle: charme du nom du restaurant	*Caveau François Villon*
charme du nom du restaurant	
décor/ambiance	
prix	
qualité de la cuisine	
sorte de cuisine (italienne, mexicaine, classique, nouvelle)	
spécialités de la maison	
quartier de la ville	
divertissements (musique, danse, spectacle, bar, etc.)	

investir: *to invest*

C. Imaginer votre propre restaurant. Imaginez que vous avez l'occasion d'investir° dans un nouveau restaurant. Considérez les qualités que vous recherchez dans un restaurant pour votre investissement.

- Quel est le nom de ce restaurant?
- Quelle sorte de cuisine va-t-on servir?
- Quels plats vont être les spécialités de la maison?
- Décrivez le décor et l'ambiance.
- Est-ce qu'il y a de la musique, des vidéos, etc.?
- Où se trouve ce restaurant? Dans un quartier chic? Un quartier commerçant?
- Enfin, combien va-t-on payer dans ce restaurant? Est-ce que les repas vont coûter très cher, ou vont-ils être plutôt bon marché?

Mon Restaurant	
Attribut	Détails
nom du restaurant	
décor/ambiance	
prix	
qualité de la cuisine	
sorte de cuisine (italienne, mexicaine, classique, nouvelle)	
spécialités de la maison	
quartier de la ville	
divertissements (musique, danse, spectacle, bar, etc.)	

D. **Négocier vos projets.** En travaillant avec un(e) partenaire, comparez vos décisions sur le nouveau restaurant. Imaginez que vous décidez de collaborer dans cette entreprise. Discutez vos préférences pour vous accorder sur les qualités de votre nouveau restaurant. Remplissez le tableau pour rapporter vos décisions.

Notre Restaurant	
Attribut	Détails
nom du restaurant	
décor/ambiance	
prix	
qualité de la cuisine	
sorte de cuisine (italienne, mexicaine, classique, nouvelle)	
spécialités de la maison	
quartier de la ville	
divertissements (musique, danse, spectacle, bar, etc.)	

E. **Écrire une annonce publicitaire.** Enfin votre restaurant est ouvert. Maintenant, vous et votre partenaire devez écrire une annonce publicitaire. Utilisez les exemples dans la lecture *Restaurants recommandés* comme modèle pour votre publicité.

Où on va pour acheter...

à la boulangerie	at the bakery
une baguette	French bread
un pain complet	whole wheat bread
un petit pain	roll
un croissant	croissant

à la pâtisserie	at the pastry shop
une tarte...	pie
aux cerises	cherry pie
aux fraises	strawberry pie
au citron	lemon pie
une tartelette	individual pie
aux framboises	raspberry tart
aux abricots	apricot tart
un gâteau...	cake
au chocolat	chocolate cake

au marché	at the market
des légumes (m.)	vegetables
des asperges (f.)	asparagus
des carottes (f.)	carrots
des champignons (m.)	mushrooms
des courgettes (f.)	zucchini squash
des épinards (m.)	spinach
des haricots verts (m.)	green beans
des oignons (m.)	onions
des petits pois (m.)	peas
des pommes de terre (f.)	potatoes
de la salade	lettuce
des tomates (f.)	tomatoes
des fruits (m.)	fruits
des bananes (f.)	bananas
des cerises (f.)	cherries
des citrons (m.)	lemons
des fraises (f.)	strawberries
des framboises (f.)	raspberries
des oranges (f.)	oranges
des pamplemousses (m.)	grapefruit
des pêches (f.)	peaches
des pommes (f.)	apples

à la fromagerie	at the cheese shop
du fromage	cheese
du lait	milk
du beurre	butter
du yaourt	yogurt
de la crème	cream

LEXIQUE D'EXPANSION

un pain de campagne	round loaf
un pain au chocolat	roll with a strip of chocolate through it
un pain de mie	loaf of white bread
un pain de seigle	rye bread
un pain aux céréales	multigrain bread
un baba au rhum	rum pastry
un gâteau aux amandes	almond cake
une tarte aux myrtilles	blueberry pie
un biscuit	cookie
à soda	cracker
un éclair	éclair

de l'ail (m.)	garlic
des aubergines (f.)	eggplants
des brocolis (m.)	broccoli
des choux (m.)	cabbage
des concombres (m.)	cucumbers
des endives (f.)	endives
du maïs	corn
des poivrons verts (m.)	green peppers
des radis (m.)	radishes

des abricots (m.)	apricots
des ananas (m.)	pineapple
des poires (f.)	pears
du raisin	grapes
des raisins secs	raisins

de la raclette	a cheese served melted
de la Gourmandise	a packaged dessert cheese, usually containing kirsch
du Boursin	a packaged soft cheese containing herbs and garlic or pepper

du camembert	a popular cheese from Normandy
du brie	a mild, semi-soft cheese
du roquefort	a strong, blue cheese
du chèvre	goat cheese
de l'Emmenthal	Swiss cheese with holes, also made in France

à la poissonnerie	**at the fish market**
du poisson	fish
un homard	lobster
une crevette	shrimp
une huître	oyster

à la boucherie	**at the butcher shop**		
du bœuf	beef	du jambon du pays	cured ham
du porc	pork	des côtelettes (f.)	cutlets
du veau	veal	du bifteck	steak
de l'agneau (m.) / du gigot	lamb/leg of lamb	du rosbif	roast beef
un poulet	chicken		

à la charcuterie	**at the delicatessen**		
des aliments préparés	prepared foods	du saucisson	salami
du jambon	ham	des saucisses	sausages
du pâté	pâté	une salade niçoise	chef salad with tuna
du saumon fumé	smoked salmon	des carottes râpées	grated carrots
des quiches	quiches (egg and cream pies)		

à l'épicerie	**at the grocery store**		
du sel	salt	du miel	honey
du poivre	pepper	de la confiture	jam
de la moutarde	mustard	de la mayonnaise	mayonnaise
des céréales (f.)	cereal	du riz	rice
(une boîte) de café/de thé	packaged coffee/tea	des pâtes (f.)	pasta
au rayon volaille	**at the poultry counter**		
de la dinde	turkey		
du canard	duck		
du poulet	chicken		
au rayon boissons	**in the beverages section**		
du vin (rouge/blanc)	wine (red/white)	de l'eau	water
de l'eau minérale	mineral water	**plate**	non-carbonated
au rayon produits surgelés	**in the frozen food section**	gazeuse	carbonated
de la glace	ice cream		
du sorbet	sorbet/sherbet		
de la pizza	pizza		

Les repas du jour

le petit-déjeuner	breakfast
le déjeuner	lunch
le dîner	dinner

le souper	supper
l'entrée (f.)	first course
le plat principal	main course
la salade	salad
le fromage	cheese
le dessert	dessert
le café	coffee

Des expressions à table

Bon appétit.	Have a nice meal.
Terminé(e)(s)?	Finished?
Ça suffit.	That's plenty.
L'addition, s.v.p.	Check, please.
Deux couverts, s.v.p.	A table for two, please.

une assiette	plate	une nappe	tablecloth
une cuillère	spoon	un napperon	placemat
une fourchette	fork		
un couteau	knife		
une serviette	napkin		
un verre	glass	un morceau de	a piece of
une tasse	cup	un plateau de	a platter of
une soucoupe	saucer	une corbeille de	a basket of
une tranche de	a slice of	un bout de	an end of, a crust of,
un kilo de	a kilogram of	un décilitre de	one-tenth of a liter of
un litre de	a liter of	une cuillère à café de	a teaspoon of
		une cuillère à soupe de	a tablespoon of

Pour indiquer des actions habituelles dans le passé

autrefois	formerly
en ce temps-là	at that time
à cette époque-là, à l'époque	at that time, back then
pendant ma jeunesse	during my youth
d'habitude	generally, as a habit
fréquemment	frequently

LES SOUVENIRS
Les gens et les événements dans la vie

Communicative Objectives

- To narrate past events of your life
- To talk about people you remember and activities you have just completed
- To describe different stages of your life: where you were living, your routine activities, what was going on around you

Thematic Objectives

✓ To identify the events of your life that have created lasting memories

✓ To identify the people who have made lasting impressions on your memories

✓ To look back on the different stages of your life, describing them in terms of their personal significance to you

OUVERTURE EN VIDÉO: La nostalgie

La mise en scène

«Nous nous sommes rencontrés en '49.»

A. **Un peu de nostalgie.** In this chapter you will identify people and events that have made lasting impressions on you. The video shows a charming French couple reminiscing about how they met, fell in love, got married, and have been together for fifty years. In anticipation of hearing how they express their fond memories in French, consider some of the memorable elements of their relationship, as listed on the grid. Categorize each element as an *event* (what happened) or as a *description* or *background information*.

memory	event (what happened)	description or background information	memory	event (what happened)	description or background information
They met each other.	X		They began to go out together.		
He was a young professor.		X	They got married.		
He was 20 years old.			They moved to a new town.		
All the students had a crush on the teacher.			Life was difficult.		
She won the top prize.			It was youth.		
She was the most interesting contender.			It was love.		
She was older than the other students.			Their children were born.		
The others were more concerned with social standing.			They lived in Paris.		

B. **Le ton et les gestes: signes d'une relation intime.** Professeur and Mme Chassigneux have been together for fifty years. They share a close intimacy that is evident in their interaction together. The first time you watch the video segment, don't try to understand what they are saying, but rather notice the linguistic features that are characteristic of the depth of their relationship. That closeness is evident as they take turns giving a joint account of their life together. Note and keep a count of the examples of the following linguistic features as they tell their story:

- look to the other person for help in expressing or completing an idea
- repeat, clarify, or embellish what the other one has said
- look to the other one with tenderness

«C'est moi qui a remporté le pompon.»

«Nous nous sommes mariés en '53.»

Les paroles et le sens

C. Nos meilleurs souvenirs. Before you listen to the complete narrative of M. and Mme Chassigneux's love story, listen to the selected excerpts. The goal is to identify which memories stand out as key events in their story (expressed with the **passé composé**), and which ones provide description or background information (expressed with the **imparfait**).

D. Les grands moments de leur histoire. Now that you have listened in detail to this beautiful love story, consider the high points of their relationship. Read through the list of some of the sentences used in the telling of their story and identify the key junctures.

memory	key junctures	memory	key junctures
Nous nous sommes rencontrés en '49.	X	Les autres jeunes filles étaient plus bourgeoises°.	
J'étais jeune professeur.		Nous avons commencé à sortir ensemble.	
Il enseignait.		Nous nous sommes mariés.	
J'avais 20 ans.		Nous avons déménagé.	
Toutes les filles lui faisaient la cour°.		La vie était un peu difficile.	
C'est moi qui ai remporté le pompon°.		C'était la jeunesse... et l'amour.	
C'était de loin la plus intéressante.		Ma première fille est née.	
J'étais plus âgée que les autres.		Nous habitions à Paris.	

---

lui faisaient la cour: *had a crush on him, flirted with him* / **C'est moi qui ai remporté le pompon:** *I'm the one who "brought home the prize."* / **bourgeoises:** *concerned with social standing*

Now go back and compare the elements you marked as "key junctures" in this chart with those that you marked as "events" in Exercise A. How well do the two correspond? Would you revise one or the other based on the insights that you've gained by working with the video?

On y réfléchit

E. Récolte (*Harvest*) des expressions. Is there someone with whom you have shared so many important experiences in your life that you could participate in a similar joint recounting of the highlights of your relationship? Select any phrases from the preceding grid that you would like to collect for recounting your own set of memories, make any minor adjustments necessary to personalize them, and list them in your portfolio.

Objective: To narrate past events in your life

PRÉSENTATION: **Un coup d'œil sur le thème**

Le moment le plus touchant de ma vie, c'est probablement le jour de mon bar-mitsva. J'étais heureux. Toute la famille était là. Mes grands-parents m'ont donné beaucoup de cadeaux. Mais—et voici l'important—à partir de° ce jour-là, ils ont commencé à me traiter° un peu comme un adulte.

à partir de: *from, since*
me traiter: *treat me*

Le plus beau cadeau que j'ai jamais offert? Je pense que c'est un voyage que j'ai offert à mes parents pour leur 25e anniversaire de mariage. J'avais 23 ans, et je venais de commencer° mon premier emploi. Enfin, j'étais capable de le faire, alors je leur ai acheté° des billets pour Rome. Vous voyez, ma mère est italienne, et à cette époque-là° toute sa famille habitait en Italie.

je venais de commencer:
I had just started

je leur ai acheté: j'ai acheté
pour mes parents

à cette époque-là: en ce
temps-là

Un des moments les plus difficiles de ma vie, c'est sans doute mon premier accident de voiture. J'avais 18 ans, et je conduisais l'auto d'un ami. Dieu merci°, personne n'a été blessé°, mais j'avais peur parce que je n'avais pas assez d'argent pour payer les réparations. Finalement, j'ai dû expliquer la situation à mon ami et trouver une façon de lui rembourser° la dette. Ça m'a donné une leçon de responsabilité.

Dieu merci: *thank God*
personne n'a été blessé: *no
one was injured*

lui rembourser: *pay him back*

Les grands moments de la vie

Dans ces paragraphes, on raconte des souvenirs.

1. Déterminez quelle histoire ressemble le plus à un de vos souvenirs.
2. Énumérez les circonstances, les sentiments ou les actions qui sont similaires aux vôtres°.
3. Faites une liste des expressions que vous pouvez utiliser pour raconter vos propres souvenirs.

°**similaires aux vôtres:** *similar to yours*

POUR DÉVELOPPER VOTRE FRANÇAIS

Structure: L'imparfait par rapport au passé composé

OBSERVATIONS

Remarquez le changement de signification entre ces deux phrases:

Mon mari m'**a téléphoné** ce matin quand il **est arrivé** au bureau à 8 heures.
*My husband **called** me this morning when he **got** to the office at 8 o'clock.*

En 1999 j'**ai eu** un héritage important.
*In 1999 I **came** into a substantial inheritance.*

Quand il **a vu** la voiture démolie, il **a été** furieux.
*When he **saw** the demolished car, he **was** furious.*

Nous **sommes partis** de la maison. Puis, nous nous **sommes promenés** dans le parc. Tout d'un coup il **a commencé** à pleuvoir. Alors, nous **avons décidé** d'aller au cinéma.
*We **left** the house. Then, we **took a walk** in the park. Suddenly it **began** to rain. So, we **decided** to go to the movies.*

Autrefois, ma sœur me **téléphonait** toujours le matin quand elle **arrivait** au travail.
*It used to be that my sister **would call** me every morning when she **would get** to work.*

Pendant les premières années de notre vie ensemble, nous n'**avions** pas beaucoup d'argent.
*During the first years of our life together, we **did not have** much money.*

Au début mon mari **était** toujours heureux.
*In the beginning my husband **was** always happy.*

Nous nous **promenions** dans le parc.
*We **were walking** in the park.*

Il **pleuvait**.
*It **was raining**.*

STRATÉGIES D'ANALYSE

1. What is the time frame of all these sentences—present, past, or future?
2. How many different tenses are used in these sentences? Do you remember what we call these tenses in French?
3. Which sentences tell about one-time happenings or events in a sequence? Which past tense is used in that group of sentences, the **passé composé** or the **imparfait**?
4. Which sentences seem to describe the background or setting for events in a story? Which past tense is used in that group of sentences, the **passé composé** or the **imparfait**?

Précisions

You have been introduced to two past tenses, the **passé composé** and the **imparfait**. Both of these tenses are concerned with past time, but they are used in different situations. They are not interchangeable. You send a different message when you use the **passé composé** than you do when you use the **imparfait**.

- To tell about an action that occurred only once, or was repeated a specific number of times, or happened in a definite period, use the **passé composé**. When a past action was habitual, or repeated an unspecified number of times, or happened over an indefinite time period, use the **imparfait**.

Passé composé: single occurrence
Samedi soir je **suis allé(e)** au théâtre avec mes amis.
Saturday evening I went to the theater with my friends.

Imparfait: habitual action
Quand j'étais au lycée, j'**allais** au théâtre avec mes amis le samedi soir.
When I was in high school, I used to go to the theater with my friends on Saturday evening.

Passé composé: action repeated a specified number of times
À la discothèque, j'**ai dansé** trois fois avec Éric.
At the disco I danced with Eric three times.

Imparfait: action repeated an unspecified number of times
Je **dansais** souvent avec Éric avant son mariage avec Monique.
I used to dance with Eric often before his marriage to Monique.

Passé composé: action in a definite time period
Nous **avons regardé** la télévision toute la nuit.
We watched TV all night long.

Imparfait: action in an indefinite time period
Nous **regardions** souvent la télévision ensemble.
We often used to watch TV together.

- To tell how things used to be, use the **imparfait**. To explain what changed in the situation, use the **passé composé**.

Imparfait: description of how things used to be
J'**allais** à Québec chaque année pour les vacances de Noël.
I used to go to Quebec City each year for the Christmas holidays.

Passé composé: what changed
Je **suis allé(e)** à Grenoble dans les Alpes françaises l'année dernière.
I went to Grenoble in the French Alps last year.

- To describe what someone was like *(physical/mental/psychological/social condition)*, use the **imparfait**. To tell what changed at a precise moment in time, use the **passé composé**:

Imparfait: description of what someone was like
J'**étais** calme et tranquille.
I was calm and tranquil.

Passé composé: what changed
J'**ai été** inquiet quand on a appelé mon nom.
I got anxious when my name was called.

- To narrate a story, use the **passé composé** to tell the sequence of events of the story (what happened). Use the **imparfait** to set the stage or describe the scene or provide the background information.

> **Imparfait:** setting the stage
> Il **faisait** froid et sombre. Il n'y **avait** pas de lumière tout près.
> *It **was** cold and dark. There **wasn't** a light nearby.*
> **Passé composé:** telling the sequence of events
> J'**ai entendu** quelqu'un derrière moi dans la nuit. J'**ai crié** aussi fort que possible et j'**ai commencé** à courir.
> *I **heard** someone behind me in the night. I **screamed** as loud as possible, and I **began** to run.*

- Use the **imparfait** to describe what was going on when something else happened. Use the **passé composé** to tell what happened that interrupted the action in progress.

> Je me **brossais** les dents quand il m'**a téléphoné**.
> *I **was brushing** my teeth when he **called** me.*
>
> Nous **regardions** un match de tennis à la télé quand notre fils **est arrivé**.
> *We **were watching** a tennis match on TV when our son **arrived**.*
>
> Elle **faisait** du bénévolat à l'hôpital quand sa fille **est née**.
> *She **was doing** volunteer work at the hospital when her daughter **was born**.*

A. **As-tu déjà fait...?** Dites à votre partenaire si vous avez fait les choses suivantes (1) une fois dans la vie, (2) jamais de la vie, ou (3) habituellement dans le passé.

Modèle: faire du ski nautique
—*As-tu déjà fait du ski nautique?*
—*Oui, j'ai fait du ski nautique une fois.*
ou   —*Non, je n'ai jamais fait de ski nautique de ma vie.*
ou   —*Oui, quand j'étais jeune, je faisais souvent du ski nautique.*

1. faire du ski nautique
2. faire du ski alpin
3. chanter dans une chorale
4. danser jusqu'à l'aube°
5. visiter la France
6. manger des escargots
7. acheter une nouvelle voiture
8. acheter une maison
9. conduire la voiture de votre patron(ne)
10. choisir un cadeau pour votre patron(ne)
11. voyager hors des États-Unis
12. travailler hors des États-Unis
13. avoir un accident de voiture

jusqu'à l'aube: *until dawn*

B. Quand je suis parti(e) de chez moi ce matin. Décrivez à votre partenaire la situation chez vous quand vous êtes parti(e) ce matin pour aller à l'université ou au travail. Dites-lui au moins cinq phrases.

> **Modèle:** *Quand je suis parti(e) de chez moi ce matin, mon camarade de chambre était toujours au lit.*

mon époux/épouse
mon/ma/mes
  camarade(s)
  de chambre
mon/ma conjoint(e)
mon/mes enfant(s)
...
	être	au lit
		dans la cuisine
		dans la salle de bains
		devant la télé
			dans la piscine
			au travail
			à l'école
			...

	faire	la cuisine la vaisselle le ménage	sa toilette ses devoirs ...
	être	heureux(-euse) malheureux(-euse) fâché(e) pressé(e) décontracté(e)	endormi(e) occupé(e) préoccupé(e) par... ennuyé(e) ...
	désirer	de l'argent le journal l'accès à la salle de bains ...	parler avec moi prendre le petit déjeuner rester à la maison m'accompagner ...
Il *(le temps)*	faire	encore nuit un temps magnifique beau mauvais	moche du soleil du vent ...
Il	être	très tôt	assez tard
Je	être	bien/mal habillé(e) bien/mal coiffé(e) de mauvaise humeur	de bonne humeur ...
Je	me sentir	inquiet(-ète) fatigué(e) content(e)	mécontent(e) motivé(e)

C. On compare nos matins. En utilisant la fiche de l'Exercice B, cherchez des situations que vous avez en commun avec votre partenaire.

> **Modèle:** —*Quand je suis parti(e) de chez moi, ce matin, mes enfants étaient devant la télé. Où étaient tes enfants quand tu es partie?*
> —*Mes enfants étaient toujours au lit. Ma femme aussi. J'étais de mauvaise humeur quand je suis parti.*
> —*Moi aussi, j'étais de mauvaise humeur quand je suis parti(e).*

D. On fait un rapport. Dites à vos camarades de classe ce que vous et votre partenaire aviez en commun ce matin.

>   **Modèle:** *Mon/Ma partenaire et moi étions de mauvaise humeur quand nous sommes parti(e)s de la maison ce matin.*

E. Et quand je suis arrivé(e). Maintenant décrivez à votre partenaire la situation à l'école ou au travail quand vous y êtes arrivé(e) ce matin. Dites-lui au moins quatre phrases. (Notez bien que c'est **l'imparfait** qu'on utilise pour les descriptions.)

>   **Modèle:** *Quand je suis arrivé(e) au travail (à l'université) ce matin, **il faisait** du vent.*

le parking	être	complet presque vide cher	gratuit loin de mon bâtiment près de mon bâtiment
il	faire	froid chaud beau	mauvais du vent ...
l'ascenseur l'escalier roulant	être	en panne° occupé très loin	vide complet
mon/ma patron(ne) le/la secrétaire mon professeur mes collègues mes camarades de classe mes ami(e)s	être	de bonne humeur de mauvaise humeur très occupé(e) hors du bureau	dans le couloir inquiet(-ète) nerveux(-euse) fâché(e)
la porte de...	être	ouverte fermée	fermée à clé°

en panne: *out of order /* **fermée à clé:** *locked*

F. On compare à nouveau nos matinées *(mornings).* En utilisant la fiche de l'Exercice E, cherchez des situations que vous avez en commun avec votre partenaire.

>   **Modèle:** *—Quand je suis arrivé(e) à l'école ce matin, le parking était presque vide. Et toi?*
>   *—Non, quand je suis arrivé(e), le parking près de mon bâtiment était complet. Finalement, j'ai trouvé une place loin d'ici.*
>   *—Oh, moi aussi. Je laisse toujours ma voiture au parking qui est loin du bâtiment. J'ai besoin de marcher un peu.*
>   *—Alors, nous utilisons le même parking: le parking près d'ici était complet, mais le parking plus loin était presque vide.*

G. **On fait un deuxième rapport.** Dites à vos camarades de classe ce que vous et votre partenaire aviez en commun ce matin quand vous êtes arrivés à l'université ou au travail.

> **Modèle:** *Quand mon partenaire et moi sommes arrivés à l'université ce matin, le parking près d'ici était complet, mais le parking plus loin était presque vide.*

H. **On peut beaucoup comprendre.** Assis à une table à la terrasse d'un café, vous entendez la plupart de la conversation d'un couple à la table à côté de vous. Vous avez étudié assez de français pour compléter les blancs. (Faites attention au choix entre **le passé composé** et **l'imparfait.**)

—Comment ___*s'est passée*___ (se passer) ton interview hier avec Intel?
—Assez bien, je crois. Quand je/j' _____ (arriver) au bureau, le parking _____ (être) déjà complet. Je/ J'_____ (chercher) un parking pendant dix minutes. Heureusement, quelqu'un qui _____ (avoir) une bonne place _____ (partir).
—Tu _____ (avoir) de la chance.
—Ben, oui. Et heureusement parce que je/j'_____ (être) déjà assez nerveux.
—Est-ce que le patron _____ (être) sympathique?
—Plus ou moins. Il est certain qu'il _____ (être) intelligent et bien informé. Il _____ (connaître) bien sa société et mon dossier. Il m'_____ (poser) beaucoup de bonnes questions.
—Tu _____ (répondre) à toutes ses questions avec clarté et beaucoup d'assurance?
—J'espère que oui.

I. **Qu'est-ce qui est arrivé?** Décrivez pour votre partenaire trois événements qui ont changé votre vie ou vos attitudes. Utilisez les expressions suivantes pour stimuler vos idées.

> **Modèle:** *Quand j'étais jeune, je n'aimais pas la musique classique. Puis je suis allé à un concert de l'orchestre de ma ville avec ma tante, et j'ai beaucoup aimé. Maintenant j'apprécie bien la musique classique.*

1. j'aimais ou je n'aimais pas	la musique les sports la cuisine	les gens qui... faire...
2. je faisais ou je ne faisais pas	la musique les sports la cuisine	le travail les études
3. j'étais ou je n'étais pas	timide sportif(-ve) généreux(-euse) avare	ambitieux(-euse) sérieux(-euse) riche pauvre
4. je savais ou je ne savais pas	les langues étrangères jouer d'un instrument de musique	jouer aux sports faire...

J. **Ce qui est arrivé à mon partenaire.** Rapportez à un(e) autre camarade de classe un détail de votre discussion de l'Exercice I. Mentionnez une chose qui est arrivée à votre partenaire et qui a changé un peu sa vie.

Modèle: *Mon partenaire était pauvre. Puis une tante inconnue est morte, et il a eu un héritage important. Maintenant mon partenaire est riche.*

NOTE CULTURELLE

«Moi, je mangeais beaucoup de steaks, surtout aux Halles°, quand j'étais jeune. Je travaillais de nuit, et à 7 heures du matin, je prenais un grand steak pour me maintenir en forme! Aujourd'hui, je ne mange plus de viande, à cause de la vache folle°. Maintenant je préfère manger thaï. J'aime préparer la cuisine moi-même. Quand je tournais «les Saigneurs», le film que j'ai tourné après «Vidange», je suis allé dans une petite ville de Provence où j'ai acheté des girolles° magnifiques au prix des champignons ordinaires à Paris. J'ai trouvé ça bizarre, et quelqu'un m'a confirmé qu'il ne fallait pas en manger parce qu'on les avait emportées de Tchernobyl.» (Metteur en scène Jean-Pierre Mocky dans *Télérama*)

Réfléchissons: M. Mocky a un sens de l'humour typiquement français. De qui est-ce que Mocky se moque?

---

les Halles: *public market in Paris, formerly in the central city, open very early in the morning*
la vache folle: *mad cow disease /* **une girolle:** *common name given to a chanterelle mushroom*

PRONONCIATION: Les consonnes occlusives

Place your hand in front of your mouth and read the following sentence aloud:
Dorrie's purple balloon got caught in the treetop.
Did you feel the puffs of air as you pronounced the sounds [b], [d], [g], [k], [p], and [t]? In linguistics, these consonants are known as "occlusives." While the sound of these consonants is similar in both languages, the English pronunciation is somewhat more "explosive" than the French. When speaking French, you can avoid these bursts of air by spreading your lips wide, as if smiling.

À vous! Holding your hand in front of your mouth again, read the French sentences below. Try to minimize the amount of air exhaled while pronouncing the occlusive consonants!

1. Aujourd'hui, il fait beau. Demain, il va pleuvoir.
2. Pour le déjeuner, j'ai mangé du poisson, des carottes et un petit pain avec du beurre.
3. Qu'est-ce que tu préfères comme sport, le tennis ou le golf?
4. Je n'ai pas pu répondre au professeur quand il m'a posé la question.

POUR DÉVELOPPER VOS IDÉES

Thematic objective: To identify the events of your life that have created lasting memories

Présentation: L'histoire d'une femme

POUR SAISIR L'ESSENTIEL:

Voici des extraits de la Table des matières d'une biographie d'Isabelle Eberhardt (1877–1904), une voyageuse et femme de lettres qui a cherché l'aventure en Afrique.

le contenu: *content*

- Examinez les titres et choisissez les trois que vous trouvez les plus intéressants.
- Essayez d'imaginer un peu le contenu° de ces chapitres.
- Puis, écrivez une phrase pour résumer le contenu que vous avez imaginé pour chacun de vos choix.

> **Modèle:** *J'aimerais lire le chapitre qui s'appelle «La vie à El Oued». Je pense qu'on va y faire une description de la vie dans cette ville africaine.*

- Communiquez vos choix et vos phrases à un partenaire. Comparez vos interprétations des titres. Avez-vous choisi les mêmes chapitres? Avez-vous interprété les titres de la même façon? Voulez-vous ajouter un chapitre choisi par votre partenaire à votre liste?
- Soyez prêt(e) à rapporter vos réponses à ces questions à la classe.
- Choisissez un ou deux titres que vous pouvez utiliser ou adapter pour votre propre autobiographie.

Nomade j'étais
une biographie d'Isabelle Eberhardt
PAR EDMONDE CHARLES-ROUX
EXTRAITS DE LA
Table des matières

1. Le grand départ.
2. Isabelle découvre le désert.
3. Un automne dans le Sahel tunisien.
4. L'amour en Sardaigne.
5. Isabelle à Paris.
6. Isabelle et les explorateurs.
7. Isabelle va s'établir à El Oued.
8. La vie à El Oued. Le temps d'un bref bonheur.
9. Isabelle écrit aux journaux. Sa lettre fait sensation.
10. Tragique rupture avec son frère aimé.
11. Un voyage aventureux. Sa rencontre avec Lella Zéineb.
12. Une longue retraite mystique.
13. La catastrophe.

K. Les moments de ma vie. En vous appuyant sur les tableaux°, réfléchissez à vos souvenirs les plus vifs° pour identifier les événements et les sentiments qu'ils ont évoqués. Identifiez au moins cinq expériences.

en vous appuyant sur les **tableaux:** *using the grids to help you*
vif: *vivid*

un accident	un premier emploi	une réunion de famille
un mariage	**un déménagement**	l'achat d'une voiture
un voyage	des vacances	**un anniversaire de** **mariage ou de naissance** ???

L'expérience	Quel âge vous aviez
1. Le moment le plus fier de ma vie, c'est (quand)...	J'avais... ans.
2. Le moment le plus heureux de ma vie, c'est (quand)...	J'avais... ans.
3. Le moment le plus difficile de ma vie, c'est (quand)...	J'avais... ans.
4. Le moment le plus décevant° de ma vie, c'est (quand)...	J'avais... ans.
5. Le moment le plus touchant de ma vie, c'est (quand)...	J'avais... ans.
6. Le moment le plus triste de ma vie, c'est (quand)...	J'avais... ans.
7. Le moment de ma vie où j'ai eu le plus de chance°, c'est (quand)...	J'avais... ans.
8. Le moment où j'ai eu le plus peur, c'est (quand)...	J'avais... ans.
9. Le plus beau cadeau que j'ai jamais offert, c'est (quand)...	J'avais... ans.

décevant: *disappointing*

la chance: *luck*

Modèle: —*Le moment le plus heureux de ma vie, c'est quand je suis allé en Europe avec quelques amis. J'avais dix-huit ans.*

L. Élaborez un peu. Dans l'Exercice K, (1) vous avez identifié cinq souvenirs particulièrement vifs, (2) vous avez indiqué vos sentiments à l'égard de ces souvenirs et (3) vous avez mentionné l'âge que vous aviez à l'époque. Maintenant continuez à élaborer trois de ces souvenirs en donnant encore trois ou quatre détails pour chacun. Appuyez-vous sur les questions ci-dessous pour formuler vos idées. Choisissez seulement les questions qui sont significatives pour votre mémoire.

Questions pour formuler les idées

- Où habitiez-vous en ce temps-là?
- Où étiez-vous quand l'événement s'est passé?
- Quelles autres personnes étaient impliquées? Où étaient-elles? Que faisaient-elles, ou bien, qu'est-ce qu'elles ont fait?
- Quel temps faisait-il?
- Quel mois ou quelle saison est-ce qu'on était?
- Qu'est-ce que vous avez fait pendant cette expérience?
- Comment est-ce qu'on a réagi à l'événement?
- Quel a été le résultat de cette expérience?
- Quels autres détails est-ce que vous vous rappelez?

Organisez les détails de vos souvenirs afin d'avoir un paragraphe à raconter sur chaque événement.

M. **La table des matières de mon autobiographie.** Choisissez au moins cinq événements qui vont figurer dans votre autobiographie. Pour chacun de ces événements, écrivez le titre du chapitre où vous allez le discuter. Pour chaque chapitre, écrivez une description assez brève° du sujet.

brève: pas longue

N. **Échange de souvenirs.** À tour de rôle, communiquez deux de vos souvenirs à votre partenaire. Écoutez ses histoires et choisissez celle que vous voudriez raconter à une autre personne.

DÉCOUVERTE

At a fundamental level, memories are perceptions of our experiences. We filter information about events and situations to make it fit with the other perceptions that compose our world view. Thus, members of a society often have a "collective memory" that fosters unity and connects them with a shared history or a cultural heritage.

Québec license plates bear the inscription *Je me souviens.*

Read the **DÉCOUVERTE** note. Considering what you know about the history of Québec, suggest the cultural heritage that might be the subject of its people's collective memory. (See the *À propos* note on page 354.)

2ᴱ THÈME: Les gens de mes souvenirs

Objectives: To talk about people you remember and activities you have just completed

PRÉSENTATION: Un coup d'œil sur le thème

Un souvenir de Marie-Claire: Me voici à l'âge de six ans avec ma meilleure amie Annie. Elle habitait à côté de chez nous quand j'étais petite. La première fois que nous nous sommes rencontrées, nous étions avec nos parents, et elle avait l'air plutôt snob. À ce moment-là, j'ai décidé que je ne l'aimais pas beaucoup. Mais quelques jours plus tard, nous sommes allées au parc ensemble. Mon frère était là avec quelques amis, et quand nous les avons rencontrés, je me suis rendu compte° qu'Annie n'était pas arrogante. En réalité elle était simplement très timide. C'était une réalisation assez importante pour moi. Après cela, nous sommes devenues de meilleures amies.

je me suis rendu compte: *I realized*

Je n'ai pas vu Annie depuis que je suis partie pour l'université, mais elle reste une personne importante dans mes souvenirs.

Un souvenir de Jacques: Me voici avec Mireille. C'est une jolie fille, n'est-ce pas? On s'est rencontré pour la première fois au lycée. Et je l'ai tout de suite aimée parce qu'elle était très charmante. Puis, quand nous avons travaillé ensemble sur un projet pour notre cours d'archéologie, il est devenu évident qu'elle était aussi très intelligente. Nous avons commencé à étudier ensemble régulièrement, et puis à sortir au cinéma, etc. Après quelque temps, on se parlait de tout, de nos projets et de nos déceptions°. Nous nous téléphonions presque tous les jours.

la déception: *disappointment*

Maintenant, nous sommes toujours bons amis, et on se téléphone deux ou trois fois par an.

Les gens qui font partie de mes souvenirs

Réfléchissez aux personnes qui font partie de vos souvenirs. Quand est-ce que vous avez fait leur connaissance? Quelle était votre opinion de ces gens à l'époque? Que pensez-vous d'eux maintenant?

Faites une liste des expressions utilisées dans ce **Coup d'œil** que vous pouvez employer pour raconter vos souvenirs.

POUR DÉVELOPPER VOTRE FRANÇAIS

Structure: Le verbe irrégulier venir

OBSERVATIONS

Je **viens** de Paris. Je **suis venu(e)** aux États-Unis en 1995 pour travailler à Chicago.
I am from Paris. I came to the United States in 1995 to work in Chicago.

Nous **venons** au cours de français trois fois par semaine. Nous y **sommes venus**
une quatrième fois la semaine dernière.
We come to French class three times per week. We came a fourth time last week.

Mes collègues **viennent** de plusieurs pays: du Canada, d'Haïti, de France et de
Belgique. Ils **sont venus** ici pour continuer leurs études à l'université ainsi que
pour travailler.
*My colleagues come from several countries: from Canada, Haiti, France, and Belgium.
They came here to continue their university studies as well as to work.*

STRATÉGIES D'ANALYSE

1. Look at the first sentence in each of the examples. Based on these present
   tense forms of **venir,** can you complete the grid, filling in the remaining
   forms of the verb?

je	viens	nous	venons
tu		vous	
il/elle/on		ils/elles	viennent

2. Which two present-tense forms of the verb **venir** are based directly on the
   infinitive stem **(ven-)**?
3. How does the spelling of the stem change in the other four forms?
4. Now can you complete the following sentences with the present tense of
   venir?

   D'où _____-tu, de Québec ou de Montréal? Quand es-tu venu(e) aux
   États-Unis?

   *Where are you from, Quebec City or Montreal? When did you come to the United
   States?*

   Sylvie _____ de Bruxelles. Elle est venue de Belgique avec son fiancé, un
   Américain.

   Sylvia is from Brussels. She came from Belgium with her fiancé, an American.

   M. Richard, est-ce que vous _____ à mon bureau après le meeting avec
   IBM?

   Mr. Richard, are you coming to my office after the meeting with IBM?

5. Now look at the second sentence in each example. Does **venir** use **avoir** or **être** as the auxiliary verb in the **passé composé?**

6. What happens to the past participle in the **passé composé?**

7. Knowing that all verbs (except **être**) are regular in the imperfect tense, can you chart the forms of **venir** in the **imparfait?**

je		nous	
tu		vous	
il/elle/on		ils/elles	

PRÉCISIONS

- The irregular verb **venir** *(to come)* has the following forms in the present tense:

je **viens**	nous **venons**
tu **viens**	vous **venez**
il/elle/on **vient**	ils/elles **viennent**

- The **passé composé** of **venir** uses **être** as the auxiliary verb. Therefore, the past participle must agree in gender and number with the subject of the verb.

je suis **venu(e)**	nous sommes **venu(e)s**
tu es **venu(e)**	vous êtes **venu(e)(s)**
il est **venu**	ils sont **venus**
elle est **venue**	elles sont **venues**

- The forms of **venir** in the **imparfait** are regular.

je **venais**	nous **venions**
tu **venais**	vous **veniez**
il/elle/on **venait**	ils/elles **venaient**

A. **Je viens de...** À tour de rôle avec votre partenaire, lisez les phrases suivantes. Remplacez les mots en italique par les mots entre parenthèses, puis faites les changements nécessaires.

1. *Je* viens de Miami. (nous / Georges / Marie et Claire / tu / vous)

2. *Paul* vient au bureau de M. Jacquot avec les autres. (je / vous / nous / tu / Sylvie et Bernard)

3. *Mme Lebrun* vient à Menton pour passer sa retraite. (vous / tu / nous / je / Christine et Jules)

4. *Jacques* est venu de Peugeot à IBM. (vous / je / Marc et Claude / tu / nous)

5. *Nous* sommes venus de Rouen à Paris pour travailler à la Banque de France. (je / tu / vous / Pierre / Pierre et Robert)

6. *Je* suis venu en ville pour chercher un poste d'architecte. (tu / vous / nous / François / Jean et son cousin)

B. D'où viennent nos invités? Vous êtes responsable de l'organisation des places à table à un dîner international pour votre société. Afin de placer chaque individu avec ses compatriotes, vous demandez à votre partenaire la nationalité de chaque invité(e).

> **Modèle:** M. Leblanc (Genève)
> —*D'où vient M. Leblanc?*
> —*M. Leblanc vient de Genève. Ainsi, il doit être à la table des Suisses.*

1. M. Lacroix (Lucerne)
2. Mme Brandenburg (Berlin)
3. Mlle Hong (Hô Chi Minh-Ville)
4. M. et Mme Thompson (San Francisco)
5. M. Garza (Mexico)
6. M. et Mme Champlain (Montréal)
7. Mme Montpellier (Strasbourg)
8. Mlle Gutenburg (Vienne)
9. M. et Mme Azar (Casablanca)
10. Mlle Deneuve (Paris)
11. M. Milano (Rome)
12. Mme Romanov (Moscou)
13. M. et Mme Li (Beijing)
14. Mme Woolworth (New York)

C. D'où viens-tu? Dans le temps indiqué par votre professeur, demandez d'où viennent vos camarades de classe. Trouvez le plus grand nombre de villes possible.

> **Modèle:** —*D'où viens-tu?*
> —*Je viens de Chicago. Et toi?*
> —*Moi, je viens de Miami en Floride.*

D. Quand es-tu venu(e) ici? Puis demandez à chaque étudiant(e) de votre liste dans l'Exercice C quand il/elle est venu(e) dans votre ville.

> **Modèle:** —*Quand est-ce que tu es venu(e) à... ?*
> —*J'y suis venu(e) l'année dernière. Et toi?*
> —*Moi, j'y suis venu(e) il y a trois ans.*

Vocabulaire: Des verbes comme venir

OBSERVATIONS

Mon amie Alice va en France chaque décembre, mais elle **revient** toujours avant Noël.
*My friend Alice goes to France each December, but she always **comes back** before Christmas.*

À l'âge de quatre ans, les petits garçons **deviennent** de plus en plus indépendants.
*At the age of four, little boys **become** more and more independent.*

Je voudrais acheter une nouvelle maison. Je **tiens à**
avoir une piscine dans le jardin.
*I would like to buy a new house. I **have my heart set
on** having a swimming pool in the yard.*

Je **me souviens de** mes grands-parents. Ils sont
venus de Colmar dans l'est de la France.
*I **remember** my grandparents. They came from Colmar
in the eastern part of France.*

STRATÉGIES D'ANALYSE

1. The caption with each picture includes a verb that changes form in the same way as **venir.** With this information, can you spell the infinitive form of each of these verbs?

2. Which one of these verbs uses a reflexive pronoun? How can you tell? What word does that verb use after it?

3. What word is used after the verb **tenir** when it means *to have one's heart set on* something?

PRÉCISIONS

- Several other verbs are conjugated like **venir,** including the following:

revenir	*to come back*
devenir	*to become*
se souvenir de	*to remember*
tenir	*to hold, to take*
tenir à	*to insist on, have one's heart set on*

E. Je tiens à... À tour de rôle avec votre partenaire, lisez les phrases suivantes. Remplacez les mots en italique par les mots entre parenthèses, et faites les changements nécessaires.

1. Après de longues heures de travail, *Paul* devient de plus en plus habile° avec les logiciels. (tu / vous / je / nous / les employés)

   habile: *skilled*

2. *Dominique* revient de Nice ce soir après quinze jours de vacances. (Paul et Marc / vous / tu / nous / je)

3. Est-ce que *vous* vous souvenez de votre premier patron? (Christine / tu / Georges et Jean / je)

4. *Je* tiens à devenir PDG° d'une grande société. (tu / vous / Marie-Louise / mon frère)

   un PDG: *président directeur général (CEO)*

À propos de la structure: Note the use of the preposition **de** with **se souvenir.** Note also that **lui** and **elle** are used for *him* and *her* after prepositions. They correspond to **moi** and **toi**.

E. **Je me souviens de lui/d'elle.** À tour de rôle avec votre partenaire, nommez cinq individus importants dans votre vie de qui vous vous souvenez, et donnez une petite description de chacun. Utilisez la liste suivante comme aide-mémoire.

Modèles: —*Est-ce que tu te souviens de ton arrière-grand-père?*
—*Oui, je me souviens de lui. Il avait une barbe blanche.*
ou —*Non, je ne me souviens pas de lui.*

—*Est-ce que tu te souviens de ton arrière-grand-mère?*
—*Oui, je me souviens d'elle. Elle était très âgée mais vive et sympathique.*
ou —*Non, je ne me souviens pas d'elle.*

1. arrière-grand-père
2. arrière-grand-mère
3. grand-mère paternelle
4. grand-père maternel
5. premier(-ère) maître/maîtresse d'école
6. premier(-ère) maître/maîtresse de musique
7. premier(-ère) maître/maîtresse de danse
8. premier Père Noël que vous avez vu
9. premier individu célèbre que vous avez vu
10. premier(-ère) petit(e) ami(e)
11. premier(-ère) patron(ne)
12. première personne que vous avez connue qui ne parlait pas anglais
13. meilleur(e) ami(e) de l'école primaire
14. ???

un but: *goal*

G. **Je tiens à...** Employez l'expression **tenir à** pour communiquer votre but° dans les situations suivantes.

Modèle: prendre un cours de français
Je voudrais prendre un cours de français. Je tiens à avoir de bonnes notes.

1. prendre un cours de...
2. prendre un dîner au restaurant ce soir
3. aller au théâtre ce week-end
4. aller au cinéma cet après-midi
5. aller à la bibliothèque
6. acheter un nouveau pull-over
7. acheter une maison
8. acheter une nouvelle voiture
9. trouver un(e) camarade de chambre
10. trouver un(e) petit(e) ami(e)

H. **Et tu es revenu(e) quand?** Décrivez à votre partenaire au moins deux voyages personnels, professionnels ou scolaires que vous avez faits. Dites-lui quand vous êtes parti(e) et quand vous en êtes revenu(e).

Modèle: —*Pendant le mois de mars, j'ai passé quinze jours dans nos bureaux à Montréal. Je suis parti le 7 mars.*
—*Et tu es revenu(e) quand?*
—*Je suis revenu(e) le 21 mars, après les vacances de printemps.*

Structure: L'expression venir de + infinitif

OBSERVATIONS

Je **viens d'**acheter une nouvelle voiture rouge. Elle est belle, n'est-ce pas?
*I **have just** bought a new red car. It's beautiful, isn't it?*

Quand j'ai fait cette photo, mes amis français, Alfred et Marguerite Stengel, **venaient de** fêter leurs noces de diamant après soixante ans de mariage.
*When I took this picture, my French friends, Alfred and Marguerite Stengel, **had just** celebrated their diamond wedding anniversary after 60 years of marriage.*

STRATÉGIES D'ANALYSE

1. What special expression is used to communicate the idea that something *has just* happened?
2. What form of the verb do we use after the expression **venir de?**
3. Which of the past tense forms of **venir** (**passé composé** or **imparfait**) do we use to say that something *had just* happened before another event took place?

PRÉCISIONS

• In the present tense, **venir de** followed by an infinitive tells about an action that *has just taken place*. It gives a sense of the immediate past.

Je **viens de** parler avec la patronne. Elle ne revient pas avant le week-end.
*I **have just** talked with the boss. She is not coming back before the weekend.*

Nous **venons de** finir le projet pour les écoles publiques.
*We **have just** finished the project for the public schools.*

Que je suis heureux! Mon fils **vient de** trouver son premier emploi.
*I am so happy! My son **has just** found his first job.*

• In the imperfect tense, **venir de** followed by an infinitive refers to an action that *had just taken place* before something else happened.

Je **venais de** prendre la photo quand on a éteint les lumières.
*I **had just** taken the picture when someone turned out the lights.*

Nous **venions de** payer la voiture quand notre fille a eu l'accident.
*We **had just** paid for the car when our daughter had the accident.*

I. Moi, je viens de faire... À tour de rôle avec votre partenaire, mentionnez trois choses que vous venez de faire. Utilisez les idées suivantes comme aide-mémoire. Répondez de façon logique à ce que votre partenaire vous dit.

Modèle:
—*Je viens d'acheter une nouvelle maison.*
—*C'est formidable! Où est cette maison?*

---

acheter une maison   servir le dîner aux parents de mon époux(-se)

voir un bon film   **visiter l'école de mon enfant**   avoir un accident

lire un livre intéressant   assister à un bon concert   **faire un voyage**

trouver une bonne vidéo   *acheter une voiture*   ???

J. Mon/Ma partenaire vient de faire... Dites à un(e) autre étudiant(e) dans la classe une des choses que votre partenaire vient de faire. Répondez de façon logique au rapport qu'on vous fait.

déguster: *to taste*

Modèle:
—*Mon/Ma partenaire vient de déguster° des escargots pour la première fois.*
—*Il/Elle les aime?*
—*Oui, beaucoup.*

Note Culturelle

Gérard Depardieu, comédien célèbre du cinéma français, se souvient de la mort de son chat:

J'ai juste pu reprendre nos derniers signes: une caresse, un regard, toucher son mu-seau. Il n'y a que moi qui pouvais le faire. J'ai pris sa tête dans ma main, dans mon poing°. Il était malade parce qu'il ne disait rien. Il n'avait aucune réaction. C'est là que je me suis rendu compte° de ce qu'était l'impuissance°. J'ai souffert de mon impuis-sance par rapport aux êtres vivants.

Réfléchissons: Avez-vous déjà vu mourir un animal? Quelle réaction avez-vous eue?

---

un poing: *fist* / **je me suis rendu compte:** *I realized* / **une impuissance:** *powerlessness, helplessness*

PRONONCIATION: Les suffixes **-sion** et **-tion**

The combinations **-sion** and **-tion** often pose a problem for native English speakers learning French. This is largely due to the fact that the languages share so many Latin-based cognates that end with these suffixes. In English, they are pronounced with a *-sh* sound and it is tempting to transfer that into one's pronunciation of French. However, **-tion** should always be pronounced with a clear [s], unless preceded by an **s.** Then, pronounce [st]. The suffix **-sion** should also be pronounced with an [s], unless preceded by a vowel. Then, pronounce [z].

Repeat the following words after your instructor.

[s]	[z]	[st]
l'expansion	la fusion	la question
la diversion	la décision	la gestion
la répétition	la corrosion	le bastion
la direction	la division	

POUR DÉVELOPPER VOS IDÉES

Thematic objective: To identify the people who have made lasting impressions on you

Présentation: On se souvient des gens qu'on a aimés

POUR SAISIR L'ESSENTIEL: La lecture est basée sur un article sur Gao Xingjian, un écrivain chinois qui travaille à Paris. Dans cette interview, Xingjian parle de sa vie, de son art et de sa mère. Évidemment cette femme occupe une place importante dans ses souvenirs, et elle continue à influencer ses décisions.

1. Parcourez le premier paragraphe, et notez les informations sur Xingjian que vous trouvez intéressantes.

2. Puis, lisez les deux paragraphes où il parle de sa mère pour déterminer les correspondances entre ces deux aspects importants de la vie de l'artiste et la description de sa mère. Écrivez «A» devant les phrases qui correspondent à «Il est dissident» et «B» devant celles qui correspondent à «Il est artiste».

Aspects de la vie de Gao Xingjian	Description de la mère
A. Il est dissident. B. Il est artiste.	1. _____ Elle se rendait compte à quel point la vie d'un écrivain était dangereuse.
	2. _____ Elle était comédienne.
	3. _____ Elle a été envoyée dans une de ces fermes de «rééducation».
	4. _____ Elle était très ouverte et compréhensive.
	5. _____ Elle a écrit une pièce° pour son fils.

une pièce (de théâtre): *play*

3. Faites des inférences concernant l'influence du souvenir de sa mère sur la vie de cet écrivain.

Un Chinois de Paris à New York

Gao Xingjian est un dramaturge et artiste chinois qui poursuit sa carrière en France. Ses parents ont été victimes de la Révolution culturelle° et Xingjian est devenu un dissident courageux. Décoré Chevalier de l'Ordre des Arts et des Lettres, il jouit à présent d'une réputation internationale. Récemment il est venu à New York pour monter sa pièce «Entre la vie et la mort». C'est le monologue d'une actrice qui «présente» le personnage de l'archétype féminin.

Xingjian parle de sa mère:
«En Chine, guidé par ma mère qui se rendait compte° à quel point la vie d'un écrivain consciencieux était dangereuse, j'ai exercé le métier de traducteur, et j'ai vécu° dans deux langues simultanément.

«Pendant la Révolution culturelle, mon père travaillait pour la Banque Nationale de Chine. Ma mère, une comédienne, a été envoyée dans une de ces fermes de «rééducation», la version chinoise du Goulag. Elle n'était pas habituée à la vie de la campagne, et on dit qu'elle s'est noyée° par accident. Qui sait? Maman était très ouverte, compréhensive. Elle a même écrit une pièce pour moi lorsque j'avais cinq ans.»

C'est sans doute en souvenir de cet être admirable que le dramaturge a célébré la Femme dans «Entre la vie et la mort».

[adapté de «Un Chinois à New York» www.france-amérique.com]

ai vécu: *passé composé de* vivre

Révolution culturelle: un mouvement commencé par Mao Zedong en 1966 et destiné à décourager les intellectuels de critiquer le gouvernement

se noyer: *be drowned or drown oneself*

se rendre compte: comprendre, réaliser

K. Des personnes remarquables. Quelles sont les personnes qui vous ont mar-qué(e)? Où est-ce que vous avez fait la connaissance de ces personnes? Est-ce qu'elles vous ont fait bonne ou mauvaise impression? Qu'est-ce qu'elles faisaient ou qu'est-ce qu'elles ont fait pour créer° cette impression? Répondez à ces questions en suivant le modèle. Mentionnez au moins trois personnes.

créer: faire

Modèle: —*Je me souviens toujours de Guy Martin. C'était un camarade de classe quand j'étais à l'école primaire. À vrai dire, il m'a donné une mauvaise impression parce qu'il était très suffisant°. Il était méchant aussi; il avait l'habitude de se moquer de° mes amis.*

suffisant: smug
se moquer de: to make fun of

L. Pour organiser les détails d'un souvenir. Réfléchissez au souvenir que vous avez des personnes identifiées dans l'activité précédente. Que pensiez-vous de ces personnes à l'époque? Avez-vous changé d'avis au fil des années°, ou avez-vous toujours la même opinion d'elles? Utilisez les expressions ci-dessous pour élaborer les portraits que vous avez déjà commencés. Écrivez un minimum de trois phrases.

au fil des années: over the years

La première phrase:

La première fois que nous nous sommes rencontré(e)s, (nom de la personne)...

me semblait...	peu...	intelligent(e).
avait l'air...	plutôt...	doué(e).
était...	très...	dévoué(e).
	vraiment...	chaleureux(-euse).
		méchant(e).
		snob.
		pleurnicheur(-euse)°.
		tragique.
		(voir d'autres adjectifs aux page 116–117)

pleurnicheur(-euse): whiny, inclined to feel sorry for him/herself

La deuxième phrase:

Depuis ce temps-là,...	j'ai changé d'avis	parce que...
	j'ai changé d'opinion	
	j'ai toujours la même opinion	
	je n'ai pas changé d'opinion	

La troisième phrase:

Maintenant...	
je le/la trouve...	(encore...)
je pense qu'il/elle est...	
il/elle me semble...	

M. Quelques personnes de ma connaissance. Communiquez à votre partenaire les souvenirs que vous avez reconstruits dans les activités précédentes. Écoutez les souvenirs de votre partenaire, et choisissez la personne que vous aimeriez connaître. Expliquez pourquoi.

DÉCOUVERTE

The shared memories of a society are often reflected in the artistic expression of its writers, musicians, and visual artists. Sometimes such works reflect a pride of spirit and an ideal self-image. The following passage is spoken by the heroine of a historical novel by Louise Simard, an author from Montréal.

J'appartiens à un peuple conquis° qui a dû se taire° devant la dépossession°. On a élevé une frontière entre mon pays et ma terre. [...] Les vainqueurs croient avoir tout pris, mais quoi qu'ils disent ou fassent°, cette terre m'appartiendra° toujours.

LA TRÈS NOBLE DEMOISELLE, Montréal, Libre Expression, 1992

J'appartiens à un peuple conquis: *I belong to a conquered people*
qui a dû se taire: *who were forbidden to speak*
la dépossession: *a reference to the* Grand Dérangement
quoi qu'ils disent ou fassent: *whatever they say or do*
m'appartiendra: *will belong to me*

1. Read the DÉCOUVERTE note. What do you think the speaker's tone is in this quote?
   a. Matter-of-fact
   b. Submissive
   c. Defiant

2. Identify the sentences that support your perception.

3. Discuss your opinions with classmates to confirm or reconsider your interpretation of the excerpt.

3ᴱ THÈME: Souvenirs de ma vie

Objective: To describe different stages of your life: where you were living, your routine activities, what was going on around you

PRÉSENTATION: Un coup d'œil sur le thème

pour toujours: *forever*

Le bonheur de la jeunesse: La meilleure époque de ma vie? Je crois que c'est la période où nous habitions à Saint-Germain-en-Laye. Nous y avons habité pendant dix ans, jusqu'au divorce de mes parents. Nous étions tous ensemble alors, et on s'amusait beaucoup. Presque tous les week-ends, Papa nous a amenés au parc. Cet endroit a marqué mes souvenirs de cette époque de ma vie. C'est là que mon père m'a appris à faire du vélo. Et nous y allions souvent pour faire un pique-nique ou simplement pour nous promener et bavarder. J'étais tellement heureuse. Quand mes parents ont divorcé, tout a changé pour toujours° dans ma vie.

décroché: *obtenu*

une bourse: *a scholarship*

s'entraider: *help one another*

La vie d'une lycéenne ambitieuse: Quand j'avais seize ans, ma mère a décroché° un poste à la Guadeloupe. Alors nous avons déménagé. J'ai dû quitter mes amis et toutes mes habitudes. Ce déménagement était encore plus difficile parce que je voulais faire mes études supérieures aux États-Unis, et pour cela il me fallait obtenir une bourse°. Je devais étudier nuit et jour, et j'avais très peu de temps pour m'amuser. Cependant, je n'étais pas tout à fait malheureuse. J'y ai fait la connaissance de Michel Martin, et il est devenu un très bon ami. Nous étudiions beaucoup ensemble, et nous nous entraidions°. Enfin, nous avons, tous les deux, obtenu une bourse. Oui, c'était une époque difficile, mais aussi satisfaisante.

Un peu d'autobiographie. Quelles sont les «grandes époques» de votre vie? Quels adjectifs s'appliquent à ces moments?

POUR DÉVELOPPER VOTRE FRANÇAIS

Structure: Les pronoms d'objet indirect lui et leur

OBSERVATIONS

M. Hervé parle **à Mme Flaubert** avant la cérémonie.
M. Hervé **lui** parle avant la cérémonie.

Mme Bethéa a montré les documents **aux autres professeurs du lycée.**
Mme Bethéa **leur** a montré les documents.

La jeune fille vend des marrons **aux gens dans la rue.**
La jeune fille **leur** vend des marrons.

Dominique va servir encore du vin **à ses invitées.**
Dominique va **leur** servir encore du vin.

STRATÉGIES D'ANALYSE

1. In the preceding examples, which two words are used to replace phrases that begin with **à**?
2. What is the difference in meaning between these two words?
3. Can you determine where **lui** and **leur** are placed in a sentence, in relation to the verb? In the present tense? In the **passé composé**? When an infinitive follows the conjugated verb?

PRÉCISIONS

Recall that a direct object is a word or phrase that answers the question *What?* or *Whom?* after the verb of the sentence. You have already studied the direct object pronouns for *him, her, it,* and *they*—**le, la, l',** and **les.**

- An indirect object is a word or phrase that is linked to the verb by a preposition (most frequently **à**, occasionally **pour**). The indirect object makes reference *to* people (or animals) and answers the question *To whom?* or *For whom?*
- **Lui** and **leur** are the indirect object pronouns for *to him or her* and *to them.*

> J'ai écrit une lettre **à mon frère** ce matin. Je **lui** ai écrit une lettre.
> *I wrote a letter **to my brother** this morning. I wrote a letter **to him.***

> Nous posons beaucoup de questions **à notre patronne.** Nous **lui** posons beaucoup de questions.
> *We ask **our boss** lots of questions. We ask **her** lots of questions.*

> Autrefois en décembre M. Laval envoyait des cartes de vœux **à ses employés.** Il **leur** envoyait des cartes de vœux.
> *Formerly, in December Mr. Laval would send greeting cards **to his employes.** He would send greeting cards **to them.***

À propos de la structure: Place an object pronoun in front of the verb *with which it is connected by meaning.* Examples:

Je veux **lui** parler.	*I want **to talk to him.***
Je **lui pose** des questions.	*I am asking him some questions.*
Je **lui montre** les documents.	*I am showing him the documents.*

- Like direct object pronouns **(le, la, l', les), lui** and **leur** usually go in front of the conjugated verb. However, if an infinitive follows the verb, **lui** and **leur** generally go before the infinitive.

> L'enfant désirait parler à sa mère. L'enfant désirait **lui** parler.
> *The child wanted to talk to his mother. The child wanted to talk **to her.***

- The verbs that tend to have indirect objects can be classified into two categories: *verbs of giving and receiving* and *verbs of communication.* The following are some of the most common verbs.

Verbs of giving and receiving

apporter à	J'ai apporté du café à mon époux.
	Je **lui** ai apporté du café.
donner à	Le patron donne des renseignements à ses employés.
	Il **leur** donne des renseignements.
envoyer à	Nous envoyons des cadeaux à nos meilleurs clients.
	Nous **leur** envoyons des cadeaux.
louer à	Nous avons loué notre appartement au nouveau président.
(to rent)	Nous **lui** avons loué notre appartement.
prêter à	J'ai prêté ma voiture à mon neveu une fois.
(to lend)	Je **lui** ai prêté ma voiture une fois.
servir à	Au bureau on ne sert pas de vin aux employés.
	Au bureau on ne **leur** sert pas de vin.
vendre à	Des gens dans les rues vendent des t-shirts aux touristes.
	Des gens dans les rues **leur** vendent des t-shirts.
acheter pour	Qui a acheté des souvenirs pour les enfants?
	Qui **leur** a acheté des souvenirs?

Verbs of communication

parler à	Quand j'étais avec mes amis, je ne parlais jamais à mon père, prof à l'université.
	Quand j'étais avec mes amis, je ne **lui** parlais jamais.
téléphoner à	Je téléphone à ma mère tous les dimanches.
	Je **lui** téléphone tous les dimanches.
écrire à	Mon conjoint écrit une lettre à ses parents chaque semaine.
	Mon conjoint **leur** écrit une lettre chaque semaine.
décrire à	Le professeur a décrit l'examen aux étudiants.
	Le professeur **leur** a décrit l'examen.
lire à	La secrétaire lit la lettre à son patron maintenant.
	La secrétaire **lui** lit la lettre maintenant.
dire à	Dites-vous toujours la vérité à vos employés?
	Leur dites-vous toujours la vérité?
montrer à	J'ai montré le nouveau répondeur à ma secrétaire.
	Je **lui** ai montré le nouveau répondeur.
demander à	Nous avons demandé les prix au représentant de vente.
	Nous **lui** avons demandé les prix.
poser à	Qui a posé les questions aux candidats?
	Qui **leur** a posé les questions?
répondre à	Moi, je respire profondément avant de répondre au patron.
	Moi, je respire profondément avant de **lui** répondre.
indiquer à	Nous avons indiqué aux visiteurs où se trouve le restaurant.
	Nous **leur** avons indiqué où se trouve le restaurant.

A. **À qui parlez-vous?** Demandez à votre partenaire à qui il/elle parle souvent.

Modèle: à tes parents
—*Est-ce que tu parles souvent à tes parents?*
—*Oui, je leur parle souvent.*
ou —*Non, mais je leur parle de temps en temps.*
ou —*Non, je ne leur parle pas souvent.*
ou —*Oui, je leur parle souvent, quand j'ai besoin d'argent.*

1. à tes parents
2. à ton frère ou à ta sœur
3. à ton/ta petit(e) ami(e)
4. à tes ami(e)s de lycée
5. aux autres employé(e)s au travail
6. à ton/ta patron(ne)
7. à tes profs en dehors des cours
8. au président de ton université

B. **Les communications dans la vie.** Demandez à votre partenaire avec qui il/elle communique regulièrement. Utilisez la liste suivante pour développer vos questions.

Modèle: —*Est-ce que tu téléphones regulièrement à ton patron?*
—*Non, je ne lui téléphone pas regulièrement.*

téléphoner à écrire à parler à	parents mère/père/frère/sœur petit(e) ami(e) époux(-se) enfant(s) patron(ne) collègue(s) ami(e)(s)	regulièrement souvent de temps en temps de l'école du bureau à l'école au bureau pour causer (*to chat*) pour demander quelque chose
poser des questions à demander à	patron(ne) collègue(s) ami(e)(s) époux(-se) camarade de chambre conjoint(e) prof(s) bibliothécaire° directeur de laboratoire	souvent tous les jours au sujet de... de l'argent des informations des renseignements des détails des explications
montrer à décrire à	invité(e)s ami(e)s enfant(s) touristes en ville touristes dans ta région visiteurs dans ton université patron(ne) collègue(s)	les sites de la région le(s) musée(s) de la ville la bibliothèque de l'université les discos ton appartement ou ta maison tes collections de...
dire à	époux(-se) conjoint(e) petit(e) ami(e)	la vérité des mensonges° l'histoire de la ville l'histoire de la famille

bibliothécaire: *librarian*

un mensonge: *a lie, fib*

C. Je vais communiquer ce soir. En utilisant le lexique de la liste de l'Exercice B, demandez à votre partenaire avec qui et de quoi il/elle va communiquer ce soir.

Modèle: —*Ce soir est-ce que tu vas dire la vérité à ton époux(-se)?*
—*Oui, je vais lui dire la vérité ce soir.*
ou —*Non, je ne vais pas lui dire la vérité ce soir.*

Structure: Les pronoms d'objet direct et indirect me, te, nous, vous

OBSERVATIONS

Je donne des conseils à mon collègue, mais il ne **m'**écoute jamais.
*I give advice to my colleague, but he never listens **to me.***

Tu es en retard; je **t'**attends depuis une demi-heure.
*You are late; I have been waiting **for you** for half an hour.*

Le patron **nous** a demandé de rester au bureau jusqu'à 18 heures.
*The boss has asked **us** to stay at the office until 6 o'clock.*

Je voudrais **vous** poser une question.
*I would like to ask **you** a question.*

STRATÉGIES D'ANALYSE

1. Are the pronouns in boldface used as the subjects (doers) or objects (receivers) of verbs?
2. In relation to the verbs with which they are connected by meaning, where are these pronouns located?

PRÉCISIONS

You have already used both direct object pronouns (**le, la, l', les**) and indirect object pronouns (**lui, leur**) in the third person (referring to *him, her,* or *them*).

- In the first and second persons, the same pronouns are used for both direct and indirect objects:

me (m')	me, to me	**nous**	us, to us
te (t')	you, to you	**vous**	you, to you

Objet direct	*Objet indirect*
Georges **m'**attend.	Georges **m'**a téléphoné hier soir à minuit.
*George is waiting for **me**.*	*Georges called **me** last night at midnight.*
Je **vous** comprends.	Je vais **vous** écrire une lettre.
*I understand **you**.*	*I am going to write a letter **to you**.*

- These pronouns go before the conjugated verb unless that verb is followed by an infinitive.

Paul **m'**attend toujours.	Il va **m'**attendre à la bibliothèque ce soir.
*Paul always waits for **me**.*	*He is going to wait for **me** at the library this evening.*

D. Les jours de fête dans ma vie. Choisissez un jour de fête qui vous est important depuis votre jeunesse. Dites à votre partenaire un détail de votre façon de le célébrer à trois époques différentes de votre vie. (Faites attention aux pronoms avant les verbes.)

Modèle: *Ma famille fête toujours Noël. Quand j'étais tout petit, le Père Noël nous apportait des cadeaux. Pendant mes années de lycée, ma grand-mère nous téléphonait de Rome où elle habitait en ce temps-là. Maintenant j'ai des enfants; ils me demandent des cadeaux.*

NOTE CULTURELLE

Marguerite Yourcenar, première femme élue à l'Académie française, raconte des souvenirs d'un livre qu'elle a lu quand elle était jeune:

C'était un jour de déménagement, et mon père m'avait laissée seule dans sa chambre pendant qu'il s'occupait à fer-mer les malles°. Il m'avait donné le premier livre qu'il avait trouvé sur la table: un roman d'une femme oubliée, tout à fait inconnue main-tenant, [...] Renée Montlaur. [...] Il y a un passage sur lequel je suis tombée, où les personnages montaient en barque sur le Nil, au soleil couchant. Grande impression: un coucher de soleil sur le Nil, à l'âge de six ou sept ans. Impression qui n'a pas été perdue [...].

Réfléchissons: Quels livres avez-vous lus quand vous étiez jeune et qui restent dans vos souvenirs? Pourquoi est-ce que ces livres vous ont impressionné(e)?

une malle: *trunk*

E. **Avec moi il/elle est comme ça.** Expliquez à votre partenaire la relation entre vous et votre époux(-se), votre conjoint(e), votre petit(e) ami(e) ou un(e) de vos ami(e)s. Vous pouvez dire à votre partenaire les qualités et les attitudes de l'autre que vous appréciez aussi bien que celles que vous n'aimez pas. (Faites attention aux pronoms avant les verbes.)

Modèle: *Mon petit ami m'aime. Il me téléphone tous les jours. Il m'apporte de petits cadeaux pour rien aussi bien que pour mon anniversaire. Il m'écrit des lettres et, de temps en temps, de la poésie. Il m'écoute toujours et il me comprend, du moins presque toujours.*

Vocabulaire: Le corps

OBSERVATIONS

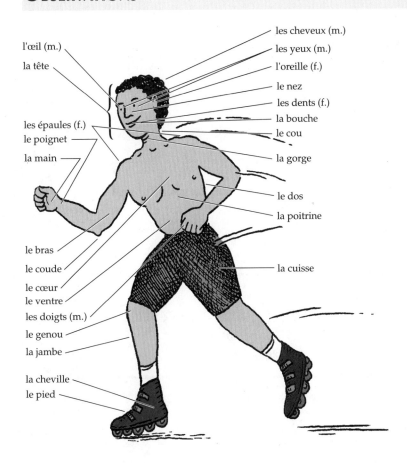

les cheveux (m.)
l'œil (m.)
la tête
les yeux (m.)
l'oreille (f.)
le nez
les dents (f.)
la bouche
le cou
les épaules (f.)
le poignet
la main
la gorge
le dos
la poitrine
le bras
le coude
le cœur
le ventre
les doigts (m.)
le genou
la jambe
la cheville
le pied
la cuisse

Lexique d'expansion

le cerveau	*brain*
la langue	*tongue*
les ongles (m.)	*nails*
le pouce	*thumb*
les reins (m.)	*kidneys*
le foie	*liver*
les doigts de pied	*toes*
la peau	*skin*
les poumons (m.)	*lungs*

Quand je fais du sport, j'ai souvent mal aux jambes, aux genoux, aux coudes, au dos et à la tête.

STRATÉGIES D'ANALYSE

1. In *Chapitre 3* you learned the vocabulary for parts of the face. How many of those words can you recall?
2. What fixed expression do you notice that is used in French to say that some part of the body hurts?

• To indicate that a part of the body hurts, we use the expression **avoir mal à**.

J'ai mal à la tête.	*I have a headache.*
	My head hurts.
J'ai mal à la gorge.	*My throat hurts.*
Paul **a mal aux reins.**	*Paul has lower-back pain.*
	Paul's lower back hurts.
Elle **avait mal au cœur.**	*She was nauseated.*

À propos de la structure: Note that although **reins** literally means *kidneys,* the French use **avoir mal aux reins** to refer to lower-back pain. Similarly, although **cœur** literally means *heart,* **avoir mal au cœur** means *to have indigestion, to be nauseated,* similar to the English expression *to have heartburn.*

• We can also use the expression **me faire mal** to express that a part of the body is giving us pain.

Le genou **me fait mal.**	*My knee is hurting (me).*
Les muscles **me font mal.**	*My muscles are hurting (me).*

• Note the impersonal manner with which French refers to the parts of the body, using the definite article (**le, la, l', les**) rather than a personal possessive adjective (*my, her, his*).

Georges a mal à **la** tête.	*George's head hurts.*
J'ai mal à **l'**épaule.	*My shoulder hurts.*
La cheville me fait mal.	*My ankle hurts.*

F. Êtes-vous malade? Dites à votre partenaire ce qui vous fait mal quand il/elle vous demande comment vous allez aujourd'hui.

> **Modèle:** —*Tu n'as pas bonne mine aujourd'hui. Es-tu malade?*
> —*Oui, j'ai mal à la gorge.*

la gorge	*la tête*	le coude	**les oreilles**
la main	**la jambe**		l'épaule
les dents	la cheville		**les reins**
le bras		**les poumons**	**le pied**

G. J'ai mal partout. Dites à votre partenaire où vous avez mal dans chacune des situations suivantes.

> **Modèle:** travailler dans le jardin
> *Quand je travaille beaucoup dans le jardin, j'ai mal à l'épaule.*

lourd: *heavy*

1. travailler dans le jardin
2. jouer au football avec des amis
3. faire la vaisselle après un dîner extraordinaire
4. faire le ménage
5. laver la voiture
6. faire un long voyage en avion
7. faire un long voyage en voiture

8. soulever quelque chose de lourd°
9. jouer au basket
10. faire une longue promenade
11. jouer au tennis
12. faire du patin aligné°
13. faire du ski
14. faire du ski nautique

le patin aligné: *roller blading, in-line skating*

H. **Je me souviens du temps où...** Racontez à votre partenaire un épisode de votre jeunesse où vous vous êtes fait mal. Votre partenaire vous pose des questions pour avoir des détails.

Modèle: —*Je me souviens du temps où je me suis cassé la jambe.*
—*Qu'est-ce que tu faisais?*
—*Je faisais du ski.*
—*Où étais-tu?*
—*J'étais à Grenoble, dans les Alpes françaises.*

PRONONCIATION: Les diphtongues et la diérèse

When two consecutive vowels are pronounced in one continuous sound (glide), as in the English word *boy*, this is called a diphthong.

When the opposite is true—two consecutive vowels are to be pronounced individually, each retaining their own sound—it is known as dieresis.

Some common French diphthongs include:

ui	nuit	lui
oi	moi	froid
ei(l)	soleil	réveiller
ai(l)	travail	caillou°
ie	fier	bien

un caillou: *pebble*

Dieresis is much more common in French. This is because a vowel sound in French constitutes a syllable.

A dieresis is sometimes marked by a **tréma** [¨]:

oï	égoïste	astéroïde
aï	naïf	maïs
uï	ambiguïté	

. . . but is also common in words containing **-é:**

Chloé   aéroport   israélien

. . . and in other combinations which would be difficult to pronounce as one sound:

boa   ponctuel

À vous! Practice reading the following sentences aloud, being sure to pronounce the vowel combinations either as one smooth sound (diphthong) or as two distinct sounds (dieresis):

1. J'adore la cuisine française, surtout les croissants et les salades niçoises.
2. Il est un peu égoïste. Il n'aime pas partager des détails personnels.
3. Il faut avoir de la patience à l'aéroport.
4. Tournez le kaléidoscope et vous verrez une mosaïque.

POUR DÉVELOPPER VOS IDÉES

Thematic objective: To look back on the different stages of your life, describing them in terms of their personal significance for you

Présentation: Les expériences de l'enfance

POUR SAISIR L'ESSENTIEL:

Détresse et l'enchantement: *"Enchantment and Sorrow"*

La lecture est un extrait de *La Détresse et l'enchantement°*, par Gabrielle Roy. À l'époque de ce souvenir, elle habitait une petite ville francophone tout près de Winnipeg, capitale de la province de Manitoba (au Canada). Elle raconte la routine de ses excursions avec sa mère dans la grande ville, où elles faisaient des achats. Elle nous fait part° aussi de l'humiliation (la détresse) qu'elle éprouvait° quand les gens de Winnipeg se retournaient° pour regarder cette fille et sa mère qui parlaient français dans ce milieu anglophone.

nous fait part: *informs us*
éprouvait: *felt, experienced*
se retournaient: *turned (to stare)*

1. Notez leurs sentiments au début de leurs excursions (dans le premier paragraphe). Faites une liste des expressions qu'elle utilise pour décrire ces sentiments.
2. Faites une deuxième liste avec les expressions utilisées pour détailler ce qu'elles ressentaient en arrivant à Winnipeg.
3. Avez-vous des histoires (similaires)?

La Détresse et l'enchantement

chiche: *peu abondant*

L'humiliation de voir quelqu'un se retourner sur moi

nous rapprocher l'une de l'autre: *draw nearer to one another*
une ombre: *shadow*

un espoir: *hope*

se retourner sur moi: *turn and stare at me*

aboutissait: *ended up*

Nous partions presque toujours animées par un espoir° et d'humeur gaie. [...] Toujours, au-devant de nous, [brillait] au départ de ces courses dans les magasins, l'espoir doux au cœur des pauvres gens [de trouver] à bon marché quelque chose de [désirable]. Il me revient maintenant que nous [ne sommes presque jamais allées] dans la riche ville voisine que pour acheter. C'est là qu'aboutissait° une bonne part de notre argent si [difficilement] gagné—et c'était le chiche° argent de gens comme nous qui faisait de la grande ville une arrogante nous intimidant. [...] C'était donc en riches, toutes les possibilités d'achat intactes encore dans nos têtes que nous traversions le pont [pour entrer dans Winnipeg].

Mais aussitôt après, s'opérait en nous je ne sais quelle transformation qui nous faisait nous rapprocher l'une de l'autre° comme pour mieux affronter ensemble une sorte d'ombre° jetée sur nous. Ce n'était pas seulement parce que nous [arrivions] dans le quartier sans doute le plus affligeant de Winnipeg, cette sinistre rue Water [...]. Le malaise nous venait aussi de nous-mêmes. Tout à coup, nous étions moins sûres de nos moyens, notre argent avait diminué, nos désirs prenaient peur. [...] Nous continuions à parler français, bien entendu, mais peut-être à voix moins haute déjà. [...] Cette humiliation de voir quelqu'un se retourner sur moi° qui parlais français dans une rue de Winnipeg, je l'ai tant de fois [ressentie] dans mon enfance que je ne savais plus que c'était de l'humiliation.

I. **Les âges de la vie.** Quelles sont les divisions qui marquent les diverses époques de votre vie? Est-ce que vous les identifiez par votre âge à l'époque, par la ville ou la maison où vous habitiez alors, ou par d'autres critères? Imaginez que vous allez esquisser° l'histoire de votre vie. Déterminez les majeures parties (au moins trois) de votre histoire et donnez un titre à chacune.

esquisser: *sketch*

> **Modèle:** *L'histoire de ma vie comprend quatre parties:*
> *Première partie: La patinoire° à Fairfield: Le samedi avec des amis*
> *Deuxième partie: Les vacances au paradis: Nos étés à la montagne*
> *Troisième partie: Les grandes décisions: L'adolescence*
> *Quatrième partie: Un début professionnel: Mes premiers emplois*

patinoire: *skating rink*

J. **Pour élaborer les idées.** Écrivez deux ou trois phrases pour expliquer le contenu que vous avez envisagé pour chaque partie de l'histoire de votre vie (dans l'Exercice I).

> **Modèle:** *Dans la première partie de mon autobiographie, je vais parler de mon enfance. J'habitais avec mes grands-parents dans la ville de Fairfield. Ils avaient une petite maison en face de la patinoire où j'ai connu mon meilleur ami. Je vais parler des samedis que nous passions à la patinoire. Et je vais expliquer comment j'y ai gagné un trophée.*

K. **On partage des souvenirs.** Donnez les titres des parties de votre autobiographie à votre partenaire. En écoutant sa table des matières, dites-lui quelle partie vous intéresse le plus et demandez-lui des détails sur cette époque de sa vie.

> **Modèle:** —*Voici les quatre parties de mon autobiographie:*
> *Première partie: La patinoire à Fairfield: Les samedis avec des amis*
> *Deuxième partie: Les vacances au paradis: Nos étés à la montagne*
> *Troisième partie: Les grandes décisions: L'adolescence*
> *Quatrième partie: Un début professionnel: Mes premiers emplois*
> —*Oh, le premier titre m'intéresse. Qu'est-ce que vous allez raconter dans cette partie de votre histoire?*
> —*Dans la première partie de mon autobiographie, je vais parler de mon enfance. J'habitais avec mes grands-parents dans la ville de Fairfield. Ils avaient une petite maison en face de la patinoire où j'ai connu mon meilleur ami. Je vais parler des samedis que nous passions à la patinoire. Et je vais expliquer comment j'y ai gagné un trophée.*

ÉCOUTONS: Un événement important dans ma vie

le récit = *la narration*

A. **On identifie les événements principaux.** Écoutez le récit° suivant qui décrit un événement important dans la vie d'une jeune fille. Ensuite, identifiez l'événement principal de chacun des quatre paragraphes (cochez ✓ la bonne réponse).

1st paragraph:

a. The narrator became a college student.

b. She got her first job.

c. She moved to an apartment.

2nd paragraph:

a. Her friend David also got a job.

b. He fell while helping her.

c. He slept on the sofa.

3rd paragraph:

a. They had a party.

b. She learned to drive a truck.

c. She had an accident.

4th paragraph:

a. They finished the job.

b. They got hungry.

c. He went home.

The narrator recalls this experience with a sense of:

a. anger.

b. satisfaction.

c. disappointment.

B. **On anticipe le temps des verbes.** Avant d'écouter de nouveau le récit, cochez (✓) la bonne colonne (**passé composé** pour les événements ou **imparfait** pour les détails descriptifs) pour indiquer le temps du verbe que vous anticipez entendre dans chaque expression donnée. Pensez aux informations que vous avez identifiées dans l'Exercice A pour vous aider à décider.

Expression	Passé composé	Imparfait
Déménager pour la première fois		
Avoir dix-neuf ans		
Travailler la nuit		
Tomber		
Partir		
Être difficile		
Avoir un accident		
Arriver à l'appartement		
Terminer le travail		
Être heureuse		

C. Dictée. Écoutez une troisième fois le récit et cette fois, complétez les phrases suivantes avec les verbes que vous entendez. Prenez en considération les temps des verbes (**passé composé** ou **imparfait**) que vous avez déjà anticipés.

1. Je me souviens de la première fois que je/j' _____.
2. Quand je/j' _____ dix-neuf ans,...
3. Mais David _____ la nuit, et il était très fatigué.
4. C'est pourquoi il _____...
5. Finalement, nous _____.
6. Le trajet entre la maison de mes parents et mon nouvel appartement _____ plutôt difficile.
7. Voilà pourquoi nous _____ un petit accident.
8. À six heures du soir nous _____ à l'appartement,...
9. Alors David était un peu fatigué quand nous _____ le travail vers dix heures.
10. Mais l'appartement était joli, et je/j' _____ vraiment heureuse.

D. On réfléchit. Réfléchissez à un déménagement auquel vous avez participé dans votre vie. Nommez trois événements principaux de cette expérience. Pour chaque événement que vous choisissez, donnez un détail descriptif.

    Modèle: **événement:** *Nous avons choisi une petite maison modeste.*
                      détail descriptif: *Elle était près du campus.*

ÉLABORATION DE PERSPECTIVE

The reading in this section is excerpted from the same work as the reading on page 414, *La Détresse et l'enchantement*, by Gabrielle Roy. Here, the author gives more specific details about her shopping excursions in Winnipeg with her mother.

1. Read the first sentence of each paragraph to get a general idea of what the author is talking about. Based on your expectations of the story at this point, write a one-sentence summary of the story she recounts here.
2. Next, skim through the reading for additional information that confirms— or invalidates—your expectations.
3. Read the excerpt more thoroughly. This time, highlight the statements or expressions that you feel are particularly relevant to the passage on page 414. Then examine the phrases you highlighted to determine how they are relevant. That is, what do they communicate that helps you grasp the author's message?
4. Discuss your ideas with your classmates, taking notes on their interpretations of the material.
5. Write a paragraph in English with the following components:
   - a thesis statement, summarizing the insights that you gained into the tensions that arise when different cultures interact
   - several sentences in which you offer detailed support for your views
   - a conclusion, in which you tell what additional sources of insight or information you know of on the subject

La Détresse et l'enchantement (suite)

Eaton: *A major department store chain in Canada*
lutte: *battle, struggle*
réclamait: *demandait avec force*
commis: *vendeur*

C'était à notre arrivée chez Eaton° que se décidait si nous allions oui ou non passer à la lutte° ouverte. Tout dépendait de l'humeur de maman. Quelquefois elle réclamait° un commis° parlant notre langue pour nous servir. Dans nos moments patriotiques,[...] on prétendait que c'était notre droit, et même de notre devoir de le faire valoir, qu'à cette condition nous obligerions l'industrie et les grands magasins à embaucher de nos gens.

Si maman était dans ses bonnes journées, le moral haut, [...] elle passait à l'attaque. Autant maman était énergique, autant [...] le chef de rayon était obligeant. Il envoyait vite [chercher] une dame ou une demoiselle [...] qui [était] souvent de nos connaissances, parfois même une voisine. [...]

vaincue: *defeated*

Mais [quelquefois] il arrivait à maman de se sentir vaincue° [...] À ces occasions, elle [le] trouvait plus simple, moins fatigant de «sortir», comme elle disait, son anglais.

Nous allions de comptoir en comptoir. Maman ne se débrouillait pas trop mal, gestes et mimiques aidant. [...]

[Mais quand] un commis ne la comprenait pas, il en appelait un autre à son aide, et celui-là un autre encore, parfois. Des «customers» s'arrêtaient pour aider aussi, car cette ville, qui nous traitait en étrangers, était des plus promptes à [venir] à notre secours [quand il était évident que nous avions un problème]. Ces [discussions] autour de nous pour nous tirer d'affaire° nous mettaient à la torture. [...]

tirer d'affaire: *aider, to help out*

fuyant: *fleeing*
ouvrit: *opened*
secouées de rire: *shaken with laughter*

Une fois, [à une occasion particulièrement énervante par tous ces efforts pour nous aider] maman, en fuyant°, ouvrit° son parapluie au milieu du magasin que nous avons parcouru au trot, comme sous la pluie, les épaules secouées de rire°. À la sortie seulement, puisqu'il faisait grand soleil, maman [a décidé] de fermer son parapluie, ce qui [a donné] à l'innocente aventure une allure de provocation. Ces fous rires° qu'elle me communiquait malgré moi, aujourd'hui je sais qu'ils étaient un bienfait, nous repêchant° de la tristesse, mais alors j'en avais un peu honte.

ces fous rires (m.): *cette hilarité*
nous repêchant: *nous protégeant*

INTÉGRATION

un corps enseignant: *faculty*

L'administration de votre université désire honorer un membre important de la région qui l'entoure. Ce citoyen sera invité à parler au corps enseignant° et aux étudiants au sujet de son travail dans la communauté. L'université a désigné votre classe de français pour choisir la personne à honorer. Travaillez en groupes de trois ou quatre étudiants et faites une recommandation à votre classe.

A. **On cherche des possibilités.** D'abord, individuellement, faites une liste des candidats potentiels qui habitent ou travaillent dans les environs de votre université. Si nécessaire, cherchez des possibilités dans les journaux de votre région.

B. **On compare les listes.** Comparez votre liste aux listes de vos partenaires. Discutez du raisonnement pour chaque personne suggérée et décidez si elle est digne d'être choisie. Choisissez le candidat que votre groupe considère le meilleur pour cet honneur universitaire.

C. **On décrit le candidat.** Faites une liste des talents personnels ou professionnels de la personne recommandée par votre groupe. Si vous voulez, indiquez aussi quelques détails de sa vie personnelle.

D. **On crée la publicité.** Enfin, avec vos partenaires, créez un communiqué de presse comme annonce publicitaire de cette occasion. N'oubliez pas d'indiquer la date, l'heure et le lieu de la conférence que l'invité(e) va donner à votre université.

LEXIQUE DE BASE

LEXIQUE D'EXPANSION

Pour parler du corps

la tête	head	le cerveau	brain
les cheveux (m. pl.)	hair	la langue	tongue
l'œil (m.)	eye	l'ongle (m.)	nail
les yeux (m.pl.)	eyes	le pouce	thumb
le nez	nose	le rein	kidney
la bouche	mouth	le foie	liver
la dent	tooth	le doigt de pied	toe
la gorge	throat	la peau	skin
l'oreille (f.)	ear	le poumon	lung
le cou	neck		
le poignet	wrist		
l'épaule (f.)	shoulder		
le bras	arm		
le doigt	finger		
la main	hand		
la poitrine	chest		
le dos	back		
le ventre	stomach, abdomen		
le cœur	heart		
le coude	elbow		
la cuisse	thigh		
le genou	knee		
la jambe	leg		
la cheville	ankle		
le pied	foot		

Pour décrire des attitudes

chanceux(-euse)	lucky	conquis(e)	conquered
doué(e)	gifted, talented	décevant(e)	disappointing
dévoué(e)	devoted	chaleureux(-euse)	warm, inviting
snob	snobbish	pleurnicheur(-euse)	inclined to feel sorry for oneself, whiny

Déjà vu

(mal)heureux(-euse)	(un)happy
fâché(e)	angry, mad
pressé(e)	hurried, pressed for time
décontracté(e)	relaxed, at ease
endormi(e)	asleep
occupé(e)	busy
préoccupé(e) avec	preoccupied with
ennuyé(e)	bored
anxieux(-euse)	anxious
fatigué(e)	tired
(mé)content(e)	(un)happy, (dis)pleased
de bonne humeur	in a good mood

de mauvaise humeur	in a bad mood		
fier (fière)	proud		
triste	sad		
méchant(e)	bad, naughty		

Pour indiquer des actions

louer	to rent	avoir bonne mine	to look healthy
prêter	to lend		
venir	to come		
devenir	to become		
revenir	to come back, to return		
tenir	to hold, to take		
tenir (à)	to have one's heart set on		
se souvenir (de)	to remember		
venir (de)	to have just (done something)		

Des pronoms objets indirects

me	to me
te	to you *(fam.)*
lui	to him, to her
nous	to us
vous	to you
leur	to them

CHOISIR UN LOGEMENT:
Le goût et les besoins

Communicative Objectives

- To prioritize housing features in terms of desirability or unacceptability

- To identify personal preferences in rooms and furnishings

- To discuss plans and aspirations

Thematic Objectives

✓ To identify the variety of considerations that determine choices in housing

✓ To associate features of your lifestyle with features of housing

✓ To examine your plans and interests and how they influence your choices in where you want to live

OUVERTURE EN VIDÉO

La mise en scène

—Une maison, c'est un jardin, c'est une autonomie, c'est beaucoup de choses qui font parler sa personnalité.

A. On cherche un nouveau logement (lodging). In this chapter you will prioritize housing features in terms of desirability or unacceptability and examine how your lifestyle influences your choices in what you want in a home. On the video, you hear Xavier interview some Parisians about their preferences on living in an apartment or a house. Then you listen in on a young French couple as they shop for a new home and discuss the features of a home that are important to them. In anticipation, what are the criteria and features that you might consider in selecting a residence? Rank the following choices (with #1 being the most important) as you consider their importance to your own lifestyle.

criteria in housing	priority #	features in housing	priority #
affordability		size	
aesthetics (pleasing appearance)		style and decor	
comfort		location	
status		amenities (modern kitchen, pool, garden, garage, etc.)	
practicality		other	

I prefer to live in (a) an apartment or (b) a house, primarily because _____. The most important feature to me is _____

Les paroles et le sens

B. Une maison ou un appartement? Watch the video to hear a few Parisians state which type of residence they prefer to live in: a house **(une maison)** or an apartment **(un appartement).** You may also hear someone answer **un immeuble,** for an apartment building. As you listen to their answers, check off on your worksheet which choice you hear each person make.

Personne interviewée ⇨	1ère femme	2e femme	3e femme	1er homme	femme avec bébé	1er jeune garçon	2e jeune garçon	dernier homme
Choix ⇩								
maison								
appartement / immeuble								

C. **À cause de quoi?** Now listen to the interviews a second time. This time, verify what you heard about apartment or house preferences, and see if you can pick up the reasons that the people who prefer a house give for their choices. Do you hear them say that is it for the space, **l'espace,** for the independence, **l'autonomie,** for a yard or garden, **un jardin,** for being in the country, **... à la campagne,** or for expressing one's personality, **... font parler sa personnalité?**

Personne interviewée ⇨	1ère femme	2e femme	3e femme	1er homme	femme avec bébé	1er jeune garçon	2e jeune garçon	dernier homme
Raison ⇩								
l'espace								
l'autonomie								
le jardin								
être à la campagne								
faire parler sa personnalité								

D. **Chez l'agent immobilier.** In the next segment of the video, Xavier's sister Élisabeth and her husband Jean-Maurice visit a real estate agent, **un agent immobilier,** and then tour a home they are thinking about buying.

On y réfléchit

E. **Ce que je cherche en priorité dans un logement.**
Now that you have heard some considerations that certain Parisians have about a residence, consider your own priorities once more. Read through the two lists of the French phrases that you have just become acquainted with for talking about choices in residences, and select as many items as apply to you.

—C'est la maison que nous avons vue en vitrine chez l'agent immobilier.

À propos de la culture: While Americans *rent* apartments and *buy* condominiums, the French do not make that lexical distinction between the two. Hence, the French would say **acheter un appartement** rather than **acheter un condominium**.

Je préfère		pour	
louer un appartement		avoir plus d'espace	
louer une maison		avoir plus d'autonomie	
acheter une maison		avoir plus de responsabilité	
acheter un appartement		avoir un jardin	
habiter au centre-ville		ne pas faire de jardinage	
être à dix minutes du centre-ville		avoir une piscine	
être à une demi-heure du centre-ville		mes enfants	
habiter hors de la ville		ma famille	
habiter à la campagne		faire parler ma personnalité	

Je voudrais avoir	
une cuisine moderne	
une grande cuisine	
une petite cuisine	
un jardin	
des chambres spacieuses	
une grande salle à manger	
un garage	
une maison bien construite	
une maison à deux étages	
un appartement dans un grand immeuble	

—C'est une belle maison. Elle est bien construite, et puis la cuisine est moderne.

1ᴱᴿ THÈME: Précisons nos goûts

Objective: To prioritize housing features in terms of desirability or unacceptability

PRÉSENTATION: Un coup d'œil sur le thème

RÉSIDENCES: VENTES ET LOCATION°

la location: *rental*

En Bretagne

Cette maison ancienne, entièrement rénovée, conserve tout son charme rustique; meublée° avec bon goût selon le style de la région. Elle est située en pleine campagne sur un terrain boisé° à dix kilomètres du village. La terrasse, avec ses meubles de jardin, offre un lieu de détente° idéal. Environnement calme, idéal pour ceux qui aiment la nature.

À Paris

Cet appartement de prestige et de grand confort est situé au 15ᵉ étage d'un immeuble moderne et luxueux. Meublé avec goût, il offre une vue magnifique de la ville. Dans le même édifice, il y a un club de santé avec sauna. Situé dans un quartier chic à dix minutes du centre-ville, il est tout près de nombreux magasins et restaurants.

meublée: *furnished*

terrain boisé: *wooded lot*

lieu de détente: *place to relax*

Préférences personnelles

En lisant les descriptions de ces deux résidences, préparez une liste des qualités que vous aimez et une autre liste des qualités qui ne conviennent° pas à vos goûts. Puis, organisez toutes les qualités que vous avez indiquées dans le tableau.

Faites un sondage parmi vos camarades de classe pour déterminer les qualités les plus et les moins recherchées.

ne conviennent pas (du verbe **convenir**): ne sont pas appropriées

	J'aime bien...	Je n'aime pas beaucoup...
Qualités de la maison en Bretagne		
Qualités de l'appartement à Paris		

POUR DÉVELOPPER VOTRE FRANÇAIS

Vocabulaire: Les résidences

OBSERVATIONS

Mon camarade de chambre et moi nous habitons dans un appartement au deuxième étage d'un grand immeuble en ville.

M. et Mme Chabrol habitent avec leurs enfants dans une maison ancienne à Riquewihr, un petit village en Alsace.

Jacqueline habite une chambre dans une résidence universitaire.

Monique Le Strat habite avec son mari André dans une maison moderne à Samois-sur-Seine, une banlieue de Fontainebleau.

STRATÉGIES D'ANALYSE

1. Can you name three different types of residences shown in the pictures?
2. Where is each of these residences located: in a city, a suburb, a village; on a farm, a ranch; at a university?

PRÉCISIONS

- Many of the names that identify different types of residences have English cognates:

un appartement	**un logement**	**une ferme**
un chalet	**un bungalow**	**un ranch**
une villa	**un cottage**	**une résidence**

- The generic word for *house* is the exception: **une maison.**

- The word **studio** as applied to apartments specifically means a one-room (efficiency) apartment in French.

- The expression **hôtel particulier** also means a *private residence.*

- A basic description of a residence usually includes information about its location.

au centre-ville	*in the center of town*
en banlieue	*in the suburbs*
au cœur de...	*in the heart of . . .*
à proximité de (d')...	*near . . .*
un terrain de golf	*a golf course*
un lac	*a lake*
la plage	*the beach*
les montagnes	*the mountains*
l'université	*the university*
un centre commercial	*a shopping center*
dans un secteur...	*in an area, section . . .*
de choix	*of choice*
de nouvelles constructions	*of new buildings*
recherché	*sought out*
tranquille	*quiet*
renommé	*well-known*
commercial	*business*
industriel	*industrial*
sur un terrain...	*on a lot . . .*
boisé	*wooded*
fleuri	*with flowers*
à la campagne	*country*
aménagé	*landscaped, cared for*
de rêve	*"dream"*

A. Où j'habite... Finissez les phrases suivantes en choisissant un des éléments donnés pour donner à votre partenaire de l'information de base au sujet de votre résidence.

Modèle: *J'habite seule une maison dans un secteur de choix. Ma résidence se trouve sur un terrain aménagé en banlieue à proximité de l'université.*

1. J'habite _____ seul(e)
   avec ma famille
   avec mon/ma/mes camarade(s)
     de chambre
   avec mon époux(-se)
   avec mon/ma conjoint(e)
   _____ une chambre
   un studio
   un appartement
   une maison
   dans un secteur _____ tranquille
   de choix
   recherché
   renommé
   de nouvelles constructions
   commercial
   industriel

tout: everything

rien du tout: nothing at all

2. Ma résidence se trouve sur un
   terrain _____ fleuri
   aménagé
   boisé
   à la campagne
   de rêve
   _____ au centre-ville
   en banlieue
   à la campagne
   dans une grande ville
   dans un village
   à proximité de (d') _____ l'université
   un centre commercial
   un centre médical
   un terrain de golf
   la plage
   tout°
   rien du tout°

Vocabulaire: Les pièces d'une maison

OBSERVATIONS

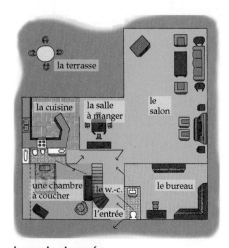

le rez-de-chaussée

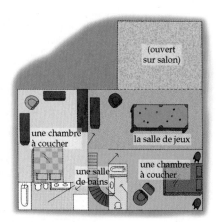

le premier étage

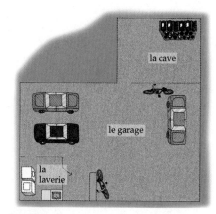

le sous-sol

le salon

la salle à manger

la chambre à coucher

la cave

la laverie

STRATÉGIES D'ANALYSE

1. Can you find the French word for entrance hall?
2. In which rooms would you expect the family to receive guests?
3. Where are meals prepared?
4. In traditional French homes, the **W.-C.** (or **cabinet de toilette** [also referred to as **les toilettes**]) is separated from the bathroom. If a French house is advertised as having **une salle de bains américaine,** what would you expect to find in it?

PRÉCISIONS

- In Francophone countries, the floors of a house (or hotel or other building) are numbered differently from the way they are counted in the United States.

Francophone countries	U.S.
le rez-de-chaussée	*ground floor or first floor*
le premier étage	*second floor*
le deuxième étage	*third floor*
le troisième étage	*fourth floor*
etc.	*etc.*

- Homes of varying sizes and styles may have one or more of the following rooms **(pièces)** or areas:

l'entrée (f.)	*entrance hall*
le salon	*living room*
la salle de séjour	*den*
la salle à manger	*dining room*
la cuisine	*kitchen*
la chambre à coucher	*bedroom*
la salle de bains	*bathroom*
le W.-C., le cabinet de toilette	*"water closet" or toilet*
la salle de jeux	*game room*
la laverie	*laundry room*
la terrasse	*patio*
la cave	*wine cellar, basement*
le sous-sol	*basement*
le garage	*garage*

B. Ma résidence est grande/moyenne/petite. Décrivez votre résidence pour votre partenaire. Dites-lui les pièces que vous avez. Mentionnez aussi au moins une pièce que vous n'avez pas chez vous.

> **Modèle:** *En ce moment, j'habite une petite maison. Il y a un salon, deux chambres à coucher, une cuisine et une salle de bains/W.-C. Il y a un garage, mais il n'y a pas de cave.*

C. Une résidence admirée. Décrivez à votre partenaire la résidence que vous admiriez le plus quand vous étiez petit(e). Par exemple, dites-lui:
- le style de la résidence
- qui habitait la résidence
- si la résidence était grande/moyenne/petite/minuscule
- combien d'étages elle avait
- combien de pièces elle avait (si vous le savez)
- dans quel secteur elle était
- comment était le terrain
- la qualité que vous aimiez le plus dans cette résidence

> **Modèle:** *Quand j'étais jeune, j'admirais beaucoup la maison de mes voisins. Elle était...*

Note Culturelle

En France il y a une amélioration° de confort résidentiel depuis les années cinquante. En voici des exemples:

- En 1962, **28,9%** des logements possédaient une baignoire° ou une douche° et **40,5%** des WC intérieurs; en 1990 ces équipements ensemble sont présents dans **93,5%** des logements.

- En 1963, le nombre moyen de personnes par logement était **3,2;** en 1992, ce nombre moyen a diminué à **2,5.**

- Entre 1963 et 1992, le nombre de pièces par logement a augmenté de 3,2 à 4,0.

- Pendant ces trente ans, le nombre de personnes par pièce principale a diminué de **1,0** à **0,6.**

Réfléchissons: À votre avis: Pensez-vous qu'on ait aussi vu une amélioration de confort résidentiel aux États-Unis entre 1960 et 2000? Citez quelques changements importants de ces quarante années. Quels changements ont le plus amélioré le cadre de vie° des familles américaines?

une amélioration: *improvement*
une baignoire: *bath tub*
une douche: *shower*
le cadre de vie: *standard of living*

Structure: Les expressions négatives

OBSERVATIONS

Avez-vous vu l'appartement de Marc? *Have you seen Marc's apartment?*	Non, je **ne** l'ai **pas** vu. *No, I haven't seen it.*

Est-ce que cela coûte cher d'habiter à Deauville? *Is it expensive to live in Deauville?*	Je **ne** sais **pas**. Je n'habite **plus** à Deauville. *I don't know. I no longer live in Deauville.*
Aimez-vous avoir le W.-C. séparé de la salle de bains? *Do you like to have the toilet separated from the bathroom?*	Je **ne** sais **pas**. Je n'ai **jamais** habité une maison où le W.-C. était séparé de la salle de bains. *I don't know. I have never lived in a house where the toilet was separated from the bathroom.*
Dominique passe beaucoup de temps à nettoyer les trois salles de bains chez elle. *Dominique spends lots of time cleaning the three bathrooms in her house.*	Heureusement, je n'ai **qu'**une salle de bains. *Fortunately, I have only one bathroom. (I don't have but one bathroom.)*
Allez-vous louer cette maison? *Are you going to rent this house?*	Non. Elle n'a **ni** cave **ni** garage. *No. It has neither a basement nor a garage.*
Qui vous a montré la maison? *Who showed you the house?*	**Personne ne** m'a montré la maison. *Nobody showed me the house.*
Aimez-vous tout de votre appartement? *Do you like everything about your apartment?*	Je n'aime **rien** de mon appartement. *I like nothing about my apartment. (I don't like anything about my apartment.)*
Avez-vous déjà fini le journal? *Have you already finished the paper?*	Non, je n'ai **pas encore** lu les petites annonces. *No, I haven't read the classifieds yet.*
Est-ce que l'entrée de votre maison a des fleurs partout? *Does your entrance hall have flowers everywhere?*	Chez moi, il n'y a des fleurs **nulle part**. *At my house, there are flowers nowhere. (At my house, there are not any flowers anywhere.)*
Où se trouvent mes clés? *Where are my keys?*	Je n'ai **aucune** idée! *I have no idea! (Not a clue!)*

STRATÉGIES D'ANALYSE

1. In French it takes two words to express a negative. One of these words is always the same. Which one? Where does this word go in relation to the verb of the sentence?

2. The other part of the negative varies, based on meaning. Which second word can you identify from the sample sentences that corresponds to each of the following negative expressions?

   - nothing
   - no one
   - never
   - no longer
   - not yet
   - only
   - nowhere
   - neither . . . nor
   - not any

3. When the verb of the sentence is in the **passé composé**, around which part of the **passé composé** construction does the two-part negative usually go?

quatre cent trente et un   431

PRÉCISIONS

- You have already learned to use the negative forms **ne... pas.** Other negative expressions in French generally follow the same pattern: a negative word placed on either side of the verb.

- Other negative expressions replace the **pas** with a different word to give the intended meaning.

ne...	**rien**	*nothing*
...	**jamais**	*never*
...	**personne**	*nobody, no one*
...	**plus**	*no longer, no more*
...	**pas encore**	*not yet*
...	**nulle part**	*nowhere*
...	**que**	*only, just, not but*
...	**ni... ni**	*neither . . . nor*
...	**aucun(e)**	*not a, not any*

- When using the **passé composé**, put the **ne** and **plus, rien, jamais,** and **pas encore** on either side of the auxiliary verb; the past participle follows.

Il **n'a jamais** visité mon appartement.	*He has **never** visited my apartment.*
Je **n'ai rien** trouvé dans les annonces.	*I found **nothing** in the ads.*
Paul **n'a pas encore** vendu la maison.	*Paul has **not yet** sold the house.*

- However, **personne, nulle part,** and **que** are placed *after* the past participle.

Je **n'ai** trouvé **que** deux studios à louer.	*I have found **only** two studios for rent.*
Je **n'ai** vu **personne** dans la maison.	*I saw **nobody** in the house.*

- **Ne... rien** and **ne... personne** can also be used as subjects of a sentence. In this case, the subject comes first but the **ne** still precedes the verb.

Personne n'est arrivé avant moi.	*Nobody arrived before I did.*
Rien n'a l'air important.	*Nothing seems important.*

- Some negative expressions may be used *without* the **pas** as short comments (without verbs).

—Qui est venu avec toi?	*Who came with you?*
—**Personne.**	*No one.*
—Qu'est-ce que tu as trouvé?	*What have you found?*
—**Rien.**	*Nothing.*
—Tout va bien?	*Is everything ok?*
—**Aucun** problème.	*No problem.*

À propos de la structure: Note that, when **personne** is used as a subject to mean *nobody*, the past participle of a verb conjugated with **être** does not change form to agree with the subject: ***Personne** n'est **arrivé** avant moi.*

- The **ne... ni... ni...** construction is similar to *neither . . . nor . . .* in English. Each **ni** precedes the element it negates. Indefinite articles are not used in the expression **ne... ni... ni.**

> Je **n'**ai **ni** maison **ni** appartement. Je loue une chambre dans une résidence près de l'université.
> *I have **neither** a house **nor** an apartment. I rent a room in a residence near the university.*

- When the expression **ne... ni... ni...** is used in the **passé composé,** the **ni... ni...** still precede the elements they negate. If they are negating objects, they follow the past participle but they precede the objects:

> Je **n'**ai vu **ni** la victime **ni** l'accident.
> *I saw **neither** the victim **nor** the accident.*

- However if the **ni... ni...** are negating verbs, they precede the past participles of the verbs they are negating.

> Je **n'**ai **ni** vu **ni** entendu l'accident.
> *I **neither** saw **nor** heard the accident.*

D. **Je n'y suis allé(e) que deux fois.** Pensez à quelqu'un chez qui vous n'êtes allé(e) que deux ou trois fois, peut-être un(e) de vos ami(e)s, un(e) cousin(e) quelque part°, un beau-frère ou une belle-sœur, par exemple. Votre partenaire va vous poser des questions au sujet de vos visites chez lui/elle. Utilisez une variété d'expressions négatives dans vos réponses.

quelque part: *somewhere*

> **Modèle:** —*À qui est-ce que tu penses?*
> —*Je pense à mon amie Sylvie.*
> —*Combien de fois as-tu visité la résidence de Sylvie?* (ne... que)
> —*Je **n'**ai visité sa résidence **que** deux fois.*

1. À qui est-ce que tu penses?
2. Combien de fois as-tu visité la résidence de...? (ne... que)
3. Qui est allé chez... avec toi? (ne... personne)
4. Combien de fois as-tu pris le dîner chez...? (ne... que)
5. As-tu dé sà fait le ménage chez...? (ne... jamais)
6. Combien de salles de bains est-ce que... a dans sa résidence? (ne... que)
7. Dans quelle pièce as-tu fait tes devoirs chez...? (ne... nulle part)

E. **On cherche un logement convenable** *(suitable).* Lisez les petites annonces suivantes. Pour chaque petite annonce, déterminez (1) à quel groupe de la liste la résidence convient° et pourquoi. De plus, (2) indiquez pourquoi la résidence ne convient pas à un autre groupe de la liste. Faites attention aux expressions négatives.

convient: *suits*

Les groupes qui cherchent une résidence:
  a. une mère et ses deux filles de 5 et de 7 ans
  b. un jeune couple professionel, sans enfants
  c. une famille: père qui travaille, mère qui reste à la maison, un fils de 13 ans
  d. un couple retraité°, de plus de 70 ans
  e. un(e) étudiant(e) universitaire
  f. deux jeunes hommes célibataires, 20–25 ans
  g. le président-directeur-général (PDG) d'une société importante, sa femme, leur fils et leur belle-fille, leur petit-fils

retraité: retired

Les petites annonces

1

Superbe hôtel particulier au cœur de la ville, situé dans une cour calme de la rue principale. Surface habitable de 330 m²° sur 3 niveaux. Splendides salons de réception, un bureau et 4 chambres somptueusement meublées d'antiquités ainsi que des salles de bains modernes, une cuisine et une salle de gymnastique. À proximité immédiate des musées et des parcs. Le vrai confort d'une maison particulière avec les prestations d'un hôtel de luxe.

2

Cette maison très conviviale dans un quartier résidentiel est meublée avec beaucoup de goût et est d'une très grande propreté. Cette maison d'un grand confort est entièrement refaite à neuf et est sur 2 étages: cuisine entièrement équipée, 4 chambres, 3 salles de bains dont 2 en marbre + une terrasse donnant accès à un petit jardin.

m² = mètres carrés = square meters

3

NON FUMEURS SEULEMENT– Petit appartement coquet bien équipé et joliment décoré situé au 2ème étage d'un immeuble placé entre deux hôtels. La rue est calme et desservie par de nombreux commerces. La chambre est indépendante et donne sur une cour. Pas de baignoire dans salle de bains; une douche seulement. Près du métro.

4

Très coquet petit appartement situé au centre-ville. 2ème étage sans ascenseur. Deux divan-lits dans le salon et salle de bains complète. Cet appartement est décoré avec beaucoup de goût et est très chaleureux. Nombreux commerces à proximité. Propriétaire disponible sur place. 3 personnes maximum. NON FUMEURS seulement.

5

Très bel appartement (36 m²) dans maison traditionnelle du propriétaire avec accès direct au jardin. Coin salon séparé de la salle à manger, cuisine donnant sur jardin. Dans la salle de bains, il y a une douche sans baignoire. Accès facile à un parc. Près du métro.

6

Appartement très convivial de très grand confort, soigné et bien décoré. Dans une petite rue calme dans un excellent quartier. Au 5ème étage avec ascenseur. Moyens de transport et tous commerces à proximité. Idéal pour 3 personnes (2 chambres, 1 lit 2 places + 1 lit 1 place).

7

Appartement deux pièces très sympa dans quartier très vivant, rue de la Gaité. Le métro est au pied de l'immeuble et de nombreux commerces sont à proximité. Au 4ème étage sans ascenseur. À noter qu'il n'y a qu'une toute petite baignoire dans la salle de bains. Idéal pour étudiants ou jeune couple.

8

Ce joli studio (32 m²) situé au 6ème étage avec ascenseur, est confortable et entièrement rénové. Appartement idéal pour une personne, jeune couple, étudiants. Douche à l'étage. L'ameublement est joli, l'endroit est calme. Marché en plein air les jeudis et samedis. Excellent rapport qualité-prix.

PRONONCIATION: h aspiré, h muet

The letter **h** is never pronounced in French and is usually treated as a vowel, necessitating elision (l'habitude) and liaison (des heures). In some words, usually of foreign origin, the **h** acts as a consonant. While still silent, the **h** in such cases prohibits elision (**le homard**) and liaison (**des / haricots verts**), and is known as **h aspiré**. Words containing **h aspiré** are marked in various dictionaries by an asterisk (*), an apostrophe ('), or a cross (†).

The following is a list of common French words that contain an **h aspiré**. Repeat each after your instructor, being sure not to make an elision or liaison.

1. le hockey
2. le hamburger
3. le homard
4. la Hollande
5. la Hongrie
6. la honte°
7. le héros
8. la hâte°
9. le hasard
10. la haine°

la honte: *shame*

la hâte: *haste*

la haine: *hate; hatred*

À vous! With a partner, practice reading the following sentences aloud. Be sure to make a distinction between **h muet** and **h aspiré**.

1. Hervé est de mauvaise humeur. Il s'est blessé pendant un match de hockey et doit aller à l'hôpital.
2. Hier, j'ai mangé des huîtres et du homard. J'adore les fruits de mer!
3. Moi, j'ai pris un hamburger et des haricots verts avec de l'huile d'olive.
4. D'habitude, l'air est sec en hiver. Il n'y a pas beaucoup d'humidité.
5. La honte et la haine sont deux émotions humaines très fortes.
6. La Hongroise a passé quelques heures à l'hôtel de ville.

POUR DÉVELOPPER VOS IDÉES

Thematic objective: To identify the variety of considerations that determine choices in housing

Présentation: On considère les avantages et les inconvénients

POUR SAISIR L'ESSENTIEL: Lisez les annonces pour des logements en France tout en réfléchissant à vos goûts personnels. En lisant, décidez le pour et le contre° de chaque résidence. Puis placez-les dans le tableau.

le pour et le contre: *the pros and cons*

	Pour	Contre
Alsace		
Paris		
Provence		

Immobilier en France

Cette belle maison traditionnelle d'Alsace est située à 40 minutes au nord de Strasbourg. Au rez-de-chaussée il y a un salon avec cheminée, une salle à manger, une cuisine équipée et un W.-C. À l'étage se trouvent deux grandes chambres, aussi avec cheminée, une salle de bains à l'américaine, et une troisième pièce, qui peut servir de bureau. Possibilité de garer la voiture dans la cave. Chauffage central au gaz.

Ce magnifique appartement, très confortable et spacieux, est au beau milieu de la vie culturelle de Paris (théâtres, restaurants, cinémas). Situé au deuxième étage (sans ascenseur), il comprend un salon, un coin cuisine, une chambre et un cabinet de toilette avec douche. Idéal pour ceux qui aiment une ambiance traditionnelle.

à louer: *for rent*

Cette petite villa à louer° est située à 15 km de Nîmes et à trente minutes de la mer. Elle comprend une chambre à coucher et une salle de séjour. Coin repas ensoleillé dans le séjour. La cuisine donne sur la terrasse meublée et la jolie piscine. W.-C. avec douche seulement.

F. Pour identifier ses goûts. En réfléchissant aux aspects que vous aimez dans une résidence et à ceux que vous n'aimez pas, notez vos goûts dans un tableau comme dans le modèle.

Modèle:

	Grandeur et Style	Emplacement	Attributs supplémentaires
J'aime bien...	1. les maisons traditionnelles	1. la campagne	1. les balcons
	2. les maisons spacieuses	2. près de la plage	2. les piscines
			3. les terrasses (à côté de la piscine)
Je n'aime pas...	1. les petits appartements dans les grands immeubles	1. la banlieue	1. un grand terrain à entretenir
		2. les régions froides	
		3. près d'un centre commercial	

G. On précise ses goûts. Écrivez deux paragraphes où vous précisez (1) les caractéristiques que vous cherchez et (2) celles que vous n'acceptez pas dans une résidence. Employez les informations que vous avez enregistrées dans le tableau comme base, et écrivez un minimum de trois phrases pour chaque paragraphe. N'oubliez pas de pratiquer l'usage des expressions négatives; utilisez au moins deux expressions négatives différentes dans vos paragraphes.

À propos du vocabulaire: You may want to look back at the **Lexique** for *Chapitres 4* and *7,* as well as the descriptions in this chapter on pages 425, 427, 429, 434, and 436 for additional vocabulary to express your preferences in these activities.

Modèle: *J'aime bien les maisons traditionnelles. Je voudrais donc avoir une assez grande maison à deux étages avec une cheminée dans le salon. Ma chambre va être à l'étage et je vais avoir un balcon. De plus, je veux habiter à la campagne, près de la plage. S'il n'est pas possible d'habiter près de la plage, je veux avoir une piscine parce que j'adore nager.*

Je n'ai jamais aimé les petits appartements dans les grands immeubles. Personne ne connaît ses voisins dans les grands immeubles. C'est pourquoi je ne veux habiter ni en banlieue ni dans une grande ville.

H. Une petite annonce. Échangez votre devoir de l'Exercice G contre celui de votre partenaire. (1) Lisez les paragraphes où il/elle précise ses préférences. Essayez de comprendre exactement ce qu'il/elle recherche. (2) Posez-lui des questions (par exemple, Combien de pièces désires-tu? Tu veux une cheminée? Une cave? Un grand terrain? Est-ce qu'il est important d'habiter près d'une grande ville? Près d'un lac?) (3) Écrivez une annonce pour l'Internet où vous décrivez la maison que *votre partenaire* recherche. Utilisez les exemples des pages 425, 434 et 436 comme modèles.

DÉCOUVERTE

Before the days of central heating, air conditioning, and modern insulating materials, the design of houses tended to reflect the nature—quite literally—of the region where they were located. To begin with, construction materials had to be drawn from native resources. Wood structures were built in the vicinity of forests, masonry was used where there were better supplies of stone or clay. The local climate also influenced architectural design. Steep roofs were used in areas where heavy rains or snowfalls might cause a roof to cave in. Thick masonry walls protected the interior of a building from extreme temperatures, and small windows also helped keep inclement weather outside. In mild climates, large, unencumbered openings allowed breezes to cool the interior. And while gardens, porches, and balconies are found in most places, verandahs that wrap around a house like an apron are particularly popular in warm regions, where shade and unfettered breezes are valued.

Some of these practices are reported in a document entitled «Inventaire général: L'architecture rurale du Tarn-et-Garonne°», hosted on the Internet by the *Ministère de la culture et de la communication* of France.

Aucune clôture°, à l'exception de quelques haies° vives ou rangées d'arbres, ne les isole°, mais leur orientation sud, est ou sud-est les protège des vents froids et de la pluie.

une clôture: *fence, enclosure*
une haie: *hedge*
isole: *insulate*

C'est la nature du sous-sol qui, en déterminant le choix des matériaux de construction, a joué un rôle essentiel dans la formation des différents types d'habitations.

Even though modern materials and technology have brought striking homogeneity to the look of buildings around the world, people still tend to think in traditional terms when they envision a Swiss chalet, a Mediterranean villa, or a cottage in Brittany.

1. Read the  **DÉCOUVERTE** note.

2. Look back through the photographs of French homes in this *Thème* that reflect traditional architecture of the region. Some possible choices include:

> page 425: *maison de campagne*
> page 436: *maison d'Alsace*
> page 436: *villa provençale*

3. Basing your judgment on the appearance of the buildings (and the surrounding grounds) as well as on the descriptions of their rooms and amenities, what inferences can you draw about the climate of the area where each is located?

4. For each inference, identify the visible features of the buildings/grounds and the phrases in the description that support your conclusions.

5. Discuss your inferences with classmates to broaden or reinforce your interpretation of the clues.

Voici la maison de mes rêves!

Objective: To determine personal preferences in rooms and furnishings

Une situation exceptionnelle à la Guadeloupe. À une demi-heure de Pointe-à-Pitre, des plages et de tous les commerces, cette maison est à proximité de tout, mais reste° très calme. Elle comprend une salle de séjour, une cuisine (avec lave-vaisselle, cuisinière, four à micro-ondes), deux grandes chambres, une salle de bains (avec baignoire) et une véranda-salle à manger.

Cette maison chaleureuse située dans un quartier tranquille de Québec a une terrasse avec des meubles de jardin. Au rez-de-chaussée il y a un séjour disposant de tous les équipements audio-visuels, une salle à manger et une grande cuisine équipée. À l'étage se trouvent deux chambres à coucher et une salle de bains. Il y a une salle de jeux et une buanderie° avec un lave-linge et un sèche-linge au sous-sol.

reste: *remains (from the verb* **rester***)*

une buanderie: *laundry room*

Le logement que je cherche
En lisant les annonces, choisissez les qualités mentionnées comme qualités positives de ces deux résidences. Puis rangez-les dans un tableau pour indiquer vos besoins personnels.

Essentiels	Utiles	Inutiles

POUR DÉVELOPPER VOTRE FRANÇAIS

Vocabulaire: Des abréviations

OBSERVATIONS

Appt 40 m², cuis. éq., coin repas, belle sdb, état neuf. 2 220F + ch. Tél: 03 88 66 18 83	Appartement de 40 mètres carrés, cuisine équipée, coin repas, belle salle de bains, état neuf. 2 220 francs par mois plus charges. Téléphone: 03 88 66 18 83
Rue de la Somme, 5 P., 100 m², 3 ch., terrasse sud 10 m², 2 sdb, gar. et cave. 5 500F + ch. Tél. 03 88 78 20 58	Rue de la Somme, 5 pièces, 100 mètres carrés, 3 chambres à coucher, terrasse sud 10 mètres carrés, 2 salles de bains, garage et cave. 5 500 francs par mois plus charges. Téléphone: 03 88 78 20 58
Prop. loue petite copropr. calme, 2e ét., asc., libre, 3 P., cuis., sdb, wc, 70 m², t.b.état, terr., chauf., gar., 3 200 F + ch 350F. T. 03 88 69 66 43	Propriétaire loue petite copropriété calme, deuxième étage, ascenseur, libre, 3 pièces, cuisine, salle de bains, cabinet de toilette, 70 mètres carrés, très bon état, terrasse, chauffage, garage, 3 200 francs par mois plus 350F charges. Téléphone: 03 88 69 66 43
60 m², 1er ét., calme, verdure, cuis., sdb, wc, b. ét, chauf. ind. gaz, cave. 2 950F + 300F ch. Tél. 03 88 33 12 50	60 mètres carrés, premier étage, calme, verdure, cuisine, salle de bains, cabinet de toilette, bon état, chauffage individuel au gaz, cave. 2 950 francs par mois plus 300 francs charges. Téléphone: 03 88 33 12 50
Prop. loue 3P., cuis. éq., sdb., gar., cave, chauf. élect. 3 200F + ch. T. ap. 19h. 03 88 96 07 13	Propriétaire loue 3 pièces, cuisine équipée, salle de bains, garage, cave, chauffage électrique. 3 200 francs par mois + charges. Téléphone après 19 heures 03 88 96 07 13

STRATÉGIES D'ANALYSE

1. Look at the classified ads in the left column. How are they different from those in the right column?
2. Which of these ads (those on the left or those on the right) do you think were taken from a newspaper? Why are newspaper ads written this way?
3. The descriptions of houses for sale or for rent in Exercise E on page 434 of *1er Thème* were taken from the Internet. Which are easier to read, the Internet ads or these newspaper ads?
4. Based on your knowledge of the telephone zones in France, can you tell what part of the country these ads are from?

- Since newspaper ads are priced based on their length, advertisers have developed a special shorthand. The following abbreviations are some of the most commonly used in descriptions of apartments and houses for sale and for rent.

ap.	après	grat.	gratuit(e)
appt	appartement	imm.	immeuble
arr./arrdt.	arrondissement	jard.	jardin
asc.	ascenseur	M./M°	Métro
banl.	banlieue	m²	mètres carrés
(t.) b. ét.	(très) bon état	min.	minimum
cft	confort	mod.	moderne
ch./chbre	chambre(s)	P.	pièce
ch.	charges	pers.	personnes
ch./chauf.	chauffage	RdC.	rez-de-chaussée
cuis.	cuisine	rés.	résidences
élect.	électrique	sdb	salle de bains
éq.	équipé(e)	séj.	salle de séjour
ét.	étage	t./tél.	téléphone
exc.	excellent(e)	terr.	terrasse
gar.	garage	tt(e)	tout(e)
gd(e)	grand(e)	ts	tous
		wc	cabinet de toilette

A. Pour lire les petites annonces. Pour étudier les petites annonces qu'on trouve dans les journaux, il faut° d'abord les comprendre. En travaillant avec votre partenaire, interprétez ces annonces pour les écrire sans abréviations. Utilisez les annonces dans *Observations* à la page précédente comme modèles.

il faut: *one must, it is necessary*

11e arr. Appt t. convivial de t. grd cft. 5ème ét., asc. Rue calme, exc. quartier. Près M°. Cuis. éq., sdb, wc. 3 pers. 4 000 F/613 E + ch. Tél. 01 48 44 35 22

À Clichy, près Paris. M° direct pour Champs-Élysées. Appt. RdC. dans bel imm. 45 m². Cuis. mod., sdb, wc, séj, 2 ch. Gar. grat. 4 500 F/690 E + ch. Tél. 01 49 32 68 83

Studio modeste (20 m²) dans 16ème arr. 2ème ét. sans asc. Appt refait à neuf. Coin cuis. Très petit bain + douche. Gde fenêtre, très clair. Près M°. 3 500 F/537 E + ch. Tél. 01 45 34 99 72

T. joli appt 11e arr. 4ème ét. sans asc. Cuis t. bien éq. Salon, salle à manger, 1 chbre, espace bureau, sdb, wc. Près ts commerces. 3 500 F/537 E + ch. Tél. 01 48 79 77 54

5ème arr. à la limite du 13ème. Joli petit studio RdC avec patio privé. Cuis. avec 2 plaques élec, évier°, mini-four°. Douche, wc. Près commerces et laverie°. 2 800 F/512 E + ch. Tél. 01 42 99 07 31

80 m² 4 P. RdC à St-Germain-des-Prés dans le 6ème arr. Cour privée de 60 m². Meublé à l'ancienne. 2 ch, cuis. mod., sdb, wc. Cheminée. À louer 6 mois min. 7 500 F/1 150 E + ch. Tél. 01 45 66 72 14

un évier: *sink*
un mini-four: *toaster oven*

une laverie: *can also mean laundromat*

B. **On loue un appartement.** Vous et votre partenaire désirez passer deux mois à Paris l'été prochain. Avec votre partenaire, (1) choisissez un des appartements dans l'Exercice A pour vous deux. (2) Donnez au moins deux raisons pour justifier votre choix. (3) Indiquez aussi l'appartement qui convient le moins bien pour votre stage à Paris. (4) Expliquez pourquoi.

Vocabulaire: Les meubles

OBSERVATIONS

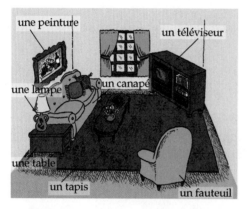

un salon

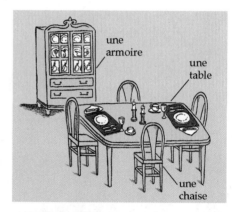

une salle à manger

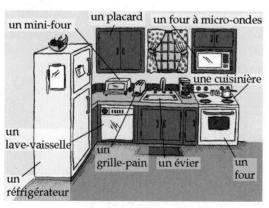

une cuisine

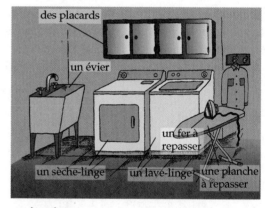

une laverie

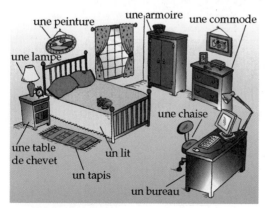

une chambre à coucher

une salle de bains

STRATÉGIES D'ANALYSE

1. Look at the items and the labels on the items in each room. Which are English cognates?
2. What is the name of the big piece of furniture used for storage both in the dining room and in the bedroom?
3. What piece of furniture in the bedroom is a false cognate with an English word?

PRÉCISIONS

- Many of the French terms for common household furnishings and objects look familiar because of their English cognates. The following are some examples:

une lampe	*lamp*	un réfrigérateur	*refrigerator*
une chaise	*chair*	une armoire	*armoire*
une table	*table*	des toilettes°†	*toilet*
un téléviseur	*television set*		

des toilettes: *W.-C. or* cabinet de toilette

- On the other hand, we have to be alert to some false cognates, words that look similar in both languages but have different meanings.

une commode	*small chest*
une douche	*shower*
un bureau	*desk, office*

C. La chambre de mon ami(e). Malheureusement, un(e) de vos ami(e)s est tombé(e) malade et a quitté l'université avant la fin du semestre. Ses parents vous ont demandé de faire une liste de tous les meubles dans sa chambre à coucher. Étudiez le dessin de sa chambre pour faire votre liste.

↑ **D.** **Une comparaison avec ma chambre.** Faites une comparaison entre la chambre de votre ami(e) (Exercice C) et votre chambre à coucher.

Les meubles qu'il y a uniquement dans ma chambre	Les meubles que nous avons tou(te)s les deux dans nos chambres	Les meubles qu'il y a uniquement dans la chambre de mon ami(e)

E. **Il faut faire un choix.** Quelquefois il n'est pas possible d'avoir tout ce qu'on désire; il faut faire un choix. Avec votre partenaire, indiquez votre choix entre chaque paire d'objets.

Moi		Mon/Ma partenaire
une douche	une baignoire *ou* une douche	
	un four *ou* un four à micro-ondes	
	un canapé *ou* deux fauteuils	
	un grand lit *ou* deux lits jumeaux°	
	une armoire *ou* deux commodes	
	un lave-vaisselle *ou* un lave-linge	
	un téléviseur *ou* un lecteur de CD	
	une cuisinière à gaz *ou* une cuisinière électrique	
	un mini-four *ou* un grille-pain	
	un téléphone *ou* un ordinateur	

lits (m.) jumeaux: *twin beds*

↑ **F.** **Nous comparons nos choix.** Comparez vos choix avec ceux de votre partenaire. Avez-vous plus de choix en commun ou plus de choix différents?

Modèle: —*Moi, je préfère une douche à une baignoire.*
—*Moi aussi. Qu'est-ce que tu as choisi—un four ou un four à micro-ondes?*
...
—*Alors, nous avons fait six choix en commun et quatre choix différents.*

À propos du vocabulaire: When referring to twin beds in a home, use the term **des lits jumeaux.** However, when referring to single beds at a hotel, say **des lits simples.**
Example: J'ai mis **des lits jumeaux** dans la chambre de mes fils. Je voudrais réserver une chambre avec **deux lits simples.**

G. **Mes priorités pour une maison.** Imaginez que vous allez acheter une maison ou un appartement. D'abord, il faut déterminer les nécessités que vous recherchez et les choses que vous ne voulez pas du tout avoir. Faites deux listes: (1) les caractéristiques à rechercher et (2) les éléments à éviter°.

éviter: *to avoid*

À rechercher	À éviter
une grande fenêtre dans le salon	une salle de bains sans douche

H. Une comparaison de priorités. Faites une comparaison entre vos listes et les listes de votre partenaire. Maintenant faites deux listes entre vous deux; nommez (1) cinq qualités que vous deux recherchez et (2) trois éléments que vous deux désirez éviter dans une maison ou un appartement.

Note Culturelle

Traditionnellement, la nourriture est une priorité importante pour les Français. Dans les familles traditionnelles, on passe beaucoup de temps à table avec la famille. Ainsi, souvent on trouve plus d'une table où on peut prendre un repas dans une maison ou un appartement.

Chez Marguerite et Alfred Stengel en Alsace, on peut prendre le repas à plusieurs tables différéntes. Bien sûr, il y a une grande table pour les occasions spéciales dans la salle à manger. Il y a aussi une petite table à manger dans la pièce où on peut en même temps regarder la télévision. De plus, on prend souvent le petit déjeuner dans la cuisine ou même dans une petite pièce à côté de la cuisine, avec une vue sur le jardin.

En été, quand il fait beau, Marguerite sert beaucoup de repas dehors° sur la table de la terrasse.

Réfléchissons: À votre avis: Si le nombre de meubles d'un certain type indique vos priorités, qu'est-ce qu'on pourrait dire sur vos priorités après avoir passé du temps chez vous?

dehors: *outside*

Chez les Stengel, quand il y a une occasion spéciale, on dîne dans la salle à manger.

Mais on prend les repas ordinaires dans la salle de séjour.

Quand il fait chaud, Alfred et Marguerite adorent manger sur la terrasse.

Structure: Le futur

OBSERVATIONS

—Quand j'**aurai** un enfant, j'**achèterai** une maison.
*When I **have** a child, **I'll buy** a house.*

—Tu ne **seras** pas contente dans un appartement avec un enfant?
*You **won't be** happy in an apartment with a child?*

—Mais non. Mon enfant **jouera** dans un beau jardin derrière une grande maison.
*Oh, no. My child **will play** in a beautiful garden behind a big house.*

—Tu rêves.
You are dreaming.

—Pas du tout. Dès que mon mari et moi **finirons** nos études, nous **chercherons** des emplois bien rémunérés. Puis nous **pourrons** penser à un enfant.
*Not at all. As soon as my husband and I **finish** our education, we'll **look for** well-paying jobs. Then we'**ll be able** to think about a child.*

—Vous **ferez** une belle famille.
*You **will have** a fine family.*

—On **verra**. Mes parents **seront** contents de nos bons emplois et aussi d'avoir un petit-fils ou une petite-fille.
*We'**ll see**. My parents **will be** happy with our good jobs as well as with a grandson or a granddaughter.*

STRATÉGIES D'ANALYSE

1. What part of speech are the words in bold letters? Are they nouns or verbs?
2. What time frame do these verbs refer to, the present, the past, or the future?
3. Look at the endings on the verbs. Do they look familiar to you?
4. Now examine the stem of each verb. What letter is on the end of each stem before the ending?
5. What meaning do these verbs convey?

PRÉCISIONS

- You already know how to use **aller** + *infinitive* to indicate a planned or anticipated action in the near future.

  Nous **allons regarder** une vidéo ce soir.   *We **are going to watch** a video this evening.*

- In French we also have a future tense that is the equivalent of the English *will* (or *shall*) + verb. As in English, the future tense is used to predict or explain what someone will do or what will happen.

- To form the future tense, we add the following set of endings to a verb stem ending in **-r**:

-ai	-ons
-as	-ez
-a	-ont

You should recognize the endings as being the present-tense conjugation of **avoir** (minus the **av-** in the **nous** and **vous** forms).

- The **-r** stem comes from the infinitive form of the verb. For regular **-er** and **-ir** verbs, use the entire infinitive. For **-re** verbs, drop the final **-e**.

Je **chercherai** un appartement convenable.
Tu **choisiras** un appartement de luxe, sans doute.
Nous **vendrons** notre maison à la campagne avant d'acheter un appartement au centre-ville.

parler	finir	attendre
parler-	finir-	attendr-
je parler**ai**	je finir**ai**	j'attendr**ai**
tu parler**as**	tu finir**as**	tu attendr**as**
il/elle/on parler**a**	il/elle/on finir**a**	il/elle/on attendr**a**
nous parler**ons**	nous finir**ons**	nous attendr**ons**
vous parler**ez**	vous finir**ez**	vous attendr**ez**
ils/elles parler**ont**	ils/elles finir**ont**	ils/elles attendr**ont**

- Many irregular verbs have irregular stems in the future. However, these stems will always end in **r**, and the future endings will always be the same.

aller	**ir-**	j'irai, tu iras...
avoir	**aur-**	j'aurai, tu auras...
être	**ser-**	je serai, tu seras...
faire	**fer-**	je ferai, tu feras...
savoir	**saur-**	je saurai, tu sauras...
envoyer	**enverr-**	j'enverrai, tu enverras...
pouvoir	**pourr-**	je pourrai, tu pourras...
voir	**verr-**	je verrai, tu verras...
pleuvoir	**pleuvr-**	il pleuvra
convenir	**conviendr-**	cela me conviendra, elles vous conviendront...
devenir	**deviendr-**	je deviendrai, tu deviendras...
revenir	**reviendr-**	je reviendrai, tu reviendras...
tenir	**tiendr-**	je tiendrai, tu tiendras...
venir	**viendr-**	je viendrai, tu viendras...

- Although the uses of the future tense are generally the same in French and in English, there is one clear difference between the two languages. In clauses introduced by **quand** *(when)*, **lorsque** *(when)*, and **dès que** *(as soon as)*, we use the future tense in French since the action is yet to happen. English uses the present tense in these situations.

> **Dès que** la pizza **arrivera**, nous déjeunerons.
> *As soon as the pizza **arrives (will arrive)**, we'll have lunch.*
>
> **Lorsque** nous **habiterons** une maison, je planterai des fleurs partout.
> *When we **(will) live** in a house, I'll plant flowers everywhere.*

I. **À l'avenir** (Au futur)... Dites à votre partenaire ce que vos proches espèrent que vous ferez dans l'avenir. Utilisez les expressions suivantes pour stimuler vos idées. Pour chaque groupe, formez au moins trois phrases.

Modèle: *Mon patron espère que je trouverai beaucoup de nouveaux clients.*

mon/ma patron(ne) mon/ma partenaire mon/ma secrétaire	espérer que je	trouver de nouveaux clients travailler mieux finir mon projet arriver au bureau à l'heure être en bonne santé faire mon possible ...
mon époux(-se) mon/ma petit(e) ami(e) mon/ma conjoint(e) mon/ma/mes camarade(s) de chambre mes parents mon père ma mère mes enfants	espérer que je	finir mes études continuer mes études gagner beaucoup d'argent trouver un emploi faire le ménage faire la vaisselle aimer bien sa famille avoir une maison louer un nouvel appartement acheter des meubles chercher un nouveau frigo jouer mieux au golf aller au supermarché aller à l'église être heureux(-se) ...

mon prof	espérer	être en classe tous les jours
mon/ma partenaire	que je	être préparé(e) pour les examens
les étudiants de mon cours		finir les devoirs
		parler bien le français
		faire mon possible
		arriver à l'heure
		étudier plus
		voir les vidéos au laboratoire
		avoir du succès

J. Et moi, j'espère que... Maintenant dites à votre partenaire ce que vous espérez que vos proches feront dans l'avenir. Utilisez les expressions suggérées dans l'Exercice I.

> **Modèle:**   *J'espère que mon patron sera en bonne santé.*

K. Quand je ferai..., on sera content. Refaites vos phrases des Exercices I et J d'après le modèle.

> **Modèle:**   *Quand je trouverai beaucoup de nouveaux clients, mon patron sera content.*

PRONONCIATION: e caduc, e muet

In *Chapitre 4, Thème 2,* you learned to pronounce the sound [ə], as it appears in the words **je** and **dedans,** for example. Very often in spoken French, this unaccented e, known as **e caduc** or **e instable** will be dropped, resulting in a mute **e,** or **e muet.** The following rules will help you to determine whether an e should be silent or pronounced [ə].

E caduc should *not* be pronounced:

- When it appears at the end of a word, followed by a vowel sound:

    un livre intéressant   une plante exotique

- When it appears at the end of a clause or phrase:

    J'ai écrit un poème.   Ce semestre, j'ai acheté dix livres.

- When it is preceded by a single consonant sound, unless its omission makes the word difficult to pronounce:

    petit   semaine   Je veux bien!

À vous! Your instructor will read the following sentences. Take note of when the **e caduc** is silent **(e muet)** and when it is pronounced. Then, practice reading them with a partner.

1. Je suis revenu ce matin à onze heures.
2. Cet arbre a des feuilles immenses!
3. Ma petite amie s'appelle Sophie.
4. J'ai retenu beaucoup de souvenirs de ma jeunesse.
5. Mme de Taillefer n'habite plus à Marseille.
6. Je me couche tôt pendant la semaine, parce que j'ai un cours le matin.

À propos de la structure: In informal written French, the **e muet** is sometimes replaced with an apostrophe: **Mon p'tit ami.**

POUR DÉVELOPPER VOS IDÉES

Thematic objective: To associate features of your lifestyle with features of housing

Présentation: Service d'hébergement° international

un hébergement: *lodging*

POUR SAISIR L'ESSENTIEL: La lecture suivante est basée sur les publicités pour les résidences d'échange. Ces échanges permettent aux habitants d'une région ou d'un pays de passer leurs vacances dans un chalet, un appartement, etc., dans un autre endroit pendant une période où les propriétaires n'utilisent pas cette résidence. Par exemple, une famille parisienne peut habiter l'appartement d'un couple québécois pendant que les Québécois passent une semaine dans le bungalow d'une famille martiniquaise, qui, à son tour, est en Bretagne.

1. En lisant les annonces pour les résidences d'échange, soulignez les éléments que vous trouvez les plus attirants.
2. Faites une liste des éléments que vous avez soulignés et classez-les par ordre de vos priorités personnelles. Le numéro 1 sera le plus important.

Résidences d'échange

Le Club Bienvenue vous propose un service d'échange et de location de résidences qui ont généralement été visitées par un membre de notre équipe. Nos conseillers, qui sont présents dans plusieurs pays, vous aideront à préparer l'échange idéal ou à trouver des locations qui vous conviendront.

À la Guadeloupe: Un bungalow en banlieue, tout près de la plage, à dix minutes d'un centre commercial et à cinq minutes à pied d'un excellent terrain de golf. Il comprend un grand séjour ouvrant sur la terrasse, une cuisine équipée (lave-vaisselle inclus), deux petites chambres à coucher et une salle d'eau avec douche.

Au Québec: Bel appartement spacieux situé en banlieue de Montréal. À une demi-heure des pistes de ski. Vous y trouverez un salon, une salle à manger, une cuisine toute équipée, une chambre avec un grand lit et une petite chambre avec canapé-lit et une salle de bains. Accès à la laverie dans l'immeuble.

Endroit exotique. Cette maison située dans un cadre de verdure et de calme offre une vue magnifique sur la mer. Avec ses 330 m² elle offre une grande salle de séjour, une salle à manger, quatre chambres, deux salles de bains, deux W.-C., une cuisine équipée et une véranda avec une belle vue de tous côtés. Un des plus jolis paysages de Guadeloupe. Service de nettoyage° inclus.

un service de nettoyage: *cleaning service*

L. **Pour déterminer les priorités.** Quand on pense à investir dans un logement, en général on considère certains critères. Il doit être confortable, pratique pour son style de vie et abordable° pour son budget. De plus, on cherche un logement qui s'accorde avec son sens de l'esthétique ou avec son statut parmi ses proches. Numérotez les critères par ordre de priorité pour vous.

abordable: *affordable*

_____ abordable	_____ pratique
_____ confortable	_____ statut
_____ esthétique	_____ ??? (autre)

M. **Les attributs qui correspondent à mes priorités.** Classez les critères de l'Exercice L dans la grille par ordre de priorité. Vous pouvez y ajouter d'autres critères que vous trouvez importants. Puis indiquez des attributs que vous cherchez pour chaque critère comme dans le modèle.

Modèle:

Attributs ⇩	Priorité n° 1: *abordable*	Priorité n° 2: *pratique*	Priorité n° 3: *esthétique*	Priorité n° 4: *confortable*	Priorité n° 5: *sécurité*	Priorité n° 6: *statut*
Grandeur et style	*pas trop grand*	*trois chambres*	*style traditionnel*	*chauffage central*		
Emplacement		*en ville*		*climat modéré*		*quartier agréable*
Attributs supplémentaires			*balcon et jardin*		*système de sécurité*	

N. **Développement des priorités.** Choisissez trois de vos priorités de l'Exercice M à développer dans une rédaction où vous décrirez un logement idéal pour vous. Commencez par énumérer les trois priorités que vous choisissez. Ensuite, en tenant compte° des informations que vous avez enregistrées dans la grille, écrivez un paragraphe pour chacune des trois priorités.

en tenant compte: *taking into account*

Modèle: *Mes trois priorités: esthétique, confortable, pratique*

> *Quand j'aurai mon logement idéal, il sera très élégant. Ce sera un grand appartement dans un quartier chic d'une grande ville. Les fenêtres de ma chambre donneront sur un balcon avec une vue magnifique sur le parc à côté de l'immeuble. J'aurai une salle à manger formelle parce que j'aime inviter mes amis à dîner.*
>
> *Mon appartement devra être confortable aussi. Il aura trois chambres à coucher parce que j'ai une fille, et je veux avoir une chambre pour les amis. Il y aura une cheminée dans la salle de séjour, où nous passerons des soirées en famille.*
>
> *Enfin, il faut être pratique. Alors je tiens à avoir une laverie avec un lave-linge et un sèche-linge parce que mon enfant a beaucoup de vêtements.*

O. **À la recherche du logement idéal.** Échangez vos paragraphes avec votre partenaire. En lisant ses paragraphes, cherchez un logement pour lui/elle, parmi les annonces dans ce chapitre. Puis expliquez pourquoi vous le trouvez approprié.

au lieu de: *instead of*

Modèle:
> —*Je crois que tu aimeras la maison à la Guadeloupe à la page 439 parce qu'elle est grande et très élégante. Au lieu d'un° balcon elle a une grande véranda avec une belle vue sur la mer.*
>
> *Elle a quatre chambres, mais tu auras plus d'amis. Et elle n'a pas de cheminée, mais il ne fait pas froid en Guadeloupe.*
>
> *Enfin, elle est très pratique parce qu'il y a un service de nettoyage!*

DÉCOUVERTE

In the **Découverte** section in the *1ᵉʳ Thème*, you considered the traditional relationship between architecture and local environment. Though it is true that technological developments have led to the creation of an "international" style, many designers still value harmony between architectural design and nature. Notice how this excerpt from a real estate advertisement (based in the Caribbean) highlights these features.

Une architecture en harmonie avec l'environnement
Le plan général, son intégration au terrain, les volumes et circulations intérieures ainsi que les choix des matériaux offrent à ses occupants un confort, une sécurité et une harmonie de vie qui associent cadre privé et convivialité.

À 140 m d'altitude, à mi-pente°, face aux alizés°, elle bénéficie d'un micro-climat et d'une ventilation idéale en toutes saisons.

à mi-pente: *on a slope*
alizés (m.): *trade winds*

1. Read the ![] **DÉCOUVERTE** note. Then look through photographs of buildings in this chapter. Decide which appear to profit from the features of their environment.

2. Identify the features that support your opinion.

3. Discuss your opinions with classmates to broaden or reinforce your interpretation.

3^E THÈME: Une résidence qui convient à mes projets

Objective: To discuss plans and aspirations

Dès que j'aurai mon diplôme, je trouverai un bon emploi. Alors je chercherai un appartement en ville, dans un quartier assez dynamique. Il sera tout près d'une laverie et de plusieurs restaurants. J'aurai une chambre, naturellement, et un séjour. Mais je n'aurai pas besoin de salle à manger ni de cuisine, parce que je ne fais jamais la cuisine.

Quand le bébé grandira un peu, nous aurons besoin d'une chambre d'enfant. Ce sera une pièce claire et ensoleillée. Nous y mettrons un lit d'enfant, une commode et peut-être un petit bureau. Et bien sûr, il y aura beaucoup de jouets°.

un jouet: *toy*

ON FAIT DES PROJETS

dans les deux cas: *in both cases*

Dans les paragraphes de la **Présentation,** on réfléchit à l'avenir. Dans les deux cas°, les projets de logement dépendent de la situation anticipée: l'un attend son diplôme, l'autre la jeunesse de son enfant.

À quelle(s) situation(s) pensez-vous lorsque vous pensez à un changement dans votre habitation? Quelles sortes de changements font partie de vos projets? Faites (1) une phrase au sujet de vos projets à court terme, et (2) une phrase où vous parlez de vos projets à (plus) long terme. Vous pouvez vous appuyer sur les **Suggestions.**

nettoyer à fond: *clean thoroughly*

> **Modèle:** **Projet à court terme:** *Dès que les examens seront terminés, je nettoierai à fond° la salle de bains.*
> **Projet à plus long terme:** *Quand j'aurai un bon emploi, j'achèterai un nouveau canapé et un fauteuil pour la salle de séjour.*

déménager: *move, change residences*

Suggestions

Situations	Changements
* Dès que le semestre se terminera...	* nettoyer à fond les placards
* Lorsque mon/ma camarade de chambre déménagera°...	* acheter un téléviseur
* Quand je trouverai un bon emploi...	* remplacer le grille-pain
* Dès qu'on finira ce projet...	* faire construire une salle de jeux
* Lorsque je serai marié(e)...	* rénover la salle de bains
* Quand j'aurai des enfants...	* changer de décor dans la salle de séjour
* Lorsque les enfants iront à l'université...	* déménager
* Quand nous gagnerons à la loterie...	* avoir une piscine chauffée
* ???	* chercher une plus grande/petite maison
	* ???

POUR DÉVELOPPER VOTRE FRANÇAIS

Structure: Le futur (suite)

OBSERVATIONS

—**Si** je **trouve** un bon emploi, je **chercherai** un nouvel appartement.
—Sois plus optimiste! **Quand** tu **trouveras** un bon emploi, tu **chercheras** un nouvel appartement.
—*If I **find** a good job, I'll **look for** a new apartment.*
—*Be more optimistic! **When** you **find** a good job, you'll **look for** a new apartment.*

—**Si** Claire **a** un enfant, elle **aura** besoin d'une deuxième chambre à coucher.
—Sois plus optimiste! **Lorsque** Claire **aura** un enfant, elle **aura** besoin d'une deuxième chambre à coucher.
—*If Claire **has** a baby, she **will need** a second bedroom.*
—*Be more optimistic! **When** Claire **has** a baby, she **will need** a second bedroom.*

1. Study each set of sentences. The first sentence and the last sentence in each set begin with different words. What are these two beginning words? What do they mean?

2. Is there a change in expectation from the first sentence to the last sentence in each set? Can you articulate the change in attitude?

3. Study the verbs in the sentences again. Compare the first sentence to the last sentence in each set one more time. What change occurs? What tense of the verb is used following **si?** What tense of the verb is used following **quand** or **lorsque?**

PRÉCISIONS

- You have just learned (in *2ᵉ Thème*) to use the future tense after **quand** *(when)*, **lorsque** *(when)*, and **dès que** *(as soon as)* to indicate that an action is yet to happen.

  Dès que Jean-Luc nous **téléphonera,** nous partirons.
  As soon as Jean-Luc calls us, we'll leave.

- However, in sentences with a **si** *(if)* clause, use the present tense in the **si** clause (that establishes the hypothetical condition) and the future tense in the result clause (that tells what will happen).

  S'il pleut, nous **resterons** à la maison.   *If it rains, we'll stay at home.*
  Si je **trouve** un appartement convenable,   *If I find a suitable apartment,*
      tu me **rendras** visite.   *you will visit me.*

- Note the subtle difference in the meaning of these two types of sentences. A **si** *(if)* clause expresses a hypothetical situation or a condition in the present tense that will have a future result. A **quand/lorsque** *(when)* or **dès que** *(as soon as)* clause implies an expectation that the condition will be met in the future.

  S'il pleut, nous resterons à   *If it rains, we'll stay at home.*
      la maison.   *(We don't know, hypothetically, whether*
                                                              it will rain.)

  Dès qu'il pleuvra, nous   *As soon as it rains, we'll return home.*
      rentrerons à la maison.   *(We expect it to rain.)*

A. Dès que je finirai mes études. À tour de rôle avec votre partenaire, dites ce que vous ferez dans les situations suivantes en remplaçant les mots en italique par les mots entre parenthèses. Faites les changements nécessaires.

1. Dès que je finirai mes études, j'*irai en Europe.* (travailler pour mon père / acheter une maison / chercher des meubles / avoir un enfant)

2. Lorsque Paul trouvera un bon travail, il *achètera une nouvelle voiture.* (demander à sa petite amie de se marier / faire un voyage / rendre visite à sa famille)

3. Quand nous trouverons l'appartement idéal, nous *chercherons une table pour la salle à manger.* (acheter un canapé / choisir un téléviseur / inviter des amis)

B. **Je cherche une maison convenable.** Vous cherchez une maison à louer. Vous avez certaines préférences des qualités et des éléments que vous désirez trouver dans la maison. Expliquez à votre partenaire quelles maisons vous accepterez. Exprimez vos conditions dans des phrases qui commencent avec **si.**

Modèles: au centre-ville; en banlieue; un terrain boisé; un terrain fleuri
Si la maison est au centre-ville, je ne l'accepterai pas.
Mais, si elle se trouve en banlieue, je l'aimerai mieux.

Si la maison a un terrain boisé, je l'accepterai.
Mais, si elle a un terrain fleuri, je l'aimerai mieux.

1. au centre-ville; en banlieue; à la campagne
2. un terrain boisé; un terrain fleuri; un grand terrain; un petit terrain
3. une piscine; une maison sans piscine
4. une salle de bains; trois salles de bains
5. une salle de bains américaine; un W.-C. séparé de la salle de bains
6. une cuisine équipée au gaz; une cuisine électrique
7. une chambre à coucher; deux chambres à coucher; trois chambres à coucher
8. un garage au sous-sol; une maison sans garage
9. une laverie au sous-sol; aucune laverie
10. un ascenseur; des escaliers
11. une maison avec beaucoup de voisins; une maison isolée
12. une maison près des commerces; une maison à la campagne loin des commerces

C. **Ce que nous cherchons en commun.** Faites une comparaison entre ce que vous désirez dans une maison et ce que votre partenaire y cherche. Préparez ensemble une liste des conditions et des éléments que vous avez en commun.

Modèle: *Si une maison a une salle de bains américaine, nous l'accepterons. Mais, si elle a les W.-C. séparés des salles de bains, nous ne l'aimerons pas.*

D. **Sois optimiste.** Lorsque votre partenaire vous parlera d'un projet qu'il/elle considère pour le futur, encouragez-le(la). Utilisez les expressions suivantes pour vous donner des idées. (Variez vos choix entre **lorsque, quand** et **dès que.**)

Modèle: —*Si je finis mes études, je ferai un voyage en Europe.*
—*Sois optimiste.* **Lorsque** *tu finiras tes études, tu feras un voyage en Europe.*

finir les études ⟶	*faire un voyage...*
	aller à...
	acheter...
	chercher un emploi
	avoir du temps pour...
	passer du temps avec...
	étudier...
	...

trouver un bon emploi ———→	*se marier*
	avoir des enfants
	faire la retraite à... ans
	aller à...
	acheter...
	...
avoir des enfants ———→	*continuer les études*
	rester à la maison
	travailler
	continuer la carrière
	passer plus de temps...
	passer moins de temps...
	faire...
	acheter...
gagner beaucoup d'argent ———→	*aller à...*
	acheter...
	travailler...
	passer du temps...
	chercher...
	considérer...
	se marier
	avoir des enfants
	offrir... à...
	...
louer/acheter un appartement ———→	*chercher...*
louer/acheter une maison ———→	*acheter...*
	passer du temps...
	planter...

E. Mes ami(e)s iront bien aussi. Dites à votre partenaire au moins cinq change-ments qui auront lieu° dans la vie de vos ami(e)s et/ou les membres de votre famille. Utilisez le lexique de l'Exercice D pour stimuler vos idées.

auront lieu: *will take place*

Modèle: *Lorsque mon ami Robert louera un appartement, il achètera des meubles.*

Structure: Les verbes **voir** et **croire**

OBSERVATIONS

—Allons **voir** le nouveau film de Mel Gibson ce soir.
*Let's **go see** the new Mel Gibson movie this evening.*

—Je l'**ai** déjà **vu.**
*I've already **seen** it.*

—Zut! J'ai envie de le **voir**. Alors, veux-tu le **revoir** encore?
*Darn! I really want **to see** it. Well, do you want **to see** it again?*

—On **verra**. **Voyons**, si tu m'accompagnes pour rendre visite à ma mère, je **verrai** le film avec toi après.
*We'll **see**. **Let's see**, if you come with me to visit my mom, I'll **see** the movie with you afterward.*

Stratégies d'analyse

1. How many of the forms of the verb **voir** *(to see)* can you identify from the brief dialogue?
2. What is its stem for the future tense?
3. What is the past participle of **voir**, which is used for the **passé composé**? Which auxiliary verb is used with **voir** in the **passé composé**, **avoir** or **être**?
4. Look at the way the French say, "I've already seen it." **(Je l'ai déjà vu.)** How is the expression **déjà vu** used in English? What connection do you see between the two?
5. There is a **y** in the **nous** form in the present tense and the imperative **(voyons)**. In which other form might you expect to see a **y?**
6. Since the **nous** form includes a **y,** can you determine the imperfect stem?
7. If you know that **croire** is conjugated like **voir** in the present, **passé composé,** and imperfect tenses, can you figure out the conjugations of **croire?**

Précisions

- The irregular verb **voir** has the following conjugation in the present tense:

je **vois**	nous **voyons**
tu **vois**	vous **voyez**
il/elle/on **voit**	ils/elles **voient**

- The past participle of **voir** is **vu. Voir** uses **avoir** as its auxiliary verb in the **passé composé.**

  j'**ai vu,** tu **as vu,** etc.

- The future stem of **voir** is **verr-.**

  je **verrai,** tu **verras,** etc.

- The imperfect stem of **voir** is **voy-.**

  je **voyais,** tu **voyais,** il/elle/on **voyait,** nous **voyions,** etc.

- **Voir** has two especially helpful uses in conversation:

  1. You can postpone a decision or avoid giving a direct answer to a question by using the expression **On verra** *(We'll see)*.
  2. You can give yourself a little time to think about what to say next by using the expression **Voyons** *(Let's see)*.

- The verb **croire** *(to believe)* is conjugated like **voir** with one exception: the future stem is **croir-**.

je **crois**	nous **croyons**
tu **crois**	vous **croyez**
il/elle/on **croit**	ils/elles **croient**

Past participle: **cru** (**avoir** as auxiliary)
Future stem: **croir-**
Imperfect stem: **croy-**

- The verb **croire** also provides us with a useful, high-frequency expression:

Je **crois** que oui.	Je **crois** que non.
*I **think** so.*	*I don't **think** so.*

F. **Je crois que oui/non.** À tour de rôle avec votre partenaire, lisez les phrases suivantes en donnant votre opinion. Cochez (✓) pour rapporter les résultats de votre discussion.

Modèle: —*Je crois que la cuisine est la pièce la plus importante de la maison.*
—*Je crois que non. Pour moi, c'est la salle de bains.*
ou —*Je crois que oui. Je suis d'accord avec toi.*

Je crois que...			Mon/Ma partenaire croit que...	
oui	non		oui	non
		1. La cuisine est la pièce la plus importante de la maison.		✓
		2. Une nouvelle maison est préférable à une maison ancienne.		
		3. La surface (mètres carrés) d'une maison est l'attribut le plus important pour établir la valeur d'une maison.		
		4. On peut déterminer la valeur d'une maison en regardant la modernité de la cuisine.		
		5. Moderniser la salle de bains augmentera le prix d'une maison.		
		6. Un terrain fleuri est plus recherché qu'un terrain boisé.		
		7. Un hôpital à proximité de la maison est désirable.		
		8. Un centre commercial à proximité de la maison est désirable.		
		9. Une maison à la campagne coûte plus cher que la même maison au centre-ville.		
		10. Je peux acheter une maison en consultant sa description détaillée et sans avoir vu la maison elle-même.		

G. **Une analyse des qualités.** Faites une analyse des qualités des appartements et des maisons présentés dans ce chapitre. Choisissez le meilleur exemple pour chaque qualité de la liste suivante. Choisissez le texte dans les annonces pour appuyer° votre décision. Préparez-vous à discuter de vos choix avec votre partenaire.

appuyer: *to support*

1. être le plus impressionnant
2. avoir le plus beau terrain
3. être le plus grand
4. être le mieux situé
5. avoir les plus beaux meubles
6. être le plus petit
7. être le plus convenable pour un étudiant
8. avoir le meilleur rapport qualité-prix
9. être le plus recherché
10. avoir la cuisine la mieux équipée
11. avoir la plus petite salle de bains
12. se trouver le plus loin d'une ville
13. coûter le plus cher
14. coûter le moins cher

H. **On verra.** À tour de rôle avec votre partenaire, mentionnez chaque choix de meilleur exemple dans l'Exercice G. Expliquez votre opinion.

Modèle: —*Je crois que cet appartement au centre de Paris est le plus impressionnant. Écoutez pourquoi:...*
—*On verra. Voilà une maison qui a... À mon avis, elle est la plus impressionnante.*

I. **La plus belle maison que j'ai vue de toute ma vie.** À tour de rôle avec votre partenaire, rapportez trois résidences spéciales que vous avez déjà vues. Expliquez votre raisonnement.

À propos de la structure: A past participle agrees in gender and number with its preceding direct object. Example: Tes livres?
Je les ai vus dans la cuisine.

Modèle: la plus belle maison
La plus belle maison que j'ai vue de toute ma vie est la maison de mon patron. Elle se trouve à la campagne, pas trop loin d'ici. Elle est très grande, assez moderne, bien meublée et située sur un grand terrain boisé.

1. la plus belle maison
2. la plus grande résidence
3. le plus petit appartement
4. l'appartement le mieux meublé
5. la maison avec le terrain le plus intéressant
6. la résidence la mieux située
7. l'appartement le moins cher
8. la résidence la plus chère
9. la résidence avec le meilleur rapport qualité-prix
10. la résidence la plus désirable

NOTE CULTURELLE

La somme annuelle dépensée en moyenne par les ménages français pour leur logement pèse° de plus en plus lourd. En 1996 le logement représentait environ 23% du budget des Français; en 1990 il était d'environ 20%. Ces dépenses comprennent les loyers des locataires°, l'estimation de la valeur d'usage° des logements des propriétaires° occupants, les impôts°, charges° et travaux d'entretien°.

Réfléchissons: À votre avis: Avez-vous une idée de ce que votre famille paie chaque mois pour le logement (les impôts, charges et travaux d'entretien inclus)? Payez-vous une somme qui représente plus d'un quart de votre salaire total pour le logement? Avez-vous d'autres dépenses plus importantes que celles pour votre logement?

peser: to weigh, (account for a heavy portion of . . .) / **un locataire:** renter / **valeur d'usage:** depreciation / **un propriétaire:** owner, landlord / **les impôts:** taxes / **les charges:** related expenses / **les travaux d'entretien:** maintenance work

PRONONCIATION: e caduc, e muet [suite]

In the previous *Thème,* you learned that an unaccented **e** (**e caduc,** or **e instable**), is often dropped in spoken French (**e muet**). There are times when the **e caduc** must be retained in pronunciation. The following rules will help you to determine whether an **e** should be silent or pronounced [ə].

E caduc should be pronounced:

- Whenever its omission would result in three or more consecutive consonant sounds, since this would make words difficult to pronounce. For example, the **e caduc** in the following words must be pronounced [ə]:

  vendr**e**di   tart**e**lette   appart**e**ment

[Note that there is a distinction between three consonants and three consonant *sounds.* For example, although the **e caduc** is surrounded by three consonants in the word **cheville,** the **ch** constitutes only one consonant sound. The **e caduc** may then be dropped in such cases.]

- when it appears before an aspirated **h:**

  l**e** homard   une équipe d**e** hockey   un**e** Hollandaise

- before the numbers **un, huit,** and **onze:**

  le chapitr**e** un   Jean part l**e** huit février.   Il revient l**e** onze.

À vous! With a partner, read the following sentences, being sure to pronounce or omit the **e caduc** where necessary.

1. Les cultures du monde francophone sont très diverses.
2. Mon anniversaire est le onze décembre. C'est un mercredi.
3. J'ai mangé un plat de haricots verts avec un peu de beurre.
4. Le huitième exemple n'est pas bon, parce que les données sont fausses.
5. Je vais acheter un nouveau sèche-linge.
6. Pour mon cours de psychologie, je dois lire le chapitre un.

POUR DÉVELOPPER VOS IDÉES

Thematic objective: To examine your plans and interests and how they influence your choices of where you want to live

Présentation: On réfléchit à ses projets

> **POUR SAISIR L'ESSENTIEL:** Dans ce texte, vous lirez les réflexions de deux personnes qui pensent à l'avenir. Pour chacun des deux, identifiez les idées principales et organisez-les dans un tableau.
>
> **L'homme**
> - La situation anticipée: _____
> - Effet de la situation sur son logement: _____
> - Priorités personnelles de l'individu (budget, confort, esthétique, pratique, etc.): _____
>
> **La femme**
> - La situation anticipée: _____
> - Effet de la situation sur son logement: _____
> - Priorités personnelles de l'individu (budget, confort, esthétique, pratique, etc.): _____

Si je trouve un bon emploi après mes études universitaires, j'aurai plus d'argent. Alors je pourrai chercher un appartement. Ça me donnera plus d'autonomie. Il ne sera plus nécessaire de partager la salle de bains avec les autres et personne° ne rangera ses affaires dans mon armoire.

Je serai pratique, bien sûr. Je choisirai un bon quartier, près des commerces et de plusieurs restaurants. Et si j'achète des meubles d'occasion°, ça conviendra à mon budget.

Je sais que je ne serai pas riche—pas au début—mais je ne voudrai rien de très moche°. Je chercherai un assez joli appartement avec un balcon qui donne sur la rue. Quel rêve!

Si je peux prendre ma retraite à l'âge de soixante-deux ans, j'aurai beaucoup de temps pour mes occupations personnelles. À ce moment-là je n'aurai plus besoin d'habiter en ville. Alors je partirai aux Antilles parce que je n'aime pas beaucoup les régions froides. Puisque j'aime la nature et le calme, j'achèterai une maison de campagne. Vous voyez, le confort est très important.

Il me faudra penser à mon budget, bien sûr. La maison ne sera pas très grande, mais elle aura une chambre d'amis° pour mes petits-enfants. Et elle aura une jolie véranda immense. Je mettrai des chaises et une table sur la véranda, et j'y passerai beaucoup de temps. Je n'aurai pas besoin de climatisation°.

Ma maison devra être pratique aussi. Je voudrai un lave-linge et un séchoir. Mais, je n'ai aucune intention de passer beaucoup de temps dans la cuisine. Alors elle sera assez petite.

---

personne: *no one* / **d'occasion:** *secondhand* / **moche:** *ugly* / **la chambre d'amis:** *guest room* / **la climatisation:** *air conditioning*

On considère les éventualités. Quelles situations est-ce que vous anticipez pour votre style de vie dans les prochaines années? Quels seront les effets de cette situation sur votre logement? Quelles seront, probablement, vos priorités? Notez vos réponses à ces questions, pour deux périodes différentes, comme indiqués dans la grille. Vous pouvez consulter les **Suggestions** suivantes et la lecture à la page précédente, si vous voulez, pour trouver des idées.

| Ma situation dans l'avenir ||
Dans deux ans	*Dans cinq ans*
* La situation anticipée: _____ * Effet de la situation sur mon logement: _____ * Priorités personnelles: _____	* La situation anticipée: _____ * Effet de la situation sur mon logement: _____ * Priorités personnelles: _____

Suggestions

Situation anticipée	Effet sur votre logement	Priorités personnelles
• Si je trouve un bon emploi • Si je gagne assez/plus d'argent • Si je ne suis pas encore marié(e) • Si mon/ma petit(e) ami(e) et moi nous nous marions • Si j'ai un/des enfant(s) • Si la famille s'agrandit° • Si mon (mes) enfant(s) n'habite(nt) plus chez moi • Si je change d'emploi • Si je ne change pas d'emploi • Si on augmente mon salaire • Si je peux prendre ma retraite • Si je gagne à la loterie • Si j'ai l'occasion de... • Si je dois m'occuper de... • ? ? ?	• déménager à... • rénover... • faire construire°... • changer la décoration de... • acheter de nouveaux meubles pour... • remplacer... • ? ? ?	• le budget • la beauté • le confort • l'aspect pratique • l'autonomie • faire parler ma personnalité • ? ? ?

_____
s'agrandit: *from* **s'agrandir:** *to grow /* **faire construire:** *have . . . built*

J. Dans dix ans (*Ten years from now*). Écrivez deux ou trois paragraphes où vous envisagez un logement idéal pour votre vie dans dix ans. Quelle sorte de résidence sera-t-elle? Un studio au centre-ville? Un appartement pour un jeune couple? Une maison de famille? Un chalet près du lac? Employez les exemples aux pages 453 et 462 comme modèles pour vos paragraphes.

À propos du vocabulaire: Remember to take full advantage of the reading as a model not only for its format and organization but also for specific expressions that apply to your own thoughts. For example, you might want to use **Puisque j'aime, Il me faudra penser à, Je n'ai aucune intention de, Il ne sera plus nécessaire de.** If these apply to what you want to say, use them as ready-made vocabulary.

ÉCOUTONS: Au bureau de l'agent immobilier

À l'agence immobilière LeFarge les assistants accueillent et posent des questions aux nouveaux clients pour préparer des rapports pour le chef de l'agence. Comme nouvel(le) assistant(e), aujourd'hui vous observez quelques interviews. Employez la méthode suivante pour développer vos compétences.

A. Anticipez les interviews. Avant d'écouter les interviews, étudiez le modèle à la page suivante, remarquez l'organisation du formulaire et identifiez le type d'informations recherchées.

B. Notez les détails. Écoutez la première interview. Cochez ou prenez des notes sur votre formulaire pour indiquer les réponses données par les clients. Cette fois, ne traitez pas la section «Autres». Réservez ces informations pour la prochaine étape.

C. Identifiez les informations supplémentaires. Écoutez l'interview encore une fois pour identifier quelques autres informations données par les clients. Notez au moins *deux* éléments dans la section «Autres» de votre formulaire.

D. Recommencez. Répétez les étapes B et C pour la deuxième interview.

E. Résumez une interview. Écrivez une note à votre patron, Monsieur LeFarge, où vous décrivez le domicile recherché par ce client.

Modèle:

AGENCE IMMOBILIÈRE LeFarge

Interview préliminaire du client

Résidence principale		Maison	✓	Vente	
Résidence secondaire	✓	Appartement		Location	✓

Profil du client:

Nom du propriétaire:	AUBIN, Denis	Nombre de personnes dans la famille:		5
Adresse:	3 rue de la Paix	Autres membres de la famille:		
Téléphone:	02.45.87.36.92	• fils	âge:	16 ans
Âge (approx.):	40 ans	• fils	âge:	8 ans
État civil:	marié	• belle-mère	âge:	

Essentiels:			Emplacement:	
Nombre de chambres	3		Centre-ville	
Nombre de salles de bains	2		Quartier résidentiel	
Jardin	✓		Banlieue	
Cuisine équipée			Campagne	✓
Coin cuisine	✓		Lac	
Au rez-de-chaussée			Près de:	
À l'étage			Village	
			Marché/Magasin d'alimentation	

AUTRES

- terrasse
- lave-vaisselle
- meublé

À: Jean-Yves LeFarge
De: (votre nom) Marianne Clémy
Référence: (nom des clients) AUBIN Denis
Date: le 3 septembre 2000

M. Aubin cherche une maison à louer à la campagne comme résidence secondaire. Il lui faut trois chambres et deux salles de bains, un coin cuisine avec lave-vaisselle et un beau jardin. La maison doit être meublée. Il désire avoir une belle terrasse où on peut prendre des repas en plein air quand il fait beau.

C'est pour l'été, la proximité des écoles n'a donc pas d'importance, mais M. Aubin ne voudrait être loin ni d'un village ni d'un magasin d'alimentation.

Puisque la belle-mère habite avec la famille, M. Aubin préfère avoir une des chambres séparée des autres.

UNE ARCHITECTURE COLONIALE ADAPTÉE AUX CONDITIONS CLIMATIQUES DU CAMEROUN

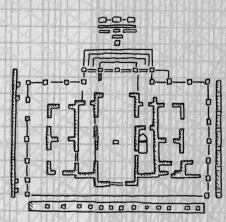

Plan de la «pagode», avec son orientation est-ouest typique pour une meilleure protection du soleil

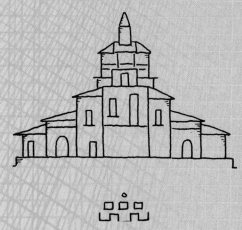

Coupe est-ouest de la «pagode»

ayant: *having*
un pilier: *pillar*

le toit: *roof*
un pan: *panel*

le midi: sud

L'architecture coloniale [européenne] a su répondre aux exigences climatiques et mettre à profit les techniques de construction locales, tout en développant un style ayant° une valeur esthétique et fonctionnelle. Les bâtiments sont en règle générale constitués d'un alignement linéaire de piliers° robustes en maçonnerie, autour d'un plan rectangulaire. L'étage, généralement aménagé selon le plan du rez-de-chaussée, est construit en bois. Les vérandas d'angle et les toits° à quatre pans° accentuent la profondeur de l'espace.

Les principes qui ont guidé ces constructions demeurent valables aujourd'hui:

1. Orientation est-ouest du corps du bâtiment, façade [longue] tournée vers le midi°;
2. Aération transversale des pièces accessibles par une galerie extérieure;
3. [Le centre de l'habitation] réalisé en maçonnerie massive avec des murs qui ne s'échauffent que lentement;
4. Construction des toits à double couverture;
5. Utilisation de couleurs claires pour améliorer la réflexion et réduire l'absorption de chaleur.

1. Read the article, noting any information or ideas that relate to your discussions of the **Découverte** notes on pages 437 and 452.

2. Examine the passages that you noted in the reading about colonial architecture to determine their significance for your conclusions regarding the **Découverte**. Writing complete sentences (in English), articulate your perceptions, so that you can communicate them clearly in class discussion. Remember to include references to words in the article on colonial architecture and from your **Découverte** discussions to support your assertions.

3. Discuss your insights with your classmates, taking notes on their interpretations of the information.

4. Write a paragraph with the following components:
   - a thesis statement, summarizing your views
   - several sentences in which you offer detailed support for your views
   - a conclusion, in which you tell what additional information you would like to have on the subject.

INTÉGRATION

Situation: Imaginez que vous travaillez dans la succursale° d'une société dont le siège° est à Paris. Le PDG a récemment promis d'aider l'organisation humanitaire DAL, «Droit Au Logement.» C'est pourquoi les employés de toutes les succursales autour du monde organiseront leurs efforts bénévoles cette année pour aider une famille mal logée de leur communauté.

une succursale: *branch office*
un siège: *home office*

Mission: Vous aurez la responsabilité de subventionner° la construction d'une maison à offrir à une certaine famille défavorisée°.

subventionner: *sponsor*
défavorisée: *underprivileged*

Démarche: Votre bureau préparera son projet et remettra le rapport de ses décisions au PDG du bureau à Paris (en français, bien sûr). C'est lui qui prendra la décision de quel projet sera adopté par votre bureau. C'est à vous et à vos collègues d'organiser vos efforts pour ce projet.

Un Toit° pour Tous / Tous pour un Toit

Un Toit, c'est un Droit°

Et, avec DAL, vous pouvez l'assurer pour une famille mal logée° de votre communauté!
Qu'est-ce que DAL?

Droit Au Logement est une association qui a pour but d'unir les familles et les individus mal logés ou sans-logis° pour la défense du droit à un logement décent pour tous. Créé en 1990, **DAL** continue aujourd'hui son développement en France et se tourne également vers d'autres pays. Des contacts ont été pris avec plusieurs pays d'Europe (Italie, Belgique, Angleterre...) et nous étions présents à la conférence des Nations Unies **HABITAT II** en juin 1996, ce qui nous a permis de nouer des liens° avec d'autres organisations qui ont des objectifs semblables aux nôtres.

Travaillez en groupe de trois ou quatre pour préparer votre projet.

A. Choisissez la famille mal logée qui vous convient.

- une famille de quatre personnes: un père, une mère, un fils de 10 ans, une fille de 8 ans
- un couple retraité: lui a 75 ans, elle a 72 ans
- une mère et ses trois enfants: une fille de 7 ans, des fils jumeaux de 4 ans
- une famille de six personnes: père, mère, trois fils (âgés de 9, de 7 et de 5 ans) et une fille de 3 ans
- un couple âgé de 35 ans avec la belle-mère (62 ans)
- un couple âgé de 50 ans et leur fils handicapé (en fauteuil roulant°) de 25 ans

B. Décidez les éléments fondamentaux pour un logement qui conviendra à la famille choisie. Les aspects à considérer seront: la composition de la famille, le nombre de pièces, le chauffage/climatisation nécessaire pour votre région, les appareils électroménagers (lave-vaisselle, sèche-linge, etc.) nécessaires, l'emplacement dans la ville, jardin ou non.

C. Dessinez le plan de la maison que vous envisagez de faire construire pour votre famille. Indiquez l'emplacement des appareils électroménagers et de quelques meubles nécessaires qui seront installés dans votre maison.

D. Préparez le rapport à remettre au PDG du siège en France. Organisez votre rapport comme indiqué dans le modèle.

À: Jacques Langlois, PDG
De: (Noms des membres), Équipe de la Succursale de... (ville)
Référence: Projet DAL
Date:

I. Description de la famille à subventionner
II. Brève description du cadre naturel de votre région
III. Besoins de logement identifiés par l'équipe (avec justification) pour la famille spécifique
IV. Plan de la maison

E. Présentez un rapport oral aux employés de votre bureau. Chaque membre de votre équipe devra avoir la responsabilité d'une section de votre rapport (description de la famille, ou explication des besoins ou exposition du plan).

Les résidences

un appartement	apartment	un bungalow	bungalow
un chalet	chalet	un cottage	cottage
une ferme	farm	un ranch	ranch
un hôtel particulier	private residence	une villa	villa
un immeuble	apartment building	un pied-à-terre	a hang-out, small temporary residence
un logement	lodging, housing		
une maison	house		
une résidence secondaire	a vacation home		
un studio	efficiency apartment		

Les niveaux

le rez-de-chaussée	ground floor
le premier étage	second floor
le deuxième étage	third floor
un sous-sol	basement

Les terrains

boisé	wooded
fleuri	with flowers
à la campagne	country landscape
aménagé	landscaped, cared for
de rêve	"dream"

Les secteurs

de choix	of choice
de nouvelles constructions	of new buildings
recherché	sought out
renommé	well-known

Les pièces d'une maison

une entrée	entrance hall	une salle de jeux	game room
un salon	living room	un bureau	office
une salle à manger	dining room	une salle de gymnastique	exercise room
une salle de séjour	den, family room		
une cuisine	kitchen		
une chambre à coucher	bedroom		
une salle de bains	bathroom		
un W.-C., un cabinet de toilette, les toilettes (f.)	water closet, toilet (as a room), restroom		
une laverie	laundry room		
un garage	garage		
un sous-sol	basement		
une cave	basement, wine cellar		

Les meubles

un canapé	sofa, divan	un placard	cupboard, closet
un fauteuil	comfortable armchair	un évier	sink

une chaise	chair	une cuisinière	stove
une table	table	une cafetière	coffee maker
une lampe	lamp	un mini-four	toaster oven
un bureau	desk; office	un grille-pain	toaster
une peinture	painting	une planche à repasser	ironing board
un tapis	rug	un fer (à repasser)	iron
une armoire	armoire	un lave-linge	washing machine
un lit	bed	un sèche-linge	dryer
une commode	small chest	un lave-vaisselle	dishwasher
un téléviseur	television set	un lavabo	basin
un magnétoscope	VCR	un miroir	mirror
un lecteur de CD	CD player	des lits jumeaux	twin beds
une étagère	bookcase	un réveil-matin	alarm clock
un four (à micro-ondes)	oven (microwave)	une table de chevet	bedside table
un réfrigérateur (un frigo)	refrigerator (fridge)		
une baignoire	bathtub		
une douche	shower		
un bidet	bidet		

Les expressions d'aménagement

déménager	to move (change residences)	le loyer	the rent (payment)
aménager	to furnish, equip, arrange furnishings		
louer	to rent		
vendre	to sell		
s'installer	to move in, get settled		
ranger (les meubles)	to arrange (the furniture or things)		
à louer	for rent		
à vendre	for sale		
de location	rental		

Les expressions négatives

ne... rien	nothing
ne... jamais	never
ne... personne	nobody, no one
ne... plus	no longer, no more
ne... pas encore	not yet
ne... nulle part	nowhere
ne... que	only, just
ne... ni... ni	neither . . . nor
ne... aucun(e)	not a, not any

Les verbes

appuyer	to support, lean on
croire	to believe
s'agrandir	to grow
voir	to see

Les conjonctions

dès que	as soon as
lorsque	when
quand	when

LE BUDGET:
Les dépenses et les priorités

Communicative Objectives

- To identify budgetary categories and to add a tentative or polite tone to statements
- To express need in relation to day-to-day expenses
- To hypothesize decisions based on given situations

Thematic Objectives

✓ To identify and categorize the ways you choose to spend your income

✓ To prioritize your expenses and spending goals

✓ To examine views of personal tendencies in relation to budgeting and spending

OUVERTURE EN VIDÉO:
Comment on dépense son argent

La mise en scène

Si je fais des économies, je pourrai me permettre de nouveaux bâtons de golf.

À propos de la communication: The activities in this chapter are designed to allow you to talk about your own budget. However, any time you are concerned about privacy, feel free to make up information for the activity.

A. **Comment je dépense (spend) mon argent.** In this chapter you will identify and categorize the ways you spend your income, prioritize your expenses, and create a personal budget. On the video we see people going about activities in which they make spending decisions and we will decide how those practices relate to our own lives.

In anticipation of hearing how people discuss their budgetary concerns in French, think about how you spend money. If you were interviewed by someone from another country who was making a video about Americans and their spending habits, what are some of the areas that you would mention?

Start off by watching some brief scenes of people involved in spending money. Use those images to create a list in English of ways you spend money, not only to purchase products, but to pay for services and leisure activities as well.

B. **On compare nos habitudes avec celles de notre partenaire.** Compare your list of the ways you spend money with that of your partner. Add to your list any items your partner thought of that you forgot to include.

C. **On détermine des catégories.** Using the lists from you and your partner, group as many items as possible into categories. For example, car payment, gas, car maintenance, car insurance, bus pass, and parking permit could all be grouped under "transportation."

Vous me demandez comment mon argent a tendance à s'évaporer? Bien, c'est parce que je ne peux pas me passer de° m'acheter un nouveau tableau de temps en temps.

me passer de: *to pass up, to do without*

Items we spend on	Category	Items we spend on	Category

Les paroles et le sens

D. **Qu'est-ce que vous achetez généralement?** Watch Xavier interview a few Parisians at a shopping mall. He asks them what kinds of things they shop for when they come to the mall: «**Qu'est-ce que vous achetez généralement?**» Some of the items you might hear people mention are listed on the chart. Listen first to a demonstration of how those items are pronounced and what they mean; then listen to the people interviewed give their answers. Check off the item(s) you hear each person mention.

Personne interviewée ⇨	garçon en t-shirt gris	deux femmes	deux jeunes filles	homme en chemise violette	femme aux cheveux roux	femme en blanc	2e femme en blanc	femme avec jeune fille en bleu
Achats ⇩								
cadeaux								
vêtements								
lunettes								
bijoux								
nourriture								
[tout] pour l'entretien de la maison								
besoins								
pour faire des courses d'alimentation								

On y réfléchit

E. **Mes dépenses régulières.** Decide which category of your routine expenses takes the greatest "piece of the pie" of your monthly budget. Number the expense categories listed in order of priority as they relate to your personal budget (with #1 representing your greatest expense). Add others that are significant to the bottom of the chart.

Mes dépenses régulières	L'importance de la somme
Alimentation	
Logement	
Habillement	
Transport	
Communications	
Loisirs	
Crèche/garderie	
Frais de scolarité°	
Besoins personnels	
Santé	
autre:	
autre:	

Frais de scolarité: *school expenses, tuition*

Une de mes plus grandes dépenses chaque mois, c'est la garderie° pour ma fille de deux ans. Mais ça vaut la peine°. J'ai trouvé une garderie de bonne qualité, et elle est très heureuse là-bas. Ça me permet d'aller à mes cours sans stress.

garderie: *child-care facility*
ça vaut la peine: *it's worth it*

F. Lorsqu'il me restera une somme assez importante... *(When I have a substantial amount left over . . .)* Consider how you'd like to spend that special pot you've saved. Put a check mark by no more than three items on the chart. Note that there is room to add some items that may not be listed.

Lorsqu'il me restera une somme assez importante, je voudrais pouvoir me permettre:	
un meilleur logement	
une nouvelle voiture	
un meilleur ordinateur	
de nouveaux vêtements	
une alimentation plus saine	
plus d'équipement de sports	
certains services médicaux	
les médicaments nécessaires	
une meilleure crèche/garderie pour les enfants	
autre:	
autre:	

Objective: To identify budgetary categories and to add a tentative or polite tone to statements

PRÉSENTATION: **Un coup d'œil sur le thème**

Vous me demandez comment je dépense mon argent? La réponse est «Très soigneusement!». D'abord il y a mes frais de scolarité, les inscriptions, les livres, le matériel pour mes cours d'art—et ça coûte assez cher. C'est presque un quart de mon budget. Mais la plus grande dépense, c'est pour la voiture, y compris l'essence°, l'entretien° et l'assurance. Je dirais° que cela me coûte trente-cinq, même quarante pour cent de mon salaire. Ça coûte les yeux de la tête°!

Naturellement, il faut manger. Mes parents paient pour la nourriture à la maison, mais je prends pas mal de mes repas «sur le pouce°» aux fast-foods. Ça fait un peu moins de quinze pour cent. Je verse° encore quinze pour cent de ma paie pour des vêtements et mes besoins personnels. Alors, il ne me reste pas beaucoup de sous° pour mes loisirs. Je dirais presque dix pour cent. Heureusement, j'habite chez mes parents, et je n'ai pas de loyer à payer. Alors j'essaie d'économiser cinq pour cent de mon chèque chaque mois. Je voudrais faire mieux... mais voilà. Je fais mon possible.

y compris l'essence: *including gasoline*
l'entretien (m.): *maintenance*
Je dirais: *I would say*
coûte les yeux de la tête: coûte très cher

(manger) sur le pouce: *(eat) on the run*
verse: *pay (Literally, the verb means pour [as a liquid].)*
pas beaucoup de sous: très peu d'argent

Notre budget? Ah. On le surveille° constamment. La maison constitue la plus grande dépense, si on compte les meubles, les factures° d'électricité, de gaz, etc. Ça représente sans doute vingt-cinq pour cent de nos revenus. Après la maison, c'est l'alimentation. Je dirais que nous dépensons presque vingt pour cent de notre paie au supermarché. Puis, il y a les frais de santé, d'assurance, des médecins et tout ça. Ça fait plus de quinze pour cent. La voiture, l'essence, l'entretien coûtent à peu près dix pour cent. Nous économisons quinze pour cent de notre paie à la banque chaque mois—on pense à l'éducation des enfants. Le quinze pour cent qui nous reste a tendance à s'évaporer.

surveille: examine consciencieusement *(cognate with* **surveillance)**
une facture: *bill*

Les dépenses importantes

Dans ces paragraphes, on parle de son budget. En lisant, faites une liste des dépenses qui comptent pour vous aussi. Puis organisez-les par ordre d'importance dans votre budget. Est-ce qu'il y a d'autres expressions que vous aimeriez ajouter à votre lexique personnel?

POUR DÉVELOPPER VOTRE FRANÇAIS

Vocabulaire: La consommation des ménages°

La consommation des ménages: *household budget*

OBSERVATIONS

Habillement (m.):
Clothing

Secteurs de consommation en France	% de budget
Alimentation, boissons, tabac	18%
Habillement°	5%
Logement, chauffage, électricité	22%
Équipement du logement	7%
Santé	10%
Transports, communications	17%
Loisirs, culture	8%
Autres biens et services	13%
	100%

Quand je fais des courses, je compte mes sous. Je fais bien attention à mes dépenses. Après tout, un sou est un sou!

À propos du vocabulaire: The word **sou** refers to the 5-centime coin in the post-revolutionary French monetary system dating from 1793. The coin had very little value. Some expressions using this term are:

être sans le sou	*to be penniless*
être près de ses sous	*to be miserly, stingy*
(un manteau) de quatre sous	*something (a coat) of little value (cheap), of little importance*
économiser sou à sou	*to scrimp and save*
Un sou est un sou.	*Every penny counts.*
C'est une affaire de gros sous.	*There's big money involved.*

STRATÉGIES D'ANALYSE

1. What does this chart tell you? What do these categories represent?
2. In which category do the French spend the largest percent of their money?
3. Does 18% of the budget seem in line with your expenditures on food, drinks, and tobacco?
4. What about the 5% spent on clothes—does that seem high or low to you?
5. Would you have used the same categories to explain your budget? Would you have combined or split any of these categories?
6. Is any significant category missing from the list?

PRÉCISIONS

• Budgetary analysis requires categorization of expenses. The following categories are often used in reporting spending:

Alimentation, boissons, tabac	*Food, drinks, tobacco*
Habillement	*Clothing*
Logement, chauffage, électricité	*Housing, heat, electricity*
Équipement du logement	*Household furnishings*
Santé	*Health*
Transports, communications	*Transportation, communication (telephone, cell phone, fax, modem)*
Loisirs, culture	*Leisure, culture*
Frais de scolarité	*Education expenses*
Frais de crèche/garderie	*Infant-/child-care expenses*
Impôts et assurances	*Taxes and insurance*
Autres biens et services	*Other goods and services*

- The following expressions are often used in talking about spending money:

Ça coûte les yeux de la tête.	*That costs an arm and a leg.*
Je cherche un bon prix.	*I am looking for a good price.*
C'est une somme importante.	*That's a lot of money.*
Je compte mes sous.	*I'm counting my pennies.*
Je suis fauché(e).	*I'm broke.*
Je n'ai pas un sou!	*I don't have a cent (to my name)!*
	I'm completely broke.
Je n'ai pas de sous.	*I don't have any money.*

A. **On catégorise les dépenses.** Voici une liste de dépenses. Avec votre partenaire, mettez-les dans les catégories des grilles suivantes.

Les dépenses

une cassette	du poisson	un bifteck
des légumes	un dîner au restaurant	une boîte de thé à l'épicerie
un pullover	le loyer	une tasse de thé au café
des billets de cinéma	la location d'une voiture	un disque compact
une visite chez le coiffeur	de l'essence	une baguette
un canapé	des bouteilles d'eau minérale	un grille-pain
des aspirines	un livre	du vin
une cafetière	le chauffage de l'appartement	un jean
la location d'une vidéo	l'entretien de la voiture	les frais d'assurance
une visite chez le dentiste	des jus de fruit	les frais du téléphone cellulaire
des cigarettes	l'éclairage de la maison	les frais de séjour à l'hôpital
du lait	une lampe	un téléphone
des tickets de métro	une visite chez le médecin	un journal

Alimentation, boissons, tabac	Habillement	Logement, chauffage, électricité	Équipement du logement

Santé	Transports, communications	Loisirs, culture	Autres biens et services

1ᴱᴿ THÈME: Analyse de mes dépenses

B. **Je suis responsable.** Dans le tableau suivant, indiquez (avec un *X*) la personne qui est responsable de ces dépenses dans chaque catégorie.

	Moi tout(e) seul(e)	Partagé avec...	Mes parents	Autres
Alimentation, boissons, tabac	X			
Habillement				
Logement, chauffage, électricité				
Équipement du logement				
Santé				
Transports, communications				
Loisirs, culture				
Frais de scolarité				
Frais de crèche/garderie				
Impôts et assurances				
Autres biens et services				

C. **Pour organiser un budget.** Faire un budget n'est pas simple. D'abord, il faut faire attention à la situation financière. Utilisez les catégories de l'Exercice B. À tour de rôle avec votre partenaire, répondez aux questions suivantes.

Modèle: dépenser le plus d'argent
—*Dans quelle catégorie dépenses-tu le plus d'argent?*
—*Je dépense toujours le plus d'argent pour le logement, pour mon appartement. Et toi?*
—*Moi, je dépense le plus d'argent chaque mois pour les transports/ communications. Je paie une voiture à crédit.*

Dans quelle catégorie...
1. dépenser le plus d'argent
2. dépenser le moins d'argent
3. préférer dépenser ton argent
4. ne pas aimer dépenser de l'argent
5. beaucoup contrôler tes dépenses
6. ne pas contrôler tes dépenses
7. dépenser de l'argent seulement pour toi-même
8. dépenser de l'argent pour les autres
9. dépenser une somme raisonnable
10. dépenser une somme ridicule

NOTE CULTURELLE

Selon *l'Observatoire de la vie étudiante*, le budget mensuel° d'un étudiant de 20 ans en France est de 5 000 francs (765 euros). Généralement, une partie de ces ressources vient des parents. L'État° attribue aussi une aide au logement et des bourses° d'études. Mais, pour acheter d'autres «essentiels», tels que les sorties sociales, les disques et les livres, plus de 40% des jeunes qui vont à la fac° sont obligés de travailler durant l'année scolaire. Les étudiants qui travaillent consacrent° environ 1500 francs (228 euros) à leurs loisirs; ceux qui ne travaillent pas ne dépassent guère° les 500 francs (76 euros).

Réfléchissons: À votre avis: Est-ce que votre budget mensuel est plus ou moins de 5 000 francs (765 euros)? D'où vient votre argent: de vos parents, de votre salaire, des bourses, de l'État? Est-ce que vous travaillez pour payer les «essentiels»? Qu'est-ce que vous considérez comme «essentiel»?

mensuel: *monthly* / **l'État:** *le gouvernement* / **à la fac:** *à l'université* / **une bourse:** *scholarship* /
consacrer: *allocate* / **ne dépassent guère:** *hardly surpass*

Structure: Le conditionnel

OBSERVATIONS

—Je **voudrais** acheter une nouvelle voiture.
*I **would like** to buy a new car.*

—Est-ce que tu **pourrais** acheter une voiture <u>et</u> payer tes frais de scolarité?
***Would** you **be able** to buy a car <u>and</u> pay your educational expenses?*

—Non, bien sûr. Mais une nouvelle voiture me **ferait** plaisir.
*Of course not. But a new car **would please** me.*

—Je comprends. Mon mari et moi **aimerions** bien avoir une maison. Mais nous sommes tous les deux étudiants, et nous **aimerions mieux** finir nos études sans beaucoup de dettes.
*I understand. My husband and I **would like** to have a house. But we are both students, and we **would prefer** to finish our education without a lot of debt.*

—Vous et votre mari **seriez**-vous contents d'habiter un appartement jusqu'à la naissance de vos enfants?
Would you and your husband be satisfied to live in an apartment until the birth of your children?

—Je crois que oui. Mais des enfants **changeraient** la situation immédiatement. Dès que nous aurons des enfants, je **voudrais** avoir une maison.
I think so. But children would change the situation immediately. As soon as we have kids, I would want to have a house.

Stratégies d'analyse

1. Look at the verbs in boldface in the sentences. Which of these verb forms have you already used to make a request (as in politely ordering something to drink at a café)?
2. These verbs in the conditional tense use the same stem as another tense that you have studied. Which other tense uses this stem?
3. The endings on these conditional verbs are the same as the endings on another tense that you have studied. Which other tense uses these endings?
4. What is the equivalent English structure of the French **conditionnel?**

Précisions

- Using the conditional allows us to be polite as we:

  express wishes,
  > **J'aimerais** bien rembourser mes cartes de crédit.
  > *I would really like to pay off my credit cards.*

  make requests,
  > Est-ce que tu **pourrais** m'aider à préparer le budget?
  > *Would you be able to help me plan the budget?*

  give advice,
  > À ta place, je **mettrais** de l'argent de côté.
  > *If I were you, I would put some money aside.*

  extend and/or accept invitations.
  > **Voudriez**-vous nous accompagner à la visite chez le comptable?
  > *Would you like to go with us to the session with the accountant?*

- The French conditional tense usually has the English equivalent of *would* (occasionally *should* or *could*).

- The conditional tense is formed by using the same stem as the future (the infinitive stem ending in **r**) and the same endings as the imperfect (**-ais, -ais, -ait, -ions, -iez, -aient**).

| arriver | choisir | vendre |
arriver-	choisir-	vendr-
j'arriver**ais**	je choisir**ais**	je vendr**ais**
tu arriver**ais**	tu choisir**ais**	tu vendr**ais**
il/elle/on arriver**ait**	il/elle/on choisir**ait**	il/elle/on vendr**ait**
nous arriver**ions**	nous choisir**ions**	nous vendr**ions**
vous arriver**iez**	vous choisir**iez**	vous vendr**iez**
ils/elles arriver**aient**	ils/elles choisir**aient**	ils/elles vendr**aient**

- Irregular verbs have the same stem in the conditional as they do in the future tense.

aller	**ir-**	j'irais, tu irais...
avoir	**aur-**	j'aurais, tu aurais...
être	**ser-**	je serais, tu serais...
faire	**fer-**	je ferais, tu ferais...
savoir	**saur-**	je saurais, tu saurais...
envoyer	**enverr-**	j'enverrais, tu enverrais...
pouvoir	**pourr-**	je pourrais, tu pourrais...
voir	**verr-**	je verrais, tu verrais...
falloir	**faudr-**	il faudrait
pleuvoir	**pleuvr-**	il pleuvrait
convenir	**conviendr-**	cela me conviendrait, elles vous conviendraient...
devenir	**deviendr-**	je deviendrais, tu deviendrais...
revenir	**reviendr-**	je reviendrais, tu reviendrais...
tenir	**tiendr-**	je tiendrais, tu tiendrais...
venir	**viendr-**	je viendrais, tu viendrais...

D. **Être poli, ça compte beaucoup.** Il est important d'être poli dans les situations professionnelles aussi bien que dans les situations personnelles. À tour de rôle avec votre partenaire, refaites les phrases suivantes d'une manière un peu plus polie.

Modèle: Pouvez-vous m'indiquer où se trouve la banque?
Pourriez-vous m'indiquer où se trouve la banque?

1. Pouvez-vous m'indiquer où se trouve le bureau de poste?
2. Voulez-vous acheter un téléviseur dans ce magasin?
3. Est-ce que je peux vous demander un petit service°?
4. Tu as le temps de m'expliquer comment ça marche°?
5. Je peux vous poser une question?
6. Est-ce que tu peux me dire quelle heure il est?
7. Pouvons-nous vous accompagner au concert?
8. Est-ce que tu es content(e) de payer ce prix?

un petit service: *a little favor*

comment ça marche: *how this works*

E. **À sa place, je...** Dites à votre partenaire ce que vous feriez dans les situations suivantes.

Moi	Les situations	Mon/Ma partenaire
À sa place, j'achèterais une pizza et j'étudierais.	1. Votre amie a assez d'argent pour louer des vidéos ou pour acheter une pizza ce soir. À sa place, que feriez-vous?	
	2. Georges se trouve dans une situation difficile. Il doit payer le loyer de son appartement et régler la note des réparations de sa voiture. Il a l'argent pour faire l'un ou l'autre, mais pas les deux. À sa place, que feriez-vous?	
	3. Christine désire un téléviseur et un four à micro-ondes pour son appartement. Elle peut payer l'un ou l'autre. À sa place, que feriez-vous?	
	4. André voudrait inviter Sophie à l'accompagner au restaurant. Mais, s'il dépense son argent comme ça, il ne pourra pas acheter de billets pour le concert de jazz. À sa place, que feriez-vous?	
	5. Mme Tristan voudrait acheter des livres pour son fils qui a sept ans. Le garçon désire une vidéo. À sa place, que feriez-vous?	
	6. Un de vos amis pense offrir une peinture à sa petite amie comme cadeau de Noël. La peinture qu'il préfère coûte 100 dollars de plus que son budget ne lui permet. À sa place, que feriez-vous?	
	7. Le père de Paul lui a donné un choix pour fêter son 19e anniversaire: une motocyclette ou quinze jours de vacances en France. À sa place, que feriez-vous?	
	8. Quand Jacques a ouvert un compte à la banque, on lui a offert un cadeau: une cafetière ou un grille-pain. À sa place, que choisiriez-vous?	

F. **Un avenir de rêve.** Avec votre partenaire, imaginez un avenir préférable au présent. Discutez vos priorités et ensuite, écrivez ensemble au moins huit phrases pour décrire cet avenir de rêve. Utilisez les suggestions suivantes pour vous donner des idées.

Selon...: *According to*

Modèle: —*Selon° moi, la condition la plus importante est qu'il n'y aurait pas de familles sans les deux parents.*
—*Oui, je suis d'accord avec toi. Et pour la deuxième condition en importance, on ne ferait pas de guerre.*

1. ne pas y avoir de familles sans les deux parents
2. ne pas y avoir de guerre
3. ne pas détruire l'environnement
4. donner un toit aux sans-abris
5. ne pas avoir faim
6. savoir lire et écrire

7. être heureux
8. ne pas y avoir de chômage°

le chômage: *unemployment*

9. finir les études universitaires
10. gagner beaucoup d'argent
11. respecter les droits de tous
12. trouver un remède contre le cancer
13. trouver un remède contre le SIDA

G. Un avenir de rêve (suite). Avec votre partenaire, décidez quelles cinq conditions de la liste dans l'Exercice F vous considérez les plus importantes dans votre avenir de rêve.

Modèles: ne pas y avoir d'enfants sans les deux parents
Dans un avenir de rêve, il n'y aurait pas de familles sans les deux parents.

ne pas y avoir de guerre
Dans un avenir de rêve, il n'y aurait pas de guerre.

H. Si on pouvait améliorer (*improve*) l'avenir. Dites à votre partenaire au moins trois choses que vous feriez pour améliorer l'avenir.

Modèle: *Je travaillerais à "Habitat for Humanity" pour améliorer l'avenir des sans-abris.*

PRONONCIATION: La combinaison **th**

While in English, *th* may be pronounced two ways (as in *those things*), in French it is pronounced [t]. This combination is relatively rare in French, and most of the words containing it are Greek-based cognates in French and English. To help improve your accent, you should carefully practice pronouncing this sound *à la française*.

Repeat the following words after your instructor.

1. thème
2. thé
3. thermomètre
4. éthique
5. philanthrope
6. méthode

À vous! With a partner, read the following sentences, being sure to pronounce "th" *à la française*:

1. Mon orthodontiste, c'est un vrai misanthrope! Il n'utilise jamais d'anesthésie!
2. J'étudie la théologie. J'écris une thèse sur l'orthodoxie catholique.
3. Le théâtre se trouve à côté de la bibliothèque.
4. L'athlète recommande les bienfaits de la kinésithérapie.
5. Cette cathédrale monolithique date des temps très anciens.
6. La glande thyroïde contient la thyroglobuline.

POUR DÉVELOPPER VOS IDÉES

Thematic objective: To identify and categorize the ways you choose to spend your income

Présentation: Nos besoins de jour en jour

POUR SAISIR L'ESSENTIEL: Le tableau suivant résume les dépenses des Français dans les années 96–97.

1. Faites une liste des sept catégories traitées dans le tableau.
2. Organisez les catégories par ordre d'importance dans votre budget.
3. Est-ce qu'il y a des dépenses mentionnées dans le tableau qui ne comptent pas du tout dans votre budget?
4. La catégorisation des éléments conviendrait-elle à votre budget? Par exemple, à votre avis, est-ce que la facture du téléphone figure dans les frais de transport, dans les frais de logement avec le chauffage et l'éclairage, ou la mettriez-vous plutôt° dans la catégorie des loisirs?

plutôt: *rather*

un milliard: *a billion*

dont: *which include*

La consommation des ménages français dans les années 96–97

Catégories des dépenses	Valeur en milliards° de francs	Pourcentage
Alimentation, boissons, tabac dont°:	**850,9**	18
Ensemble alimentation	658,9	
Boissons nonalcoolisées	28,9	
Boissons alcoolisées	90,8	
Habillement dont:	**248,2**	05
Articles d'habillement	198,1	
Chaussures	50,1	
Logement, chauffage, électricité dont:	**1060,0**	22
Location de logement	759,0	
Chauffage et éclairage	178,6	
Équipement du logement dont:	**349,8**	07
Meubles, tapis	97,6	
Équipement électroménager	50,7	
Santé dont:	**489,6**	10
Médicaments	124,4	
Médecins	108,2	
Dentistes	42,9	
Autres	44,4	

Transports, communications	795,5	17
dont:		
Automobiles	164,5	
Carburants, lubrifiants	168,1	
Transports en commun	100,1	
Télécommunications	65,0	
Loisirs, culture	352,2	08
dont:		
Matériel électronique (T.V., Vidéo, etc.)	32,2	
Disques, cassettes	24,9	
Cinéma, spectacles, jeux de hasard	91,3	
Livres, quotidiens, périodiques	65,7	
Autres biens et services	621.8	13
dont:		
Soins personnels (coiffeurs, esthétique, parfumerie)	89,5	
Consommation finale des ménages	**4768,0**	100

I. **Les principales catégories dans mon budget.**
Réfléchissez à votre budget personnel. Comment est-ce que vous dépensez votre argent? Quelles sont les principales catégories de votre budget? Quelle part de votre revenu final est-ce que vous consacrez à chaque catégorie? Vous pouvez rechercher du vocabulaire dans le tableau intitulé «Quelques dépenses» ci-dessous ainsi que dans le tableau ci-dessus de l'activité précédente.

Organisez vos informations dans un tableau comme «Le budget général». Notez bien que la somme° des pourcentages doit être de 100%.

J'ai un ami qui habite à la Martinique. Alors, pour moi, ce sont les factures de téléphone qui coûtent cher.

À propos du vocabulaire: In arithmetic, **somme** is feminine, but there is a masculine **somme** that means *nap*. It is related to the word **sommeil**.

la somme: *the sum*

Le budget général

Catégories des dépenses	Pourcentages

un compte d'épargne: *savings account*
menues dépenses: *petty cash*

Quelques dépenses

- frais de scolarité
- achats de logiciels
- achats de livres, de magazines
- entretien de la voiture (essence)
- frais de crèche/garderie

- impôts
- assurances
- frais de santé
- logement
- bonnes œuvres
- compte d'épargne°
- dettes diverses

- cinéma
- location de vidéos
- achat de disques
- cadeaux
- dépenses de coiffure
- soins personnels
- paiements à…

- factures de gaz, d'eau, d'électricité, de téléphone, de télévision par câble
- téléphone cellulaire
- menues dépenses°
- dépenses diverses

revenu actuel: *current income*

J. **Plus on est riche, plus on...** Imaginez que vous arrivez à doubler votre revenu actuel°. Dans ce scénario, vous auriez deux fois plus d'argent chaque mois. Comment est-ce que vos habitudes financières changeraient? Refaites le tableau que vous avez créé pour l'Exercice I, en ajoutant les changements que vous feriez dans votre budget.

La révision de mon budget

Catégories des dépenses	Pourcentages actuels	Nouveaux pourcentages

K. **Discussion des choix budgétaires.** En groupes de trois ou quatre, discutez les révisions que vous avez faites dans votre budget pour l'Exercice J. À la fin de la discussion, décidez ensemble comment décrire la «personnalité financière» de votre groupe. Vous pouvez vous aider des expressions dans la grille.

Pour parler du budget révisé:
Avec cette somme d'argent,...
je pourrais...
je voudrais acheter...
je donnerais...
j'aimerais...
je pourrais contribuer... à
il serait possible de...
je ferais un voyage...
j'apprendrais à...
j'irais... avec...
j'offrirais...

Pour décrire le groupe:
On dirait que notre groupe est plutôt/peu...
sobre
frivole
humanitaire
pratique
aventureux
???

DÉCOUVERTE

The visual presentation of data helps focus the reader's attention on significant information. It is a little like drawing a picture of the statistics.

Basically, tables display the intersections of two or more lists. Thus, in consulting data in a table, we usually read down one list to find a particular entry, then we read across to find the corresponding information in another list. As an example, consider the data on pages 484–485 representing how French people spend their money. The arrangement of the data in a table makes it easier to see how the expenses are categorized and how much money each subcategory represents. In this case, the table shows the list of goods and services that the French buy in relation to the list of the amounts of money that they spend and the list that separates the percentages of their annual expenses into different categories. If you imagine how that information might look in paragraph form, you get a better sense of the value of tables.

Use these data on American households to try your hand at constructing a similar table for households in the United States. Your table will not show the expenses divided into subcategories.

Les données pour les ménages américains: Les Américains dépensent une somme d'argent énorme chaque année. Au milieu des années 90, c'était 4.378,2 milliards de dollars. En particulier, ils ont payé 700,3 milliards (16%) pour leur alimentation (y compris les boissons et le tabac). Pour l'habillement, c'était 293,3 milliards (7%). Le logement, le chauffage et l'électricité représentaient 788,3 milliards (18%) de leurs revenus, et l'équipement du logement encore 280,7 milliards (6%). La santé (médecins, séjours à l'hôpital, médicaments, assurance, etc.) leur coûte 760,5 milliards (17%) de leur salaire. Les transports et communications prennent 572,4 milliards (13%) et les loisirs 339,9 milliards (8%). Enfin, ils consacrent 642,2 milliards de dollars (15%) pour leurs autres besoins.

La consommation des ménages américains au milieu des années 90

2ᴱ THÈME: Pour établir des priorités

Objective: To express need in relation to day-to-day expenses

Un coup d'œil sur le thème

il a fallu: *passé composé de «il faut»*
un prêt: *loan, from the verb* **prêter**

rembourser: *reimburse, repay*
un compte d'épargne: *savings account*

se passer de: *do without, abstain from*
atteindre: *attain*

Être étudiant, ça coûte cher. Heureusement, j'ai reçu une bourse qui paie ma scolarité. Mais il m'a fallu° aussi demander un prêt° pour payer les frais supplémentaires. Lorsque j'obtiendrai mon diplôme, cela fera une somme assez importante. Alors, un de mes objectifs à moyen terme sera de rembourser° cette dette. Je fais déjà des économies. J'ai un compte d'épargne° à la banque, et chaque mois je décide combien d'argent je peux mettre de côté. Quelquefois, je dois me passer du° déjeuner au café ou du cinéma pour atteindre° mon but pour le mois. Mais je sais qu'il faut établir des priorités dans la vie… et persévérer.

Depuis quelques mois, nous avons besoin d'un nouveau réfrigérateur. Je voulais attendre un peu pour l'acheter, parce que nous avions l'intention de nous offrir un téléviseur. Malheureusement, on n'a pas assez d'argent pour ces deux grosses dépenses avant Noël. Mais, notre frigo ne marche plus maintenant. Alors, cet appareil devient notre priorité numéro un. Il faudra l'acheter cette semaine; on ne peut pas se passer du frigo. Je suppose que nous pourrions attendre quelques mois pour l'achat du téléviseur. Après Noël, peut-être, on les trouvera en solde°. Enfin, il faut être raisonnable pour régler° les factures à la fin du mois.

en solde: *on sale*
régler: *pay (a bill), settle (an account)*

Les désirs et les besoins: On prend des décisions

En lisant les monologues, (1) faites une liste des expressions que vous aimeriez utiliser pour parler de votre propre situation financière ou des choix que vous devez faire. (2) Écrivez au moins cinq phrases où vous utilisez ces expressions. (3) Communiquez vos phrases à votre partenaire, en ajoutant quelques-unes de ses phrases à votre liste.

POUR DÉVELOPPER VOTRE FRANÇAIS

Vocabulaire: Les vêtements

OBSERVATIONS

Le placard de Richard

un complet, un costume — une veste — un gilet — un pantalon — un jean — un jogging — un maillot de bain — un short — un tee-shirt — des sous-vêtements (m.) — une chemise — une ceinture — une cravate — un pardessus — un imperméable — un anorak — des chaussures (f.) — des baskets (m.) — des chaussettes (f.)

Le placard de Brigitte

un tailleur — un chemisier — une veste — un pull(over) — une robe — un jean — un pantalon — un gilet — une jupe — un chapeau — un short — un parapluie — un imperméable — une écharpe — des gants (m.) — un sac à main — des bottes (f.) — un maillot de bain — un manteau — des sous-vêtements — un collant — des chaussures (f.) — un bikini

STRATÉGIES D'ANALYSE

1. Several items of clothing have similar names in French and in English. Make a list of these cognates from the drawings.

2. Do the cognates seem to be primarily casual clothes or business attire?

3. Most clothing items are named alike for men and for women. What items can you find that have different names, depending on whether they are for men or for women?

4. Can you find articles of clothing that are referred to in the singular in French but in the plural in English?

5. Pay special attention to the meanings of words that may surprise you:

Une veste is not *a vest;* rather it is a _____.

The French word for *vest* is _____.

Des baskets can be worn for _____, not just for basketball.

PRÉCISIONS

- The names of some clothing items, expecially casual or sports clothes, are cognates in French and English.

un **short**	un **pullover**
un **t-shirt (tee-shirt)**	un **pantalon**
un **jean**	un **bikini**

- Most items of clothing have the same names whether they are designed for men or women. However, a few have different names.

un **pardessus**	*man's overcoat*	un **complet**	*man's suit*
un **manteau**	*woman's overcoat*	un **tailleur**	*woman's suit*
une **chemise**	*man's shirt*		
un **chemisier**	*woman's shirt*		

- Some clothing items are used as singular in French and plural in English.

un **pantalon**	*pants*	un **pyjama**	*pajamas*
un **jean**	*jeans*	un **slip**	*panties, briefs*
un **short**	*shorts*		

un billet: *ticket*

A. On fait vite sa valise. Votre cousin vient de vous téléphoner. Il a un billet° pour vous pour l'accompagner à la plage à Cancún (au Mexique) ce week-end. Le seul problème, c'est qu'il faudra partir dans un quart d'heure. Il faut vite faire la valise. Dites à votre partenaire (1) ce que vous apporteriez pour le week-end à Cancún et (2) ce que vous pourriez acheter à Cancún.

Modèle: *J'apporterais un short, mon maillot de bain, ma brosse à dents et...*
À Cancún je pourrais acheter des t-shirts.

B. On a le choix. Quelle surprise! Imaginez que vous recevez cinq invitations pour le week-end. (1) Dites à votre partenaire quelle invitation vous accepteriez. (2) Puis dites-lui une destination que vous ne choisiriez jamais. (3) Enfin dites-lui ce que vous auriez besoin d'avoir dans votre valise pour le week-end.

Les invitations: à Londres en Angleterre; à Jonquière dans le nord du Québec; à Managua au Nicaragua; à Pointe-à-Pitre en Guadeloupe; à Rome en Italie

Modèle: *Moi, j'accepterais l'invitation à...*
Je ne choisirais jamais d'aller...
J'aurais besoin de (d')... pour mon week-end à...

C. Mais, si je dois payer... Avoir une invitation, c'est une chose. Payer les frais d'un voyage, c'est autre chose. (1) D'abord, dites à votre partenaire quelle ville vous voudriez visiter. (2) Puis, dites-lui s'il vous faudrait faire des économies pour payer le voyage. (3) Ensuite, dites-lui sur quoi vous pourriez économiser. (4) Enfin, dites-lui sur quoi il serait impossible d'économiser.

Modèle: *Je voudrais visiter Cannes, dans le sud de la France. Il me faudrait faire des économies pour payer le voyage. Je pourrais économiser sur les frais de coiffeur, mais je ne pourrais pas me passer d'un nouveau bikini pour la plage.*

Je pourrais économiser sur les frais de coiffeur, mais il serait impossible de me passer d'un nouveau maillot de bain pour la plage.

D. Je voudrais de nouveaux vêtements. Vous voudriez avoir quelque chose de nouveau à porter. Faites deux listes: les vêtements pour lesquels vous pourriez faire des économies et ceux dont vous pourriez vous passer.

Modèle: *Je voudrais avoir quelque chose de nouveau à porter. Pour m'acheter un manteau en cuir, je pourrais faire des économies. Je pourrais facilement me passer d'un imperméable.*

Je pourrais faire des économies pour...	Je pourrais (facilement) me passer de...

un manteau en cuir°	*un pullover en cachemire*	**en cuir:** *leather*
un imperméable **un jean**	**une bague en or°**	**en or:** *gold*
un maillot de bain qui me va bien°		**qui me va bien:** *that looks good on me*
des bottes en cuir	un complet/tailleur en laine°	**en laine:** *wool*
un anorak	une veste rouge **des baskets confortables**	

E. Une comparaison de goût. Consultez les deux listes que vous avez préparées dans l'Exercice D pour rapporter vos choix à votre partenaire.

Modèle: *J'aimerais avoir quelque chose de nouveau à porter. Je voudrais m'acheter un manteau en cuir, mais il me faudrait faire des économies. Pour l'avoir, je pourrais me passer d'un imperméable.*

Structure: Des expressions impersonnelles + infinitif

OBSERVATIONS

Pour pouvoir travailler sans trop de stress, **il me faut** trouver une garderie qui est excellente mais pas trop chère.

*In order to be able to work without too much stress, **I have to** find a child-care center that is excellent but not too expensive.*

Dès que j'aurai mon diplôme, **il me faudra** trouver un bon travail pour rembourser au gouvernement mes prêts d'étudiant.

*As soon as I have my degree, **I'll have to** find a good job in order to pay the government back for my student loans.*

Pour devenir sculpteur, **il est essentiel de** mettre de côté assez d'argent pour acheter du marbre.

*To become a sculptor, **it is essential** to put aside enough money to buy marble.*

Au supermarché, **il faut** peser les légumes vous-même avant d'aller à la caisse.

*In the supermarket, **it is necessary** to weigh the vegetables yourself before going to the checkout counter.*

Il n'est pas nécessaire d'avoir beaucoup d'argent français quand on arrive en France. **Il vaut mieux** changer des dollars en francs en France qu'aux États-Unis.

It isn't necessary *to have lots of French money when you arrive in France.* ***It is better*** *to change dollars to francs in France than in the United States.*

Il ne faut pas fumer dans le Louvre.
One must not *smoke in the Louvre.*

STRATÉGIES D'ANALYSE

1. Find three ways to express the notion of obligation in the captions to the photos.

2. What verb form follows all of these expressions?

3. Which of these expressions use **de** before the following infinitive?

4. Which expression do we use to indicate that one action is preferable to another although either is possible?

5. Pay special attention to the meanings in the negative forms. We can express the idea of obligation or necessity with **il faut** or **il est nécessaire de.** However, what is the difference in meaning between **il ne faut pas** and **il n'est pas nécessaire de**?

PRÉCISIONS

- We can use a variety of phrases to express obligation or to make recommendations about what one should do. To make a general statement (rather than talking to or about a specific person), we use an infinitive after these phrases.

Il faut...	*One must, one has to, it is necessary to . . .*
Il est essentiel de...	*It is essential to . . .*
Il est nécessaire de...	*It is necessary to . . .*
Il est important de...	*It is important to . . .*
Il est indispensable de...	*It is indispensable to, it is critical to . . .*
Il vaut mieux...	*It's better to . . .*

- Of course, all these expressions can be used in a variety of tenses.

Il faudra...	*One will have to, it will be necessary to . . .*
Il faudrait...	*One would have to, it would be necessary to . . .*
Il a fallu...	*One had to, it became necessary to . . .*
Il vaudrait mieux...	*It would be better to . . .*
Il était essentiel de...	*It was essential to . . .*
Il sera important de...	*It will be important to . . .*

- **Il faut** and **il vaut mieux** are followed directly by an infinitive.

   Il faut payer les frais de scolarité pour rester à l'université.
   One must pay the academic tuition to stay in school.

   Il vaudrait mieux mettre de l'argent de côté chaque mois.
   It would be better to put some money aside each month.

- The other expressions (**il est nécessaire/essentiel/important/indispensable**) require **de** before the infinitive.

   Il est nécessaire de payer le chauffage.
   It is necessary to pay for the heating.

   Il est important de payer l'électricité aussi.
   It is also important to pay for electricity.

À propos de la structure: *Il est nécessaire/important/essentiel/indispensable de...* are followed by a verb telling whatever it is that must be done. *C'est nécessaire/important/essentiel/indispensable* can be used alone to express a complete thought, referring to something already mentioned. However, in colloquial French, it is becoming common also to hear *C'est nécessaire/important/essentiel/indispensable de...*

- Note the difference in meaning between **il ne faut pas** (a strong warning: *one must not . . .*) and **il n'est pas nécessaire de** (*it is not necessary*).

> **Il ne faut pas** prendre de photos au ballet. C'est dangereux pour les danseurs.
> *You **must not** take photos at the ballet. It's dangerous for the dancers.*

> **Il n'est pas nécessaire d'**apporter ton manteau. Il ne fait jamais très froid ici.
> *It **isn't necessary** to bring your coat. It's never very cold here.*

- With the expression **il faut**, you can use an indirect object pronoun to indicate who has to do the action.

Il me faut mettre de l'argent de côté.	*I **must** put some money aside.*
Il te faut faire des économies.	*You **must** economize.*
Il nous faut payer les frais de la garderie.	*We **have to** pay the child-care costs.*

F. **Il vaut mieux porter...** À tour de rôle avec votre partenaire, dites ce qu'il vaudrait mieux porter dans les situations suivantes.

> **Modèle:** quand il pleut *(un parapluie/un pardessus)*
> *Quand il pleut, il vaut mieux prendre un parapluie.*

1. quand il pleut et il fait du vent *(un parapluie/un imperméable)*
2. quand on prend le déjeuner avec le patron *(un complet ou un tailleur/ un jogging)*
3. quand on a une interview *(un complet ou un tailleur/un jogging)*
4. quand on fait du ski *(un maillot de bain/un anorak)*
5. quand on fait du ski nautique *(un maillot de bain/un anorak)*
6. quand on fait la connaissance des parents de son (sa) petit(e) ami(e) *(un jean et des baskets/un pantalon et des chaussures)*
7. quand on dîne dans un restaurant chic *(un pantalon ou une jupe/un short)*
8. quand on va à la plage *(un maillot de bain/un pardessus ou un manteau)*
9. quand on porte une jupe *(des baskets sans chaussettes/un collant et des chaussures)*

G. **J'ai des responsabilités financières.** Dites à votre partenaire au moins huit responsabilités financières que vous avez. Vous pouvez utiliser la fiche de l'Exercice A ou de l'Exercice B du *1er Thème* de ce chapitre (pages 477–478) pour stimuler votre mémoire.

> **Modèles:** *Il me faut payer le loyer.*
> *Il est essentiel d'acheter mes livres de texte.*

H. **Ça coûte les yeux de la tête.** Dites à votre partenaire au moins cinq choses que vous voudriez faire ou avoir l'année prochaine. Puis, dites-lui les choses pour lesquelles il vous faudrait faire des économies.

> **Modèle:** *Je voudrais aller au Mont Blanc dans les Alpes pour faire du ski. Mais ça coûte les yeux de la tête. Il me faudrait faire des économies pour pouvoir payer le voyage.*

I. **Ce qu'il faut faire.** Donnez des conseils à votre partenaire pour améliorer l'organisation de son budget. Dites-lui au moins six phrases pour expliquer votre situation personnelle ou votre philosophie financière. Servez-vous de° la fiche suivante pour vous donner des idées.

Servez-vous de: *Make use of*

Modèle: *Pour avoir de l'argent à la fin du mois, il n'est pas nécessaire d'établir un budget strict, mais il ne faut pas gaspiller° votre argent.*

gaspiller: *to waste*

Pour...		
avoir de l'argent à la fin du mois	il vaudrait mieux	mettre de l'argent de côté
payer les cartes de crédit	il faut	(ne pas) payer les yeux de la tête pour...
payer le loyer	il n'est pas nécessaire de	faire attention au budget
aller au cinéma deux fois par mois	il ne faut pas	faire des économies
mettre les enfants dans la meilleure garderie de la ville		établir un budget strict
		dépenser l'argent soigneusement
		dépenser très peu pour les loisirs
payer les frais de scolarité		habiter chez les parents
payer la voiture et l'assurance		(ne pas) gaspiller de l'argent
mettre de l'argent de côté		organiser les éléments du budget
		avoir un(e) camarade de chambre
		chercher des prix intéressants
		dépenser une somme importante pour ...
		rembourser...
		demander de l'argent à...
		faire attention à...

NOTE CULTURELLE

Chaque année les Français dépensent 50 milliards de francs dans la vente par correspondance en France. Ce mode de distribution progresse lentement mais sûrement: 53% des foyers français ont acheté quelque chose sur catalogue en 1997 contre 50% en 1990. Autrefois, les ventes de vêtements étaient très importantes. Aujourd'hui ces ventes stagnent. C'est surtout grâce à des secteurs comme la micro-informatique que la VPC (vente par correspondance) séduit de nouveaux clients. Les deux sociétés qui dominent dans ce domaine sont **la Redoute** (28 milliards de francs) et **les Trois Suisses** (15 milliards de francs).

Réfléchissons: À votre avis: Est-ce que vous faites des achats par correspondance? Pourquoi ou pourquoi pas? Qu'est-ce que vous achetez par correspondance? Qu'est-ce que vous n'avez aucune intention d'acheter par correspondance? Pourquoi? Si vous faites des achats par correspondance, préférez-vous les faire par la poste ou sur l'Internet?

PRONONCIATION: La combinaison **gn**

In French, the combination **gn** is pronounced [ɲ]. It is similar to the sound in the English words *onion* or *canyon*.

Repeat the following words after your instructor.

Michel de Montaigne (1533–1592): philosophe moraliste; auteur des *Essais*

1. vigne
2. agneau
3. renseignement
4. caisse d'épargne
5. campagne
6. espagnol
7. soigneux
8. Montaigne°

À vous! With a partner, read the following sentences, being sure to pronounce the sound [ɲ] correctly:

1. La chaîne de montagnes qui séparent la France de l'Espagne s'appelle les Pyrénées.
2. Elle a gagné un magnétoscope à la loterie!
3. S'il vous plaît, signez sur la ligne en bas du contrat.
4. Est-ce que tu voudrais un filet mignon avec des oignons et des champignons?
5. Les vignobles de Bourgogne produisent du vin magnifique.
6. J'ai foulé mon poignet° en sortant de la baignoire.

fouler le poignet: *to sprain one's wrist*

POUR DÉVELOPPER VOS IDÉES

Thematic objective: To prioritize your expenses and spending goals

Présentation: Les objectifs financiers

À propos: Note that the dollar sign follows the amount in French, as in this French Canadian site alluding to Canadian dollars, 1500$.

épargne (f.): *saving (money)*

que tu veuilles: *whether you want*
un cheval: *horse*
inscris: *write, cognate of inscribe*
affiche: *display*
retiens: *garde*

a mis au point: *devised, developed*

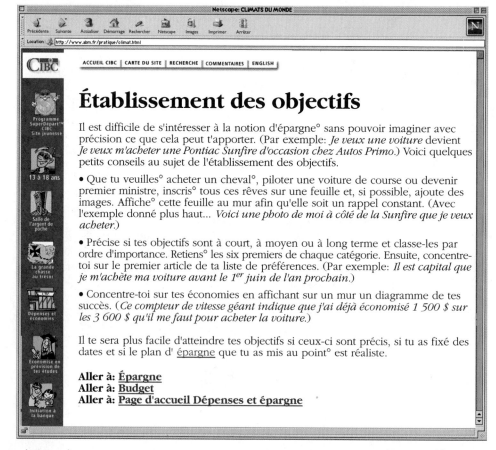

Établissement des objectifs

Il est difficile de s'intéresser à la notion d'épargne° sans pouvoir imaginer avec précision ce que cela peut t'apporter. (Par exemple: *Je veux une voiture* devient *Je veux m'acheter une Pontiac Sunfire d'occasion chez Autos Primo.*) Voici quelques petits conseils au sujet de l'établissement des objectifs.

• Que tu veuilles° acheter un cheval°, piloter une voiture de course ou devenir premier ministre, inscris° tous ces rêves sur une feuille et, si possible, ajoute des images. Affiche° cette feuille au mur afin qu'elle soit un rappel constant. (Avec l'exemple donné plus haut... *Voici une photo de moi à côté de la Sunfire que je veux acheter.*)

• Précise si tes objectifs sont à court, à moyen ou à long terme et classe-les par ordre d'importance. Retiens° les six premiers de chaque catégorie. Ensuite, concentre-toi sur le premier article de ta liste de préférences. (Par exemple: *Il est capital que je m'achète ma voiture avant le 1ᵉʳ juin de l'an prochain.*)

• Concentre-toi sur tes économies en affichant sur un mur un diagramme de tes succès. (*Ce compteur de vitesse géant indique que j'ai déjà économisé 1 500 $ sur les 3 600 $ qu'il me faut pour acheter la voiture.*)

Il te sera plus facile d'atteindre tes objectifs si ceux-ci sont précis, si tu as fixé des dates et si le plan d' épargne que tu as mis au point° est réaliste.

Aller à: Épargne
Aller à: Budget
Aller à: Page d'accueil Dépenses et épargne

POUR SAISIR L'ESSENTIEL: La lecture à la page 496 est tirée d'un site Internet qui propose des conseils et des services bancaires aux jeunes.

1. Résumez les idées principales de la lecture en trois phrases aussi brèves° que possible.

2. Comparez vos trois phrases avec celles d'un(e) partenaire. Travaillez ensemble pour les développer autant que possible.

3. Décidez ensemble quel conseil est le plus utile.

brève: *brief The masculine form is* **bref.**

J. On se fait des objectifs. Faites une liste de vos objectifs budgétaires dans plusieurs domaines. Vous pouvez consulter les **Suggestions** ainsi que le **Coup d'œil** pour vous donner des idées. Mentionnez au moins six objectifs.

Suggestions pour les objectifs

- m'acheter une voiture
- payer les cartes de crédit
- m'offrir un téléphone cellulaire
- faire un voyage en Europe
- acheter une bague de fiançailles

- offrir un téléviseur à mes parents
- déménager
- acheter une maison
- payer les études universitaires de mes enfants

- rénover mon appartement
- acheter de nouveaux vêtements
- m'abonner à un service Internet
- avoir un nouvel ordinateur
- mettre de l'argent de côté pour ma retraite

K. Combien de temps me faudra-t-il attendre? Catégorisez vos objectifs selon le temps qu'il vous faudra pour les atteindre. Rangez-les par ordre d'importance dans un tableau.

Objectifs à court terme	Objectifs à moyen terme	Objectifs à long terme
N° 1	N° 1	N° 1

L. Un de mes objectifs financiers. Écrivez un petit paragraphe sur un des objectifs de l'Exercice K. Précisez l'objectif, indiquez s'il est à court, à moyen ou à long terme, puis expliquez un peu son importance pour vous. Vous pouvez utiliser les exemples dans le **Coup d'œil** comme modèle.

Objective: To hypothesize decisions based on given situations

Un coup d'œil sur le thème

distributeur automatique de billets: *ATM machine*
gaspiller: *waste*
dépensière: *spendthrift, extravagant*

Je suis très consciencieuse en ce qui concerne mon budget. Je n'achète rien sans me demander si j'ai vraiment besoin de cet article. Je ne gaspille° pas mon argent. Après tout, il faut penser aux besoins de mes frères aussi.

Mais quelquefois je voudrais être moins disciplinée. Quelquefois je voudrais m'offrir un petit luxe, quelque chose de spécial pour me féliciter d'un succès au travail, ou quelque chose comme ça. Mais ma conscience est plus forte que mon sens du luxe. Peut-être que ça vaut mieux après tout.

Il me semble que je cherche un distributeur automatique de billets° cent fois par jour! Je suis un peu dépensière°, c'est vrai, mais pas gaspilleuse. Quand je vois quelque chose que je voudrais avoir, je me demande si j'ai assez d'argent pour l'acheter. Si je n'ai pas d'argent, je ne l'achète pas.

Mais je sais que je devrais être plus organisée en ce qui concerne mon budget. Ça m'aiderait à anticiper mes besoins... et si je planifiais mes dépenses, j'aurais un peu d'argent à la fin du mois. Peut-être que j'essaierai un jour.

À propos de la structure: In casual usage, **peut-être** is followed by **que** when it introduces a sentence (or clause). In more formal usage, invert the subject and verb.]

 ## Nos tendances budgétaires

Lequel des deux «autoportraits budgétaires» vous ressemble le plus? En lisant les descriptions, faites deux listes. Dans la première, copiez les expressions des deux autoportraits qui vous correspondent. Dans la deuxième, copiez les expressions qui ne correspondent pas à vos tendances budgétaires.

> **Modèle:**   *Je suis:*
> *consciencieuse*
>
> *Je ne suis pas:*
> *dépensière*

POUR DÉVELOPPER VOTRE FRANÇAIS

Structure: si + l'imparfait

OBSERVATIONS

—**Si** je **travaillais** sept jours sur sept, je **gagnerais** assez d'argent pour acheter une voiture.
*If I **worked** seven days a week, I **would earn** enough money to buy a car.*
—**Si** tu **achetais** une voiture, qui **payerait** l'assurance?
*If you **bought** a car, who **would pay** for the insurance?*
—Aucune idée. Voilà le problème. **Si** je **dépensais** mon argent pour acheter une voiture, je ne **pourrais** pas payer l'assurance.
*Not a clue. There's the problem. **If I were to spend** my money for a car, I **would** not **be able** to pay for the insurance.*

STRATÉGIES D'ANALYSE

1. What word do we use in French to introduce a hypothetical situation? What is its English equivalent?
2. What is the tense of the verb in the clause that expresses the hypothetical situation?
3. What is the tense of the verb in the result clause, the one that tells what would happen under the imagined circumstances?
4. Do you remember what tense we use in the result clause when the **si** (*if*) clause is in the present tense?

PRÉCISIONS

You have already used **si** (*if*) clauses in the *present* tense with a following result clause in the *future*.

> **Si** tu **achètes** les billets pour l'opéra, je **payerai** le dîner au restaurant.
> *If you (**will**) **buy** the opera tickets, I **will pay** for dinner at the restaurant.*

- To describe a hypothetical situation, use a clause introduced by **si** with a verb in the *imperfect* tense. To tell what would happen as a result of the hypothetical situation, use a clause with the verb in the *conditional*.

> **Si** j'**avais** beaucoup d'argent, je **ferais** un voyage en Chine.
> *If I **had** a lot of money, I **would take** a trip to China.*

> Si j'**étais** toi, je **mettrais** l'argent à la banque.
> *If I **were** you, I **would put** the money in the bank.*

A. **Moi, je ferais...** À tour de rôle avec votre partenaire, dites ce que vous feriez dans les situations suivantes.

> **Modèle:** trouver de l'argent dans la rue
> *le mettre dans la poche, l'apporter au commissariat de police, chercher la personne qui l'a perdu, mettre une petite annonce dans le journal,...*
>
> —*Si tu trouvais de l'argent dans la rue, que ferais-tu?*
> —*Moi, si je trouvais de l'argent dans la rue, je le mettrais dans la poche. Et toi?*
> —*Moi, je chercherais la personne qui l'a perdu.*

1. trouver un franc dans la rue
   le mettre dans la poche, l'apporter au commissariat de police, chercher la personne qui l'a perdu, mettre une petite annonce dans le journal,...

2. trouver cent dollars dans la rue
   les mettre dans la poche, les apporter au commissariat de police, chercher la personne qui les a perdus, mettre une petite annonce dans le journal,...

3. trouver dix mille dollars dans un W.-C. public
   les mettre dans la poche, les apporter au commissariat de police, chercher la personne qui les a perdus, mettre une petite annonce dans le journal,...

4. gagner de l'argent pendant les vacances
   acheter des vêtements, payer les cartes de crédit, le mettre à la banque,...

5. trouver un bon travail
   chercher un nouvel appartement, acheter une nouvelle voiture, habiter tout(e) seul(e),...

6. ne pas avoir de travail
   habiter chez les parents, vendre la voiture, demander de l'argent à... ,...

7. perdre cent dollars
   utiliser les cartes de crédit, aller à la banque, demander de l'argent à... ,...

B. **Ça dépend.** À tour de rôle avec votre partenaire, dites ce que vous feriez dans les situations suivantes si vous n'aviez pas d'assurance médicale. Choisissez parmi les **Actions possibles** indiquées à la page suivante.

> **Modèle:** —*Si tu n'avais pas d'assurance médicale et que tu te cassais le bras, qu'est-ce que tu ferais?*
> —*Si je n'avais pas d'assurance médicale et que je me cassais le bras, je me rendrais au service des urgences à l'hôpital.*

1. se casser le bras
2. avoir mal à la tête
3. se casser la jambe
4. avoir mal à la gorge
5. avoir une crise cardiaque
6. avoir mal au cœur
7. souffrir d'un mal de dos
8. avoir besoin d'une opération
9. avoir mal aux dents
10. être enceinte°
11. se fouler° le poignet°
12. avoir une pneumonie
13. être enrhumé(e)°

enceinte: *pregnant*

se fouler: *to sprain*
le poignet: *wrist*

être enrhumé(e): *to have a cold*

Actions possibles

... je choisirais mes propres médicaments.

... je me présenterais à la clinique de l'université.

... je consulterais un pharmacien.

... je prendrais rendez-vous chez le médecin.

... je demanderais au médecin de faire une consultation à domicile.

... je me rendrais au service des urgences à l'hôpital.

... je ferais un séjour à l'hôpital.

... j'aurais une opération pour corriger le problème.

... j'irais chez le dentiste.

... je resterais au lit.

... je prendrais deux aspirines et je me coucherais.

Si j'héritais d'une somme importante, j'irais au casino.

Moi, si j'héritais de beaucoup d'argent, je le mettrais à la caisse d'épargne°.

caisse d'épargne: *savings and loan association*

C. Si j'héritais d'une somme importante. Dites à votre partenaire que vous rêvez d'hériter de l'argent. Puis, dites-lui au moins quatre choses que vous feriez si vous héritiez d'une somme importante.

Modèle: *Je rêve d'hériter de l'argent. Si j'héritais d'une somme importante, j'irais en France cet été, j'offrirais des bijoux à ma mère, et...*

Si j'héritais d'une somme importante, je...

aller (à, en, au)...	
acheter	une voiture
	une maison
	des bijoux
	des vêtements
offrir... à...	un hôpital
	une université
	une bonne cause
	un membre de la famille
	des sans-abris

rembourser	un membre de la famille
	les cartes de crédit/mes dettes
	le gouvernement
	la banque
payer	les frais de scolarité
	la facture de téléphone
	le chauffage et l'électricité
	les consultations chez...
pouvoir	voyager...
	acheter...
	rembourser...
	payer...
	offrir...

 **D. Mais si ma famille recevait cet héritage...** Peut-être y a-t-il des membres de votre famille ou des ami(e)s qui ne sont pas d'accord avec vos idées pour dépenser l'argent. Dites à votre partenaire au moins quatre personnes qui dépenseraient une somme importante d'une manière différente de la vôtre.

Modèle: *Si mon frère héritait d'une somme importante, il mettrait tout l'argent à la caisse d'épargne.*

E. On est d'accord. Écoutez bien ce que dit votre partenaire au sujet des idées de ses ami(e)s et de sa famille. Choisissez la personne qui vous ressemble le plus. Expliquez ce que vous deux feriez avec une somme importante.

À propos de la structure: Note that the subject of the verb in "la personne qui vous ressemble" is "la personne."

Modèle: *Parmi les ami(e)s et les membres de la famille de mon partenaire, je ressemble le plus à son/sa... Si nous héritions d'une somme importante, nous achèterions une nouvelle maison.*

Note Culturelle

En France (comme partout dans le monde), des inégalités persistent en matière de rémunérations entre hommes et femmes, malgré de nombreuses actions législatives. En France, l'écart° de salaires varie entre 20% et 30%.

Pourquoi est-ce que cet écart persiste? C'est compliqué à expliquer. D'abord, les femmes n'occupent pas les mêmes emplois que les hommes. Elles ne sont pas concentrées dans les mêmes secteurs d'activités, comme les professions libérales. Les femmes sont concentrées dans les secteurs les moins rémunérateurs, notamment le commerce de détail°, l'hôtellerie-restauration, la santé et le secteur de la petite enfance.

De plus, en général, plus le degré de responsabilité et d'autorité augmente, moins l'on trouve de femmes. Et plus on monte dans la hiérarchie de n'importe quelle catégorie professionnelle, plus les écarts de salaire sont élevés. Il est même de trois ou quatre fois plus élevé entre employé(e)s et cadres: les hommes employés gagnent 8% de plus que les femmes employées, mais les hommes cadres gagnent de 20% à 35% de plus que les femmes cadres.

l'écart (m.): *discrepancy* / le commerce de détail: *retail sales*

Salaires féminins non agricoles comparés aux salaires masculins (en %)

Australie	90.8%
France	81
États-Unis	75
Belgique	74.5
Suisse	67.6
Luxembourg	65.2
Canada	63

Réfléchissons: Êtes-vous surpris(e) que l'écart entre le salaire des hommes et celui des femmes soit plus prononcé aux États-Unis qu'en France? Pouvez-vous suggérer des raisons pour expliquer cette situation? Pourquoi est-ce que cet écart est même plus élevé au Canada? Pensez-vous que la situation s'améliorera à long terme, à court terme ou jamais?

PRONONCIATION: Les lettres **g** et **j**

While in French the pronunciation of the letters **j** and (soft) **g** is similar to that of their English counterparts ("zh"), a somewhat softer sound is produced.

Repeat the following pairs of words after your instructor. Do you hear the difference between the English and French pronunciation of **g** and **j**?

1.	age	âge
2.	generate	générer
3.	giraffe	girafe
4.	juice	jus
5.	major	majeur

> Remember that **g** is pronounced "soft" when followed by the vowels **e** or **i** (**gestion, agitation**) and "hard" when followed by **a**, **o**, or **u** (**gâteau, égoïste, aigu**).

À vous! With a partner, read the following sentences, being sure to pronounce **g** and **j** correctly. Remember that **g** is "soft" only when followed by **e** or **i**.

1. Je ne joue plus de la guitare.
2. Aujourd'hui, il gèle et il fait nuageux.
3. Ce gigot d'agneau a un mauvais goût.
4. Quand j'ai déménagé, j'ai cassé l'étagère.
5. Je me suis fait un budget pour acheter une bague de fiançailles.
6. J'ai versé du jus d'orange sur ma nouvelle jupe.

«Une priorité dans mon budget mensuel est de faire coiffer ma petite Fifi.»

POUR DÉVELOPPER VOS IDÉES

Thematic objective: To examine views of personal tendencies in relation to budgeting and spending

Présentation: L'argent et la personnalité

POUR SAISIR L'ESSENTIEL: Lisez les extraits tirés d'un site bancaire sur l'Internet.

1. Lesquels de ces commentaires correspondent le mieux—ou le moins bien—à vos attitudes envers l'argent et les budgets? Indiquez-en au moins deux.
2. Comment est-ce que ces attitudes se manifestent dans vos actions, votre situation financière, vos objectifs personnels? Écrivez une phrase d'explication pour chaque commentaire que vous notez.

> **Modèle:** *Le dixième commentaire correspond bien à mon style de vie parce que j'adore m'acheter de nouveaux vêtements et offrir des cadeaux. Mais le premier commentaire ne correspond pas du tout à mon style de vie parce que je n'ai jamais préparé de budget. Le troisième correspond un peu à ma situation parce que j'ai un compte d'épargne où je mets presque 10% de mon revenu chaque mois.*

Commentaires sur l'argent et les budgets

1. Préparer un budget et le respecter sont les bases d'une bonne planification financière. Acquise° jeune, cette bonne habitude vous rapportera° toute votre vie.
2. C'est lundi matin, tu n'as pas un sou. Si tu avais fait des économies, il te resterait quelque chose de ton argent de poche pour te permettre de tenir° le reste de la semaine.
3. Une bonne gestion financière doit permettre de trouver le juste équilibre entre la jouissance° de la vie et la planification de l'avenir.
4. La vie coûte cher.
5. Le magasinage° intelligent pourrait même te permettre d'épargner beaucoup d'argent. Par exemple, le même pantalon peut être vendu dans plusieurs magasins à différents prix.
6. [Un budget t'aidera] à distinguer tes priorités pour tes dépenses, ce que tu peux te permettre tout de suite, ce que tu dois remettre° à plus tard et, enfin, quand tu vas parvenir° à tout te payer.
7. … Par-dessus tout°, avant de chercher à obtenir° le [meilleur prix possible pour un produit], tu dois te demander si tu en as vraiment besoin.
8. Il n'est jamais trop tôt pour commencer à cotiser° tous les ans à [une caisse de retraite] pour assurer la liberté et l'indépendance financières [… à] l'âge de la retraite.
9. N'oublie pas que la valeur d'un produit ne doit pas dépasser la somme que tu es prêt à payer!
10. N'oubliez pas que la vie est courte et que le plaisir de se gâter° ou de gâter les autres est aussi une idée importante.

acquise: *acquired*
rapporter: *have financial rewards*

tenir: *hold on, tide you over*

la jouissance: *enjoyment*

le magasinage: *shopping (in Québec)*

remettre: *postpone*
parvenir: *arriver, pouvoir*

par-dessus tout: *above all*
obtenir: *obtain*

cotiser: *pay into*

gâter: *pamper*

F. **Les dépenses et les traits de personnalité.** Décrivez votre personnalité en termes de vos habitudes budgétaires. Êtes-vous économe, pratique, généreux(-se), intelligent(e), frivole, juste, soigneux(-se), extrême, modéré(e), avare, etc.? (Vous pouvez chercher d'autres expressions aux pages 486 et 513.) Puis indiquez le domaine de votre vie où ces aspects de votre caractère sont particulièrement évidents. Écrivez ces informations dans un paragraphe.

> **Modèle:** *Si je devais décrire ma personnalité en termes de mes habitudes budgétaires, je dirais que je suis plutôt économe et pratique, mais pas strict. Cette tendance est surtout évidente au supermarché. Je compare les prix et les quantités pour trouver les produits les moins chers. En général, je n'hésite pas à remettre un achat ou à aller dans un autre magasin pour trouver de meilleurs prix. Quand même°, j'apprécie la qualité, et je paie ce qu'il faut payer pour bien manger.*

Quand même: *Anyway*

G. **Les habitudes financières et les relations personnelles.** Pensez aux tendances financières que vous aimeriez—ou n'aimeriez pas—trouver chez les gens qui font partie de votre vie. Choisissez trois personnes de la liste suivante et indiquez un trait que vous aimeriez trouver dans sa «personnalité financière» et un autre que vous n'aimeriez pas y trouver. Pour chaque trait, écrivez une phrase où vous expliquez pourquoi vous le trouvez bon ou mauvais pour les rapports aux finances.

> **Modèle:** *Les camarades de chambre devraient être responsables. S'ils n'étaient pas responsables, ils ne paieraient pas leur part des factures. Ils ne devraient pas être trop distraits, parce que s'ils étaient trop distraits, ils ne feraient jamais attention aux dépenses.*

- un(e) petit(e) ami(e)
- un(e) camarade de chambre
- les collègues
- un(e) comptable
- le maire de votre ville

- un(e) époux/épouse
- les parents
- un employeur
- un(e) employé(e)
- ??? autres idées

H. **Comparaison d'opinions.** Comparez vos idées de l'Exercice G avec celles de votre partenaire. Quels sont les points sur lesquels vous vous ressemblez dans votre attitude envers l'argent et les relations personnelles? Sur quels points avez-vous des perspectives différentes?

I. **Autoportrait budgétaire.** Écrivez deux paragraphes sur votre «personnalité financière». Dans le premier, décrivez vos tendances actuelles. (Ce paragraphe peut être le même que vous avez écrit pour l'Exercice F.) Dans le deuxième, décrivez les changements que vous aimeriez faire, en expliquant comment ils se manifesteraient dans votre vie. Vous pouvez utiliser les descriptions dans le **Coup d'œil** du *3ᵉ Thème* à la page 498 pour vous inspirer.

DÉCOUVERTE

In the **Découverte** section in the *1ᵉʳ Thème,* you looked at how tables help people access data. But tables are not the only way to provide graphic representation of data, and each type of graphic has its own strengths. Whereas tables do well for complex lists, pie charts more clearly show the "part-whole" relationship among percentages.

Consider the chart showing the categories of goods and services and percentages of income spent in the United States during the mid-1990s. The advantages of a pie chart are evident. The problem is deciding how to size the wedges easily. The following reading offers a few rules of thumb for drawing pie charts off the cuff. Read the guidelines, then make a pie chart for the French percentages presented on pages 484–485.

Pourcentages des dépenses dans les ménages aux États-Unis*

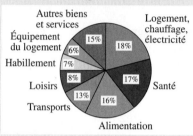

*SOURCE: U.S. BUREAU OF THE CENSUS.

---

un diagramme circulaire sectorisé: *pie chart*

une horloge: *clock*

Les diagrammes circulaires sectorisés°

Ces diagrammes sont assez faciles à fabriquer. Regardons quelques idées de base.

Commencez par faire un cercle sur une feuille de papier. Puis imaginez que le cercle est la face d'une horloge°.

Pour représenter la moitié (50%), tracez une ligne de 12h00 à 6h00.

Tracez encore une ligne de 9h00 jusqu'au centre pour indiquer les quarts (25%).

Pour diviser le cercle en tiers (33%), faites un Y avec des lignes du centre à 10h00, à 2h00 et à 6h00.

Si vous voulez représenter des dixièmes, vous pouvez compter «six minutes» pout chaque dixième. Ainsi 20% égale «douze minutes» sur l'horloge.

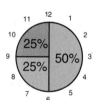

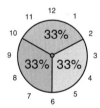

Maintenant, utilisez les données dans le tableau aux pages 484–485 pour faire un diagramme circulaire sectorisé. Votre diagramme va ressembler un peu au graphique «Pourcentages des dépenses dans les ménages aux États-Unis».

La consommation des ménages français au milieu des années 90 en pourcentages des revenus annuels

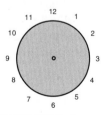

ÉCOUTONS: De nouvelles situations financières

Moi, je m'appelle Jean-Jacques Charpentier et je me prépare à devenir avocat.

Bonjour, je suis Marie-Louise Tremblay et je travaille dans une grande banque internationale au centre-ville.

Je me présente: Moi, je suis Marc Dufour, et voilà ma charmante épouse Christiane. Nous sommes mariés depuis 35 ans et les enfants sont finalement grands.

Vous allez écouter trois monologues où ces personnes discutent de nouveaux événements dans leur vie qui auront une influence importante sur leur budget. Écoutez les monologues au moins deux fois, en cherchant chaque fois à identifier des détails différents.

A. **On identifie les dépenses.** La première fois que vous écoutez les trois monologues, identifiez les sortes de dépenses (au moins trois pour chaque personne) qui seront influencées par le changement dans leur vie. Notez que la même sorte de dépense peut s'appliquer à plus d'une personne.

La personne ⇨ Les dépenses qui changeront ⇩	Jean-Jacques	Marie-Louise	M. et Mme Dufour
éducation			
alimentation			
logement			
santé			
habillement			
loisirs			
transport			
retraite			

B. **On identifie comment les budgets seront affectés.** Écoutez encore les trois monologues. Cette fois-ci, identifiez au moins deux effets que chaque personne anticipe à cause de sa nouvelle situation financière.

How new budget will be affected ⇩	Jean-Jacques	Marie-Louise	M. et Mme Dufour
will be taking on new expenses			
will need to cut expenses			
will be getting more income			
will be getting less income			
plan(s) to build savings			

C. **On réfléchit à notre budget personnel.** Considérez les changements qui se présenteront dans votre vie lorsque vous aurez votre diplôme universitaire. Pour quels types de dépenses pouvez-vous anticiper des changements? Indiquez-les dans la partie à gauche de la fiche. Ensuite, dans la partie à droite de la fiche, identifiez au moins deux effets que vous anticipez à cause de votre nouvelle situation financière.

Les dépenses qui changeront dès que j'aurai mon diplôme		Quelques effets sur mon budget	
frais de scolarité		J'aurai des dépenses supplémentaires.	
alimentation		J'aurai moins de dépenses.	
logement		J'aurai plus de revenus.	
santé		J'aurai moins de revenus.	
habillement		Il me faudra faire plus d'économies pour payer mes dettes.	
loisirs		Je pourrai faire plus d'économies pour l'avenir.	
transport		Je pourrai me permettre quelques luxes.	
(autre...)		Je pourrai réduire mes dettes.	
(autre...)		Je pourrai accepter plus de responsabilités financières.	

ÉLABORATION DE PERSPECTIVE

In the **Découverte** sections, you looked at how tables and pie charts—each in its way—give clarity and impact to the presentation of data. Bar graphs provide yet another focus, that of contrasting similar data for two or more entities. The particular strength of this sort of display is the visual impact it gives to the contrast.

The following pie charts and bar graph use the same percentages you worked with in the pie charts for the *3ᵉ Thème*.

Les données pour les Français   **Les données pour les Américains**

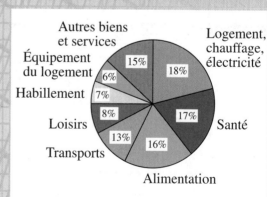

Notice how much easier it is to compare these data when they are displayed in a bar graph.

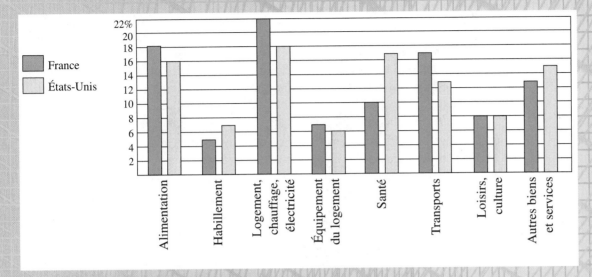

Though this chart demonstrates the mechanics of the method, these data—because they lack significant contrast—fail to show the impact a bar graph can deliver.

Use the data in the chart below comparing the rate of savings in several different countries to complete the bar graph. Notice how the spread in the numbers shows more dramatically in your graph.

Taux d'épargne de certains pays

Pays	Taux d'épargne
États-Unis	9,6%
Japon	17,9%
France	10,3%
Allemagne	11,9%
Royaume-Uni	6,2%

Royaume-Uni: *United Kingdom*

Source: État de la France, 1992

Use the data from the table to complete the bar graph.

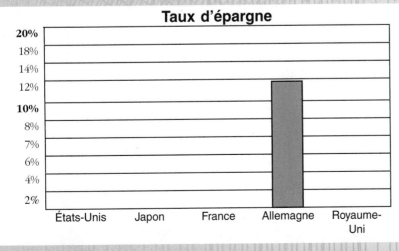

1. Examine the contrasts displayed in your bar graph and consider differences that the rates of savings might reflect in the respective cultures. Bear in mind that the inferences that you draw from these limited data can be only tentative.

2. With your initial inferences in mind, look back at the data that you worked with in the table on pages 484–485 and in the **Découvertes** sections (pages 487 and 506). How might this additional information affect your preliminary conclusions? Write complete sentences to articulate your perceptions so that you can communicate them clearly in class discussion. Remember to include references to the data to support your assertions.

3. Discuss your insights with your classmates, taking notes on their interpretations of the information.

4. Write a paragraph with the following components:
   * a thesis statement, summarizing your views
   * several sentences in which you offer detailed support for your views (Cite data from this chapter, insights gained from discussions, as well as your general knowledge.)
   * a conclusion, in which you tell what additional information you would like to have on the subject.

INTÉGRATION

subvention: *grant*

Situation: Imaginez que votre université a reçu une subvention° du gouvernement français. C'est pour faire venir un professeur expert en culture française contemporaine pour un stage de six mois. À part les billets d'avion, la subvention paiera 400 dollars par mois pour contribuer aux frais de subsistance° du professeur en visite. C'est à l'université de payer tout ce qui reste.

frais (m.) de subsistance: *living expenses*

Mission: Vous aurez la responsabilité de préparer un budget détaillé pour les frais de subsistance anticipés. Votre rapport servira à déterminer cet aspect du coût du projet pour l'université.

Démarche: Votre équipe préparera un budget et remettra ses recommandations au président de l'université qui l'enverra au bureau du Ministre de la Culture à Paris (en français, bien sûr). Votre budget sera organisé en quatre catégories de dépenses: l'hébergement (logement), le transport, l'alimentation et les dépenses personnelles.

Travaillez en groupes de trois ou quatre pour préparer votre projet.

Étape A. Déterminez trois niveaux de confort pour les frais de subsistance dans chaque catégorie, selon le modèle. Pour les dépenses personnelles, indiquez seulement une somme d'argent à fournir.

	Étape A	Étape B	Étape A	Étape B	Étape A	Étape B
	Qualité de luxe	Montant par mois (niveau luxe)	Qualité moyenne	Montant par mois (niveau moyen)	Qualité médiocre	Montant par mois (niveau médiocre)
Modèle: *Hébergement*	*L'hôtel Worthington*	$3.000	*l'immeuble Quail Run*	$600	YMCA	$400
Hébergement		$		$		$
Transport		$		$		$
Alimentation		$		$		$
Dépenses personnelles	Généreux	$	Raisonnable	$	Modeste	$
Étape C: Total		$		$		$

Étape B. Indiquez le montant prévu par mois (en dollars américains) pour les trois différents niveaux de confort dans chaque catégorie de frais.

Étape C. Calculez la totalité des frais par mois pour chaque niveau de confort.

Étape D. Supposez que l'université accepte de payer la somme moyenne (totalité de la qualité moyenne), après les $400 par mois de subvention. Étant donné cette somme, établissez le budget que vous recommandez. Vous pouvez varier les niveaux de confort dans les catégories pour vous permettre plus de possibilités (par exemple, pour ajouter des excursions aux dépenses personnelles).

	Recommandations (descriptions spécifiques)	Montant par mois
Hébergement		$
Transport		$
Alimentation		$
Dépenses personnelles		$
Total par mois		$
Montant payé par la subvention		−$ 400
Ce que votre université devra payer		$

LEXIQUE DE BASE

Catégories de dépenses

l'alimentation (f.)	food
l'habillement (m.)	clothing
le logement	housing
l'équipement (m.) du logement	household furnishings
les frais (m.) de scolarité	education expenses, tuition
les frais de crèche/garderie	infant-/child-care expenses
les impôts (m.)	taxes
les assurances (f.)	insurance
les autres biens et services (m.)	other goods and services

Dépenses ménagères

le loyer	rent	l'entretien (m.)	maintenance, upkeep
la facture de téléphone	telephone bill	le gaz	gas
le chauffage	heating	l'essence (f.)	gasoline
l'électricité (f.)	electricity		

Dépôts monétaires

un compte (chèque)	checking account	un site bancaire	banking site (on the Internet)
une banque	bank	(sur l'Internet)	
une caisse d'épargne	savings and loan association		
un héritage	inheritance		
un distributeur automatique de billets	ATM (automatic teller machine)		

Actions budgétaires

améliorer	to improve		
coûter	to cost	compter ses sous	to count one's pennies
les yeux de la tête	. . . an arm and a leg		
dépenser	to spend	économiser sou à sou	to scrimp and save
économiser	to save money on, to pay less for	laisser s'évaporer	to let go up in smoke
gaspiller	to waste		
mettre de côté	to put aside, to save		
louer	to rent		
offrir	to offer, to give		
se passer de	to do without		
payer	to pay (for)		
rembourser	to pay back		
se permettre	to afford, to allow oneself		
se payer	to reward oneself		
avoir les moyens de	to have the means to, to be able to		
faire un budget	to set up a budget		
dépasser son budget	to go beyond one's budget		

Pour décrire les dépenses

un prix intéressant	a good price	c'est un luxe	it is a luxury
une somme importante	a substantial amount	être en solde	to be on sale
abordable	affordable	un prix compétitif	a competitive price
cher (chère)	expensive	coûteux(-euse)	costly
bon marché	inexpensive, a good buy	dispendieux(-ieuse)	expensive

Pour décrire les habitudes budgétaires

économe	economical	frivole	frivolous
pratique	practical	juste	fair
généreux(-euse)	generous	soigneux(-euse)	careful
avare	miserly	modéré(e)	moderate
raisonnable	reasonable	gaspilleux(-euse)	wasteful
être fauché(e)	to be broke	extrême	extreme
		dépensier(-ère)	spendthrift
		ne pas avoir un sou	to be completely broke
		ne pas avoir de sou	not to have any money
		être sans le sou	to be penniless
		être près de ses sous	to be miserly, stingy
		(une chose) de quatre sous	(a thing) of little value
		Un sou est un sou.	A penny is a penny.
		C'est une affaire de gros sous.	There is big money involved.

Des vêtements

un complet, un costume	man's suit	un anorak	ski jacket
une veste	sport coat, suit coat, blazer	un jogging	jogging suit
un gilet	vest, light knit top	un short	shorts
un pantalon	pair of pants	des bottes (f.)	boots
un jean	jeans	des gants (m.)	gloves
une cravate	tie	un foulard, une écharpe	scarf
une chemise	shirt	des sous-vêtements (m.)	underwear
un tee-shirt	T-shirt	un collant	pantyhose
des chaussures (f.)	shoes	un pardessus	man's overcoat
des baskets (m.)	running/basketball shoes	un manteau	woman's overcoat
des chaussettes (f.)	socks	une bague	ring
une robe	dress	une alliance	wedding ring
un chapeau	hat	une bague de fiançailles	engagement ring
une casquette	cap	des bijoux (m.)	jewelry
un chemisier	blouse, woman's shirt	des boucles d'oreille (f.)	earrings
une ceinture	belt	une chemise de nuit	nightshirt/gown
une jupe	skirt	un col	collar
un pull(over)	pullover sweater	un collier	necklace
un imperméable	raincoat	un col roulé	turtleneck
un parapluie	umbrella	une combinaison	underwear, slip; outerwear, jumpsuit
un maillot de bain	swimsuit		
un tailleur	woman's suit	un pyjama	pajamas
		un slip	panties, briefs
		un soutien-gorge	bra

à manches courtes	short-sleeved
à manches longues	long-sleeved
sans manches	sleeveless
en coton	cotton
en laine	wool
en cachemire	cashmere
en soie	silk
en cuir	leather
en or	gold
en argent	silver
rayé(e)	striped
imprimé(e)	print
uni(e)	solid-colored
à fleurs	floral
écossais(e)	plaid

Pour parler des dépenses médicales

une assurance médicale	medical insurance
médicaments (m.)	medication, medicines
se présenter à la clinique de l'université	to go to the university infirmary
demander conseil à un pharmacien	to request advice from the pharmacist
prendre rendez-vous chez le médecin	to make an appointment at the doctor's
se rendre au service des urgences de l'hôpital	to go to the emergency room of the hospital
faire un séjour à l'hôpital	to stay in the hospital
faire une crise cardiaque	to have a heart attack
être enceinte	to be pregnant
aller chez le dentiste	to go to the dentist
les frais de santé	health cost

demander au médecin de faire une consultation à domicile	to ask the doctor to make a house call
se faire opérer pour corriger le problème	to have surgery to correct a problem
faire une crise de nerfs	to become hysterical
faire une dépression	to have a nervous breakdown
trouver un remède contre...	to find a cure for . . .
le cancer	cancer
le SIDA	AIDS

À LA DÉCOUVERTE DU MONDE FRANCOPHONE

Communicative Objectives

- To express necessary conditions for comfort while traveling
- To express preferences and recommendations for travel
- To discuss sites of historical, artistic, and cultural significance in Paris

Thematic Objectives

- ✓ To evaluate the attractions of major cities in terms of the quality of life they offer tourists and residents
- ✓ To gain insight into heritage and culture through sightseeing experiences
- ✓ To identify the historical processes that influence the construction of landmarks in a city

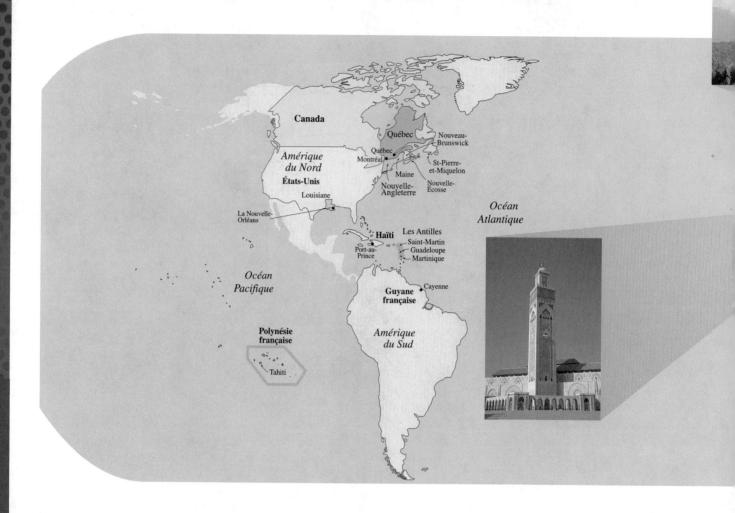

La mise en scène

As a student of French, you now have many doors open to you, not only in France but all over the French-speaking world. In *Chapitre 12* you will evaluate the attractions of major francophone cities, both in France and beyond, in terms of the quality of life they offer tourists and residents. You will also examine some of the insights into heritage and culture to be gained through sightseeing experiences. The video segment focuses on some of the rich historical, cultural, and geographical range of **la francophonie** beyond France.

You will see some scenes from three vastly different francophone sites in the world: Switzerland, the small country (principality) of Monaco, and Morocco. As you watch the scenes, you will be asked to make observations. They will help you anticipate some phrases that you will learn for talking about the geography and cultural heritage of the locations.

A. On fait la préparation. Before watching the video, examine the three photographs of well-known sites in Switzerland, Monaco, and Morocco. Then

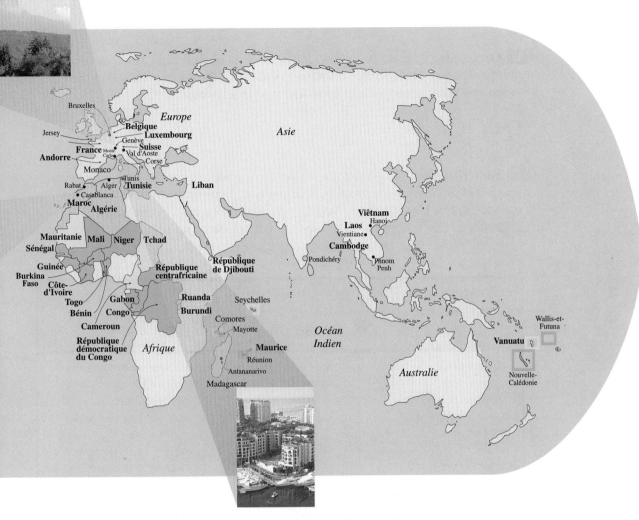

identify the features in the following list that you would associate with each of the three sites. Next to each item, write *S* for Switzerland, *M* for Monaco, and/or *A* for North Africa, where Morocco is located. Remember, these are just your impressions of these places *before* you start to study them. Each item can be associated with more than one of the three sites.

_____ 1. old-world architecture
_____ 2. arabesque architecture
_____ 3. chrome and glass architecture
_____ 4. snowy, winter weather
_____ 5. hot, dry weather
_____ 6. waterfront
_____ 7. desert terrain
_____ 8. mountainous terrain
_____ 9. international commerce

_____ 10. international car rallies
_____ 11. multicultural population
_____ 12. exotic settings
_____ 13. cosmopolitan lifestyle
_____ 14. fountains as public art
_____ 15. formal parks and gardens
_____ 16. open-air markets
_____ 17. snake charmers
_____ 18. ethnic costumes

B. On anticipe le vocabulaire. The first time you watch the video segment, focus on the visual elements. You will be asked to identify descriptive elements from a list on the screen that will help you anticipate the French you will hear on your second viewing.

Les paroles et le sens

C. On écoute. As you view the video segment a second time, listen for and identify the key phrases that are used to tell about the places you see in the video and other sites you will learn about in this chapter.

On y réfléchit

D. Réfléchissons. Now think back over the sights you saw and the expressions you heard to describe geographic, economic, and cultural features of the francophone cities. How do they compare with your own city? From the list of expressions that follow, check (✓) each one that you could use to describe your own city (either your hometown or where you live now).

Situation géographique	Situation géographique/ culturelle	Situation culturelle
la capitale de l'état ou du pays un paysage montagneux à la frontière entre deux états ou pays une ville au bord d'un lac dans un décor naturel magnifique plus de 100.000 habitants moins de 100.000 habitants une ville au bord d'un fleuve	une population multi- culturelle une société bilingue	fait une contribution spéci- fique à la culture nationale des parcs célèbres l'œuvre d'un architecte renommé un héritage historique célébrité historique née dans notre ville une statue/un monument en l'honneur d'un citoyen important

Situation culturelle/économique	Situation économique
une diversité d'activités culturelles une université un centre touristique une ville animée jour et nuit de l'artisanat régional une renommée mondiale une équipe sportive renommée une diversité d'activités sportives des marchés aux puces très appréciés	siège d'un commerce respecté une économie stable un centre de services médicaux toutes sortes de marchés un grand stade des produits régionaux un centre bancaire et commercial beaucoup de sociétés internationales siège d'un organisme important

DÉCOUVERTE

To know a place (*connaître*) and to know facts about it (*savoir*) are two perspectives of the same information. The first form of "knowing" has more to do with mental images; the second has more to do with data. But both are important when you need to tell someone about it. These are the concepts you will use in the **Découverte** sections of this chapter.

À propos de la structure: Remember that facts are data; impressions are mental images. When pressed to justify our impressions, we usually support them with facts. For example, "I'll bet Guadeloupe is a great place to spend a vacation" is an impression. The speaker has a mental image of having fun in Guadeloupe. The impression can be justified by listing the sites and activities available to tourists.

1. Which one of the cities presented in the **Ouverture** would you most like to visit: Genève, Lausanne, Monte-Carlo, Marrakech, or Casablanca?

2. Make a list of the most interesting details given in the presentation for the city you selected. Identify each detail as either a fact or an impression.

3. What else do you know about this city? Make an additional list of facts and impressions based on your previous knowledge of the place.

4. Categorize the information in your lists according to whether it relates to (a) the size and location of the city, (b) the economy, or (c) the culture. Note that some information may fall into more than one category.

5. Use the following chart to create a profile of the city. (You do not need to include information for every category.)

6. Working in a group with other students who have profiled the same city, pool your knowledge of the place. Then together write a one- or two-paragraph description of the city, illustrating your key points with information from your profiles.

Categories of information	A profile of: _____
Geography Country: Terrain: Climate: Physical size: Approximate population: (other) ???	
Economy Technology: Agriculture: Industry: Tourism: Crafts: (other) ???	
Culture Ethnic heritages: Religions: Costumes: Customs: Holidays: Heroes: Place names that commemorate people or events: (other) ???	

1ᴱᴿ THÈME: Les grands centres urbains

Objective: To express necessary conditions for comfort while traveling

PRÉSENTATION: Un coup d'œil sur le thème

La capitale de la Suisse est Berne. Mais quand on pense à ce pays, on pense surtout à Genève. Située au bord du lac Léman, dans l'extrême sud-ouest de la Suisse, Genève est aujourd'hui une ville internationale. Des 400.000 gens qui habitent ses environs, plus de 40% sont étrangers°. Pourquoi viennent-ils à Genève? Voici les raisons mentionnées dans les informations distribuées par l'administration municipale de la ville.

un étranger: personne d'un autre pays

- Genève est caractérisée par le dynamisme et l'ouverture d'esprit°.
- Elle a un énorme pouvoir d'intégration. C'est une ville où les étrangers se sentent vite chez eux.
- La qualité de vie est excellente. Les Genevois ont tenu à préserver leur cadre de vie°. Contrairement à quelques autres villes internationales, cette communauté est restée à taille humaine°.

une ouverture d'esprit: tendance à accepter de nouvelles idées

Genève, ville internationale, au bord du lac Léman

un cadre de vie: espace où on habite, environnement personnel
la taille humaine: *human scale*

- Une grande proximité d'équipements sportifs et de centres artistiques favorise l'harmonie des activités professionnelles, sociales et culturelles.
- Les Genevois ont à leur disposition un dense réseau° de transports publics. Les enfants y sont autonomes et en toute sécurité.

un réseau: *network*

Ce que j'apprécie surtout dans les grandes villes

Faites deux listes basées sur les qualités mentionnées dans la lecture. Dans la première, mettez les qualités que vous trouvez assez importantes. Dans la seconde, mettez celles qui ne vous intéressent pas beaucoup.

Les trois qualités les plus importantes	Les deux qualités les moins importantes

NOTE CULTURELLE

1864: La première Convention de Genève est adoptée: la *Croix rouge sur fond blanc* est reconnue comme signe distinctif des services de santé des forces armées.

1982: La *Fédération internationale des Sociétés de la* *Croix-Rouge et du Croissant-Rouge* adopte comme emblème la croix et le croissant rouge sur fond blanc.

Les emblèmes de la *Croix-Rouge* ou du *Croissant-Rouge* sont la base de toute activité humanitaire: ils doivent protéger les victimes et ceux qui leur portent secours.

L'emblème symbole... de Protection... de l'Appartenance au mouvement... d'Humanité, d'Impartialité, de Neutralité, d'Indépendance, de Bénévolat, d'Unité et d'Universalité.

POUR DÉVELOPPER VOTRE FRANÇAIS

Structure: Le présent du subjonctif

OBSERVATIONS

—Est-ce que tu travailles cet été?

—Non, pas cet été. Je voudrais parler mieux le français. Il vaut mieux **que je passe** les trois mois de vacances dans un pays francophone.

—C'est parce qu'il faut **que tu réussisses** à l'examen oral en français pour obtenir ton diplôme?

—Oui. Et mon professeur préfère **que chaque candidat** au certificat d'études internationales **se rende** à l'examen avant sa dernière année d'études. Pour moi, l'examen sera en septembre.

—Pour moi aussi. Vaut-il mieux **que nous allions** ensemble en France?

—Toi et tes amis, vous êtes riches. Il n'est pas nécessaire **que vous cherchiez** un voyage bon marché, comme moi. Je pense aller à Montréal, au Canada.

—C'est une bonne idée. Je voudrais y aller avec toi, et il vaut mieux **que les autres** nous **accompagnent.**

Are you working this summer?

No, not this summer. I would like to speak French better. It would be better for me to spend the three months of vacation in a French-speaking country.

Is it because you have to pass the oral exam in French to earn your degree?

Yes. And my professor prefers that each candidate for a certificate in international studies sit for the exam before his/her last year of courses. For me, the exam will be in September.

For me too. Would it be better for us to go together to France?

You and your friends are rich. It isn't necessary for you to look for an inexpensive trip, like me. I am thinking about going to Montreal, Canada.

That's a good idea. I think I'll go there with you, and it would be better for the others to accompany us.

1. Each sentence containing words in boldface is composed of two clauses. Can you find the end of the first clause (and thus the beginning of the second clause) in each of these sentences?
2. What word introduces each of the second clauses?
3. Using the verbs in boldface, can you determine the set of endings for the new verb forms?

    je -_____   nous -_____

    tu -_____   vous -_____

    il/elle/on -_____   ils/elles -_____

4. Look at the verbs used in the first clause of each sentence that call for the use of the new verb form in the second clause. What kind of attitude or opinion is expressed in those first clauses?

PRÉCISIONS

You have been using verbs in the indicative mood to tell what happens. Another verb mode, **the subjunctive mood,** allows you to express **attitudes** or **opinions** about what is happening or about to happen.

- The **subjunctive mood** is used in the clause of a sentence that *follows* the first clause expressing an attitude or opinion. The two clauses are connected by **que.**

    Il faut **que nous parlions** avec Charles avant l'arrivée du vol.
    We have to talk with Charles before the flight gets in.

    Il vaut mieux **que nous achetions** les billets à la gare.
    It would be better for us to buy the tickets at the train station.

- In French, the expression of necessity in the first clause is followed by a verb in the subjunctive in the second clause. The following expressions are used to express the notion of necessity:

il faut que	*one has to, one must*
il vaut mieux que	*it would be better to*
il est nécessaire que	*it's necessary to*
il est préférable que	*it's preferable to*
il est important que	*it's important to*
il est essentiel que	*it's essential to*
il est indispensable que	*it's indispensable to*

- You have already used these impersonal expressions followed by an *infinitive* to show obligation or necessity of a general nature.

    Que **faut-il** faire pour organiser un voyage?
    *What **must** be done to organize a trip?*

Il **faut** choisir une destination, chercher un moyen de transport et trouver de l'argent et du temps. **Il est important** aussi d'étudier des brochures ou d'autres informations. Et **il est indispensable** de choisir un compagnon convenable.
*It **is necessary** to choose a destination, to look for a means of transportation, and to find money and time. It's also **important** to study brochures or other information. And it **is indispensable** to select a suitable companion.*

- Using these expressions followed by a clause in the subjunctive allows you to express obligation or necessity for specific persons.

  Il faut **que nous visitions** tous les musées.
  We must visit all the museums. (or)
  It is necessary that we visit all the museums.

  Il est important **que vous réserviez** une chambre à l'hôtel.
  It is important for you to reserve a room at the hotel. (or)
  It is important that you reserve a room at the hotel.

- All verbs except **avoir** and **être** use the following endings in the subjunctive:

-e	-ions
-es	-iez
-e	-ent

- All regular **-er** verbs get the stem of the subjunctive by dropping the **-ent** ending of the **ils/elles** form of the present indicative.

  example: **ils parl**ent
            que je parl**e**
            que tu parl**es**
            qu'il/elle/on parl**e**
            que nous parl**ions**
            que vous parl**iez**
            qu'ils/elles parl**ent**

Note that for **-er** verbs in the subjunctive, only the **nous** and **vous** forms look and sound different from their indicative counterparts. The **nous** and **vous** forms are like their counterparts in the imperfect tense.

A. **Il faut que...** À tour de rôle avec votre partenaire, remplacez les mots en italique par les mots entre parenthèses et faites les changements nécessaires.

1. Il faut que *nous* voyagions pendant les vacances scolaires. (je / tu / nous / ils)
2. Il est préférable que *je* cherche des restaurants à un prix raisonnable. (nous / vous / elles / tu)
3. Il n'est pas nécessaire que *nous* visitions tous les musées. (vous / tu / je / ils)
4. Il vaut mieux qu'*ils* comparent les prix. (je / tu / vous / nous)

À propos du vocabulaire: Remember the differences in meaning among the following expressions:

il faut	*it is necessary, you must*
il ne faut pas	*you must not*
il est nécessaire	*it is necessary*
il n'est pas nécessaire	*it isn't necessary*

B. Pour organiser un voyage. Avant de voyager avec un(e) ami(e), il est nécessaire que vous parliez, tou(te)s les deux, franchement de vos préférences pour le voyage. Donnez à votre partenaire vos recommandations pour faire un bon voyage. Utilisez une de ces expressions dans chaque phrase, et variez vos choix.

il faut que	il est nécessaire que	il vaut mieux que
il ne faut pas que	il n'est pas nécessaire que	il est préférable que

Modèle: voyager pendant une période où il n'y a pas beaucoup de touristes
—*Il faut que nous voyagions pendant une période où il n'y a pas beaucoup de touristes.*

1. voyager pendant une période où il n'y a pas beaucoup de touristes
2. voyager pendant les vacances scolaires
3. chercher le meilleur hôtel de la ville
4. réserver une chambre à l'avance
5. visiter le syndicat d'initiative *(tourist office)* pour trouver une chambre
6. demander une chambre avec W.-C. et salle de bains
7. demander une chambre sans W.-C. et salle de bains
8. dîner dans les meilleurs restaurants
9. louer une voiture

C. Pour payer un voyage. Avant de voyager avec un(e) ami(e), il est aussi nécessaire que vous soyez, tou(te)s les deux, d'accord sur les dépenses. Faites vos recommandations à votre partenaire pour économiser pendant votre voyage ensemble. Utilisez une de ces expressions dans chaque phrase, et variez vos choix.

il faut que	il est nécessaire que	il vaut mieux que
il ne faut pas que	il n'est pas nécessaire que	il est préférable que

Modèle: voyager jamais/quelquefois en première classe
—*Pour économiser, il vaut mieux que nous ne voyagions jamais en première classe.*

1. voyager jamais/quelquefois en première classe
2. comparer les prix des vols
3. chercher un hôtel le moins cher possible
4. économiser aux repas
5. utiliser les transports publics
6. payer avec une carte de crédit
7. payer toujours en espèces°

en espèces: *in cash*

PRÉCISIONS

- All regular **-ir** and **-re** verbs get the stem of the subjunctive by dropping the **-ent** ending of the **ils/elles** form of the present indicative.

ils **finiss**ent	ils **sort**ent	ils **vend**ent
que je finiss**e**	que je sort**e**	que je vend**e**
que tu finiss**es**	que tu sort**es**	que tu vend**es**
qu'il/elle/on finiss**e**	qu'il/elle/on sort**e**	qu'il/elle/on vend**e**
que nous finiss**ions**	que nous sort**ions**	que nous vend**ions**
que vous finiss**iez**	que vous sort**iez**	que vous vend**iez**
qu'ils/elles finiss**ent**	qu'ils/elles sort**ent**	qu'ils/elles vend**ent**

Note that for these verbs, unlike regular **-er** verbs, there is a difference in the pronunciation of the singular forms in the indicative and subjunctive moods. Listen to your teacher pronounce the following:

je finis	que je finisse
tu sors	que tu sortes
elle vend	qu'elle vende

D. **Il vaut mieux que…** À tour de rôle avec votre partenaire, remplacez les mots en italique par les mots entre parenthèses et faites les changements nécessaires.

1. Il est préférable que *nous* choisissions les meilleurs restaurants de la ville. (vous / je / tu / ils)

2. Il faut que *je* finisse mes recherches des monuments historiques. (tu / nous / vous / elles)

3. Il est essentiel que *vous* réfléchissiez bien aux détails de l'itinéraire. (je / nous / tu / ils)

4. Il vaut mieux que *nous* partions avant midi. (je / tu / vous / elles)

5. Il ne faut pas que *je* dorme trop tard. (nous / vous / ils / tu)

6. Il est indispensable que *vous* répondiez aux messages. (je / tu / elles / nous)

7. Il n'est pas nécessaire que *nous* rendions visite à mes parents. (vous / je / tu / ils)

E. **Pour visiter une ville.** Donnez à votre partenaire vos recommandations pour bien visiter une ville. Utilisez une de ces expressions dans chaque phrase, et variez vos choix. Réfléchissez bien pour déterminer si vous voulez utiliser une expression affirmative ou négative.

il faut que	il est nécessaire que	il vaut mieux que
il ne faut pas que	il n'est pas nécessaire que	il est préférable que
il est essential que	il est indispensable que	

Modèle: sortir tous les soirs
Il n'est pas nécessaire qu'on sorte tous les soirs.

1. sortir tous les soirs
2. dormir jusqu'à midi tous les jours
3. partir après 24 heures dans une ville
4. choisir les meilleures places au théâtre
5. finir chaque jour par prendre un verre au café de l'hôtel
6. remplir les valises avec des souvenirs

une loi: *law*

7. obéir aux lois° du pays
8. bien réfléchir aux excursions
9. établir chaque matin un programme pour la journée
10. grossir pendant le voyage
11. rendre visite à un(e) résident(e) célèbre
12. perdre du temps devant la télévision
13. répondre aux lettres des ami(e)s
14. vendre les billets d'avion de retour

PRÉCISIONS

There are a few high-frequency irregular verbs that are also irregular in the subjunctive, including **avoir** and **être**.

- The present subjunctive forms of **avoir** and **être** are irregular:

avoir	être
que j'**aie**	que je **sois**
que tu **aies**	que tu **sois**
qu'il/elle/on **ait**	qu'il/elle/on **soit**
que nous **ayons**	que nous **soyons**
que vous **ayez**	que vous **soyez**
qu'ils/elles **aient**	qu'ils/elles **soient**

The forms **aie, aies, ait,** and **aient** are all pronounced like the **ai** in **j'ai.** Likewise, the forms **sois, soit,** and **soient** are all pronounced alike.

À propos de la structure: The subjunctive forms of **avoir** and **être** are the sources of the imperative forms of these verbs that you have already studied.

Aie	**Sois**
Ayons de la patience.	**Soyons** sage.
Ayez	**Soyez**

Remember that the **tu** form of **avoir** in the imperative, like its **-er** verb counterparts, drops its **-s.**

E. **Une ville intéressante.** Dites à votre partenaire ce qu'une ville doit avoir pour vous intéresser. Pendant votre discussion, faites une fiche comme l'exemple pour rapporter vos préférences.

Modèle: —*Pour m'intéresser, il faut qu'une ville ait un quartier historique.*
—*Et pour moi, il est essentiel qu'il y ait une équipe sportive professionnelle dans la ville.*

---

un opéra   plusieurs cinémas   **une symphonie**   un ballet renommé
un casino   un festival célèbre   **des monuments historiques**   *un musée*
une équipe sportive professionnelle   une université prestigieuse
un quartier historique   des espaces verts   *une bibliothèque*
un métro   un aéroport   **de beaux parcs**   un centre-ville animé

Moi	Nous deux	Mon/Ma partenaire

G. Une ville attirante. Dites à votre partenaire si une ville doit avoir certaines autres caractéristiques pour vous attirer. Ajoutez vos préférences à votre fiche de l'Exercice F.

Modèle: *Pour m'attirer, il faut qu'une ville soit francophone.*
Il n'est pas nécessaire qu'elle soit moderne.

1. en Europe
2. en Asie
3. en Amérique
4. moderne
5. historique
6. près des montagnes
7. près d'un lac
8. près d'une plage
9. riche en musées
10. pleine de théâtres
11. pleine de cinémas
12. touristique
13. dynamique
14. grande

H. Une ville: à habiter ou à visiter? En utilisant les expressions des activités précédentes, identifiez pour votre partenaire au moins cinq différences entre ce que vous aimez dans une ville que vous habitez et dans une ville que vous visitez.

Modèle: *Pour moi, il est important que la ville où j'habite soit moderne. Si je vais visiter une ville, il vaut mieux qu'elle soit historique.*

NOTE CULTURELLE

Quand on voyage, si on franchit° plus de quatre fuseaux horaires°, on souffrira probablement du décalage horaire (ou *jet lag*). Le décalage horaire entraîne des symptômes gênants°: somnolence, irritabilité, fatigue. Les voyages vers l'est sont les plus fatigants.

Voici les conseils du «Docteur Vacances» pour des vacances réussies:

1. Dans l'avion, reposez-vous: demandez couverture, appuie-tête°, masque, chaussons°.
2. Sur place, adoptez immédiatement les horaires du pays d'accueil.
3. Prenez vos repas aux heures locales en privilégiant le petit déjeuner: protides°, jus de fruit, pain.
4. Exposez-vous au soleil ou à une lumière artificielle de forte intensité.
5. Exercez une activité physique (promenade, sport).
6. En cas de fatigue intense, faites de courtes siestes d'une vingtaine de minutes.
7. La première nuit, dormez le plus possible.
8. Le lendemain, reposez-vous le plus possible.

Réfléchissons: Avez-vous fait l'expérience° du décalage horaire? Quel voyage faisiez-vous? Combien de fuseaux horaires avez-vous franchis pendant ce voyage? Combien de temps vous a-t-il fallu pour retrouver votre équilibre?

---

franchir: *to cross* / **fuseaux horaires:** *time zones* / **gênant:** *bothersome, annoying* / **appuie-tête:** *pillow, head support* / **chaussons:** *slippers* / **protides:** *protein* / **Avez-vous fait l'expérience de... ?:** *Have you experienced . . . ?*

PRONONCIATION: Le son [k] 🔊

The sound [k] may be written several ways in French: **k, qu(e), c,** and **ch** (rare).

Repeat the following examples after your instructor.

- **k**   *kir*   *kilomètre*   *képi°*
- **qu(e)**   *question*   *qualifier*   *unique*
  (Note that there is no [w] sound as there is in English!)
- **c** (without a **cédille**), when preceding a consonant sound or the vowels **a, o,** or **u**
  casse-croûte   *construction*   *accusation*
- **ch** (usually [sh], but pronounced [k] in certain words of Greek origin)
  chaotique   *psychologie*   *écho*   *orchestre*

un képi: *a round, flat-topped hat with a viser worn as part of the French military uniform*

À vous! With a partner, practice reading the following sentences, focusing on your pronunciation of the sound [k].

1. Quand j'étais en Australie, j'ai vu des kangourous qui sautaient et des koalas qui mangeaient des feuilles d'eucalyptus. J'ai même cueilli° des kiwis des arbres en Nouvelle-Zélande.

   cueillir: *to gather; to pick*

2. Moi, j'ai visité la capitale du Mali qui s'appelle Bamako. Il y a eu beaucoup de construction à Bamako pendant la période coloniale, comme la Mosquée de Hamdalaye.

3. Les Acadiens habitaient au Nouveau-Brunswick et à la Nouvelle-Écosse au Canada, près du Québec. Quand l'Angleterre a conquis° cette région au dix-huitième siècle, certains Acadiens sont allés vivre en Louisiane et s'appellent les *cajuns*.

   conquérir: *to conquer; to take over*

4. Au Cameroun, il y a un volcan actif qui s'appelle Mont Cameroun. C'est le point le plus haut de la côte ouest de l'Afrique, mesurant plus de quatre kilomètres de hauteur.

POUR DÉVELOPPER VOS IDÉES

Thematic objective: To evaluate the attractions of major cities in terms of the quality of life they offer tourists and residents

Présentation: Montréal: Portrait de la ville

POUR SAISIR L'ESSENTIEL: La lecture est extraite d'une page personnelle sur l'Internet. Évidemment l'auteur est fier de sa ville, Montréal. En lisant les informations, faites une liste des phrases dans le texte qui représentent les attributs que vous trouvez les plus importants pour une ville internationale. Puis travaillez avec un(e) partenaire pour classer les attributs que vous deux avez identifiés par ordre de priorité.

Modèle: —*À mon avis, la chose la plus importante est l'influence des cultures internationales.*
—*Mais le coût de la vie° est très important aussi, n'est-ce pas?*

coût de la vie: *cost of living*

Montréal est une métropole° multiculturelle très touristique. Les immigrants provenant de tous les pays du monde ont contribué au charme et à l'énergie de cette ville cosmopolite. La vie à Montréal est palpitante et est, en plus, moins chère que d'autres villes d'Europe ou des États-Unis. Ses rues, ses théâtres, ses quartiers sont les témoins de festivals, d'évènements culturels par lesquels les touristes se laissent séduire. Fins gourmets ou oiseaux de nuit, vous trouverez votre bonheur dans la métropole québécoise. La vie nocturne à Montréal est électrisante. Dépaysement garanti!

une métropole: ville importante

Si vous êtes perdus, allez directement au boulevard Saint-Laurent, c'est le point de repère° pour retrouver le centre-ville.

point de repère: *landmark*

Montréal est la ville des festivals, des divertissements par excellence. Le Festival de jazz et le Festival Juste pour Rire en juillet en sont des exemples. Les visiteurs succombent° à l'ambiance extraordinaire de ces fêtes. C'est une expérience unique.

succomber: *to succumb*

Les équipes professionnelles font aussi la fierté des Montréalais: l'équipe de hockey des Canadiens de Montréal, l'équipe de baseball des Expos et *Les Alouettes*, équipe de football canadien.

Montréal, ville moderne, ville historique

I. Qu'est-ce qu'une ville internationale? Quelles sont les caractéristiques les plus importantes d'une ville internationale? Écrivez un paragraphe basé sur les phrases dans la partie jaune de la grille ci-dessous.

Modèle: *Quelles sont les qualités indispensables d'une ville internationale? Bon, à mon avis il faut qu'une ville internationale ait l'esprit ouvert, une économie dynamique et un centre-ville animé. Il est aussi nécessaire qu'elle ait un aéroport international. Il est important qu'elle soit moderne et propre. De plus, il faut que les habitants aient une qualité de vie satisfaisante et un cadre de vie agréable. Enfin il faut qu'ils aient un choix de distractions et qu'ils vivent en sécurité.*

Indiquez les dix qualités les plus importantes pour une ville internationale. Utilisez des expressions des trois sections de la grille ici et à la page suivante.

Aspects de l'esprit de la ville	Ressources de la communauté	Culture et distractions	Infrastructures
Phrase n° 1: *Il faut/est nécessaire/est important qu'une ville internationale ait...*			
—l'esprit ouvert —du prestige —une excellente réputation —une population multiethnique —une appréciation de son histoire / patrimoine —un caractère unique —un charme individuel —une beauté régionale —??? (d'autres idées)	—une économie dynamique —une université prestigieuse —une bibliothèque renommée —un centre médical important —des espaces verts —de beaux parcs —des places publiques —un quartier historique —??? (d'autres idées)	—un centre-ville animé —une symphonie —un musée —un opéra important —un ballet —un casino —un hippodrome —une vie nocturne —des festivals communautaires —des théâtres —une équipe sportive professionnelle —??? (d'autres idées)	—un aéroport international —un port maritime —un métro moderne et propre —une police consciencieuse —peu de pollution —un gouvernement compétent —des services sanitaires efficaces —un coût de la vie modéré —des écoles progressives —??? (d'autres idées)

Phrase n° 2: *Il faut/est nécessaire/est important qu'une ville internationale soit...*		
moderne propre	prestigieuse multiethnique	dynamique esthétique

Phrase n° 3: *Dans une ville internationale, il faut/est nécessaire/est important que les habitants...*			
—aient une qualité de vie satisfaisante —respectent leurs voisins —participent à des activités communautaires —??? (d'autres idées)	—aient un cadre de vie agréable —trouvent de bons emplois —??? (d'autres idées)	—aient un choix de distractions culturelles —apprécient leurs artistes —??? (d'autres idées)	—vivent en sécurité —respectent l'environnement —participent aux décisions municipales —??? (d'autres idées)

J. **Planifier un centre urbain.** Expliquez vos idées de l'Exercice I à votre partenaire. Puis essayez de déterminer les qualités de votre ville internationale idéale. Ensemble, prenez des décisions sur ses caractéristiques dans les catégories suivantes.

Notre ville internationale idéale	
Localisation:	(Par exemple, *près de la mer, près des montagnes, dans le désert, dans une île, etc.*)
Climat:	
Esprit de la ville:	
Ressources communautaires:	
Centres culturels:	
Distractions:	
Infrastructures:	
? ? ?	

DÉCOUVERTE

1. Which one of the cities presented in this *Thème* would you most like to visit: Genève or Montréal?

2. Make a list of the most interesting details given in the presentation for the city you selected. Identify the details as either facts or impressions.

3. What else do you know about this city? Make an additional list of facts and impressions.

4. Categorize the information in your lists according to whether they relate to (a) the size and location of the city, (b) the economy, (c) the culture. Note that some information may fall into more than one category.

5. Use the chart on page 519 to create a profile of the city. (You do not need to include information for every category.)

6. Working in a group with other students who have profiled the same city, pool your knowledge of the place. Then write a one- or two-paragraph description of the city, illustrating your key points with information from your profiles.

2ᴱ THÈME: Faisons du tourisme

Objective: To express preferences and make recommendations for travel

PRÉSENTATION: Un coup d'œil sur le thème

Faire du tourisme c'est découvrir un peu une ville, son histoire, sa splendeur, son esprit. C'est connaître un peu ce qu'elle est fière d'offrir aux étrangers. Bien que cela ne constitue pas une connaissance profonde d'un endroit, c'est quand même un bon début. Dans ce thème nous allons faire des mini-tours guidés par des habitants (ou des amateurs) qui parlent avec affection et fierté d'une ville qu'ils aiment.

Capitale spirituelle, culturelle, artisanale, perle° du monde arabe, Fès est véritablement une ville impériale enivrante et saisissante par ses bruits, ses odeurs, ses couleurs. Fès est le trésor d'une civilisation, tout comme Florence ou Athènes.

Vous tomberez sous la magie tel un serpent envoûté par un charmeur. Ses musiques enchanteresses, sa gastronomie unique et extraordinaire, ses palais, ses habitants vous feront des souvenirs inoubliables. Vos yeux s'éblouiront devant la mosquée La Qaraouiyyin, magnifique au toit scintillant de tuiles° émeraude. Les ornements sont somptueux: boiseries° sculptées, bronzes ciselés, zelliges° polichromes, colonnes et plâtres sculptés. Elle reste, encore de nos jours, le plus vaste et le plus ancien centre d'enseignement religieux du Maghreb°.

La luxueuse décoration d'une mosquée

La Nouvelle-Orléans

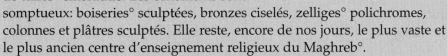

Un petit coin des USA qui sent bon la France...

L'endroit de la Nouvelle-Orléans où il faut aller est le quartier français. Notre langue est bien présente dans ce quartier et l'intonation américaine lui donne encore plus de charme. Le Vieux Carré vit° la nuit, on ne compte plus les bars, les restaurants ni les cafés-concerts. Évidemment la Nouvelle-Orléans est la ville du jazz. Vous voulez voir un concert, choisissez le Preservation Hall. Les concertistes semblent faire partie de l'histoire. En effet, la ville regorge° de musées et d'histoire. Chaque maison au balcon en fer forgé° est un témoignage° du passé de *New Orleans*.

À propos de la culture: The description of Fez refers to this city as the intellectual and artistic capital of Morocco, but Rabat is the administrative capital of the country.

À propos de la structure: If you wonder why *émeraude* isn't plural to agree with *tuiles*, it's because nouns used as colors are not altered for agreement. Common examples of this are the color names *orange* and *marron*.

perle: *pearl*

scintillant toit de tuiles: *sparkling tile roof*
boiserie (f.): *paneling*
zellige (m.): *ornement en céramique*
Maghreb (m.): *the northwest African countries Morocco, Algeria, and Tunisia*

vit: s'anime, devient animé

regorge: être plein
fer forgé: *wrought iron*
témoignage: *testimony*

Cherchons des idées

En lisant les descriptions de Fès et de la Nouvelle-Orléans, cherchez des phrases ou des expressions qui évoquent un sens de l'histoire, de la splendeur ou de l'esprit de ces villes. Trouvez au moins une expression pour chaque catégorie.

Modèle: Histoire: *comme à Florence ou à Athènes, le trésor d'une civilisation*
Splendeur: *le trésor d'une civilisation,*
              l'inépuisable richesse
Esprit: *le Vieux Carré vit la nuit*

POUR DÉVELOPPER VOTRE FRANÇAIS

Structure: Le présent du subjonctif (suite)

OBSERVATIONS

—Est-ce que tu vas prendre des cours cet été?

Are you going to take courses this summer?

—Non, pas cet été. Je n'ai pas beaucoup voyagé hors des États-Unis, et mon père veut **que j'aille** en Europe.

No, not this summer. I haven't traveled much outside the United States, and my father wants me to go to Europe.

—Quelle chance! Il n'est pas nécessaire **que tu travailles?**

What luck! Isn't it necessary for you to work?

—Non. Papa m'a offert ces vacances parce que j'ai très bien réussi à tous mes cours. Alors, je vais faire le voyage. Je veux **qu'il soit** heureux!

No. Dad offered me this vacation because I did very well in all my courses. So, I'm going to take the trip. Certainly, I want him to be happy!

—Oh, que je voudrais **que nous fassions** ce voyage ensemble! Mais je n'ai pas assez d'argent en ce moment.

Oh, how I would like us to take that trip together! But I don't have enough money right now.

—Tu m'as dit une fois que ta grand-mère parlait de vous offrir une partie de votre héritage à toi et à tes sœurs. Tu peux lui demander si elle préfère **que vous profitiez** de ce don maintenant plutôt qu'après sa mort.

You told me once that your grandmother used to talk about giving a part of your inheritance to you and your sisters. You can ask her if she prefers you to benefit from this gift now instead of after her death.

—C'est une idée. Ce n'est pas mal. Mais je souhaite **que mes sœurs** lui **fassent** la proposition. Elles sont plus courageuses que moi.

Not a bad idea. But I wish my sisters would propose it to her. They are more courageous than I.

1. The verbs in boldface are in the subjunctive mood. One of these sentences expresses necessity. Can you tell what other attitude or opinion is expressed in the others?

2. Can you find two verbs that are irregular in the subjunctive in addition to **être?**

PRÉCISIONS

- In French, the expression of volition (wish or desire) in the first clause is followed by a verb in the subjunctive in the second clause. The following verbs are often used to express the notion of volition:

désirer	*to desire, to want*
vouloir	*to want, to wish*
souhaiter	*to wish*
préférer	*to prefer*
aimer (mieux)	*to like (better)*

- You have already used these verbs followed by an *infinitive* to indicate that the subject of the sentence wants something for himself or herself.

  Je désire **finir** mes études aux États-Unis.
  I want to finish my studies in the United States.

  Nous voudrions **habiter** en France cet été.
  We would like to live in France this summer.

- Using these verbs followed by a clause in the subjunctive allows the subject of the sentence to express desire for *someone else* to do something.

  Mon père désire **que je finisse** mes études aux États-Unis.
  My father wants me to finish my studies in the United States.

  Nous voudrions **que tu habites** en France cet été.
  We'd like for you to live in France this summer.

- The present subjunctive stems of **aller** and **faire** are irregular.

aller	faire
que j'**aille**	que je **fasse**
que tu **ailles**	que tu **fasses**
qu'il/elle/on **aille**	qu'il/elle/on **fasse**
que nous **allions**	que nous **fassions**
que vous **alliez**	que vous **fassiez**
qu'ils/elles **aillent**	qu'ils/elles **fassent**

A. Je veux que... À tour de rôle avec votre partenaire, remplacez les mots en italique par les mots entre parenthèses et faites les changements nécessaires.

1. Je veux que *vous* voyagiez avec la famille pendant les vacances d'été. (tu / nous / elle / ils)

2. Mon patron préfère que *je* reste en ville pendant les vacances scolaires. (nous / les employées / vous / sa secrétaire)

3. Mon/Ma camarade de chambre aimerait que *nous* choisissions une chambre avec W.-C. et salle de bains. (je / vous / tu / les autres)

4. Le guide désire que *tu* visites tous les musées. (vous / nous / je / tout le monde)

5. Le guide ne veut pas que *vous* vendiez les billets aux autres. (je / tu / nous / les clients)

B. Pour partager les responsabilités. Pour chaque paire de responsabilités, dites à votre partenaire ce que vous voulez faire et ce que vous préférez qu'il/elle fasse.

> **Modèle:** chercher un hôtel convenable
> comparer les prix des vols
> *Moi, je vais comparer les prix des vols. Je préfère que tu cherches un hôtel convenable.*

1. chercher un hôtel convenable
   comparer les prix des vols

2. choisir les restaurants
   choisir les hôtels

3. payer les vols
   payer les restaurants

4. organiser les visites aux musées
   organiser les visites des monuments

5. acheter les billets de train
   réserver les chambres d'hôtel

6. conduire la voiture
   naviguer avec le plan de la ville

7. porter les valises
   étudier le plan de la ville

8. commander les dîners au restaurant
   demander les directions en ville

9. choisir les souvenirs
   payer les souvenirs

10. parler au chauffeur du taxi
    parler au serveur au restaurant

À propos de la culture: Note that the French usually use the expression *huit jours* when making reference to a week. They count both the first and the last days. Likewise, they say *quinze jours* in reference to a period of two weeks, again counting both the first and last days.

C. Je veux qu'une ville soit... Quand on choisit une ville pour passer les vacances, on cherche des caractéristiques spécifiques. Dites à votre partenaire quelle caractéristique de chaque groupe vous préférez trouver dans une ville où vous ferez un séjour d'au moins huit jours.

Modèle: tranquille / dynamique
—*Moi, je veux que la ville soit tranquille. Et toi?*
—*Moi aussi, je veux que la ville soit tranquille.*
ou   —*Pas moi, je préfère que la ville soit dynamique.*

1. tranquille / dynamique
2. artisanale / élégante
3. industrielle / agricole
4. rurale / cosmopolite
5. accueillante° / intellectuelle

6. charmante / futuriste
7. pleine de charme / pleine de discothèques
8. intéressante en architecture / pleine de casinos
9. historique / pleine d'activités
10. pleine d'artistes / pleine de politiciens

accueillante: *welcoming, friendly*

D. **Je veux qu'une ville ait...** Quand on choisit une ville pour passer les vacances, on cherche des lieux et des activités spécifiques. Dites à votre partenaire ce que vous préférez trouver dans une ville où vous ferez un séjour d'au moins huit jours.

Modèle: *Je veux (préfère, souhaite) que la ville ait beaucoup de petites boutiques.*

petites boutiques	**musées**	*fêtes*	parcs
casinos	**gratte-ciel°**	**RESTAURANTS**	
cafés	théâtres	marchés aux puces°	
cinémas	grands magasins		**concerts**

un gratte-ciel: *skyscraper(s) (This noun does not change for the plural.)*
un marché aux puces: *flea market*

E. **Qu'est-ce que tu recommandes que je fasse?** Demandez à votre partenaire ce qu'il/elle recommande que vous fassiez pendant un séjour dans chaque endroit. On peut trouver des idées dans la liste ci-dessous et dans l'Exercice D.

Modèle: à Paris
—*Si je vais à Paris, qu'est-ce que tu recommandes que je fasse?*
—*Si tu vas à Paris, je recommande que tu ailles aux musées.*

1. à Paris
2. à Rome
3. à Londres
4. à Monte Carlo
5. à New York
6. à Mexico
7. à Québec
8. à Montréal
9. à la Nouvelle-Orléans
10. à Fès

- faire du shopping
- faire beaucoup de promenades
- faire une excursion à...
- faire un pique-nique à...
- faire du sport (tennis, foot, ski, etc.)
- visiter les palais/musées/cathédrales, etc.
- passer du temps dans les parcs/cafés/musées, etc.
- chercher les petites boutiques/cafés/théâtres, etc.
- parler français/espagnol, etc.
- faire attention° à ton sac à main/à ton argent/à ton appareil photo/ au passeport, etc.
- être sage/chaleureux/généreux/sympathique, etc.
- sortir aux restaurants/théâtres/cinémas, etc.
- aller aux marchés aux puces/grands magasins/petites boutiques

faire attention à: *to watch out for*

F. **Il vaudrait mieux qu'on aille...** À tour de rôle avec votre partenaire, demandez où on doit aller pour faire chaque activité.

Modèle: pour voir des gens célèbres
—*Où est-ce qu'on doit aller pour voir des gens célèbres?*
—*Pour voir des gens célèbres, il vaudrait mieux (je recommande) qu'on aille à New York.*

1. pour voir des gens célèbres
2. pour trouver de bons casinos
3. pour voir les meilleures plages
4. pour faire du ski
5. pour faire du shopping
6. pour faire des courses automobiles
7. pour apprécier la belle architecture
8. pour voir le beau paysage
9. pour visiter une belle cathédrale
10. pour trouver la meilleure vie nocturne
11. pour trouver un métro moderne
12. pour voir de bons films
13. pour sortir au théâtre

NOTE CULTURELLE

Quand on est à l'étranger°, on doit faire attention à ce qu'on mange. Pour passer des vacances en bonne santé, le «Docteur Vacances» offre au voyageur quelques conseils sur les aliments permis et interdits.

1. Une règle d'or°: Fruits et légumes: Cuisez°-les ou faites les bouillir°, pelez°-les ou... oubliez-les!
2. Lavez-vous les mains à l'eau chaude et au savon avant chaque repas.
3. Évitez avant tout:
   • les fruits de mer,
   • les glaces et laitages, le pudding,
   • les hamburgers, sandwiches et pastèques° vendus dans les rues
4. Évitez aussi:
   • les aliments réchauffés,
   • la viande et le poisson froids,
   • les crudités,
   • les sauces froides
5. Vous pouvez manger:
   • la nourriture cuite à point° et servie chaude,
   • les fruits et légumes que vous pouvez peler ou éplucher°,
   • la nourriture locale préparée devant vous,
   • les fruits ou des légumes lavés par vous-même avec une eau rendue potable,
   • les viandes qui ont été congelées

Réfléchissons: Avez-vous jamais été malade pendant un voyage? Où étiez-vous? Savez-vous pourquoi? Dans quels pays est-ce que vous buvez l'eau de robinet°? Dans quels pays est-ce que vous buvez toujours de l'eau minérale? Faites-vous attention à vos habitudes de santé chez vous?

à l'étranger: *abroad, in foreign lands* / **une règle d'or:** *a golden rule* / **cuire:** *to cook* / **bouillir:** *to boil* / **peler:** *to peel* / **pastèques:** *watermelon* / **cuite à point:** *thoroughly cooked, well done* / **éplucher:** *to peel* / **l'eau de robinet:** *tap water*

PRONONCIATION: À la découverte du monde francophone!

À vous! With a partner, practice reading the names of the francophone countries and states and their capital cities below.

1. Rabat, le Maroc
2. Yaoundé, le Cameroun
3. Bamako, le Mali
4. Abidjan, la Côte d'Ivoire
5. Dakar, le Sénégal
6. Niamey, le Niger°
7. Paris, la France
8. Bruxelles, la Belgique
9. Berne, La Suisse
10. Ajaccio, La Corse
11. Ottawa, Le Canada
12. Baton Rouge, La Louisiane
13. Port-au-Prince, Haïti
14. Fort-de-France, La Martinique
15. Basse-Terre, La Guadeloupe
16. Cayenne, La Guyane française

À propos de la structure: The French-speaking peoples of **Le Niger** *(Niger)* are **nigérien(ne)s,** while the English speakers of **La Nigeria** *(Nigeria)* are referred to as **nigérian(e)s.**

POUR DÉVELOPPER VOS IDÉES

Thematic objective: To gain insight into heritage and culture through sightseeing experiences

Présentation: L'esprit des Bamakois

POUR SAISIR L'ESSENTIEL:

Cet article sur l'esprit bamakois est extrait d'un site Internet sur le Mali. En lisant, essayez de donner une impression de l'esprit de la ville et de ses habitants. Puis complétez une de ces deux phrases:
• *Il me semble que les Bamakois apprécient...*
• *J'ai l'impression que Bamako (n')est (pas)...*
Expliquez un peu votre opinion en citant un ou deux commentaires de la lecture. *Selon° la lecture,...*

À propos de la culture: Bamako is the capital of Mali. Although its existence can be traced back many centuries, it does not tout a history of splendorous empire. Whereas some African capitals are bejeweled with ancient palaces and royal traditions, Bamako acquired its importance late, during the colonial period, as a result of its strategic location.

selon: *according to*

Modèle: *J'ai l'impression que les Bamakois apprécient la vie sociale. Selon la lecture, les jeunes passent des journées entières à discuter.*

Bamako, fruit de la colonisation et capitale du Mali est la plus africaine des capitales africaines. Si vous êtes Londoniens ou Parisiens, vous ne serez pas dépaysés à la vue de jeunes Africains qui derrière chaque enceinte° ou parfois autour d'un manguier°, sirotent° du thé durant des journées entières. Ces jeunes aiment prolonger leurs soirées dans les bars à parler entre amis.

Bamako n'a pas la longue histoire des grands empires. Mais née avec la colonisation, elle a réussi à devenir le symbole de la résistance culturelle des Maliens.

une enceinte: *enclosure (But beware! It also means, as an adjective, "pregnant.")*
un manguier: *mango tree*
siroter: *to sip*

Les Bamakois ne se sont pas laissés influencer par la vie urbaine. L'opulence et la modernité ne les ont pas changés, ils conservent leur âme de villageois. Les bars restent toujours aussi bondés° malgré l'abondance des boîtes de nuit et des somptueux hôtels. Une extraordinaire richesse et une tradition de grandeur engagent les touristes à l'humilité. C'est ce qui explique qu'à Bamako, les visiteurs qui cherchent un simple exotisme se sentent désorientés. Les Bamakois ont toujours défendu leur pays contre la puissance du tourisme international.

Bamako, Mali

G. Des villes que je connais. Décrivez deux ou trois villes que vous connaissez bien. Pour chaque description, faites au moins deux phrases. Vous pouvez les baser sur les exemples dans le tableau.

Modèle: *Québec est une ville charmante et historique. Les habitants sont chaleureux et accueillants. C'est un endroit plein d'activités et de divertissements.*

1. (Ville) est une ville...	2. En général, les habitants de (ville) sont...	3. (Ville) est un endroit plein...
accueillante°	chaleureux	d'activité
artisanale	accueillants	de charme (classique, rural, traditionnel)
industrielle	engagés	de belle architecture
intellectuelle	conservateurs	de musées
rurale	libéraux	de contrastes
charmante	généreux	d'artistes
cosmopolite	sympathiques	de petites boutiques
dynamique	fiers de leur héritage	d'histoire
élégante	??? (d'autres idées)	de divertissements
ensoleillée		de fêtes
étendue°		de bons cafés (restaurants, théâtres)
fascinante		de luxe
futuriste		de musique
mythique		de beauté
touristique		de discothèques
tranquille		de casinos
où on s'amuse bien		de gratte-ciel
??? (d'autres idées)		??? (d'autres idées)

H. Une de mes villes préférées. Écrivez un paragraphe sur une des villes que vous aimez le mieux dans le monde. Cela peut être la ville où vous habitez ou une ville que vous aimez visiter. Faites des recommandations touristiques en décrivant ce que cette ville offre aux visiteurs. Identifiez quelques sites qu'il faut absolument aller voir. Indiquez ce qu'on découvrira si on y va.

Château Frontenac

Modèle: *Ma ville préférée est Québec. C'est un endroit plein de contrastes. Il y a des gratte-ciel très modernes et de grands centres commerciaux très à la mode, mais il y a aussi des quartiers historiques, pleins de charme traditionnel. Les gens sont très chaleureux et accueillants, et ils sont très fiers de leur héritage français.*

Vous pourrez bien apprécier cela si vous faites la visite des Plaines d'Abraham. C'est le site d'une fameuse bataille entre les armées française et anglaise dirigées par Montcalm et Wolfe en 1759. Aujourd'hui il y a de beaux jardins où on peut se promener ou faire un pique-nique.

Ne manquez surtout pas de visiter le Château Frontenac. Maintenant c'est un hôtel de luxe. Mais autrefois c'était le château particulier du comte de Frontenac. Prenez des photos pour impressionner vos amis, parce que tout le monde connaît ce symbole international de la ville de Québec.

À côté du château vous y trouverez la Terrasse Duferrin. Promenez-vous le long de la terrasse. Il y a souvent des clowns, des kiosques et de petits orchestres. On peut danser, s'amuser ou simplement apprécier la vue panoramique du fleuve Saint-Laurent.

Et finalement il faudra que vous fassiez la visite de la Citadelle. Chaque matin à dix heures on peut regarder la relève de la garde°. C'est une vraie découverte pour les Américains qui pensent que cette cérémonie a lieu seulement en Angleterre.

relève de la garde: *changing of the guard*

DÉCOUVERTE

1. Which one of the cities presented in this **Thème** would you most like to visit: Fès or Bamako?

2. Make a list of the most interesting details given in the presentation for the city you selected. Identify the details as either facts or impressions.

3. What else do you know about this city? Make an additional list of facts and impressions.

4. Categorize the pieces of information in your lists according to whether they relate to (a) the size and location of the city, (b) the economy, or (c) the culture. Note that some information may fall into more than one category.

5. Use the chart on page 519 to create a profile of the city. (You do not need to include information for every category.)

6. Working in a group with other students who have profiled the same city, pool your knowledge of the place. Then write a one- or two-paragraph description of the city, illustrating your key points with information from your profiles.

Synthèse des idées sur les *Découvertes.* Review the profiles you have done in the **Découverte** sections of this chapter. Using the map on pages 516–517, tell what continent each city is in. Which of the features mentioned in your profile do you think are particular to places in that part of the world? Do these features relate to climate and topography or to cultural heritage?

3ᴱ THÈME: Paris: Métropole de la francophonie

Objective: To discuss sites of historical, artistic, and cultural significance in Paris

Un coup d'œil sur le thème

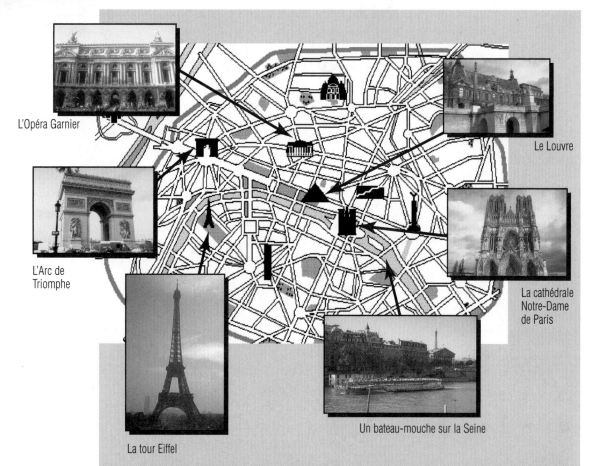

L'Opéra Garnier

Le Louvre

L'Arc de Triomphe

La cathédrale Notre-Dame de Paris

La tour Eiffel

Un bateau-mouche sur la Seine

Paris est l'une des villes les plus visitées du monde. On la voit dans les revues chics ainsi que dans les films d'Hollywood. Cherchons des informations sur quelques-uns de ses sites les plus renommés.

Le Louvre est un ancien palais qui s'est transformé en musée de renommée mondiale. Cet édifice a commencé son existence en 1190 comme château fort. En 1546, on a décidé de transformer l'antique forteresse en palais luxueux. En 1678, Louis XIV a choisi Versailles comme résidence royale; en 1793, l'ancien palais est devenu musée. Aujourd'hui c'est l'un des musées les plus renommés du monde.

La cathédrale Notre-Dame de Paris, qui a plus de 800 ans, est située sur une île en plein milieu de la Seine. On dit que la cathédrale Notre-Dame est le cœur de Paris. En fait, à côté de la cathédrale il y a une étoile qui marque le centre de Paris. La distance de la capitale à toute autre ville du pays est mesurée à partir de ce point.

Une promenade sur **la Seine en bateau-mouche** offre une perspective spéciale de la ville. Ce fleuve divise Paris en deux parties complémentaires. Au nord, sur la rive droite, on peut observer le Paris chic. On y trouve les plus beaux monuments, les grands hôtels, les restaurants élégants, les théâtres et les grands magasins. Au sud, sur la rive gauche, on découvre le Paris universitaire et artistique, les boîtes de nuit et les cafés animés.

La tour Eiffel est le symbole par excellence de la ville. Lors de son inauguration, c'était la plus haute construction de la ville. À l'époque l'opinion publique à son égard était très partagée. L'écrivain Guy de Maupassant a déclaré qu'il devait quitter Paris pour éviter la vue de cette «carcasse métallique». Heureusement, des artistes tels que Seurat et Le Douanier Rousseau l'ont représentée dans leurs tableaux. Aujourd'hui certains tentent de l'escalader à mains nues, sans corde, ou bien de sauter du 3ᵉ étage en parachute. Il faut noter que ces exploits se terminent inévitablement au commissariat de police.

L'Arc de Triomphe abrite la tombe du Soldat Inconnu. Les douze avenues qui rayonnent autour de ce monument évoque l'image d'une étoile, ce qui explique le nom de cet endroit: «Place de l'Étoile».

L'Opéra Garnier, chef-d'œuvre de Charles Garnier, représente une image typique de l'architecture parisienne. Comme vous avez remarqué au début de ce chapitre, ce même architecte a créé le casino classique à Monte-Carlo.

Ma carte postale de Paris. Chacun de nous a sa vision personnelle de cette ville célèbre. Imaginez que vous créez une carte postale de Paris. Quelle(s) image(s) emploierez-vous pour faire votre portrait de la ville? Écrivez la phrase de description de l'image que vous utiliserez au dos de° votre carte.

au dos de: *on the back of*

POUR DÉVELOPPER VOTRE FRANÇAIS

Structure: Les verbes comme ouvrir

OBSERVATIONS

En général, il est assez rare de trouver un bon restaurant dans une gare. Mais à Paris, *le Train Bleu* à la Gare de Lyon **ouvre** ses portes à une clientèle qui cherche à **s'offrir** un des meilleurs repas de la ville.

Pas toutes les gares de Paris **offrent** un restaurant célèbre. Mais on peut trouver facilement des restaurants fast-food. La chaîne *Pains à la ligne* **offre** des sandwiches et des pâtisseries. Les voyageurs peuvent les manger à la gare ou plus tard dans le train.

À la Gare de l'Est j'**ai découvert** la chaîne *Croq Voyage* qui **offre** des sandwiches chauds, des frites et des boissons fraîches. Ce n'est pas un restaurant élégant. On ne **couvre** pas les tables avec des nappes°. Il n'y a même pas de chaises!

Autrefois, si on **souffrait** de la chaleur à Paris, il fallait chercher un café ou un bar pour trouver une boisson. Aujourd'hui, on **découvre** des distributeurs automatiques avec des boissons fraîches dans les gares et les stations de métro.

une nappe: *tablecloth*

STRATÉGIES D'ANALYSE

1. The verbs in boldface are all formed in the same way. **S'offrir** appears in its infinitive form. Can you determine the infinitive form of the other verbs in this group?

2. How many different verbs did you find that fit this category? Using the context of the photo captions, can you determine the meaning of these verbs?

3. The infinitive form of these verbs ends in **-ir**. Does it appear that these verbs conjugate like the other **-ir** verbs that you have studied (verbs like **finir** or **sortir**)? Why or why not?

4. Look at the verb endings in the present tense. What other set of verbs have similar endings?

5. Can you find the past participle of **découvrir** in the examples? Based on this model, can you form the past participle of the other verbs?

6. Can you determine the tense of the form **souffrait** from the context of the caption? Using this verb as a model, can you form the imperfect tense of the other verbs?

PRÉCISIONS

You have already studied a set of verbs that have an infinitive ending in **-ir** (verbs like **finir** and **choisir**). These verbs are conjugated in the present tense with the endings **-is, -is, -it, -issons, -issez, -issent.**

• Not all verbs whose infinitives end in **-ir** use this set of endings. For example, the verbs **partir, sortir, servir,** and **dormir** use a different set of endings **(-s, -s, -t or -d, -ons, -ez, -ent).**

• The group of verbs like **ouvrir** *(to open)* **(-rir** verbs) is conjugated like regular **-er** verbs in the present tenses of the indicative and subjunctive.

ouvrir

j'ouvre	nous ouvr**ons**	que j'ouvre	que nous ouvr**ions**
tu ouvr**es**	vous ouvr**ez**	que tu ouvr**es**	que vous ouvr**iez**
il/elle/on ouvre	ils/elles ouvr**ent**	qu'il/elle/on ouvre	qu'ils/elles ouvr**ent**

• Other verbs conjugated like **ouvrir** include:

couvrir	to cover
découvrir	to discover
offrir	to offer
s'offrir	to allow (or indulge) oneself
souffrir	to suffer

• To form the past participle of these verbs, remove the **-rir** from the infinitive and add **-ert.**

En cherchant le Panthéon, nous avons **découvert** l'église Saint-Étienne-du-Mont, où se trouve le tombeau de Sainte Geneviève, la sainte patronne de Paris.
While looking for the Panthéon, we discovered the church Saint-Étienne-du-Mont, where the tomb of Sainte Geneviève, the patron saint of Paris, is located.

- To form the imperfect tense of these verbs, remove the final **-ir** from the infinitive, and add the regular imperfect endings.

j'ouvr**ais**	nous ouvr**ions**
tu ouvr**ais**	vous ouvr**iez**
il/elle/on ouvr**ait**	ils/elles ouvr**aient**

En été le marchand **ouvrait** son kiosque à dix heures; maintenant que c'est l'hiver, il ne l'ouvre pas avant onze heures et demie.
In summer the merchant used to open his stand at 10 o'clock; now that it is winter, he doesn't open it before 11:30.

A. **Ouvrir les yeux.** À tour de rôle avec votre partenaire, remplacez les mots en italique par les mots entre parenthèses et faites les changements nécessaires.

1. Quand *je* souffre de la chaleur, *je* veux de l'eau minérale. (vous / nous / tu / il / elles)
2. *Le patron* ouvre la crêperie à onze heures. (je / nous / vous / Marc et Paul)
3. *Lisette* couvre la tête quand il fait du vent. (nous / je / vous / les garçons)
4. À Noël *on* offre des cadeaux aux amis. (la famille / je / nous / vous)
5. Chaque jour à Paris *nous* découvrons quelque chose d'intéressant. (je / vous / on / les étudiants)

B. **Une touriste souffrante.** Assise à une table sur la terrasse d'un café, vous entendez une partie de la conversation entre deux personnes à la table à côté de vous. Vous avez étudié assez de français pour pouvoir compléter la conversation avec la forme convenable des verbes suivants: *couvrir, découvrir, offrir, ouvrir, souffrir.*

Touriste: Oh là là! Il faut avoir beaucoup d'énergie pour être touriste à Paris! Je _____ des pieds après avoir marché toute la matinée dans la ville. Ne peut-on pas continuer le tour en voiture ou en autobus?

Guide: Je regrette que vous _____, mademoiselle, mais j'insiste, quand même, qu'il nous faut continuer à pied pour pouvoir _____ la ville comme il faut°. La ville de Paris vous _____ mille lieux touristiques, pas seulement la tour Eiffel, le Louvre, et la cathédrale de Notre-Dame!

comme il faut: *properly, as one should*

Touriste: Mais que les escaliers dans le métro sont fatigants! Pourquoi est-ce que vous ne _____ pas de mal aux pieds comme moi?

Guide: Parce que je fais chaque jour des kilomètres dans ces rues et dans le métro. Pour moi, c'est essentiel comme guide. Après trois ou quatre jours à Paris, vous serez en meilleure forme. Bon, dépêchons-nous. Le Grand Palais _____ ses portes pour notre séance dans une demi-heure.

Structure: Les verbes connaître et savoir

OBSERVATIONS

Vous **connaissez,** sans doute, la cathédrale Notre-Dame de Paris. Il y a beaucoup d'autres belles églises dans la ville. En voici un exemple: **l'église Saint-Sulpice** dans le 6ᵉ arrondissement, bien moins **connue** que la cathédrale, mais très jolie et accueillante.

Tout le monde **connaît** le musée du Louvre, le musée le plus **connu** du monde. Paris est remplie d'autres musées où on peut trouver des trésors artistiques. **Le musée Rodin** dans le 7ᵉ arrondissement est superbe. Même les jardins sont remplis de sculptures, telles que les *Bourgeois de Calais.*

Nous **connaissons** les fontaines de la place de la Concorde. Elles sont souvent dans les photos des cartes postales de Paris. **J'ai connu les fontaines de Tinguely** un jour quand je me promenais près du Centre Pompidou.

vivant: *alive*

On **connaît** la Basilique du Sacré-Cœur et la place du Tertre comme des lieux touristiques célèbres à Paris. Je **sais** que si on continue à se promener jusqu'à derrière la place du Tertre, on trouvera un endroit, pas bien **connu,** mais très romantique. Cet endroit s'appelle **les escaliers des Anglais.**

Les touristes à Paris **connaissent** la place Vendôme avec sa colonne des Victoires de Napoléon Bonaparte. Et les habitants de Paris **connaissent** aussi **la place des Vosges.** Ils **savent** que la maison de Victor Hugo, aujourd'hui un musée, se trouve ici.

Tous les gens intéressants à Paris ne sont pas toujours vivants°. Quand j'**ai su** que le tombeau du musicien américain Jim Morrison se trouvait au cimetière du **Père Lachaise,** j'ai visité ce lieu fascinant plusieurs fois.

STRATÉGIES D'ANALYSE

1. **Connaître** and **savoir** have the same English equivalent. What do you think these verbs mean in English?
2. Which one of these verbs is used in the sense of *to be familiar* or *acquainted with*?
3. Which one of these verbs is used in the sense of *to know a fact* or *to have been informed about something*?
4. Can you figure out the special meaning of **savoir** in the *passé composé* by studying its use in context?

PRÉCISIONS

The verbs **connaître** and **savoir** both mean *to know*. However, these verbs cannot be used interchangeably.

connaître

je **connais**	nous **connaissons**
tu **connais**	vous **connaissez**
il/elle/on **connaît**	ils/elles **connaissent**

- Use **connaître** when you mean *to be familiar with* or *to be acquainted with* a person, place, or broad subject that no one would be expected to master completely.

Je **connais** Marie-Claire. Elle était étudiante au lycée La Fontaine où j'ai fait mes études secondaires.	*I **know** Marie-Claire. She was a student at the Lycée La Fontaine where I went to secondary school.*
Nous ne **connaissons** pas du tout les Alpes. Nous avons toujours passé les vacances en Alsace.	*We don't **know** the Alps at all. We have always spent our vacations in Alsace.*
Je **connais** un peu l'histoire de la France, au moins jusqu'à la fin de la monarchie.	*I **know** a little about the history of France, at least until the end of the monarchy.*

- The indicative present of the verb **savoir**

savoir

je **sais**	nous **savons**
tu **sais**	vous **savez**
il/elle/on **sait**	ils/elles **savent**

- Use **savoir** to mean that you *have been informed* about something, *have learned or memorized* something, *know how to do* something, or *are in the know* about something.

Je **sais** les noms de toutes les capitales des pays francophones.
*I **know** the names of all the capitals of francophone countries.*

Nous **savons** lire le plan du métro de Paris.
*We **know how** to read the map of the Paris subway system.*

Savez-vous à quelle heure le Grand Palais ouvre ses portes?
*Do you **know** what time the Grand Palais opens?*

- Both **connaître** and **savoir** have special meanings in the *passé composé*.

J'**ai connu** des artistes à la fête dans les jardins des Tuileries.
*I **met** (became acquainted with) some artists at the festival in the Tuileries Gardens.*

Nous **avons su** la date de la fête à l'hôtel.
*We **found out** the date of the festival at the hotel.*

C. **Est-ce que tu connais... ?** Dites à votre partenaire les endroits historiques à Paris que vous connaissez.

Modèle:
—Quels endroits historiques sur ces photos est-ce que tu connais?
—Moi, j'ai visité Paris une fois. Je connais le Louvre, Notre-Dame et le Sacré-Cœur. Et toi?
—Moi, je n'ai pas encore voyagé en France, mais je connais le Louvre, le musée d'Orsay et le Grand Palais.
—Ah oui? Comment?
—J'ai étudié l'histoire de l'art l'année dernière.

1

2

3

4

5

6

7

8

D. **Connaître ou savoir.** Utilisez correctement **connaître** ou **savoir** pour demander à votre partenaire les renseignements indiqués. Votre partenaire vous répondra *oui* ou *non* et ensuite justifiera sa réponse.

Modèles:
où se trouve l'ambassade américaine à Paris
    —Sais-tu où se trouve l'ambassade américaine à Paris?
    —Bien sûr. L'ambassade américaine se trouve à la place de la Concorde.
ou   *—Ça non. Je ne sais pas.*

le musée Rodin
    —Connais-tu le musée Rodin?
    —Bien sûr. C'est le musée où se trouvent les sculptures d'Auguste Rodin.
ou   *—Non. Je ne le connais pas.*

1. où se trouve l'ambassade américaine à Paris
2. où se trouve la cathédrale Notre-Dame de Paris
3. le Quartier latin
4. le Louvre
5. à quelle heure le Louvre ouvre ses portes aux visiteurs

6. le musée Rodin

7. s'il y a un restaurant dans le Grand Palais

8. si on peut faire des photos dans le musée d'Orsay

9. combien de statues se trouvent à la place de la Concorde

10. la tour Eiffel

11. la hauteur° de la tour Eiffel

12. combien de personnes habitent Paris

13. Paris

14. le métro de Paris

hauteur: *height* (with an aspirate **h**)

Note Culturelle

rêver: *to dream*
la bijouterie: *jewelry*
un adhérent: *member*

Si vous passez tout votre temps à Paris à étudier l'architecture, les arts et l'histoire de la ville, vous n'en aurez pas beaucoup pour faire des achats. Alors, si vous disposez de peu de temps, les grands magasins vous proposent tout ce dont vous pouvez rêver° dans les domaines de la mode, de la parfumerie, de la bijouterie°, des arts de la table, etc. Vous pouvez acheter tout dans un seul magasin. Les grands magasins suivants sont adhérents° de l'Office de Tourisme et des Congrès de Paris. Ils sont parmi les magasins les plus connus du monde.

Le Bon Marché Rive Gauche
22, rue de Sèvres
75007 Paris
Métro: Sèvres-Babylone
Tél: 01 44 39 80 00

Le Printemps
http://www.printemps.fr
64, boulevard Haussmann
75009 Paris
Métro: Havre Caumartin
RER: Auber
Tél: 01 42 82 50 00

Galeries Lafayette
http://www.galerieslafayette.com
40, boulevard Haussmann
75009 Paris
Métro: Havre Caumartin,
     Chaussée d'Antin
Tél: 01 42 82 34 56

La Samaritaine
19, rue de la Monnaie
75001 Paris
Métro: Louvre, Châtelet, Pont Neuf
RER: Châtelet-Les Halles
Tél: 01 40 41 20 20

la douane: *customs*

Dans le Marché Commun d'Europe il y a une taxe, la T.V.A. (taxe sur la valeur ajoutée), qui augmente tous les prix d'environ 20 pour cent. Si vous avez un passeport américain, si vous voyagez comme touriste et si vous achetez au moins 200 euros de marchandises dans un seul magasin, vous pouvez demander la détaxe quand vous partez de la France. Il faut que vous demandiez les documents nécessaires dans le magasin, puis il faut que vous remettiez ces documents à la douane° à l'aéroport le jour du départ. Plus tard, vous recevrez la somme de la taxe que vous avez payée.

Réfléchissons: Organiser tous ses documents pour faire une demande de détaxe peut prendre longtemps. À votre avis, est-ce que cela en vaut la peine? Pour quelle somme de détaxe est-ce que vous seriez content(e) d'attendre une heure? Une demi-heure?

À vous! With a partner, take turns reading the following sentences, focusing on your pronunciation of the Parisian landmarks and sites of interest.

le funiculaire: *a cable-car (such as that which scales the steep slope of Montmartre)*
la coupole dorée: *the golden dome*
les Invalides: *a military museum and site of Napoleon Bonaparte's tomb*
fouiller: *to rummage (through)*
les bouquinistes: *used book merchants, many of whom display their wares streetside near the Seine in Paris*
(des) bateau(x)-mouche(s): *small passenger steamers that offer tours of Paris along the Seine*

1. L'Arc de Triomphe se trouve dans l'Avenue des Champs-Élysées.
2. À Montmartre, on peut monter à la Basilique du Sacré-Cœur en funiculaire°.
3. Du haut de la tour Eiffel, on aperçoit la coupole dorée° des Invalides°.
4. Beaucoup des étudiants de la Sorbonne habitent au Quartier latin.
5. Si vous êtes bibliophile, n'oubliez pas de fouiller° les trésors des bouquinistes° le long de la Seine.
6. À Beaubourg, il faut absolument visiter le Centre Pompidou!
7. La cathédrale Notre-Dame de Paris domine l'Île de la Cité.
8. Combien coûte le tour de Paris en bateau-mouche°?

POUR DÉVELOPPER VOS IDÉES

Thematic objective: To identify the historical processes that influence the construction of landmark sites in a city

Présentation: Le nouveau visage de Paris

POUR SAISIR L'ESSENTIEL:

Vous connaissez déjà plusieurs grands monuments de Paris. Mais savez-vous pourquoi ils sont là? En lisant le texte à la page suivante, notez les raisons données pour l'existence de ces sites. Puis pour chaque monument identifiez une raison de la liste suivante qui a influencé sa construction. Quels passages du texte justifient vos choix?

Discutez vos idées avec votre partenaire. Êtes-vous d'accord sur votre interprétation?

Liste des sites	Raisons qui ont influencé leur construction
1. l'Arc de Triomphe: ...	A. Une réponse aux besoins d'une région en pleine croissance
2. la Grande Arche: ...	B. Une réponse aux besoins des progrès technologiques
3. l'Opéra Garnier: ...	C. Un héritage politique qui commémore des événements
4. l'Opéra Bastille: ...	D. Une réponse aux nouveaux besoins de la ville
5. la Bibliothèque Nationale, site Richelieu: ...	E. Un bijou d'une rénovation municipale
6. la Bibliothèque Nationale, site François Mitterrand: ...	F. Un héritage politique au service du public
	G. Une commémoration de la Révolution

Les deux visages de Paris

Paris classique

L'Arc de Triomphe

Déjà en 1730 on recherchait un monument central pour la place de l'Étoile. Mais il a fallu attendre l'arrivée de Bonaparte qui avait l'idée d'y faire bâtir l'Arc de Triomphe, un monument à la gloire de sa Grande Armée. C'est un arc triomphal de style classique.

L'Arc de Triomphe et ses pieds monumentaux sont décorés avec des bas-reliefs qui décrivent des scènes de l'époque révolutionnaire. Sur le côté qui fait face aux Champs-Élysées se trouve «la Marseillaise» de Rude représentant le départ des volontaires vers le front en 1792. Les scènes sur les autres côtés sont «le Triomphe de Napoléon en 1810», «la Résistance de 1814» et «la Paix de 1815».

L'Opéra Garnier

Ce magnifique bâtiment a été commandé par Napoléon III pendant la grande rénovation de la ville menée par le baron Haussmann. L'architecte Charles Garnier a gagné le concours, et les travaux ont duré de 1860 à 1875.

Vaste et richement décoré, le grand foyer ressemble aux châteaux de l'âge classique. La salle de spectacle, en rouge et or, est éclairée par un immense lustre en cristal pesant huit tonnes. Et pour combler ces beaux décors, le plafond de Marc Chagall, peint en 1964, évoque de grandes œuvres lyriques du répertoire.

La Bibliothèque Nationale de France: le site Richelieu

C'est Louis XI, roi de 1461 à 1483, qui a fondé la Bibliothèque de France. Elle s'est installée à Paris en 1570. Et elle a eu un grand développement à partir de 1666 sous Colbert, qui avait pour ambition d'en faire un instrument à la gloire de Louis XIV.

En 1720 la Bibliothèque est arrivée à ses locaux sur le site Richelieu. Napoléon III a demandé à l'architecte Henri Labrouste de faire la reconstruction d'une partie des bâtiments. Il a créé la grande Salle des imprimés—qu'on appelle aussi la salle Labrouste—dans le style architectural du Second Empire. Elle a été inaugurée en 1868.

Le nouveau visage de Paris

La Grande Arche

Dans les années 50 la recrudescence de circulation automobile a stimulé une concentration des entreprises dans l'ouest de Paris. Cette condition a nécessité le développement de ce secteur de la ville. En 1982, le Président Mitterrand a eu l'idée de lancer un concours° pour la construction d'un monument qui prolongera la perspective qui passe par le Louvre et l'Arc de Triomphe. L'architecte danois Otto von Sprekenben a gagné le concours avec «la Grande Arche». Les travaux ont été finis en 1989, deux cents ans après la Révolution.

C'est un immense cube évidé° de béton° recouvert de verre et de marbre blanc. Elle fait 108m de côté, 110m de haut, 112m de profondeur et son toit terrasse fait plus d'un hectare. Son espace vide central pourrait aisément tenir la cathédrale Notre-Dame.

L'Opéra Bastille

Inauguré le 13 juillet 1989—la veille du bicentenaire de la Révolution—l'Opéra-Bastille est l'œuvre de Carlos Ott, un architecte canadien-uruguayen. Ott a été parmi les 1700 architectes à participer au concours international.

Ce monument est appelé «un chef d'œuvre de la technologie». Son architecture est marquée par l'emploi de matériaux identiques à l'intérieur comme à l'extérieur. Cette modernité présente un contraste frappant avec les riches décors de l'Opéra-Garnier et le rend l'un des opéras les plus controversés d'Europe.

La Bibliothèque Nationale de France: le site François-Mitterrand

En 1537, François Ier a introduit une ordonnance qui obligeait qu'un exemplaire de toute production imprimée° soit déposé à la bibliothèque. Cette ordonnance s'appelle «le dépôt légal». Au fil du temps, cette obligation s'est étendue pour couvrir les périodiques, les gravures, les affiches et les partitions musicales. Depuis 1925 elle couvre aussi les photographies, les films et les phonogrammes. Et en 1992 on a ajouté les documents en multimédia.

Étant donné la grandeur des collections et le fait qu'il y a plus de 500.000 étudiants universitaires dans la région de Paris, il est naturel qu'on cherche un nouveau site pour la Bibliothèque nationale. Ainsi, en 1988, on a décidé la création d'un nouveau bâtiment au 13e arrondissement, sur le site maintenant appelé François-Mitterrand.

---

lancer un concours: *have a contest* / **évidé:** *hollow* / **le béton:** *concrete* / **imprimé:** *printed*

E. Des points de repère (landmarks). Il y a des endroits qui font partie de l'image d'une ville. Pour les habitants, ces points de repère rappellent souvent des «leaders» ou des événements importants. Parfois ils reflètent une époque importante dans l'histoire de la ville, ou ils signalent le progrès vers l'avenir.

Réfléchissez aux sites significatifs de votre ville et identifiez cinq ou six points de repère principaux.

F. L'esprit d'une ville. En général, on peut classer les raisons de l'existence d'un point de repère dans plusieurs catégories. Voici quelques exemples:

- le prestige politique ou public d'une personne:

  le château de Versailles pour Louis XIV; le musée J. Paul Getty à Los Angeles

- un événement important nécessite la construction d'un site:

  le Stade de France, construit pour «la dernière Coupe du Monde de football du siècle» en 1998; la tour Eiffel, construite à l'occasion du centenaire de la Révolution; le Space Needle à Seattle, construit pour l'Exposition Internationale de 1962

- le progrès ou la croissance de la ville exige une nouvelle construction:

  le développement du secteur de la ville appelé la Défense, à Paris, exigé par les progrès économiques suite à la Seconde Guerre mondiale

- commémoration d'un événement ou d'une personne:

  le Lincoln Memorial à Washington, D.C.; la place de la Concorde à Paris

- une époque dans l'histoire de la ville ou d'un quartier:

  Les Halles, autrefois un grand marché de viandes, de légumes, etc. (qui s'appelait le «ventre de Paris»), se sont transformées en un grand centre commercial touristique, tout en retenant son identité historique.

Catégorisez les points de repère de votre liste pour l'Exercice E. Utilisez les catégories dans le modèle et ajoutez vos idées.

Catégories	Ville: *Paris*	Explication
Un site qui est l'héritage° politique ou personnel d'un leader		
Un site construit à l'occasion d'un événement important	le stade	construit à l'occasion de la coupe mondiale de football
Un site important dans le passé de la ville	Les Halles/Beaubourg	
Un site qui témoigne de la croissance de la ville	La Défense	
??? (d'autres idées)		

un héritage: *legacy*

G. L'esprit de notre ville. Travaillez en groupe de deux ou trois pour préparer un guide touristique de votre ville. Choisissez des sites qui représentent l'esprit de votre ville. Chaque personne du groupe doit rechercher un des sites pour la brochure. Pour chaque site:

1. Dites où il se trouve.
2. Expliquez son importance. Mentionnez l'histoire, les dates, des personnes ou des événements.
3. Décrivez un peu son apparence (sa taille, son âge, son architecture).
4. Discutez l'attitude des habitants de la ville envers cet endroit.

Finalement, travaillez ensemble pour écrire l'introduction et les informations générales de votre brochure.

ÉCOUTONS: FAISONS UN PETIT TOUR

Si vous allez à Paris, il faut absolument que vous alliez voir la cathédrale Notre-Dame. On recommande aussi que vous fassiez la visite du Louvre. Et il ne faut surtout pas que vous manquiez la tour Eiffel et l'Arc de Triomphe. Selon les guides touristiques, ce sont les «incontournables», les lieux qu'il faut absolument visiter. En effet, ce sont les images traditionnelles de Paris. C'est le Paris des cartes postales. C'est le Paris des tableaux des impressionnistes et le Paris des films d'Hollywood. Enfin, c'est le Paris des rêves. Alors, faisons-en un petit tour.

A. **On identifie les détails historiques.** Avant d'écouter, étudiez le tableau suivant afin de déterminer quels détails vous cherchez pour chaque monument de votre visite. Ensuite, pendant que vous écoutez les commentaires du guide, prenez au moins deux notes pour chaque monument.

Des notes sur la visite guidée

Monument	Il date du... siècle	Une qualité associée à ce monument	Une personne associée à ce monument	Un événement associé à ce monument
Modèle: Notre-Dame	*XIIe*		*les Parisiens*	*destruction des sculptures*
Notre-Dame				
Le Louvre				
L'Arc de Triomphe				
La tour Eiffel				

B. **Pour retenir les points d'intérêt.** Imaginez que vous cherchez un emploi comme guide touristique à Paris. (1) Relisez vos notes de la visite guidée, et (2) organisez les informations afin de les rendre aussi claires que possible. Ensuite, (3) mémorisez les trois faits° que vous trouvez les plus intéressants. Enfin, (4) fermez votre cahier, expliquez vos trois faits à votre partenaire. Essayez de retenir les informations communiquées par votre partenaire pour les rapporter à la classe.

faits (m.): *facts*

Modèle: —*Dis! savais-tu que la cathédrale Notre-Dame et le musée du Louvre ont presque le même âge? Les deux monuments datent du XIIe siècle.*

ÉLABORATION DE PERSPECTIVE

Review the city profiles that you wrote for the **Découverte** sections in this chapter. Using your previous work as a guide, draft a profile of your city. Provide as much information as possible for each category. When you have your draft ready, work with one or two partners to prepare a detailed profile. Then decide which features of your city identify it with the region where it is located. Do these features relate to climate and topography, to cultural heritage, or to the course of economic development in your region? (Note that these explanations may overlap one another.)

Use the chart on page 519 to create a profile of the city. (You do not need to include information for every category.)

INTÉGRATION: Un projet de jumelage°

un jumelage: *matching, pairing up (as in sister cities)*

une ville jumelle: *twin city*

Situation: Le conseil municipal cherche à créer des rapports internationaux dans le but de favoriser les échanges scolaires, sportifs, culturels, économiques, touristiques et sociaux avec des villes étrangères. Ainsi, on a demandé à votre classe de recommander une ville francophone comme ville jumelle° de la ville universitaire.

Mission: Proposez une ville jumelle. Vous cherchez une ville où les habitants possèdent un point de vue, des intérêts et/ou une vision pour l'avenir qui correspondent à ceux de votre ville.

Démarche: Travaillez en groupe de trois ou quatre pour préparer votre projet.

Étape A. Examinez les profils que vous avez créés dans les sections **Découverte** de ce chapitre afin de choisir la meilleure jumelle pour votre ville. Basez la décision sur ce que ces villes ont en commun avec la vôtre et sur les contributions mutuelles que vous pouvez imaginer entre ces villes et la vôtre.

Étape B. Faites des recherches supplémentaires sur la ville que vous choisissez.

Étape C. Faites une liste des échanges qu'on pourrait faire entre les deux villes. Pour chaque échange que vous proposez, identifiez les bénéfices que les habitants pourraient en tirer.

Quelques idées à considérer:

- des échanges scolaires—étudiants ou professeurs, camps de vacances, projets spéciaux pour les enfants dans les musées/les Scouts
- des échanges culturels—expositions d'art régional, ateliers d'artisanat, troupes de théâtre ou de danse, équipes sportives, fêtes multiculturelles
- des échanges économiques—foires internationales, expositions commerciales, délégations de quelques entreprises, études de marchés mutuels, tourisme
- des échanges sociaux—accueils des membres des églises, contacts directs entre les habitants

Étape D. Présentez vos suggestions au conseil municipal.

LEXIQUE DE BASE

LEXIQUE DÉJÀ VU

Pour voyager

un cimetière	cemetery
une courte sieste	short nap
le décalage horaire	jet lag
la douane	customs
un itinéraire	itinerary
un marché aux puces	flea market
un moyen de transport	means of transportation
la T.V.A. (taxe sur la valeur ajoutée)	VAT (value added tax)
comparer les prix	to compare prices
disposer de peu de temps	to have little time
économiser	to spend less money, to economize
faire attention	to pay attention, to be careful
louer une voiture	to rent a car
payer en espèces	to pay cash

acheter les billets	to buy the tickets
chercher un hôtel	to look for a hotel
réserver les chambres	to reserve the rooms
utiliser les transports publics	to use public transportation

Pour exprimer la nécessité

il faut que	one has to, must
il vaut mieux que	it would be better to
il est nécessaire que	it's necessary to
il est préférable que	it's preferable to
il est important que	it's important to
il est essentiel que	it's essential to
il est indispensable que	it's indispensable to

Pour exprimer la volition

souhaiter	to wish

désirer	to want, to desire
vouloir	to want
préférer	to prefer
aimer (mieux)	to like (better)

Des verbes

couvrir	to cover
découvrir	to discover
offrir	to offer
s'offrir	to allow or indulge oneself
souffrir	to suffer
connaître	to be acquainted or familiar with
savoir	to know; to know how to

INFINITIF	PRÉSENT	PASSÉ COMPOSÉ	IMPARFAIT

Verbs in -er, ir, -re

chercher	je cherche	j'ai cherché	je cherchais
	tu cherches	tu as cherché	tu cherchais
	il cherche	il a cherché	il cherchait
	nous cherchons	nous avons cherché	nous cherchions
	vous cherchez	vous avez cherché	vous cherchiez
	ils cherchent	ils ont cherché	ils cherchaient
finir	je finis	j'ai fini	je finissais
	tu finis	tu as fini	tu finissais
	il finit	il a fini	il finissait
	nous finissons	nous avons fini	nous finissions
	vous finissez	vous avez fini	vous finissiez
	ils finissent	ils ont fini	ils finissaient
attendre	j'attends	j'ai attendu	j'attendais
	tu attends	tu as attendu	tu attendais
	il attend	il a attendu	il attendait
	nous attendons	nous avons attendu	nous attendions
	vous attendez	vous avez attendu	vous attendiez
	ils attendent	ils ont attendu	ils attendaient

Reflexive verbs

se coucher	je me couche	je me suis couché(e)	je me couchais
	tu te couches	tu t'es couché(e)	tu te couchais
	il se couche	il s'est couché	il se couchait
	nous nous couchons	nous nous sommes couché(e)s	nous nous couchions
	vous vous couchez	vous vous êtes couché(e)(s)	vous vous couchiez
	ils se couchent	ils se sont couchés	ils se couchaient

Verbs with spelling changes in the stem

acheter (like acheter: se lever, se promener)	j'achète	j'ai acheté	j'achetais
	tu achètes		
	il achète		
	nous achetons		
	vous achetez		
	ils achètent		
préférer (like préférer: espérer)	je préfère	j'ai préféré	je préférais
	tu préfères		
	il préfère		
	nous préférons		
	vous préférez		
	ils préfèrent		
appeler	j'appelle	j'ai appelé	j'appelais
	tu appelles		
	il appelle		
	nous appelons		
	vous appelez		
	ils appellent		

FUTUR	SUBJONCTIF	CONDITIONNEL	IMPÉRATIF
	que (qu')		
je chercherai	je cherche	je chercherais	cherche
tu chercheras	tu cherches	tu chercherais	cherchons
il cherchera	il cherche	il chercherait	cherchez
nous chercherons	nous cherchions	nous chercherions	
vous chercherez	vous cherchiez	vous chercheriez	
ils chercheront	ils cherchent	ils chercheraient	
je finirai	je finisse	je finirais	finis
tu finiras	tu finisses	tu finirais	finissons
il finira	il finisse	il finirait	finissez
nous finirons	nous finissions	nous finirions	
vous finirez	vous finissiez	vous finiriez	
ils finiront	ils finissent	ils finiraient	
j'attendrai	j'attende	j'attendrais	attends
tu attendras	tu attendes	tu attendrais	attendons
il attendra	il attende	il attendrait	attendez
nous attendrons	nous attendions	nous attendrions	
vous attendrez	vous attendiez	vous attendriez	
ils attendront	ils attendent	ils attendraient	
	que (qu')		
je me coucherai	je me couche	je me coucherais	couche-toi
tu te coucheras	tu te couches	tu te coucherais	couchons-nous
il se couchera	il se couche	il se coucherait	couchez-vous
nous nous coucherons	nous nous couchions	nous nous coucherions	
vous vous coucherez	vous vous couchiez	vous vous coucheriez	
ils se coucheront	ils se couchent	ils se coucheraient	
	que (qu')		
j'achèterai	j'achète	j'achèterais	achète
	tu achètes		achetons
	il achète		achetez
	nous achetions		
	vous achetiez		
	ils achètent		
je préférerai	je préfère	je préférerais	préfère
	tu préfères		préférons
	il préfère		préférez
	nous préférions		
	vous préfériez		
	ils préfèrent		
j'appellerai	j'appelle	j'appellerais	appelle
	tu appelles		appelons
	il appelle		appelez
	nous appelions		
	vous appeliez		
	ils appellent		

Conjugaison des verbes

INFINITIF	PRÉSENT	PASSÉ COMPOSÉ	IMPARFAIT
payer (like **payer**: s'ennuyer, essayer)	je paie tu paies il paie nous payons vous payez ils paient	j'ai payé	je payais
commencer	je commence tu commences il commence nous commençons vous commencez ils commencent	j'ai commencé	je commençais
manger (like **manger**: exiger, voyager)	je mange tu manges il mange nous mangeons vous mangez ils mangent	j'ai mangé	je mangeais

Other verbs

aller	je vais tu vas il va nous allons vous allez ils vont	je suis allé(e)	j'allais
avoir	j'ai tu as il a nous avons vous avez ils ont	j'ai eu	j'allais
boire	je bois tu bois il boit nous buvons vous buvez ils boivent	j'ai bu	je buvais
connaître (like **connaître**: reconnaître)	je connais tu connais il connaît nous connaissons vous connaissez ils connaissent	j'ai connu	je connaissais
devoir	je dois tu dois il doit nous devons vous devez ils doivent	j'ai dû	je devais
dire	je dis tu dis il dit nous disons vous dites ils disent	j'ai dit	je disais

FUTUR	SUBJONCTIF	CONDITIONNEL	IMPÉRATIF
je paierai	je paie tu paies il paie nous payions vous payiez ils paient	je paierais	paie payons payez
je commencerai	je commence tu commences il commence nous commencions vous commenciez ils commencent	je commencerais	commence commençons commencez
je mangerai	je mange tu manges il mange nous mangions vous mangiez ils mangent	je mangerais	mange mangeons mangez
	que (qu')		
j'irai	j'aille tu ailles il aille nous allions vous alliez ils aillent	j'irais	va allons allez
j'aurai	j'aie tu aies il ait nous ayons vous ayez ils aient	j'aurais	aie ayons ayez
je boirai	je boive tu boives il boive nous buvions bous buviez ils boivent	je boirai	bois buvons buvez
je connaîtrai	je connaisse tu connaisses il connaisse nous connaissions vous connaissiez ils connaissent	je connaîtrais	connais connaissons connaissez
je devrai	je doive tu doives il doive nous devions vous deviez ils doivent	je devrais	dois devons devez
je dirai	je dise tu dises il dise nous disions vous disiez ils disent	je dirais	dis disons dites

Conjugaison des verbes

INFINITIF	PRÉSENT	PASSÉ COMPOSÉ	IMPARFAIT
écrire (like écrire: décrire)	j'écris tu écris il écrit nous écrivons vous écrivez ils écrivent	j'ai écrit	j'écrivais
être *(to be)*	je suis *I am* tu es *you are* il est *he is* nous sommes *we are* vous êtes *they are* ils sont *they are*	j'ai été	j'étais
faire	je fais tu fais il fait nous faisons vous faites ils font	j'ai fait	je faisais
lire	je lis tu lis il lit nous lisons vous lisez ils lisent	j'ai lu	je lisais
mettre (like mettre: permettre, promettre)	je mets tu mets il met nous mettons vous mettez ils mettent	j'ai mis	je mettais
ouvrir (like ouvrir: offrir)	j'ouvre tu ouvres il ouvre nous ouvrons vous ouvrez ils ouvrent	j'ai ouvert	j'ouvrais
partir (like partir: dormir, sentir, servir, sortir)	je pars tu pars il part nous partons vous partez ils partent	je suis parti(e)	je partais
pouvoir *to be able to have permission*	je peux tu peux il peut nous pouvons vous pouvez ils peuvent	j'ai pu	je pouvais
prendre (like prendre: apprendre, comprendre)	je prends tu prends il prend nous prenons vous prenez ils prennent	j'ai pris	je prenais

FUTUR	SUBJONCTIF	CONDITIONNEL	IMPÉRATIF
j'écrirai	j'écrive tu écrives il écrive nous écrivions vous écriviez ils écrivent	j'écrirais	écris écrivons écrivez
je serai	je sois tu sois il soit nous soyons vous soyez ils soient	je serais	sois soyons soyez
je ferai	je fasse tu fasses il fasse nous fassions vous fassiez ils fassent	je ferais	fais faisons faites
je lirai	je lise tu lises il lise nous lisions vous lisiez ils lisent	je lirais	lis lisons lisez
je mettrai	je mette tu mettes il mette nous mettions vous mettiez ils mettent	je mettrais	mets mettons mettez
j'ouvrirai	j'ouvre tu ouvres il ouvre nous ouvrions vous ouvriez ils ouvrent	j'ouvrirais	ouvre ouvrons ouvrez
je partirai	je parte tu partes il parte nous partions vous partiez ils partent	je partirais	pars partons partez
je pourrai	je puisse tu puisses il puisse nous puissions vous puissiez ils puissent	je pourrais	(n'existe pas)
je prendrai	je prenne tu prennes il prenne nous prenions vous preniez ils prennent	je prendrais	prends prenons prenez

Conjugaison des verbes

INFINITIF	PRÉSENT	PASSÉ COMPOSÉ	IMPARFAIT
savoir	je sais tu sais il sait nous savons vous savez ils savent	j'ai su	je savais
suivre	je suis tu suis il suit nous suivons vous suivez ils suivent	j'ai suivi	je suivais
venir (like venir: devenir, revenir)	je viens tu viens il vient nous venons vous venez ils viennent	je suis venu(e)	je venais
voir (like voir: croire)	je vois tu vois il voit nous voyons vous voyez ils voient	j'ai vu	je voyais
vouloir	je veux tu veux il veut nous voulons vous voulez ils veulent	j'ai voulu	je voulais

FUTUR	SUBJONCTIF	CONDITIONNEL	IMPÉRATIF
je saurai	je sache tu saches il sache nous sachions vous sachiez ils sachent	je saurais	sache sachons sachez
je suivrai	je suive tu suives il suive nous suivions vous suiviez ils suivent	je suivrais	suis suivons suivez
je viendrai	je vienne tu viennes il vienne nous venions vous veniez ils viennent	je viendrais	viens venons venez
je verrai	je voie tu voies il voie nous voyions vous voyiez ils voient	je verrais	vois voyons voyez
je voudrai	je veuille tu veuilles il veuille nous voulions vous vouliez ils veuillent	je voudrais	

Français-anglais

A

à in; at; to
abominable abominable
abordable affordable
abricot (*m*) apricot
absent(e) absent
absenter : s'— du travail to be absent from work
accent (*m*) accent; stress
accepter to accept
accident (*m*) accident
accomplir to accomplish
accord (*m*) agreement; **d'—** okay; **être d'—** to agree
accumuler to accumulate
acheter to buy
acteur(-trice) (*m, f*) actor; actress
actuel(le) curent
actuellement currently
adapter : s'— (à) to adapt oneself to; to get used to
addition (*f*) check; bill (at a restaurant); addition
adieux : faire ses — say good-bye
admirer to admire
adorer to love
adresse (*f*) address
aéroport (*m*) airport
affaires (*f pl*) belongings; business; **homme d'—** businessman; **femme d'—** businesswoman
affectueux(-euse) affectionate
affiche (*f*) poster
afin de in order to
africain(e) African
Afrique (*f*) Africa
âge (*m*) age
âgé(e) old
agence (*f*) agency; **— de voyage** travel agency
agent(e) (*m, f*) agent; **— de police** police officer; **—de voyage** travel agent; **—immobilier** real estate agent
agir to act
agneau (*m*) lamb
agréable pleasant
aide (*f*) help
aider (à) to help
ail (*m*) garlic
aile (*f*) wing
aimer to like; **— mieux** to prefer
aîné(e) eldest
ainsi thus; **— que** as well as
air : avoir l'— to seem; to look
ajouter to add
alimentation (*f*) food
aliments (*m pl*) food
Allemagne Germany
allemand(e) German
aller to go; **s'en —** to go away
allergie (*f*) allergy
aller-retour (*m*) round trip

aller-simple (*m*) one-way
alliance (*f*) wedding ring
allô hello (on the telephone)
alors so; then
ambitieux(-euse) ambitious
améliorer to improve; **s'—** to improve oneself
aménagé(e) landscaped; cared for
aménager to furnish; to equip; to arrange furnishings
amener to bring (someone); to take (someone)
amer(-ère) bitter
américain(e) American
Amérique (*f*) America
ami(e) (*m, f*) friend
amour (*m*) love
amoureux(-euse) in love with
amusant(e) amusing; fun
amuser : s'— to have a good time; **s'— le week-end** to enjoy oneself on the week-end
an (*m*) year; **Le Nouvel —** New Year's
ananas (*m*) pineapple
ancêtres (*m pl*) ancestors
ancien(ne) old; former; ancient
andouille (*f*) sausage made of chitterlings
anglais(e) English
Angleterre (*f*) England
année (*f*) year
anniversaire (*m*) birthday
annoncer to announce
annuler to cancel
anonyme anonymous
anorak (*m*) ski jacket
anthropologie (*f*) anthropology
anxieux(-euse) anxious
apéritif (*m*) before-dinner drink
appareil (*m*) apparatus; **— photo** camera
appartement (*m*) apartment
appartenir (à) to belong (to)
appel (*m*) roll call
appeler to call; **s'—** to be called; **Je m'appelle** My name is . . .
appétit (*m*) appetite; **Bon appétit!** Enjoy your meal!
appliquer : s'— (à) to apply oneself
apporter to bring (something)
apprécier to appreciate; to value
apprendre to learn
après after
après-midi (*m*) afternoon
arbre (*m*) tree
archéologie (*f*) archeology
architecte (*m, f*) architect
argent (*m*) silver;
armoire (*f*) armoire
arranger to arrange; **s'—** to get organized; to work itself out
arrêt (*m*) stop; **sans —** non-stop; **— de bus** bus stop

arrêter: s'— to stop
arrivée (*f*) arrival
arriver to arrive; to happen
art (*m*) art; **beaux—s** fine arts
artiste (*m, f*) artist
ascenseur (*m*) elevator
asiatique Asian
Asie (*f*) Asia
asperges (*f pl*) asparagus
asseoir : s'— to sit down
assez rather; **— de** enough
assiette (*f*) plate
assis(e) seated
assistance (*f*) assistance; help
assistant(e) (*m, f*) assistant
assister (à) to attend
assurance (*f*) assurance; confidence; insurance
astronaute (*m, f*) astronaut
astronomie (*f*) astronomy
athlétisme (*m*) track and field
attendre to wait (for)
attention : faire — be careful; pay attention
aubergine (*f*) eggplant
aucun(e) not a one; **ne...—** none whatsoever
aussi also; **—...que** as . . . as
Australie (*f*) Australia
australien(ne) Australian
autant que as much as
auto (*f*) car
autobus (*m*) bus
automne (*m*) autumn, fall; **en —** in the autumn; in the fall
autoroute (*f*) highway
autre other
autrefois formerly
Autriche (*f*) Austria
autrichien(ne) Austrian
avancer : s'— to advance
avant before
avant-hier the day before yesterday
avare (*m*) miser
avare miserly
avec with
avocat(e) (*m, f*) lawyer
avoir to have

B

baba au rhum (*m*) rum pastry
bac = baccalauréat
baccalauréat (*m*) exam taken at the end of secondary school studies
bague (*f*) ring
baguette (*f*) French bread
baigner : se — to go swimming
baignoire (*f*) bath tub
balader: se — to take a stroll
balayeur (*m*) janitor; sweeper
balcon (*m*) balcony
ballon (*m*) ball; balloon

banane *(f)* banana
banc *(m)* bench
banque *(f)* bank
banquier(-ière) *(m, f)* banker
barbe *(f)* beard
bas *(m)* bottom
basket *(m)* running shoe; basketball shoe
basse *(f)* string bass
bataille *(f)* battle
bateau *(m)* boat
bâtiment *(m)* building
batterie *(f)* drums
bavarder to make conversation
beau (bel, belle) beautiful
beaucoup a lot
beau-frère *(m)* brother-in-law; step-brother
beau-père *(m)* father-in-law; step-father
bébé *(m)* baby
beigne *(f)* slap
belge Belgian
Belgique Belgium
belle-mère *(f)* mother-in-law; step-mother
belle-soeur *(f)* sister-in-law; step-sister
besoin *(m)* need; **avoir —** to need; **-s financiers** financial needs
beurre *(m)* butter
bibliothèque *(f)* library
bicyclette *(f)* bicycle
bidet *(m)* bidet (low sink used for personal hygiene)
bien well; **— entendu** of course
bientôt soon; **À —.** See you soon.
bière *(f)* beer
bifteck *(m)* steak
bijouterie *(m)* jewelry store
bijoux *(m pl)* jewelry
billet *(m)* ticket; bill (money)
biographie *(f)* biography
biologie *(f)* biology
biscuit *(m)* cookie
blanc(he) white
blesser to wound; to injure
bleu(e) blue
blond(e) blond
blouson *(m)* jacket
bœuf *(m)* beef
boire to drink
bois *(m)* wood
boisson *(m)* drink
boîte *(f)* box; can; **— de nuit** nightclub
bol *(m)* bowl
bon(ne) good; **Bon appétit!** Enjoy your meal!; **—marché** inexpensive, a good buy; **une bonne présentation** quality of presenting oneself well in demeanor as well as dress
bonbon *(m)* (a piece of) candy
bonheur *(m)* happiness
bonjour hello
bord *(m)* edge; **au — de** along; **— de la mer** seashore
botanique *(f)* botany
bottes *(f pl)* boots
bouche *(f)* mouth

boucher(-ère) butcher
boucherie *(f)* butcher shop
boucle d'oreille *(f)* earring
bouillir to boil
boulanger(-ère) *(m, f)* baker
boulangerie *(f)* bakery
bourse *(f)* scholarship
Boursin *(m)* a packaged soft cheese containing herbs and garlic or pepper
bout *(m)* end; piece; **au — du monde** at (to) the end of the world
bouteille *(f)* bottle
boutique *(f)* boutique
bras *(m)* arm
bref (brève) brief
bricoler to tinker; to putter
brie *(m)* a mild, semi-soft French cheese
brique *(f)* brick
britannique British
brocoli *(m)* broccoli
bronzer: se faire — to get a suntan
brosse *(f)* brush; **— à dents** toothbrush
brosser : se — les dents to brush one's teeth; **se — les cheveux** to brush one's hair
brouillard *(m)* fog; **Il fait du brouillard.** It's foggy.
bruit *(m)* noise
brûler to burn
brume *(f)* mist
budget *(m)* budget
bungalow *(m)* bungalow
bureau *(m)* desk; office; **— de poste** post office; **— de tabac** tobacco shop
but *(m)* goal

C

ça that; **— va?** How's it going?
cabine téléphonique *(f)* phone booth
cachemire *(m)* cashmere
cadeau *(m)* gift
cadre *(m)* business executive
café *(m)* café; coffee; **— au lait** coffe with hot milk; **— crème** coffee with cream
cafétéria *(f)* cafeteria
cafetière *(f)* coffee maker
cahier *(m)* notebook
caisse *(f)* cash register; **— d'épargne** savings and loan
caissier(-ère) cashier
calculatrice *(f)* calculator
calculer to calculate
caleçon *(m)* boxer shorts
calendrier *(m)* calendar
calme calm
calmer : se — to calm down
camarade : — de classe classmate; **— de chambre** roommate
cambrioler to rob
camembert *(m)* a popular Normandy cheese
caméra *(f)* movie camera; camcorder
campagne *(f)* country; **à la —** in the country

camping *(m)* camping
Canada *(m)* Canada
canadien(ne) Canadian
canapé *(m)* sofa
canard *(m)* duck
capacité *(f)* ability
car *(m)* bus
car because
carnet *(m)* note pad
carotte *(f)* carrot; **-s rapées** grated carrots
carrefour *(m)* crossroads; intersection
carrière *(f)* career
carte *(f)* map; **— de crédit** credit card; **— de visite** business card; **— de vœux** greeting card; **— postale** postcard
casquette *(f)* cap
casser to break; **se — la jambe** to break one's leg
casserole *(f)* saucepan
cassette *(f)* cassette tape
catégorie *(f)* category
cathédrale *(f)* cathedral
caution *(f)* deposit
cave *(f)* wine cellar
ce (cet, cette) this, that
ceinture *(f)* belt
célèbre famous
célébrer to celebrate
célibataire single
cendrier *(m)* ashtray
cent hundred
centime *(m)* centime (one one-hundredth of a franc)
centre *(m)* center; **— commercial** shopping center; **— d'étudiants** student center; **le — -ville** downtown
céramique *(f)* ceramics
céréales *(f pl)* cereal
cerise *(f)* cherry
certain(e) certain
certainement certainly
cerveau *(m)* brain
ces these; those
chacun(e) each one
chaîne *(f)* chain; **— de montagnes** mountain range; **— stéréo** stereo
chaise *(f)* chair
chalet *(m)* chalet
chaleur *(f)* heat
chaleureux(-euse) warm; inviting
chamailler : se — to bicker
chambre (à coucher) *(f)* bedroom
champ *(m)* field
champignon *(m)* mushroom
chanceux(-euse) lucky
change : bureau de — foreign currency exchange office
chanson *(f)* song
chanter to sing
chanteur(-euse) *(m, f)* singer
chapeau *(m)* hat
chapitre *(m)* chapter
chaque each
charcuterie *(f)* pork butcher's shop; delicatessen
charger : se — (de) to take charge of; to take responsibility for

charme *(m)* charm
chat *(m)* cat
châtain light brown (hair)
château *(m)* castle
chaud warm; hot; **Il fait —** It (the weather) is hot.
chauffage *(m)* heating
chauffer to heat
chaussette *(f)* sock
chaussetterie *(f)* sock shop
chaussure *(f)* shoe
chauve bald
chef *(m)* leader; **— d'entreprise** company president (C.E.O.); **— d'œuvre** masterpiece
chemise *(f)* shirt; **— de nuit** night-shirt; nightgown
chemiserie *(f)* shirt shop
chemisier *(m)* blouse; woman's shirt
chèque *(m)* check
cher (chère) expensive; dear
chercher to look for; **aller —** to go get
cheveux *(m pl)* hair
cheville *(f)* ankle
chèvre *(m)* goat; goat cheese
chez at the house of; **— le medecin** at the doctor's office
chien *(m)* dog
chiffre *(m)* number; digit
chimie *(f)* chemistry
Chine *(f)* China
chinois(e) Chinese
chocolat *(m)* chocolate
choisir to choose
choix *(m)* choice
chômage *(m)* unemployment; **être au —** to be unemployed
chose *(f)* thing; **quelque —** something
chou *(m)* cabbage
chou-fleur *(m)* cauliflower
chute (d'eau) *(f)* waterfall
cidre *(m)* cider
ciel *(m)* sky; **Le — est couvert.** It's cloudy.
cimetière *(m)* cemetery
cinéma *(m)* movie theater
circonstance *(f)* circumstance
citron *(m)* lemon; **— pressé** lemonade (freshly squeezed)
clair(e) clear; **bleu —** light blue
clarinette *(f)* clarinet
classe *(f)* class; **première —** first class
classer to file (documents)
clé *(f)* key
client(e) *(m,f)* customer
climat *(m)* climate
Coca *(m)* Coca-Cola
cochon *(m)* pig
cœur *(m)* heart; **avoir mal au —** to be nauseated
coiffer : se — to fix one's hair
coiffeur(-euse) *(m, f)* hairdresser
coin *(m)* corner
col *(m)* collar; **— roulé** turtleneck
colère *(f)* anger
collant *(m)* pantyhose
collège *(m)* intermediate or middle school

collègue *(m, f)* colleague
collier *(m)* necklace
colline *(f)* hill
colocataire *(m, f)* roommate; housemate
combien (de) how many; how much
combinaison *(f)* (underwear) slip; (outerwear) jumpsuit
comédie *(f)* comedy
comédien(ne) *(m, f)* stage actor; stage actress
commander to order
comme like; as; for; since; **comme ci comme ça** so-so; **Et — boisson?** And (what would you like) to drink?
commencer to begin
comment how
commerçant(e) *(m, f)* shopkeeper
commerce *(m)* shop; business; **les -s** business sector
commode *(f)* small chest; dresser
communiquer to communicate
comparer to compare
complet *(m)* man's suit
compléter to complete
compliqué(e) complicated
comportement *(m)* behavior
comprendre to understand
comptabilité *(f)* accounting
comptable *(m, f)* accountant
compte *(m)* account; **— de dépôt** checking account; **se rendre — de** to realize
compter to count
concentrer to concentrate
concert *(m)* concert
concombre *(m)* cucumber
condo *(m)* condominium
conduire to drive
conférence *(f)* lecture
confiance trust; confidence; **— en soi** self-confidence
confiture *(f)* jam
confort *(m)* comfort
congé *(m)* time off
conjoint(e) *(m, f)* live-in partner
conjoint(e) living together as a couple
connaissance *(f)* knowledge
connaître to be acquainted or familiar with
conquis(e) conquered
conseil *(m)* (piece of) advice
conseiller to suggest
consensus *(m)* agreement
conséquent : par — consequently
consonne *(f)* consonant
constamment constantly
construire to build
consultation à domicile *(f)* house call
consulter to consult
content(e) happy; pleased
continent *(m)* continent
continuer to keep going
contraire *(m)* opposite
contre against; **par —** on the other hand
contribuer to contribute

contrôler to control; monitor
coordonner to coordinate
copain (copine) *(m, f)* friend
copieur *(m)* photocopier
corbeille *(f)* basket
corps *(m)* body
corriger to correct
costume *(m)* man's suit
côte *(f)* coast; rib
côté *(m)* side; **à — de** next to; beside
côtelette *(f)* cutlet
coton *(m)* cotton
cou *(m)* neck
coucher : — de soleil *(m)* sunset
coucher : se — to go to bed
coude *(m)* elbow
coudre to sew
couleur *(f)* color
couloir *(m)* hallway
coup d'œil *(m)* glance
coupe *(f)* haircut
couper to cut
courageux(-euse) courageous
courgette *(f)* zucchini squash
courrier *(m)* mail; **— électronique** e-mail
cours *(m)* course; **— magistral** lecture course
course *(f)* errand; **faire les -s** to run errands
court *(m)* court; **—de tennis** *(m)* tennis court
court(e) short
cousin(e) *(m, f)* cousin
couteau *(m)* knife
coûter to cost
coûteux(-euse) costly
coutume *(f)* custom
couturier(-ière) *(m, f)* fashion designer
couvert(e) covered; **Le ciel est —.** It's cloudy.
couvrir to cover
cravate *(f)* tie
crayon *(m)* pencil
créer to create
crème *(f)* cream
crémerie *(f)* creamery, dairy store
crevette *(f)* shrimp
crime *(m)* crime
crise *(f)* crisis
critiquer to criticize
croire to believe; to think
croissant *(m)* croissant
croque-madame *(m)* a hot ham and cheese sandwich, topped with a fried egg
croque-monsieur *(m)* a hot ham and cheese sandwich, topped with grilled cheese
crudités *(f pl)* raw vegetables
cuillère *(f)* spoon; **— à café** a teaspoon
cuir *(m)* leather
cuire : faire — to cook
cuisine *(f)* kitchen; cuisine; **faire la —** to cook
cuisiner to cook
cuisinière *(f)* stove
cuisse *(f)* thigh

cuit(e) cooked
cultiver to cultivate
curieux(-euse) curious
curriculum vitae (C.V.) *(m)* résumé
cycliste *(m, f)* cyclist
cyclone *(m)* hurricane

D

D.A.B. (Distributeur Automatique de Billets) *(m)* A.T.M. (Automatic Teller Machine)
d'abord first
dame *(f)* woman
dans in
danser to dance
début *(m)* beginning
décalage horaire *(m)* jet lag
décevant(e) disappointing
déchirer to tear
décider (de) to decide
décilitre *(m)* one-tenth of a liter
décision *(f)* decision; **prendre une —** to decide
déclarer to declare
décontracté(e) relaxed; at ease
décourager to discourage
découvrir to discover
décrire to describe
déçu(e) disappointed
degré *(m)* degree (temperature)
dégustation *(f)* tasting
dehors outside
déjà already
déjeuner *(m)* lunch
déjeuner to have lunch
demain tomorrow
demander to ask (for); **se —** to wonder
déménager to move (change residences)
demi *(m)* a glass of draft beer
demi-frère *(m)* half-brother
demi-sœur *(f)* half-sister
dénivellation *(f)* difference in level; difference in altitude
dense dense
dent *(f)* tooth
dentifrice *(m)* toothpaste
dentiste *(m, f)* dentist
départ *(m)* departure
dépasser to go past
dépêcher : se — to hurry (up)
dépenser to spend
dépensier(-ère) spendthrift
déprimant(e) depressing
depuis since
dernier(-ère) last; latest
derrière behind; in back of
dès : — que as soon as
des some
descendre to go down (stairs, for example) ; **— la rue...** to go down . . . street
désert *(m)* desert
désir *(m)* desire; wish
désirer to want; to desire
dessert *(m)* dessert
dessin *(m)* drawing
dessiner to draw

détail *(m)* detail
détendre : se — to relax
détester to detest; to hate
devant in front of
développer to develop
devenir to become
deviner to guess
devoir to have to; must; should; to owe
devoirs *(m pl)* homework
dévoué(e) devoted
dialogue *(m)* dialogue
dinde *(f)* turkey
dîner *(m)* dinner
dîner to have dinner
diplôme *(m)* diploma, degree
dire to tell; to say; **— des gaudrioles** to tell raunchy stories
directeur(-trice) *(m, f)* director
discothèque *(f)* discotheque
discuter (de) to discuss
dispendieux(-ieuse) expensive
disponible available
disposer (de) to have at one's disposal; **— de peu de temps** to have little time
disputer : se — to argue; to quarrel
disque *(m)* record
disque compacte *(m)* CD
distribuer to distribute
divers miscellaneous
diviser to divide
divorcé(e) divorced
divorcer to (get a) divorce
doctorat *(m)* doctoral degree
doigt *(m)* finger; **— de pied** toe
dommage : C'est — It's a shame.
donc therefore
donner to give; **— des conseils** to give advice
dont about whom; of which; whose
dormir to sleep
dos *(m)* back
dossier *(m)* file
douane *(f)* customs
doute *(m)* doubt; **sans —** probably
douter to doubt
douche *(f)* shower
doué(e) gifted; talented
doux (douce) soft; mild
douzaine *(f)* dozen
dramatique dramatic
droit *(m)* law; **— de l'enfant** children's law; **— de la famille** family law; **— fiscal** financial law; **— international** international law; **— social** social law;
droit : tout — straight ahead
droite right
drôle funny
dur(e) hard
durée *(f)* length
durer to last
dynamique dynamic

E

eau *(f)* water; **— minérale** mineral water; **— gazeuse** water with bub-

bles (Perrier); **— plate** water without bubbles (Évian)
éblouir to dazzle
échanger to exchange
écharpe *(f)* scarf
échecs *(m pl)* chess
échelle *(f)* ladder
échouer (à) to fail; **— à un examen** to fail a test
éclair *(m)* a chocolat eclair (pastry)
éclairage *(m)* lighting
école *(f)* school; **— des beaux-arts** School of Fine Arts
économe economical
économie *(f)* economy; economics
économiser to save money; **— sou à sou** to scrimp and save
écossais(e) plaid; Scottish
écouter to listen to
écran *(m)* screen
écrire to write
écrivain *(m)* writer; **femme —** woman writer
éducation *(f)* education
effectivement effectively
effet *(m)* effect
église *(f)* church
égoïste selfish
élastique *(f)* rubber band
électricité *(f)* electricity
électrique electric
élève *(m, f)* high school student
embarrassant(e) uncomfortable; awkward
embrasser to kiss
émotif(-ive) emotional
emploi *(m)* employment; job; use; **— du temps** schedule
employé(e) *(m, f)* employee
employer to use
employeur(-euse) *(m, f)* employer
emporter to take; to bring along
en in; at; to; made of; **— avion** by plane; **— ce temps-là** at that time; **— face de** across from; facing
enceinte pregnant
enchanté(e) delighted; **— de faire votre connaissance.** Delighted to meet you.
encore again
encourager to encourage
endive *(f)* endive
endormi(e) asleep
endroit *(m)* place
énergique energetic
énerver : s'— to get upset
enfance *(f)* childhood
enfant *(m, f)* child
enfin finally
ennui *(m)* problem
ennuyé(e) bored
ennuyer to bore; **s'—** to be bored
ennuyeux(-euse) boring; annoying
enseigner to teach
ensemble together
ensoleillé(e) sunny
ensuite then; next

entendre to hear
enterrement *(m)* burial
enthousiaste enthusiastic
entier(-ière) whole; entire
entraîner : s'— to work out
entre between
entrecôte *(f)* rib steak
entrée *(f)* entrance hall; first course
entreprise *(f)* company; business
entrer to enter; to go in
entretien *(m)* maintenance; upkeep
envie : avoir — de to want, to feel like
envoyer to send
épaule *(f)* shoulder
épée *(f)* sword
épicerie *(f)* grocery store
épicier(-ière) *(m, f)* grocer
épinards *(m pl)* spinach
époque *(f)* period; era; **à l'— de** at the time of
épouser to marry
époux(-ouse) *(m, f)* spouse; husband; wife
équilibrer to balance
équipe *(f)* team
équipement *(m)* equipment; **— du logement** household furnishings
escalier *(m)* stairs; **— roulant** escalator
escargot *(m)* snail
Espagne *(f)* Spain
espagnol(e) Spanish
espérer to hope
essayer to try
essence *(f)* gasoline
essentiel(le) essential
est *(m)* east
estomac *(m)* stomach
et and
établir to establish; to set up
étage *(m)* floor; **deuxième —** third floor **premier —** second floor
étagère *(f)* bookcase
étape *(f)* stage or leg of a journey
état *(m)* state
été *(m)* summer; **en —** in the summer
étendre : s'— to stretch out; to extend
éternuer to sneeze
étiquette *(f)* label; tag
étoile *(f)* star
étonner to astonish
étranger : à l'— abroad
étranger(-ère) foreign
être to be
étudier to study
euh... um . . .
européen(ne) European
eux them
événement *(m)* event
évident(e) obvious
évier *(m)* sink
éviter to avoid
exactement exactly
examen *(m)* test
examiner to examine
exemple *(m)* example
exercice *(m)* exercise

exotique exotic
expliquer to explain
express *(m)* espresso
extrême extreme

F

fac = faculté
face : en — de across from
fâché(e) angry; mad
facile easy
facilité *(f)* ease; **la — des contacts** quality of "having a way with people"
facture *(f)* bill; **— téléphonique** telephone bill
faculté *(f)* school (university)
faible weak
faim *(f)* hunger; **avoir —** to be hungry
faire to do; to make; **— attention** to pay attention; be careful; **— de l'exercice** to do exercises; **— de la lecture** to do some reading; **— de la paperasse** to do paperwork; **— de la planche à voile** to windsurf; **— de son mieux** to do one's best; **— des courses** to run errands; **— des devoirs** to do homework; **— dodo** to sleep (baby talk); **— du basket** to play basketball; **— du camping** to go camping; **— du foot(ball)** to play soccer; **— du golf** to play golf; **— du hockey** to play hockey; **— du jardinage** to do some gardening; **— du jogging** to jog; **— du magasinage** to go shopping (Québec); **— du shopping** to go shopping; **— du ski (nautique)** to (water) ski; **— du sport** to do sports; **— du tennis** to play tennis; **— du vélo** to go bike riding; **— la cuisine** to cook; **— la grasse matinée** to sleep late; **— la moyenne** to make average grades; **— la queue** to stand in line; **— la vaisselle** to do the dishes; **— le marché** to do the grocery shopping; **— le ménage** to do housework; **— le nécessaire** to do whatever it takes; **— sa part** to do one's part (of work); **— un coup de téléphone** to make a phone call; **— un séjour à l'hôpital** have a stay in the hospital **— un voyage** to take a trip; **— une crise cardiaque** to have a heart attack; **— une crise de nerfs** to become hysterical; **— une dépression** to have a nervous breakdown; **— une promenade** to take a walk; **Il fait...** The weather is . . . ; **se — un budget** to set up a budget
fait : en — in fact
falloir to have to; must; **Il faut que...** It is necessary that . . . ; **Il ne faut pas...** One must not . . .
famille *(f)* family
fantastique fantastic
fatigué(e) tired
faubourg *(m)* suburb
fauché broke (out of money)

faut = falloir
fauteuil *(m)* armchair
faux (fausse) false
femme *(f)* woman; wife
fer *(m)* iron; **— à repasser** (clothes)iron
ferme *(f)* farm
fermer to close
festival *(m)* festival
fêter to celebrate; to party
feu *(m)* fire; **-x d'artifice** fireworks
feuillage *(m)* foliage
fiabilité *(f)* reliability
fiancé(e) *(m, f)* fiancé(e)
fier(-ère) proud
fièvre *(f)* fever
figure *(f)* face
fille *(f)* girl; daughter
film *(m)* film
fils *(m)* son
fin *(f)* end
finir to finish
flamboyant(e) flamboyant
fleur *(f)* flower
fleuve *(m)* major river (leading to the sea)
flexible flexible
flûte *(f)* flute
foie *(m)* liver; **— gras** liver pâté
fois *(f)* time; **des —** at times
foot(ball) *(m)* soccer; **— américain** (American) football
force *(f)* strength
forêt *(f)* forest
fort(e) strong
fou (fol, folle) crazy
foulard *(m)* scarf
four *(m)* oven; **— à micro-ondes** microwave oven
fourchette *(f)* fork
foyer *(m)* hearth; home; **femme de —** housewife
fragile fragile
frais *(m pl)* expenses; **les — de crèche/garderie** infant-/child-care expenses; **les — de scolarité** education expenses; **les — d'inscription** tuition and fees
frais (fraîche) cool
fraise *(f)* strawberry
framboise *(f)* raspberry
franc *(m)* franc
français *(m)* French (language)
français(e) French
France *(f)* France
francophone French-speaking
frapper to hit; to knock
fréquemment frequently
fréquenter to frequent (a place)
frère *(m)* brother
frigo *(m)* fridge
frisé(e) curly
frites *(f pl)* French fries
frivole frivolous
froid *(m)* cold; **avoir —** to be cold
froid(e) cold; **Il fait —.** It (the weather) is cold.
fromage *(m)* cheese

fromagerie (f) cheese shop
fruit (m) fruit; **-s de mer** seafood
fumée (f) smoke
fumer to smoke
fumeur (non-fumeur) smoking
(non-smoking)

G

gagner to win; **— de l'argent** to earn
money
gant (m) gloves; **— de toilette**
washcloth
gar (m) guy
garage (m) garage
garçon (m) boy; waiter
garder to keep
gare (f) train station
gare : — à toi watch it!
gaspiller to waste
gaspilleux(-euse) wasteful
gastronomique gastronomical
gâté(e) spoiled
gâteau (m) cake
gauche left
gaz (m) gas
gazeux(-euse) with bubbles
général(e) : en — in general
généreux(-euse) generous
genou (m) knee
gens (m pl) people
gentil(le) nice; kind
géographie (f) geography
géologie (f) geology
gérant(e) (m, f) manager
gestion (f) management
gifle (f) slap (in the face)
gigot (m) leg of lamb
gilet (m) vest; light knit top
glace (f) ice cream
golf (m) golf
golfe (m) gulf
gorge (f) throat
goût (m) taste
goûter to taste
gouvernement (m) government
grâce : — à thanks to; as a result of
gracieusement graciously
grammaire (f) grammar
grand(e) tall; big; **— magasin** department store
Grande-Bretagne (f) Great Britain
grandir to get big; to grow up
grand-mère (f) grandmother
grand-père (m) grandfather
gras(se) fat
gratuit(e) free
grave serious
gré: au — de according to; depending
on
grille-pain (m) toaster
grippe (f) flu
gris(e) gray
gronder to scold
gros(se) big; fat
grossir to get fat; to gain weight
groupe (m) group
guère : ne...— hardly

guerre (f) war
guichet (m) (ticket) window
guitare (f) guitar

H

habile clever
habillement (m) clothing
habiller : s'— to get dressed
habitant(e) (m, f) inhabitant
habiter to live
habitude (f) habit; **d'—** generally; as a
habit
habituer : s'— (à) to become accustomed (to)
haricot (m) bean; **-s verts** green
beans
héritage (m) inheritance
hésiter to hesitate
heure (f) hour; **Quelle heure est-il?**
What time is it?; **À tout à l'—**; See
you later.; **à l'—** on time
heureux(-euse) happy
hier yesterday
histoire (f) history; story
hiver (m) winter; **en —** in the winter
hollandais(e) Dutch
homard (m) lobster
homme (m) man
honnête honest
hôpital (m) hospital
horaire (m) timetable; schedule
horreur : avoir — de to hate; **film
d'—** horror movie
hors d'oeuvre (m) appetizer
hôtel (m) hotel; **— de ville** city hall;
— particulier private residence
huile (f) oil
huître (f) oyster
humain(e) human
humeur (f) mood; **de bonne —** in a
good mood; **de mauvaise —** in a
bad mood
humidité (f) humidity
hygiène (f) hygiene

I

idée (f) idea
identifier to identify
île (f) island
image (f) image; picture
imaginer to imagine
immeuble (m) apartment building; **—
de bureaux** office building
impatient(e) impatient
imperméable (m) raincoat
important(e) important
impôts (m pl) taxes
impressionnant(e) impressive
imprimer to print
incroyable unbelievable
indépendant(e) independent
indifférent(e) indifferent; lacking in
intellectual curiosity
indispensable indispensable
industrie (f) industy
infirmier(-ière) (m, f) nurse

influençable easily influenced;
impressionable
informaticien(ne) (m, f) computer
expert
informatique (f) computer science
informer : s'— (sur) to get information (on)
ingénieur (m) engineer
inquiéter to worry; **s'—** to be worried
inscrire : s'— to register; to enroll
installer : s'— to move in; to get settled
instituteur (-trice) (m, f) grade school
teacher
insupportable unbearable
intelligent(e) intelligent
intéressant(e) interesting
intéresser to interest; **s'— (à)** to be
interested (in)
interview (f) interview
interviewer to interview
intolérant(e) intolerant
inviter to invite; to offer to pay for; **—
des amis** to invite friends over
irlandais(e) Irish
israélien(ne) Israeli
Italie (f) Italy
italien(ne) Italian
itinéraire (f) itinerary

J

jamais ever; **ne... —** never
jambe (f) leg
jambon (m) ham
Japon (m) Japan
japonais(e) Japanese
jardin (m) garden; **— botanique**
botanical garden
jaune yellow
jazz (m) jazz
jean (m) jeans
jeu (m) game
jeune young
jeunesse (f) youth
jogging (m) jogging suit
joli(e) pretty; handsome
jouer to play; **— à** to play (a sport);
— de to play (an instrument)
jour (m) day; **huit —s** a week; **quinze
—s** two weeks; **tous les —s** every
day
journal (m) newspaper
journalisme (m) journalism
journaliste (m, f) journalist
journée (f) day
jumeau (jumelle) (m f) twin; **lit —**
twin bed
jupe (f) skirt
jus (m) juice; **— de fruits** fruit juice
jusqu'à to; until
juste fair
justement exactly

K

kilo (m) kilogram
kir (m) before-dinner drink of white
wine with cream of Cassis liqueur

L

là there; **ce jour-là** that day; **là-bas** over there
lac *(m)* lake
lacustre lakeside
laid(e) ugly
laine *(f)* wool
laisser to leave; **— quelqu'un faire quelque chose** to let someone do something; **— vaporiser** to let go up in smoke
lait *(m)* milk
laitue *(f)* lettuce
lampe *(f)* lamp
langue *(f)* tongue; language; **—s modernes** modern languages; **—s mortes** classical languages
lavabo *(m)* washbasin; washbowl
lave-linge *(m)* washing machine
laver to wash; **se —** to wash up; **se — les mains** to wash one's hands
laverie *(f)* laundry room
lave-vaisselle *(m)* dishwasher
lave-voitures *(m)* car wash
leçon *(f)* lesson
lecteur(-trice) *(m, f)* reader; **lectrice laser** CD player
lecture *(f)* reading
légume *(m)* vegetable
lendemain *(m)* the next day
lettre *(f)* letter
leur (to, for) them
lever : se — to get up
lèvre *(f)* lip
librairie *(f)* bookstore
lieu *(m)* place; **avoir —** to take place
limonade *(f)* lemon soda
linguistique *(f)* linguistics
lire to read
lit *(m)* bed
litre *(m)* liter
littérature *(f)* literature
livre *(m)* book
location : de — rental
logement *(m)* housing
loin far; **— de** far from
long(ue) long; **les cheveux longs,** long hair
lorsque when
louer to rent
lourd(e) heavy; oppressive
loyer *(m)* rent
lui (to, for) him; (to, for) her
lunettes *(f pl)* eyeglasses; **— de soleil** sunglasses
lycée *(m)* high school

M

Madame (Mme) *(f)* madam (Mrs.)
Mademoiselle (Mlle) *(f)* miss
magasin *(m)* store
magnétoscope *(m)* video cassette recorder (VCR)
magnifique wonderful; marvelous
maigrir to get thin; to lose weight
maillot : — de bain *(m)* swimsuit

main *(f)* hand
maintenant now
maïs *(m)* corn
mais but
maison *(f)* house
maîtrise *(f)* master's degree
mal bad; wrong; poorly; **avoir —** to hurt; to ache; **avoir — à la tête** to have a headache; **avoir du — à** to have trouble
malade sick; ill
malheureux(-euse) unhappy
manche *(f)* sleeve; **La Manche** The English Channel
manger to eat
mannequin *(m)* fashion model
manteau *(m)* coat
maquiller : se — to put on makeup
marché *(m)* market; **— aux puces** *(m)* flea market
marché : bon — inexpensive
marcher to walk
mari *(m)* husband
marié(e) married
marier : se — to get married
marketing *(m)* marketing
Maroc *(m)* Morocco
marocain(e) Moroccan
marque *(f)* brand
marron brown
mathématiques *(f pl)* mathematics
maths = mathématiques
matin *(m)* morning
mauvais(e) bad; **Il fait —.** The weather is bad.
mayonnaise *(f)* mayonnaise
me (to, for) me, myself
mécanicien(ne) *(m, f)* mechanic
méchant(e) bad; naughty; mean
mécontent(e) unhappy; displeased
médecin *(m)* doctor; **femme —** woman doctor
médecine *(f)* medicine
médicament *(m)* medication; medicine
meilleur(e) better (as adjective); **le (la) —** the best (as adjective)
mélanger to mix
même same; even; **lui —** himself; **quand —** anyway
mer *(f)* sea
merci thank you
mère *(f)* mother
merveilleux(-euse) marvelous
message *(m)* message
météo *(f)* weather report
méthodique methodical
mètre *(m)* meter
mettre to put; **— à côté** to put aside; to save
meubles *(m pl)* furniture
mexicain(e) Mexican
Mexique *(m)* Mexico
midi noon
miel *(m)* honey
mieux better (as adverb); **le —** the best (as adverb)
milieu *(m)* middle

militaire *(m, f)* serviceman; servicewoman
mille thousand
mince thin
mini-four *(m)* toaster oven
minuit midnight
miroir *(m)* mirror
misérable miserable
moche ugly
mode *(f)* fashion
modéré(e) moderate
moderne modern
modeste modest
moi me; **chez —** (at) my house; **—-même** myself
moins less; **le —** the least; **moins...que** less...than
mois *(m)* month
moitié *(f)* half
monde *(m)* world
Monsieur (M.) *(m)* mister (Mr.); sir
monstre *(m)* monster
montagne *(f)* mountain
monter to go up (stairs, for example); **— la rue...** go up ... street
montrer to show
morceau (de) *(m)* a piece (of)
mort *(f)* death
mosquée *(f)* mosque
mot *(m)* word
motiver to motivate
motocyclette *(f)* motorcycle
mourir to die
mousse *(f)* mousse
moustache *(f)* moustache
moutarde *(f)* mustard
mouton *(m)* sheep; mutton
moyen *(m)* means; **— de transport** means of transportation
mur *(m)* wall
musée *(m)* museum
musicien(ne) *(m, f)* musician
musique *(f)* music
myrtille *(f)* blueberry

N

nager to swim
naïf (naïve) naïve
naissance *(f)* birth
naître to be born; **Je suis né(e)** I was born
nappe *(f)* tablecloth
napperon *(m)* placemat
nationalité *(f)* nationality
nature *(f)* nature
ne : —...pas (do) not; **ne...aucun(e)** none; not one; **ne...jamais** never; **ne...ni...ni** neither . . . nor; **ne...nulle part** nowhere; **ne...pas (du tout)** not (at all); **ne...pas encore** not yet; **ne...personne** no one; nobody; **ne...plus** no more; no longer; **ne...que** only; **ne...rien** nothing; **ne...rien que** nothing but; **n'est-ce pas?** right?
né(e): être né(e) to be born
nécessaire necessary

négocier to negotiate
neige (f) snow
neiger to snow
nerveux(-euse) nervous
nez (m) nose
ni : ne...—...— neither . . . nor
Noël (m) Christmas
noir(e) black; **les yeux —s** dark eyes
noix (f) nut
nom (m) name; noun
nombre (m) number
non no
nord (m) north
nord-américain(e) North American
normal(e) normal
note (f) note; grade
noter to note
nourriture (f) food
nous we; us
nouveau (nouvel, nouvelle) new
nouvelles (f pl) news
nuage (m) cloud
nuageux(-euse) cloudy
nutrition (f) nutrition
numéro (m) number; **— de téléphone** telephone number

O

obéir (à) to obey (someone or something)
objet (m) object
obligatoire mandatory; obligatory
obtenir to get; to obtain
occupé(e) busy
occuper : s'— (de) to attend (to); to busy oneself (with)
œil (m) (pl **yeux**) eye
œuf (m) egg
offrir to offer; to give; **s'—** to allow oneself; to indulge oneself
oignon (m) onion
omelette (f) omelet; **— au fromage** cheese omelet; **— nature** plain omelet
on one; you; we; they; people
oncle (m) uncle
ondulé(e) wavy
ongle (m) fingernail
opinion (f) opinion
optimiste optimistic
or (m) gold
orange (f) orange; **— pressée** freshly squeezed orange juice
Orangina (m) orange soda
ordinateur (m) computer
oreille (f) ear
organisation (f) organization
organisé(e) organized
organiser to organize; **s'—** to get organized
original(e) original
ou or
où where
oublier to forget
oui yes
ours (m) bear
ouvrir to open

P

page (f) page
pain (m) bread; **— au chocolat** bread with a strip of chocolate through it; **— aux céréales** multi-grain bread; **— complet** whole wheat bread; **— de campagne** round loaf; **— de mie** white sandwich bread; **— de seigle** rye bread
paire (f) pair
palmier (m) palm tree
pamplemousse (m) grapefruit
panini (m) a hot, pressed sandwich, with a variety of grilled ingredients, such as cheese, tomatoes, or tuna, as selected by the customer
panne : être en — to be broken down
panpan expression indicating that a child is going to get a spanking
pantalon (m) pair of pants
papier (m) paper
Pâques (f pl) Easter
par by; per
paragraphe (m) paragraph
parapluie (m) umbrella
parc (m) park
parce que because
pardessus (m) (man's) overcoat
pardonner to forgive; to pardon; **Pardon!** Excuse me!
parent (m) parent; relative
paresseux(-euse) lazy
parfait(e) perfect
parfois sometimes
parfumerie (f) perfume shop
parking (m) parking garage; parking lot
parler to speak; **— français** to speak French
parler to talk; to speak; **se —** to talk to each other
part (f) piece; **nulle —** nowhere
partager to share
partenaire (m, f) partner
participer (à) to participate (in)
partir to leave; to depart; to go away
pas not; **ne...pas (du tout)** not (at all); **ne... pas encore** not yet
passé (m) past
passer to pass; to spend; **— du temps** to spend time; **— la soirée** to spend the evening; **— un examen** to take a test; **— un film** to show a film; **se —** to happen
pâté (m) pâté
pâtes (f pl) pasta
patience (f) patience
patient(e) patient
pâtisserie (f) pastry shop
patron(ne) (m, f) boss
pauvre poor
payer to pay (for); **— en espèces** to pay cash; **se —** to reward oneself
pays (m) country
paysage (m) countryside
peau (f) skin
pêche (f) peach

pêcher to fish
pédagogie (f) pedagogy
peigne (m) comb
peine (f) trouble
peinture (f) painting
pendant during
perdre to lose; **— (son) temps** to waste (one's) time; **— patience** to lose patience
père (m) father
perle (f) pearl
permettre to permit; to allow
persévérance (f) perseverance
persévérant(e) persevering
personnage (m) character
personne (f) person; **ne...—** nobody
peser to weigh
pessimiste pessimistic
petit(e) small; little; **— ami** boyfriend; **— déjeuner** breakfast; **—e amie** girlfriend; **—s enfants** grandchildren; **— pain** roll; **petits pois** green peas
petite-fille (f) granddaughter
petit-fils (m) grandson
petits enfants (m pl) grandchildren
peu : un — a little
peur (f) fear; **avoir —** to be afraid
peut-être maybe
pharmacie (f) drug store
pharmacien(ne) (m, f) pharmacist
philosophie (f) philosophy
photo (f) photograph
photographe (m, f) photographer
photographer to photograph
physiologie (f) physiology
physique (f) physics
physique physical
piano (m) piano
pièce (f) room; **— de théâtre** play
pied (m) foot
pied-à-terre (m) hang-out, small temporary residence
pique-nique (m) picnic
pittoresque picturesque
pizza (f) pizza
placard (m) cupboard; closet
place (f) seat; lace; central square
plage (f) beach
plaindre : se — to complain
plaisir (m) pleasure
plaît : s'il vous (te) — please
planche (f) board; **— à repasser** ironing board; **— à voile** windsurf
planifier to plan
plante (f) plant
plat (m) dish (of a meal); **— principal** main course
plat(e) flat; **eau —e** water without bubbles
plateau (m) platter
pleurnicheur(-euse) (m, f) person inclined to feel sorry for him/herself
pleuvoir to rain
pluie (f) rain
plus more; **de — en —** more and more; **en —** besides; **le —** the most; **ne...—** no more; **non —** neither; **—...que** more... than; **— tard** later

plusieurs several
plutôt rather
pneu *(m)* tire
poche *(f)* pocket
poêle *(f)* frying pan
poignet *(m)* wrist
poing *(m)* fist
pointu(e) pointed
poire *(f)* pear
pois : petits — *(m pl)* green peas
poisson *(m)* fish
poissonnerie *(f)* fish market
poitrine *(f)* chest (anat.)
poivre *(m)* pepper
poivron *(m)* sweet pepper; **— vert** green pepper
poli(e) polite
politicien(ne) *(m, f)* politician
pomme *(f)* apple; **— de terre** *(f)* potato
ponctuel(le) punctual
pont *(m)* bridge
populaire popular
porc *(m)* pork
porte *(f)* door
porter to wear; to carry
poser to place; to pose; **— une question** to ask a question
pouce *(m)* thumb
poulet *(m)* chicken
poumon *(m)* lung
pour for
pourquoi why
pourtant yet; neverthelsee
pouvoir to be able to; to have permission to
pratique practical
préciser to specify; to clarify
préférable preferable
préférer to prefer
prendre to take; **— la rue...** to take...street; **— rendez-vous au cabinet du médecin** to get an appointment at the doctor's office; **— son petit déjeuner** to have breakfast
prénom *(m)* first name
préoccupé(e) (avec) preoccupied (with)
préparer to prepare; **se — (pour)** to get ready (for)
près (de) near
présentation *(f)* presentation; **une bonne —** quality of presenting oneself well in demeanor as well as dress
présenter to present; to introduce; **se — à la clinique** to go to infirmary
presque almost
pressé(e) hurried; pressed for time
prêt(e) ready
prêter to lend
printemps *(m)* spring
prix *(m)* price; **— compétitif** competitive price; **— intéressant** good price
probablement probably
problème *(m)* problem
prochain(e) next
proche close to; nearby
produit *(m)* product

professeur *(m)* professor
profiter (de) to take advantage of
programme *(m)* program
progrès *(m)* progress
projet *(m)* plan
promenade *(f)* walk; **faire une —** to take a walk
promener : se — to take a walk
pronom *(m)* pronoun
propre clean; own
protéger to protect
province *(f)* province
psychologie *(f)* psychology
public (publique) public
publier to publish
puis then; next
pull(over) *(m)* pullover sweater
punir to punish
pyjama *(m)* pyjama(s)

Q

quand when
que what; whom; which; that; **ne...—** only
quelque chose something
quelqu'un someone
quelquefois sometimes
quelques a few
question *(f)* question
qui who
quiche *(f)* quiche
quitter to leave (a person or place)
quoi what

R

raclette *(f)* a cheese served melted
raconter to tell (a story)
radio *(f)* radio
radis *(m)* radish
raide straight (hair)
raisin *(m)* grapes
raison *(f)* reason; **avoir —** to be right
raisonnable reasonable
ramener to bring back
ranch *(m)* ranch
randonnée : faire une — to go for a hike
rang *(m)* rank
ranger to arrange things; to put things away
rapidement quickly
rappeler to call again
rapport *(m)* relation
rapporter to report
raquette *(f)* racket
rarement rarely
raser : se — to shave
rater to fail; to miss (a train, for example); **— un examen** to flunk a test
rattraper to catch up with; **se —** to get caught up
ravi(e) delighted
rayé(e) striped
rayon *(m)* department (of a store)
réaction *(f)* reaction
réagir (à) to react (to)

réaliste realistic
recette *(f)* recipe
recevoir to receive
réchauffer to heat
recherche *(f)* research; **faire des —s** to do research
recherché sought-after; sought-out
reconnaître to recognize
réfléchir (à) to think (about); to reflect (on)
réfrigérateur *(m)* refrigerator
refuser to refuse
regard *(m)* look
regarder to watch; to look at; **— la télé** to watch T.V.
reggae *(m)* reggae
règle *(f)* rule
regretter to be sorry
rein *(m)* kidney
relations *(f pl)* relations
relax relaxed
remarquer to notice
rembourser to pay back
remercier to thank
remplacer to replace
remplir to fill out (a form)
rendez-vous *(m)* appointment
rendre to give back; **— visite à** to visit (a person); **se — (à)** to go (to)
renommé(e) well-known
renseignements *(m pl)* information
renseigner to give information; **se — (sur)** to find out (about); to enquire (about)
rentrer to return (home); to go back; to go home
répondre (à) to answer
réponse *(f)* answer
reposer : se — to rest
reprendre to take back; to regain; to rehire
réputation *(f)* reputation
réserver to reserve
résidence *(f)* residence; **— secondaire** vacation home
résister to resist; **— au stress** bear up under stress
respirer to breathe
responsabilité *(f)* responsibility
ressources *(f pl)* resources
restaurant *(m)* restaurant
rester to stay; to remain; **— à la maison** to stay home
retourner to return
retrouver to meet; to meet up with
réussir (à) to succeed; **— à un examen** to pass a test; to do well on a test
rêve *(m)* dream
réveiller : se — to wake up
réveil-matin *(m)* alarm clock
revenir to come back; to return
rêver to dream
rêveur(-euse) *(m, f)* dreamer
rez-de-chaussée *(m)* ground floor
rhume *(f)* cold
riche rich
richesse *(f)* wealth
rien : ne — nothing

rire to laugh
rive (f) shore; riverbank
rivière (f) river
riz (m) rice
robe (f) dress
rocheux(-euse) rocky
rock (m) rock and roll
ronfler to snore
ronger to gnaw; **se — les ongles** to bite one's nails
roquefort (m) a strong, blue cheese
rosbif (m) roast beef
rose pink
rouge red
rougir to turn red; to blush
route (f) road; **en — pour** on the way to
roux (rousse) red (hair)
russe Russian

S

sac (m) bag; **— à dos** backpack
saison (f) season
salade (f) lettuce; salad; **— mixte** tossed salad; **— niçoise** mixed salad with tuna, eggs, and olives, typical of the south of France and named after the city of Nice
sale dirty
salle (f) room; **— à manger** dining room; **— de bains** bathroom; **— de gymnastique** exercise room; **— de jeux** game room; **— de séjour** den; family room
salon (m) living room
saluer to greet
salut hello; good-bye
sandwich (m) sandwich
sandwicherie (f) sandwich shop
sang (m) blood
sans without; **— manches** sleeveless
santé (f) health; **— de la prévention** (f) preventive medicine
sauce (f) sauce
saucisse (f) (link) sausage
saucisson (m) (slicing) sausage; **— sec** salami
sauf except
saumon (m) salmon; **— fumé** smoked salmon
sauter to jump
savoir to know; to know how to
savon (m) soap
saxophone (m) saxophone
sciences (f pl) science; **les — économiques** economics; **les — politiques** political science
sculpture (f) sculpture
se passer de to do without
séance (f) session
sec (sèche) dry
sèche-linge (m) dryer
secrétaire (m, f) secretary
sel (m) salt
selon according to
Sénégal (m) Senegal
sénégalais(e) Senegalese

sens (m) sense; direction
sensibilité (f) sensitivity
sensible sensitive
sentimental(e) sentimental
sentir to smell; **se — bien** to feel well; **se — mal** to feel bad
serveur(-euse) (m, f) waiter, waitress
service (m) service
serviette (f) napkin
servir to serve; **se — (de)** to make use of
seul(e) alone
seulement only
shampooing (m) shamoo
shopping (m) shopping
short (m) shorts
si if
signifier to signify; to mean
sincère sincere
site (m) site; **— bancaire (sur Internet)** bank site (on the Internet)
ski : faire du — to ski
slip (m) panties; briefs
snob snobbish
sociologie (f) sociology
sœur (f) sister
soie (f) silk
soif (f) thirst; **avoir —** to be thirsty
soigneux(-euse) careful
soir (m) evening
solde : être en — to be on sale
soleil (m) sun; **— couchant** setting sun; **Il fait du —** It's sunny.
somme (f) nap; snooze; sum; **— importante** substantial amount
son (m) sound
sonner to ring
sophistiqué(e) sophisticated
sorbet (m) sorbet
sortir to leave; to go out;
sou (m) penny; **Un — est un —**. A penny is a penny.
soucoupe (f) saucer
soudain suddenly
souffrir to suffer
souhaiter to wish
soupçonner to suspect
souper (m) supper
soupirer to sigh
sous-sol (m) basement
sous-vêtements (m, pl) underwear
soutenir to support
soutien-gorge (m) bra
souvenir : se — (de) to remember
souvent often
spécialisation (f) (university) major
spontané(e) spontaneous
spontanément spontaneously
sportif(-ive) athletic; **équipement —** sports equipment
sports (m pl) sports
stade (m) stadium
station (f) station; **— balnéaire** seaside resort; **-service** gas station
stocker to stock
studio (m) efficiency apartment
stylo (m) pen
suggérer to suggests

Suisse (f) Switzerland
suisse Swiss
sujet (m) subject
superbe superb
supermarché (m) supermarket
supporter to bear; to stand; to put up with
sur on top of; on; about
sûr(e) sure; **bien —** of course
surgelé frozen (food)
surprendre to surprise
surveillant(e) (m, f) supervisor
surveiller to supervise
sweaterie (f) sweater shop
sympa = sympathique
sympathique nice
synagogue (f) synagogue

T

T.V.A. (taxe sur la valeur ajoutée) (f) VAT (Value Added Tax)
table (f) table
tableau (m) chart; table; chalkboard; painting
taille (f) size
tailleur (m) suit
taire : se — to hush; to get quiet
tante (f) aunt
taper to type
tapis (m) rug
tard late
tarte (f) pie
tartelette (f) individual pie
tasse (f) cup
taxi (m) taxi
te (to) you (familiar)
technique (f) technique; **— de communication** speech and communication theory
téléphoner (à) to call; to telephone
téléviseur (m) television set
télévision (f) television
temps (m) time; weather; **de — en —** from time to time
tenir to hold; to take; **— à** to have one's heart set on
tennis (m) tennis
terminé(e) finished
terminer to finish
terrain (m) terrain; ground; **— de golf** golf course
terrasse (f) terrace
tête (f) head
têtu(e) stubborn
TGV (Train à Grande Vitesse) (m) French high-speed train
thé (m) tea; **— au lait** tea with milk; **— citron** lemon tea; **— nature** plain tea
théâtre (m) theater
théologie (f) theology
thon (m) tuna
timbre (f) postage stamp
timide timid
toilette (f) toilet; **faire sa —** to wash up; **—s** bathroom
tolérant(e) tolerant

tolérer to tolerate
tomate *(f)* tomato
tomber to fall (down)
toucher to touch; — **un chèque** to cash a check
toujours always
tourner to turn; — **à droite** to turn right; — **à gauche** to turn left; — **un film** to shoot a film
tous : — **les jours** every day
tout : pas du — not at all; — **droit** straight ahead
tout(e) all
train *(m)* train
tranche *(f)* slice
transport *(m)* transportation; —**s publics** public transportation
travail *(m)* work
travailler to work; — **en équipe** to work on a team; — **seul(e)** to work alone
travailleur(-euse) hard-working
traverser to cross
très very
triste sad
trombone *(m)* trombone
tromper : se — to be mistaken
trompette *(f)* trumpet
trop (de) too much
tropical(e) tropical
trouver to find; **se** — to be located
t-shirt *(m)* t-shirt

U

uni(e) plain; solid colored
université *(f)* university
urgence : en cas d'— in case of emergency
utile useful
utiliser to use

V

vacances *(f pl)* vacation
vache *(f)* cow

valise *(f)* suitcase
vallée *(f)* valley
valoir to be worth; **Il vaut mieux que...** It would be better to . . .
variété *(f)* variety
veau *(m)* veal
végétation *(f)* vegetation
vélo *(m)* bicycle
vendeur(-euse) sales person
vendre to sell
venir to come; — **de** to have just (done something)
vent *(m)* wind; **Il y a du** — It's windy.
ventre *(m)* stomach; abdomen
verglas *(m)* black ice
verifier to verify; — **les stocks** to check the inventory
verre *(m)* glass; **prendre un**— to have a drink; — **de blanc** glass of white wine; — **de champagne** glass of champagne; — **de rouge** glass of red wine
vers toward
vert(e) green
veste *(f)* sportcoat
vêtements *(m pl)* clothes
veuf (veuve) widowed
viande *(f)* meat
vide empty
vie *(f)* life
vieillir to grow older
Viêt-Nam *(m)* Vietnam
vietnamien(ne) Vietnamese
vieux (vieil, vieille) old
villa *(f)* villa
village *(m)* village
ville *(f)* city
vin *(m)* wine; — **rouge** red wine; — **blanc** white wine
violet *(m)* purple
violon *(m)* violin
violon-celle *(m)* cello
visage *(m)* face
visiter to visit (a place)
vite quickly

vivant(e) living
vocabulaire *(m)* vocabulary
voici here's; **Le** —. Here it (he) is.
voilà there's
voir to see
voisin(e) *(m, f)* neighbor
voiture *(f)* car; — **de sport** sports car
voix *(f)* voice
vol *(m)* flight
volaille poultry
voler to steal
volley *(m)* volleyball
vomir to vomit
vouloir to want; **Je veux bien.** OK, sure, with pleasure
vous you (plural and formal)
voyager to travel
vrai(e) true
vraiment really
vue *(f)* sight
vue *(f)* view; — **panoramique** panoramic view

W

W.-C. *(m)* water closet; toilet
week-end *(m)* weekend

Y

y there; **il** — **a** there is; there are
yaourt *(m)* yogurt

Z

Zut! Darn!

A

a un(e)
abdomen ventre *(m)*
ability capacité *(f)*
able : to be — to pouvoir
abominable abominable
absent absent(e); **to be —** s'absenter
to accept accepter
accountant comptable *(m, f)*
accounting comptabilité *(f)*
to accumulate accumuler
accustomed : to get — (to) s'habituer (à); **to become — (to)** s'habituer (à)
across from en face de
actor acteur *(m)*
actress actrice *(f)*
to adapt (to) s'adapter (à)
to admire admirer
to adore adorer
to advance s'avancer
advantage : to take — (of) profiter (de)
advice conseils *(m pl)*
affectionate affecteux(-euse)
afraid : to be — avoir peur
Africa Afrique *(f)*
African africain(e)
agent agent(e) *(m, f)* **travel —** agent(e) de voyage; **real estate —** agent(e) immobilier
agreement consensus *(m)*
aid assistance *(f)*
airport aéroport *(m)*
all tout(e)
almond amande *(f)*; **— cake** gâteau aux amandes *(m)*
almost presque
always toujours
ambiance ambiance *(f)*
America Amérique *(f)*
American américain(e)
amusing amusant(e)
to analyze analyser
and et
angry fâché(e)
ankle cheville *(f)*
annoying ennuyeux(-euse)
to answer répondre à *(répondu)*
anthropology anthropologie *(f)*
anxious anxieux(-euse)
apartment appartement *(m)*; **— building** immeuble *(m)*
apple pomme *(f)*
to apply oneself s'appliquer (à)
to appreciate apprécier
apricot abricot; **— tart** tarte aux abricots *(f)*
archeology archéologie *(f)*
architect architecte *(m, f)*
to argue se disputer
arm bras *(m)*
around autour; **— the world** autour du monde

to arrive arriver; **I arrived** je suis arrivé(e)
art art *(m)*; **art history** histoire de l'art *(f)*
artist artiste *(m, f)*
as comme; **—...—** aussi...que; **— a result of** grâce à; **— well** ainsi que
Asia Asie *(f)*
Asian asiatique
asleep endormi(e)
asparagus asperge *(f)*
assistant assistant(e) *(m, f)*
astronaut astronaute *(m, f)*
astronomy astronomie *(f)*
to attend assister (à); **attend (to)** s'occuper (de)
aunt tante *(f)*
autumn automne *(m)*; **in the —** en automne

B

back : in — of derrière
back dos *(m)*
bad (not good) mauvais(e)
bad (wicked) méchant(e)
bakery boulangerie *(f)*
to balance équilibrer
banana banane *(f)*
bank banque *(f)*
banker banquier(-ière) *(m, f)*
basket corbeille
basketball basket *(m)*; **to play —** faire du basket
to be être *(été)*
beach plage *(f)*
bean haricot *(m)*; **green —s** haricots verts *(m pl)*
to bear up (under) résister (à)
beard barbe *(f)*
beautiful beau; bel; belle
to become devenir; **I became** je suis devenu(e)
bed lit; **to go to —** se coucher
beef bœuf *(m)*; **roast —** rosbif *(m)*
beer bière *(f)*
behind derrière
Belgian belge
Belgium Belgique *(f)*
beside à côté de
besides à part; en plus de
best (adjective) **the —** le (la) meilleur(e)
best (adverb) le mieux; **the —** le mieux; **to do one's —** faire de son mieux
better (adjective) meilleur(e)
better (adverb) mieux
between entre
bicycle vélo *(m)*
big grand(e); **to get —** grandir
bike vélo *(m)*; **to go — riding** faire du vélo

biology biologie *(f)*
black noir(e)
blond blond(e)
blue bleu(e)
blueberry myrtille *(f)*; **— pie** tarte aux myrtilles *(f)*
to blush rougir
bored : to be — s'ennuyer
bored ennuyé(e)
boring ennuyeux(-euse)
born : to be naître; être né(e); **I was born** je suis né(e)
boss patron(ne) *(m, f)*
botanical botanique; **— garden** jardin botanique *(m)*
botany botanique *(f)*
boulevard boulevard *(m)*
boutique boutique *(f)*
boy garçon *(m)*
boyfriend petit ami *(m)*
brain cerveau *(m)*
bread pain *(m)*; **French —** baguette *(f)*; **whole wheat —** pain complet *(m)*; **round loaf of —** pain de campagne *(m)*; **— with strip of chocolate through it** pain au chocolat *(m)*; **loaf of white —** pain de mie *(m)*; **rye —** pain de seigle *(m)*; **multi-grain —** pain aux céréales
breakfast petit déjeuner *(m)*
British britannique
broccoli brocoli *(m)*
brother frère *(m)*
brother-in-law beau-frère *(m)*
brown marron; châtain
brush brosse *(f)*; **tooth—** brosse à dents *(f)*
to brush se brosser
bubbles : with — gazeux(-euse); **without —** plat(e)
budget budget *(m)*
building immeuble *(m)*
bus autobus *(m)*; **— stop** arrêt d'autobus *(m)*
business commerce *(m)*
business executive cadre *(m, f)*
business sector commerces *(f pl)*
businessman homme d'affaires *(m)*; **businesswoman** femme d'affaires *(f)*
busy occupé(e); **to — oneself (with)** s'occuper (de)
butcher boucher(-ère) *(m, f)*; **— shop** boucherie *(f)*
butter beurre *(m)*
to buy acheter

C

cabbage chou *(m)*
café café *(m)*
cake gâteau *(m)*; **chocolate —** gâteau au chocolat *(m)*
calendar calendrier *(m)*

to call téléphoner (à); **— each other** se téléphoner
calm calme
to calm down se calmer
calmly avec calme
to camping : to go — faire du camping
can (to be able to) pouvoir *(pu)*
Canada Canada *(m)*
Canadian canadien(ne)
to cancel annuler
candidate candidat *(m)*
car voiture *(f)*; **sports —** voiture de sport
car wash lave-voitures *(m)*
card carte *(f)*; **greeting —** carte de vœux
career carrière *(f)*
carrot carotte *(f)*
to cash (a check) toucher (un chèque)
cashier caissier(-ière) *(m, f)*
cat chat *(m)*
cathedral cathédrale *(f)*
caught : get — up se rattraper
to celebrate fêter
cello violon-celle *(m)*
ceramics céramique *(f)*
cereal céréales *(f pl)*
chair chaise *(f)*
charge : to take — (of) se charger (de)
check addition *(f)*
to check verifier; **— the inventory** vérifier les stocks
cheese fromage *(m)*; **— shop** fromagerie *(f)*; **popular Normandy —** camembert *(m)*; **mild, semi-soft —** brie *(m)*; **strong, blue —** roquefort *(m)*; **goat —** chèvre *(m)*; **Swiss — with holes, also made in France** emmenthal *(m)*; **— served melted** raclette *(f)*; **packaged dessert —, usually containing kirsch** gourmandise *(f)*; **packaged soft — containing herbs and garlic or pepper** Boursin *(m)*
chemistry chimie *(f)*
cherry cerise *(f)*; **— pie** tarte aux cerises *(f)*
chest (anat.) poitrine *(f)*
chicken poulet *(m)*
child enfant *(m)*; **— psychology** psychologie de l'enfant *(f)*
China Chine *(f)*
Chinese chinois(e)
chocolate chocolat *(m)*; **— cake** gâteau au chocolat *(m)*; **— éclair** éclair *(m)*
choir chorale *(f)*
to choose choisir
church église *(f)*
city hall hôtel de ville *(m)*
city ville *(f)*; **picturesque —** ville pittoresque
to clarify préciser
clarinet clarinette *(f)*
client client(e) *(m, f)*
clientele clientèle *(f)*
clothes vêtements *(m pl)*
cloud nuage *(m)*; **It's cloudy.** Il y a des nuages; C'est nuageux; Le ciel est couvert.

club club *(m)*
coast côte *(f)*
coffee café *(m)*; **packaged —** une boîte de café
cold froid *(m)*
cold froid(e); **to be —** avoir froid
colleague collègue *(m, f)*
color couleur *(f)*
comb peigne *(m)*
to come back revenir; **I came back** je suis revenu(e)
to come venir; **I came** je suis venu(e)
comedian comédien(ne) *(m, f)*
to communicate communiquer
computer ordinateur *(m)*; **— expert** informaticien(ne) *(m, f)*; **— science** informatique *(f)*
concept concept *(m)*
concert concert *(m)*
confidence confiance *(f)*; **self- —** confiance en soi (moi)
conquered conquis(e)
to consult consulter
continent continent *(m)*
to contribute contribuer
to cook faire la cuisine
cookie biscuit *(m)*
cool frais (fraîche)
to coordinate coordonner
corn maïs *(m)*
corner coin; **at the — of** au coin de
country pays *(m)*
countryside paysage *(m)*
course : first — (of a meal) entrée *(f)*; **main —** plat principal *(m)*
course cours *(m)*; **lecture —** cours magistral
cousin cousin(e) *(m, f)*
cracker biscuit à soda *(m)*
cream crème *(f)*
creamery crémerie *(f)*
to create créer
crescent roll croissant *(m)*
croissant croissant *(m)*
to cross traverser
crust bout *(m)*
cucumber concombre *(m)*
to cultivate cultiver
cup tasse *(f)*
curious curieux(-euse)
curly frisé(e); bouclé(e)
customer client(e) *(m, f)*
cutlet côtelette *(f)*

D

to dance danser
dark sombre; **— eyes** les yeux noirs
daughter fille *(f)*
day jour *(m)*
degree degré (temperature); **It is...-s.** Il est de . . . degrés.
delicatessen charcuterie *(f)*
dense dense; **— vegetation** végétation dense *(f)*
dentist dentiste *(m, f)*
to depart partir; **I departed** je suis parti(e)
department rayon *(m)*

department store grand magasin *(m)*
depressing déprimant(e)
desert désert *(m)*
to desire désirer
dessert dessert *(m)*
detail détail *(m)*
to detest détester
to develop développer
devoted dévoué(e)
to die mourir; **he (she) died** il (elle) est mort(e); **he (she) is dead** il (elle) est mort(e)
different différent(e)
difficult difficile
to dinner dîner *(m)*; **to have —** dîner
disappointing décevant(e)
dishes vaisselle *(f)*; **to do the —** faire la vaisselle
displeased mécontent(e)
divorced divorcé(e)
to do faire; **— homework** faire des devoirs; **— some reading** faire de la lecture; **do well** réussir à; **do whatever it takes** faire le nécessaire
doctor médecin *(m)*; femme médecin *(f)*
document document *(m)*
dog chien *(m)*
door porte *(f)*
down : to go — descendre; **to go — . . . street** descendre la rue...
drama l'art dramatique *(m)*
draw dessiner
drawing dessin *(m)*
dream rêver
dreamer rêveur(-euse) *(m, f)*
dressed : to get — s'habiller
drink(s) boisson *(f)*
drug store pharmacie *(f)*
drums batterie *(f)*
duck canard *(m)*
during pendant
Dutch hollandais(e)
dynamic dynamique

E

ear oreille *(f)*
to earn gagner
ease : at ease décontracté(e)
easy facile
to eat manger
éclair éclair *(m)*
economics économie *(f)*; sciences économiques *(f pl)*
education éducation
egg œuf *(m)*
eggplant aubergine *(f)*
egotistical égoïste
elbow coude *(m)*
e-mail courrier électronique *(m)*
emotional émotif(-ive)
employee employé(e) *(m, f)*
employer employer(-euse) *(m, f)*
end bout *(m)*; fin; **at the — of** au bout de
endive endives *(f)*
energetic énergique
engineer ingénieur *(m)*

England Angleterre *(f)*
English anglais(e)
to enjoy oneself s'amuser
to enroll s'inscrire
to enter entrer; **I entered** je suis entré(e)
errands courses *(f pl)*; **to run —** faire des courses
to establish établir
Europe Europe *(f)*
European européen(ne)
exam examen *(m)*; **final —s** examens de fin de semestre
to examine examiner
excursion excursion *(f)*
exercice exercice *(m)*; **to do —s** faire de l'exercice
exhibit exposition *(f)*
to exit sortir; **I exited** je suis sorti(e)
exotic exotique; **— plant** plante exotique *(f)*
extreme extrême
eye œil *(m)*; **eyes** yeux *(m pl)*
eyeglasses lunettes *(f pl)*

F

face visage *(m)*
facing en face de
to fail a test échouer à un examen
to fall (down) tomber; **I fell** je suis tombé(e)
fall automne *(m)*; **in the —** en automne
family famille *(f)*
far loin; **— from** loin de
fascinating fascinant(e)
fashion designer couturier(-ière) *(m, f)*
fat gros(se); **to get —** grossir
father père *(m)*
father-in-law beau-père *(m)*
fiancé(e) fiancé(e) *(m, f)*
to file classer
file dossier *(m)*
financial financier(-ière)
finger doigt *(m)*
to finish finir; terminer
fish poisson *(m)*; **— market** poissonnerie *(f)*
flamboyant flamboyant(e)
to flunk a test rater un examen
flute flûte *(f)*
foggy : It's —. Il y a du brouillard
foliage feuillage *(m)*
food cuisine *(f)*; aliments *(m pl)*; **prepared —** aliments préparés
foot pied *(m)*
football football américain *(m)*; **to play —** faire du football américain
forest forêt *(f)*
fork fourchette *(f)*
formerly autrefois
fragile fragile
France France *(f)*
French français(e); **French (language)** français *(m)*; **— bread** baguette *(f)*; **— fries** frites *(f)*; **—-speaking world** monde francophone *(m)*

to frequent fréquenter
frequently fréquemment
friend ami(e) *(m, f)*; copain *(m)*; copine *(f)*; **best —** meilleur(e) ami(e)
frivolous frivole
from de
front : in — of devant
frozen surgélé(e); **— foods** produits surgelés
fruit fruits *(m pl)*
fun amusant(e); **to have —** s'amuser
funny drôle, amusant(e)

G

to gain weight grossir
garden jardin *(m)*; **botanical —** jardin botanique
gardening jardinage *(m)*; **to do some —** faire du jardinage
garlic ail *(m)*
gas station station-service *(m)*
generally d'habitude, en général
generous généreux(-euse)
geographical géographique; **— map** carte géographique *(f)*
geography géographie *(f)*
geology géologie *(f)*
German allemand(e)
Germany Allemagne *(f)*
to get obtenir; **go —** aller chercher; **— accustomed to** s'habituer à; **— big** grandir; **— caught up** se rattraper; **— dressed** s'habiller; **— fat** grossir; **— information (about)** se renseigner (sur); **— information (on)** s'informer (sur); **— married** se marier; **— organized** s'arranger; **— quiet** se taire; **— ready** se préparer; **— settled** s'installer; **— thin** maigrir; **— up** se lever; **— upset** s'énerver; **— used (to)** s'adapter (à)
gifted doué(e)
girl fille *(f)*
girlfriend petite amie *(f)*
to give donner; offrir (offert)
glass verre *(m)*; **— of champagne** verre de champagne; **— of draft beer** demi *(m)*; **— of red wine** verre de rouge; **— of white wine** verre de blanc
to go aller; **I went** je suis allé(e); **— away** partir; s'en aller; **— camping** faire du camping; **— down . . . street** descendre la rue...; **— downstairs** descendre; **— grocery shopping** faire le marché; **— out** sortir; **I went out** je suis sorti(e); **— past (to)** dépasser; **— shopping** faire du shopping; (Québec) faire du magasinage; **— straight** aller tout droit; **— to bed** se coucher; **— to the movies** aller au cinéma; **— up** monter; **I went up** je suis monté(e); **— up . . . street** monter la rue...
goat chèvre *(f)*; **— cheese** chèvre *(m)*
golf golf *(m)*; **to play —** faire du golf; **— course** terrain de golf *(m)*
good bon(ne)

graciously gracieusement
grade note *(f)*
grandchildren petits enfants *(m pl)*
granddaughter petite-fille *(f)*
grandfather grand-père *(m)*
grandmother grand-mère *(f)*
grandson petit-fils *(m)*
grape raisin *(m)*
grapefruit pamplemousse *(m)*
grated râpé(e)
gray gris; **— hair** les cheveux blancs *(m pl)*
green vert(e); **— beans** haricots verts *(m pl)*
greeting salutation *(f)*
grocery : to go — shopping faire le marché
grocery store épicerie *(f)*
to grow older vieillir; **— up** grandir
guitar guitare *(f)*
gym gym *(m)*

H

habit habitude *(f)*; **as a —** d'habitude; **to be in the — of** avoir l'habitude de
hair cheveux *(m pl)*
hairdresser coiffeur(-euse) *(m, f)*
half-brother demi-frère *(m)*
half-sister demi-sœur *(f)*
ham jambon *(m)*; **cured —** jambon du pays *(m)*
hand main *(f)*
handsome joli(e)
happy heureux(-euse); content(e)
hard dur(e)
hard-working travailleur(-euse)
to hate détester
to have avoir *(eu)*; **— a good time** s'amuser; **— a way with people** avoir la facilité des contacts; **— dinner** dîner; **— to** devoir
head tête *(f)*
health sante *(f)*; hygiène *(f)*
to hear entendre
heart cœur *(m)*
heat chaleur *(f)*
heavy lourd(e)
hello salut; bonjour; âllo
to help aider
help assistance *(f)*; aide *(f)*
here ici
high school lycée *(m)*
hill colline *(f)*
history histoire *(f)*; **art —** histoire de l'art
hockey hockey *(m)*; **to play —** faire du hockey
home : to stay — rester à la maison
homework devoirs *(m pl)*; **to do —** faire des devoirs
honey miel *(m)*
hospital hôpital *(m)*
hot chaud(e); **to be —** avoir chaud
hotel hôtel *(m)*
hour heure *(f)*
house maison *(f)*
housemate colocataire *(m, f)*
housework ménage; **to do —** faire le ménage

human relations relations humaines
humidity humidité (f)
hungry : to be — avoir faim
hurried pressé(e)
to hurry (up) se dépêcher
husband mari (m); époux (m)
to hush se taire (tu)
hygiene hygiène (f)

I

ice cream glace (f)
icy : It's — Il y a du verglas; **The road is —.** La route est verglacée.
idea idée (f)
if si
importance importance (f)
impressionable influençable
impressive impressionnant(e)
to improve oneself s'améliorer
indifferent (lacking in intellectual curiosity) indifférent(e)
influenced : easily — influençable
information renseignements (m pl); **to get — about** se renseigner sur; **to get — on** s'informer sur; **to provide —** renseigner
to install installer
intelligent intelligent(e)
intelligently avec intelligence
to intend avoir l'intention (de)
interested : to be — in s'intéresser à
international international(e); **— relations** relations internationales
interview entretien (m); interview (f)
to interview interviewer
intolerant intolérant(e)
inventory stocks (m pl)
to invite inviter
Ireland Irlande (f)
Irish irlandais(e)
island île (f); **tropical —** île tropicale
Israeli israélien(ne)
Italian italien(ne)
Italy Italie (f)

J

jam confiture (f)
Japan Japon (m)
Japanese japonais(e)
jazz jazz (m)
job travail (m)
to jog faire du jogging
journalism journalisme (m)
journalist journaliste (m, f)

K

to keep going continuer
kidney rein (m)
kilogram kilo (m)
kind gentil(le)
to kiss embrasser; **— each other** s'embrasser
knee genou (m)
knife couteau (m)
knowledge connaissance (f)

L

lab session séance de travaux pratiques (f)
lake lac (m)
lamb agneau (m); **leg of —** gigot (m)
language langue (f); **modern —s** langues modernes; **classical —s** langues mortes
law droit (m) **social —** droit social; **financial —** droit fiscal; **children's —** droit de l'enfant; **international —** droit international; **family —** droit de la famille
lawyer avocat(e) (m, f)
lazy parasseux(-euse)
to lead (a team) animer une équipe
to learn apprendre (appris)
least le moins
to leave sortir; **I left** je suis sorti(e); partir; **I left** je suis parti(e); **— (a person or place)** quitter
lecture conférence (f)
left gauche; **to the — of** à gauche de; **to turn —** tourner à gauche
leg jambe (f)
lemon citron (m); **— pie** tarte au citron (f); **—tea** thé citron (m)
less moins; **— than** moins que
lettuce salade (f), laitre
library bibliothèque (f)
to like aimer; aimer bien; **to — a lot** aimer beaucoup
linguistics linguistique (f)
to listen to écouter
liter litre (m); **one-tenth of a —** décilitre (m)
literature littérature(f)
little : a — un peu
live-in-partner conjoint(e) (m, f)
liver foie (m)
lobster homard (m)
located : to be — se trouver
long long(ue)
to look at regarder ; **— at each other** se regarder
to look for chercher
to lose perdre; **— patience** perdre patience; **— weight** maigrir
lot : a — beaucoup
to love adorer; aimer
lucky chanceux(-euse); **to be —** avoir de la chance
to lunch déjeuner (m) **to have —** déjeuner
lung poumon (m)
luxurious de luxe

M

mad fâché(e)
main course plat principal (m)
major spécialisation (f)
to make faire (fait); **— a phone call** faire un coup de téléphone; **— average grades** faire la moyenne; **— conversation** bavarder; **— use (of)** se servir (de)

makeup maquillage (m); **to put on —** se maquiller
man homme (m)
management gestion (f)
map carte (f); **geographical —** carte géographique
marital status état civil (m)
market marché (m)
marketing marketing (m)
married marié(e); **to get —** se marier (avec)
marvelous magnifique; merveilleux (-euse)
math maths (f pl)
mathematics mathématiques (f pl)
may (to be allowed to) pouvoir (pu)
mayonnaise mayonnaise (f)
mean méchant(e)
mechanic mécanicien(ne) (m, f)
medicine médecine (f)
to meet rencontrer; **— friends at the café** retrouver des amis au café
message message (m)
methodical méthodique
Mexican mexicain(e)
Mexico Mexique (m)
midnight minuit (m)
mild doux; douce
milk lait (m)
miserable misérable
miserly avare
modest modeste
money argent (m)
to monitor contrôler
month mois (m)
mood humeur (f); **in a bad —** de mauvaise humeur; **in a good —** de bonne humeur
more plus; **— than** plus que
Moroccan marocain(e)
Morocco Maroc (m)
mosque mosquée (f)
most le plus
mother mère (f)
mother-in-law belle-mère (f)
to motivate motiver
mountain montagne (f) **— range** chaîne de montagnes (f)
moustache moustache (f)
mouth bouche (f)
movie film (m); **go to the movies** aller au cinéma
movie theater cinéma (m)
museum musée (m)
mushroom champignon (m)
music musique (f); **classical —** musique classique; **— store** magasin de musique (m)
musician musicien(ne) (m, f)
must devoir; **one —** il faut
mustard moutarde (f)

N

nail ongle (m)
naïve naïf; naïve
name nom (m); **first —** prénom; **my — is . . .** je m'appelle...

napkin serviette (f)
natural science sciences naturelles (f pl)
naughty méchant(e)
near près de
necessary : it is— il est nécessaire; il faut
neck cou (m)
to need avoir besoin (de)
need besoin (m)
to negotiate négocier
neighbor voisin(e) (m, f)
never ne....jamais
new nouveau; nouvel; nouvelle
news nouvelles (f, pl)
newspaper journal (m)
next ensuite; prochain
next to à côté de
nice gentil(le)
no non
noon midi (m)
nose nez (m); **to have a turned-up** — avoir le nez retroussé
not ne...pas; — **at all** pas du tout
now maintenant
nurse infirmier(-ière) (m, f)
nutrition nutrition (f)

O

o'clock heure(s)
to obey obéir (à)
to offer offrir (offert)
office bureau (m); — **building** immeuble de bureaux (m); **post** — bureau de poste
often souvent
OK d'accord; Je veux bien
old vieux; vieil; vieille; **to grow older** vieillir
omelet omelette (f); **ham** — omelette au jambon; **cheese** — omelette au fromage; **plain** — omelette nature
onion oignon (m)
oppressive lourd(e)
optimistic optimiste
orange orange (f)
to order commander; — **supplies** commander du matériel
organization organisation (f)
to organize organiser
organized organisé(e); **to get** — s'arranger
other autre; **on the** — **side of** de l'autre côté de
out : to go — sortir; **I went** — je suis sorti(e)
oval ovale
oyster huître (f)

P

painting peinture (f)
palm tree palmier (m)
panoramic panoramique; — **view** vue panoramique (f)
paperwork paperasse (f); **to do** — faire de la paperasse

parent parent (m)
park parc (m)
parking garage parking (m)
parking lot parking (m)
part part (f); **to do one's** — faire sa part
to participate (in) participer (à)
to party fêter
to pass (a test) réussir à (un examen)
past passé (m); **to go** — dépasser
pasta pâtes (f pl)
pastry shop pâtisserie (f)
pâté pâté (m)
patience patience (f)
patient patient(e)
patiently avec patience
to pay a visit to (a person) rendre visite à
to pay for payer
peach pêche (f)
pear poire (f)
peas petits pois (m)
pedagogy pédagogie (f)
pen stylo (m)
pencil crayon (m)
people gens (m pl)
pepper poivre (m); **sweet** — poivron vert (m)
perfume parfum (m); — **shop** parfumerie (f)
perseverance persévérance (f)
persevering persévérant(e)
person personne (f)
personal personnel(le)
pessimistic pessimiste
pharmacist pharmacien(ne) (m, f)
philosophy philosophie (f)
phone téléphone (m); **make a** — **call** faire un coup de téléphone
photograph photo (f)
physical physique; — **education** éducation (f) physique
physics physique (f)
physiology physiologie (f)
piano piano (m)
picturesque pittoresque; — **city** ville pittoresque (f)
pie tarte (f); **cherry** — tarte aux cerises; **individual** — tartelette (f); **strawberry** — tarte aux fraises
piece morceau (m)
pineapple ananas (m)
pizza pizza (f)
placemat napperon (m)
to plan planifier
plant plante (f); **exotic** — plante exotique
plate assiette (f)
platter plateau (m)
to play jouer; — **soccer** jouer au foot; — **piano** jouer du piano
plaza place (f)
please S'il vous plaît.
pleased content(e)
pointed pointu(e)
police officer agent(e) de police (m, f)
political science sciences politiques (f pl)

politician politicien(ne) (m, f)
poor pauvre
popular populaire
pork porc (m)
post office bureau de poste (m)
potato pomme de terre (f)
practical pratique
to prefer préférer
preoccupied (with) préoccupé(e) (avec)
to prepare préparer
prepared préparé(e); —**d foods** aliments préparés
to present présenter
presentation présentation (f)
pressed for time pressé(e)
pretty joli(e)
preventive medicine santé de la prévention (f)
priority priorité (f)
product produit (m)
professor professeur
professional school faculté des études professionnelles (f)
program programme (m)
project projet (m)
proud fier(-ère)
to provide information renseigner
province province (f)
psychology psychologie (f); **child** — psychologie de l'enfant (f)
punctual ponctuel(le)
to put mettre (mis); — **away** ranger; — **on makeup** se maquiller; — **up** ranger
to putter bricoler

Q

to quarrel se disputer
quiche quiche (f)
quiet : to get — se taire

R

radish radis (m)
rain pluie (f); **It's raining.** Il pleut.
range : mountain — chaîne de montagnes (f)
rarely rarement
raspberry framboise (f); — **tart** tarte aux framboises (f)
rather assez
to react réagir (à)
to read lire (lu)
reading lecture (f); **to do some** — faire de la lecture
ready : to get — se préparer
real estate agent agent(e) immobilier (m, f)
realistic réaliste
receive recevoir
red rouge; — **hair** les cheveux roux; — **wine** vin rouge (m)
to reflect (on) réfléchir (à)
to regain reprendre (repris)
reggae reggae (m)
to register s'inscrire (inscrit)
to rehire reprendre (repris)

relations rapports (m pl)
relative parent (m)
to relax se détendre
relaxed décontracté(e)
reliability fiabilité (f)
to remain rester; I remained je suis resté(e)
to rent louer
report rapport (m)
to report rapporter
reputation réputation (f)
responsibility : to take — (for) se charger (de)
to rest se reposer
restaurant restaurant (m)
restful reposant(e)
result résultat (m)
to return retourner; I returned je suis retourné(e)
to return home rentrer; I returned home je suis rentré(e)
rice riz (m)
rich riche
right : to be — avoir raison
right droite; to the — of à droite de; to turn — tourner à droite
river rivière (f); major — to the sea fleuve (m)
rock and roll rock (m)
rocky rocheux(-euse)
roll petit pain (m)
roommate colocataire (m, f)
round rond(e)
rum rhum (m); — pastry baba au rhum (m)
Russian russe

S

sad triste
salad salade (f); tossed — salade mixte; mixed — with tuna, eggs, and olives, typical of the south of France and named after the city of Nice salade niçoise
salami saucisson (m) sec
sales person vendeur(-euse) (m, f)
salmon saumon (m); smoked — saumon fumé
salt sel (m)
sandwich sandwich (m); ham — sandwich au jambon (m); cheese — sandwich au fromage (m); hot ham and cheese — topped with grilled cheese croque-monsieur (m); hot ham and cheese — , topped with a fried egg croque-madame (m); hot, pressed — with grilled ingredients panini (m); — shop sandwicherie (f)
saucer soucoupe (f)
sausage saucisse (f)
saxophone saxophone (m)
to say dire (dit)
schedule emploi du temps (m)
school école (f); faculté (f); high — lycée (m); — of exact science école des sciences exactes (f); — of fine arts école des beaux-arts (f); — of language and literature école des lettres

science science (f); computer — informatique; exact — sciences exactes; natural — sciences naturelles; political — sciences politiques; social — sciences humaines
sculpture sculpture (f)
seashore bord de la mer (m); at the — au bord de la mer
secretary secrétaire (m, f)
to see voir (vu)
to seem avoir l'air
selfish égoïste
to sell vendre
to send envoyer
Senegal Sénégal (m)
Senegalese sénégalais(e)
sense sens (m)
sensitive sensible
sensitivity (to) sensibilité (à)
sentimental sentimental(e)
to serve servir
serviceman militaire (m); servicewoman femme militaire (f)
session séance (f); lab — séance de travaux pratiques
settled : to get — s'installer
to shave se raser
shirt chemise (f); — shop chemiserie (f)
shoe chaussure (f)
shopkeeper commerçant(e) (m, f)
shopping shopping (m); to go — faire du shopping; (Québec) faire du magasinage; — center centre commercial (m)
short court(e)
shorts short (m)
should devoir
shoulder épaule (f)
shrimp crevette (f)
sick malade
side côté (m); on the other — of de l'autre côté de
sincere sincère
to sing chanter; — in a choir chanter dans une chorale
singer chanteur(-euse) (m, f)
single célibataire
sister sœur (f)
sister-in-law belle-sœur (f)
to sit down s'asseoir (assis)
situation situation (f)
to ski faire du ski; to water — faire du ski nautique
skin peau (f)
sky ciel (m)
to sleep dormir (dormi); — late faire la grasse matinée
sleepy : to be — avoir sommeil
slice tranche (f)
small petit(e)
to smoke fumer
snobbish snob
snow neige (f); It's snowing. Il neige.
soccer foot (m); to play — faire du foot
social sciences sciences humaines (f pl)
sociology sociologie (f)
sock chaussette (f); — shop chaussetterie (f)

software program logiciel (m)
solitude solitude (f)
sometimes quelquefois
son fils (m)
sophisticated sophistiqué(e)
sorbet sorbet (m)
sound son (m)
Spain Espagne (f)
Spanish espagnol(e)
to speak parler; to — French parler français
special spécial(e)
to specify préciser
to spend (the evening) passer (la soirée); — (money) dépenser (de l'argent)
spinach épinards (m pl)
spontaneous spontané(e)
spontaneously spontanément
spoon cuillère (f)
sports sports (m pl); to do — faire du sport
spring printemps (m); in the — au printemps
square carré(e)
squash courgette (f)
stadium stade (m)
to stand in line faire la queue
state état (m)
to stay rester; I stayed je suis resté(e); — home rester à la maison
steak bifteck (m)
step-brother beau-frère (m)
step-father beau-père (m)
step-mother belle-mère (f)
step-sister belle-sœur (f)
to stock (a department) stocker (un rayon)
stock stock (m)
stomach ventre (m)
store magasin (m); grocery — épicerie; music — magasin de musique; video — magasin de vidéos
straight : to go — aller tout droit
straight raide
strawberry fraise (f); — pie tarte aux fraises (f)
stress stress (m)
string bass basse (f)
strong fort(e)
stubborn têtu(e)
student étudiant(e) (m, f); — center centre d'étudiants (m)
studies études (f pl)
to study étudier
to succeed réussir à; I succeeded in J'ai pu
summer été (m); in the — en été
sun soleil (m); setting — soleil couchant (m)
sunny ensoleillé(e); It is —. Il fait du soleil; Il y a du soleil.
sunset coucher de soleil (m)
superb superbe
supermarket supermarché (m)
to supervise surveiller
supervisor surveillant(e) (m, f)
supper souper (m)

sure bien sûr; Je veux bien
sweater pull(over) (m); — **shop** sweaterie (f)
to swim nager
Swiss suisse
Switzerland Suisse (f)
synagogue synagogue (f)

T

table table (f)
tablecloth nappe (f)
to take prendre (pris); — **a test**; passer un examen; — **a trip** faire un voyage; — **a walk** se promener; — **advantage (of)** profiter (de); — **back** reprendre; — **charge (of)** se charger (de); — **messages** prendre des messages; noter des messages; — **responsibility (for)** se charger (de); — **. . . street** prendre la rue...
talented doué(e)
to talk parler; — **to each other** se parler
tall grand(e)
tea thé (m); **packaged** — une boîte de thé
to teach enseigner
team équipe (f); —**work** travail en équipe (m)
teaspoon cuillère à café (f)
technology technologie (f)
telephone téléphone (m)
to telephone téléphoner (à)
tennis tennis (m); — **court** court de tennis (m); **play** — jouer au tennis; faire du tennis
test examen (m); **do well on a** — réussir à un examen; **fail a** — échouer à un examen; **flunk a** — rater un examen; **pass a** — réussir à un examen; **take a** — passer un examen
thanks to grâce à
theology théologie (f)
thigh cuisse (f)
thin mince; maigre; **to get** — maigrir
to think (about) penser (à, de); réfléchir (à)
thirsty : to be — avoir soif
throat gorge (f)
thumb pouce (m)
time temps; **at that** — en ce temps-là, à cette époque-là, à l'époque; **from** — **to** — de temps en temps; **pressed for** — pressé(e); **to spend** — passer du temps; **to waste one's** — perdre (son) temps; **What** — **is it?** Quelle heure est-il?
timid timide
to tinker bricoler
tired fatigué(e)
tobacco shop bureau de tabac (m)
today aujourd'hui
toe doigt de pied (m)
tolerant tolérant(e)
to tolerate tolérer
tomato tomate (f)

tongue langue (f)
tooth dent (f); —**brush** brosse à dents (f)
train train (m); — **station** gare (f)
to travel voyager; — **agent** agent(e) de voyage (m, f)
tree arbre (m)
trip voyage (m)
trombone trombone (m)
tropical tropical(e); — **island** île tropicale (f)
trumpet trompette (f)
tuna thon (m)
turkey dinde (f)
to turn tourner; — **left** tourner à gauche; — **right** tourner à droite
TV télé (f)
twins jumeaux (m); jumelles (f)
to type taper

U

ugly laid(e), moche
um . . . euh...
unbearable insupportable
unbelievable incroyable
uncle oncle (m)
to understand comprendre
unhappy malheureux(-euse); mécontent(e)
university université (f)
until jusqu'à
up : to get — se lever
up : to go — monter; **I went** — je suis monté(e); **to go** — **. . . street** monter la rue...
upset : to get — s'énerver
usually d'habitude

V

vacation vacances (f pl)
valley vallée (f)
to value apprécier
veal veau (m)
vegetable légume (m)
vegetation végétation (f); **dense** — végétation dense
very très
video vidéo (f); — **store** magasin de vidéos (m)
Vietnam Viêt-Nam (m)
Vietnamese vietnamien(ne)
view vue (f); **panoramic** — vue panoramique
village village (m)
violin violon (m)
to visit (a place) visiter; — **(a person)** rendre visite à

W

to wait for attendre (attendu)
to wake up se réveiller
walk promenade (f); **to go for a** — faire une promenade; **to take a** — se promener
wall mur (m)

to want désirer, vouloir (voulu), avoir envie (de)
war guerre (f)
warm chaud(e)
to wash laver; — **up** se laver
to waste (one's) time perdre (son) temps
to watch regarder
water eau (f); **mineral** — eau minérale (f) — **with bubbles** eau gazeuse; — **without bubbles** eau plate
waterfall chute d'eau (f)
wavy ondulé(e)
weak faible
weather : the — **is...** il fait...; il fait un temps...; — **report** météo (f)
weekend week-end (m)
weight : to gain — grossir; **to lose** — maigrir
well bien
what qu'est-ce que...
when quand
where où
white blanc(he); — **wine** vin blanc (m)
who qui
why pourquoi
widowed veuf(-euve)
wife femme (f); épouse (f)
to windsurf faire de la planche à voile
windy : It is —. Il fait du vent; Il y a du vent.
wine vin (m); **red** — vin rouge; **white** — vin blanc
winter hiver (m); **in the** — en hiver
with avec; — **pleasure** avec plaisir; Je veux bien
without sans
woman femme (f)
wonderful magnifique
work travail (m)
to work travailler; — **individually** travailler seul(e); — **on a team** travailler en équipe; — **out** s'entraîner
world monde (m); French-speaking — monde francophone (m)
worried : to be — s'inquiéter
wrist poignet (m)
to write écrire (écrit)
writer écrivain (m); femme-écrivain (f)
wrong : to be — avoir tort

Y

year an (m); **to be . . . —s old** avoir...ans
yes oui
yogurt yaourt (m)
young jeune
youth jeunesse (f)

Z

zucchini courgette (f)

Anglais-français

à
  contractions with 126–128
abbreviations 440–441
adjectives 97–98
  agreement 37–38
  comparative 200–202
  demonstrative 157–158
  placement 198–199
  possessive 81–82
  superlative 213–214, 312–313
adverbs 131–132
age 93–94
agreement
  adjective 37–38
aller 129
  to form immediate future 133–134
articles
  definite with **de** 138–139
  definite + geographical names 286–287
  indefinite 13
  partitive 348–349
avoir 87–88
  expressions with 88
  to describe someone 95–96
  to form the **passé composé** 232–233,
    250–251

body 411–412

ce, cet, cette, ces 157–158
celebrations 215–217
city *see* town
clothing 489–490
comparative 200–202
conditional 479–481
connaître 544–545
contractions
  with **à** 126–128
croire 457–458

dates 42–43
days of the week 62
de
  preposition 21–22
  + prepositions of place 140–142
  + definite article 138–139
describing someone 95–96
devoir 202–203
directions 147–149
dormir 209–210

education
  university 192–197
en 361–363

être 20
  to form the **passé composé** 251–255
everyday activities 105–106
expenses 476–477

faire 104–105
  expressions with 105–106, 107, 108–109
family 83–85
food 11–12
  grocery shopping 329–335
  meals 345–347
  ordering 10–12
furniture 442–443
future 446–448, 454–455
futur immédiat 133–134

geographic names, 286–290
greetings 4–7

hotel 307–309
household tasks 107
housing 426–429

imperative 144–146
  with pronominal verbs 182–183
imparfait 336–338
  vs. **passé composé** 383–385
infinitive
  with impersonal expressions 492–494
  with pronominal verbs 180–181
interrogation 67–68

jamais 237
  ne... jamais 237
jouer 207–208

languages 39–40
leisure activities 63–64

marital staus (*état civil*) 41
months 42–43

nationalities 36–37
nature 284–285
necessity 185–186
negation 56–57, 430–433
  ne...jamais 237
  with passé composé 235–236
  with pronominal verbs 179
numbers 42–43, 93–94

opinion, verbs of 23–25
ouvrir 541–543

partir 209–212
passé composé
  interrogation with 236–237

irregular verbs 240
  negation with 235–236, 266
  pronominal verbs 261–262, 266
  regular verbs 232–233, 250–251, 251–255, 311
  vs. **imparfait** 383–385
past, talking about the 238–239
possessive adjectives 81–82
pouvoir 313–315
prendre 158–159
prepositions
  de 21–22, 138–139, 140–142
  of place 140–142
  with city names 287
  with country, province, and state names 288–289
professions 49–52
pronouns
  direct object 364–365, 409–410
  en 361–363
  indirect object 405–408, 409–410
  le, **la**, **les** (direct object) 364–365
  lui, **leur** (indirect object) 405–408
  me, **te**, **nous**, **vous** (object) 409–410
  reflexive 178–179
  subject 18–19
  y 301–302
pronunciation
  alphabet 8
  consonants 45, 203, 218, 315, 389, 483, 496, 503, 528
  diacritical signs (accent marks) 26
  elision 90
  francophone countries 536
  "h" 434–435
  intonation 187
  liaison 58, 69–70, 339, 352–353, 365
  nasals 162–163, 303
  places in Paris 547
  rhythm and accentuation 15
  suffixes "-sion" and "-tion" 400
  vowels 101, 110, 135, 150, 241, 256, 268, 290, 413, 449, 461

quantity, expressions of 358–360
questions 22–23, 67–68
  question words 160–161
  with **passé composé** 236–237
quitter 211–212

savoir 544–545
se sentir 209–210
seasons 295–299
servir 209–210
si + imperfect 499
sortir 209–212
sports 108–109
subjunctive 521–526, 532–533
superlative 213–214, 312–313

table 350–352
thanking someone 215–216
time 153–155
town
  directions in 147–149
  places in 124–125

venir 394–395
  venir de + infinitive 399–400
verbs
  -er 54–55, 86
  -ir 246–249
  -re 309–310, 311
  irregular, like **ouvrir** 541–543
  irregular, like **venir** 396–397
  pronominal 177–179, 180–181, 182–183, 184, 261–262, 266
  reciprocal 184
  reflexive 177–179, 180–181, 182–183
  + infinitive 64–65
voir 457–459
vouloir 313–315

weather 295–299

y 301–302

Credits

Photo credits

Photos furnished by the authors:
18 (L); 48; (T); 63; 64 (L); 83; 85 (TL, TR, BL); 86; 88; 92; 96; 104; 105; 108; 126; 141 (C, R); 160; 180; 232; 250; 251; 284 (TR, BL); 296 (B); 307; 309 (R); 326; 327; 328; 341; 350; 396; 397; 399; 405; 426 (TR, BR); 428 (L, C); 429; 436 (T); 445; 472 (B); 492 (TL, CL, CR, BL, BR); 501; 541; 544; 546 (TL, TCL, TCR, BL, BCR)

All other photos, with the exception of the following, were taken by Jonathan Stark, for the Heinle & Heinle Image Resource Bank.

4 (BR) Corbis/Adamsmith Productions; 49 (L) Corbis/Mitchell Gerber; (R) Corbis/Hulton–Deutsch Collection; 157 Corbis/Dave Bartruff; 207 (L) (Corbis/Wally McNamee, (C) Corbis/Warren Morgan; 231 (C) Corbis/Ken Redding, (B) Corbis/Kevin R. Morris; 238 (L) Corbis/Adamsmith Productions, (C) Corbis/Mark Stephenson; 283 (TL) Corbis/Marc Garanger; 289 (L) Corbis/Bob Krist; 306 (TR) Corbis/Dean Conger, (B) Corbis/The Purcell Team; 344 Corbis/Owen Franken; 357 (B) Corbis/Owen Franken; 358 FoodPix; 367 Corbis; 426 (BL) Corbis/Bob Krist; 474 A.S.K. Images/Viesti Collection; 529 Corbis; 531 (T) Corbis/Jamie Harron, (B) Corbis/Morton Beebe, S.F.; 537 Corbis/Marc Garanger; 538 Corbis/Wolfgang Kaehler; 550 Corbis/Paul Almasy;

Text/Realia Credits

59, 90, 180 Le Journal de Montréal/Sondages Léger & Léger; 136, *Télégraphe de Québec*; 150, *www.pagemontreal.qu.ca*; 189, Insitut de la statistique du Québec; 206, 219, La Redoute/IFOP; 222, *l'Expansion* online; 230, 243, 259, *CV Magazine*/Agence Presse CVM SARL; 235, 289, 389, 479, 495 *www.le-petit-bouquet.com*; 271, *Le magazine de l'emploi* ; 291-92, Jérôme & Fabien Maurice; 304, 496 *www.abm.fr*; 328, *Saveurs du monde*; 342, Institut québecois de l'érable; 344, *The Evolution of Cajun and Creole Cuisine*, John Folse & Company; 367, *Du côté de chez Swann*, Marcel Proust; 372-73, *Pariscope*, Nov. 1997; 390, *Nomade j'étais*, Edmonde-Charles-Roux, Éditions Bernard Grasset; 400, *Lettres volées*, Gerard Depardieu, Éditions JC Lattès; 401, *www.france-amérique.com*; 403, *La très noble demoiselle*, Montréal: Libre Expression, 1992; 410, *Yeux ouverts*, Marguérite Yourcenar, Éditions Bayard Presse; 414,418, *La détresse et l'enchantement*, Gabrielle Roy, Éditions Arléa; 430, Marion Segaud, "Cadre de vie: grandes tendances," *L'État de la France*, Édition 97-98, Paris: Éditions La Déccouverte & Syros, 1997; 466, Wolfgang Lauber; 468, club-internet.fr; 487, 506, U.S. Bureau of the Census; 502-03, Rachel Silvera, "Les inégalités de salaires entre hommes et femmes." *État de la France*, Édition 97-98. Paris: Édition La Découverte, 1997; 509, *État de la France*, 1992; 521, Comité International de la Croix-Rouge; 531, www.unimedia.fr

Est-ce qu'il est une femme ou un homme?
D'où vient-til? where is he from
Quelle couleur de cheveaux a-telle?
Jeune ou plus âger
    belle ou

(f) hôtess de l'air → flight attendant
(m) steward

cochon
  Tu mange commes un cochon
  Je suis
   J'ai de couton